CONCORDIA UNIVERSITY

3 4211 00119 8764

SO-BNW-515

MULTICULTURAL EDUCATION 96/97

Third Edition

Editor

Fred Schultz
University of Akron

Fred Schultz, professor of education at the University of Akron, attended Indiana University to earn a B.S. in social science education in 1962, an M.S. in the history and philosophy of education in 1966, and a Ph.D. in the history and philosophy of education and American studies in 1969. His B.A. in Spanish was conferred from the University of Akron in May 1985. He is actively involved in researching the development and history of American education with a primary focus on the history of ideas and social philosophy of education. He also likes to study languages.

Annual Editions
A Library of Information from the Public Press

Cover illustration by Mike Eagle

KLINCK MEMORIAL LIBRARY
Concordia University
River Forest IL 60305-1499

Dushkin Publishing Group/
Brown & Benchmark Publishers
Sluice Dock, Guilford, Connecticut 06437

The Annual Editions Series

Annual Editions is a series of over 65 volumes designed to provide the reader with convenient, low-cost access to a wide range of current, carefully selected articles from some of the most important magazines, newspapers, and journals published today. Annual Editions are updated on an annual basis through a continuous monitoring of over 300 periodical sources. All Annual Editions have a number of features designed to make them particularly useful, including topic guides, annotated tables of contents, unit overviews, and indexes. For the teacher using Annual Editions in the classroom, an Instructor's Resource Guide with test questions is available for each volume.

VOLUMES AVAILABLE

Abnormal Psychology
Africa
Aging
American Foreign Policy
American Government
American History, Pre-Civil War
American History, Post-Civil War
American Public Policy
Anthropology
Archaeology
Biopsychology
Business Ethics
Child Growth and Development
China
Comparative Politics
Computers in Education
Computers in Society
Criminal Justice
Developing World
Deviant Behavior
Drugs, Society, and Behavior
Dying, Death, and Bereavement
Early Childhood Education
Economics
Educating Exceptional Children
Education
Educational Psychology
Environment
Geography
Global Issues
Health
Human Development
Human Resources
Human Sexuality

India and South Asia
International Business
Japan and the Pacific Rim
Latin America
Life Management
Macroeconomics
Management
Marketing
Marriage and Family
Mass Media
Microeconomics
Middle East and the Islamic World
Multicultural Education
Nutrition
Personal Growth and Behavior
Physical Anthropology
Psychology
Public Administration
Race and Ethnic Relations
Russia, the Eurasian Republics,
    and Central/Eastern Europe
Social Problems
Sociology
State and Local Government
Urban Society
Western Civilization,
    Pre-Reformation
Western Civilization,
    Post-Reformation
Western Europe
World History, Pre-Modern
World History, Modern
World Politics

Cataloging in Publication Data
Main entry under title: Annual editions: Multicultural education. 1996/97.
    1. Intercultural education—Periodicals. I. Schultz, Fred, *comp.* II. Title: Multicultural education.
ISBN 0–697–31576–2   370.19′341′05

© 1996 by Dushkin Publishing Group/Brown & Benchmark Publishers, Guilford, CT 06437

Copyright law prohibits the reproduction, storage, or transmission in any form by any means of any portion of this publication without the express written permission of Dushkin Publishing Group/Brown & Benchmark Publishers, and of the copyright holder (if different) of the part of the publication to be reproduced. The Guidelines for Classroom Copying endorsed by Congress explicitly state that unauthorized copying may not be used to create, to replace, or to substitute for anthologies, compilations, or collective works.

Annual Editions® is a Registered Trademark of Dushkin Publishing Group/
Brown & Benchmark Publishers, a Times Mirror Higher Education Group company.

Third Edition

Printed in the United States of America

Printed on Recycled Paper

Editors/ Advisory Board

EDITOR

Fred Schultz
University of Akron

Members of the Advisory Board are instrumental in the final selection of articles for each edition of Annual Editions. Their review of articles for content, level, currentness, and appropriateness provides critical direction to the editor and staff. We think you'll find their careful consideration well reflected in this volume.

ADVISORY BOARD

Martha Allexsaht-Snider
University of Georgia

Julie Bao
Shippensburg University

Ruth Benns-Suter
Millersville University

Timothy J. Bergen
University of South Carolina
Columbia

Anna Lou Blevins
University of Pittsburgh

Janice White Clemmer
Brigham Young University

Michael L. Fischler
Plymouth State College

Mary Ann Flowers
Cleveland State University

Mary G. Harris
Bloomsburg University

Inez A. Heath
Valdosta State University

Gwendolyn W. Henderson
University of North Carolina
Asheville

Jacqueline J. Irvine
Emory University

E. Joseph Kaplan
Florida International University

Edith W. King
University of Denver

Rebecca Oxford
University of Alabama

Patricia T. Rooke
University of Alberta

Quirico S. Samonte, Jr.
Eastern Michigan University

David Strom
San Diego State University

Mary R. Sudzina
University of Dayton

Joan Thrower Timm
University of Wisconsin
Oshkosh

STAFF

Ian A. Nielsen, Publisher
Brenda S. Filley, Production Manager
Roberta Monaco, Editor
Addie Raucci, Administrative Editor
Cheryl Greenleaf, Permissions Editor
Deanna Herrschaft, Permissions Assistant
Diane Barker, Proofreader
Lisa Holmes-Doebrick, Program Coordinator
Charles Vitelli, Designer
Shawn Callahan, Graphics
Lara M. Johnson, Graphics
Laura Levine, Graphics
Mike Campbell, Graphics
Libra A. Cusack, Typesetting Supervisor
Juliana Arbo, Typesetter
Jane Jaegersen, Typesetter
Marie Lazauskas, Word Processor

To the Reader

In publishing ANNUAL EDITIONS we recognize the enormous role played by the magazines, newspapers, and journals of the *public press* in providing current, first-rate educational information in a broad spectrum of interest areas. Within the articles, the best scientists, practitioners, researchers, and commentators draw issues into new perspective as accepted theories and viewpoints are called into account by new events, recent discoveries change old facts, and fresh debate breaks out over important controversies.

Many of the articles resulting from this enormous editorial effort are appropriate for students, researchers, and professionals seeking accurate, current material to help bridge the gap between principles and theories and the real world. These articles, however, become more useful for study when those of lasting value are carefully *collected, organized, indexed,* and *reproduced* in a *low-cost format,* which provides easy and permanent access when the material is needed. That is the role played by ANNUAL EDITIONS. Under the direction of each volume's *Editor,* who is an expert in the subject area, and with the guidance of an *Advisory Board,* we seek each year to provide in each ANNUAL EDITION a current, well-balanced, carefully selected collection of the best of the public press for your study and enjoyment.

We think you'll find this volume useful, and we hope you'll take a moment to let us know what you think.

As an ever more multicultural society, we need to recall that we are moving toward a common national destiny. What is that destiny to be? As the 96/97 edition of *Annual Editions: Multicultural Education* goes to press, the debate regarding multicultural issues in American society is intense.

The concept of multicultural education evolved and took shape in the United States out of the social travail that wrenched the nation in the late 1960s, through the 1970s and 1980s, and into the present decade. The linkages between diverse and coexisting ethnic, racial, and socioeconomic heritages are explored in these readings. There has been enthusiastic support for the idea of a volume in this series exclusively devoted to multicultural education. Having taught and studied multicultural education for 27 years, it is a pleasure for me to serve as editor of *Annual Editions: Multicultural Education 96/97.*

The critical literature on gender, race, and culture in educational studies increases our knowledge base regarding the multicultural mosaic that so richly adorns North America. When the first courses in multicultural education were developed in the 1960s, the United States was in the midst of urban and other social crises, and there were no textbooks available. Educators who taught in this area had to draw heavily from academic literatures in anthropology, sociology, social psychology, social history, sociolinguistics, and psychiatry. Today, there are textbooks available in the area, but there is also a need for a regularly published volume that offers samples from the recent journal literature in which the knowledge bases for multicultural education are developed. This volume is intended to address that need.

The National Council for the Accreditation of Teacher Education (NCATE) in the United States has in place national accreditation standards requiring that accredited teacher education programs offer course content in multicultural education. A global perspective of the subject is usually recommended, in which prospective teachers are encouraged to develop empathetic cultural sensitivity to the demographic changes and cultural diversity that continue to appear in the public schools as a result of dramatic shifts in the population.

In this volume, we first explore the national and global social contexts for the development of multicultural education. Its role in teacher education is then briefly defined in the essays in unit 2. In unit 3, the nature of multicultural education as an academic discipline is discussed, and several issues related to this topic are explored. The readings in unit 4 look at multicultural education from the perspective associated with the enculturation and acculturation of persons in the process of developing their own unique personal identities in the context of their interactions with their own as well as others' cultural heritages and personal life experiences. The readings in unit 5 focus on curriculum and instruction in multicultural perspective. Unit 6 addresses special topics relevant to development of multicultural insight, and the essays in unit 7 explore alternative visions for multicultural education and the need for a critically conscious quest for emancipatory educational futures for all persons of all cultural heritages.

This year I would like to acknowledge the very helpful contributions of the members of the advisory board to this volume in finding useful sources. I would also like to acknowledge one of my students, Victoria Ortiz-Castro Aron, for her help in finding useful essays for inclusion in the volume, as well as Stephen H. Aby, research librarian at the University of Akron, whose assistance is greatly valued.

This volume will be useful in courses in multicultural education at the undergraduate and graduate levels. It will add considerable substance to the sociocultural foundations of education, educational policy studies, and leadership, as well as to course work in other areas of preservice and in-service teacher education programs. We hope you enjoy this volume, and we would like you to help us improve future editions. Please complete and return the postage-paid *article rating form* at the back of the book. We look forward to hearing from you.

Fred Schultz

Fred Schultz
Editor

Contents

Unit
1

The Social Contexts of Multicultural Education

Eight articles discuss the importance of a multicultural curriculum in sensitizing students to an integrated world society.

To the Reader   iv
Topic Guide   2

Overview   4

1. **Diversity without Equality = Oppression,** Meyer Weinberg, *Multicultural Education,* Spring 1994.   6
Meyer Weinberg reviews major struggles and events in the *civil rights movement* in the United States and how *multicultural education* grew out of this struggle for *human rights* and *social justice.* He argues that social equality must be attained for all persons in order to avoid social oppression.

2. **Toward a Common Destiny,** Sandee Brawarsky, *Carnegie Quarterly,* Fall 1994/Winter 1995.   9
This article reports on a study of how to improve *intercultural and race relations* in the United States. The article focuses on issues related to the common destiny of the American population, which is becoming even more multicultural with each passing year.

3. **The Importance of Education . . . and How His Education Helped Turn the Tide for Indian People,** John Echohawk, *Children Today,* Volume 23, Number 1, 1994.   12
John Echohawk, a Native American attorney, discusses the *importance of education* and how he has been able to be a constructive force in the defense of the legitimate interests of *Native Americans.*

4. **One Nation, One Language?** *U.S. News & World Report,* September 25, 1995.   15
Several *U.S. News & World Report* writers cover the current debate over whether or not *English* ought to be declared the *official language* in the United States. The debate centers around the question of whether this would unite or divide the nation. Of the students in American schools in the fall of 1995, more than a third speak a "first" language other than English.

5. **Tongue-Tied in the Schools,** *U.S. News & World Report,* September 25, 1995.   18
Susan Headden describes the debate occurring over *bilingual education* across the United States. The author discusses some of the reasons behind the debate as to whether or not bilingual educational programming is appropriate for all "limited English proficient" (LEP) students.

6. **A "Glorious Mongrel,"** *U.S. News & World Report,* September 25, 1995.   20
The author points out that three out of four words in standard American English are derived from other languages. He goes on to show how English has become a truly international language.

7. **Go North, Young Man,** Richard Rodriguez, *Mother Jones,* July/August 1995.   22
Richard Rodriguez discusses the new trends in *immigration into the United States* from south *(Latin America)* to north. He notes the old movement from east to west has given way to the new mass migrations of Latin Americans to the United States.

8. **Intermarried . . . with Children,** Jill Smolowe, *Time,* Special Issue, Fall 1993.   26
Jill Smolowe discusses the challenges that come to couples who intermarry across cultures. America's *cultural pluralism* is giving birth to a greater frequency of marriage among persons of different *cultural heritage,* and a growth in the number of children who share more than one cultural heritage as a result.

The concepts in bold italics are developed in the article. For further expansion please refer to the Topic Guide and the Index.

Unit 2

Teacher Education in Multicultural Perspective

Five selections examine some of the major issues being debated on how to effectively integrate the multicultural dynamic into teacher education programs.

Unit 3

Multicultural Education as an Academic Discipline

Seven selections examine the dynamics of integrating multicultural education into the discipline of education.

Overview   28

9. **Why Do We Need This Class? Multicultural Education**   30
   for Teachers, Valerie Ooka Pang, *Phi Delta Kappan*, December 1994.
   The author discusses her beliefs about how multicultural education ought to be conducted in *teacher education programs.* She cites Paulo Freire's ideas and relates her ideas about the practice of teacher education to *critical theoretical perspectives.*

10. **Questions and Answers about Inclusion: What Every**   34
    Teacher Should Know, Bonnie B. Greer and John G. Greer, *The Clearing House,* July/August 1995.
    The authors present a cogent and sympathetic summary of the main principles underlying *inclusion of handicapped learners* in classroom settings. They discuss the sources of support for the movement for inclusive classroom practice as well as the issues and problems involved in implementing this policy.

11. **Time to Talk Back,** Michael L. Fischler, *Phi Delta Kappan,*   38
    April 1992.
    The author identifies the problem of ethnocentric and racist behavior among many American college students, and he focuses on the necessity of directly confronting *racism and prejudice* on the college campus. Many college students need to be confronted about unhealthy and antisocial forms of prejudiced behavior, and many need to confront the prejudices they bring with them to college.

12. **The Ideology of Star Teachers of Children in Poverty,**   40
    Martin Haberman, *Educational Horizons,* Spring 1992.
    The author identifies what he believes to be the essential attitudes and styles of successful *urban teachers.* In doing so, he also suggests alternative ways to *recruit and train teachers* for *urban schools.*

13. **Building Cultural Bridges: A Bold Proposal for Teacher**   45
    Education, Geneva Gay, *Education and Urban Society,* Volume 25, Number 3, May 1993.
    Geneva Gay presents recommendations for changes in *teacher education* that would prepare teachers to deal constructively with *cultural diversity.* She addresses the demographic changes occurring in American culture and the idea of teachers as cultural brokers and change agents.

Overview   52

14. **Bridging Multicultural Theory and Practice,** Geneva Gay,   54
    Multicultural Education, Fall 1995.
    The author discusses the issues involved in bridging the gap between *theory and practice in multicultural education.* She uses some of the theoretical constructs from *critical theoretical perspectives* to indicate her views as to where the field ought to be directed.

15. **Affirmation, Solidarity, and Critique: Moving beyond**   59
    Tolerance in Multicultural Education, Sonia Nieto, *Multicultural Education,* Spring 1994.
    Sonia Nieto reviews a model of *multicultural education* to explore how it would be reflected in *school policies and practices.* She argues for greater acceptance of cultural diversity in schools and stresses that we must move beyond *"tolerance"* to full *acceptance of cultural diversity.*

The concepts in bold italics are developed in the article. For further expansion please refer to the Topic Guide and the Index.

16. **Multicultural Education: A Movement in Search of Meaning and Positive Connections,** Leonard Davidman, *Multicultural Education,* Spring 1995.   66
The author identifies key questions that need to be addressed in developing a meaningful and constructive approach to *multicultural curriculum development.* He addresses important values and concepts that ought to be imbedded in directing future efforts at the development of multicultural studies in schools. He discusses the *meaning of multicultural education* as well as the importance of *ethnic and cultural self-disclosure.*

17. **Multicultural Education as an Academic Discipline,** James A. Banks, *Multicultural Education,* Winter 1993.   71
James Banks discusses the development of *multicultural education as an academic discipline* and the challenges that the field will face as it moves into the next century. Banks supports a *"multicultural education + integration model" (MCE + integration model)* for teaching multicultural education.

18. **Multicultural Education and Culture Change: An Anthropological Perspective,** Stanton W. Green and Stephen M. Perlman, *Multicultural Education,* Summer 1995.   76
The authors discuss the *concepts of culture and change,* and they explore how people learn cultures and the processes involved in cultural change. They argue that multicultural education must include helping people to understand how human cultures develop and why it is important to understand the processes of cultural change from an *anthropological perspective.*

19. **White Racism,** Christine Sleeter, *Multicultural Education,* Spring 1994.   79
Christine Sleeter explores the phenomenon of *white racism* and how it continues to be a serious issue that we must confront in our efforts as educators. Sleeter argues that some educators fail to see or to acknowledge their own cultural biases. She maintains that white educators need to be in ongoing and sincere dialogue with persons of color in order to develop genuine *multicultural education programming.*

20. **Cultural Pluralism, Multicultural Education, and Then What?** Elaine C. Hagopian, *Multicultural Education,* Summer 1994.   83
Elaine Hagopian provides an insightful analysis of the present status of dialogue regarding *"cultural pluralism"* and the present and future directions of *multicultural education.* Important issues in the struggle to achieve *equality of educational opportunity* in *polyethnic societies,* such as the United States, are identified.

Overview   90

21. **The Inside Story,** David Aronson, *Teaching Tolerance,* Spring 1995.   92
David Aronson points out that persons can be *taught tolerance* and helped to unlearn or to avoid acceptance of *prejudice,* something the psychiatric community has known since the 1940s at least. Aronson argues that counseling children to be *tolerant, accepting persons* in their early years is extremely important.

22. **The Intersections of Gender, Class, Race, and Culture: On Seeing Clients Whole,** Tracy Robinson, *Journal of Multicultural Counseling and Development,* January 1993.   98
Tracy Robinson explores the vital *contextual relationships between a person's cultural heritage,* gender, and social location in his or her daily life. Her insights can inform educators and assist them in better seeing their clients (students) in the wholeness of their humanity.

Unit
4

Identity and Personal Development: A Multicultural Focus

Eight articles consider the interconnections between gender, social class, racial or ethnic heritage, and primary cultural values.

The concepts in bold italics are developed in the article. For further expansion please refer to the Topic Guide and the Index.

23. **Can Separate Be Equal?** James Traub, *Harper's,* June 1994.   103
The dialogue over **racial integration in schools** since **Brown v. Board of Education** in 1954 is examined. James Traub discusses issues relating to various forms of **racial separation** that have developed in the field of education.

24. **Contradictions of Identity: Education and the Problem of Racial Absolutism,** Cameron McCarthy, *The Clearing House,* May/June 1995.   111
The author provides an excellent research-based discussion of **human identity formation** and the impact that **racism** can have on this critical process in each human life. He cites some important **critical theoretical perspectives** in his argument against **ethnic absolutism**.

25. **All-Black Schools Provide Role Models: Is This the Solution?** Russell Bradshaw, *The Clearing House,* January/February 1995.   115
The author discusses how to create school environments where African American youth, especially black males, have responsible black **role models** that defy racist stereotypes. Focusing on personal identity development, he asks whether or not separate all-black schools might enhance healthy **identity development** among African American youth. The shortage of black teachers, he says, inhibits this as a permanent solution.

26. **On Being a Mexican American,** Joe I. Mendoza, *Phi Delta Kappan,* December 1994.   120
The author argues that it is important for **Mexican Americans** to realize that they have a dynamic and uniquely developing identity as a cultural group in the United States. Mexican Americans are approaching a crossroads in their **cultural experience** within the United States.

27. **Respect, Cultural Sensitivity, and Communication,** Jinhee K. Hyun and Susan A. Fowler, *Teaching Exceptional Children,* Fall 1995.   123
The authors present insightful suggestions for ways to help the **parents and children of different cultures** to feel welcome and supported at school. They discuss **culturally acceptable family outcomes** and several other interesting ideas.

28. **Lessons of Vancouver: Immigration Raises Fundamental Questions of Identity and Values,** Andrew Phillips and Chris Wood, *Maclean's,* February 7, 1994.   127
This report examines the experience of citizens in Vancouver, British Columbia, as they continue to receive more and more new immigrants. The phenomenon of **immigration** challenges the intercultural skills of newcomers as well as older residents.

Overview   132

29. **Curriculum Guidelines for Multicultural Education,** *Social Education,* September 1992.   134
The **Curriculum Guidelines for Multicultural Education** were originally adopted by the National Council for the Social Studies (NCSS) in 1976 and revised in 1991. This article addresses the **revised guidelines** in schools (K–12). There are 23 standards to be met with their respective corollary questions to which school personnel must satisfactorily respond.

30. **Empowering Children to Create a Caring Culture in a World of Differences,** Louise Derman-Sparks, *Childhood Education,* Winter 1993/94.   155
Research findings on how children develop a sense of **personal identity** and on how they learn about **cultural diversity and race** are reviewed in this essay. Louise Derman-Sparks presents research on **racism** and the impact it has on **personal identity development** in childhood. She identifies several things we can do to **empower children** to develop caring, affirmative conceptions of themselves and others.

Unit 5

Curriculum and Instruction in Multicultural Perspective

Five articles review how curriculum and instruction must be formulated to sensitize young people to the multicultural reality of a national civilization.

Unit 6

Special Topics in Multicultural Education

Nine articles explore some of the ways students succeed
or fail in culturally pluralistic school settings.

31. **"The Party": Role Playing to Enhance Multicultural Understanding,** Ellen N. Junn, *College Teaching,* Volume 42, Number 3, Summer 1994. 162

    Ellen Junn describes a role-play simulation experience that can be used to help students examine intercultural and interracial issues in schools. Intercultural simulation experiences like this one can be designed to help students become sensitized to *gender, racial, cultural, and social status issues in school settings.* It is a classroom activity that can help students to understand the destructive impact of *stereotyping* groups of persons.

32. **Classrooms without Borders,** Kathleen Ralph, *Childhood Education,* Annual Theme Issue, 1995. 164

    Kathleen Ralph's argument is that the use of *multicultural literature* in the classroom along with learning activities that help students to confront cultural, racial, and gender borders in society can lead them to become tolerant and accepting of *gender, racial, and cultural diversity.* She calls for *collaborative classroom environments* to empower students.

33. **Teaching: The Challenge of Change; Reclaiming Democracy through Schooling,** Sudia Paloma McCaleb, *Multicultural Education,* Spring 1995. 167

    The author describes her efforts to use *critical theoretical perspectives* designed to create democratic school and classroom environments that liberate and *empower students and teachers* to take control of their own visions for their lives. She tells about this new emphasis in the *teacher education* program at New College in San Francisco.

Overview 174

34. **The Dynamic Demographic Mosaic Called America,** Leobardo F. Estrada, *Education and Urban Society,* May 1993. 176

    The dramatic *demographic changes* occurring in the cultural composition of the population of the United States are documented by Leobardo Estrada. We are becoming an even more uniquely *multicultural society* than we are already.

35. **Black Hawk's *An Autobiography*: The Production and Use of an "Indian" Voice,** Mark Wallace, *American Indian Quarterly,* Fall 1994. 182

    Mark Wallace examines the 1833 autobiography of Black Hawk to confront the issues surrounding the struggle of Native Americans to be heard, for their *voice* to become a part of the American national experience. The author of this essay treats Black Hawk's autobiography as a *text* representing Black Hawk's *resistance* to attempts to impose an *"Anglo-Indianist"* vision of the *Native American* experience on his writing.

36. **Behind the Model-Minority Stereotype: Voices of High- and Low-Achieving Asian American Students,** Stacey J. Lee, *Anthropology & Education Quarterly,* December 1994. 188

    Stacey Lee examines the differences between how Asian American students look at their cultural experience and prevalent American social stereotypes of them. The author cites John Ogbu's distinction between voluntary and involuntary cultural minorities, and questions the use of this distinction because *Asian Americans* come from several national cultures. Lee seeks to blow away the myth of Asian Americans as a *"model minority."*

The concepts in bold italics are developed in the article. For further expansion please refer to the Topic Guide and the Index.

37. **Multicultural Education: Reflections on** *Brown* **at 40,**   **197**
Debbie G. Thomas, Phil Chinn, Fran Perkins, and David
G. Carter, *The Journal of Negro Education,* Summer 1994.
The authors of this article offer some introspective assessments
of the effects of the U.S. Supreme Court decision in *Brown v.
Board of Education of Topeka* in its fortieth anniversary year.
Evaluating the effects of this decision, the authors argue that there
has been much *resegregation* in the United States. They argue
for more focus on *multicultural curricula* as the American student
body becomes more culturally pluralistic.

38. **The Road to Auschwitz: What's So Funny about**   **202**
Schindler's List? Bernard Beck, *Multicultural Education,*
Spring 1995.
Bernard Beck offers a reflective analysis of the Jewish experience
in the post-Holocaust years and the use of *mass media,* in this
case the popular film *Schindler's List,* in portraying Jewish culture. Beck offers an insightful, sensitive, and much-needed ap-
praisal of Jewish concerns regarding how they are portrayed in
film and other mass media.

39. **New Colors,** Melissa Steel, *Teaching Tolerance,* Spring   **206**
1995.
Melissa Steel reports on the increase of *interracial marriages* in
the United States as well as the continuing challenges and social
resistance that *multiracial families* can meet. She describes
struggles that children of interracial marriages still confront. More
American youth are choosing to date and to marry interculturally.
Crossing racial boundaries is a theme of this article.

40. **Another School's Reality,** Jeffrey Raison, Lee Anna Han-   **210**
son, Cheryl Hall, and Maynard C. Reynolds, *Phi Delta Kappan,* February 1995.
The authors focus on what has gone into an exceptional attempt
to maintain the standards of "inclusion" under very challenging
conditions. They help to clarify the educational issues relating to
the inclusion of *the physically and mentally handicapped in the
multicultural educational effort.*

41. **How School Materials Teach about the Middle East,**   **212**
Barry Rubin, *American Educator,* Summer 1994.
Barry Rubin describes some of the issues involved in attempts to
get *accurate information about the Middle East* into the hands
of teachers and parents. This essay is a good contribution to
thought about how controversial cultural matters should be dealt
with in schools. The author explores major errors in the representation of present-day Middle Eastern social and political reality
in American secondary school textbooks.

42. **The AAUW Report: How Schools Shortchange Girls,**   **219**
American Association of University Women Report, 1992.
This report on the status of girls and young women in American
education shows that there is still much work to be done to ensure
equality of educational opportunity for *female students.* Gender issues in schooling are related to racial, ethnic, and socioeconomic factors; 40 recommendations for dealing with gender issues
in schools are made.

The concepts in bold italics are developed in the article. For further expansion please refer to the Topic Guide and the Index.

Unit 7

For Vision and Voice: A Call to Conscience

Four selections address the concerns that must be kept in mind for the future improvement of our educational system.

Overview   **224**

43. Home Was a Horse Stall, Jim Carnes, *Teaching Tolerance,* Spring 1995.   **226**
The author describes the ordeal of a ***Japanese American*** family in California from the time of their arrival in America in 1905 through their experiences in World War II and thereafter. Their experiences and feelings at being forced to leave their home and to live in ***Japanese American internment camps*** under extremely harsh circumstances are recounted.

44. Turning the Tide: A Call for Radical Voices of Affirmation, Bakari Chavanu, *Multicultural Education,* Fall 1995.   **230**
Bakari Chavanu gives eloquent ***voice*** to his experience as an African American who was bused into a predominantly white secondary school in the 1970s. He speaks of the ***"cultural silence"*** that exists in most American classrooms today. He calls for critical reflection on one's identity and vision as a person.

45. Knocking on Heaven's Door, Jonathan Kozol, *Teacher,* October 1995.   **232**
Jonathan Kozol interviews ***children and youth of the South Bronx*** in New York City and eloquently records ***their voices*** as they express their feelings regarding the conditions of their lives. This article is from Kozol's ***Amazing Grace: The Lives of Children and the Conscience of a Nation,*** published in October 1995 by Crown Publishers.

46. Investing in Our Children: A Struggle for America's Conscience and Future, Marian Wright Edelman, *USA Today Magazine (Society for the Advancement of Education),* March 1993.   **238**
In this article, the author argues that we must transcend our traditions of ***racial and cultural prejudice*** and not leave any of our children behind in our efforts to become more effective competitors in a global economy. We must educate all of our children for ***effective public service,*** and we need to rebuild a sense of national community and put our children first.

Index   **241**
Article Review Form   **244**
Article Rating Form   **245**

The concepts in bold italics are developed in the article. For further expansion please refer to the Topic Guide and the Index.

Topic Guide

This topic guide suggests how the selections in this book relate to topics of traditional concern to students and professional educators involved with the study of education. It is useful for locating articles that relate to each other for reading and research. The guide is arranged alphabetically according to topic. Articles may, of course, treat topics that do not appear in the topic guide. In turn, entries in the topic guide do not necessarily constitute a comprehensive listing of all the contents of each selection.

TOPIC AREA	TREATED IN	TOPIC AREA	TREATED IN
African American Youth	23. Can Separate Be Equal? 24. Contradictions of Identity 25. All-Black Schools Provide Role Models 44. Turning the Tide 45. Knocking on Heaven's Door	**Curriculum and Instruction**	29. Curriculum Guidelines for Multicultural Education 31. "The Party" 32. Classrooms without Borders 33. Teaching: Challenge of Change
Anthropology and Education	18. Multicultural Education and Culture Change	**Democracy and Education**	33. Teaching: Challenge of Change
Anti-Semitism	38. Road to Auschwitz	**English Language**	4. One Nation, One Language 5. Tongue-Tied in the Schools 6. "Glorious Mongrel"
Asian Americans	36. Behind the Model-Minority Stereotype 43. Home Was a Horse Stall	**Gender Issues**	31. "The Party" 32. Classrooms without Borders 42. How Schools Shortchange Girls
Bilingual Education	5. Tongue-Tied in the Schools	**Guidelines**	14. Bridging Multicultural Theory and Practice 17. Multicultural Education as an Academic Discipline 29. Curriculum Guidelines for Multicultural Education
Brown v. Board of Education	1. Diversity without Equality = Oppression 23. Can Separate Be Equal? 37. Multicultural Education		
Children and Poverty	12. Ideology of Star Teachers of Children in Poverty 45. Knocking on Heaven's Door	**Identity**	21. Inside Story 22. Intersections of Gender, Class, Race, and Culture 23. Can Separate Be Equal? 24. Contradictions of Identity 25. All-Black Schools Provide Role Models 26. On Being a Mexican American 27. Respect, Cultural Sensitivity, and Communication 28. Lessons of Vancouver
Civil Rights Movement	1. Diversity without Equality = Oppression 23. Can Separate Be Equal?		
Cultural Bridges	13. Building Cultural Bridges 32. Classrooms without Borders 33. Teaching: Challenge of Change		
Cultural Change	18. Multicultural Education and Culture Change	**Immigration**	7. Go North, Young Man 28. Lessons of Vancouver 34. Dynamic Demographic Mosaic Called America
Cultural Diversity in Schools	9. Why Do We Need This Class? 11. Time to Talk Back 12. Ideology of Star Teachers of Children in Poverty 13. Building Cultural Bridges 23. Can Separate Be Equal? 27. Respect, Cultural Sensitivity, and Communication 29. Curriculum Guidelines for Multicultural Education 30. Empowering Children to Create a Caring Culture 31. "The Party" 32. Classrooms without Borders 33. Teaching: Challenge of Change 36. Behind the Model-Minority Stereotype 37. Multicultural Education 44. Turning the Tide	**Inclusion**	10. Questions and Answers about Inclusion 32. Classrooms without Borders
		Japanese Americans	43. Home Was a Horse Stall
		Language	4. One Nation, One Language 5. Tongue-Tied in the Schools 6. "Glorious Mongrel" 35. Black Hawk's _An Autobiography_
		Latin American Immigration	7. Go North, Young Man
		Mexican American Youth	26. On Being a Mexican American
		Model Minority	36. Behind the Model-Minority Stereotype

TOPIC AREA	TREATED IN	TOPIC AREA	TREATED IN
Multicultural Education as an Academic Discipline	14. Bridging Multicultural Theory and Practice 15. Moving beyond Tolerance 16. Multicultural Education 17. Multicultural Education as an Academic Discipline 18. Multicultural Education and Culture Change 19. White Racism 20. Cultural Pluralism, Multicultural Education, and Then What?	**Social Context**	1. Diversity without Equality = Oppression 2. Toward a Common Destiny 3. Importance of Education 4. One Nation, One Language 5. Tongue-Tied in the Schools 6. "Glorious Mongrel" 7. Go North, Young Man 8. Intermarried . . . with Children 39. New Colors
Native Americans	3. Importance of Education 35. Black Hawk's *An Autobiography*	**Special Topics**	35. Black Hawk's *An Autobiography* 36. Behind the Model-Minority Stereotype 37. Multicultural Education 38. Road to Auschwitz 39. New Colors
Parents	27. Respect, Cultural Sensitivity, and Communication		
Population and Multicultural Education	28. Lessons of Vancouver 34. Dynamic Demographic Mosaic Called America	**Teacher Education in Multicultural Perspective**	9. Why Do We Need This Class? 10. Questions and Answers about Inclusion 11. Time to Talk Back 12. Ideology of Star Teachers of Children in Poverty 13. Building Cultural Bridges 33. Teaching: Challenge of Change
Race and Education	1. Diversity without Equality = Oppression 31. "The Party" 32. Classrooms without Borders 44. Turning the Tide	**Tolerance**	1. Diversity without Equality = Oppression 15. Moving beyond Tolerance 19. White Racism 21. Inside Story 25. All-Black Schools Provide Role Models 31. "The Party" 32. Classrooms without Borders
Racial Intermarriage	8. Intermarried . . . with Children 39. New Colors		
Racism	1. Diversity without Equality = Oppression 11. Time to Talk Back 19. White Racism 21. Inside Story 22. Intersections of Gender, Class, Race, and Culture 24. Contradictions of Identity 44. Turning the Tide	**Visions and Voice**	43. Home Was a Horse Stall 44. Turning the Tide 45. Knocking on Heaven's Door

The Social Contexts of Multicultural Education

We cannot ignore the power of culture in shaping conceptions of social reality and the phenomenology of their visions of their own lives and the lives of others around them. Every person needs to develop her or his own social vision of life as it relates to actual cultural realities.

The United States is rapidly becoming an ever more multiculturally unique nation-state. Canada is also experiencing major changes in its cultural composition, due to its very generous immigration policies. Both nations face multicultural futures. From its beginnings, the United States has been a multicultural nation. Some demographic projections indicate that, within five years, a majority of the total American elementary and secondary school student body will be composed of "persons of color," the children of the rainbow coalition (Native American, African American, Asian American, and Latino American).

Multicultural national communities have special challenges associated with the dynamics of daily life among their diverse cultural groups. Such societies also have unique opportunities to develop great, culturally pluralistic civilizations, in which the aesthetic, artistic, literary, and moral standards of each cultural group can contribute to the creation of new standards of national civilization. Cultural groups can learn from one another, benefit from their respective strengths and achievements, and help one another to transcend problems and injustices of the past. Furthermore, there are several major multicultural national social orders worldwide, and they can learn from and help each other even more than they have heretofore. We, therefore, ought to see the multicultural national fabric that is our social reality as a circumstance of promise and hope, one of which we can be proud.

In examining the social context of multicultural education, we need to help teachers and education students to sense the promise, the great social opportunity, that our multicultural social reality presents. There are many serious challenges to the social and economic well-being of children and young adults. We are heirs to social conditions yet to be rectified. We have the task of empowering students with a constructive sense of social consciousness and a will to transcend the social barriers to safety, success, and personal happiness that confront, in one form or another, almost one-third of them. It is

essential that we invest in all the children and young adults of multicultural nations, in order that great social promise and hope may be brought to fulfillment in our near-term future as nations.

We can ask ourselves certain very important questions as we work with children and young adults in our schools. Are they unsafe? Are they hungry? Are they afraid? Are they angry? Do they have a sense of angst; are they filled with self-doubt and uncertainty as to their prospects in life? For far too many children and adolescents from all socioeconomic groups, social classes, and cultural groups, the answers to these questions are "yes." Far greater numbers of children from minority cultural groups answer "yes" to at least some of these questions than do children from higher socioeconomic groups.

Having asked these questions, we, as educators and civic leaders, ought to pose a few others. What are the purposes of schooling? Are schools limited to their acknowledged mission of intellectual development? Or, are schools also capable of serving to advance, as classical Greek and Roman education did, education in honor, character, courage, resourcefulness, civic responsibility, and social service? This wider concept of the mission of schooling is still today the brightest hope for the full achievement of our great promise as a multicultural society embraced in an interdependent world community of nations.

What are the problems we face in achieving this end? We need to enable each child to advance intellectually in school as far as may be possible for that child. At the same time, we need to help develop a child's sense of self-respect and pride in his or her own cultural heritage as a part of a national community. We need to do what we can to help all students develop a sense of honor, pride, and self-respect that will lead them in their adult years to want to serve, help, and heal the suffering of others. We need intellectually curious and competent graduates who are both knowledgeable about their own ethnic heritages and committed to social justice for all persons, in their own nation as well as in the community of nations.

The problems we face in achieving such an intellectual and social end are not insignificant. Developing multicultural curriculum materials for schools and integrating them throughout the course content and activities of the

school day and year can help to sensitize all students to the reality of the inherent worth of all persons. Also, the safety and security needs of all school-aged children must be better served. All youth deserve the opportunity to learn about their own cultural heritages, and they deserve the right to know the culturally unique reality of their nation from an objective, socially scientific perspective that is *not* seen through Eurocentric cultural lenses alone.

Many people believe that in todayís social reality we must help all persons to better comprehend the interdependence of humanity and those shared interests and concerns that all human cultures embrace.

North American nations have qualitative issues to face in the area of intercultural relations. Our problems differ because of very different national experiences and very different school systems. Around the world, other nations have to wrestle with providing adequate opportunity structures for minority populations while maintaining high intellectual standards. The articles in this unit attempt to

discuss these problems and the thoughtful concerns of those who have studied the rhetoric of debate over multiculturalism in school curricula.

Dramatic demographic changes are taking place in the characteristics of the world's population as well as in the interdependence of the world's nations in a global economy. We must reconsider how we develop human talent in our schools, for the young people are the ones who will be the most basic resource in the near term. Some unit essays also give important background on the history of the civil rights movement in the United States as well as on the origins of many racial and cultural stereotypes that have inhibited the efforts of educators to help young people become more accepting of cultural diversity.

Young adults have the right to learn that the struggle for freedom, and against tyranny, is not really over everywhere in the world, in spite of the great advances that democratic forces have made in recent years. Young persons need to be able to accept and to value cultural diversity. This unit seeks to offer a concise discussion of the nature of the social context in which efforts to expand multicultural education has occurred.

The unit essays are relevant to courses in cultural foundations of education, educational policy studies, multicultural education, social studies education, and curriculum theory and construction.

Looking Ahead: Challenge Questions

What should every student learn about cultural diversity and her or his own cultural heritage?

What facets of the history of the human struggle for civil rights should be taught to students?

What should students learn about other nations and other democratic traditions?

How can the mass media more effectively inform the public on issues related to cultural diversity?

What can educators do to help students to better understand the social contexts in which they live?

What should every student know about equality of opportunity?

What should everyone know about our common humanity?

—F. S.

Diversity Without Equality
=
Oppression

Meyer Weinberg

Meyer Weinberg is a professor in the Graduate School of Education, California State University, Long Beach.

Civil rights are legally enforceable claims to equal treatment. Under the United States Constitution, many such rights are enjoyed by citizen and noncitizen alike. One example is the Fourteenth Amendment, under which a state is forbidden to "deny any **person** within its jurisdiction the equal protection of the laws."

Any government can grant rights to persons or groups, or it may choose to annul such rights after a time. For many years, Americans had the legal right to own other human beings. The prospect of withdrawing this right led to the outbreak of the Civil War. The Thirteenth Amendment ended slavery.

Possessors of certain civil rights frequently are hesitant about extending such rights to others. The right to vote in America was for decades closely held by a tight little group of white, property-holding men. Large-scale movements of African-Americans and women arose to ultimately extend this right. The results of such efforts are embodied in the Fourteenth, Fifteenth, and Nineteenth Amendments (1868, 1870, 1920) and the Voting Rights Act (1965).

The Civil Rights movement of the 1950s through 1970s was a largely successful effort to solve certain enduring weaknesses of American democracy. It was conceived, organized, and led principally by African-Americans. In the North, some whites also joined in.

What were the aims of this movement?

In the area of civil rights, to be equal does not mean being the **same**. Rather, equal means to be of the **same worth**. In other words, people striving for civil rights insist that they be treated with the same respect as anyone else. The word dignity derives from the Latin word *dignus*, worthy. Being treated with dignity is thus to have one's human worth acknowledged. During the historic Civil Rights demonstrations of the 1960s, one was often struck by the overwhelming dignity of demonstrators whose message was simply: we are as good as you and deserve the same human consideration.

The Civil Rights movement thrived in the streets where imposing numbers were obvious. They had to resort to the streets because all the other arenas of power were closed to them. The courts, legislatures, executive offices—almost all were lily-white. The viewpoints of millions of people were simply not being heard and certainly they were not being consulted. Blacks, Hispanics, and other excluded people objected in the name of democracy. This keynote strengthened their stature as it appealed to many Americans outside the movement.

How was this growing support translated into specific laws and regulations that extended democracy in the United States? Six lines of action were discernible.

1. Create fairer patterns of living. Simply talking about better living would no longer do. Actual changes in day-to-day affairs needed to materialize.

2. Establish a more just distribution of political and community power. Having others speak for you would need to be replaced by people representing themselves.

3. Enforce the actual application of new patterns. Government would not remain content with the passage of resounding measures but would require practical implementation.

4. Broaden the types of activities meriting government protection. Governmental measures will be enacted to protect the rights of women, the disabled, of privacy, and others.

5. Minimize barriers to change. Education and information through mass media and school and colleges will deepen popular understanding.

6. Develop a politics of fairness. Insist that political parties discuss problems of creating a more just society and require that mass media repay their privileges by opening their facilities to broad ranges of opinion. Facilitate organization of congressional caucuses for a fairer society.

During the 1960s and 1970s, these lines of action penetrated many institutions, including schools and colleges.

Foremost was an effort to abolish racial discrimination based on segregation. New laws forbade the use of federal funds to discriminate against minorities. School districts were directed to desegregate when evidence in court established that the segregation was deliberately created. Segregation meant separateness, but it also almost always led to shortchanging minority children educationally.

Courts sought to make all public schools open to every child. After equal access was assured, other steps were taken: faculties were desegregated, compensatory education was made available to children who had been denied an equal education, special educational programs were opened to hitherto-excluded students, and discriminatory rules governing promotion and transfer were abolished.

. . . .

Between 1954 and 1973, the U.S. Supreme Court turned aside all appeals involving northern school segregation. The latter year, in a case involving Denver, the court extended its 1954 *Brown v. Board of*

From *Multicultural Education*, Spring 1994, pp. 13-16. © 1994 by the National Association for Multicultural Education. Reprinted by permission.

Education decision. Thereafter, a number of northern and western cities saw their segregated school systems undergo significant change. The greatest changes, North and South, occurred whenever federal courts, Congress, and the executive officer acted in the same spirit. This happened especially during the years 1968 through 1972.

Looking back at historical events, there is often a tendency to imagine that a certain inevitability was at work. Opposition to the changes is passed over, and thus the ease with which the new course occurred is exaggerated. It should not be forgotten, for example, that the central impetus for desegregation was the people whose children suffered most from segregation. Professional organizations of educators remained silent or even antagonistic. Professional journals of education, published by well-known universities, found little or no space to analyze the problems of segregation. In cities undergoing or facing desegregation battles, teacher unions most often supported school-board resistance to desegregation. Local newspapers and other mass media usually criticized desegregation advocates. Mayor Richard J. Daley of Chicago called Dr. Martin Luther King a Communist when the latter turned his attention to segregation in the North.

During the 1970s and 1980s, congressional ardor for civil rights cooled considerably. Federal agencies in charge of enforcement of civil rights statutes were pressed to ease up on school districts and other recipients of federal aid. Regulations governing procedures whereby new laws were to be implemented were watered down at congressional request. Always hanging over the heads of federal agencies concerned was a threat—frequently exercised—to cut agency budgets and thus hobble altogether a capacity to enforce the laws concerned. In state legislatures, parallel trends could be discerned.

During the 1980s, the federal courts retreated along a broad front of civil rights. The Supreme Court laid down standards for governmental action against racial discrimination that were almost impossible to document. These involved the manner in which a court needed to prove intention of officials to discriminate. By the close of the 1980s, the U.S. Department of Justice more frequently represented school officials than aggrieved minority parents in desegregation proceedings.

Major political candidates continue to avoid the subject of civil rights. In the election campaign of 1992, neither the Democrats nor the Republicans initiated any programmatic demand in the area of desegregation. Professional educators more or less follow the same pattern of inattention. You can search the texts of one school reform proposal after another and still not come up with a single demand in this area.

Inevitably, the meaning of civil rights has changed. For many years, mention of the term brought to mind Blacks and Whites. Thus, everyday controversy as well as more academic discourse assumed a black-white framework. Not only is this incorrect today; it has been so for decades.

During the first half of the present century, Mexican-American children and youth were educated under conditions of extreme segregation, especially in Texas. School boards did not hesitate to build three schools within a few blocks of each other, designating them explicitly for African-Americans, Mexican-Americans, and Whites. Schools built for the Blacks and Mexican-Americans were inferior to those for whites. Mexican-American parents and residents organized local protests, but little heed was paid them. Meanwhile, the children were subjected to various forms of discrimination inside the schools. It was a common practice to compel them to repeat early grades for their ethnicity rather than academic ability. In a number of districts, they were excluded from high schools. I.Q. exams were administered in English without an allowance for the unfamiliar language. Throughout the Southwest, school children were forbidden to speak Spanish, even while at play.

During World War II, some Mexican-Americans gained seats on local government agencies, where they could blunt at least some of the worst practices. After the war, Mexican-American veterans formed the American GI Forum which, during the next quarter-century, filed over 200 lawsuits against segregated schools. Parents protested at the unequal funding by the state of Texas of segregated elementary schools. Segregation and unequal funding were also attacked by the League of United Latin American Citizens (LULAC), the first Mexican-American national ethnic-protest organization. LULAC, founded in 1949, was a civil rights group that used legal and demonstrative tactics extensively.

• • • • • • • • • • • • •

Civil rights demonstrations were conducted throughout Mexican-American communities during the late 1960s and 1970s. Many dealt with school issues related to special ethnic themes, but as many or more were aimed at introducing democratic practices into the schools.

In March 1968, for example, thousands of students in five Los Angeles high schools boycotted the schools and made a number of demands. Some called for Mexican-American administrators in predominantly Mexican-American schools, com-

pulsory bilingual and bicultural education for Mexican-American students in such schools, and textbooks that would accurately and truthfully portray the life and history of Mexican-Americans, as well as other similar issues. In addition, however, they requested an end to homogeneous grouping, abolition of corporal punishment, and elimination of ROTC. The combination was characteristic of demands made by African-American students in contemporaneous civil rights actions.

Some five years after enactment of the Civil Rights Act of 1964, Mexican Americans began to benefit from the measure. Title VI of the law had outlawed the discriminatory use of federal funds on the grounds of national origin as well as race and color. Late in 1969, the federal Office for Civil Rights (OCR) began systematic exploration of discrimination against national origin minority group children. The next year, OCR issued a memorandum assigning school districts the affirmative obligation to provide special instruction whenever "inability to speak and understand the English language excludes national origin-minority group children from effective participation" in a district's educational program.

First applying this rule in Texas, OCR recommended errant districts offer bilingual programs. Because, however, the districts almost always regarded these measures as "extra," they sought outside funds rather than provide support from their regular budget. When federal funding for bilingual education fell far short of requests, little changed in the classrooms.

During the 1968 to 1972 period, the U.S. Commission on Civil Rights conducted the most detailed survey ever made of Mexican-American education. Its findings confirmed the essential characteristics of Mexican-American education in the United States: (1) a high degree of segregation, (2) an extremely low academic achievement, (3) a predominance of exclusionary practices by schools, and (4) a discriminatory use of public finance to the detriment of Mexican-American children. A quarter-century later, the situation continues to be marked by similar characteristics.

Asian Americans constitute another group which has pursued civil-rights methods in its century and a half of American history.

During the years 1850 to 1900, Chinese Americans were subjected to sweeping racial discrimination by federal, state, and local governments. Until 1882, Chinese were free to enter the United States as immigrants. They could not, however, become naturalized citizens as the federal Naturalization Act of 1790 reserved this right to Whites only. This law remained in force for more than a century and a half.

Only Asian-Americans born here could be citizens. In 1882, the Chinese Exclusion Act barred the further immigration of Chinese laborers and certain others. It was the first time in United States history that a specific racial-ethnic group was excluded by law. Further enactments were made by Congress to regulate or restrict Chinese-American immigrants, including a provision that they must carry an identification card; no other people were so required.

• • • • • • • • • • • • • •

Asian Americans sought protection of their civil rights in the courts. Historian Sucheng Chan reports that "tens of thousands of Asians sought justice through legal action." (See Asian Americans: An Interpretive History, Twayne, 1991, p. 90). According to Chan, over 90 percent of the cases dealt with the issue of immigrant exclusion. Two other subjects—naturalization and economic discrimination—covered the remaining cases. Chinese-Americans were also deprived of an equal opportunity to gain an education for most of their years here. California public schools for decades excluded Chinese students by state law. Nevertheless, Chinese continued to pay school taxes to support white attendance where their own children were turned away. Finally, Chinese-Americans were permitted to attend California schools, but not with white students. In the 1920s, a Chinese-American girl was refused admission to a white-only school in Mississippi. the U.S. Supreme Court upheld the exclusion.

Other Asian-Americans suffered similarly. During World War II, when some 120,000 Japanese Americans—most American citizens—were arrested and incarcerated in concentration camps, their children were given a sub-standard educa-

tion. This cataclysm was preceded by decades of discrimination in many areas of ordinary living. Both Chinese- and Japanese-Americans were not employed by large or small U.S. enterprises, even if they had earned a university degree in a field of relevant to such employment. In 1924, the latter were also excluded from further immigration.

As a result of the Spanish-American War, which ended in 1898, the American suppression of the Philippine revolt for independence, which followed immediately, a secular public school system was installed in the Philippines. The United States, however, refused to provide funds for operating it. Also withheld from the Philippines were any federal land grants to help finance the public schools. Previously, every new state had received such aid, which was indispensable in building a school system. As a result, only a weak foundation had been provided for the schools by 1946, when the Philippines became independent.

Asian Americans benefited in a major way from the civil rights movement after World War II. State laws restricting land ownership by them were stricken from the books. Asian Americans were no longer barred from naturalized-citizenship. The growth of the civil rights movement, including the Civil Rights Acts of 1964 and 1965, created a favorable atmosphere for a very major improvement in immigration law: In 1965, Congress passed a law ending discriminatory immigration quotas of Asian Americans and others. Until then, western Europeans were favored with high quotas and eastern Europeans, Asians, and Africans received low ones. Now, all countries receive the same basic quotas. Many civil rights groups fought for this change as did a number of ethnic and

immigrant organizations. Not least important, Asian Americans started to organize civil rights groups.

In the Japanese-American community, an effort was launched to bring about reparations payments to those who had been victimized during World War II. The campaign was successful. Chinese-Americans organized groups aiming to abolish discrimination in employment, particularly in public employment. Under affirmative-action requirements, Asian Americans were entitled to remedial action. The U.S. Commission on Civil Rights published reports documenting areas of American life in which discrimination against Asian Americans could still be found.

• • • • • • • • • • • • • •

This historical review suggests that a strong tie exists between the civil rights movement and multicultural education. Both are based on a powerful movement towards equality.

Multicultural education is teaching and learning about the equal human worth of distinctive groups of people acting in customary spheres of social life. As indicated in the opening paragraphs of this article, equal human worth is the core of civil rights concerns. So, too, is it of multicultural education. Mere plurality of cultures is not the heart of the matter. Diversity without equality is oppression. Nazi Germany contained Jews, Poles, foreign workers, and Serbs, as well as Germans. That did not make Germany a truly multicultural society. During the course of American history, multiculturalism has waxed and waned. It has never been stronger than it is today. But its future is far from assured.

TOWARD A COMMON DESTINY

Sandee Brawarsky

Is prejudice inevitable in America? Can young people learn tolerance and respect, instead of misunderstanding and hatred?

At a 1993 conference held under the auspices of the Common Destiny Alliance and supported by Carnegie Corporation, leading scholars in the behavioral and social sciences grappled with these and other questions. Their focus was on current research: what has been proven about the sources of prejudice and which strategies can work to prevent and ameliorate its poisonous impact.

Toward a Common Destiny: Improving Race and Ethnic Relations in America, edited by Willis D. Hawley and Anthony W. Jackson (San Francisco: Jossey-Bass Publishers, 496 pp., $45.00), grew out of that conference. A collection of seventeen papers, it presents the most up-to-date knowledge about the problem of racial and ethnic prejudice in the United States and identifies ways that individuals and organizations can act to reduce intolerance and discrimination. The book is written from a scholarly point of view, combining theoretical and develop-

mental perspectives with studies of effective practices. Its insights may be especially useful to researchers in pointing out an agenda for scientific inquiry, to educators and employers seeking to improve intergroup relations, and to decision makers who now have a more reliable basis for making wise social policy.

Admirably, *Toward a Common Destiny* is unusually coherent for a collection of essays written by experts in disparate fields. Hawley, a professor of education at the University of Maryland, and Jackson, a program officer at Carnegie Corporation, both express the hope that their volume will rekindle research interest in this field, which has dwindled since the early 1980s — mainly due to a lack of government and foundation commitment and funding.

In the 1990s, a generation after the Watts Riots and the Civil Rights Act of 1964, race relations are once again a national preoccupation as renewed debate over discrimination and affirmative action rages, and journalists and experts churn out popular books

with widely differing views. But as Jackson cautions: "One of the concerns we have is that the discussion of race and ethnic relations be based on knowledge — not just opinions or anecdotes." Serious study of racial and ethnic bias among young people is of urgent interest because of a growing tendency toward violence in the schools. Conflicts, as Jackson explains, "are exacerbated by the accessibility of weaponry."

America still seems to be a place where the skin color of people is of more interest than what Martin Luther King, Jr., labeled the "content of their character." As a report published by the National Academy of Sciences notes, "The status of black Americans today can best be characterized as a glass that is half full — if measured by progress since 1939 — or as a glass that is half empty — if measured by the persisting disparities between black and white Americans since the early 1970s."[1]

Hawley echoes: "There's no question that things are getting better . . .

From *Carnegie Quarterly,* Fall 1994/Winter 1995, pp. 1-4. Reprinted by permission of the Carnegie Corporation of New York, 437 Madison Avenue, New York, NY 10022.

but we still have a long way to reach our goal."

Developmental Processes in Children

What is known about how prejudice is acquired? Is it basic to human nature? How do young children pick up messages about people different from themselves? When are the key moments when young people are most open to positive messages about others?

Unfortunately, as Hawley remarks, there is nothing as simple as a vaccine to innoculate children against prejudice. For children, learning to differentiate among objects and to categorize is essential in cognitive development and perhaps, in ancient times, was necessary for survival. From a young age, as they learn the differences between "floor" and "ceiling" or "table" and "chair," they can also learn to distinguish between "us" and "them." Those first distinctions can be the roots of stereotypic thinking.

But as research demonstrates, there is a positive aspect, too. With early intervention, children can learn to be more "inclusive" in their categorizations. Studies show that the continuous exposure of young children, under favorable conditions, to people who differ from each other in language, culture, or ethnic origins can be influential in countering negative bias. Such positive interactions encourage children to feel greater empathy and to overlook unwarranted distinctions. Parents as well as teachers can play a key role in modeling such positive attitudes.

Hawley notes that most programs that start from the premise that "promoting positive relations among young children has positive consequences" are effective. However, only a limited number of such programs now exist, so that the chances of any but a few children benefiting from them are presently quite low.

---

¹ *A Common Destiny*, by J. Jaynes and R. Williams (Washington, D.C.: National Academy of Sciences, 1989).

Adolescence and Identity Formation

In the developmental chain from early childhood to adolescence, the possibilities multiply for both learning and intensifying prejudice. In fact, adolescence is the critical time for the formation of racial and ethnic identity. Influenced by parents, teachers, peers, and the media, individuals challenge views they internalized earlier, form opinions, make decisions, and may altogether reshape the way they perceive themselves, the world, and their futures.

In an illuminating chapter, "Race, Ethnicity, and the Defiance of Categories," linguistic anthropologist Shirley Brice Heath of Stanford University illustrates how racial and ethnic identification is not clear-cut for many urban youngsters. The young people she interviewed recognize "diversities within diversity"; they see themselves as "of color" or "kinda' all ethnic."

Although some educators believe that group differences should be minimized to reduce tensions, others believe that such an approach is unlikely to foster true "color blindness" and that it is healthier for adolescents to be anchored in an understanding and appreciation of their ethnic and racial background. As Jackson points out, a dialogue between cultures is more authentic when every group is aware of its own culture.

But recognizing the importance of strong racial and ethnic identification raises a paradox: How can parents and educators encourage the development of a strong racial and ethnic identity, with the accompanying feelings of pride, connectedness, and self-respect, that does not result in the denigration of other races and groups?

How can ethnicity be supported without encouraging intergroup tensions? How can young people be helped through this sensitive and complicated quandary?

As the contributors point out, there are some answers — or the beginnings of answers — but much additional research is needed. As suggested,

meaningful intergroup contact on an ongoing basis is the key to positive identification with a particular group and to improved relations with other groups. Single meetings that have more to do with expressing feelings than with working together are not effective, and can even backfire.

Cooperative Learning and Multicultural Education

One technique that does work is cooperative learning. Proven successful in reducing prejudice as well as improving students' academic achievement, cooperative learning emphasizes teamwork. Within small, diverse groups that meet regularly to work on joint projects, group members share equal status and get to know one another as individuals, with friendship an additional benefit. Social contacts, whether in extracurricular school activities, like athletics, or in community-based programs, can also provide young people opportunities for high-quality cross-race contacts.

Other findings demonstrate gains from school programs that promote the "ideology of multiculturalism" — not just for minority youth but for all. If "multicultural competence" is to be a goal of education, what, exactly, does multiculturalism refer to? In general usage, it has become a catch-all term for acceptance of cultures that stand outside of the mainstream. In his chapter, "Multicultural Education and the Modification of Students' Racial Attitudes," James A. Banks, professor of education and director of the Center for Multicultural Education at the University of Washington, Seattle, offers a lucid definition of multicultural education: "A restructuring and transformation of the total school environment so that it reflects the racial and cultural diversity that exists within U.S. society and helps children from diverse groups to experience educational equality."

More than just curricular reform, multicultural education involves using content from a variety of cultures as illustrations in every subject area, teaching students how knowledge is created and influenced, encouraging the development of democratic attitudes and values, and employing techniques to facilitate the academic achievement of students from diverse backgrounds.

Much depends on the teachers. To engage their students in cooperative learning, they need specialized training: to address the needs of a diverse student population, teachers need to be multiculturally literate. As Kenneth Zeichner, professor of teacher education at the University of Wisconsin, writes in his essay, "Preparing Educators for Cross-Cultural Teaching," very little is being done to prepare teachers to work with culturally and linguistically diverse students. He charges that teacher education for diversity necessitates significant change at the teacher training institutes.

In the book's final section, Hawley and four other contributors collaborate to present a set of thirteen principles of program design, to be used either to evaluate existing programs or as guidelines for creating new ones. The first principle, which Hawley emphasizes, is that context means a lot. Strategies should address both institutional and individual sources of prejudice in the situations in which participants live, learn, and work.

Other principles emphasize the importance of the involvement of those in authority, careful training, the inclusion and consideration of all racial and ethnic groups, and ongoing evaluation of outcomes.

More Questions for Research

Editors Hawley and Jackson, along with all of the contributing scholars, assert the need for ongoing, serious research to create a solid foundation for new programs to foster positive intergroup relations. Most of the important studies are now fifteen years old and require updating to take into consideration societal changes. Significantly, much previous research focuses on black-white relations, without addressing multicultural identities and settings.

Aspiring "to achieve a common destiny worth striving for," Jackson focuses the research agenda on young people and opportunities in school and other places they frequent. He believes there is much to be learned from young people themselves about how they have already found ways to get along with others. "It's important to draw lessons from them," he explains, "and not just impose on them."

What patterns of contact already exist, and how can they be replicated on larger scales? Why are some children more successful than others in developing complex, integrated identities? What is the impact of the environment? How can a holistic approach to effective educational policy be designed? Can intergroup relations be improved without also addressing the basic economic and social inequalities of American society? In his essay, Jackson targets several priority areas for future research: curriculum, school organization, teacher development, student assessment, school governance, and the involvement of parents and community leaders.

Both Hawley and Jackson express optimism about chances for positive change. "It's inevitable," Jackson says, "that people from diverse backgrounds will need to be involved and engaged with each other. . . . New strategies can be crafted to create good relations. There's nothing on the horizon that makes it seem that negative outcomes are inevitable." Hawley agrees, adding: "There's no question if we put any effort into it, things would get better."

Jackson's own experience as an adolescent underlines his hopeful point of view. Growing up in California, he encountered "culture shock" when he switched from elementary school — which was 95 percent African-American — to middle school — which was 95 percent Anglo-American. That he quickly formed friendships, which proved to be long-lasting, with students from different cultures made him realize that conflicts were avoidable. "There's got to be a way to have cross-cultural positive relationships extended on a larger scale."

The Corporation, Jackson explains, is considering initiating a program of grantmaking to stimulate new research in intergroup relations focusing on children and adolescents. It may try to develop collaborations with foundations and government agencies to stimulate both research and program development.

As several contributors to *Toward a Common Destiny* maintain, the dearth of research and the indifference of policymakers to what is known about the formation of racial attitudes is foolhardy. Much is at stake. In the year 2020, about 46 percent of the nation's school-age youths will be of color. Understanding the origins of bias and working to eliminate it — breaking the cycle of distrust, prejudice, and violence — may determine whether the nation is strengthened or its very fabric is torn.

For information:

Anthony W. Jackson, Carnegie Corporation of New York, and Willis D. Hawley, Dean, College of Education and Professor of Education, University of Maryland, College Park, MD 20742.

The Importance of Education...

...and how his education helped turn the tide for Indian people.

John Echohawk, JD

John Echohawk, a Pawnee, is the Executive Director of the Native American Rights Fund. He was the first graduate of the University of New Mexico's special program to train Indian lawyers, and, while in law school, was a founding member of the American Indian Law Students Association. He serves on the Boards of the American Indian Resources Institute, the Association on American Indian Affairs, the National Committee for Responsive Philanthropy, the National Resources Defense Council, and the National Center for American Indian Enterprise Development. He has received numerous service awards and other recognition for his leadership in the Indian law field. He has been named one of the 100 most influential lawyers in the United States by the National Law Journal.

I want to tell you about the importance of education from my experience and hope that it will help all youth in achieving their education. I tell Indian youth that becoming an educated person is the most important thing that they can ever do for themselves, their families and their Tribes.

My parents always stressed the importance of an education. There are six children in our family and we all received an education. So our parents must have taught us well.

They told us that we had to prepare to support ourselves and be self-sufficient when we grew up. The best way to do that, they said, was to get an education. They taught us that with a good education we could get good jobs to support ourselves and our families. They told us that someone without an education would have a hard time doing that.

I think the reasons my parents taught us this were that neither of them had a great deal of education and they knew how difficult it was to provide for a family.

My father, a full-blood Pawnee from Oklahoma, had two years of college, and gradually built a successful land surveying business that sustained the family. My mother, a non-Indian, had a high school education.

I grew up in Farmington, New Mexico, a small town in the northwestern part of the state surrounded by the Navajo, Ute Mountain, Southern Ute, and Jicarilla Apache reservations. Since most Indian students attended Bureau of Indian Affairs schools or missionary schools, I was one of the few Indian students in the public schools that I attended. As a result, I learned to compete in school with non-Indians.

I kept pace with my schoolwork and made good grades. I wanted to do well enough to be able to enter college, which I did in 1963. I also realized that I could be a lawyer, so I set my goal to go to law school after I finished college. In 1967, I graduated from the University of New Mexico with a bachelor's degree in Government, and in 1970 I graduated from the University of New Mexico (UNM) School of Law.

It would have been much more difficult for me if I had not had scholarship assistance from the Santa Fe Railway Foundation in undergraduate school and the federal Office of Economic Opportunity (the precursor to the Administration for Native Americans in the Administration for Children and Families) in Law School. I also worked part-time during undergraduate school. I believe that I would have worked more and gone to school part-time if necessary, even though it would have taken longer to graduate.

I strongly encourage Indian youth to seek out grants, take out loans, work part-time, or go to school part-time in order to get their college educations. I point out that youths must be determined not to let financial difficulties stop them from getting an education.

I often worried that I was not as smart as the other students and would not be able to compete with them intellectually. I learned that good study habits and hard work often prevailed because some students just were not willing to put in the time necessary to be successful in college. I would sometimes think of the time that I spent studying as clearly preferable to spending that same time working at some menial, dead-end job that I could have without an education.

I was the first Indian to graduate from UNM, even though New Mexico has always had a substantial Indian population. I also learned that I was one of only a handful of Indian lawyers in the whole country.

To be proportionately represented in the legal profession at that time, there should have been a thousand Indian lawyers. It was this need that the Federal Office of Economic Opportunity was trying to address in offering scholarships to Indian college graduates to go to law school. I was

From *Children Today*, Vol. 23, No. 1, 1994, pp. 30-32. Reprinted by permission of *Children Today*, a publication of the Administration for Children and Families, U.S. Department of Health and Human Services.

fortunate to receive such a scholar-ship.

One of the subjects in law school that the Indian law students were introduced to was a new, developing field of law called Indian Law. It dealt with Indian treaties and other Federal laws governing the rights of Indian people.

I had never studied or been exposed to this field of law and its legal history and neither had the other Indian law students. As we studied Indian law and also learned more about the legal process, we realized that Indians had substantial rights that were going unaddressed. These rights were not being enforced largely because Indians did not have lawyers.

Since most Indians are poor, they simply could not afford legal represen-tation, which is necessary under this legal system to enforce their rights.

I realized that I was one of the few Indians in the country who was educated about the Indian legal situation, and I felt a special responsi-bility to help our Indian people legally. The other Indian students felt the same way.

After graduating from law school in 1970, I worked with some non-Indian lawyers and Tribal leaders to organize the Native American Rights Fund (NARF), a national Indian legal organization that would eventually raise funds as a non-profit charity, hire lawyers expert in Indian law, and make them available to those Tribes with the most important cases who could not afford attorneys. In the 24 years since that time, millions of dollars have been raised to make legal representation possible in thousands of major cases upholding Indian rights.

I currently serve as Executive Director of the Native American Rights Fund in Boulder, Colorado. Because most Indian Tribes are situated in the West, our offices are located in a central western location. NARF also has an office in Washington, D.C., in order to deal with the Federal govern-ment and serve Eastern Tribes, as well as an office in Anchorage, Alaska, to better serve Alaska Native clients.

We have an annual budget of $6.7

million and a staff of 45 people, which includes 16 lawyers, 11 of whom are Native American attorneys. We are the largest law firm devoted to Indian law in the country. NARF has more Indian attorneys than any other firm or organization.

The NARF Board of Directors consists of 13 Indian people from different parts of the country who are knowledgeable and involved in Indian and legal and political affairs. The Board represents about 75 Tribes and has cases in about 25 states.

The Native American Rights Fund is commemorating its 25th anniver-sary next year. I believe that the organization has played a major role in the Indian rights movement, which began in the 1960s and has resulted in the recognition of Indian rights today.

Much of this recognition of Native American rights has come through the courts, where there has been more Indian litigation in the last 25 years than there was in the previous 200 years. The courts have reviewed treaties and other federal laws that benefit Indians, and they have, for the most part, enforced those promises in favor of the Indians. The Native American Rights Fund has been involved in most of the major Indian litigation during this time.

Education has been important not only to me personally, but to the Indian Tribes across the country.

Before learning how to use the legal process and a litigation strategy to help Indian people in the 1960s, Indian Tribes had been powerless to stop a Federal Indian policy in Washington that was gradually terminating Tribes, one by one. The white political leaders thought that they knew what was best for Indians. This type of paternalistic policy ignored the wishes of Tribal leaders to maintain their Tribes and to have the Federal government fulfill the treaty promises to protect and assist the Tribes. Litigation finally forced the Federal government to do that for the benefit of the Tribes.

As a result of these changes, a modern day definition and understand-ing of Indian Tribes has emerged.

Indian Tribes are governments within the American political system, along with state governments and their subdivisions and the Federal govern-ment.

Everyone is familiar with the concept of Indian treaties, which were made between sovereign governments. Legally, Indian Tribes were then, and still are, recognized as sovereign governments with the power to govern their own affairs.

Treaties and Federal laws did place some limits on this sovereign Tribal governmental authority that the Tribes have had since time immemorial, but Tribal governmental status exists today. Government-to-government relationships exist today between the Tribal governments and the Federal government, and between the Tribal governments and the state govern-ments.

Tribal governments have developed rapidly since the 1960s, when the courts began upholding Tribal sover-eignty in Indian court cases, and Congress accepted Indian self-determination as the new Federal Indian policy replacing the old Tribal termination and assimilation policy.

These Tribal governments have largely displaced Federal Bureau of Indian Affairs officials as the decision-makers on Indian reservations — bringing back the period when Indian Nations managed their own affairs before non-Indian control was im-posed. Tribal legislators, Tribal courts, Tribal police, and Tribal bureaucrats now routinely carry out governmental functions and increasingly provide governmental services to reservation residents.

Elected Tribal leaders are called upon to make all of the social, eco-nomic, and political decisions for their Tribal governments, just as state and Federal elected officials must do for their governments.

The importance of education for Native youth and their Tribes has taken on new dimensions in this modern era of Indian self-determina-tion, in which Indian Tribes have taken their rightful place among the councils of governments in this country. Tribal governments are becoming increasingly sophisticated and are involved in a growing range of governmental functions, including taxation and environmental regulation.

To properly carry out these responsibilities and programs, tribal governments need trained, educated Indian people who can perform the Tribal jobs and do them in ways that respect and integrate Tribal tradition and culture. College educated Indians have increasingly filled those jobs for Tribal governments, but more college educated youths are needed as the challenges grow.

I believe there are terrific opportunities out there for young Indian students who want to get an education and use it to help their own Indian people in these modern times.

There was a time when people thought that Indians could not be educated or did not want to be educated. As more and more Indians graduate from college today, that myth is destroyed. Indian students are just as capable of getting a college degree as other students.

The key to getting that degree is **motivation.** Wherever they are in schools across the nation, Indian students should be motivated to participate in the opportunities and challenges that exist for their Tribal governments in this modern era, where the Indian world still exists, is gaining recognition, and will play an increasingly important role nationally and internationally in the future.

ONE NATION, ONE LANGUAGE?

Would making English the nation's official language unite the country or divide it?

For a Sherman Oaks, Calif., election worker, the last straw was hanging campaign posters in six languages and six alphabets. For a taxpayer in University Park, Texas, it was a requirement that all employees of the local public utility speak Spanish. For a retired schoolteacher from Mount Morris, N.Y., it was taking her elderly and anxious mother to a Pakistani doctor and understanding only a fraction of what he said.

As immigration, both legal and illegal, brings a new flood of foreign speech into the United States, a campaign to make English the nation's official language is gathering strength. According to a new *U.S. News* poll, 73 percent of Americans think English should be the official language of government. House Speaker Newt Gingrich, Senate Majority Leader Bob Dole and more than a third of the members of Congress support proposed federal legislation that would make English America's official tongue; twenty-two states and a number of municipalities already have English-only laws on the books.

Like flag burning and the Pledge of Allegiance, the issue is largely symbolic. Without ever being declared official, American English has survived—and enriched itself from—four centuries of immigration. It is not much easier for today's Guatemalan immigrant to get a good education and a good job without learning English than it was for his Italian, Polish or Chinese predecessors. And at best, eliminating bilingual education might save about a dollar per student per day. But many Americans are feeling threatened by a triple whammy of growing economic uncertainty, some of it caused by foreign competition; rising immigration, much of it illegal; and political pressure to cater to the needs of immigrants rather than letting them sink or swim. "Elevating English as an icon," says author and bilingual expert James Crawford, "has appeal for the insecure and the resentful. It provides a clear answer to the question: Who belongs?"

Nation of strangers. There is no question that America is undergoing another of its periodic diversity booms. According to the Census Bureau, in 1994 8.7 percent of Americans were born in other countries, the highest percentage since before World War II. More tellingly, at least 31.8 million people in the United States speak a language other than English at home. Of the children returning to urban public schools this fall, a whopping one third speak a foreign language first. "It blows your mind," says Dade County, Fla., administrator Mercedes Toural, who counts 5,190 new students speaking no fewer than 56 different tongues.

English-only advocates, whose ranks include recent immigrants and social liberals, believe that accommodating the more than 300 languages spoken in the United States undercuts incentives to learning English and, by association, to becoming an American. Massachusetts offers driver's tests in 24 foreign languages, including Albanian, Finnish, Farsi, Turkish and Czech. Federal voting rights laws provide for ballots in multiple translations. Internal Revenue Service forms are printed in Spanish.

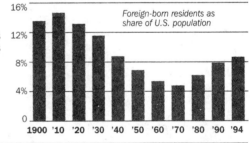

A LANDSLIDE FOR OFFICIAL ENGLISH

Coming to America. *An immigrant family at Ellis Island in 1920*

A rising tide
A larger share of Americans were foreign born earlier in this century, but the percentage is again on the rise.

Foreign-born residents as share of U.S. population

16%
12%
8%
4%
0

1900 '10 '20 '30 '40 '50 '60 '70 '80 '90 '94

USN&WR—Basic data: U.S. Census Bureau
ROBERT KEMP—USN&WR

■ **American voters who favor making English the official language of government (for instance, printing government forms only in English):**

FAVOR: 73% OPPOSE: 23%

■ **Voters who favor legislation that would prohibit bilingual election ballots and swearing-in ceremonies:**

FAVOR: 50% OPPOSE: 43%

U.S. News poll of 1,000 registered voters conducted by Celinda Lake of Lake Research and Ed Goeas of the Tarrance Group on Sept. 11-13, 1995. Margin of error: plus or minus 3.1 percent. Percentages may not add up to 100 because some respondents answered, "Don't know."

And in Westminster, Calif., members of Troop 2194 of the Boy Scouts of America can earn their merit badges in Vietnamese. "It's completely insane," says Mauro Mujica, the chairman of the lobbying group U.S. English and himself an immigrant from Chile. "We are not doing anybody any favors."

Pulling the plug. The proposed official-

From *U.S. News & World Report,* September 25, 1995, pp. 38-42. © 1995 by U.S. News & World Report. Reprinted by permission.

English laws range from the barely noticeable to the almost xenophobic. A bill introduced by Missouri Republican Rep. Bill Emerson would mandate English for government use but provide exceptions for health, safety and civil and criminal justice. Although it is the most viable of the bunch, it would change the status quo so little that it begs the question of why it is needed at all. The most extreme official-English measures would pull the plug on what their sponsors consider linguistic welfare, ending bilingual education and bilingual ballots.

Advocates of official-English proposals deny that their measures are draconian. Says U.S. English's Mujica: "We are simply saying that official documents should be in English and money saved on translations could go to help the people learn English. We're saying you could still take a driver's test in another language, but we suggest it be temporary till you learn English."

U.S. English, which reports 600,000 contributors, was founded by the late U.S. Sen. S. I. Hayakawa, a Japanese-American linguistics professor, and boasts advisory board members such as Saul Bellow and Alistair Cooke. The group was tarred eight years ago when its founder, John Tanton, wrote a memo suggesting that Hispanics have "greater reproductive powers" than Anglos; two directors quit, Tanton was forced out and the group has been rebuilding its reputation ever since. Its competitor, English First, whose founder, Larry Pratt, also started Gun Owners of America, is more hard-line.

Defenders of bilingual education, multilingual ballots and other government services ask whether legal immigrants will vote if there are no bilingual ballots. If foreign speakers can't read the street signs, will they be allowed to drive? Such thoughts bring Juanita Morales, a Houston college student, to tears. "This just sets up another barrier for people," she says. "My parents don't know English, and I can hardly speak Spanish anymore and that's painful to me."

Go it alone, the hard-liners reply, the way our grandfathers did. But these advocates don't mention that there is little, if any, evidence that earlier German or Italian immigrants mastered English any faster than the current crop of Asians, Russians and Central Americans. And it's hard to argue that today's newcomers aren't trying. San Francisco City College teaches English to 20,000 adults every semester, and the waiting list is huge. In De Kalb County, Ga. 7,000 adults are studying English; in Brighton Beach, N.Y., 2,000 wait for a chance to learn it.

The economic incentives for learning English seem as clear as ever. Yes, you can earn a good living in an ethnic enclave of Chicago speaking nothing but Polish. But you won't go far. "Mandating English," says Ron Pearlman of Chicago, "is like mandating that the sun is going to come up every day. It just seems to me that it's going to happen."

What worries many Americans are efforts to put other languages on a par with English, which often come across as assaults on American or Western culture. Americans may relish an evening at a Thai restaurant or an afternoon at a Greek festival, but many are less comfortable when their children are celebrating Cinco de Mayo, Kwanzaa and Chinese New Year along with Christmas in the public schools. In Arlington, Va., a classically trained orchestra teacher quit the public school system rather than cave in to demands to teach salsa music.

But diversity carries the day. The U.S. Department of Education policy is not simply to promote learning of English but also to *maintain* immigrants' native tongues. And supporters of that policy make a good case for it. "People ask me if I'm embarrassed I speak Spanish," says Martha Quintanilla Hollowell, a Dallas County, Texas, district attorney. "I tell them I'd be more embarrassed if I spoke only one language."

Language skills. That may be what's most disturbing about the English-only sentiment: In a global economy, it's the monolingual English speakers who are falling behind. Along with computer skills, a neat appearance and a work ethic, Americans more and more are finding that a second language is useful in getting a good job. African-Americans in Dade County, now more than half Hispanic, routinely lose tourism positions to bilingual Cubans. Schoolteachers cry foul because bilingual teachers earn more money while monolingual teachers are laid off. "There is no way I could get a job in the Los Angeles public schools today," says Lucy Fortney, an elementary school teacher for 30 years.

The proliferation of state and local English-only laws has led to a flurry of language-discrimination lawsuits and a record number of complaints with the U.S. Equal Employment Opportunity Commission. Ed Chen, a lawyer with the San Francisco office of the American Civil Liberties Union, says clients have been denied credit and insurance because they don't speak English. But courts increasingly have endorsed laws that call for exclusive use of English on the job. Officials at New York's Bellevue Hospital, where the vast majority of nurses are Filipino, say an English-only law was necessary because nurses spoke Tagalog among themselves.

Other employers have wielded English-only laws as a license to discriminate, giving rise to fears that a national law would encourage more of the same. A judge in Amarillo, Texas, claimed a

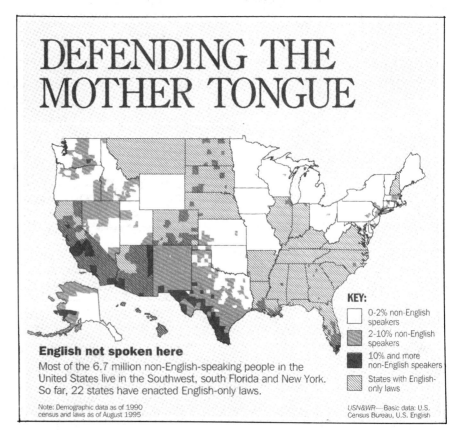

DEFENDING THE MOTHER TONGUE

English not spoken here

Most of the 6.7 million non-English-speaking people in the United States live in the Southwest, south Florida and New York. So far, 22 states have enacted English-only laws.

Note: Demographic data as of 1990 census and laws as of August 1995

KEY:

☐ 0-2% non-English speakers

▨ 2-10% non-English speakers

■ 10% and more non-English speakers

▧ States with English-only laws

USN&WR—Basic data: U.S. Census Bureau, U.S. English

mother in a custody case was committing "child abuse" by speaking Spanish to her child at home. Another Texas judge denied probation to a drunk driver because he couldn't benefit from the all-English Alcoholics Anonymous program. In Monterey Park, Calif., a citizens' group tried to ban Chinese signs on businesses that served an almost all-Asian clientele. In Dade County, a since-repealed English-only law was so strict that it forbade using public funds to pay for court translations and bilingual signs to warn metrorail riders against electrocution.

Though it is not intended as such, the English-first movement is a reminder of a history of prejudice toward speakers of foreign tongues. Many American Indians were prohibited from speaking their own languages. The Louisiana Legislature banned the use of Cajun French in public schools in 1912, but instead of abandoning their culture, many Cajuns dropped out of school and never learned English.

French was finally allowed back in the schools in the 1960s. As recently as 1971, it was illegal to speak Spanish in a public school building in Texas, and until 1923 it was against the law to teach foreign languages to elementary school pupils in Nebraska. At Ellis Island, psychologists tested thousands of non-English-speaking immigrants exclusively in English and pronounced them retarded.

Champions of diversity say it's high time Americans faced the demographic facts. In Miami, with leading trade partners Colombia and Venezuela, businesses would be foolish to restrict themselves to English. If emergency services suffer because of a shortage of foreign-speaking 911 operators, it is downright dangerous not to hire more. As for embattled teachers, Rick Lopez of the National Association of Bilingual Education says: "Why should we expect students to learn a new language if teachers can't do the

same? We have to change the product to fit the market. The market wants a Toyota and we're still building Edsels."

Many Americans still value the melting pot: General Mills's new Betty Crocker is a digitized, multiethnic composite. But Skokie, Ill., educator Charlene Cobb, for one, prefers a colorful mosaic. "You don't have to change yourself," she says, "to make a whole thing that's very beautiful." The question is whether the diverse parts of America still make up a whole.

BY SUSAN HEADDEN WITH LINDA RODRIGUEZ BERNFELD AND SALLY DENEEN IN MIAMI, MISSY DANIEL IN BOSTON, MONIKA GUTTMAN IN LOS ANGELES, BARBARA BURGOWER HORDERN IN HOUSTON, SCOTT MINERBROOK IN NEW YORK, DEBRA A. SCHWARTZ IN CHICAGO AND JILL JORDAN SIEDER IN ATLANTA

THE IMMIGRATION BATTLE

Closing the golden door

California Gov. Pete Wilson's bid for re-election last year was in trouble. Polls had him behind by as much as 23 percent. Then the Republican discovered Proposition 187, a ballot measure that sought to cut off most government services for illegal immigrants. Wilson's popularity soared, and he breezed to victory in November.

Many politicians are now trying to appeal to the nation's uneasiness about immigrants. "When we got here," says White House aide Rahm Emanuel, "the border looked like swiss cheese. We've spent two years plugging holes." But some legislators and presidential hopefuls want to reduce the flow of legal, as well as illegal, immigrants. In June, the U.S. Commission on Immigration Reform concluded that re-

ducing legal immigration is in the "national interest." President Clinton surprised immigration advocates by calling the commission's findings "consistent with my views."

Congress, too, is following the commission's lead. The House Judiciary Committee this week considers a bill by Republican Rep. Lamar Smith of Texas that would crack down on illegal immigration — through steps such as doubling the Border Patrol and stiffening penalties for bogus documents — and would reduce legal immigration by about 20 percent, to 535,000 a year. GOP Sen. Alan Simpson of Wyoming held hearings last week on legislation that closely resembles Smith's bill.

Undue burden? Critics say there is no evidence that legal immigrants are placing an undue burden on society. Frank

Sharry of the National Immigration Forum, a pro-immigration group, says the commission "is still trying to come up with a rationale for their cuts." Michael Fix of the Urban Institute says data on the costs and benefits of legal immigration are scarce and unreliable. As a result, he says: "These limits are culturally or politically driven choices."

Still, Smith and Simpson think the numbers are on their side. "Over the past 12 years, the number of legal immigrants applying for supplemental security income has increased by 580 percent," Smith says. Simpson, meanwhile, feels the country needs a "breathing space" to absorb a recent uptick in new residents. Indeed, the Census Bureau reported last month that 20 percent of the country's foreign-born population arrived in the past five years.

The Smith and Simpson bills also would eliminate several visa categories. Both give priority to "nuclear family"

members — spouses and minor children of current citizens and legal residents — but parents, siblings and adult children would no longer be eligible for permanent residency. Last week Doris Meissner, head of the Immigration and Naturalization Service, said the Clinton administration opposes that strategy: "We are arguing for parents to be in the scheme, along with adult married and unmarried children, so that the core family unit is maintained."

A crackdown on illegal immigration is a virtual certainty; restrictions on legal immigration are not so certain. More than 100 co-sponsors have signed on to Smith's bill. But House Majority Leader Dick Armey of Texas believes legal immigration is good for the economy, and other prominent Republicans such as Jack Kemp and Texas Gov. George W. Bush also support legal immigration. The battle is just beginning.

DAVID BOWERMASTER

Tongue-tied in the schools

Bilingual education began as a good idea. Now it needs fixing

Javier Sanchez speaks English like the proud American he is. Born in Brooklyn, N.Y., the wiry 12-year-old speaks English at home, and he speaks it on the playground. He spoke it in the classroom, too—until one day in the third grade, when he was abruptly moved to a program that taught him in Spanish all but 45 minutes a day. "It was a disaster," says his Puerto Rican-born mother, Dominga Sanchez. "He didn't *understand* Spanish." Sanchez begged the teacher to return her son to his regular class. Her request was met with amazement. "Why?" the teacher asked. "Don't you feel proud to be Hispanic?"

Along with crumbling classrooms and violence in the hallways, bilingual education has emerged as one of the dark spots on the grim tableau of American public education. Started 27 years ago to help impoverished Mexican-Americans, the program was born of good intentions, but today it has mushroomed into a $10 billion-a-year bureaucracy that not only cannot promise that students will learn English but may actually do some children more harm than good. Just as troubling, while children like Javier are placed in programs they don't want and may not need, thousands more children are foundering because they get no help with English at all.

Bilingual education was intended to give new immigrants a leg up. During earlier waves of immigration, children who entered American schools without speaking English were left to fend for themselves. Many thrived, but others, feeling lost and confused, did not. Their failures led to Title VII of the Elementary and Secondary Education Act, which ensured supplementary services for all non-English-speaking newcomers to America.

Armenian to Urdu. Significantly, the law did not prescribe a method for delivering those services. But today, of the funds used to help children learn English, 75 percent of federal money—and the bulk of state and local money—goes toward classes taught in students' native tongues; only 25 percent supports programs rooted in English. That makes bilingual education the de facto law of the land.

Historically, Hispanics have been the largest beneficiaries of bilingual education. Today, however, they compete for funding with new immigrant groups whose urge to assimilate, some educators say, may be stronger. Further, not many school districts can offer classes in such languages as Armenian and Urdu. So for practical reasons, too, children of other nationalities are placed in English-based classes more often than children of Hispanics. The problem, as many see it, is that students are staying in native-language programs far too long. In a typical complaint, the mother of one New York ninth grader says her daughter has been in "transitional" bilingual education for nine years. "We support bilingual education," says Ray Domanico of the New York Public Education Association. "But it is becoming an institutionalized ghetto."

Learning Chinese. In theory, bilingual education is hard to fault. Students learn math, science and other "content" subjects in their native tongues, and they take special English classes for a small part of the day. When they are ready, ideally within three or four years, they switch to classes taught exclusively in English. The crucial advantage is that students don't fall behind in their other lessons while gaining competence in English. Further, supporters claim, bilingual education produces students fluent in two languages.

That would be great, if it were true. Too often it is not. What is sometimes mistaken for dual-language instruction is actually native-language instruction, in which students hear English for as little as 30 minutes a day. "Art, physical education and music are supposed to be taught in English," says Lucy Fortney, a third-grade teacher from Sun Valley, Calif. "But that is absolutely not happening at all."

Assignments to bilingual programs are increasingly a source of complaint. Many students, parents say, are placed in bilingual classes not because they can't understand English but because they don't read well. They need remedial, not bilingual, help. Others wind up in bilingual programs simply because there is no room in regular classes. Luz Pena says her third-grade son, born in America, spoke excellent English until he was moved to a bilingual track. Determined to avoid such problems with her daughter, she registered her for English kindergarten—only to be told the sole vacancies were in the Spanish class.

In some cases, the placements seem to defy common sense. In San Francisco, because of a desegregation order, some English-speaking African-Americans end up in classes taught partly in Chinese. Chinese-speakers, meanwhile, have been placed in classes taught partly in Spanish. Presented with evidence that blacks in bilingual programs scored well below other blacks on basic skills tests, school officials recently announced an end to the practice.

Whether a child is placed in a bilingual program can turn on criteria as arbitrary as whether his name is Miller or Martinez. In Utah, federal records show that the same test scores that identified some students as "limited English proficient" (LEP) were used to identify others as learning disabled. The distinction depended on the student's ethnic group: Hispanics were designated LEP, while Native Americans who spoke Navajo or

From *U.S. News & World Report*, September 25, 1995, pp. 44-46. © 1995 by U.S. News & World Report. Reprinted by permission.

Ute were labeled learning disabled. In New York City, where public schools teach children in 10 different languages, enrollment in bilingual education has jumped by half since 1989, when officials raised the cut-off on a reading test. Critics say that 40 percent of *all* children are likely to fail the test—whether they speak English or not.

Misplacement, however, is only part of the problem. At least 25 percent of LEP students, according to the U.S. Department of Education, get no special help at all. Other children are victims of a haphazard approach. In Medford, Ore., LEP students received English training anywhere from three hours a day, five days a week to 30 minutes a day, three days a week. The results? Of 12 former LEP students reviewed by education department officials, seven had two or more F's and achievement scores below the 20th percentile. Four more had D's and test scores below the 30th percentile. In Twin Falls, Idaho, three high-school teachers had no idea that their students needed any help with English, despite their obvious LEP background and consistently failing grades.

Poorly trained teachers further complicate the picture. Nationwide, the shortage of teachers trained for bilingual-education programs is estimated at 170,000. The paucity of qualified candidates has forced desperate superintendents to waive some credentialing requirements and recruit instructors from abroad. The result is teachers who themselves struggle with English. "You can hardly understand them," said San Francisco teacher Gwen Carmen. In Duchesne, Utah, two teachers' aides admitted to education department inspectors that they had no college credits, no instructional materials and no idea what was expected of them.

What all these problems add up to is impossible to say precisely, but one statistic is hard to ignore. The high-school dropout rate for Hispanic students is nearly 30 percent. It remains by far the highest of any ethnic group—four times that of whites, three times that of blacks—and it has not budged since bilingual education began.

Although poverty and other problems contribute to the disappointing numbers, studies suggest that confining Hispanic students to Spanish-only classrooms also may be a significant factor. A New York study, published earlier this year, determined that 80 percent of LEP students who enrolled in English-immersion classes graduated to mainstream English within three years, while only half the students in bilingual classes tested out that quickly. A similar study released last fall by the state of

A COSTLY SURGE IN BILINGUAL COURSES

A growth industry
About 3 million students are designated as limited English proficient (LEP), 45% of them in California. Some $156 million in federal money supports an estimated 600,000 LEP students; others are funded by states and local agencies.

Pupils enrolled in language-assistance programs (estimated)

1972 '74 '76 '78 '80 '82 '84 '86 '88 '90 '92

USN&WR–Basic data: U.S. Dept. of Education
ROBERT KEMP–USN&WR

English, Spanish and others
Of the students in the nation's two largest cities, the native languages spoken are–

New York: 1.03 million total students

English 84.2%
Spanish 10.7%

Total other: 5.1%	
Chinese	1.3%
Russian	0.8%
Haitian	0.3%
Korean	0.3%
Other	2.4%

Los Angeles: 632,973 total students

English 53.4%
Spanish 42.7%

Total other: 3.9%	
Armenian	0.9%
Korean	0.7%
Cantonese	0.4%
Filipino	0.4%
Other	1.5%

USN&WR–Basic data: California Dept. of Education; New York City Board of Education

■ U.S. voters who say bilingual education programs should be continued so children don't fall behind in other subjects **55%**

■ Voters who say bilingual education programs slow down learning English and should be eliminated **35%**

■ Even if bilingual education slows down the learning of English, is it valuable in order to preserve a student's heritage? **YES: 49% NO: 44%**

California concluded that students stayed in native-language instruction far too long. It followed an independent investigation in 1993 that called native-language instruction "divisive, wasteful and unproductive."

Not everyone agrees. More than half of American voters, according to a new *U.S. News* poll, approve of bilingual education. Jim Lyons, executive director of the Bilingual Education Association, says the recent studies are flawed because they fail to measure mastery of academic content: "They don't even pretend to address the issue of the *full* education," he says. Learning English takes time, insists Eugene Garcia of the education department. "And it's well worth the wait."

Practical approach. The alternative to native-language instruction is to teach children exclusively in English, pulling them out of class periodically for lessons in English as a second language. Lucy Fortney taught exclusively white American-born children when she started her career 30 years ago; now her classroom is

almost entirely Vietnamese, Cambodian and Armenian. "I can't translate one single word for them," she says, "but they learn English."

Today, bilingual education is creeping beyond impoverished urban neighborhoods to rural and suburban communities likely to expose its failings to harsher light. Until now, no constituency has been vested or powerful enough to force the kind of reforms that may yet come with civil-rights lawsuits. "Everybody's appalled when they find out about the problems," says Linda Chavez, onetime director of the Commission on Civil Rights and a dogged opponent of bilingual education, "but the fact is, it doesn't affect their kids." That may have been true in the past. But as a rainbow-hued contingent of schoolchildren starts filling up the desks in mostly white suburbia, it is not likely to be the case for long.

BY SUSAN HEADDEN

A 'Glorious Mongrel'

The language that some Americans want to defend against foreign invasions is itself a multicultural smorgasbord of borrowed words

Back in 1780, John Adams urged the creation of an American academy with a lofty mission–to keep the English language pure. The Continental Congress, preoccupied with other challenges (such as winning independence from Britain), let the proposal die. And wisely so. It would have been like giving a courtesan a chastity belt for her birthday. "The English language," as Carl Sandburg once observed, "hasn't got where it is by being pure." Not from the get go.

Three out of four words in the dictionary are foreign born.

The language that many now seek to shore up against the babel of America's multicultural masses is itself a *smorgasbord* (Swedish) of words borrowed from foreign tongues. Three out of four words in the dictionary, in fact, are foreign born. Sometimes anglicized, sometimes not, many loan words are so familiar that most English speakers are aware of their exotic origins only vaguely if at all. We can borrow *sugar* from a neighbor only because English borrowed the word from Sanskrit centuries ago. Ask your *pal* (Romany) to go to the *opera* (Italian), and he may prefer instead to go hunting in the *boondocks* (Tagalog), to play *polo* (Tibetan) or to visit the *zoo* (Greek) to test his *skill* (Danish) at milking a *camel* (Hebrew), after which he may need a *shampoo* (Hindi). Whether silly or scholarly, many sentences have equally rich lineages, illustrating Dorothy Thompson's *aphorism* (Greek) that English is a "glorious and imperial mongrel" (*mongrel*, fittingly, being pure English).

English itself is one of history's most energetic immigrants. Three northern European tribes, the Angles, the Saxons and the Jutes, got the enterprise started by invading Britain around A.D. 449. The Vikings arrived from Scandinavia in A.D. 793 to mix it up, battle-ax against battle-ax, adverb against adverb. The Norse and Anglo-Saxon tongues melded, enriching the word hoard. Example: You *reared* a child (Anglo-Saxon) or *raised* a child (Norse). As every schoolchild used to know, the Norman French conquered England in 1066. The language of the Saxon peasantry then conquered the Norman aristocracy. The result was a tongue that kept its Germanic structure but took a huge new vocabulary of French words and through it Latin and Greek terms. Traders, warriors, scholars, pirates and explorers all did their part to advance English's cosmopolitan destiny.

The language was happily spiced with words from 50 languages even before the opening of the New World offered fresh avenues. Americans quickly became known for their own coinages, the many "Americanisms" they invented–words like *groundhog, lightning rod, belittle* (minted by Thomas Jefferson), *seaboard*–new words for a new land. But American English also adopted American Indian terms (mostly place names) and welcomed useful words brought across the water by immigrants. The Dutch supplied *pit* (as found in fruit) and *boss* (as found in the front office), *sleigh, snoop* and *spook.* Spanish supplied *filibuster* and *bonanza;* Yiddish enabled Americans to *kibitz schmucks* who sold *schlock* or made *schmaltz.*

Big dictionary. Today, after 1,500 years of promiscuous acquisitiveness, the vocabulary of English is vast. The Oxford English Dictionary lists more than 600,000 words; German has fewer than one third that number, French fewer than one sixth. What makes English mammoth and unique is its great sea of syn-

 From *U.S. News & World Report*, September 25, 1995, p. 48. © 1995 by U.S. News & World Report. Reprinted by permission.

onyms, words with roughly the same meaning but different connotations, different levels of formality and different effects on the ear. Anglo-Saxon words are blunt, Latin words learned, French words musical. English speakers can calibrate the tone and meter of their prose with great precision. They may *end* (Anglo-Saxon), *finish* (French) or *conclude* (Latin) their remarks. A girl can be *fair* (Anglo-Saxon), *beautiful* (French) or *attractive* (Latin). A bully may evoke *fear* (Anglo-Saxon), *terror* (French) or *trepidation* (Latin).

Its depth and precision have helped make English the foremost language of science, diplomacy and international business—and the medium of T-shirts from Tijuana to Timbuktu. It is the native tongue of 350 million people and a second language for 350 million more. Half the books being published in the world are in English; so is 80 percent of the world's computer text. While Americans debate bilingualism, foreigners learn English. Its popularity is fed by U.S. wealth and power, to be sure. But Richard Lederer, author of *The Miracle of Language* and other books on the peculiarities of English, believes the language's "internationality" has innate appeal. Not only are English's grammar and syntax relatively simple, the language's sound system is flexible and "user friendly"—foreign words tend to be pronounced the same as in their original tongues. "We have the most cheerfully democratic and hospitable language that ever existed," Lederer says. "Other people recognize their language in ours."

Gerald Parshall

GO NORTH, YOUNG MAN

We all speak of North America. But has anyone ever actually met a North American? I know one.

Richard Rodriguez

Richard Rodriguez, an editor with Pacific News Service in San Francisco, is the author of Days of Obligation *(Penguin). He delivered an earlier version of this essay at an international gathering of writers, "A New Moment in the Americas," sponsored by the United States Information Service.*

TRADITIONALLY, AMERICA HAS BEEN AN EAST-WEST COUNTRY. WE HAVE read our history, right to left across the page. We were oblivious of Canada. We barely noticed Mexico, except when Mexico got in the way of our westward migration, which we interpreted as the will of God, "manifest destiny."

In a Protestant country that believed in rebirth (the Easter promise), land became our metaphor for possibility. As long as there was land ahead of us—Ohio, Illinois, Nebraska—we could believe in change; we could abandon our in-laws, leave disappointments behind, to start anew further west. California symbolized ultimate possibility, future-time, the end of the line, where loonies and prophets lived, where America's fads necessarily began.

Nineteenth-century real estate developers and 20th-century Hollywood moguls may have advertised the futuristic myth of California to the rest of America. But the myth was one Americans were predisposed to believe. The idea of California was invented by Americans many miles away.

ONLY A FEW EARLY VOICES FROM CALIFORNIA EVER WARNED against optimism. Two decades after California became American territory, the conservationist John Muir stood at the edge of California and realized that America is a finite idea: We need to preserve the land, if the dream of America is to survive. Word of Muir's discovery slowly traveled backward in time, from the barely populated West (the future) to the crowded brick cities of the East Coast (the past).

I grew up in California of the 1950s, when the state was filling with people from New York and Oklahoma. Everyone was busy losing weight and changing hair color and becoming someone new. There was, then, still plenty of cheap land for tract houses, under the cloudless sky.

The 1950s, the 1960s—those years were our golden age. Edmund G. "Pat" Brown was governor of optimism. He created the University of California system, a decade before the children of the suburbs rebelled, portraying themselves as the "counterculture." Brown constructed freeways that permitted Californians to move farther and farther away from anything resembling an urban center. He even made the water run up the side of a mountain.

By the 1970s, optimism was running out of space. Los Angeles needed to reinvent itself as Orange County. Then Orange County got too crowded and had to reinvent itself as North County San Diego. Then Californians started moving into the foothills or out to the desert, complaining all the while of the traffic and of the soiled air. And the immigrants!

Suddenly, foreign immigrants were everywhere—Iranians were buying into Beverly Hills, the Vietnamese were moving into San Jose; the Chinese were taking all the spaces in the biochemistry courses at UCLA. And Mexicans, poor Mexicans, were making hotel beds, picking peaches in the Central Valley, changing diapers, even impersonating Italian chefs at Santa Monica restaurants.

The Mexicans and the Chinese had long inhabited California. But they never resided within the golden myth of the state. Nineteenth-century California restricted the Chinese to Chinatowns or to a city's outskirts. Mexicans were neither here nor there. They were imported by California to perform cheap labor, then deported in bad economic times.

The East Coast had incorporated Ellis Island in its myth. The West Coast regarded the non-European immigrant as doubly foreign. Though Spaniards may have colonized the place and though Mexico briefly claimed it, California took its meaning from "internal immigrants"—Americans from Minnesota or Brooklyn who came West to remake their parents' version of America.

From *Mother Jones*, July/August 1995, pp. 31-35. © 1995 by Richard Rodriguez. Reprinted by permission of Georges Borchardt, Inc.

But sometime in the 1970s, it became clear to many Californians that the famous blond myth of the state was in jeopardy. ("We are sorry to intrude, señor, we are only looking for work.") Was L.A. "becoming" Mexican?

Latin Americans arrived, describing California as "el norte." The "West Coast" was a finite idea; el norte in the Latin American lexicon means wide-open. Whose compass was right?

Meanwhile, with the lifting of anti-Asian immigration restrictions, jumbo jets were arriving at LAX from Bangkok and Seoul. People getting off the planes said about California, "This is where the United States begins." Californians objected, "No, no. California is where the United States comes to an end—we don't have enough room for you." Whose compass was truer?

IT HAS TAKEN TWO MORE DECADES FOR THE EAST COAST TO GET THE point. Magazines and television stories from New York today describe the golden state as "tarnished." The more interesting possibility is that California has become the intersection between comedy and tragedy. Foreign immigrants are replanting optimism on California soil; the native-born know the wisdom of finitude. Each side has a knowledge to give the other.

Already, everywhere in California, there is evidence of miscegenation—Keanu Reeves, sushi tacos, blond Buddhists, Salvadoran Pentecostals. But the forces that could lead to marriage also create gridlock on the Santa Monica freeway. The native-born Californian sits disgruntled in traffic going nowhere. The flatbed truck in front of him is filled with Mexicans; in the Mercedes next to him is a Japanese businessman using a car phone.

PUERTO RICANS, MEXICANS: EARLY IN THIS CENTURY WE WERE immigrants. Or not immigrants exactly. Puerto Ricans had awakened one day to discover that they suddenly lived on U.S. territory. Mexicans had seen Mexico's northern territory annexed and renamed the southwestern United States.

We were people from the South in an east-west country. We were people of mixed blood in a black and white nation. We were Catholics in a Protestant land. Many millions of us were Indians in an east-west country that imagined the Indian to be dead.

Today, Los Angeles is the largest Indian city in the United States, though Hollywood filmmakers persist in making movies about the dead Indian. (For seven bucks, you can see cowboys slaughter Indians in the Kevin Costner movie—and regret it from your comfortable chair.) On any day along Sunset Boulevard you can see Toltecs and Aztecs and Mayans.

Puerto Ricans, Mexicans—we are the earliest Latin American immigrants to the United States. We have turned into fools. We argue among ourselves, criticize one another for becoming too much the gringo or maybe not gringo enough. We criticize each other for speaking too much Spanish or not enough Spanish. We demand that politicians provide us with bilingual voting ballots, but we do not trouble to vote.

Octavio Paz, the Mexican writer, has observed that the Mexican-American is caught between cultures, thus a victim of history—unwilling to become a Mexican again, unable to belong to the United States. Michael Novak, the United States writer, has observed that what unites people throughout the

ALREADY, EVERYWHERE IN CALIFORNIA, THERE IS EVIDENCE OF MISCEGE-NATION—KEANU REEVES, SUSHI TACOS, BLOND BUDDHISTS, SALVADORAN PENTECOSTALS. EACH SIDE HAS A KNOWLEDGE TO GIVE THE OTHER.

There are signs of backlash. Pete Wilson has become the last east-west governor of California. In a state founded by people seeking a softer winter and famous internationally for being "laid back," Californians vote for Proposition 187, hoping that illegal immigrants will stay away if there are no welfare dollars.

But immigrants are most disconcerting to California because they are everywhere working, transforming the ethos of the state from leisure to labor. Los Angeles is becoming a vast working city, on the order of Hong Kong or Mexico City. Chinese kids are raising the admission standards to the University of California. Mexican immigrant kids are undercutting union wages, raising rents in once-black neighborhoods.

Californians used to resist any metaphor drawn from their state's perennial earthquakes and floods and fires. Now Californians take their meaning from natural calamity. People turn away from the sea, imagine the future as existing backward in time.

"I'm leaving California, I'm going to Colorado."

"I'm headed for Arizona."

After hitting the coastline like flies against glass, we look in new directions. Did Southern California's urban sprawl invent NAFTA? For the first time, Californians now talk of the North and the South—new points on our national compass.

"I've just bought a condo in Baja."

"I'm leaving California for Seattle."

"I'm moving to Vancouver. I want someplace cleaner."

"Go North, young man."

Americas is that we all have said goodbye to our motherland. To Europe. To Africa. To Asia. *Farewell!*

The only trouble is: Adios was never part of the Mexican-American or Puerto Rican vocabulary. There was no need to turn one's back on the past. Many have traveled back and forth, between rivals, between past and future, commuters between the Third World and First. After a few months in New York or Los Angeles, it would be time to head "home." After a few months back in Mexico or Puerto Rico, it would be time to head "home" to the United States.

We were nothing like the famous Ellis Island immigrants who arrived in America with no expectation of return to the "old country." In a nation that believed in the future, we were a puzzle.

We were also a scandal to Puerto Rico and Mexico. Our Spanish turned bad. Our values were changing—though no one could say why or how exactly. "Abuelita" (grandmother) complained that we were growing more guarded. Alone.

There is a name that Mexico uses for children who have forgotten their true address: "pocho." The pocho is the child who wanders away, ends up in the United States, among the gringos, where he forgets his true home.

THE AMERICAS BEGAN WITH A CONFUSION ABOUT MAPS AND A JOKE about our father's mistake. Columbus imagined himself in a part of the world where there were Indians.

We smile because our 15th-century "papi" thought he was in India. I'm not certain, however, that even today we know where in the world we live. We are only beginning to look at the map. We are only beginning to wonder what the map of the hemisphere might mean.

Latin Americans have long complained that the gringo, with characteristic arrogance, hijacked the word "American" and gave it all to himself—"the way he stole the land." I remember, years ago, my aunt in Mexico City scolding me when I told her I came from "America." Pocho! Didn't I realize that the entire hemisphere is America? "Listen," my Mexican aunt told me, "people who live in the United States are norteamericanos."

Well, I think to myself—my aunt is now dead, God rest her soul—I wonder what she would have thought a couple of years ago when the great leaders—the president of Mexico, the president of the United States, the Canadian prime minister—gathered to sign the North American Free Trade Agreement. Mexico signed a document acknowledging that she is a North American.

I predict that Mexico will suffer a nervous breakdown in the next 10 years. She will have to check into the Betty Ford Clinic for a long rest. She will need to determine just what exactly it means that she is, with the dread gringo, a norteamericana.

Canada, meanwhile, worries about the impact of the Nashville music channel on its cable TV; Pat Buchanan imagines a vast wall along our southern flank; and Mexican nationalists fear a Clinton bailout of the lowly peso.

We all speak of North America. But has anyone ever actually met a North American? Oh, there are Mexicans. And there are Canadians. And there are so-called Americans. But a North American?

I know one.

Let me tell you about him—this North American. He is a Mixteco Indian who comes from the Mexican state of Oaxaca. He is trilingual. His primary language is the language of his tribe. His second language is Spanish, the language of Cortés. Also, he has a working knowledge of U.S. English, because, for several months of the year, he works near Stockton, Calif.

He commutes over thousands of miles of dirt roads and freeways, knows several centuries, two currencies, two sets of hypocrisy. He is a criminal in one country and an embarrassment to the other. He is pursued as an "illegal" by the U.S. border patrol. He is preyed upon by Mexican officers who want to shake him down because he has hidden U.S. dollars in his shoes.

In Oaxaca, he lives in a 16th-century village, where his wife watches blond Venezuelan soap operas. A picture of la Virgen de Guadalupe rests over his bed. In Stockton, there is no Virgin Mary, only the other Madonna—the material girl.

He is the first North American.

A JOURNALIST ONCE ASKED CHOU EN-LAI, THE CHINESE PREMIER UNDER Mao Zedong, what he thought of the French Revolution. Chou En-lai gave a wonderful Chinese reply: "It's too early to tell."

I think it may even be too early to tell what the story of Columbus means. The latest chapter of the Columbus saga may be taking place right now, as Latin American teenagers with Indian faces violate the U.S. border. The Mexican kids standing on the line tonight between Tijuana and San Diego—if you ask them why they are coming to the United States of America, they will not say anything about Thomas Jefferson or *The Federalist Papers*. They have only heard that there is a job in a Glendale dry cleaner's or that some farmer is hiring near Fresno.

They insist: They will be returning to Mexico in a few months. They are only going to the United States for the dollars. They certainly don't intend to become gringos. They don't want anything to do with the United States, except the dollars.

But the months will pass, and the teenagers will be changed in the United States. When they go back to their Mexican village, they will no longer be easy. They will expect an independence and an authority that the village cannot give them. Much to their surprise, they will have been Americanized by the job in Glendale.

For work in the United States is our primary source of identity. There is no more telling question we Americans ask one another than "What do you do?" We do not ask about family or village or religion. We ask about work.

The Mexican teenagers will return to Glendale.

MEXICANS, PUERTO RICANS—MOST OF US END UP IN THE UNITED States, living in the city. Peasants end up in the middle of a vast modern metropolis, having known only the village, with its three blocks of familiar facades.

The arriving generation is always the bravest. New immigrants often change religion with their move to the city. They need to make their peace with isolation, so far from relatives. They learn subway and bus routes that take them far from home every day. Long before they can read English, they learn how to recognize danger and opportunity. Their lives are defined by change.

Their children or their grandchildren become, often, very different. The best and the brightest, perhaps, will go off to college—become the first in their family—but they talk about "keeping" their culture. They start speaking Spanish, as a way of not changing; they eat in the cafeteria only with others who look like themselves. They talk incessantly about "culture" as though it were some little thing that can be preserved and kept in a box.

The unluckiest children of immigrants drop out of high school. They speak neither good English nor Spanish. Some end up in gangs—family, man—"blood." They shoot other kids who look exactly like themselves. If they try to leave their gang, the gang will come after them for their act of betrayal. If they venture to some other part of the city, they might get shot or they might merely be unable to decipher the freeway exits that speed by.

They retreat to their "turf"—three blocks, just like in their grandmother's village, where the journey began.

ONE OF THE THINGS THAT MEXICO HAD NEVER ACKNOWLEDGED about my father—I insist that you at least entertain this idea—is the possibility that my father and others like him were the great revolutionaries of Mexico. Pocho pioneers. They, not Pancho Villa, not Zapata, were heralds of the modern age in Mexico. They left for the United States and then they came back to Mexico. And they changed Mexico forever.

A childhood friend of my father's—he worked in Chicago in the 1920s, then returned one night to his village in Michoacán with appliances for mamasita and crisp dollars. The village gathered round him—this is a true story—and asked, "What is it like up there in Chicago?"

The man said, "It's OK."

That rumor of "OK" spread across Michoacán, down to Jalisco, all the way down to Oaxaca, from village to village to village.

Futurists and diplomats talk about a "new moment in the Americas." The Latin American elite have condos in Miami and send their children to Ivy League schools. U.S. and Canadian businessmen project the future on a north-south graph. But for many decades before any of this, Latin American peasants have been traveling back and forth, north and south.

Today, there are remote villages in Latin America that are among the most international places on earth. Tiny Peruvian villages know when farmers are picking pears in the Yakima valley in Washington state.

I am the son of a prophet. I am a fool. I am a victim of history. I am confused. I do not know whether I am coming or going. I speak bad Spanish. And yet I tell Latin America this: Because I southern invasion. I say this to California: Immigration is always illegal. It is a rude act, the leaving of home. Immigration begins as a violation of custom, a youthful act of defiance, an insult to the village. I know a man from El Salvador who has not spoken to his father since the day he left his father's village.

IMMIGRATION IS ALWAYS ILLEGAL. IT IS A RUDE ACT, THE LEAVING OF HOME, A VIOLATION OF CUSTOM, A YOUTHFUL ACT OF DEFIANCE. BUT IMMIGRANTS HAVE ALSO BEEN OUR CIVILIZATION'S PROPHETS.

grew up Hispanic in California, I know more Guatemalans than I would if I had grown up in Mexico, more Brazilians than if I lived in Peru. Because I live in California, it is routine for me to know Nicaraguans and Salvadorans and Cubans. As routine as knowing Chinese or Vietnamese.

My fellow Californians complain loudly about the uncouth Immigrants horrify the grandmothers they leave behind.

Illegal immigrants trouble U.S. environmentalists and Mexican nationalists. Illegal immigrants must trouble anyone, on either side of the line, who imagines that the poor are under control.

But they have also been our civilization's prophets. They, long before the rest of us, saw the hemisphere whole.

INTERMARRIED . . . WITH CHILDREN

For all the talk of cultural separatism, the races that make up the U.S. are now crossbreeding at unprecedented rates

Jill Smolowe

Hostile stares and epithets were the least of their problems when Edgar and Jean Cahn first dated. Twice the couple—he a white Jew, she a black Baptist—were arrested simply for walking the streets of Baltimore arm in arm. When they wed in 1957, Maryland law barred interracial marriages, so the ceremony was held in New York City. Although Jean had converted by then, the only rabbi who would agree to officiate denied them a huppah and the traditional breaking of glass. As law students at Yale in the 1960s, the couple lived in a basement because no landlord would rent them a flat.

In 1963 the Cahns moved to Washington, D.C., where they raised two sons, Reuben and Jonathan. By 1971, as co-deans of the Antioch School of Law, the high profile couple had received so many death threats that they needed bodyguards. The boys' mixed ancestry caused near riots at their public school. One principal said they "brought a dark force to the school" and called for their expulsion.

Now the generational wheel has turned. In 1990 young Reuben married Marna, a white Lutheran from rural Pine Grove, Pennsylvania. Although both a rabbi and a minister officiated, none of Marna's relatives, except her mother, attended the wedding. Her father fumed, "I can't believe you expect me to accept a black person, and a Jewish one at that!" But with the birth last year of towheaded Aaron, Marna's family softened considerably.

Intermarriage, of course, is as old as the Bible. But during the past two decades, America has produced the greatest variety of hybrid households in the history of the world. As ever increasing numbers of couples crash through racial, ethnic and religious barriers to invent a life together, Americans are being forced to rethink and redefine themselves. For all the divisive talk of cultural separatism and resurgent ethnic pride, never before has a society struggled so hard to fuse such a jumble of traditions, beliefs and values.

The huddled masses have already given way to the muddled masses. "Marriage is the main assimilator," says Karen Stephenson, an anthropologist at UCLA. "If you really want to affect change, it's through marriage and child rearing." This is not assimilation in the Eurocentric sense of the word: one nation, under white, Anglo-Saxon Protestant rule, divided, with liberty and justice for some. Rather it is an extended hyphenation. If, say, the daughter of Japanese and Filipino parents marries the son of German and Irish immigrants, together they may beget a Japanese-Filipino-German-Irish-Buddhist-Catholic-American child. "Assimilation never really happens," says Stephenson. "Over time you get a bunch of little assimilations."

The profusion of couples breaching once impregnable barriers of color, ethnicity and faith is startling. Over a period of roughly two decades, the number of interracial marriages in the U.S. has escalated from 310,000 to more than 1.1 million; 72% of those polled by TIME know married couples who are of different races. The incidence of births of mixed-race babies has multiplied 26 times as fast as that of any other group. Among Jews the number marrying out of their faith has shot up from 10 to 52% since 1960. Among Japanese Americans, 65% marry people who have no Japa-

nese heritage; Native Americans have nudged that number to 70%. In both groups the incidence of children sired by mixed couples exceeds the number born into uni-ethnic homes.

Some critics fret that all this criss-crossing will damage society's essential "American" core. By this they usually mean a confluence of attitudes, values and assumptions that drive American's centuries-old quest for a better life. What they fail to acknowledge is that legal, educational and economic changes continuously alter the priorities within that same set of social variables. A few generations back, religion, race and custom superseded all other considerations. When Kathleen Hobson and Atul Gawande, both 27, married last year, however, they based their vision of a shared future on a different set of common values: an upper-middle-class upbringing in tight-knit families, a Stanford education and love of intellectual pursuits.

Unlike many other mixed couples, Gawande, an Indian American, and Hobson, a white Episcopalian of old Southern stock, have always enjoyed a warm reception from both sets of parents. Still, when Hobson first visited the Gawandes in October not every one of their friends was ready to celebrate. "One Indian family didn't want to come because they were concerned about their children being influenced Hobson says. Their wedding in Virginia was a harmonious blend of two cultures though Kathleen wore a white gown and her minister officiated, the ceremony included readings from both Hindu and Christian texts.

Tortured solutions to mixed-marriage ceremonies are common. Weddings, funerals, are a time when family resent-

 From *Time*, Special Issue, Fall 1993, pp. 64-65. © 1993 by Time Inc. Magazine Company. Reprinted by permission.

ments, disappointments and expectations bubble to the surface. The tugging and tussling over matters that may seem frivolous set the stage for a couple's lifelong quest to create an environment that will be welcoming to both families, yet uniquely their own.

Accommodation and compromise only begin at the altar. The qualities that attracted Dan Kalmanson, an Anglo of European extraction, to Yilva Martinez in a Miami reggae club—her Spanish accent, exotic style of dance and playfulness—had a more challenging echo in their married life. After they wed in 1988, Ignacio, Yilva's then eight-year-old son by a previous marriage, moved from Venezuela to join the couple. Dan, 33, spoke no Spanish, the boy no English. The couple decided to compel Ignacio to speak English. He caught on so fast that his Spanish soon degenerated. Says Yilva: "We have literally forced him to learn Spanish again."

For Yilva, 35, the struggle is not just to preserve her native tongue; she also wants to suffuse her home, which has grown with the addition of Kristen, 3, with the Latin ethic that values family above all else. "Here, you live to work. There, we work to live," she says. "In Venezuela we take a two-hour lunch break; we don't cram in a hamburger at MacDonald's."

Children also force mixed couples to confront hard decisions about religion. Blanche Speiser, 43, was certain that Mark, 40, would yield if she wanted to raise their two kids Christian, but she also knew that her Jewish husband would never attend church with the family or participate in holiday celebrations. After much soul searching, she opted for a Jewish upbringing. "I knew it would be O.K. as long as the children had some

belief," she says. "I didn't want a mishmash." Although Blanche remains comfortable with that decision and has grown accustomed to attending synagogue with her family, she admits that it pricks when Brad, 7, says, "Mommy, I wish you were Jewish." Other couples expose their families to both religions, then leave the choice to the kids.

When it comes to racial identity, many couples feel that a child should never have to "choose" between parents. The 1990 U.S. census form, with its "Black," "White" and "Other" boxes, particularly grated. " 'Other' is not acceptable, pure and simple," says Nancy Brown, 40. "It is psychologically damaging to force somebody to choose one identity when physiologically and biologically they are more than one." Nancy, who is white, thinks the census form should include a "Multiracial" box for her two daughters; her black husband Roosevelt, 44, argues that there should be no race box at all. Both agree that people should be able to celebrate all parts of their heritage without conflict. "It's like an equation," says Nancy, who is president of an interracial family support group. "Interracial marriage that works equals multiracial children at ease with their mixed identity, which equals more people in the world who can deal with this diversity."

The world still has much to learn about living with diversity. "What people say, what people do and what they say they do are three entirely different things," says anthropologist Stephenson. "We are walking contradictions." Kyoung-Hi Song, 27, was born in Korea but lived much of her youth abroad as her father was posted from one United Nations assignment to the next. Despite that cosmopolitan upbringing, her parents balked when

Kyoung-Hi married Robert Dickson, a WASP from Connecticut. They boycotted the 1990 wedding, and have not contacted their daughter since. The Dicksons hope that the birth of their first child, expected in April, will change that.

Intolerance need not be that blatant to inflict wounds. If Tony Jeffreys, 34, and Alice Sakuda Flores, 28, have a child, that hypothetical Japanese-Filipino-German-Irish-Buddhist-Catholic-American will become flesh and blood. In their one year of marriage, Tony says, "I've heard friends say stupid stuff about Asians right in front of Alice. It is real hypocritical because a lot of them have Mexican or black girlfriends or wives." Sometimes the more subtle the rejection, the sharper the sting. Says Candy Mills, 20, the daughter of black and Native American parents, who is married to Gabe Grosz, a white European immigrant: "I know that people are tolerating me, not accepting me."

Such pain is evidence that America has yet to harvest the full rewards of its founding principles. The land of immigrants may be giving way to a land of hyphenations, but the hyphen still divides even as it compounds. Those who intermarry have perhaps the strongest sense of what it will take to return America to an unhyphenated whole. "It's American culture that we all share," says Mills. "We should capitalize on that." Perhaps her two Native American-black-white-Hungarian-French-Catholic-Jewish-American children will lead the way.

—**Reported by Greg Aunapu/ Miami, Sylvester Monroe/Los Angeles, Andrea Sachs/New York and Elizabeth Taylor/Chicago**

Teacher Education in Multicultural Perspective

At a time when minority students are beginning to approach 50 percent of the national elementary and secondary school population, fewer students from cultural minorities are choosing to prepare to be teachers. As the population of U.S. college students choosing to prepare for teaching as a career becomes more white, fewer persons of the rainbow coalition are choosing teaching as a career. This social reality only underscores the need for multicultural education, as well as for course work in specific cultural studies areas in the education of American teachers.

Multicultural educational programming of some sort is now an established part of teacher education programs, but major issues are still being debated as to how it can be integrated effectively into these programs. The National Council for the Accreditation of Teacher Education (NCATE) has established a multicultural standard for the accreditation of programs for teacher education in the United States. Many educators involved in teaching courses in multicultural education have frequently wondered why multicultural education course work is so often a segregated area of teacher education curricula. And many who are involved in multicultural teacher education believe that all teacher educators should become knowledgeable in the area of multicultural education. Teaching preservice teachers to respect cultural diversity can reinforce their studies in learning to respect individual students' diversity in learning styles and beliefs. All persons who become teachers need to be sensitized to the reality of cultural diversity and to the need to learn about the values and beliefs of their students. The demographic changes in the population characteristics of Canada and the United States ensure that many North American teachers will have students from a wide array of differing cultural heritages.

There is still much misunderstanding as to what multicultural education is within the teacher education establishment. This will continue as long as many of its opponents consider it a political rather than an intellectual or educational concept. If all children and young adults are to receive their educational experiences in schools that nourish and respect their respective heritages as persons, all teachers must learn those intellectual and affective skills that can empower them to study and to learn about diverse cultures throughout their careers. Multicultural education course content in teacher education programs is, at one and the same time, both about cultural diversity and about individual students from differing cultural heritages.

Teachers will have to consider how a person's (especially their students') development is shaped by the powerful force of those values into which they are enculturated in their homes and neighborhoods. In a civilization rapidly becoming more culturally pluralistic, resistance to overwhelmingly Eurocentric domination of social studies and language arts curricula in the schools will continue. By the year 2000, about 5 billion of the projected 6 billion people on Earth will be persons with a non-Eurocentric conception of the world. Scholars in the social sciences, humanities, and teacher education in North America who study minority-majority relations in the schools now realize that the very terms "minority" and "majority" are changing when we speak of the demographic realities of the cultural configurations existent in most major urban and suburban educational systems. This is also true when we consider minority-majority relations in vast isolated rural or wilderness areas where those of western or northern European descent are minorities in the midst of indigenous peoples. Many teachers will teach students whose values and views of the world are very different from their own, hence, the relevance of teachers learning how to learn about human cultures and belief systems in order that they can study the lives and heritages of their students in the schools.

Many teachers of European ethnic heritage are having difficulty understanding the importance of the fact that our national culture in North America is becoming more culturally pluralistic. From a multicultural perspective, one of the many goals of course content is to help all prospective teachers realize the importance of becoming learners themselves throughout their lives. The knowledge base of multicultural education is further informed by the history of the struggle for civil rights in North American societies. Multicultural educational programming in teacher education programs seeks to alter the way prospective teachers perceive society as a whole, not just its current minority members. We must take a broad view, not a narrow view, of multicultural education. Culturally pluralistic themes need to be apparent throughout teacher education programs and integrated into the knowledge bases of teacher education. Broadly conceived, multicultural education seeks to help members of all ethnic and cultural backgrounds to appreciate one another's shared human concerns and interrelationships; it should not be conceived as simply the study of minority cultural groups. Teachers need to be prepared in such a manner that they learn genuine respect for cultural as well as personal diversity.

Teachers should be prepared to take a global perspective of the world and to think critically about the issues confronting them, their students, and society as a whole (seen as part of an interdependent community

of nations). Multicultural education should not be politicized. It should be a way of seeing the world as enriched by cultural and personal diversity. Preservice teachers should learn from case studies that exemplify and report on the differing learning styles that develop in differing cultural contexts. Different styles of teaching can be learned from differing cultural traditions in child rearing, entry into adulthood (rites of passage), and child-adult interaction in school settings.

The essays in this unit explore why it is important to see multicultural education not just as a political concept, but rather as an area of critical inquiry from which we can all learn alternative, diverse styles of teaching appropriate to the learning styles and cultural backgrounds of students. The articles stress the importance of teachers' being able to learn differing ways, sharing in social interaction in classroom settings, and seeing the impact of how their ideas of race, gender, and social class interact with their perceptions of themselves as teachers, of other teachers, and of their students.

This unit's articles are relevant to courses that focus on introduction to the cultural foundations of education,

educational policy studies, history and philosophy of education, and curriculum theory and construction, as well as methods courses in all areas of teacher education programs.

Looking Ahead: Challenge Questions

Why is multicultural education so frequently seen as an isolated, segregated part of teacher education programs?

What are the reasons for so much resistance to course work in the area of multicultural education?

What can we learn about teaching styles and methods from case studies of teachers from cultures other than our own?

Why can it be said that our understanding of the relevance of multicultural perspectives on teacher education emerged from the struggle for human rights in general?

What seem to be the major points of disagreement about the role of multicultural education in teacher education programs?

What attitudes need to change in much talk about multicultural education?

—F. S.

Why Do We Need This Class?

Multicultural Education for Teachers

Ms. Pang's main goal is to help teachers create a classroom that is effective for all children. To accomplish that goal, she encourages teachers to examine issues of race, class, and gender that may serve as barriers to equal opportunity to learn.

Valerie Ooka Pang

VALERIE OOKA PANG is an associate professor of teacher education at San Diego State University.

Illustration by Meg Akiyama

IT WAS THE first day of class. A new group of teachers conversed noisily as I looked for my attendance sheet. I could hear a loud voice saying, "Why do we have to take *this* class? I'm not prejudiced. I don't need to be in here. I like all kids." I could hear someone else answer in a low voice, "I don't need it either. This is going to be a waste of time."

I smiled to myself and thought, "There are always doubting Thomases or Tomasitas. That's great. They will make my work easier."

After calling names on the class roster, I said, "I want to welcome you to the class. I am excited that I will have the opportunity to get to know you over the next 15 weeks. I realize that some of you feel the class will be a waste of time because you aren't prejudiced. Let's talk a little about this."

I turned to a broadly built woman with horn-rimmed glasses who was chatting in the back of the classroom. With a smile I said gently, "Joan, I was just wondering why you don't think you need this class."

Many of the teachers had been talking while I read through the class roster, but all of a sudden the room was quiet. The teachers turned toward Joan, waiting to see what she would say. Joan didn't want to back down. Just like the children in her classroom, she was cool and stood her ground. "Well, I just don't need to hear about prejudice and discrimination. I'm tired of hearing about the things we have done to blacks and Indians."

I smiled and replied, "I realize that many of you have thought a lot about prejudice and that you would never knowingly discriminate against any of your students." Joan's broad shoulders relaxed. "Let's hear from someone else. Why do you think we have this class?" I asked.

A tall male student wearing a gray sweat suit said, "I want to know how to teach black kids."

I looked at Larry in a puzzled way. "You need to respect, care, and believe in every student," I ventured.

"No, that's not what I mean," Larry said, his forehead wrinkling in frustra-

   From *Phi Delta Kappan*, December 1994, pp. 289-292. © 1994 by Phi Delta Kappa, Inc. Reprinted by permission.

tion. "I want you to tell me about black culture. You know — their music, history, foods. Things like that."

"Why do you think you need information about black culture?" I asked.

"Because then I will appreciate their culture more," Larry said, smiling.

"What do you know about your own culture?" I asked.

This was the beginning of another wonderful semester in multicultural education. And I knew that this class would be exciting because these teachers were already willing to share their honest views with one another. We were off to a great start.

Preparing Teachers for Diversity

Preparing teachers for a culturally diverse society is one of the most exciting and rewarding endeavors in education. I love what I do because most teachers are caring and dedicated people. I see teachers as America's national treasures. They do not go into teaching to get rich. Many teachers feel that teaching is more than a job; it is a commitment and a calling.

In my semester-length class on multicultural education, I try to model the kind of classroom that I hope the teachers in my class will create. I believe that modeling is the most powerful strategy in teaching. I try to create a learning atmosphere that says to each teacher, "You are a precious and worthy person. All of us in the class need your input to grow. Help us be the best people we can be." During the first class session, I begin memorizing the names of each teacher. I learn the teachers' names quickly because I want each one to know that he or she is an important member of our team.

I also try to create an interesting and lively classroom climate. If I expect teachers to motivate their students, I must get teachers involved in their own learning. Though the content and the activities I use in a college class are different from those in a fourth-grade classroom, I can still get teachers excited about learning. Teachers can become enthusiastic and animated about the ideas and solutions they develop to solve classroom problems.

I have developed my class around some of the beliefs of Paulo Freire, the Brazilian educator. I asked myself, "How can I develop a community of learners where everyone works together to create a free and just society?" I like Freire's idea of "problem-posing education," which means centering learning on social is-

sues and problems. He thinks that students who are truly free bring what they know into the classroom. Students make connections between their lives, others' lives, and themes in society. True freedom occurs when teachers and young people tackle a problem and come to collective decisions about what action can be taken. The teacher does not act as the person in control; rather he or she shares leadership and the responsibility for learning. The "light bulb" goes on in both teachers' and students' minds, because through their dialogue they struggle together to arrive at solutions to social problems.

In contrast Freire sees most teachers making deposits in the minds of children. In this "banking" approach to education, students are passive learners, receiving and memorizing information so that they can recite it back to the teacher.[1] This passive role, Freire believes, conditions students to accept the status quo. Because the environment of the classroom teaches students not to challenge ideas or to create new ways to think, they will blindly accept the unfairness of society.

I attempt to provide a challenging and engaging learning environment by using lots of dialogue. I believe that the teachers in my classes learn more from one another than from me. In this shared learning process, they ask one another many questions, which forces them to clarify their values. They also ask me difficult, soul-searching questions.

Since I believe in "problem-posing" or issues-centered education, I know it is crucial to get teachers to talk about their ideas. I try to create a classroom in which we trust and respect one another, a place of caring.[2] It is a safe place where mistakes are the "fertilizer of success." I believe that every teacher should have the opportunity to find his or her "voice" and to express it. I explain to my teachers that we need each person's input because we will not grow as individuals or as a learning community unless we help one another see new aspects of issues. This point is extremely crucial in a class like multicultural education, which deals with a complex mix of emotions, attitudes, misconceptions, and ignorance about race, class, gender, and other cultural differences. I want my teachers to be "hooked" on dialogue so that their classrooms will become "think tanks" of committed students who work together. Each classroom can reflect a democratic community in which each student is an active and respected learner.

Three Phases of Instruction

My main goal is to help teachers create a classroom that is effective for all children. Teachers need to know that multicultural education is the study of schooling aimed at providing all children with an equal opportunity to learn in a culturally affirming and caring environment.[3] I help teachers look at issues of race, class, and gender that may serve as barriers to that goal. In building my class I divide the instruction into three phases.

1. *Who am I? Am I prejudiced?* In the beginning of the class, I want teachers to better understand themselves. I ask them to examine who they are by identifying their own values and goals. I am convinced that no matter how much information I give teachers about other cultural groups, if they are not prepared to understand others, they will not be ready to hear and receive the information.

Since most of those who enter the teaching profession are white and middle class, we read the book *White Teacher*, by Vivian Gussin Paley.[4] This book is a wonderful resource because Paley writes about her own prejudices and the mistakes she made as a kindergarten teacher. Reading this book helps teachers examine their own biases in a nonthreatening way; they look at racism in schools while learning effective teaching strategies that worked for Paley in her classroom.

I believe that teachers do not want to be prejudiced, but, because prejudice is often part of the hidden curriculum, they may be acting or thinking in ways that limit their own growth or that of their students. For example, a teacher might say, "I don't know why those black kids can't sit still." Then I ask the teacher, "Do you hear what you are saying? Do you also say, 'I don't know why those white kids can't sit still'?" Another teacher may point out the first teacher's unconscious prejudices by noting the tone of voice and the use of the term "those" children.

2. *What do I think about culturally diverse communities?* The second phase of my class focuses on getting to know culturally diverse neighborhoods. I ask the teachers, "Do you hold stereotypes about different communities? Do you believe that Mexican parents from low-income areas do not care about their children? And do you believe that rich white parents from Beverly Hills are more concerned than black parents about their youngsters? Where did you get those ideas?" In order to help teachers think

about their misconceptions, I take my class on field trips and require teachers to donate time to a community organization of their choice.

I believe that teachers will feel more connections with children in their classes when they know the school neighborhood and the issues that are most important to the community. In large urban areas, teachers may live in the suburbs and commute an hour to their schools in the inner city. Yet in teaching children, teachers can be more effective when they can make connections between the school curriculum and students' lives.

On one of our field trips, I take my classes to visit a community center in San Diego. The center serves several hundred low-income families. The drug traffic in the community has been limited because the neighbors worked with the police and forced the drug pushers out. I want the teachers to get to know the community and to learn that the parents and children in this neighborhood have the same desires for education, homes, and jobs as the teachers do.

At one point in the semester, we put on a learning carnival. The teachers set up booths with science experiments, math games, reading activities, and art projects. In discussions after the carnival, one teacher said, "I expected the kids from this neighborhood to be rude and wild. But they were all polite. In fact I was surprised that so many older siblings — some only as old as 6 — were taking younger brothers and sisters from booth to booth making sure that they had fun and got prizes. Many of the younger kids spoke only Spanish and so their older brothers or sisters translated and encouraged them to try each booth. I never knew how much family meant to some children."

Though the teachers thought they had created the carnival for the community, they benefited too. Members of the class began to feel personal connections with parents and children from low-income African American and Mexican American families — people whom they had initially seen as so different and separate from themselves. The walls of isolation were slowly crumbling.

During the debriefing discussion, Joan, one of the teachers in the class, mentioned, "There's a family in the neighborhood with two boys in junior high. These boys aren't going to school because they don't have any shoes. Is there anyone

willing to donate so the community center can buy them shoes?"

The teachers generously contributed. We then began to discuss what kinds of shoes the kids wanted. Larry commented, "I know that my students are very label-conscious. Do you think we should put any stipulations on how expensive the shoes are that the center buys for the boys?"

A teacher who was usually quiet raised her hand and said, "Just because these boys are poor, why should they want anything less than other children?" Several other teachers agreed. Though we hoped the money would be spent in a reasonable way, we felt that the students and the center would know what was best.

The social worker called me several weeks later to thank us for the donation. He told me that he had taken the boys to the store, and they had decided not to buy the designer tennis shoes but to buy a more moderately priced brand, because that would leave them a few dollars to buy new shirts too.

Since we all went on the field trip and were part of the carnival, everyone could share observations about our common experiences. One of the most damaging assignments a college professor can give teachers in a multicultural education class is to send them to various gatherings in ethnic communities — for example, services at black churches, Vietnamese festivals, or Latino political rallies — which may reinforce stereotypes that outsiders hold about culturally different groups. I have heard teachers come back from an African American Baptist church service and say, "Those people are so warm. I was scared to go to the church, and I didn't want to leave my car on the street, but the people made me feel so accepted. And the people are great gospel singers." Many times teachers need a chance to talk about what they have observed so that their encounters with other cultures do not become "zoo" experiences. Going to view another neighborhood can be dangerous if teachers do not understand what they are seeing. Many cultural traditions are rooted in deep values, but these values may not be obvious because of differences in dress and behaviors.

I want teachers to go beyond knowing that "we are all people" or being satisfied with only superficial contact with members of other communities. In a community service project, such as tutoring children after school or teaching English to newly arrived adult immigrants, teachers

are able to have real discussions of ideas and to learn about the world view of people who are culturally different from themselves, because they visit the neighborhoods of those people repeatedly. In addition, teachers are more likely to see beyond cultural stereotypes and learn about individual differences. Again, dialogue with their peers is crucial because it gives teachers the opportunity to clarify their beliefs and to better understand what they felt and saw.

3. *What does multicultural education look like in a classroom?* In the third portion of the semester we explore the teaching of multiculturalism. I help teachers to look at what happens in the classroom by asking such questions as, What is multicultural education? What do you know about the historical experience of women, Native Americans, Asian Americans, Latino Americans, and African Americans in the United States? Why is a child's home language important to keep? What strengths does culture give children? What impact does culture have on learning? What does racism, sexism, or classism look like in schools?

Many teachers do not realize that culture can affect the learning environment. Students bring beliefs from home to school. One teacher asked a Vietnamese student to work with a new Cambodian immigrant. The Vietnamese student told the teacher, "I don't think he will accept my help." The teacher dismissed his concerns, believing that, since both students were from Southeast Asia, they would have natural connections. "I don't think you will have any trouble," she told the Vietnamese student.

Soon after this exchange, the Cambodian student came to the teacher with fire in his eyes and said, "I respect you because you are the teacher, but I won't work with a Vietnamese." This teacher learned that animosities from the past affected her classroom. After this incident, she did not assume that all Asian students got along well.

In addition to bringing up the questions listed above, I encourage teachers to incorporate ethnic content into their curriculum. Teachers are often unsure how to begin. One said, "I'm afraid I'll offend a Navajo student by talking about Navajo culture, because I don't know much about the culture." I suggest that they begin by getting to know each student as a person.

A teacher can also use literature to provide windows into the lives and cultures of others. In order to model the importance of literature, I read to my students almost every week. Since I am a former first-grade teacher, reading stories is one of my greatest pleasures. My teachers are just like young students. Their eyes sparkle when I read *The Knight Who Was Afraid of the Dark* or *Honey, I Love*. Their faces become clouded with sadness when I read *The Children We Remember* — a book about the Holocaust — or *Teammates*, which tells about the pain Jackie Robinson and Pee Wee Reese endured fighting racism. Teachers feel the desperation in Langston Hughes' poems "Dream Deferred" and "American Heartbreak." The book *Grandfather's Journey* helps them sense the closeness of family and understand the emotional bonds we have to our country.[5] I discuss how to choose multicultural literature that can enrich the curriculum and how to use it in the classroom. I believe that literature is one of the most wonderful gifts we can share with our students.[6]

Another aspect of curriculum that I focus on is how to build a problem-posing unit. I ask teachers, "How can you provide ways for your students to look at a social issue? What questions can you ask students that will let them investigate and come to their own conclusions?" Older students might examine the civil rights movement as they consider the question,

Are there times when people should challenge their government? Other students might examine the importance of diversity in the United States, seeking to answer the questions, Do you think the emphasis on cultural diversity separates Americans or brings them together? Why? Younger children can struggle with the question, What is fairness? Or they might be asked, Why do children call each other mean names? Wise teachers create lessons on issues that their students have chosen to investigate.

On the last day of class, after most of the teachers had left, a young teacher named Delia sat down next to me. "This has been the most difficult and yet most fun class I've had. You made me think. I learned more about who I was in this class. I never knew I had so many preconceived notions about people from other cultures. Sometimes I went home from class with a terrible headache. I had to own up to my prejudices and ignorance. I want to make a difference with all kids, and now I know I should never deny any children their culture."

Teachers like Delia created a real family of learners because they shared themselves with their peers and with me. I celebrate the important work that she and the other teachers do because they care for our most precious people, our children.

1. Paulo Freire, *Pedagogy of the Oppressed* (New York: Herder & Herder, 1971).

2. Nel Noddings, *The Challenge to Care in Schools* (New York: Teachers College Press, 1992).

3. The phrase "study of schooling" was taken from the wonderful book by John Goodlad, *A Place Called School: Prospects for the Future* (New York: McGraw-Hill, 1984). I use the phrase because Goodlad documents the importance of looking at the entire ethos of schools in order to better understand what reforms must be undertaken.

4. Vivian Gussin Paley, *White Teacher* (Cambridge, Mass.: Harvard University Press, 1979).

5. Barbara Shook Hazen, *The Knight Who Was Afraid of the Dark* (New York: Dial Books, 1989); Eloise Greenfield, *Honey, I Love* (New York: Thomas Y. Crowell, 1977); Chana Abells, *The Children We Remember* (New York: Greenwillow Press, 1986); Peter Golenbock, *Teammates* (New York: Harcourt Brace Jovanovich, 1990); Langston Hughes, *The Panther and the Lash* (New York: Alfred A. Knopf, 1967); and Allen Say, *Grandfather's Journey* (Boston: Houghton Mifflin, 1993).

6. The Council on Interracial Books for Children published a pamphlet called "10 Quick Ways to Analyze Children's Books for Racism and Sexism," which has been reprinted in Bill Bigelow et al., eds., *Rethinking Our Classrooms: Teaching for Equity and Justice* (Milwaukee: Rethinking Schools, 1994). For lists of children's books that are multicultural and appropriate for the discussion of social issues, see Ronald Evans and Valerie Ooka Pang, "Resources and Materials for Issues-Centered Social Studies Education," *The Social Studies*, May/June 1992, pp. 118-19; and Valerie Ooka Pang et al., "Beyond Chopsticks and Dragons: Selecting Asian-American Literature for Children," *Reading Teacher*, November 1992, pp. 216-24.

Questions and Answers about Inclusion: What Every Teacher Should Know

BONNIE B. GREER and JOHN G. GREER

Bonnie B. Greer and John G. Greer are professors in the Department of Instruction and Curriculum Leadership, University of Memphis, Memphis, Tennessee.

Since the passage of the landmark Education for All Handicapped Children Act (Public Law 94-142) in 1975, the special education profession and the school community have been guided by the concept of the least restrictive environment. Whenever possible, children with disabilities must be, and to an ever-growing extent have been, educated with children who are not disabled. However, Public Law 94-142 also stipulates that a continuum of placement options, ranging from institutionalization to education in the regular class, be employed. Traditionally, children with mild learning problems have been mainstreamed into general education classes while those with more serious problems have been sent to the resource room, educated in self-contained classrooms, or placed outside the regular school environment.

In recent years, the continuum of placement has come under fire (Will 1986). The Regular Education Initiative (REI), a philosophy developed in the 1980s, envisioned a fundamental restructuring of the relationship between special and regular education. Proponents of the REI argued for the elimination of the special education eligibility process and the questioned practice of labeling children. Calling for close collaboration between regular and special education personnel, proponents sought to require that schools educate the majority of children with disabilities in the regular classroom.

Today, the inclusion movement is at the forefront of reform and has many of the same objectives as REI—with one very significant difference. Although some reformers continue to believe that the continuum of services and placement options must still be used for those children with the severest problems (Gersten and Woodward 1990; Jenkins, Pious, and Peterson 1988), many others in the inclusion movement demand that all children, regardless of their dis-abilities or special needs, be educated in the regular class (Lipsky and Gartner 1991; Stainback and Stainback 1992). They consider it the right of every child to be included in all aspects of school life alongside their nondisabled peers. Thus, they advocate the elimination of the present dual system of regular education and "pullout" special education alternatives in favor of a more unified, coordinated, and inclusive system. Responsibilities for the planning, delivery, and evaluation of every child's instruction would be shared in a multidisciplinary, school-based setting. If it is fully implemented, inclusion, which is based on principles that have long guided the special education profession, will have a profound impact on virtually every teacher in America.

Why Is Inclusion Being Proposed?

Those people who are most vocal in their support of full inclusion cite their disenchantment with the current system. Despite a proliferation of "special" or "compensatory" programs developed over the years, the special education effort has had only limited success, with many serious and widely recognized shortcomings. Instructional results have been mixed, and no consensus exists as to the effectiveness of pullout programs (Madden and Slavin 1983; Wang, Reynolds, and Walberg 1986). At the same time, those children segregated from their peers in special classes are often stigmatized and suffer from low self–esteem (Guralnick and Groom 1988).

Other problems with the present system also exist. Children are only identified as needing special services after they have failed in the regular system and have been labeled. The screening procedures and eligibility requirements used in this process often exclude many children who need extra instructional support (Reynolds, Zetlin, and Wang 1993). Overall the dual system of regular and special education is commonly described as fragmented and poorly coordinated (Jenkins, Pious, and Peterson 1988). Believing that many children fall through the cracks, advocates of inclusion look to a single system that is responsible for teaching all children, regardless of their needs or level of

From *The Clearing House*, July/August 1995, pp. 339-342. © 1995 by the Helen Dwight Reid Educational Foundation. Reprinted by permission of Heldref Publications, 1319 Eighteenth Street, NW, Washington, DC 20036-1802.

functioning. They believe that education in the regular classroom, using individualized instruction as has long been characteristic of special education, will result in more effective and more socially appropriate education for all.

Who Are the Children Involved in Inclusion?

At the heart of the inclusion debate is the question, Which children would actually be placed in the regular class and spend most or all of their time with nondisabled same-age classmates? Most people agree that students with mild and moderate disabilities who are currently served in special education classrooms will be placed in the regular class. A small but articulate, vocal group is calling for the inclusion of even those children who are profoundly retarded or who have severe behavior disorders (Snell 1991; Stainback and Stainback 1992). The instructional needs of these children are very different from those of the average youngster. Those with mental retardation, for example, learn in very small steps and need large amounts of repetition to master new material. The teacher emphasizes basic skills rather than academics. It is not uncommon for students with severe behavior disorders to bite without warning, poke someone else's eyes, and engage in other extremely violent and aggressive behaviors. Various self-stimulatory or self-injurious behaviors are also common to this group of children. Obviously, these students would be highly disruptive to the routine found in most regular classrooms.

Those of a less-extreme position believe in retaining the continuum of placement options for limited numbers of children, but they also envision children with severe disabilities in the regular class. Children with severe cerebral palsy, for example, who are wheelchair bound, with significant paralysis and distorted speech, might be provided with current technology to augment their speech and allow them to participate in appropriate, though mediated, instructional activities. Growing numbers of parents and teachers are recognizing the moral, social, and academic justification for placing such children in a regular class.

Medically fragile children represent another issue. Many children with severe disabilities have concomitant medical problems that can be very restrictive and often life threatening. If these children are placed in the regular classroom, they could be exposed to a much higher risk of infection than that to which they are accustomed. Although many would undoubtedly benefit from socialization with nondisabled classmates, a case-by-case decision-making process would seem to be the only realistic approach. It would be important to consider any medical procedures the child may need each day and whether a teacher would be qualified to carry them out.

In any case, the future promises a regular classroom population that will be far more diverse than the typical one today. Some children with disabilities will learn at a much slower rate than other students. What they do learn, they will have difficulty retaining, and they will need help generalizing skills from one situation to another. The focus, for most, will be on learning skills necessary for participating in everyday living activities.

Is There Strong Support for Inclusion?

The philosophical support for inclusion is basically the same as that which led to the passage of PL 94–142. Three factors, common to both, are especially important:

1. The principle of normalization. Originating in Scandinavia in the early 1970s, normalization holds that those with disabilities should, to whatever degree possible, be allowed to participate in the routines, the activities, and the general lifestyles enjoyed by those who are not disabled.

2. The zero-reject policy. All children, regardless of the severity of their disabilities, must be provided a free and appropriate public education. Local systems can neither choose whom to serve nor turn away any child from needed services.

3. The idea of least restrictive environment. This approach has guided the actions of special educators for two decades. Inclusion represents the culmination of this principle.

Solid legal support for inclusion also exists. The cumulative effect of legislation and litigation over the past several decades has been to clearly establish the right of every child, regardless of disability, to be educated in classes with same-age peers whenever possible. With recent advances in adaptive technology and growing expertise in the individualization of instruction, regular class placement will be possible for many, if not most, children with severe disabilities.

When Will It Be Implemented?

In some areas of the country, inclusion has already been put into practice. Several states (e.g., Vermont, Colorado, Minnesota, and Oregon) have for years supported the placement of children with disabilities in the regular class, and many more have received federal funding to develop programs that promote inclusion (Alper and Ryndak 1992). Many school systems are now fully inclusive.

The literature contains an ever growing number of articles on inclusive classrooms, and many of them report successful experiences (Johnston 1994; Leister, Koonce, and Nisbet 1993). Nevertheless, relatively few focus on the placement of children who have severe or profound retardation or severe behavior disorders. More often, the regular class experiences of children with physical disabilities are reported. In any case, little empirical support for or against inclusion exists. Although advocates claim that existing instructional models and strategies would enable the immediate implementation of inclusion (Slavin and Stevens 1991; Wang and Walberg 1988), most experts are more cautious. Pointing to the difficulties schools already have in handling the diversity of student needs, they argue that such a fundamental restructuring of American education cannot begin until there is a sound empirical basis for decision making.

How Will the Classroom Teacher's Role Change?

With the implementation of inclusion, the role of the regular classroom teacher will change dramatically. If children with disabilities are no longer pulled out for special instruction and related services, teachers will provide those forms of assistance in the regular classroom. This change will require close collaboration between the special education teacher and other professionals who will need to work with these children. Drawing on the regular teacher's expertise in content and curriculum sequence and the special education teacher's understanding of disabilities and different learning strategies, the two professionals together can adapt instruction to the individual needs of their students. Common planning and shared decision making will therefore replace the relatively independent role played by many teachers today. Furthermore, teachers must work together to encourage peer acceptance of and tolerance for individual differences. They also must have similar behavior management strategies and enforce classroom rules consistently. In the inclusive classroom, the regular teacher must be as involved with the problems of children with disabilities as is the special educator.

Will It Work?

Changing the place of instruction is more easily accomplished than changing the nature of student–teacher interactions, which are complicated by myriad instructional variables. To work, inclusion will need a highly coordinated effort from all involved. Merging the talents and resources of regular and special educators will require a partnership in which all involved are committed to a common goal.

At present, there is no consensus in the educational community. Many, if not most, teachers, from regular classrooms and special education, are not strongly opposed to the current system. The main push for full inclusion has come from a relatively small group of parents and professionals. Concerned primarily with the instructional and social–emotional needs of children with severe disabilities, they are well organized and articulate their position with great zeal. They have already had a very significant impact on state and federal policies and have heavily influenced the positions taken by important professional organizations.

Inclusion, of course, is not the only agenda facing American education. As our preeminence in commerce, industry, and science is being eclipsed by other countries, it is widely agreed that the American school curriculum must be more rigorous and challenging, with greater emphasis on math, science, and foreign language. Balancing those demands for greater academic rigor with the challenges represented by inclusion is a daunting task for the regular classroom teacher as well as everyone else in the profession. To design an educational system that more effectively meets the needs of all children, we must find a process for consensus building. Open dialogue is a prerequisite to sound decision making. The increasingly emotional rhetoric now characterizing the debate must be replaced with a more reasoned, constructive exchange of ideas. Until now largely restricted to the special education literature, with few regular educators participating, the debate is lacking a key ingredient. Because the ultimate success or failure of inclusion will depend on the commitment and willingness of the regular classroom teachers to put it into practice, their input in its design is absolutely critical. It is incumbent on all educators to become meaningfully involved—through professional organizations, local groups, state agencies, and representative government—in the process of shaping the future of American education.

REFERENCES

Alper, S., and D. L. Ryndak. 1992. Educating students with severe handicaps in regular classes. *Elementary School Journal* 92(3): 373–87.

Gartner, A., and D. K. Lipsky. 1987. Beyond special education: Toward a quality system for all students. *Harvard Educational Review* 57:367–95.

Gersten, R., and J. Woodward. 1990. Rethinking the Regular Education Initiative: Focus on the classroom teacher. *Remedial and Special* streamed and specialized classrooms: A comparative analysis. *Exceptional Children* 54:415–25.

Jenkins, J. R., C. G. Pious, and D. L. Peterson. 1988. Categorical programs for remedial and handicapped students: Issues of validity. *Exceptional Children* 55:147–58.

Johnston, W. F. 1994. How to educate all the students together. *Schools in the Middle* (May):9–14.

Leister, C., D. Koonce, and S. Nisbet. 1993. Best practices for preschool programs: An update on inclusive settings. *Day Care and Early Education* (Winter):9–12.

Lipsky, D. K., and A. Gartner. 1991. Restructuring for quality. In *The Regular Education Initiative: Alternative perspectives on concepts, issues and models,* edited by J. W. Lloyd, A. C. Repp, and N. N. Singh, 43–56. Sycamore, Ill.: Sycamore.

Madden, N. A., and R. E. Slavin. 1983. Mainstreaming students with mild handicaps: Academic and social outcomes. *Review of Educational Research* 53:519–69.

Reynolds, M. C., A. G. Zetlin, and M. C. Wang. 1993. 20/20 analysis: Taking a close look at the margins. *Exceptional Children* 59:294–300.

Slavin, R. E., and R. J. Stevens. 1991. Cooperative learning and mainstreaming. In *The Regular Education Initiative: Alternative perspectives on concepts, issues, and models,* edited by J. W. Lloyd, A. C. Repp, and N. N. Singh, 177–81. Sycamore, Ill.: Sycamore.

Snell, M. E. 1991. Schools are for all kids: The importance of integration for students with severe disabilities and their peers. In *The Regular Education Initiative: Alternative perspectives on concepts, issues and models,* edited by J. W. Lloyd, A. C. Repp, and N. N. Singh, 133–48. Sycamore, Ill.: Sycamore.

Stainback, S., and W. Stainback. 1992. *Curriculum considerations in inclusive classrooms: Facilitating learning for all students.* Baltimore: Paul Brookes.

Wang, M. C., M. C. Reynolds, and H. J. Walberg. 1986. Rethinking special education. *Educational Leadership* 55(2):128–37.

Wang, M. C., and H. J. Walberg. 1988. Four fallacies of segregation. *Exceptional Children* 55:128–37.

Will, M. C. 1986. Educating children with learning problems: A shared responsibility. *Exceptional Children* 52:411–15.

SUGGESTED RESOURCES

Fuchs, D., and L. S. Fuchs. 1994. Inclusive schools movement and the radicalization of special education reform. *Exceptional Children* 60:294–309.

This article examines the inclusive schools movement and cautions against the increasingly strident rhetoric that characterizes the debate. Critical of some positions taken by advocates of full inclusion, the authors call for more open and meaningful dialogue with general education.

Giangreco, M. F., R. Dennis, C. Cloninger, S. Edelman, and R. Schattman. 1993. "I've counted Jon": Transformational experiences of teachers educating students with disabilities. *Exceptional Children* 59:359–72.

This article describes the experiences of over thirty general education teachers who have had a child with severe disabilities in their classrooms.

Horner, H. H., S. J. Diemer, and K. C. Brazeau. 1992. Educational support for students with severe problem behaviors in Oregon: A descriptive analysis from the 1987–1988 school year. *Journal of the Association for Persons with Severe Handicaps (JASH)* 17:154–69.

Because Oregon has been identified as a leader in maintaining students with severe disabilities in the regular school environment, the authors used a survey to examine what placement options were used there with children with severe behavior problems.

Kauffman, J. M. 1993. How we might achieve the radical reform of special education. *Exceptional Children* 60:6–16.

While recognizing the current pressures for change in special education, the author of this article calls for decisions to be made on the basis of careful empirical investigation. He cautions against fashionable actions and fanaticism.

Rainforth, B., J. York, and C. MacDonald. 1992. *Collaborative teams for students with severe disabilities: Integrating therapy and educational services.* Baltimore: Paul H. Brookes.

Anticipating the placement of students with severe disabilities in the regular classroom, the authors examine strategies for collaborative teamwork and the delivery of therapy and related services.

Villa, R., J. Thousand, W. Stainback, and S. Stainback, eds. 1992. *Restructuring for caring and effective education.* Baltimore: Paul H. Brookes.

The authors critique current special education strategies and find them seriously inadequate. They emphasize the need for the inclusion of all children, regardless of the type and severity of their disabilities, in the regular education setting and argue for reform now.

Time to Talk Back

The task for higher education is to keep the "malignant representations" of bigotry above ground, to challenge bigotry's assumptions, and to challenge its expression, Mr. Fischler reminds us.

MICHAEL L. FISCHLER

MICHAEL L. FISCHLER is director of the Office of Counseling and Human Relations and a professor in the Department of Education at Plymouth (N.H.) State College.

THE SEMESTER was barely two weeks old as I sat in my counseling office with a client. Our sober interaction was punctuated by the blaring sound of a male resident from a neighboring dorm loudly singing along with the Guns 'n' Roses recording of "One in a Million": "Po-lice and niggers, get out of my way, don't need to buy none of your gold chains today. . . ."

Unable to leave my client so that I could identify the exact source of the music, I finished my session, contacted a resident assistant and later the resident director, and sought to have the individual identified so that the situation could be addressed. An investigation began, but no student was identified.

Three weeks later, I was walking hurriedly past that same residence hall. A student perched in an open window interrupted my thoughts with the electronically augmented sound of that same Guns 'n' Roses song. He was loudly singing: "Immigrants and faggots, they make no sense to me . . . they come to our country and think they'll do as they please. . . ." I approached the open window and asked him if if he knew what he was saying. He said, "Yes." I then asked him what he thought he was doing, to which he responded with mock respect, "I'm singing a song." I asked for his name (he gave a false one) and told him emphatically that I would see him later. The student then returned to his music and continued singing.

I returned that evening with the dean of student affairs to confront the student. His attitude when we confronted him was one of self-righteousness, arrogance, and heightened defensiveness. We tried to help him understand the significance of his playing and singing those lyrics. We struggled to make him aware of the song's message, of its affront to human dignity, of its divisive and inflammatory nature, and of his shared culpability when he belted out the lyrics for all to hear. The student failed to understand what we were so upset about.

"I've got the right to sing whatever I want," he said. "Anyway, it's just a song."

While we acknowledged his First Amendment rights of free expression, we nonetheless reminded him that the college had rules with regard to excessive noise, verbal harassment, and disorderly conduct. Still, the point of our confrontation was not a legal one. We simply wanted to create some understanding — an understanding of the power of words to hurt, to destroy, to frighten, to isolate, to humiliate, and to divide. We brought up examples of violence against blacks, Native Americans, immigrants, and gays. He showed but little appreciation for the connection between such violence and his own behavior, and he steadfastly maintained that his behavior was typical — that "lots of students" play Guns 'n' Roses (as well as the music of other allegedly offensive groups) and that it's "good music and we enjoy it!"

Just at that moment, as if on cue, "One in a Million" was heard blaring from a nearby room. We invited the neighbors to join our discussion group (now up to five students) on the merits of the song's message and on their involvement in projecting that message loudly from their rooms. This discussion mirrored the earlier interaction. "It's good music; why does it bother you?" one student asked. After all, none of us were members of any of the groups mentioned in the song. "I probably wouldn't play it if one of *them* was in the room," said another. "They [blacks] use nigger, too," said a third. And so it went.

The hurt, the pain, the loss of self-esteem, the divisiveness and anger that those lyrics could cause seemed at best a remote consideration for these students. They could not see that by loudly playing and/or singing them — by helping to disseminate them — they were indirectly endorsing the message. The legacy of blood and hate attached to such flash words as *nigger* and *faggot* did not seem relevant.

WHAT SEEMED to be an isolated incident may not be isolated after all. Many individuals in our society lack the historical knowledge, concern, or empathy necessary to appreciate the significance and the destructive power of messages similar to those conveyed by Guns 'n' Roses. Some people place their personal pleasure ("I really *like* the music") above the potential displeasure of others. Others honestly don't believe that a song — especially one with "catchy" lyrics and a good beat — can hurt anyone. Regardless of motivation, the behavior of those who play or sing these songs is scarcely ever questioned or challenged.

Americans have grown far too tolerant of the offensive word. In our quest to guarantee the individual his or her freedom to speak, we have neglected our solemn responsibility to speak back. The greatest threat to our First Amendment rights and to that fragile structure we call democracy is not the racist or pornographic posturings of youth. It is our silence. For it is through silence that we risk communicating assent.

 From *Phi Delta Kappan*, April 1992, pp. 634-635. © 1992 by Phi Delta Kappa, Inc. Reprinted by permission.

As members of the academic community, we must "talk back," and we must encourage our students to "talk back." We must challenge our students to listen carefully to messages like those conveyed by Guns 'n' Roses, to consider their implications, and to contemplate their potential impact. If students are offended, then they need to find constructive outlets for their expression. If students are not offended, then they need to search their hearts and minds to understand why.

Language can connect and disconnect; it can sustain and destroy. Words have the power to hurt as much as — perhaps more than — any sharpened stick or jagged stone. Yet laws that circumscribe expression, that limit one's "words," do little to inhibit the development of racism, sexism, and other malevolent prejudices.

Too often these decrees suppress only the most superficial manifestations of bigotry and drive its more malignant representations underground. The challenge for higher education is to keep the "malignant representations" of bigotry above ground, to challenge its assumptions, and to challenge its expression. Only through this essential dialectic can learning, our most cherished of outcomes, occur.

The Ideology of Star Teachers

of Children in Poverty

Star urban teachers are driven more by their desire to develop "good people" than by learning theories and classroom strategies, says this proponent of alternative accreditation. Dismissing what some schools of education say make expert teachers, Martin Haberman suggests that teachers in urban settings can be recruited from non-educational settings and receive on-the-job training from star urban teachers.

Martin Haberman

MARTIN HABERMAN is Professor of Curriculum and Instruction, University of Wisconsin-Milwaukee. His programs for preparing teachers for children in poverty include models which became The National Teacher Corps and more recently, alternative certification programs in urban school districts.

The best way to improve urban schools is to get better teachers. The best way to get better teachers is to recruit educated adults who closely resemble the star teachers already effective in urban schools. The best way to train these recruits is by having them actually teach and be coached on-the-job by star urban teachers.[1]

The knowledge new urban teachers need is derived from the procedures star urban teachers demonstrate. This knowledge base includes subject matter content. (You can't teach what you don't know.) This knowledge base also includes teaching strategies; i.e., how to organize and manage a classroom, how to interest and engage learners, how to resolve student problems. It is also imperative that beginning teachers have a working knowledge of technology-based information systems and computer-assisted instruction.

But these things are what any teacher needs in order to teach anywhere. The component which is vital for urban, multicultural teachers, and which must be the organizing theme for all their other forms of know-how, is an ideology—a set of ideas that reflect the social needs and aspirations of a people. There is no way to be an effective teacher of children in poverty by simply knowing a great deal, or by demonstrating the use of various teaching strategies.

This in no way deprecates these two very valuable components of teacher knowledge. But having a rich background of subject matter and knowing strategies of teaching are not enough for teachers to be successful with children in poverty.

The Ideology of Star Teachers

Stars teachers' ideology is directed at making good people in a society where there is less than complete agreement about what constitutes a good person. This is no mean task nor one most teachers even undertake. Star teachers perceive themselves as performing a different job from most other teachers. This distinction

Reprinted with permission from *Educational Horizons*, Spring 1992, pp. 125-129. © 1992 by Pi Lambda Theta, Inc., international honor society and professional association in education, Bloomington, IN 47407-6626.

is crucial to understanding what star teachers do that distinguishes them from the outset—before they even enter a classroom or begin interacting with youngsters. The following parable illustrates this basic part of star teacher ideology.

Three workers were doing the same job, at least objective observers agree they were performing similar tasks with equal degrees of competence. An observer asked each of the workers, "What are you doing?" The first responded, "I'm making twenty dollars an hour." The second responded, "I'm laying bricks." The third responded, "I'm building a cathedral." The question is, "Are the three workers really achieving the same things?"

The students of star teachers learn a great deal as measured by standardized tests and other means. These teachers are also adept at classroom organization, discipline and ways of engaging learners. But their perception of what they are about is really quite grand, and in many cases grandiose. Stars intend that their teaching develop good people—people with character who are to some degree inner-directed by reflection and commitments, not merely by impulse. Teaching, like bricklaying, is a craft, but one in which minute-by-minute decisions involve human interaction. The teacher's ideology undergirds the basis of every response she or he makes to a student. Every act reflects this ideology. Stars are different from other teachers in that they are aware of the connection between their behavior and their ideology, and they accept this challenge because they believe the purpose of schooling is to form good people who are knowledgeable. This is an entirely different orientation from most teachers, who believe that stacking of bricks (subjects) will somehow lead to good people.

In truth, most teachers don't believe their teaching culminates into much since they never really think about the matter. They assume it! "My job is to teach Home Economics, or Algebra II, or how to conjugate irregular verbs." The students are expected to somehow integrate the various forms of knowledge, apply them to living and thereby become good! In contrast, star teachers believe it is their responsibility to help students see meaning in knowledge, integrate and apply it to their lives and remain permanently affected by this learning. When stars ask or answer a question, listen, talk, make an assignment, show how to do the same thing, grade a piece of work, complain, discipline, suggest, approve and engage in any teaching behavior, they are consciously and actively guided by their ideology of making good people.

Star teachers don't practice their craft without reflection. Nor do they rely on any theory or research which pretends that a scientifically-derived technique can guide a teacher's behavior. Stars are well aware and accept the fact that the creation of good people is a normative process; they are comfortable deciding what "should be." Their distinction from most other teachers is that they are familiar and comfortable with practicing a moral craft. Most other teachers, particularly those who fail or quit, make just as many normative decisions as stars, but because they are not cognizant of teaching as a "should be" craft they unthinkingly implement meaningless traditions rather than a well-thought-out ideology.

Ideology in Practice

Two kindergarten teachers in Minneapolis took their respective classes on a field trip to the zoo. When the children returned they were to contribute ideas to a common experience chart. Ideas such as the biggest animal, the smallest, the funniest, the one I liked best, the baby animals, the animals I fed, would all help the children become more observant. Children would express themselves, read, write, listen, and draw pictures about what they had actually experienced. This is standard kindergarten fare. Like apple pie and motherhood it is beyond reproach.

Both of these teachers had the same experience with two different students. A Sioux child in each of their classes began to weep during the trip and would not participate in the class after returning from the zoo. The teachers subsequently learned that it is common for Native Americans to teach their children that the spirits of their dead ancestors are in animals. The children were upset that their dead relatives were locked in cages and seemed so unhappy.

One teacher responded to this incident by saying, "No way! That zoo trip is the best thing we do all semester. I'm not going to deny it to the rest of the class. I'll just leave those kids at school who don't want to come." The other teacher responded by announcing, "That takes care of that. We'll just find someplace else to go."

Incidents such as these are replayed countless times in urban, multicultural classrooms. Teachers decide, usually on their own, how to deal with such situations. Some teachers such as the two described here define the issue as a problem and then decide their future behavior. Other teachers regard such events as opportunities. They involve the children in discussing, thinking, and planning what to do next time. Such teachers see their role as raising awareness and helping children become sensitive to human differences and how to best live with them.

Regardless of how the teacher "handles" the issue, including ignoring it, we can be reasonably certain that teachers were not taught the responses they should make to these situations in their teacher training programs. Professorial expertise cannot answer these questions. Neither can knowledge of Piaget or recent research on instruction. What the teacher does is a reflection of his or her own ideology.

The most important *instructional* decisions teachers make reflect their ideology. Indeed, almost every decision they make reflects it. Typically, teachers make decisions about content, method, discipline, and evaluation, not necessarily about zoos. And because the issue is not always as clear as it was in this case many teachers misunderstand the bases of their decisions. They may believe that how they get a class to work, settle an argument, or present a lesson is value-free or neutral in its ethical implications. Giving directions reflects an ideology just as clearly and quite as powerfully as taking a trip to the zoo. Asking children to cooperate or share ideas is also a reflection of personal ideology.

Teaching is neither an art nor a science. An art is practiced for the benefit of the artist. Whether others appreciate or denigrate the artist's work is their problem. Protections and safeguards are directed at protecting the rights of the artist to engage in authentic expression. The freedom of the artist is the ultimate value to be preserved even, as frequently occurs, when there are few who appreciate the artist's work. It is preposterous to apply the metaphor of the unfettered artist to schoolteachers whose existence is judged by their impact on students who are required to attend school. Frequently, those who use the analogue of the artist to explain the work of the teacher are actually stating their belief that teachers exhibit individual personality traits, or that teaching involves making many subjective judgments, or that the qualities of good teachers cannot be described scientifically. Clearly, schoolteachers cannot be judged primarily by the authenticity of their own expression but by their influence on their students.

Science is an equally poor analogue for teaching. While art emphasizes the expression of some inner truth, science is the search for external truths which explain and predict how the universe works. These explanations are based on theories which are comprised of propositions. The propositions are, in turn, comprised of axioms which are supported or refuted by systematic, objective research. To the degree that this research culminates in axioms and propositions which accurately explain and predict some aspect of the universe, a field of scientific inquiry can be said to exist. The nature of such research is that it can be replicated (it is reliable) and that it is a true and accurate depiction of an objective reality (it is valid). To claim that school teaching can be based on this form of knowledge would require that general propositions be applicable to specific cases. For instance, if Ray won't sit down, be quiet, and do his work, there would have to exist a scientific proposition derived from valid and reliable research to explain and predict the behavior of a group of Rays. This is not possible because the myriad factors preventing Ray from sitting down and working quietly are specific to the situation and can *not* be generalized into axioms, propositions, and theories.

The best definition of teaching is that it is a craft.[2] It is a demonstration of proficiency rather than merely knowing, thinking, or feeling about things without having to *do* something. Plumbing is a craft. What the plumber may or may not know about the physics of water pressure is secondary to his or her ability to make water flow or stop leaks. The craft is learned *primarily* through experience and practice and much less by learning the formulas for computing water pressure or the physical theories which explain hydrodynamics. A secondary definition of craft is "skill in guile, cunning, and evasion." Teaching is the craft of doing things with materials, equipment, and settings and with moving people in directions they might not necessarily seek to go. Many have defined teaching as a moral craft; that is, the teacher has the know-how to teach goodness and character as well as basic skills and subject matter. Accepting this definition means that we cannot use the scientific analogue for teaching since science reveals what "is" not what "should be." At the same time, the artist metaphor deals with what the artist feels and prefers and not with sup-

porting any particular standard of goodness in human action.

Teaching as a moral craft must be built upon by an ideology that reflects the social needs and aspirations of a people. There's the rub! The aspirations of the American people are diverse. Indeed, many general American values are actually contradictory. We believe in science *and* religion, individual competition *and* individuals contributing to the common good, equality *and* status, patriotism *and* brotherhood, power *and* democratic action, pragmatism (i.e., producing results) *and* the importance of ethical means.

If these contradictions are not in themselves a sufficient obstacle to sharing a common ideology, teachers must also deal with a pluralistic society. We are composed of numerous subgroups. The rights of women, for example, are not only a set of contradictions in the larger American society but even more diverse as one considers the views of various ethnic, language, and racial subgroups regarding the rights and place of women.

Imagine, for example, a teacher who tries to interest female students in scientific questioning. The teacher has recently attended a workshop on procedures for helping females feel that scientific inquiry is not a male domain. Strategies include actually teaching female pupils to question what others say and to reward the girls who ask, "How do you know that?" The teacher has also been taught to encourage females to question the teacher and to introduce competing ideas, to raise challenging questions, and to speak up if they disagree. After a few days of such instruction the teacher is met by a father from a particular ethnic group (it might be any one of several) who states: "I've raised my little girl to be respectful and polite. She does what adults, and especially adult males, tell her. I don't like the idea of you telling her she should criticize the teacher. I'm teaching her to be respectful, quiet, and do her work."

At this point, the teacher must make a decision. Whatever action the teacher takes we can be certain that it was not specifically taught in his or her certification program and was not part of the license requirement of the state in which the teacher was certified. The teacher must now decide how to answer the father based on an ideology. One ideology may place the family above all else, in which case the teacher will assure the father that in future *his* little girl will be taught to politely follow directions. Another

teacher, whose ideology emphasizes achieving equity in the larger society, will reject the father's demand and insist that the child will be expected to function in an intellectually aggressive manner.

What guidelines may be offered teachers to help them sort through this maze? The way I have chosen is to use star teachers in urban, multicultural schools as my referent. Such teachers function in a pluralistic, multilingual society and not in a homogeneous rural or suburban setting.

In small rural schools there is such a high level of homogeneity that teachers frequently reflect the children's family values without thinking about them. In affluent suburbs, schools are also more homogeneous than in cities since parents who may object to schools which are "too diverse" have the resources to select private or parochial schools more to their liking. Currently, approximately 23 percent of children attend schools in urban, metropolitan systems, 44 percent in suburban districts, and 33 percent in rural areas. In the suburban and rural schools teachers may teach their entire careers and never realize they have been practicing any ideology. The reason for this: without personal reflection they simply know what good people are and how good people behave and so do the parents. What's more, there is general agreement. In the cases where there is not common agreement, most people will define the divergence as a problem and quickly settle the matter.

It is in the urban schools—multilingual, multiracial, and largely populated by the poor—that the teacher's role as a moral craftsperson becomes clearly evident. My approach to understanding this conflict in values has been to raise the issue with star teachers and observe their answers in practice. What do they do? How do they think about their role? On what bases do they decide particular issues?

Star Teachers Perfect Their Ideology by Practicing It

Ideology is not something teachers merely talk or think about. Instead, their ideology can be readily inferred from their behavior. Based on the two examples raised here, the trip to the zoo and the father who wanted his daughter to learn to follow directions, I am confident I have had enough interaction with star teachers to anticipate their responses. Both instances might be viewed as clashes between a subculture and the larger American society. In the case of the zoo incident, the teacher's ideology would lead him or her to protect the Native American child against the common assumption that zoo experiences are a universal good. In the latter case, their ideology would lead them to consider ways of educating females that their parents might not necessarily approve of, without causing too much stress for the child. Assuming that these interpretations are accurate, why would teachers decide in one case to support a subgroup value in opposition to the larger society and in another instance undermine a subgroup's value? As star teachers make their daily decisions they use specific questions to implement their ideologies. In interviews they report using guidelines such as the following:

1. In one way or another, I recognize that everything I do as a teacher reveals my view of how a good person behaves.

2. Since I recognize that what I do reflects my ideology and not some universal right answers, I can reconsider what I believe by looking at what I'm doing.

3. The children can understand how I decide what a good person does. I frequently share the *bases* of my decisions with them.

4. The children can understand and consider how they think a good person acts. They can share why they believe as they do.

5. Children are capable of handling contradictions in ideology. (At age two they were taught to not undress in public but were taken to the beach and undressed.)

6. Children of all ages can become aware of and sensitive to differences among cultural subgroups.

7. Children of all ages can be involved in thinking and making decisions about contradictory visions of good behavior.

Implementing the Ideology

The ideology of star teachers for children in poverty is a constant referent, a guideline for their daily interactions with children and youth.

These teachers do not use theory to guide their teaching behavior. Faced with myriad decisions in the hurly-burly environment of doing minute-to-minute teaching they do not refer to the postulates and axioms of Piaget, Skinner, or Freud. Nor do they consider the research summaries of school achievement, data support-

---

What Martin Haberman Says about Star Teachers in Urban Schools

Star teachers . . .

- perceive themselves as performing a different job from most other teachers.
- are adept at classroom organization, discipline, and ways of engaging learners.
- intend that their teaching develop good people—people with character who are to some degree inner-directed by reflection and commitments, not merely by impulse.
- are aware of the connection between their behavior and their own ideology.
- believe the purpose of schooling is to form good people who are knowledgeable.
- believe it is their responsibility to help students see meaning in knowledge, integrate and apply it to their lives and remain permanently affected by this learning.
- don't practice their craft without reflection.
- see their role as raising awareness and helping children become sensitive to human differences and how best to live with them.
- do not use theory to guide their teaching behavior.
- do not refer to the postulates and axioms of Piaget, Skinner, or Freud. Nor do they consider the research summaries of school achievement, dating supporting time on task, cooperative learning, or heterogeneous grouping.
- are generally oblivious to how experts in the various subject matters logically organize the studies of "their" disciplines.
- are more controlled by the internal organization of the subject matter (i.e., how their students organize and personalize the learning) rather than by the external logic of any body of knowledge.
- work on the assumption that what happens in their classrooms is not getting ready to live but living.
- believe that poor children cannot only learn but can think and reflect as well.
- accept the challenge of fostering high achievement but see their role as transcending this concern.

---

ing time on task, cooperative learning, or heterogeneous grouping. But theories of learning and research on instruction are not all they ignore. They are generally oblivious to how experts in the various subject matters (e.g., biology, history, English, etc.) logically organize the studies of "their" disciplines. Star teachers are more controlled by the internal organization of subject matter (i.e., how their students organize and personalize the learning) rather than by the external logic of any body of knowledge. For example, experts in math advise that division should be taught after subtraction, about third grade. This makes logical sense since division is sequential subtraction. But most children have learned the concept of division by age three. In day care and at home they have learned that a pretzel is broken into equal parts to be divided. Children sequence their learning of arithmetic psychologically, not logically. Star teachers realize that the placement of most school learning is similarly an arbitrary decision.

Where does this leave the teacher? If theory, research, and the logical organiza-

tion of subject matter do not guide teachers' classroom behavior, then what does? For many teachers their guide is a combination of tradition and experience: what they have always done, what they experienced as children in schools, and practices they have self-discovered which make their work easier.[3] Unfortunately, what makes the work of the teacher easier is not necessarily what leads to the most desirable student learning.

Thus far star ideology has been described as a process for developing good people and not as an advocacy for particular characteristics such as hard work, honesty, concern for others, and love of learning. Star teachers refer to such values but seem to believe that the best way to teach them is *not* by exhortation, moralizing, or the giving of formal lessons (for instance, reading a story and asking for the moral). The seven processes described earlier in this article are the means they use to focus and sensitize students to their own lives and experiences. Engaging in these processes leads stars to consider both the ideology undergirding the subjects they teach and the ways in which they and the students go about their studies. Their classrooms become the most self-conscious setting that either the teacher or the students are likely to experience. There is constant, endless discussion of why we are doing "X," the best way to do "X," who says so, other ways to do "X," how to assess "X," the implications of "X," what happens if we don't do "X" and where did "X" come from anyway.

Goodness does not grow and develop in a vacuum. In a democratic society it must be learned through active participation to insure future involvement. Since star teachers work on the assumption that what happens in their classrooms is not getting ready to live but living, this examination of what everyone does and why is a constant refrain. They operate on the belief that "learning taken on authority is not educative." Most teachers and principals whom I interviewed cannot explain what this phrase means since telling students things, or assigning them to read things is their operational definition of teaching. Stars, however, interpret this phrase to mean that accepting ideas in a nonreflective, uncritical way—without knowing their source, basis, or uses—inevitably leads to dependent learners who remain in need of direction and control. Star teachers believe that sharing the sources of their teaching with students, beginning in primary grades, leads to independent students. Once learners know that the teacher, the book, or any authority is based on theory, research, logic, experience, expert opinion, or common sense, the learner is empowered to evaluate what he or she is being directed to learn. In short, the ideology of stars is to transform the question, "How do you know that?" from a teacher question to a student question, and from an impoliteness to an indicator of student thought and involvement.

The position I have outlined is an attempt to portray the undergirding ideology of star teachers. Their "high expectations" for low-income students are manifested in their belief that poor children cannot only learn but that they can think and reflect as well. Such teachers utilize this belief not only in the teaching of "controversial" issues but also in the expression of every aspect of their daily interactions with students. They accept the challenge of fostering high achievement but see their role as transcending this concern. They use knowledge as an excuse to foster the development of good people rather than as an end in itself. Finally, this orientation toward the purpose of their work, which differs markedly from most teachers and particularly from ineffective and failed teachers, leads stars to perform a set of classroom behaviors which are in many ways different from other teachers. Like the casual observer of the bricklayers, it may seem to the unwary witness that teachers generally perform the same tasks. But star teachers' ideology gives their performance a different meaning—for themselves and for their students.

1. Martin Haberman, *The Dimensions of Excellence in Teacher Education* (Washington, D.C.: Office of Governmental Affairs, U.S. Department of Education, 1991).

2. Alan Tom, *Teaching as a Moral Craft* (New York: Longmans, 1984).

3. Kenneth Zeichner and Carl Grant, "Biography and Social Structure in the Socialization of Student Teachers," Journal of Education for Teaching V.1. (1981): 1.

BUILDING CULTURAL BRIDGES

A Bold Proposal for Teacher Education

Geneva Gay

University of Washington

One of the most compelling features of current school demographics is the growing sociocultural gap between teachers and students. Although the percentage of citizens and students who are Hispanic, Asian, Indian, African-American, poor, and limited English speaking is increasing significantly, the number of teachers from similar backgrounds is declining. This distribution has some major implications for the professional preparation of teachers and for how classroom instruction is conducted. The discussion that follows describes some of the specific demographic characteristics of students and teachers, explains some of the implications of these for teacher education, and offers some suggestions for how teacher preparation programs should be designed to respond to these demographic realities.

STUDENT AND TEACHER DEMOGRAPHICS

The percentage of students of color in U.S. schools has increased steadily since the 1960s. They now compose 30% of the total population of elementary and secondary schools. During the 1980s Hispanics and Asians/Pacific Islanders accounted for the greatest increases, by 44.7% and 116.4%, respectively (*The Condition of Education*, 1992). Although their percentages are not evenly distributed throughout the United States, the trend of increasing numbers of children of color in all school districts across the country is. Already, in at least 18 states and Washington, DC, between 30% and 96% of the public school students in grades K–12 are children of color (*Digest of Education Statistics*, 1992; *Education That Works*, 1990).

The increasing number of ethnically and culturally diverse students is attributable to two major factors—the relative youth of groups of color and their higher birthrates and increased immigration from non-White, non-Western European countries in Asia, the Caribbean, Central and South America, Africa, and the Middle East. By the beginning of the 1990s, more than one third of Hispanics (39%) and African-Americans (33%) were 18 years old or younger, compared to 25% of Anglos. Also, a greater proportion of the population of these groups fell within the prime childbearing years and produced a larger average number of children per family unit. The median ages of Hispanics, African-Americans, and Anglos were 25.5, 27.3, and 33.1 years, respectively (*The Condition of Education*, 1992; *Statistical Abstract of the United States*, 1991).

During the 1980s, the pattern of immigration to the United States shifted radically from previous generations. People coming from Western European nations declined to a mere trickle, whereas those from other parts of the world, such as Southeast Asia, Central and South America, and the Caribbean, increased (*Statistical Abstract of the United States*, 1991). The reunification of Germany, the fall of the USSR, the democratization of Eastern European nations formerly under communistic control, and political shifts in Arabic nations also are having a major impact on immigration patterns. As more people from these parts of the world arrive in the United States, even more strands of ethnic, religious, cultural, and language diversity are being added to the American mosaic. The overall impact of these demographic changes on U.S. society led Time magazine, in its April 9, 1990, cover story, to describe it as the "browning of America" (Henry, 1990).

Increasing levels of poverty are another salient characteristic of today's students. According to the latest statistics from the Bureau of the Census (*Statistical Abstract of the United States*, 1991), 38.4% of Hispanic and 44% of African-American children under the age of 18 live in poverty. Rather than stabilizing or declining in the near future, these rates are expected to continue to increase.

The statistics on ethnic identity, immigration, and poverty among public school students have major ramifications for teacher education because there are direct correlations between these social descriptors and the educational opportunities and outcomes of different groups of students. Also, they are significant because the ethnic, racial, and cultural diversity among school-teachers and administrators does not reflect similar trends.

From *Education and Urban Society*, Vol. 25, No. 3, May 1993, pp. 285-299. © 1993 by Sage Publications, Inc. Reprinted by permission of Corwin Press, Inc.

Ethnic minorities now compose less than 15% of the teaching force, and less than 12% of school administrators. About 8.0% of all K–12 public school teachers are African-Americans, 3.0% are Hispanics, 1.4% are Asians/Pacific Islanders, and 0.9% are American Indians/Native Alaskans (*Status of the American School Teacher,* 1992). Among public school principals and central office administrators there are 8.6% African-Americans; 3.2% Hispanics; 1.1% American Indians, Eskimos, and Aleuts; and 0.6% Asians/Pacific Islanders (*The Condition of Education,* 1992; De La Rosa & Maw, 1990; *The Hispanic Population in the U.S.,* 1991).

DEMOGRAPHIC IMPLICATIONS GREATER THAN NUMBERS

A closer scrutiny of the demographics summarized above suggests that the problem is greater than the numbers and that the solution is more complex than merely recruiting teachers of color. There is a growing cultural and social distance between students and teachers that is creating an alarming schism in the instructional process. In addition to racial disparities, other key factors accounting for these widening gaps are residence, generation, gender, social class, experiential background, and education levels.

Many teachers simply do not have frames of reference and points of view similar to their ethnically and culturally different students because they live in different existential worlds. Whereas a growing percentage of students are poor and live in large urban areas, increasing numbers of teachers are middle class and reside in small- to medium-size suburban communities (*Statistical Abstract of the United States,* 1991; *Status of the American School Teacher,* 1992). Furthermore, there is not much mobility in the profession, which means that the teaching population is aging, and relatively few opportunities are available for significant numbers of new and younger individuals to enter the profession. The most recent summary of U.S. teachers compiled by the National Education Association (*Status of the American School Teacher,* 1992) indicate that their mean age is 42 years. Although 60% live within the boundaries of the school district where they are employed, only 37% live in the attendance area of the school where they teach. This percentage drops to 17.3 for schools in large systems, where the greater number of ethnically diverse and poor children are enrolled. The overwhelming majority of teachers continue to be Anglo (86.8%). More than 72% are female. By comparison, the student population in public schools is increasingly children of color.

Disparities in educational levels also contribute to the growing social distance between students and teachers. More and more teachers are achieving higher levels of education, whereas students of color and poverty are becoming less educated. Teachers with 5 years of college education, and a master's degree, or its equivalent, are common occurrences throughout the country.

Another distancing phenomenon in who teaches and who is taught is that students are far more technologically adept than

most teachers. Thus they are accustomed to high levels of multiple sensory stimulation and mediated information processing. These conditions are rather alien in most conventional classrooms, which tend to emphasize single sensory stimulation, similarity, passivity, and mental activities (Goodlad, 1984). These orientations and dispositions challenge the basic foundations of how teaching and learning are customarily organized and practiced. This challenge is apparent in the frustrations frequently voiced by teachers throughout the United States that they can no longer teach; they have to entertain. From the vantage point of students, many of them find it difficult to become personally invested in classroom learning because too often it lacks the "special effects" that characterize the dissemination of information they are accustomed to from constant exposure to technological media. Consequently, many of the assumptions, premises, programs, and strategies that have been used previously to teach students do not work any more. Therefore, radical changes must be made in how teacher preparation programs are conceived, designed, and implemented to meet these new challenges.

In classroom interactions, these sociocultural factors can become impenetrable obstacles to effective teaching and learning. The conduits or carriers of personal meaning in teaching and learning are examples, illustrations, vignettes, and scenarios. Understandably, teachers tend to select these from their own personal experiences and frames of reference. These examples, which are supposed to make subject matter and intellectual abstractions meaningful to culturally different students, often are irrelevant, too. The experiences, values, orientations, and perspectives of middle-class, highly educated, middle-aged Anglo teachers who live in small to mid-size suburban communities are very different from those of students who are poor, under-educated, racial and ethnic minorities, living in large urban areas. Yet establishing effective communication between students and teachers is imperative for academic success. Preparing teachers to connect meaningfully is the ultimate challenge of teacher education in an ethnically and culturally pluralistic and technologically complex world. Meeting this challenge requires reform in both the conceptual frameworks and substantive components of the preparation programs.

NEW CONCEPTUAL FRAMEWORKS NEEDED

In addition to the idea of *social distance,* there are several other behavioral science and multicultural education paradigms that offer some new and challenging directions for preparing teachers to work effectively with culturally diverse students and issues. Five are discussed here: cultural discontinuities, stress and anxiety, learned helplessness, situational competence, and cultural context teaching.

A growing body of behavioral science research and scholarship suggests that the burden of school failure does not rest on individual students and teachers but is nested in the lack of "fit" or syncretization between the cultural systems of schools and diverse groups. Spindler (1987), and other contributing authors to *Education and Cultural Process,* refer to this phenomenon variously as *cultural incompatibilities, cultural discontinuities,* and *cultural mismatches.* They and others (Gibbs, Huang, & Associates, 1989; Kochman, 1981; Shade, 1989; Trueba, Guthrie, & Au, 1981) agree that many of these mismatches occur at the level of procedures rather than substance. That is, culturally diverse students often have difficulties succeeding in school because *how* they go about learning is incompatible with school expectations and norms, not because they lack desire, motivation, aspiration, or academic potential. Opportunities to participate in the substantive components of teaching and learning frequently are a condition of the extent to which students conform to the "correct procedures and social protocols" (Holliday, 1985) of teaching. Failure to master these virtually ensures academic failure as well.

Some of the most crucial cultural discontinuities in classrooms occur in the areas of cultural values, patterns of communication and cognitive processing, task performance or work habits, self-presentation styles, and approaches to problem solving. That many of these incompatibilities happen without deliberate and conscious intent does not distract from their importance. If anything, this increases their significance as obstacles to successful teaching and learning in culturally pluralistic classrooms and as variables to be targeted for inclusion in multicultural teacher preparation programs.

Living and functioning effectively in culturally pluralistic classrooms can be highly stress provoking for both students and teachers. Trying to negotiate two or more different cultural systems can take psychoemotional priority over attending to academic tasks. *Stress and anxiety* correlate inversely with task performance. As psychoemotional stress levels increase in culturally pluralistic classrooms, teaching and learning task performance declines, thereby reducing the overall quality of academic efforts and achievement outcomes (Beeman, 1978; Gaudry & Spielberger, 1971). Teachers spend inordinate amounts of time on classroom control and maintaining the Anglocentric cultural hegemonic status quo. Culturally different students spend much of their psychoemotional and mental resources defending themselves from attacks on their psychic senses of well-being. Many find themselves in what Boykin (1986) calls a "triple quandary," having to negotiate simultaneously in three often-disparate realms of experience: the mainstream school culture, their natal ethnic cultures, and the status of being members of oppressed, powerless, and unvalued minority groups.

These conditions do not create "safe and supportive" environments for learning, one of the commonly accepted requirements for effective schooling. Instead, the result is classroom climates charged with adversarial opposition, distrust, hostility, and heightened levels of discomfort and tension. Neither students nor teachers can function at their best under these circumstances. Thus being able to identify stress-provoking factors in cross-cultural instructional interactions and knowing how to alleviate them can be a vital way to improve the overall quality of teaching in pluralistic classrooms.

An assumption held by many teachers is that children from certain ethnic groups and social classes are "universally disadvantaged or incompetent" because they do not do well on school tasks. These teachers further assume that the normative ways of doing things in school, whether they deal with social adaptation or academic issues, are the only "correct" and acceptable ones. Research conducted by cultural anthropologists, social psychologists, ethnographers, and sociolinguists (Boggs, Watson-Gegeo, & McMillen, 1985; Florio & Schultz, 1979; Greenbaum, 1985; Holliday, 1985; Kochman, 1981) indicate that ethnically and socially diverse students are very capable in their own cultural communities and social contexts. But these skills do not necessarily transfer to schools. A case in point is African-American youths who are verbally adept, creative, imaginative, and fluent among other African-Americans but appear inarticulate and unthinking in the classroom. The Kamehameha Early Education Program (KEEP) demonstrates the positive benefits of modifying the schooling process to incorporate the social competences native Hawaiian children exhibit in their homes and cultural communities (Au & Jordon, 1981; Boggs et al., 1985).

Furthermore, all individuals are not equally capable in all intellectual areas. Some are artistic; others are more scientific, mechanical, literary, or musical. Gardner (1983) reaffirms this point in his work on multiple intelligences, and Barbe and Swassing (1979) explain the merits of teaching to different students' modality strengths. But teachers frequently do not extend this principle to functioning in different cultural systems. They assume that deficiency in one area extends to all others. Thus children who are poor and from racial minority groups become "culturally deprived," "at risk," "learning disabled," and "socially maladaptive," and *all* of their educational experiences are so affected. Children with limited English proficiencies are too often assumed also to have limited intellectual potential in mathematics, science, computers, and critical thinking. These orientations need to be replaced with ones that emphasize *situational competence* and the understanding that all students are competent in some things within certain environments. The challenge is for teachers to determine what individual strengths and cultural competencies different students bring to the classroom and to design learning experiences to capitalize on them.

Irrespective of their ethnic identity, socioeconomic status, gender, or cultural background, most children begin school eager to demonstrate their abilities and excited about engaging in new learnings, experiences, and interactions. However small the rest of the world might think their achievements are, these youngsters see them as major accomplishments. They do not focus their energies on what they do not have and cannot do; they naturally take great pride in showing off what they do have and can do. They have the dispositions and perspectives on their own experiences that Giovanni (1970) praised in the poem, "Nikka Rosa," and lamented about these strengths being ignored or abused by those who do not understand them. Giovanni explains that what she remembers most about her childhood is self-pride, a strong sense of accomplishment, love, and happiness, not the constraints of poverty that others outside her social network feel define her essence.

These positive perceptions of personal competence begin to erode for many culturally different students shortly after they start their formal schooling. A persistent message is sent to them, in innumerable ways, of all the things they do not have and cannot do. The longer they stay in school, the more persuasive this message becomes. They become helpless, insecure, and incompetent. This concept of *learned helplessness* is crucial to understanding the plight of these students in schools and developing teacher attitudes and behaviors to avoid its perpetuation.

Basic principles of learning (Gagne, 1985) suggest that students are more likely to master new learnings when they build on previous learnings. These principles apply to the content to be learned, as well as to the structures, conditions, and environments under which learning occurs. Ecological psychologists have found that setting, environment, and climate are important factors in fostering desired behavior (Shade, 1989). Thus students who are accustomed to work being framed in informal social relations and group structures outside school will perform better if this tradition is continued in the classroom, rather than in formal, highly competitive, and individualistic situations.

This continuity can be achieved by doing *cultural context teaching.* That is, placing the mechanics and technical components of teaching and learning into the cultural frameworks of various ethnic, racial, and social groups. Stated somewhat differently, cultural context teaching is synchronizing various cultural styles of teaching and learning and creating culturally compatible classrooms that provide genuine invitations and opportunities for all students to engage maximally in academic pursuits without any one group being unduly advantaged or penalized (Barbe & Swassing, 1979; Shade, 1989).

Cultural context teaching is somewhat analogous to *segmented marketing* in business and industry. As the United States evolved from a factory-driven to a consumer-driven economy, corporations moved rapidly from total reliance on mass media advertising to marketing strategies designed for specifically targeted segments of the population. The shift involves identifying the values, institutions, connections, concerns, experiences, and motivations of key consumer segments; affiliating with esteemed individuals, organizations, and activities that embody these features to enter into the "circles of trust" of different consumer groups; and packaging products and services to match the life-styles of the various groups (Swenson, 1990). The merits of these strategies are readily apparent—"increased consideration translates into increased sales" (Swenson, 1990, p. 12).

Educational institutions are very susceptible to the opinions of business and industry. They have a long tradition of borrowing models from the corporate world and using economic reasoning to justify program priorities. Education, like other consumer goods and services, must be marketed effectively if it is to "sell" and succeed. Just as mass, homogeneous advertising is obsolete in the economic marketplace, so is it in the educational marketplace.

The questions now are (a) What knowledge and skills do teachers need to acquire to respond to the practical implications of *consumer-segmented teaching* and other paradigms for understanding cultural pluralism in the classroom? and (b) How should teacher preparation programs be redesigned to address these needs?

TEACHERS AS CULTURAL BROKERS

No one should be allowed to graduate from a teacher certification program or be licensed to teach without being well grounded in how the dynamic of cultural conditioning operates in teaching and learning. To achieve this goal, the preparation programs should be designed to teach teachers how to be *cultural brokers* (Gentemann & Whitehead, 1983) in pluralistic classrooms and to be competent in *cultural context teaching* (e.g., *segmented marketing of pedagogy*).

A cultural broker is one who thoroughly understands different cultural systems, is able to interpret cultural symbols from one frame of reference to another, can mediate cultural incompatibilities, and knows how to build bridges or establish linkages across cultures that facilitate the instructional process. Cultural brokers translate expressive cultural behaviors into pedagogical implications and actions. They model maneuvers within and negotiations among multiple cultural systems without compromising the integrity of any. They provide mechanisms for establishing continuity between ethnically and socially diverse cultures and mainstream school culture. Cultural brokers are *bicultural actors* who are able to straddle or syncretize different cultural systems and integrate elements of ethnic cultures into classroom procedures, programs, and practices (Gentemann & Whitehead, 1983). How they function epitomizes cultural context teaching at the levels of interpersonal interactions with students, pedagogical strategies employed in the classroom, and the infusion of multiculturalism throughout the entire instructional process.

Several skills are necessary for teachers to become cultural brokers. These can be classified as acquiring cultural knowledge, becoming change agents, and translating cultural knowledge into pedagogical strategies. They should form the substantive core of all teacher preparation programs.

ACQUIRING CULTURAL KNOWLEDGE

This component of preparing teachers to be cultural brokers should have three aspects: learning factual information about the specific characteristics of different ethnic and cultural groups, understanding the pedagogical implications of these cultural characteristics, and developing a philosophy for cultural context teaching. The students enrolled in the preparation programs should declare a cultural or ethnic group for concentrated study. They also may choose more than one group to concentrate on with the understanding that this choice will extend the time they spend in the preparation program. When they finish the program, the graduates will have a culturally diverse area of specialization (e.g., African-Americans, Mexican-Americans, children of poverty), as well as a subject matter major and endorsement.

Knowledge about cultural diversity should be acquired through two primary means: studying the accumulated research and scholarship on different ethnic and cultural groups and first-hand experiences gained from participatory observations in various cultural communities. Both of these should be in-depth experiences, guided by the methodologies, orientations, conceptual frameworks, and knowledge funds generated by behavioral scientists, ethnic studies scholars, and expressive artists (such as cultural anthropologists, social psychologists, sociolinguists, ethnomusicologists, ethnographers, cultural artists, and literary authors). College of education faculties will need to establish previously unexplored instructional partnerships with some university divisions and scholars. These partnerships in search of accurate and authentic knowledge about cultural patterns and functions are as essential as the more traditional ones between educationists and social scientists designed to increase mastery of the subject matter taught in schools.

Some dimensions of culture are more applicable than others to understanding and remediating cultural conflicts in pluralistic classrooms. These include cultural values, relational patterns, learning styles and work habits, communication styles, rewards and punishments, social etiquette and decorum, cultural ethos, self-presentation styles, and patterns of ethnic identification and affiliation. Students enrolled in teacher education programs should be expected to take relevant behavioral science courses to learn specific content about each of these cultural components for specific ethnic groups. They may take courses in ethnic literature, cultural values, folklore, family, art and aesthetics, celebrations and ceremonies, customs and traditions, and developmental psychology.

The cultural content courses should be complemented with education seminars that have three primary purposes. The first is the extrapolation of pedagogical principles and practices embedded in the cultural content. Seminars should be sequenced so that students' enrollment in the content courses and the seminars coincide with each other or follow closely thereafter. The courses could even be team taught by behavioral scientists and educationists working together. A second component of the seminars is a field-based practicum in which students spend concentrated periods of time in culturally pluralistic school sites. During these experiences, students will function as participant observers to document how the cultural characteristics they are studying are expressed in actual classroom settings and interactions. The third element of the seminars should be the development of students' philosophies for cultural context teaching. The emphasis here is on developing an understanding and appreciation of cultural pluralism in the classroom as a vital, creative, and enriching phenomenon, as well as its potential for transforming the quality of schooling for students from historically disenfranchised groups. The conceptual paradigms discussed earlier should be the foundations of this philosophy.

BECOMING CHANGE AGENTS

To be effective cultural brokers and cultural context teachers, students in teacher education programs must be taught how to be change agents. This role requires a commitment to institu-tional transformation and developing skills for incorporating cultural diversity into the normative operations of schools and classrooms. A four-step process should constitute this aspect of teacher education.

First, teacher education students should be taught skills of critical analysis and self-reflection. These skills will help them learn to analyze systematically the structures and procedures in schools and classrooms and their own habitual ways of behaving in instructional settings, from various cultural vantage points; to identify points of conflict between the culture of the school and different ethnic groups; and to determine which of these offer the best and the worst opportunities for negotiation and change to serve the academic needs of culturally different students better.

Second, education students should be taught how to deconstruct mainstream hegemonic assumptions, values, and beliefs embedded in the normative structures and procedures of conventional classroom teaching. This requires a thorough understanding of how cultural values shape classroom policies, procedures, and practices; points in the instructional process that are most susceptible to cultural conflict; and the ability to discern those structural components that are most significant to incorporating cultural pluralism into routine classroom procedures.

Commitments to making teaching more culturally relevant need to be grounded in principles of organizational behavior and change (e.g., Belasco, 1990; Bowditch & Buono, 1985; Meltzer & Nord, 1980; Robbins, 1991). Many teacher education students recognize the need for change and have strong affinities for making their classroom teaching more culturally sensitive. But they do not know how to anchor it in a realistic and reliable operational framework. They seem to believe that desire alone is sufficient to bring about change. In the long run, this naïveté is a serious obstacle to real change. Students must understand the organizational culture, climate, and psychology of schools; why schools are self-perpetuating institutions; obstacles to change; cooperative strategies for planned change; and techniques to initiate and sustain change.

An integral feature of success as cultural brokers is being able to relate well to students from culturally, ethnically, and racially diverse backgrounds. Therefore, a fourth part of becoming effective change agents is developing competencies in cross-cultural communications and multicultural counseling. Both of these fields of research and scholarship have rich data bases from which students can acquire conceptual skills and practical techniques. The emphases should be on sociolinguistic and paralinguistic communication components (Cazden, John, & Hymes, 1985; Greenbaum, 1985; Hall, 1981; Kochman, 1981; Smitherman, 1977; Trueba et al., 1981). In some instances, language studies and principles of bilingual education and second language learning also are appropriate. Techniques of cross-cultural counseling are important because teachers need to know how to help students deal with the stress and strain of living and functioning in culturally pluralistic settings. Some of the specific associated needs are style shifting across cultures, self-declaration for different ethnic group members, dealing with interracial and interethnic group hostilities, editing cultural nuances out of public behaviors, and coping with traumas and anxieties related to functioning in cross-cultural settings (Beeman, 1978; Schofield, 1982; Spencer, Brookins, & Allen, 1985).

TRANSLATING KNOWLEDGE INTO PRACTICE

Finally, teacher education programs should provide ample opportunities for students to engage in supervised practice doing cultural context teaching and being cultural brokers in actual classroom settings. Through a combination of classroom simulations, sample demonstrations, media protocols, case studies, and field experiences, students should develop skills in diagnosing teaching and learning styles, matching teaching styles with learning styles, creating inviting classroom climates (Purkey, 1978), using culturally sensitive assessment tools and techniques, and integrating culturally diverse content into subject matter curricula. These action strategies will need to be accompanied by corresponding changes in beliefs about what knowledge is of greatest worth for citizenship in a pluralistic world and what are the best ways it can be acquired for students from different ethnic, cultural, racial, and social backgrounds. The overriding principles should be the cultural contextuality of teaching and learning and using alternative pedagogical means to achieve common learning outcomes.

All teacher education students also should be expected to participate in a cultural brokerage internship before completing their preparation program. This internship should take place in actual classroom settings and provide opportunities to practice all of the skills involved in being a cultural broker. It is to be a complement to, not a replacement for, the traditional student teaching experience. The duration of the experience should be long enough for the students to get a sampling of the wide variety of issues and challenges involved in the institutional culture of schools. The internship should be carefully monitored and assessed by experienced classroom teachers or university professors. Successful completion should be a condition of graduating from the teacher preparation program and receiving a license to teach.

CONCLUSION

The plight of many culturally different students in U.S. public schools is chronic and critical. Because teachers play a central role in resolving it, their preparation must be a prime target of reform. This need is becoming even more imperative, given shifts in school demographics that show rapid increases in the numbers of children who are poor, limited English speakers, immigrants, and members of ethnic groups of color, as well as a decline in teachers from similar backgrounds. The resulting social distance can be an impenetrable obstacle to effective teaching and learning.

Generic teacher education programs that are supposed to prepare teachers to function well in all types of school communities are no longer viable. Instead, preparation must be population based and contextually specific. Nor can participation in multicultural learning experiences be left to choice and

chance—it must be mandatory and carefully planned. The best way to translate these—ideas into practice is preparation programs that emphasize developing skills in cultural context teaching and how to be cultural brokers in pluralistic classrooms. The essence of these strategies is affirming the cultures of diverse students, establishing continuity and building bridges across different cultural systems, creating supportive classroom climates where diverse students feel welcome and valued, and replacing cultural hegemonic pedagogy with one that models cultural pluralism without hierarchy. Mastering the skills necessary for cultural brokering and cultural context teaching may require longer time in preparation. But it is time well spent, and the long-range payoffs are more than worth the relative short-term investments.

Preparing teachers to work better with culturally different students and communities demands action now. Conventional approaches to teacher education must be decentered and transformed at their most fundamental core, if teachers are to be maximally prepared to teach students of the 21st century who will be increasingly racially, culturally, ethnically, socially, and linguistically pluralistic.

REFERENCES

Au, K. H. P., & Jordan, C. (1981). Teaching reading to Hawaiian children: Finding a culturally appropriate solution. In H. T. Trueba, G. P. Guthrie, & K. H. P. Au (Eds.), *Culture and the bilingual classroom: Studies in classroom ethnography* (pp. 139–152). Rowley, MA: Newbury House.

Barbe, W. B., & Swassing, R. H. (1979). *Teaching through modality strengths: Concepts and practice.* Columbus, OH: Zaner-Bloser.

Beeman, P. N. (1978). *School stress and anxiety: Theory, research and intervention.* New York: Human Sciences Press.

Belasco, J. A. (1990). *Teaching the elephant to dance: Empowering change in your organization.* New York: Crown.

Boggs, S. T., Watson-Gegeo, K., & McMillen, G. (1985). *Speaking, relating, and learning: A study of Hawaiian children at home and at school.* Norwood, NJ: Ablex.

Bowditch, J. L., & Buono, A. T. (1985). *A primer on organizational behavior.* New York: Wiley.

Boykin, A. W. (1986). The triple quandary and the schooling of Afro-American children. In U. Neisser (Ed.), *The school achievement of minority children: New perspectives* (pp. 57–92). Hillsdale, NJ: Lawrence Erlbaum.

Cazden, C. B., John, V. P., & Hymes, D. (Eds.). (1985). *Functions of language in the classroom.* Prospects Heights, IL: Waveland.

The condition of education. (1992). Washington, DC: U.S. Department of Education, National Center for Education Statistics, Office of Educational Research and Information.

De La Rosa, D., & Maw, C. E. (1990). *Hispanic education: A statistical portrait.* Washington, DC: National Council of La Raza.

Digest of education statistics, 1991. (1992). Washington, DC: U.S. Department of Education, Office of Education Research and Improvement, Center for Educational Statistics.

Education that works: An action plan for the education of minorities. (1990). Cambridge: MIT, Quality of Education for Minorities Project.

Florio, S., & Shultz, J. (1979). Social competence at home and at school. *Theory Into Practice, 18,* 234–243.

Gagne, R. M. (1985). *The conditions of learning and theory of instruction* (4th ed.). New York: Holt, Rinehart & Winston.

Gardner, H. (1983). *Frames of mind: The theory of multiple intelligences.* New York: Basic Books.

Gaudry, E., & Spielberger, C. D. (1971). *Anxiety and educational achievement.* New York: Wiley.

Gentemann, K. M., & Whitehead, T. L. (1983). The cultural broker concept in bicultural education. *Journal of Negro Education, 54,* 118–129.

Gibbs, J. T., Huang, L. N., & Associates (1989). *Children of color: Psychological interventions with minority youth.* San Francisco: Jossey-Bass.

Giovanni, N. (1970). *Black feeling, Black talk and Black judgment.* New York: William Morrow.

Goodlad, John I. (1984). *A place called school: Prospects for the future.* New York: McGraw-Hill.

Greenbaum, P. E. (1985). Nonverbal differences in communication style between American Indian and Anglo elementary classrooms. *American Educational Research Journal, 22,* 101–115.

Hall, E. T. (1981). *The silent language.* New York: Anchor.

Henry, W. A., III. (1990, April 9). Beyond the melting pot. *Time,* pp. 28–31.

The Hispanic population in the U.S. (1991, March). (Current Population Reports, Series P-20, No. 455). Washington, DC: U.S. Department of the Census.

Holliday, B. G. (1985). Towards a model of teacher-child transactional processes affecting Black children's academic achievement. In M. B. Spencer, G. K. Brookins, & W. R. Allen (Eds.), *Beginnings: The social and affective development of Black children* (pp. 117–130). Hillsdale, NJ: Lawrence Erlbaum.

Kochman, T. (1981). *Black and White styles in conflict.* Chicago: University of Chicago Press.

Meltzer, H., & Nord, W. R. (1980). *Making organizations humane and productive: A handbook for practitioners.* New York: Wiley.

Purkey, W. W. (1978). *Inviting school success: A self-concept approach to teaching and learning.* Belmont, CA: Wadsworth.

Robbins, S. P. (1991). *Organizational change: Concepts, controversies and applications.* Englewood Cliffs, NJ: Prentice-Hall.

Schofield, J. W. (1982). *Black and White in school: Trust, tension, or tolerance.* New York: Praeger.

Shade, B. J. R. (Ed.). (1989). *Culture, style, and the educative process.* Springfield, IL: Charles C Thomas.

Smitherman, G. (1977). *Talkin' and testifyin': The language of Black America.* Boston: Houghton Mifflin.

Spencer, M. B., Brookins, G. K., & Allen, W. R. (Eds.). (1985). *Beginnings: The social and affective development of Black children.* Hillsdale, NJ: Lawrence Erlbaum.

Spindler, G. D. (Ed.). (1987). *Education and cultural process: Anthropological perspectives.* Prospect Heights, IL: Waveland.

Statistical abstract of the United States (111th ed.). (1991). Washington, DC: Department of Commerce, Bureau of the Census.

Status of the American school teacher 1990–1991. (1992). Washington, DC: National Education Association, Research Division.

Swenson, C. A. (1990). *Selling to a segmented market: The lifestyle approach.* New York: Quorum.

Trueba, H. T., Guthrie, G. P., & Au, K. H. P. (1981). *Culture and the bilingual classroom: Studies in classroom ethnography.* Rowley, MA: Newbury House.

Multicultural Education as an Academic Discipline

A spirited dialogue is occurring among scholars in multicultural education and critical theoretical perspectives on the future directions and the philosophical foundations of multicultural education as a field of study. The essays in this unit reflect the results of some of this dialogue. How can the emergent academic areas of cultural studies and multicultural education be integrated into professional educational studies in such a way as to optimize the liberation and social empowerment objectives of multicultural education and critical pedagogy? Scholars are critically evaluating the possible future directions of multicultural education as a field of study.

Multicultural education has had a fascinating developmental history as an emergent area of scholarship out of the social upheavals of the 1960s and the concern of many in the scholarly community that there is critical need for research-based knowledge of the cultural contexts of education. As noted in *To the Reader,* the preface to this volume, it was in the 1960s that the first courses in the academic area that would come to be called "multicultural education" developed. Much of our early knowledge base came from critically important research in anthropology and sociology (as well as from psychiatric studies of the impact of prejudice and victimization on targeted racial and cultural minorities) starting in the 1920s. These studies examined intercultural relations in all sorts of urban, suburban, small town, and rural settings in the United States. These were "field studies" using ethnographic field inquiry methods developed by anthropologists initially and later used by some sociologists and educators as well. The earliest of these studies in the 1920s through the 1950s focused on such concerns as child-rearing practices, rites of passage into adulthood, perceptions of other cultural groups, and the social stratification systems of communities and neighborhoods. Studies of how victimized and involuntarily segregated racial and cultural groups responded to being "targeted" for discriminatory treatment documented the intercultural state of affairs in American society in the 1930s and 1940s. This body of social science knowledge became very important documentation for the plaintiffs in *Brown v. Board of Education of Topeka* in 1954, the historic U.S. Supreme Court case that declared segregation on the basis of race to be unconstitutional.

As the civil rights movement of the 1950s in the United States continued to grow in momentum throughout the decade of the 1960s, continued anthropological and sociological inquiry about the education of minority cultural youth developed. Out of the urban and other social crises of the 1960s in the United States emerged a belief among those educators concerned about questions of racial and cultural justice that there was a serious need for an area of educational studies that would specifically focus on the study of intercultural relations in the schools from a "multi" cultural perspective in harmony with cultural pluralist visions of American social life. This would challenge the by-then traditional Eurocentric "melting pot" vision of how one became "American." The problem was that the Eurocentric "melting pot" was very exclusionary; not everyone was welcome to jump in it. Many cultural groups were excluded from it. The philosophy of a culturally pluralist democracy in which all cultural heritages would be treasured and none rejected, within the broader framework of a united, multicultural democratic nation state, became attractive to many who witnessed the arbitrary and cruel effects of racial and cultural prejudice in schools as well as in other areas of life in mainstream society.

The belief that all teachers should respect the cultural heritages of their students and that all students have the right to know their cultural heritages, as well as to develop self-esteem and pride in them, began to spread among socially concerned educators. The studies that had been conducted on intercultural relations among teachers and students by the early 1970s clearly demonstrated the need for an academic discipline that would specifically focus on building knowledge bases about our multicultural social reality as well as on how to teach about other cultural heritages and to improve the quality and the pedagogical effectiveness of instruction in multicultural school settings. Many of us realize today that all young Americans of our social present and future need to know about the American experience as a nation from a multicultural perspective that rejects and transcends the old Anglo- and Eurocentric presuppositions of melting pot theories of "assimilation" in American social life.

As part of the movement for civil rights, persons from linguistic minority heritages also sought to guarantee that their children would be given the opportunity to grow up both bilingual and "bicultural." By the time the U.S. Supreme Court handed down its decision in *Lau v. Nichols* in 1974, there were dozens of federal court cases pending at various stages of development concerning this matter. The causes of bilingual education and English as a second language were being argued (as well as contested).

The academic leadership of the nation's cultural minorities and many other concerned scholars have forged a competent community of scholars charged with the task of setting standards of academic practice for multicultural education as an academic discipline. There is spirited dialogue going on about what these standards should be and about the academic qualifications needed to teach multicultural education. James A. Banks, professor of multicultural education at the University of Washington, and others are concerned about the future survival and development of multicultural education as an academic discipline that must maintain its focus on classroom practice as well as on defensible theoretical constructs.

Multicultural education must develop an ongoing cadre of competent scholarly leaders to direct the further development of the field and to ensure that attempts to merely infuse multicultural content into existing teacher education courses do not dilute its academic quality or the quality of its standards of practice. Banks argues that merely integrating multicultural education content into existing teacher education course work must be resisted. He calls for a "multicultural education (MCE) + integration" model. There should be qualified academic specialists in multicultural education on school faculties. Multicultural education is an interdiscipline that draws its knowledge base from anthropology, sociology, social history, and even psychiatry. Focused, adequately prepared specialists in this new interdiscipline are necessary if it is to maintain its academic integrity.

The essays in this unit reflect concerns regarding academic standards and goals for multicultural education as the field continues to develop and to enter a new period in its history. The authors of these essays raise important qualitative issues that must be addressed as multicultural education nears the time when a majority of Americans will be from "minority" cultural heritages and traditional conceptions of "eminority" and "majority" relations in the United States will have little meaning.

The essays in this unit are relevant to courses in curriculum theory and construction, educational policy studies, history and philosophy of education, cultural foundations of education, and multicultural education.

Looking Ahead: Challenge Questions

What should be minimal "standards of practice" in multicultural education?

What should be the qualifications for specialists in multicultural education?

Why and how should all American students learn the multicultural reality of our nation?

Why is multicultural education an interdiscipline?

What issues are raised by total "infusion" models of multicultural education in teacher education programs?

What should all American students know about racism and prejudice by the time they graduate from high school?

What things can teachers do to foster acceptance of cultural differences?

—F. S.

Bridging Multicultural Theory and Practice

Geneva Gay

Geneva Gay is a professor of education and an associate with the Center of Multicultural Education at the University of Washington, Seattle, Washington.

The current state of multicultural education is at once exciting and troubling. A significant part of this dilemma—and the one of interest here—results from disparities in the developmental growth of its theory and practice. Ideally, educational theory and practice develop in tandem, and the relationship between them is complementary, reciprocal, and dialectic. This is not yet happening, in any systematic way, in multicultural education. Its theoretical development is far out-stripping its practical development, and its further refinement is stimulated more by proposals of what should be than by lessons learned from what is.

Multicultural theory is becoming more thorough, complex, and comprehensive, while its practice in K-12 and college classrooms continues to be rather questionable, simplistic, and fragmentary. This gap is growing exponentially; it fuels much of the current debate because critics fail to distinguish between the two in their critiques; and it limits the overall effectiveness of multi-cultural reform efforts.

These divergent growth patterns also make it difficult for multicultural advocates in different aspects of the educational enterprise to engage in constructive dialogue, and to work as collaboratively as they might for the achievement of common goals. As a result, multicultural classroom instruction is often not synchronized with curriculum development. Policy statements governing school practices may specify that multiculturalism must be included in instructional materials and program designs, but routinely fail to make similar requirements for hiring personnel and for assessing the performance of students and teachers. Yet, theorists consistently argue that for multicultural education to be maximally successful, all parts of the educational system must be responsive to and inclusive of cultural diversity.

The gaps between multicultural theory and practice present some serious challenges and opportunities for future directions in the field. In this discussion, I will offer some thoughts about why these gaps exist, and make some suggestions for how the challenges they present might be addressed.

INVERSE GROWTH PATTERNS

According to George Beauchamp (1968), an essential function of educational theorizing is to constantly search for new conceptual ideas, understandings, and principles to describe, explain, and predict issues of interest or study. He adds that the theorist "seeks out new relationships by combining sets of events into a new universal set and then [proceeds] with the search for new relationships and new laws in a new theory" (p. 19). This search has both internal and external dimensions. It analyzes the components of an existing paradigm to achieve greater depths and clarity of meanings, while simultaneously bringing ideas and insights from other sources to bear upon the phenomenon being studied.

For example, multicultural education was initially conceptualized as a discrete program of studies with heavy emphasis on teaching factual content about the histories, heritages, and contributions of groups of color. Over the last 25 years, this conceptualization has been re-examined, revised, and refined so that now multicultural education is conceived more as a particular ideological and methodological approach to the entire educational enterprise than a separate curriculum or program *per se.*

The relationships between culture, ethnicity, and learning, which are so central to multicultural education are continually analyzed and reinterpreted. Different ways to systematize the implementation of commonly-agreed-upon elements of multicultural education are constantly being proposed by various scholars. In the rhetoric of today's educational thinking, these processes might be coded as self-reflection, critical interrogation, knowledge reconstruction, meta-analysis or meta-cognition, and multiple perspectives. Thus, the evolvement of educational theory from inception to maturity is a self-renewing, regenerative process. One of its natural effects is the creation of subsidiary theories and conceptual models.

Even a quick and cursory look at the scholarship of leading multiculturalists (see, for example, Banks & Banks, 1993, 1995; Hollins, King, & Hayman, 1994; Bennett, 1995; Sleeter, 1992; Sleeter & Grant, 1995; Foster, 1991) provides persuasive evidence of these processes taking place. Senior scholars are revisioning and elaborating on some of their earlier thinking, as well as using knowledge and interpretive filters from other disciplines to enrich, elaborate, and extend the conceptual contours, attributes, and principles of multicultural education.

Several specific examples illustrate this trend. In a recent publication, Gay (1994) explained the relationship between canonical principles of general education commonly endorsed by United States schools and those of multicultural education. She argued that these are fundamentally the same, with the only differences being in context and constituency. Multicultural

From *Multicultural Education,* Fall 1995, pp. 4-9. © 1995 by the National Association for Multicultural Education. Reprinted by permission.

education merely translates general educational principles to fit the specific contexts of ethnic and cultural diversity. James Banks (1995) is now exploring intersections between feminist theory, knowledge reconstruction, and multicultural education, as well as ideological antecedents to it found in the thinking of early 20th century African American educators. Christine Bennett (1995) and Sonia Nieto (1992), along with Banks and many others, evoke democratic principles and ethics to support their claims about the multicultural imperative in education. Carl Grant, Christine Sleeter, Joyce King, Gloria Ladson-Billings, and Antonia Darder (1992) incorporate ideas from critical theory, post-modernism, social reconstructionism, and political empowerment into their explanations of the essential goals, purposes, and anticipated outcomes of multicultural education. Other theorists are beginning to establish direct linkages between economic development, international diplomacy, and being responsive to cultural diversity in the educational process.

This "conceptual webbing" is producing both encouraging and disturbing results for multicultural education. It is stimulating and enriching discussions among theorists about the necessities, contours, and potentialities of multicultural education. The thoughts and ideas which result from these discussions are at increasingly higher levels of sophistication, abstraction, and complexity. In this sense, the field is developing the way it should, from the perspective of theory development. As any kind of educational theory matures, its ideological contours become more complex and abstract, and thus moves further and further away from direct and immediate translation to classroom application.

Ironically, its theoretical strengths are also the nemesis of multicultural education practice. Rather than enlightening practitioners and stimulating them to higher levels of instructional action, complex theoretical explanations often have the reverse effects. They can intimidate, confuse, overwhelm, and incapacitate classroom teachers. The language used to expressed key ideas and concepts become more esoteric, thereby making them less clear to everyone except other theorists with similar developmental status and understanding. More attention is devoted to conceptualizing than to actualizing multicultural components and characteristics. That is, as theorists pre-

scribe and visualize what **should be done,** they speak increasingly in terms of ideals without clearly articulating directions for how these are to be operationalized in practice.

This situation is complicated even further by differences in the ideological ideas disciplinary emphases, and maturational levels of theorists themselves. Some multiculturalists are influenced heavily by history and sociology, while others speak through the conceptual and linguistic filters of politics, psychology, anthropology, and pedagogy. Consequently, classroom teachers and school administrators are left to their own devices to translate theory to practice. Frequently what they do in practice is inconsistent with or even violates what is meant by the theory.

Thus, while multicultural theorists argue that cultural diversity should be infused into the learning experiences of all students regardless of the ethnic demographics of specific school and classroom sites, practitioners still tend to make its implementation contingent upon the presence of specific ethnic groups of color. If there are no African-American, Latino, Native-American, or certain Asian-American students enrolled in their schools, they find it difficult to see the relevance of doing multicultural education. When theorists propose that the K-12 educational process be **transformed** by cultural diversity, they mean the most fundamental and deeply ingrained values, beliefs, and assumptions which determine all educational policies, content, procedures, and structures schooling will be **revolutionalized** by being culturally pluralized.

However, their college and university counterparts do not necessarily conceive of transformation in the same way. They, as well as many K-12 practitioners, use a more restricted notion of transformation as simply "change." They assume that multicultural transformation is accomplished by merely including information about ethnically diverse individuals and achievements into the content of instruction, or disciplinary canons. In this sense, the curriculum of a United States literature course is thought to have been transformed when writings by authors of color and females are routinely included for study. These conceptions and practices fail to realize that curriculum involves more than content, that the educational enterprise is not analogous to curriculum, and that the mere presence of ethnic information is not enough to constitute transformation.

These kinds of discrepancies in meanings between theorists and practitioners, are understandable, given their differential levels of mastery of and maturity in the field. But they also are confusing and can have negative effects on the overall advancement of multiculturalism in all levels of the educational enterprise. They place both the practitioners and the theorists in reactive, rather than pro-active positions. The practitioners are faced with having to explain away their unintended misinterpretations and possible accusations that theorists are too esoteric in their explanations of key multicultural ideas. The theorists feel the need to re-examine and re-explain their intended original meanings to avoid future misinterpretations. This "back-stepping" slows down the forward thrust and continuous development of multicultural education in both theory and practice.

A strongly endorsed theoretical idea that is often misunderstood and is another powerful illustration of the lack of **operational bridging** between multicultural educational theory and practice is **infusion.** Virtually every multicultural theorist supports the idea that cultural diversity should be an integral part of the total educational experiences of all students in all school settings. This means it should impact the contexts and structures of teaching and learning as well as their content and text. Stated somewhat differently, all policies, programs, and procedures in school curriculum, instruction, administration, guidance, assessment, and governance should be responsive to cultural diversity. This responsiveness is multidimensional, too, including recognition, knowledge, acceptance, respect, praise, and promotion. But, very few theorists explain how to actually do these all-encompassing mandates in the various dimensions of the educational enterprise.

What do school principals do to multiculturalize the different tasks which comprise their administrative and leadership functions? What are the operational steps and decision-making points involved in multiculturalizing the curriculum creation process? How can these general principles be specified to different domains of learning such as math, science, reading, and social studies? How does one make the content as well as the administrative styles of student assessment culturally pluralistic? These are the kinds of questions that remain after most theoretical pronouncements are made regarding multicultural education infusion. They must be answered more precisely in order to establish better connections between theory and practice.

The few attempts that are made to create these bridges often are unsuccessful because they tend be "finished or product examples" of what infusion looks like, instead of clearly articulated and functional explanations of the **processes** of infusion itself. For example, theorists may present illustrations of multiculturally-infused reading units, but fail to explain how decisions about their specific components were made, or why they embody and personify different principles of multicultural education.

Consequently, these samples are of limited value in empowering other educators to create similar ones, and thereby continuing to advance the development of multicultural education practice. This places practitioners in a situation of trying to imitate or replicate the sample lessons without being sufficiently informed about how the original decisions were made. The results are not very successful which can cause instructional program designers to become frustrated and discouraged. This frustration then becomes a convenient excuse for them to abandon future efforts to implement multicultural education in their classrooms.

Another tension between multicultural theory and practice is the fact that many application models suggested for classroom use are **decontextualized.** They are not connected in any systematic way to what teachers routinely do in the day-to-day operations of their curricula and classrooms. Excellent books which present authentic and accurate portrayals of different ethnic groups' cultures, contributions, and experiences are now available. A wide variety of richly textured and significant learning activities have been developed for teaching various aspects of multicultural education, such as prejudice reduction, ethnic identity development, intergroup relations, and self-esteem.

Despite their inherent worth, decontextualized multicultural activities are of limited use in classrooms because the authors do not explain where and how they fit into typical instructional tasks and responsibilities. If, for example, designers were to demonstrate how learning non-pejorative terms for ethnic groups can be incorporated into standard vocabulary lessons in reading instruction, how ethnic population statistics can be used in teaching math skills such as proportions, ratios, and graphing, and how participating in

inter-ethnic group social exchanges approximate some of the skills social studies teach about international diplomacy classroom teachers may be more willing and capable of using them.

Without this **functional contextualization,** teachers are likely to continue to perceive multicultural education as an intrusive addition to an already over-burdened workload, or something that requires extra efforts and special skills. It then becomes very easy for them to dismiss the idea of cultural diversity without due consideration because they "don't have time to teach anything else," or because "it jeopardizes other important things that must be taught, such as basic literacy skills."

Another occurrence common to a profession which causes a split between theory and practice is variability in the positional responsibilities of the membership. Educational theorists tend to be more highly specialized in selected aspects of a discipline than school practitioners. They have the luxury of concentrating their professional activities on fewer things, and becoming more thoroughly involved in exploring even deeper conceptual parameters and possibilities of their areas of expertise.

By comparison, school practitioners tend to be more generalists than specialists, and are more engaged in applying than creating new knowledge. The more deeply involved they are in a pedagogical field, the more devoted they become to improving its practical applications. It seems only natural that these positional emphases would produce more divergent than convergent developments. As the field of study advances, both groups grow in clarity and coherency, but in opposite directions—practice seeks increasing conciseness, while theory searches for greater complexity. These kinds of developments support the need for specialists who can translate theory to practice.

These **patterns of professional participation** are evident in the field of multicultural education. Most nationally-known multiculturalists are scholars and specialists whose units of study and analysis are precollegiate educational programs, processes, and practices. Their suggestions and proposals are **ideal prescriptions** about what cultural education should be.

By comparison, most school practitioners are specialists in something other than multicultural education, such as reading, history, math, or science instruction. They are concerned more with **real-

istic and functional descriptions** of what to do, and how—about cultural diversity in relation to their other pedagogical responsibilities.

When these different professionals appeal to each other to satisfy their respective needs, they are often disappointed, and may even doubt the value of each other's contributions because their quality may not be readily apparent in other domains of operations. Thus, when multicultural practitioners appeal to theorists for suggestions on how cultural diversity should be taught, they expect procedural specificities, but get conceptual guidelines instead. They are advised to be integrative, authentic, and transformative. These are great principles, but they do not have any action directives.

Conversely, when theorists look to practitioners for evidence of the application of conceptual ideas in classroom actions they expect composites and systems of varieties of methods, materials, and tools, since concepts embed a multitude of action possibilities. Instead, they frequently see isolated activities and fragmented events.

These situations are understandable from the perspective of both the theorist and the practitioner. Multicultural theorists should be pursuing deeper conceptual understandings and explanations of the field, and practitioners should be looking for more pragmatic ways to implement cultural diversity in the classroom. It does little toward advancing both theory and practice for either to indict the other for not being maximally accountable for quality performance. Theorists should not be expected to perform as practitioners do; nor should practitioners be held accountable for being theorists. Both should be valued for their respective skills and functions. Yet, the need to establish better linkages between multicultural education theory and practice is imperative. Therefore, individuals who can translate theoretical ideas to the functional operations of actual classroom instruction can contribute significantly to the overall development of the field.

BUILDING BETTER BRIDGES BETWEEN THEORY AND PRACTICE

Two ideas are discussed here to illustrate how multicultural education theory and practice can be linked closer together. One involves approaches to multicultural education implementation, and the other has to do with the personal and professional empowerment of teachers in cultural diversity. Hopefully, they are instructive of the kinds of opportunities this challenge offers for enriching current developments in the field, as well as adding new dimensions of growth in the future.

All major multicultural scholars have developed models of different approaches to implementing cultural diversity in classroom curriculum and instruction. In some form or another, they include variations of **inclusion, infusion, deconstruction,** and **transformation.** The progression of these is from teaching information about ethnic groups in rather fragmentary, haphazard, and additive ways; to incorporating cultural pluralism throughout the educational process systemically and systematically; to using culturally pluralistic knowledge, perspectives, and experiences as criteria for re-examining the basic premises and assumptions on which the United States educational system is grounded; to creating new educational and social systems that are based upon the ethics, morality, and legalities of cultural diversity.

Embedded in all of these models are ideas of historical context, developmental growth, and increasing referential and conceptual complexity. Each model also conveys the message that some approaches to dealing with cultural diversity are inherently better than others, and everyone should aim to adopt these. It will help to establish closer and more functional linkages between multicultural theory and practice if these conceptualizations were reconsidered to be more developmental than hierarchical.

Rather than continuing to argue that there is **a single best** way to do multicultural education to which everyone should adhere, it is more feasible, pragmatic, inclusive, and empowering to legitimize multiple levels appropriateness in participation. Currently the theoretical message is that efforts to do multicultural education are inadequate if they are not at least at the infusion and preferably the transformation level. To impose these expectations on everyone is unrealistic. Educators just entering the field of multiculturalism simply do not have the background information, the pedagogical skills, or the personal confidence needed to fully understand what infusion and transformation are, least of all how to translate these ideals to practice. When they try to do so, the results are disastrous for everyone concerned—the professionals, the students, and the field.

The theoretical ideas of **developmental progression and appropriateness** have far greater potential for improving the quality of participation of educators at various stages of personal growth and professional positions in the promotion of multicultural education, as well as closer synchronizing its theory and practice. Developmental progression means that people's understanding of and capabilities in multicultural education move through different stages of conceptualization and practice; that each stage has inherent worth and legitimacy; and that the emergence of more advanced stages are contingent upon the development of earlier, more basic stages. It also means that there is growth potential within each stage.

While the inclusion of ethnic content into selective curriculum lessons or units of instruction is a more rudimentary and basic approach to multicultural education than transforming the entire schooling enterprise, it has conceptual value and practical utility. Educators have to master this approach before they move on to more advanced levels of implementation. They have to learn how to do good multicultural lessons before they can design effective units on cultural diversity, or redesign topics in other subjects so that they include multicultural perspectives. Teachers most certainly cannot deconstruct the cultural hegemony ingrained in their instructional styles, or make them multiculturally responsive until they have learned a great deal about how cultural elements of different ethnic groups are embedded in the rituals and routines of teaching and learning.

Viewing multicultural education theory and practice as developmental and progressional enfranchises more people to be active advocates. Relatively few educators are ready now to actually transform the educational system so that it reflects cultural diversity in all of its content, values, and structures even though they may believe this is necessary. Therefore, if its practice were solely dependent upon them, very little would be accomplished. As others engage in practical actions at other levels of conceptualization the numbers of advocates who promote diversity increases significantly. The field needs these numbers to create a critical mass of change agents who can impact the educational system at multiple levels and in diverse ways. Diversified personnel with differentiated abilities and skills are imperative to operationalize the multicultural mandate of **systemic reform.**

This idea of individuals involved at various levels of complexity, and using a variety of techniques to incorporate cultural diversity in the educational enterprise, is highly consistent with the nature of the field. The heart of multicultural education is diversity and plurality. Just as advocates demand that these principles be applied in teaching students about cultural differences, the field should apply similar criteria to itself. If it does, then both multicultural theory and practice must provide opportunities for educators in various stages of professional development to be involved in a variety of ways in promoting cultural diversity that are legitimized and compatible with their capabilities. They also should have the chance to improve the quality of their present state of being before they are expected to move to new planes of performance. These ideas evoke the learning principles of readiness and prerequisites. Just as classroom teachers use them to help guide their students' learning, similar applications should be made to the professional growth of teachers in cultural diversity.

More systematic ways to **empower practice** are needed within each of the developmental stages of multicultural education theory. These can be accomplished by carefully analyzing essential components of teaching functions endemic to each stage, and then demonstrating how these can be modified to illustrate stage related principles of multicultural education. Four brief examples will suffice to illustrate this point. A powerful feature of the **inclusion** stage of multicultural education theory and practice is the concept of heroism. Students are introduced to a host of ethnic individuals who have made major contributions to their own cultural groups, as well as to United States society and humankind. The theoretical idea of selecting authentic ethnic individuals and artifacts to be taught can be applied in practice by teachers understanding what is a cultural hero or heroine according to the standards of different ethnic groups. Using these as criteria to select candidates for this distinction will help educators to avoid using their own cultural standards to select heroes and then imposing them upon students from other ethnic groups. Understanding cultural standards of heroism and how different candidates manifest them thus empowers teachers and curriculum designers to select better examples of ethnic heroes and contributions to teach to students.

At the **infusion** level of multicultural education, implementation educators can be empowered in practice by demonstrating how the typical components of curriculum development can be culturally diversified. For example, how can sensitivity to cultural diversity be embedded in a curriculum rationale, statement of goals and objectives, content and learning objectives, and students' performance assessment? Other natural infusion opportunities can be identified by analyzing the teaching act to determine things that teachers routinely do, and then changing them to be responsive to cultural diversity. The notions of impacting that which is habitual, routine, and fundamental in the educational process are central to the multicultural education infusion. Because teacher talk is a major component of instruction, and it affects culturally diverse students differently, it should be a primary target for multicultural infusion. But, in order to do this well, how teachers talk needs to be carefully analyzed, and then changed accordingly. This analysis might include the kinds of questions asked of which students, turn-taking rules, wait time for responses, and mechanisms used to convey praise and criticism to students.

At the essence of **deconstruction** approaches to multicultural education is what is often referred to as critique, interrogation, and knowledge reconstruction. In practice this means that students are groomed to be healthy skeptics who are constantly questioning existing claims to social and academic truths and accuracy in search of new explanations, and to determine if the perspectives of different ethnic and cultural groups are represented. Nothing is considered sacrosanct, infallible, perfect, totally finished, or purely objective. Students are taught how to discern authors' biases, determine whose story is being told and validated from which vantage point, how to engage in perspective taking, as well as how to be self-monitoring, self-reflective, and self-renewing, especially in relation to issues of cultural diversity. These are the behavioral or practical manifestations of such deconstructive principles as multiple perspectives, giving voice, and the positionality of knowledge.

In practice, **transformative** approaches to multicultural education focus on constructing new realities, new systems, and new possibilities. They are the **action response** to deconstructive processes. Whereas deconstruction focuses on thinking and imagining new explanations of culturally pluralistic social situations, transformation takes the revisioning processes to its ultimate conclusion by acting upon the mental constructions. This building of new systems that are fully culturally pluralistic may include models, facsimiles, simulations, and actual creations. In creating them students are engaged in various forms of social and political actions, both within and outside of schools, which symbolize their moral and ethical commitments to freedom, equality, and justice for culturally diverse peoples.

CONCLUSION

The challenges posed by the need to bridge multicultural education theory and practice require that one is able to think analytically about current developments to explicate their most salient intersecting possibilities. With some careful thinking from individuals with the necessary expertise, it is possible to generate a whole new body of research and scholarship in multicultural education which demonstrates, with operational clarity, how theoretical principles can be translated into actual practices in schools and classrooms.

However, the act of creating these strategies will prompt yet another generation of multicultural theorizing. But, this evolving vitality and potential should not be seen as a problem to the field. As long as multicultural education has the regenerative power to create new thoughts, critiques, possibilities, and proposals for its own refinement, it is alive and well both as a theoretical endeavor and a practical necessity.

REFERENCES

Banks, J. A. (1995). The historical reconstruction of knowledge about race: Implications for transformative teaching. *Educational Researcher,* 24 (20), 15–25.

Banks, J. A., & Banks, C. A. M. (Eds.). (1993). *Multicultural education: Issues and perspectives.* Boston, MA: Allyn & Bacon.

Banks, J. A., & Banks, C. A. M. (Eds.). (1995). *Handbook of research on multicultural education.* New York: Macmillan.

Beauchamp, G. A. (1968). *Curriculum theory* (2d. ed.). Wilmette, IL: Kagg Press.

Bennett, C. I. (1995). *Comprehensive multicultural education: Theory and practice* (3rd ed.). Boston, MA: Allyn & Bacon.

Darder, A., (1991). *Culture and power in the classroom: A critical foundation for bicultural education.* New York: Bergin & Garvey.

Foster, M. (Ed.). (1991). *Readings on equal education. Volume 11: Qualitative investigations into schools and schooling.* New York: AMS Press.

Gay, G. (1994). *At the essence of learning: Multicultural education.* West Lafayette, IN: Kappa Delta Pi.

Hollins, E. R., King, J. E., & Hayman, W. C. (Eds.). (1994). *Teaching diverse populations: Formulating a knowledge base.* Albany, NY: State University of New York Press.

Nieto, S. (1992). *Affirming diversity: The sociopolitical context of multicultural education.* New York: Longman.

Sleeter, C. E. (Ed.). (1991). *Empowerment through multicultural education.* Albany, NY: State University of New York Press.

Sleeter, C. E., & Grant, C. A. (1995). *Making choices for multicultural education: Five approaches to race, class, and gender* (2d ed.). Columbus, OH: Merrill.

Affirmation, Solidarity, and Critique:
Moving Beyond Tolerance in Multicultural Education

Sonia Nieto

Sonia Nieto is a faculty member with the Cultural Diversity and Curriculum Reform Program, School of Education, University of Massachusetts, Amherst.

Tolerance: the capacity for or the practice of recognizing and respecting the beliefs or practices of others.
     –The American Heritage Dictionary, *as quoted in* Teaching Tolerance, *Spring, 1993.*

"We want our students to develop **tolerance** of others," says a teacher when asked what multicultural education means to her. "The greatest gift we can give our students is a **tolerance** for differences," is how a principal explains it. A school's mission statement might be more explicit: "Students at the Jefferson School will develop critical habits of the mind, a capacity for creativity and risk-taking, and **tolerance** for those different from themselves." In fact, if we were to listen to pronouncements at school board meetings, or conversations in teachers' rooms, or if we perused school handbooks, we would probably discover that when mentioned at all, multicultural education is associated more often with the term tolerance than with any other.

My purpose in this article is to challenge readers, and indeed the very way that multicultural education is practiced in schools in general, to move beyond tolerance in both conceptualization and implementation. It is my belief that a movement beyond tolerance is absolutely necessary if multicultural education is to become more than a superficial "bandaid" or a "feel-good" additive to our school curricula. I will argue that tolerance is actually a low level of multicultural support, reflecting as it does an acceptance of the *status quo* with but slight accommodations to difference. I will review and expand

upon a model of multicultural education that I have developed elsewhere (See Sonia Nieto, *Affirming Diversity: The Sociopolitical Context of Multicultural Education,* Longman, 1992) in order to explore what multicultural education might actually look like in a school's policies and practices.

Levels of Multicultural Education Support

Multicultural education is not a unitary concept. On the contrary, it can be thought of as a range of options across a wide spectrum that includes such diverse strategies as bilingual/bicultural programs, ethnic studies courses, Afrocentric curricula, or simply the addition of a few "Holidays and Heroes" to the standard curriculum (See James A. Banks, *Teaching Strategies for Ethnic Studies,* Allyn & Bacon, 1991), just to name a few. Although all of these may be important parts of multicultural education, they represent incomplete conceptualizations and operationalizations of this complex educational reform movement. Unfortunately, however, multicultural education is often approached as if there were a prescribed script.

The most common understanding of multicultural education is that it consists largely of additive content rather than of structural changes in content and process. It is not unusual, then, to hear teachers say that they are "doing" multicultural education this year, or, as in one case I heard, that they could not "do it" in the Spring because they had too many other things to "do." In site of the fact that scholars and writers in multicultural education have been remarkably consistent over the years about the complexity of approaches in the field (see, especially, the analysis by Christine E. Sleeter & Carl A. Grant, "An Analysis of Multicultural Ed-

ucation in the United States," *Harvard Educational Review,* November, 1987), it has often been interpreted in either a simplistic or a monolithic way. It is because of this situation that I have attempted to develop a model that clarifies how various levels of multicultural education support may actually be apparent in schools.

Developing categories or models is always an inherently problematic venture, and I therefore present the following model with some hesitancy. Whenever we classify and categorize reality, we run the risk that it will be viewed as static and arbitrary, rather than as messy, complex, and contradictory, which we know it to be. Notwithstanding the value that theoretical models may have, they tend to represent information as if it were fixed and absolute. Yet we know too well that nothing happens exactly as portrayed in models and charts, much less social interactions among real people in settings such as schools. In spite of this, models or categories can be useful because they help make concrete situations more understandable and manageable. I therefore present the following model with both reluctance and hope: reluctance because it may improperly be viewed as set in stone, but hope because it may challenge teachers, administrators, and educators in general to rethink what it means to develop a multicultural perspective in their schools.

The levels in this model should be viewed as necessarily dynamic, with penetrable borders. They should be understood as "interactive," in the words of Peggy McIntosh (see her *Interactive Phases of Curricular Re-vision: A Feminist Perspective,* Wellesley College Center for Research on Women, 1983). Thus, although these levels represent "ideal" categories that are internally consistent and therefore set,

From *Multicultural Education,* Spring 1994, pp. 9-12, 35-38. © 1994 by the National Association for Multicultural Education. Reprinted by permission.

the model is not meant to suggest that schools are really like this. Probably no school would be a purely "monocultural" or "tolerant" school, given the stated characteristics under each of these categories. However, these categories are used in an effort to illustrate how support for diversity is manifested in schools in a variety of ways. Because multicultural education is primarily a set of beliefs and a philosophy, rather than a set program or fixed content, this model can assist us in determining how particular school policies and practices need to change in order to embrace the diversity of our students and their communities.

The four levels to be considered are: **tolerance**; **acceptance**; *respect*; and, finally, **affirmation, solidarity, and critique**. Before going on to consider how multicultural education is manifested in schools that profess these philosophical orientations, it is first helpful to explore the antithesis of multicultural education, namely, **monocultural education**, because without this analysis we have nothing with which to compare it.

In the scenarios that follow, we go into five schools that epitomize different levels of multicultural education. All are schools with growing cultural diversity in their student populations; differences include staff backgrounds, attitudes, and preparation, as well as curriculum and pedagogy. In our visits, we see how the curriculum, interactions among students, teachers, and parents, and other examples of attention to diversity are either apparent or lacking. We see how students of different backgrounds might respond to the policies and practices around them. (In another paper entitled "Creating Possibilities: Educating Latino Students in Massachusetts, in *The Education of Latino Students in Massachusetts: Policy and Research Implications*, published by the Gaston Institute for Latino Policy and Development in Boston, which I co-edited with R. Rivera, I developed scenarios of schools that would provide different levels of support specifically for Latino students.)

Monocultural Education

Monocultural education describes a situation in which school structures, policies, curricula, instructional materials, and even pedagogical strategies are primarily representative of only the dominant culture. In most United States schools, it can be defined as "the way things are."

We will begin our tour in a "monocultural school" that we'll call the George Washington Middle School. When we walk in, we see a sign that says "NO UNAUTHORIZED PERSONS ARE ALLOWED IN THE SCHOOL. ALL VISITORS MUST

REPORT DIRECTLY TO THE PRINCIPAL'S OFFICE." The principal, assistant principal, and counselor are all European-American males, although the school's population is quite diverse, with large numbers of African-American, Puerto Rican, Arab-American, Central American, Korean, and Vietnamese students. As we walk down the hall, we see a number of bulletin boards. On one, the coming Christmas holiday is commemorated; on another, the P.T.O.'s bake sale is announced; and on a third, the four basic food groups are listed, with reference to only those foods generally considered to be "American."

The school is organized into 45-minutes periods of such courses as U.S. history, English, math, science, music appreciation, art, and physical education. In the U. S. history class, students learn of the proud exploits, usually through wars and conquest, of primarily European-American males. They learn virtually nothing about the contributions, perspectives, or talents of women or those outside the cultural mainstream. U.S. slavery is mentioned briefly in relation to the Civil War, but African-Americans are missing thereafter. In English class, the students have begun their immersion in the "canon," reading works almost entirely written by European and European-American males, although a smattering of women and African-American (but no Asian, Latino, or American Indian) authors are included in the newest anthology. In music appreciation class, students are exposed to what is called "classical music," that is, European classical music, but the "classical" music of societies in Asia, Africa, and Latin America is nowhere to be found. In art classes, students may learn about the art work of famous European and European-American artists, and occasionally about the "crafts" and "artifacts" of other cultures and societies mostly from the Third World.

Teachers at the George Washington Middle School are primarily European-American women who have had little formal training in multicultural approaches or perspectives. They are proud of the fact that they are "color-blind," that is, that they see no differences among their students, treating them all the same. Of course, this does not extend to tracking, which they generally perceive to be in the interest of teaching all students to the best of their abilities. Ability grouping is a standard practice at the George Washington Middle School. There are four distinct levels of ability, from "talented and gifted" to "remedial." I.Q. tests are used to detemmine student placement and intellectually superior students are placed in "Talented and Gifted" programs, and in advanced levels of math, science, English, and social studies. Only these top students

have the option of taking a foreign language. The top levels consist of overwhelmingly European-American and Asian-American students, but the school rationalizes that this is due to either the native intelligence of these students, or to the fact that they have a great deal more intellectual stimulation and encouragement in their homes. Thus, teachers have learned to expect excellent work from their top students, but little of students in their low-level classes, who they often see as lazy and disruptive.

Students who speak a language other than English as their native language are either placed in regular classrooms where they will learn to "sink or swim" or in "NE" (non-English) classes, where they are drilled in English all day and where they will remain until they learn English sufficiently well to perform in the regular classroom. In addition, parents are urged to speak to their children only in English at home. Their native language, whether Spanish, Vietnamese, or Korean, is perceived as a handicap to their learning, and as soon as they forget it, they can get on with the real job of learning.

Although incidents of racism have occurred in the George Washington Middle School, they have been taken care of quietly and privately. For example, when racial slurs have been used, students have been admonished not to say them. When fights between children of different ethnic groups take place, the assistant principal has insisted that race or ethnicity has nothing to do with them; "kids will be kids" is the way he describes these incidents.

What exists in the George Washington Middle School is a monocultural environment with scant reference to the experiences of others from largely subordinated cultural groups. Little attention is paid to student diversity, and the school curriculum is generally presented as separate from the community in which it is located. In addition, "dangerous" topics such as racism, sexism, and homophobia are seldom discussed, and reality is represented as finished and static. In summary, the George Washington School is a depressingly familiar scenario because it reflects what goes on in most schools in American society.

Tolerance

How might a school characterized by "tolerance" be different from a monocultural school? It is important here to mention the difference between the **denotation** and the **connotation** of words. According to the dictionary definition given at the beginning of this article, tolerance is hardly a value that one could argue with. After all, what is wrong with "recognizing and respecting the beliefs or practices of others"? On the contrary, this is a quintessential part of developing a multicultural perspective. (*Teaching Tolerance*, a journal developed by the Southern Anti-Poverty Law Project, has no doubt been developed with this perspective in mind, and my critique here of tolerance is in no way meant to criticize this wonderful classroom and teacher resource.)

Nevertheless, the connotation of words is something else entirely. When we think of what **tolerance** means in practice, we have images of a grudging but somewhat distasteful acceptance. To **tolerate** differences means that they are endured, not necessarily embraced. In fact, this level of support for multicultural education stands on shaky ground because what is tolerated today can too easily be rejected tomorrow. A few examples will help illustrate this point.

Our "tolerant" school is the Brotherhood Middle School. Here, differences are understood to be the inevitable burden of a culturally pluralistic society. A level up from a "color-blind" monocultural school, the "tolerant" school accepts differences but only if they can be modified. Thus, they are accepted, but because the ultimate goal is assimilation, differences in language and culture are replaced as quickly as possible. This ideology is reflected in the physical environment, the attitudes of staff, and the curriculum to which students are exposed.

When we enter the Brotherhood School, there are large signs in English welcoming visitors, although there are no staff on hand who can communicate with the families of the growing Cambodian student population. One prominently-placed bulletin board proudly portrays the winning essays of this year's writing contest with the theme of "Why I am proud to be an American." The winners, a European-American sixth grader and a Vietnamese seventh grader, write in their essays about the many opportunities given to all people in our country, no matter what their race, ethnicity, or gender. Another bulletin board boasts the story of Rosa Parks, portrayed as a woman who was too tired to give up her seat on the bus, thus serving as a catalyst for the modern civil rights movement. (The Fall 1993 issue of *Multicultural Education* includes a powerful example of how people such as Rosa Parks have been de-contextualized to better fit in with the U.S. mainstream conception of individual rather than collective struggle, thus adding little to children's understanding of institutionalized discrimination on our society; see "The Myth of 'Rosa Parks the Tired,'" by Herbert Kohl, pages 6-10, in which Kohl reports that based on his research most stories used in American schools present Rosa Parks simply as "Rosa Parks the Tired.")

Nevertheless, a number of important structural changes are taking place at the Brotherhood School. An experiment has recently begun in which the sixth and seventh graders are in "family" groupings, and these are labeled by family names such as the Jones family, the Smith family, and the Porter family. Students remain together as a family in their major subjects (English, social studies, math, and science) and there is no ability tracking in these classes. Because their teachers have a chance to meet and plan together daily, they are more readily able to develop integrated curricula. In fact, once in a while, they even combine classes so that they can team-teach and their students remain at a task for an hour and a half rather than the usual three quarters of an hour. The students seem to like this arrangement, and have done some interesting work in their study of Washington, D.C. For instance, they used geometry to learn how the city was designed, and have written to their congressional representatives to ask how bills become laws. Parents are involved in fund-raising for an upcoming trip to the capital, where students plan to interview a number of their local legislators.

The curriculum at the Brotherhood School has begun to reflect some of the changes that a multicultural society demands. Students are encouraged to study a foreign language (except, of course, for those who already speak one; they are expected to learn English and in the process, they usually forget their native language). In addition, a number of classes have added activities on women, African Americans, and American Indians. Last year, for instance, Martin Luther King Day was celebrated by having all students watch a video of the "I Have a Dream" speech.

The majority of changes in the curriculum have occurred in the social studies and English departments, but the music teacher has also begun to add a more international flavor to her repertoire, and the art classes recently went to an exhibit of the work of Romare Bearden. This year, a "multicultural teacher" has been added to the staff. She meets with all students in the school, seeing each group once a week for one period. Thus far, she has taught students about Chinese New Year, *Kwanzaa*, *Ramadan*, and *Dia de los Reyes*. She is getting ready for the big multicultural event of the year, Black History Month. She hopes to work with other teachers to bring in guest speakers, show films about the civil rights movement, and have an art contest in which students draw what the world would be like if Dr. King's dream of equality became a reality.

Students who speak a language other than English at the Brotherhood School are placed in special E.S.L. classes, where they are taught English as quickly, but sensitively, as possible. For instance, while they are encouraged to speak to one another in English, they are allowed to use their native language, but only as a last resort. The feeling is that if they use it more often, it will become a "crutch." In any event, the E.S.L. teachers are not required to speak a language other than English; in fact, being bilingual is even considered a handicap because students might expect them to use their other language.

The principal of the Brotherhood School has made it clear that racism will not be tolerated here. Name-calling and the use of overtly racist and sexist textbooks and other materials are discouraged. Recently, some teachers attended a workshop on strategies for dealing with discrimination in the classroom. Some of those who attended expect to make some changes in how they treat students from different backgrounds.

Most teachers at the Brotherhood School have had little professional preparation to deal with the growing diversity of the student body. They like and genuinely want to help their students, but have made few changes in their curricular or instructional practices. For them, "being sensitive" to their students is what multicultural education should be about, not overhauling the curriculum. Thus, they acknowledge student differences in language, race, gender, and social class, but still cannot quite figure out why some students are more successful than others. Although they would like to think not, they wonder if genetics or poor parental attitudes about education have something to do with it. If not, what can explain these great discrepancies?

Acceptance

Acceptance is the next level of supporting diversity. It implies that differences are acknowledged and their importance is neither denied nor belittled. It is at this level that we see substantial movement toward multicultural education. A look at how some of the school's policies and practices might change is indicative of this movement.

The name of our school is the Rainbow Middle School. As we enter, we see signs in English, Spanish, and Haitian Creole, the major languages besides English spoken by students and their families. The principal of the Rainbow School is Dr. Belinda Clayton, the first African-American principal ever appointed. She has designated her school as a "multicultural building," and has promoted a number of professional development opportunities for teachers that focus on diversity. These include seminars on diverse learning styles, bias-free assessment, and bilingual education. In addition, she has hired not only Spanish- and Haitian Creole-speaking teachers for the bilingual classrooms, but has also diversified the staff in the "regular" program.

Bulletin boards outside the principal's office display the pictures of the "Students of the Month." This month's winners are Rodney Thomas, a sixth-grader who has excelled in art, Neleida Cortes, a seventh-grade student in the bilingual program, and Melissa Newton, an eighth-grader in the special education program. All three were given a special luncheon by the principal and their homeroom teachers. Another bulletin board focuses on "Festivals of Light" and features information about *Chanukah*, *Kwanzaa*, and Christmas, with examples of *Las Posadas* in Mexico and Saint Lucia's Day in Sweden.

The curriculum at the Rainbow Middle School has undergone some changes to reflect the growing diversity of the student body. English classes include more choices of African-American, Irish, Jewish, and Latino literature written in English. Some science and math teachers have begun to make reference to famous scientists and mathematicians from a variety of backgrounds. In one career-studies class, a number of parents have been invited to speak about their job and the training they had to receive in order to get those positions. All students are encouraged to study a foreign language, and choices have been expanded to include Spanish, French, German, and Mandarin Chinese.

Tracking has been eliminated in all but the very top levels at the Rainbow School. All students have the opportunity to learn algebra, although some are still counseled out of this option because their teachers believe it will be too difficult for them. The untracked classes seem to be a hit with the students, and preliminary results have shown a slight improvement among all students. Some attempts have been made to provide flexible scheduling, with one day a week devoted to entire "learning blocks" where students work on a special project. One group recently engaged in an in-depth study of the elderly in their community. They learned about services available to them, and they touched on poverty and lack of health care for many older Americans. As a result of this study, the group has added a community service component to the class; this involves going to the local Senior Center during their

weekly learning block to read with the elderly residents.

Haitian and Spanish-speaking students are tested and, if found to be more proficient in their native language, are placed in transitional bilingual education programs. Because of lack of space in the school, the bilingual programs are located in the basement, near the boiler room. Here, students are taught the basic curriculum in their native language while learning English as a second language during one period of the day with an ESL specialist. Most ESL teachers are also fluent in a language other than English, helping them understand the process of acquiring a second language. The bilingual program calls for students to be "mainstreamed" (placed in what is called a "regular classroom") as quickly as possible, with a limit of three years on the outside. In the meantime, they are segregated from their peers for most of the day, but have some classes with English-speaking students, including physical education, art, and music. As they proceed through the program and become more fluent in English, they are "exited" out for some classes, beginning with math and social studies. While in the bilingual program, students' native cultures are sometimes used as the basis of the curriculum, and they learn about the history of their people. There is, for instance, a history course on the Caribbean that is offered to both groups in their native languages. Nevertheless, neither Haitian and Latino students in the bilingual program nor students of other backgrounds have access to these courses.

Incidents of racism and other forms of discrimination are beginning to be faced at the Rainbow Middle School. Principal Clayton deals with these carefully, calling in the offending students as well as their parents, and she makes certain that students understand the severe consequences for name-calling or scapegoating others. Last year, one entire day was devoted to "diversity" and regular classes were canceled while students attended workshops focusing on discrimination, the importance of being sensitive to others, and the influence on U.S. history of many different immigrants. They have also hosted a "Multicultural Fair" and published a cookbook with recipes donated by many different parents.

The Rainbow Middle School is making steady progress in accepting the great diversity of its students. They have decided that perhaps assimilation should not be the goal, and have eschewed the old idea of the "melting pot." In its place, they have the "salad bowl" metaphor, in which all students bring something special that need not be reconstituted or done away with.

Respect

Respect is the next level of multicultural education support. It implies admiration and high esteem for diversity. When differences are respected, they are used as the basis for much of what goes on in schools. Our next scenario describes what this might look like.

The Sojourner Truth Middle School is located in a mid-size town with a changing population. There is a fairly large African-American population with a growing number of students of Cape Verdean and Vietnamese background, and the school staff reflects these changes, including teachers, counselors, and special educators of diverse backgrounds. There is, for example, a Vietnamese speech pathologist, and his presence has helped to alleviate the concerns of some teachers that the special needs of the Vietnamese children were not being addressed. He has found that while some students do indeed have speech problems, others do not, but teachers' unfamiliarity with the Vietnamese language made it difficult to know this.

When we enter the Sojourner Truth Middle School, we are greeted by a parent volunteer. She gives us printed material in all the languages represented in the school, and invites us to the parents' lounge for coffee, tea, and danish. We are then encouraged to walk-around and explore the school. Bulletin boards boast of students' accomplishments in the Spanish Spelling Bee, the local *Jeopardy* Championship, and the W.E.B. DuBois Club of African-American history. It is clear from the children's pictures that there is wide participation of many students in all of these activities. The halls are abuzz with activity as students go from one class to another, and most seem eager and excited by school.

Professional development is an important principle at the Sojourner Truth Middle School. Teachers, counselors, and other staff are encouraged to take courses at the local university and to keep up with the literature in their field. To make this more feasible, the staff gets released time weekly to get together. As a consequence, the curriculum has been through tremendous changes. Teachers have formed committees to develop their curriculum. The English department decided to use its time to have reading and discussion groups with some of the newly available multicultural literature with which they were unfamiliar. As a result, they have revamped the curriculum into such overarching themes as **coming of age**, **immigration**, **change and continuity**, and **individual and collective responsibility**. They have found that it is easier to select literature to reflect themes such as these, and the literature is by its very nature multicultural. For instance, for the theme **individual and collective responsibility** they have chosen stories of varying difficulty, including *The Diary of Anne Frank, Bridge to Terabithia* (by Katherine Paterson), *Morning Girl* (by Michael Dorris), and *Let the Circle be Unbroken* (by Mildred D. Taylor), among others. The English teachers have in turn invited the history, art, and science departments to join them in developing some integrated units with these themes. Teachers from the art and music departments have agreed to work with them, and have included lessons on Vietnamese dance, Guatemalan weaving, Jewish Klezmer music, and American Indian story telling as examples of individual and collective responsibility in different communities.

Other changes are apparent in the curriculum as well, for it has become more antiracist and honest. When studying World War II, students learn about the heroic role played by the United States, and also about the Holocaust, in which not only six million Jews, but millions of others, including Gypsies, gays and lesbians, and many dissenters of diverse backgrounds, were exterminated. They also learn, for the first time, about the internment of over a hundred thousand Japanese and Japanese Americans on our own soil.

It has become "safe" to talk about such issues as the crucial role of labor in U.S. history and the part played by African Americans in freeing themselves from bondage, both subjects thought too "sensitive" to be included previously. This is one reason why the school was renamed for a woman known for her integrity and courage.

The Sojourner Truth Middle School has done away with all ability grouping. When one goes into a classroom, it is hard to believe that students of all abilities are learning together because the instruction level seems to be so high. Upon closer inspection, it becomes apparent that there are high expectations for all students. Different abilities are accommodated by having some students take more time than others, providing cooperative groups in which students change roles and responsibilities, and through ongoing dialogue among all students.

Students who speak a language other than English are given the option of being in a "maintenance bilingual program," that is, a program based on using their native language throughout their schooling, not just for three years. Changing the policy that only students who could not function in English were eligible for bilingual programs, this school has made the program available to those who speak English in addition to their native language. Parents and other community members who speak these languages are invited in to classes routinely to talk about their lives, jobs, or families, or to tell stories or share experiences. Students in the bilingual program are not, however, segregated from their peers all day, but join them for a number of academic classes.

Teachers and other staff members at this middle school have noticed that incidents of name-calling and interethnic hostility have diminished greatly since the revised curriculum was put into place. Perhaps more students see themselves in the curriculum and feel less angry about their invisibility; perhaps more teachers have developed an awareness and appreciation for their students' diversity while learning about it; perhaps the more diverse staff is the answer; or maybe it's because the community feels more welcome into the school. Whatever it is, the Sojourner Truth Middle School has developed an environment in which staff and students are both expanding their ways of looking at the world.

Affirmation, Solidarity, and Critique

Affirmation, solidarity, and critique is based on the premise that the most powerful learning results when students work and struggle with one another, even if it is sometimes difficult and challenging. It begins with the assumption that the many differences that students and their families represent are embraced and accepted as legitimate vehicles for learning, and that these are then extended. What makes this level different from the others is that conflict is not avoided, but rather accepted as an inevitable part of learning. Because multicultural education at this level is concerned with equity and social justice, and because the basic values of different groups are often diametrically opposed, conflict is bound to occur.

Affirmation, solidarity, and critique is also based on understanding that culture is not a fixed or unchangeable artifact, and is therefore subject to critique. Passively accepting the status quo of any culture is thus inconsistent with this level of multicultural education; simply substituting one myth for another contradicts its basic assumptions because no group is inherently superior or more heroic than any other. As eloquently expressed by Mary Kalantzis and Bill Cope in their 1990 work *The Experience of Multicultural Education in Australia: Six Case Studies*, "Multicultural education, to be effective, needs to be more active. It needs to consider not just the pleasure of diversity but more fundamental issues that arise as different groups negotiate community and the basic issues of material life in the same space—a process that equally might generate conflict and pain."

Multicultural education without critique may result in cultures remaining at the romantic or exotic stage. If students are to transcend their own cultural experience in order to understand the differences of others, they need to go through a process of reflection and critique of their cultures and those of others. This process of critique, however, begins with a solid core of solidarity with others who are different from themselves. When based on true respect, critique is not only necessary but in fact healthy.

The Arturo Schomburg Middle School is located in a mid-size city with a very mixed population of Puerto Ricans, Salvadoreans, American Indians, Polish Americans, Irish Americans, Chinese Americans, Philippinos, and African Americans. The school was named for a Black Puerto Rican scholar who devoted his life to exploring the role of Africans in the Americas, in the process challenging the myth he had been told as a child in Puerto Rico that Africans had "no culture."

The school's logo, visible above the front door, is a huge tapestry made by the students, and it symbolizes a different model of multicultural education from that of either the "melting pot" or the "salad bowl." According to a publication of the National Association of State Boards of Education (*The American Tapestry: Educating a Nation*), "A tapestry is a hand-woven textile. When examined from the back, it may simply appear to be a motley group of threads. But when reversed, the threads work together to depict a picture of structure and beauty" (p. 1). According to Adelaide Sanford, one of the study group members who wrote this publication, a tapestry also symbolizes, through its knots, broken threads, and seeming jumble of colors and patterns on the back, the tensions, conflicts, and dilemmas that a society needs to work out. This spirit of both collaboration and struggle is evident in the school.

When we enter the Schomburg Middle School, the first thing we notice is a banner proclaiming the school 's motto: LEARN, REFLECT, QUESTION, AND WORK TO MAKE THE WORLD A BETTER PLACE. This is the message that reverberates throughout the school. Participation is another theme that is evident, and the main hall contains numerous pictures of students in classrooms, community service settings, and extracurricular activities. Although housed in a traditional school building, the school has been transformed into a place where all children feel safe and are encouraged to learn to the highest levels of learning. While there are typical classrooms of the kind that are immediately recognizable to us, the school also houses centers that focus on specific areas of learning. There is, for instance, a studio where students can be found practicing traditional Philippino dance and music, as well as European ballet, and modern American dance, among others. Outside, there is a large garden that is planted, cared for, and harvested by the students and faculty. The vegetables are used by the cafeteria staff in preparing meals and they have noticed a marked improvement in the eating habits of the children since the menu was changed to reflect a healthier and more ethnically diverse menu.

We are welcomed into the school by staff people who invite us to explore the many different classrooms and other learning centers. Those parents who are available during the day can be found assisting in classrooms, in the Parent's Room working on art projects or computer classes, or attending workshops by other parents or teachers on topics ranging from cross-cultural child-rearing to ESL. The bulletin boards are ablaze with color and include a variety of languages, displaying student work from critical essays on what it means to be an American to art projects that celebrate the talents of many of the students. Learning is going on everywhere, whether in classrooms or in small-group collaborative projects in halls.

What might the classrooms look like in this school? For one, they are characterized by tremendous diversity. Tracking and special education, as we know them, have been eliminated at the Schomburg Middle School. Students with special needs are taught along with all others, although they are sometimes separated for small-group instruction with students not classified as having special needs. All children are considered "talented" and special classes are occasionally organized for those who excel in dance, mathematics, poetry, or science. No interested students are excluded from any of these offerings. Furthermore, all students take algebra and geometry, and special coaching sessions are available before, after, and during school hours for these and other subjects.

Classes are flexible, with an interdisciplinary curriculum and team-teaching, resulting in sessions that sometimes last as long as three hours. The physical environment in classrooms is varied: some are organized with round work tables, others have traditional desks, and still others have scant furniture to allow for more movement. Class size also varies from small groups to large, depending on the topic at hand. Needless to say, scheduling at this school is a tremendous and continuing challenge, but faculty and students are

committed to this more flexible arrangement and willing to allow for the daily problems that it may cause.

There are no "foreign languages" at the Schomburg Middle school, nor is there, strictly speaking, a bilingual program. Rather, the entire school is multilingual, and all students learn at least a second language in addition to their native language. This means that students are not segregated by language, but instead work in bilingual settings where two languages are used for instruction. At present, the major languages used are English, Spanish, and Tagalog, representing the most common languages spoken by this school's community. It is not unusual to see students speaking these languages in classrooms, the hallways, or the playgrounds, even among those for whom English is a native language.

Students at the Schomburg Middle School seem engaged, engrossed, and excited about learning. They have been involved in a number of innovative long-range projects that have resulted from the interdisciplinary curriculum. For instance, working with a Chinese-American artist in residence, they wrote, directed, and produced a play focusing on the "Know-Nothing" Movement in U.S. history that resulted in, among other things, the Chinese Exclusion Act of 1882. In preparation for the play, they read a great deal and did extensive research. For example, they contacting the Library of Congress for information on primary sources and reviewed newspapers and magazines from the period to get a sense of the climate that led to Nativism. They also designed and sewed all the costumes and sets. In addition, they interviewed recent immigrants of many backgrounds, and found that they had a range of experiences from positive to negative in their new country. On the day of the play, hundreds of parents and other community members attended. Students also held a debate on the pros and cons of continued immigration, and received up-to-date information concerning immigration laws from their congressional representative.

The curriculum at the Schomburg Middle School is dramatically different from the George Washington School, the first school we visited. Teachers take very seriously their responsibility of **teaching complexity.** Thus, students have learned that there are many sides to every story, and that in order to make informed decisions, they need as much information as they can get. Whether in English, science, art, or any other class, students have been encouraged to be critical of every book, newspaper, curriculum, or piece of information by asking questions such as: **Who wrote the book? Who's missing in this**

story? Why? Using questions such as these as a basis, they are learning that every story has a point of view and that every point of view is at best partial and at worst distorted. They are also learning that their own backgrounds, rich and important as they may be, have limitations that can lead to parochial perceptions. Most of all, even at this age, students are learning that every topic is fraught with difficulties and they are wrestling with issues as diverse as homelessness, solar warming, and how the gender expectations of different cultures might limit opportunities for girls. Here, nothing is taboo as a topic of discussion as long as it is approached with respect and in a climate of caring.

What this means for teachers is that they have had to become learners along with their students. They approach each subject with curiosity and an open mind, and during the school day they have time to study, meet with colleagues, and plan their curriculum accordingly. Professional development here means not only attending courses at a nearby university, but collaborating with colleagues in study groups that last anywhere from half a day to several months. These provide a forum in which teachers can carefully study relevant topics or vexing problems. Some of these study groups have focused on topics such as Reconstruction and the history of the Philippines, to educational issues such as cooperative learning and diverse cognitive styles.

Especially noteworthy at this school is that **multicultural education** is not separated from **education**; that is, all education is by its very nature multicultural. English classes use literature written by a wide variety of people from countries where English is spoken. This has resulted in these classes becoming not only multicultural, but international as well. Science classes do not focus on contributions made by members of specific ethnic groups, but have in fact been transformed to consider how science itself is conceptualized, valued, and practiced by those who have traditionally been outside the scientific mainstream. Issues such as AIDS education, healing in different cultures, and scientific racism have all been the subject of study.

One of the major differences between this school and the others we visited has to do with its governance structure. There is a Schomburg School Congress consisting of students, faculty, parents, and other community members, and it has wide decision-making powers, from selecting the principal to determining reasonable and equitable disciplinary policies and practices. Students are elected by their classmates and, although at the beginning these were little more than popularity contests, in recent months it has been clear that students are beginning to take this responsibility seriously. This is probably because they are being taken seriously by the adults in the group. For instance, when students in one class decided that they wanted to plan a class trip to a neighboring city to coincide with their study of toxic wastes and the environment, they were advised to do some preliminary planning: what would be the educational objectives of such a trip? how long would it take? how much would it cost? After some research and planning, they presented their ideas to the Congress and a fund-raising plan that included students, parents, and community agencies was started.

The Schomburg School is a learning center that is undergoing important changes every day. As teachers discover the rich talents that all students bring to school, they develop high expectation for them all. The climate that exists in this school is one of possibility, because students' experiences are used to build on their learning and expand their horizons. Students in turn are realizing that while their experiences are important and unique, they are only one experience of many. A new definition of "American" is being forged at this school, one that includes everybody. Above all, learning here is exciting, engrossing, inclusive, and evolving.

Conclusion

One might well ask how realistic these scenarios are, particularly the last one. Could a school such as this really exist? Isn't this just wishful thinking? What about the reality of bond issues rejected by voters?, of teachers woefully unprepared to deal with the diversity in their classrooms?, of universities that do little more than offer stale "Mickey Mouse" courses?, of schools with no pencils, paper, and chalk, much less computers and video cameras?, of rampant violence in streets, homes, and schools?, of drugs and crime?, of parents who are barely struggling to keep their families together and can spare precious little time to devote to volunteering at school?

These are all legitimate concerns that our society needs to face, and they remind us that schools need to be understood within their sociopolitical contexts. That is, our schools exist in a society in which social and economic stratification are facts of life, where competition is taught over caring, and where the early sorting that takes place in educational settings often lasts a lifetime. Developing schools with a multicultural perspective is not easy; if it were, they would be everywhere. But schools with a true commitment to diversity, equity, and high levels of learning are difficult to achieve precisely because the problems they face are pervasive and seemingly impossible to solve. Although the many problems raised above are certainly daunting, the schools as currently organized are simply not up to the challenge. In the final analysis, if we believe that all students deserve to learn at the very highest levels, then we need a vision of education that will help achieve this end.

The scenarios above, however, are not simply figments of my imagination. As you read through the scenarios, you probably noticed bits and pieces of your own school here and there. However, because the "monocultural school" is the one with which we are most familiar, and unfortunately even comfortable, the other scenarios might seem far-fetched or unrealistic. Although they are **ideal** in the sense that they are not true pictures of specific schools, these scenarios nevertheless describe **possibilities** because they all exist to some degree in our schools today. These are not pie-in-the-sky visions, but composites of what goes on in schools every day. As such, they provide building blocks for how we might go about transforming schools. In fact, were we to design schools based on the ideals that our society has always espoused, they would no doubt come close to the last scenario.

It is not, however, a monolithic model or one that can develop overnight. The participants in each school need to develop their own vision so that step by step, with incremental changes, schools become more multicultural, and thus more inclusive and more exciting places for learning. If we believe that young people deserve to be prepared with skills for living ethical and productive lives in an increasingly diverse and complex world, then we need to transform schools so that they not only teach what have been called "the basics," but also provide an apprenticeship in democracy and social justice. It is unfair to expect our young people to develop an awareness and respect for democracy if they have not experienced it, and it is equally unrealistic to expect them to be able to function in a pluralistic society if all we give them are skills for a monocultural future. This is our challenge in the years ahead: to conquer the fear of change and imagine how we might create exciting possibilities for all students in all schools.

Multicultural

A Movement in Search

of Meaning

Leonard Davidman

Leonard Davidman is a Professor of Education with the University Center for Teacher Education at California Polytechnic State University, San Luis Obispo.

Introduction

When teacher educators responsible for conveying the meanings and rationales for multicultural education sit down to plan their courses, there are many questions to ponder. For example, several of the questions listed below are likely to be considered:

1. How many conceptions or definitions of multicultural education will I present, and whose conceptual framework will receive the most emphasis?
2. Should I begin the course with one or more definitions of culture, ethnicity, cultural group, ethnic group, minority group, etc., and if so, which definitions should be employed?
3. Which essays, texts, and on-and off-campus activities should be included?
4. Will students be expected to engage in some form of ethnic and/or cultural self-analysis and self-disclosure, and if yes, why?
5. What are the central objectives of this course of study? Am I primarily concerned with knowledge exchange, attitude formation (including commitment to multicultural education), and/or modelling how to implement multicultural education in a given setting (the school, classroom, community, or a specific level of education—elementary or secondary), or all of the above?
6. How will I perceive (label) and relate to my students, and how do I want them to perceive and relate to me?

The process of delineating these questions reminds me of the complexity professors of multicultural education face as they design their courses. It reminds me also of the need for an in-fusion approach to multicultural teacher education, one in which concepts and activities critical to an understanding of multicultural education are spread throughout all the courses and phases in a program. But, even with an infusion approach, it is likely that one or more courses will be given the special responsibility of introducing the topic of multicultural education. Therefore, some faculty will have to contemplate several of the questions enumerated above.

As might be expected, I have a point of view about each of the questions listed. All have been grappled with for over 15 years as I have created separate multicultural education courses for elementary, secondary, and graduate students at my university.

Three related beliefs have guided me in my planning:

(1) I believe that courses which cover topics related to multicultural education should involve knowledge exchange and growth, attitude formation and reformation, and modeling of strategies related to multicultural education.

(2) I also believe that prospective and inservice teachers at an early and later point in a program should have the opportunity to study and discuss themselves as individuals with a cultural identity, and, further, that these discussions should occur in small, diverse cooperative groups. This implies that students will receive instruction regarding various competing meanings of specific concepts like culture, ethnicity, race, cultural group, ethnic group, racial group, minority group, ethnic minority group, macroculture and microcultures, and core values. This also implies a flexible instructor, one who will not tell the candidates who they are, as in "You are White, lower-middle class, women with little awareness of the importance of your Whiteness," but will genuinely engage students in a process of self-exploration, self-defini-

From *Multicultural Education*, Spring 1995, pp. 8-12. © 1995 by the National Association for Multicultural Education. Reprinted by permission.

Education:

and Positive Connections

tion, self-discovery, and self-disclosure, a process informed by the idea that the concepts used and knowledge gleaned in this self-analysis activity are socially constructed. This process might wind up with the instructor politely challenging the self-definitions of a group of candidates, who, for example, refuse to see the social meaning of their own color or anyone else's color or ethnicity, but this will come after a degree of rapport has developed and will be carried out in a thoughtful, respectful way.

(3) Finally, I believe that a logical place to begin an inquiry about the design of multicultural teacher education courses is with the meaning or meanings of multicultural education. A cursory review of the multicultural education literature will show that I am not alone in making this assumption.

Most writers begin their discussion of multicultural education by sharing one or several meanings of multicultural education. One recent example of this is found in the work of Brian M. Bullivant (1993); his work will be used as a point of departure as I try to indicate why a very broad and pluralistic conception of culture and cultural group will work to the advantage of multicultural teacher educators in general, and particularly those who make use of some form of ethnic and cultural self-disclosure in their courses. After this attempt I will discuss: my definition of "cultural group;" the implications which this definition holds for multicultural education; and the importance of teachers developing a positive attitude toward multicultural education in general, and more specifically the idea of beginning a journey into the field of multicultural education. I will close this essay by taking a closer look at ethnic and cultural self-disclosure, and in this final section will provide examples of the

questions I use to initiate the process of ethnic and cultural self-disclosure in my classes.

The Meaning(s) of Multicultural Education

In his attempt to clarify the meaning of multiculturalism and multicultural education, Bullivant took the seemingly logical approach of breaking the word multicultural down into its constituent parts, prior to doing an analysis of each of the parts—"multi-" and "cultural." Because the meaning of multi-, or many, is obvious, his main analytical work was with "cultural," and for Bullivant this meant determining, in the context of multicultural education, the truest or best meaning for the term "culture." After examining several alternative meanings Bullivant defined culture "...as a social group's design for survival in and adaptation to its environment," (1993, p. 29) and with this definition in mind went on to add that one aim of multicultural education would be "...to teach about the many social groups and their different designs for living in a pluralist society."

I am concerned about the narrowness of Bullivant's definition and his general approach to defining the meanings and aims of multicultural education, particularly as this term and reform movement has evolved in the American (U.S.A.) context. While analyzing the term "multicultural," or more specifically "culture," to shed light on the meaning of multicultural education appears logical, the approach is ahistorical and somewhat presumptuous in assuming that there is one meaning of multicultural education out there. This approach would have had a stronger rationale if the early "American" creators of the multicultural education movement had moved directly from a definition of culture to their conceptions and operationalizations of multicultural education.

But, this is not what happened, at least not within the American historical context. As James A. Banks (1992) and others have pointed out, the educational movement(s) now called multicultural education was initially a set of individual and group responses to economic inequality, racism, and sexism in American culture. And, these responses, by and large, were initially located in the 20th century Negro (and now African-American) community. Indeed, in retrospect, it can be seen that all of the individuals and groups struggling for greater equality and opportunity for members of oppressed groups were laying the groundwork for the educational reform movement which in America would later be called multicultural education.

Given these realities, first, that the roots of multicultural education preceded early definitions of multicultural education, and second, that the early definitions of multicultural education did not have a one-to-one correspondence with a specific definition of culture, it may prove profitable to reverse Bullivant's procedure. Instead of selecting or creating a definition of culture to shed light on the aims of multicultural education, we can examine a pivotal goal and early influential definition of multicultural education to see what it might imply about the meaning of "cultural" in the term multicultural education. The goal referred to is educational equity; analysis of this goal will make three things clear.

First, from its beginning in the American context, multicultural education was concerned with a range of cultural and ethnic groups; second, the groups which initially fell under multicultural education's umbrella of concern were different in kind, and finally these differences can have important implications for the way we invite prospective teachers, students, parents, and lay people to enter into the conversation about multicultural education.

The influential definition referred to above stated that "Multicultural education [is] an educational reform movement that is concerned with increasing educational equity for a range of cultural and ethnic groups" (Banks, 1981). We see with this definition that educational equity has always been a pivotal concern for leading advocates of multicultural education, and further, that a central proposition in this enterprise has been the idea that **all** students regardless of gender, social class, degree of learning handicap, linguistic background, or ethnic, cultural, or religious identity should have an equal opportunity to learn in school and, by extension,

society. Put another way, in school students should not be penalized because of the various labels and social groups which together shape their "social identity." We see also that for teachers, multicultural education could mean learning as much as possible about a range of cultural and ethnic groups so as to be better able to create equitable learning environments for members of these groups.

In other words, the adjective multicultural in the term "multicultural education" refers to various social, cultural, and ethnic groups which exist within America's macroculture (total culture), and a major concern for advocates of multicultural education is equity (and excellence) for all members of these groups. To the extent that studying these different groups and their "...designs for living or program for survival" can provide ideas for maximizing the learning of members of these cultural groups, Bullivant's description of aims for multicultural education reinforces the equity focus of multicultural education. But, it is noteworthy that many groups of concern to multicultural education practitioners do not have a "survival program" which is widely shared by group members. Ironically, in Bullivant's use and definition of the term "culture," these groups lack culture, and yet in the eyes of multicultural practitioners these culture-less groups are important cultural groups. And this means that these groups—the "poor," the "homeless," learners who are "at risk," the "English learner," "women," and the "learning disabled" or "gifted" learners—do have a culture, or rather are part of a macroculture.

One Meaning of Cultural Group

At this point, it may prove helpful to discuss my understanding of the term "cultural group." As I use them the terms "social group" and "cultural group" are synonymous; if a specific social group has an identity or label which is recognized or created in a macroculture (from within or outside the social group—exonymously or autonymously), like "Gay-Americans" or "developmentally disabled/mentally retarded," "recovering alcoholics," or "African-American," then that social group can also be accurately described as a cultural group, and possibly as an ethnic or racial group as well.

This is true because in a macroculture any group that has a publicly recognized identity (label) becomes a cultural group within the macroculture; this is the case because its identity and label are facts which are negotiated or given meaning within that specific macroculture. In other words, any group in a macroculture that fits or fits itself into that macroculture's definition of "group" becomes, automatically, a cultural group.

Furthermore, cultural groups that exist in one macroculture like the "gifted" or "at-risk learners" or the "criminally insane" or "Mexican-Americans" or the "homeless" may not exist in some other macroculture. Or, if a group such as "developmentally disabled learners" does exist as a category in one macroculture, the developmentally disabled learners in this macroculture may by bureaucratic definition have different characteristics than the developmentally disabled learners in a second macroculture.

Implications for the Multicultural Education Conversation

As indicated earlier, this discussion about the meaning of culture, cultural group, and multicultural education has implications for the way we can invite future teachers, parents, students, and lay people into the multicultural education conversation. To begin with, it reminds us that multicultural education is about cultural groups of all kinds (cultural, ethnic, racial, and socio-economic) as well as culture, and that the key cultural groups of concern in one macroculture (nation) may differ from those in another. In addition, in a given society the focus of multicultural education may broaden from one decade to the next as new groups enter a society (the Hmong from Laos and Viet Nam) or are invented by legislative or bureaucratic definition (the at-risk learner or the "English learner," formerly called the limited English proficient student), or are "rediscovered" as a group which is uniquely disadvantaged by power relationships within a society (women).

This expansive meaning of cultural group, if accepted, may also have positive implications for multicultural teacher educators who are trying to help prospective and veteran teachers see that:

(a) as individuals with a cultural identity they are a part of multicultural America and the multicultural education equation; and

(b) multicultural education, broadly construed, is about equity, and empowerment, and intergroup harmony, and cultural pluralism for teachers as well as students.

In short, multicultural education is for and by teachers, as well as their students, parents, and other stakeholders.

Developing a Positive Attitude Towards Multicultural Education

In many cases when teacher educators responsible for conveying the meanings and rationales for multicultural education face their university audience, mainly prospective and in-service teachers, the majority of the group, often up to 70 or 90 percent, are White Americans or Americans of European Descent (depending on your label preference), and the majority of this group are women, particularly in elementary education classes. In addition, the students "of color" in the class, Americans of African, Asian, American Indian, Hispanic, and Pacific Island descent, often have overlapping values and social characteristics with the White Americans as well as differences. In short, the students of color and their white colleagues have commonalities and points of divergence just like most of the classes they encounter, or will encounter, in K-12 settings.

One of the commonalities pertains to their preliminary understanding or misunderstanding about multicultural education. Like many others, these students often confuse multicultural education with ethnic studies, and for many, both of these topics appear to be exclusively or largely concerned with the social and academic problems of "people of color." While somewhat understandable given the origins of multicultural education and the recent contentious public and university debate about multiculturalism, ethnic studies, and multicultural education, this perception is both erroneous and counter-productive in terms of getting a group of largely White teacher candidates and their non-white colleagues to develop a positive connection with multicultural education; and I mean here multicultural education construed as a powerful model of curriculum and instruction which addresses the aspirations and learning needs of all students, as well as their parents and teachers.

I believe that a major objective of a course or sequence of courses on multicultural education should be to develop in teacher candidates a positive personal connection with the content and goals of multicultural education. If this objective is to be realized, the course(s) should have certain characteristics. To begin with the course content should be historically accurate, reveal that multicultural education is for and about the candidates and their individual and group needs as well as groups they are not a part of, and should provide a forum in which candidates can safely explore and publicly speculate about their tentative cultural, ethnic, and racial group connections.

In addition, at the beginning of such a course the instructor should make clear that the attempt to comprehend multicultural education in all its facets is a lifelong journey. And, further, that at the beginning of such a journey it is inevitable that many students will discover that there is a lot they don't know about African-American history, Mexican-American his-

Self-Disclosure Questions

1. Your name.

2. Geographically, where are you from? Where do you live now?

3. Your mode of abode (I live with my friends, family, etc.). **This is optional**.

4. How long has your family or ancestors been on this continent?

5. Where did your family or ancestors come from before joining the drama "of the Americas"? Or, were they always here?

6. How many generations of your family, on both sides, have lived in the U.S.A.? In California?

7. What languages were or are spoken in your (childhood) home? What languages are spoken in your current domicile?

8. Please identify a favorite author, book, film, or ritual you value or have especially enjoyed, and/or a significant event in your life. An important book in your life like the Bible, Koran, or Torah, etc., should also be mentioned.

9. Given our opening definitions of race, ethnicity, ethnic group, culture, and cultural group, would you be comfortable in describing yourself as a member of a racial, ethnic and/or cultural group? If so, which **groups** would you say you are a part of at this point in your life?

10. Have you ever experienced interpersonal conflict because of your race, ethnicity, gender, cultural group, or an organization you were active in? If so, please describe one or more of these conflicts. Was this conflict resolved in any way, and if so, how?

11. Do you feel your racial, ethnic, and/or cultural group membership (and the latter includes gender) has been a positive feature in your life? If so, briefly explain why.

12. At this point in your teacher education (or graduate school) program, do you have any opinions about multicultural education which you'd like to share? If yes, please list below.

13. Do you have a favorite hobby? If so, please identify.

14. If currently employed, please describe where and what your current responsibilities are.

15. When you have the license or credential you are seeking, in what organization and region would you like to begin, or continue, your career?

tory, inequality in American life, and so on, and much to learn. But, that is the point of the journey and the course(s); it is the attitude toward the lifelong journey that is critical and practical, rather than the unrealistic hope that the candidates can master a substantial part of the increasing "multicultural" body of knowledge prior to student teaching or that they will have developed a set of correct attitudes by the end of a ten or 14 week course.

Ethnic and Cultural Self-Disclosure

In the context of such a course the opportunity to explore, describe, and share one's cultural, ethnic, and racial connec-

tions can have a positive enduring effect. Instructors and students sometimes overlook and bypass the rich diversity—religious, gender, ethnic, racial, S.E.S., age, life style, work and life experience, language, and experience with handicapping conditions—that exists in almost any classroom, as they make a sustained effort to cover some part of the traditional curriculum. But, a positive experience with cultural and ethnic self-exploration and disclosure can make a strong impression on prospective and in-service teachers.

If such teachers, working in small, diversely structured, cooperative discussion groups (five or six students to a group), can see that their efforts to study and communicate with fellow teachers are en-

...ed because of the prior knowledge ...ined from the teachers' self-disclosure, it is quite possible that these same teachers will be more likely to create opportunities for their students to discover each other as sources of cultural information and insight.

Part of the value of self-disclosure derives from the realization that the cultural information shared in small groups sets the stage for a deeper type of trust and rapport building in a classroom community. It is noteworthy that this trust and rapport is linked to the broad conception of "cultural group" discussed earlier. I want my candidates to see that their values and self-perceptions lead them to culturally connect with selected groups, and, I want them to know I am interested in all their cultural connections, just as I want them to be interested in their students' full cultural biographies.

Thus, in my courses the term "cultural group" is taken to mean any collection of people in the macroculture who share a public identity and sense of commonality. This sense of commonality is not the same as a sense of unity, or the strong sense of affinity which is felt by members of some ethnic, racial, and cultural groups. The sense of commonality merely suggests that members of the group understand that: (a) they have something in common with all members of that group, and (b) the group has a public identity or label which can be shared. A vegetarian, for example, may share some norms and behavior patterns with all other vegetarians, and may read articles and books about vegetarians, but may not, at a given point in time, know other vegetarians in his or her community, or be interested in spending time with other vegetarians. And the fact that the vegetarian's spouse and children do not choose to share vegetarianism is inconvenient but not critical.

Of course, it is likely that there are vegetarians who take their lifestyle and group more seriously; such individuals may be vegetarians on an individual as well as a group level. They may pay dues to a vegetarian organization, write articles about vegetarianism, and attend local and state meetings of vegetarians. Still, this organization-oriented vegetarian may be more connected to a healthy lifestyle and social movement than to other vegetarians as a "people." And, if he or she should desire, it would be fairly easy to stop being a vegetarian. And vegetarians have not suffered oppression because of their belief system, physical characteristics, language background, or place of origin, although being a vegetarian in some agricultural-oriented contexts could be delicate. In this sense, vegetarians are very far from being an ethnic group, a cultural group with a sense of peoplehood, shared history, common ancestry, and a common set of political and economic interests.

Nevertheless, this cultural connection should be treated seriously and respectfully; in no way should it be dismissed as a "mere" lifestyle identity. I have learned that being a vegetarian, or a divorced, working single parent, or a conservationist, or a pacifist, or a recovering alcoholic can be a critical part of a student's cultural identity for the short or long term. More importantly, this identity can become the lens through which a candidate better perceives the similarities and differences between himself or herself and others who have different types of cultural identities; furthermore, in an accepting environment the identities students start with serve as a catalyst for deeper insights into their full cultural biographies.

A key point to remember is that when I ask teachers and prospective teachers to engage in cultural and ethnic self-exploration and disclosure, I want them to report on **all** the cultural groups they see themselves as part of, and not just the important ones that are traditionally and still a major concern of multicultural education. This strategy is consistent with the idea of starting your teaching where your students are, and not where you'd have them be. Furthermore, because we encourage students to define themselves and then proceed to value those initial self-percep-

tions, it is also consistent with cultural pluralism, a major goal of multicultural education.

Finally, and quite significantly, this strategy builds positive relationships between advocates (and models) of multicultural education and our next generation of teachers. Although I have not studied this claim in a systematic way, my qualitative impression is that these positive human relationships help to produce candidates who have a more positive attitude towards the content and goals of multicultural education. If such attitudes are part of what we are after in our introductory multicultural education courses, then I think the self-disclosure strategy discussed above is worthy of more discussion, adaptation, and research.

To promote such discussion I will close by enumerating the set of questions which students respond to in the latest version of my ethnic and cultural self-disclosure form. Parenthetically, in my university courses I use the self-disclosure data in a variety of ways. For example, at the beginning of the course I use the self-disclosure data to help form heterogeneous discussion groups. The self-disclosure reports, made in the small groups, also helps each student see the rich diversity that exists in a class that could be perceived as fairly homogeneous (80-90 percent White women).

References

James A. Banks (1981). *Multiethnic Education: Theory and Practice*. Boston, MA: Allyn and Bacon, p. 32.

James A. Banks (1992), "African American Scholarship and the Evolution of Multicultural Education," *The Journal of Negro Education*, Vol. 61, No. 3, pp 273-286.

Brian M. Bullivant (1993). "Culture: Its Nature and Meaning for Educators," in *Multicultural Education: Issues and Perspectives*, 2nd edition, James A. Banks and Cherry A McGee Banks, eds., Boston, MA: Allyn and Bacon, p. 29.

Multicultural Education as an Academic Discipline

James A. Banks

James A. Banks is Professor and Director, Center for Multicultural Education, University of Washington, Seattle. His most recent book is An Introduction to Multicultural Education *(Allyn and Bacon, 1994). He is also the Editor (with Cherry A. McGee Banks) of the* Handbook of Research on Multicultural Education *(Macmillan.)*

Multicultural education is moving down the road toward academic legitimacy and institutionalization. Signs of vitality are the establishment of required multicultural teacher education courses in a large number of colleges and universities, the proliferation of multicultural education textbooks, scholarly books and articles, the brisk sales of textbooks, the establishment of a national organization (NAME) and magazine, and the publication of the first *Handbook of Research on Multicultural Education,* which will bring together the major scholarship, research, and theory that has developed since the field evolved in the seventies.

These significant markers of the development of multicultural education, a nascent and practical field, should not prevent us from recognizing and conceptualizing ways to deal with the challenges the field faces as it enters the 21st century. We should also view the progress and challenges to the field within a historical context. To provide such a context, I will briefly discuss the historical development of anthropology and sociology. (Space does not permit a discussion of the significant ways in which academic disciplines such as anthropology and sociology and fields such as multicultural education—which are grounded in practice—differ.)

During the late nineteenth and early twentieth centuries, the social science disciplines such as anthropology and sociology were in a nascent phase and had to struggle to attain academic legitimacy and institutionalization. At that time, the physical and natural sciences reigned supreme in colleges and universities. The new social sciences tried to gain legitimacy by attempting to adapt and incorporate the aims and methods of the physical and natural sciences. In fact, a number of early pioneers in these disciplines, such as anthropologist Franz Boas and sociologist Lester Frank Ward, had received their advanced degrees and training in the natural and physical sciences.

. . . .

The Legitimization of Anthropology and Sociology

The social sciences, such as anthropology and sociology, survived and eventually gained academic legitimacy. They also became institutionalized as departments in the nation's leading research universities. Several factors contributed to their success and implementation. One of the most important was the strong academic leadership provided by scholars such as Boas (US) and Bronislaw Malinowski (United Kingdom) in anthropology; and by William G. Sumner and Lester Frank Ward in sociology. The "Chicago School" sociologists at the University of Chicago also greatly enhanced the academic status of sociology in the years after Sumner and Ward published their seminal works. William I. Thomas and Robert E. Park published highly influential works at Chicago during the second decade of this century.

The academic leadership provided by scholars such as Boas, Malinowski, Thomas, and Park included the development of paradigms, concepts, and theories that grew out of empirical research in field settings conducted by themselves, their students, and by scholars they heavily influenced. The pioneering empirical and theoretical work done by these early leaders in anthropology and sociology were decisive factors in building these two disciplines. Landmark publications that contributed to the growth and legitimacy of anthropology included *The Mind of Primitive Man* by Boas (1911), and *Argonauts of the Western Pacific* by Malinowski (1922). Landmark publications in sociology included *Dynamic Sociology* by Ward (1883); *Folkways* by Sumner (1907); *The Polish Peasant in Europe and America* by Thomas and Florian Znaniecki (1918-1920); and *Introduction to the Science of Sociology* by Park and Ernest W. Burgess (1921).

From *Multicultural Education,* Winter 1993, pp. 8-11, 39. © 1993 by James A. Banks. Reprinted by permission.

The commitment by these early scholars in anthropology and sociology to empirical research and to theory-building were the most important factors that led to the academic legitimacy and institutionalization of these disciplines on college and university campuses and in the public imagination.

. . . .

Twenty-First Century Goals

The next several decades will be critical ones for multicultural education as a discipline and field of study and practice. During this period, its fate will be determined. Multicultural education will either attain academic legitimacy and become fully institutionalized within the next several decades, or it will fade away like progressive education and intergroup education.

I believe that multicultural education will survive and become fully institutionalized in the nation's universities, colleges, and school districts. However, its survival is by no means assured. We can act thoughtfully and decisively in ways that will greatly increase its possibilities for survival and institutionalization. Toward that end, I will offer, for discussion by the profession, what I think ought to be the key goals for multicultural education as it faces the 21st century.

. . . .

The Development of Scholarly Leaders

We need to develop scholarly leaders for the future. Within the next two decades, the torch must be passed to a new generation of scholars and researchers in multicultural education. We need to invest much more of our time, energy, and resources in the development of new scholars for the field.

I am concerned that the identification of future scholars, and adequate training and mentoring programs for them, are not receiving the attention in the field that is essential for its development. To continue on a path of institutionalization, leadership within a field must be continuing and consistent over several generations. Anthropology succeeded in part because Boas trained students such as Ruth Benedict and Margaret Mead, who continued to develop the field after Boas had completed his most significant works. Yet one of the most important reasons that the intergroup education movement perished is that its leaders, such as Hilda Taba and William Van Til, left the field and pursued other professional interests.

Another positive example of the survival of a field because of long, continuing, and consistent leadership is the way in which African American history developed from the early twentieth century to the present. Carter G. Woodson devoted his entire life to research, organizational, and professional work in African American history. He also inspired and influenced an entire generation of younger historians, who pursued work in African American history and continued that work beyond Woodson's time. These historians included Rayford Logan, Charles H. Wesley, Benjamin Quarles, and John Hope Franklin.

To survive and prosper, leaders must not only devote a lifetime to its development, but must make sure that younger scholars are trained so that leadership in the field will be continuous over many decades. (By *younger scholars* I am not referring to chronological age, but rather to new recruits to the field. Ruth Benedict did not receive her doctorate until she was 36, yet she became one of the nation's most widely read and influential anthropologists.)

Strong and consistent scholarly leadership is essential for an academic field to survive over the long haul. Several generations of scholars must be willing to devote lifetimes to a discipline for it to develop and become institutionalized and to gain academic legitimacy. Respect among practitioners tends to follow respect in the academy.

Scholarship and research, whose aim is to improve practice, must be the field's top priority during the remainder of the nineties and the first decades of the 21st century. The field's quest for academic legitimacy and institutionalization should be an overarching goal that is vigorously and continually pursued. Although it is essential that multicultural education develop its own journals and publications, it is also important for multicultural scholars, researchers, and practitioners to publish frequently in the most respected and influential journals in education. These journals have academic legitimacy, professional authority, and large and influential audiences.

It is going to take several decades for multicultural education to attain the academic legitimacy and respect that it deserves. However, this respect and legitimacy must be earned the hard way—the same way that it was earned by other new fields and disciplines, such as anthropology, sociology, and special education. That is why it is essential that multicultural education invest heavily in the development and mentoring of future scholars who have a deep commitment to and interest in the field.

Since 1980, a number of significant multicultural education articles and papers have been published in highly respected mainstream journals and books. These publications have contributed greatly to the academic legitimization of the field. Among them are Barbara A. Shade's 1982 paper on African American cognitive style in the *Review of Educational Research*; Carl A. Grant and Christine E. Sleeter's 1986 paper on race, class and gender in the *Review of Educational Research*; Sleeter and Grant's influential 1987 paper describing their multicultural education typology in the *Harvard Educational Review*; and my own review of research in the field in 1993, in Volume 19 of the *Review of Research in Education*.

. . . .

Formulating Standards for the Field

The field needs to discuss the feasibility of developing criteria for determining who can practice in multicultural education, the possibility of developing standards and guidelines for multicultural professionals, and of developing minimum standards for practice.

A serious problem exists within multicultural education because people with varied—and often sparse—professional education are calling themselves multicultural professionals and are conducting training for business, health care, and educational institutions on a wide and often profitable scale. In their training sessions, these individuals often violate key principles and practices in the field that are derived from theory, research, and wisdom of practice.

It is not uncommon for individuals with varying skills and abilities to proclaim expertise and to practice in nascent fields. In the early years of their discipline, sociologists became deeply concerned because of the wide range of people who called themselves "sociologists." Writes B. Bernard, in "Re-viewing the impact of women's students on sociology," in *The Impact of Feminist Research in the Academy*, 1987: "They [sociologists] sought...to achieve an identity uncontaminated by quacks who called themselves sociologists. The rapid growth of the study of sociology had created a great shortage of teachers." Bernard quotes Lundberg, writing in 1929:

> Second-rate and half-trained men have in consequence filled important positions. As a result of the demand for men, sociology has tended to be a sort of happy hunting ground for well-meaning sentimentalists, plausible charlatans, and other worthy persons unwilling or unable to weather the rigorous discipline of real scholarship.

Sociology solved the problem of professional certification and of who could practice in the field by establishing the criterion that trained sociologists must earn a doctorate from a recognized university. The solution for multicultural education will be more difficult because the field is both a research and practical field. In its early years, sociology also had a practical component. However, this component was essentially eliminated during the discipline's quest for legitimacy. Because of the nature of multicultural education, in which practice and the improvement of practice are an integral part of what we are, practice must remain a significant part of the field. However, dialogue ought to take place about the possibility of setting minimum standards for practice in multicultural education.

. . . .

The Infusion/Separate Course Problem

One of the most difficult issues that multicultural education now faces and will increasingly face in the future is the pressure by mainstream colleagues in teacher education programs to "infuse" the content of multicultural education courses into existing or newly created general teacher education courses. This pressure is likely to mount as the popularity of infused education courses increases, caused in part by the budget crisis that exists in higher education throughout the nation.

It is essential that we give well-reasoned and thoughtful responses to requests (often disguised demands) to infuse the content of multicultural education courses to avoid the appearance of mere self-interest. I strongly believe, however, that the infusion model of curriculum reform, if widely implemented nationally, will seriously threaten the existence of multicultural education as a discipline and retard the academic legitimacy and institutionalization of the field.

A total integration model must be resisted on *academic, pragmatic,* and *political* grounds. We should argue for the implementation of a *Multicultural Education + Integration Model* (MCE + Integration Model). The *MCE + Integration Model* will assure that students will learn the key paradigms, concepts, ideologies, and knowledge in multicultural education from committed experts in the field. At the same time, instructors of courses such as foundations, general curriculum, and the subject matter methods courses will be encouraged and allowed to integrate multicultural content into their courses. If multicultural content is poorly integrated into the general courses (or is not integrated beyond the course outline—both conditions frequently exist), students will have benefited from the one or two multicultural education courses taught by specialists.

. . . .

The Academic Justification

I should make my preference for the *MCE + Integration Model* explicit. First, the academic justification for this model. Multicultural education is a distinct inter-disciplinary field with a unique set of paradigms, concepts, theories, and skills. It is not highly likely that non-specialists can adequately teach the specialized content of the field to novice teachers and practitioners. They are likely to be learning the content of the field themselves, and may not have much more expertise in multicultural education than their students.

Even if non-specialists have mastered the academic content of multicultural education, they often have not had adequate opportunities to examine their attitudes, feelings, and beliefs, important factors in teaching multicultural content. We do not expect or usually permit a non-expert in reading to teach the content of the readings methods course to novice students or to infuse it into a general methods course that the non-expert is teaching. Multicultural specialists should insist that the same standards used to select instructors and to teach content in the other academic fields are used when making curricular and instructional decisions about multicultural content and courses.

. . . .

The Pragmatic Justification

Second, the pragmatic justification. Advocates of the *Infusion-Only Model* argue that by placing a multicultural specialist on a teaching team, multicultural content can be effectively integrated into the general course. This form of course integration can cause problems for the students as well as for the multicultural specialist on the team. Multicultural concepts, paradigms, and ideologies are *oppositional* to the paradigms, concepts, and theories taught in most mainstream general methods and curriculum courses. When multicultural concepts and paradigms conflict with the other concepts and paradigms in the general course, students often become angry and confused. The lone multiculturalist on the teaching team often becomes the victim of student hostility and confusion.

Multicultural education asks students to examine some of their latent and unexamined attitudes, beliefs, feelings, and assumptions about U. S. society and culture. Students often find this process a difficult and painful one. Because of the power of context, this self-introspection and self-analysis becomes even more painful and unsettling when it is experienced within the context of an integrated course in which most of the other content and concepts reinforce the students' mainstream values, attitudes, and beliefs.

. . . .

Mainstream vs. Transformative Knowledge

Most of the knowledge in teacher education courses is *mainstream academic knowledge*. Mainstream academic knowledge consists of the concepts, principles, theories, and explanations that constitute traditional and established knowledge in the behavioral and social sciences. An important tenet within mainstream academic knowledge is that it is a set of objective truths that can be verified through rigorous and objective research and is uninformed by human interests, values, and perspectives.

In reality, mainstream academic knowledge, while appearing neutral and objective, often presents propositions, concepts, and findings that reinforce dominant group hegemony and perpetuates racism, sexism, and classism. Influential examples of such mainstream knowledge are the concept of cultural deprivation that emerged in the 1960s (in David Riessman's *The Culturally Deprived Child*, 1962); Arthur Jensen's theory of Black-White intelligence, (in the 1969 article "How much can we boost IQ and scholastic achievement?" published in the *Harvard Educational Review);* and the concepts of "at-risk" youth and the "underclass" that are popular today. These concepts are heavily value-laden, yet they masquerade as neutral and objective.

Multicultural education, as conceptualized by the major theorists in the field, is a form of transformative academic knowledge. *Transformative academic knowledge* consists of the paradigms, themes, and explanations that challenge mainstream academic knowledge and that expand the historical and literary canon. Transformative scholars, unlike mainstream scholars, assume that knowledge is not neutral but is heavily influenced by human interests; that all knowledge reflects the social, economic, and political relationships within society, and that an important purpose of transformative knowledge is to help citizens improve society.

During the late 1960s and 1970s, transformative scholars (such as Baratz & Baratz in their "Early childhood intervention: The social science base of institutional racism" in the *Harvard Educational Review)* challenged some of the dominant paradigms that were heavily influencing the education of low-income students and students of color. They challenged cultural deprivation theories and theories about how mother tongue languages adversely affected the learning of standard English.

Transformative scholars such as Code, Patricia Hill Collins and Sandra Harding interrogate the assumptions, ideological positions, and political interests of the knower. Lorraine Code, in her seminal 1991 book, *What Can She Know? Feminist Theory and the Construction of Knowledge,* raises this question: "Is the gender of the knower epistemologically significant?" After a rigorous philosophical analysis of this question, she concludes that gender does have a complex influence on the knowledge produced by the knower. Harding and Collins have reached similar conclusions about the relationship between gender and the knower.

Nearly two decades before the work of Code, Collins, and Harding, Joyce Ladner explored a similar question regarding the influence of race on knowledge in her 1973 book, *The Death of White Sociology.* Ladner and her colleagues documented the effects of race on knowing in sociology. Ladner was about two decades ahead of her time. Consequently, her message was often criticized rather than praised.

Finally, the *Infusion-Only Model* must be resisted because the power of the multicultural specialist to control the content and pedagogy of the infused course is decentered and may completely disappear. Typically, the multicultural specialist is a lone member of a teacher education teaching team and is likely to have an ideology and conception of knowledge highly inconsistent with the other members of the team. The multiculturalist on such teams can easily became marginalized as the *Other.* Thus, the power relationship within the larger society and within the wider university community are likely to be reproduced on the teaching team.

The *MCE + Infusion Model* allows the multicultural specialist to control an important course and to serve as a resource person for instructors of other courses who wish to infuse their courses with multicultural concepts, paradigms, and pedagogy in a meaningful way. Many of these instructors need and want staff development in multicultural education. An important and appropriate role for the multicultural specialist is to lead an effort to implement a staff development effort within the school or college of education. Outside consultants and resources are usually required to implement such an effort. Local multicultural specialists can facilitate but can almost never conduct training within their own department, college, or school.

The ultimate fate of multicultural education as a discipline will to a large extent be determined by the kind of vision we develop and implement within the field. I believe that its fate will be more akin to anthropology and sociology than to progressive education and intergroup education. However, we must act now to set and pursue a rigorous scholarly and research agenda, develop a cadre of strong academic leaders who will shepherd the field in the future, develop standards for practice in the field, strive to improve classroom practice, and take vigorous steps to assure that multicultural education courses and programs are consistent with a transformative tradition that promotes justice, equality, and human dignity.

Multicultural Education and Culture Change

An Anthropological Perspective

Stanton W. Green & Stephen M. Perlman

Stanton W. Green is dean of the College of Arts and Sciences at Clarion University, Clarion, Pennsylvania; Stephen M. Perlman resides in Medlothian, Virginia

Introduction

Multiculturalism confronts all Americans with questions on the effects of pluralism on the American culture. Does the recognition of American subcultures divide us or does it strengthen us as a nation? Is multiculturalism a threat to the coherence of American society or does it strengthen the diverse pillars upon which this nation was built? For educators, this political argument quickly turns practical: What do we teach our children? Is there, as E. D. Hirsch would assert, "a body of information that each American should know to take part in our shared culture?" If so, how many subcultures should be included in this body of knowledge?

To anthropologists, these questions frame a crucial process confronted in all societies: the passing of culture from one generation to the next. What should be the role of the traditions, knowledge, and values of older generations in the education of succeeding generations? To approach these central and most provocative questions, we must view culture as a dynamic, historical process.

Indeed, when we view culture as a dynamic process we can see why it is so difficult to define one American Culture. To begin, the American continent has always been multicultural. The recent colonization of peoples from the Old World (Europe, Africa, Asia) complemented the already diverse cultures of the Native Americans (the first colonizers from Asia). The interaction between these cultures over time forms the mosaic of American life. If one could define an "American" culture and assess its particular history, given the changes that have occurred, we would be brought back to a central problem: which culture from which time?

The educational implications of this perspective are direct and profound. Conceptualizing culture as a process, rather than a "shared heritage," changes the way we frame the educational content and pedagogy of our schools as well as the way we conceptualize the role of the teacher, the structure of courses, and what we expect of students.

Culture

At the core of our discussion is the concept of culture. Culture is learned, it is shared by a society, and it concerns ideas, values, attitudes, and behaviors. The culture that is learned distinguishes it from the innate or instinctual aspects of human behavior, but does not, of course, imply that all learning is culture. Individual learning is done through simple trial and error as well as imitation. What makes learning cultural is the ability to use symbols to communicate. The cultural world is created by groups of people. From this culture comes a group's shared viewpoint of the ways in which the world works and ought to work. That it is shared does not denote homogeneity. Rather we would conceptualize culture as networks of created knowledge. Similarities are greater within cultures and subcultures than between them. Simple examples of cultural constructs are the definition of colors from the continuum of light and edible foods from the range of organic possibilities. More complex examples involve kinship, marriage rules, and the sexual division of labor. Central to the working of all this is language as a primary conduit between culture and behavior.

In a sense, language is the essence of human interaction or discourse, where discourse can be defined as a "socially accepted association among ways of using language, of thinking, and of acting that can be used to identify oneself in a number of socially meaningful groups or 'social networks'" (Gee 1991:3). Discourse, in this sense, frames the ways of using language socially. Discourse competency—or what some might call cultural literacy—is gained within the primary context of family socialization and secondary contexts including formal education. (As an aside, this is the basis for the great advantage to students growing up in families that converse and interact in standard English. The onus then often falls in the classroom, as teachers are expected to relate to both primary and secondary speakers of standard English).

Cultures and their associated discourses and literacy changes as a result of their own internal dynamics and in relation to other cultures. If we meld notions of culture and literacy, we can begin to see culture change as an inevitable, unavoidable historical progression and an equally inevitable and unavoidable educational process. Cultures change as shared ideas, values, attitudes, and behaviors are altered as a consequence of interaction among members of a culture and between members of different cultures. The question becomes: how can we as educators grab hold of this malleable and ever-changing phenomenon of culture so that we can teach it?

Culture Change

Although she was writing well before the multicultural/cultural literacy debate was formulated, Margaret Mead's examination of the 1960s generation gap in *Culture and Commitment* (1970) may well

From *Multicultural Education*, Summer 1995, pp. 4-6. © 1995 by the National Association for Multicultural Education. Reprinted by permission.

hold some answers to this question. Rather than assuming that the communication and education gap between generations is the result of the younger generation simply not gaining the wisdom of the former generation (either because of their inability to learn it or the elders inability to teach it), she finds the reasons in the process of culture change itself (Mead 1951, 1970). Not only do cultures change at different rates, she posits, but they change in different ways. In traditional societies, change is relatively slow (but not nonexistent). Culture is passed on from elder to younger through multiple generation households and within what Wendell Berry terms a "coherent oral tradition."

Mead sees a major disjuncture in this coherence in 20th century America. Time becomes more linear (although it can include cyclical elements) and societal boundaries now leak. Immigration breaks the continuity of experience felt in American society. Peer learning becomes more important and previous older generations provide a wider variety of viewpoints as a result of immigration.

In today's culture, change is so quick that the future can be essentially independent from the past and the present. Change is accelerated, time is fragmented, and knowledge is global and instantaneous. News is as fast as the speed of light. The history of the Persian Gulf War was viewed as it happened as millions of people watched the skies of Baghdad explode with missiles, bombs, and anti-aircraft fire. How does one teach the Gulf War as history to students who viewed parts of it?

Mead summarizes the modern condition in an insightful and haunting way: the older generation can never say they were young once, because they were never young in the world of the current generation. How do we educate students in such a time of culture change? What, indeed, do we teach them? Mead's lesson is that we cannot succeed in passing on our core cultural values unless we confront the fact that culture change is different in today's world than it was in the past. If our educational system is not attuned to the nature of our cultural dynamic—then the generations cannot communicate and the next generation cannot be reached. This contrasts with a model of traditional culture that sees learning as occurring essentially (if not solely) through the teaching of elders.

Of course one cannot eliminate the teaching of tradition and past culture nor would we argue against the view that some truths and moral sensibilities transcend generations and cultures (Wilson 1994).

But it is provocative to contrast such a belief with Mead's assertion that "older people can no longer say they were young once." Traditions teach children how to live as their parents and grandparents did, while swift culture change produces generations as "immigrants in time."

This critical analysis of cultural change is equally relevant to questions concerning cultural pluralism. If we view American culture as a coherent, well-bounded, and largely unchanging whole, then diversity can be subsumed in a melting pot metaphor. Diversity in this sense is a list of ingredients being mixed into a batter and cooked into a cake. However, if we understand culture as a dynamic historic process and cultural diversity to be a natural outcome of culture change, then diversity does not disappear (through mixing or cooking) nor does it threaten the holism of American culture. Indeed, it defines it. Tension and division, according to this view, is not the direct result of emergent subcultures and changing ways, but rather from attempts to resist diversity and culture change.

Educational Implications

What does all of this mean for multicultural education? For this we need to identify the rationale for and goals of multicultural education. Rationales include supporting the identity formation of students, recognizing other ethnic groups and giving them equal support in the curriculum, and teaching an accurate cultural history of America (Takaki 1994). What is provocative to us is how can we as educators achieve these goals within an understanding of contemporary culture change. If we view generation differences as cultural differences, then teacher/student interaction becomes intercultural. The increasing pluralistic and global dimension of today's world adds additional intercultural relationships in the classroom. One key to communication in such a classroom culture would seem to be mutuality through the active engagement of the student—that is, active learning.

In effect, active learning allows for student cultures to meet other student cultures as well as teacher cultures. Controversies surrounding active learning, outcomes-based-education and multicultural education derive from the difficulty of balancing the teaching of traditional information and values and engaging the contemporary culture of students. Although active learning does not imply that students set the agenda, it

does recognize that student and teacher discourse must be made mutually intelligible. Although multiculturalism does not imply that anything goes in the classroom (what some might call moral relativism), it does assert that all cultures need be recognized (cultural relativism). The bottom line is that the empowerment of students and the recognition of American subcultures is not immediately consonant with the teaching of tradition and the goal of creating one American culture. But let us try for the moment and in conclusion to pull away from this political thread and offer an example of how multiculturalism can work through the active learning of culture by students in the classroom.

An Experiment in Cultural Awareness

In order to gain an understanding of other cultures, anthropological approaches teach students to see others, not as essentially different, but as themselves in a different context. Culture theory teaches us that the cultural diversity we see in the world is an outcome of general principles. Students' personal histories have created many of the particulars in their life; however, much of the structural context they experience (i.e., social and economic position, and the geographic distribution of employment and educational opportunities) are outcomes of these principles. Other people and groups are behaving in response to the same principles in different contexts.

The goal is to help students understand the foundation for many parts of their lives, so that it becomes more difficult for them to reject the lifestyles of others. As a test of this proposition we did the following social experiment. A class of eighth graders was divided into groups and told to select a diet from a list of foods. They could choose as they wished as long as their menu was sufficient to feed a family of four. The only other constraint was the amount of money each group was given to accomplish the task. Group allocations ranged from just a few dollars a day to an unlimited amount. When the groups compared their diets they could see that those with few dollars to spend selected essentially the same diets. Groups with larger allocations selected a wider diversity of foods. Through discussion, students learned that family menus are not just the result of personal or cultural choice—but also related to socioeconomic factors. They also learned that they all used similar decision-making criteria. Differences in diets that they had observed and experienced in the past were no longer seen as an impenetrable behavioral and cultural barrier as they could better appreciate the basis for these choices. The "other" was, to a degree, themselves in another context.

Active learning about culture, such as illustrated in this brief example, can move us toward achieving the goals of multiculturalism, because it allows students to build bridges across cultural differences. An active understanding of culture as a process aids students in understanding the basis for cultural differences so that they can then examine and appreciate the particulars that make different cultures different.

Concluding Remarks

We must understand that cultural diversity is a part of culture process and change. The goal of multiculturalism should not just be to recognize and appreciate that other cultures exist, for this can amount to mere tokenism or making cultures into museum displays. We must understand the significance of a culture's history and tradition as a part of the dynamic and multifaceted American culture. We can do this if we understand culture as a dynamic process. Although families are the primary purveyors of culture, educators are next in line. As such, we must develop curricula and pedagogies that incorporate an understanding of cultural process and cultural continuity and change within the framework of cultural diversity and American pluralism.

References

Berry, Wendell (1970). "In Defense of Literacy." In *A Continuous Harmony: Essays Cultural and Agricultural*. New York: Harcourt Brace Jovanovich, pp. 169–173.

Carroll, Thomas (1990). "Who Owns Culture?" In *Cultural Diversity and American Education: Visions of the Future*. Edited by Thomas G. Carroll & Jean J. Schensul. *Education and Urban Society*, vol. 22, no. 4:346–355.

Gee, James Paul (1991). "What is literacy." In *Rewriting Literacy: Culture and the Discourse of the Other*. Edited by Candace Mitchell & Kathleen Weiler. New York: Bergin and Garvey, pp. 3–12.

Hirsch, E. D. (1987). *Cultural Literacy*. New York: Vintage Books, Random House.

Mead, Margaret, (1951) *The School in American Culture*. Cambridge, MA: Harvard University Press.

Mead, Margaret (1970). *Culture and Commitment*. New York: Columbia University Press.

Takaki, Ronald (1993). *A Different Mirror: A History of Multicultural America*, Boston, MA: Little, Brown.

White Racism

Christine Sleeter

Christine E. Sleeter is a professor of education, University of Wisconsin-Parkside, Kenosha, Wisconsin.

Fifteen years ago, I wondered whether my own prospective involvement in multicultural education as a White person, could be helpful or problematic. The issue as I saw it—and still see it—is that Whites tend to take over. We find it "normal" to set the direction and agenda for things we become involved in. Or, when we do not take over, we nevertheless get in the way and deflect attention away from primary concerns of people of color. I decided, however, that racial justice requires White involvement, although exactly how White people could help best was not very clear to me.

In this article, I will discuss what I believe can be a helpful role for Whites, as well as our tendency to deflect attention away from racism, which is the main problem undergirding the need for multicultural education. As a whole, Whites do not talk about White racism. Even those of us involved in multicultural education examine and critique how White racism works far less than we ought. We are much more likely to discuss cultural differences than racism or Whiteness. If multicultural education is sometimes criticized as skirting around racism (see P. R. Mattai, "Rethinking multicultural education: Has it lost its focus or is it being misused," *Journal of Negro Education,* 1992; C. McCarthy, *Race and curriculum,* Falmer Press, 1990), I believe this is a result of Whites' reluctance to address it rather than people of color's disregard for it.

The field of multicultural education could benefit, however, from a rich discourse about White racism, to which we Whites need to contribute. White people have a good deal of knowledge about rac-

ism: all of us have been well socialized to be racists, and benefit from racism constantly. I would like to challenge Whites to articulate, examine, question, and critique what we know about racism. Doing so would strengthen not only multicultural education's anti-racist stance, but also our own personal efforts to promote racial justice.

In the following, I will illustrate White silence about racism, discuss some strategies we use to deflect attention away from White racism, then provide an example of the kind of experience we should be critiquing openly. My point is that, in order to collaborate in the work of envisioning and building a just society that includes all of us, we as Whites need to engage in multifaceted and critical analyses of how White racism structures our lives, viewpoints, vested interests, and daily actions.

Naming our silence about White racism

With precious few exceptions, White people do not talk about White racism. Instead, we talk about group differences, very often in ways that simplify and devalue others while rendering Whiteness itself as invisible, or "normal." I first noticed White silence about racism about 15 years ago, although I was not able at the time to name it as such. I recall realizing, after having shared many meals with African American friends while teaching in Seattle, that racism and race-related issues were fairly common topics of dinner-table conversation, which African Americans talked about quite openly. It struck me that I could not think of a single instance in which racism had been a topic of dinner-table conversation in White contexts. Race-related issues sometimes came up, but not **racism**. For example, I could

remember short discussions about what one would do if a Black family moved next door, or about a very bigotted relative, or about policies such as desegregation or immigration. In these discussions, what was viewed as problematic was people of color themselves, changes in policies that relate to race, or outspoken bigots.

Recently, I was giving a talk about multicultural education to a group of predominantly White teachers at an inservice session. My talk centered around persistent racial, class, and gender disparities in access to various resources such as jobs and housing. My main recommendation to the teachers was that we engage directly in reciprocal dialog with people of color and poor people in our own communities, in order to decide what kind of social system and what kind of schools we actually want, then begin to work collaboratively. I argued that White professionals cannot shape the vision of a multicultural society by ourselves, although we tend to use our status as professionals to assume exactly that role; shaping a vision of multicultural education in our own communities has to be done collaboratively, and must address social inequalities. Afterward, a White teacher approached me with a very puzzled expression on her face, and commented in a rather perplexed tone of voice that she had never heard multicultural education discussed that way. At least she reacted verbally to it; most of the audience simply applauded politely, then went on to the next session. This incident struck me because, although my discussion of racism was not as direct as it might have been, I was still framing multicultural education in a way the White teachers had not even thought about and had difficulty comprehending.

At a recent women's studies conference, participants were asked to divide

From *Multicultural Education,* Spring 1994, pp. 5-8, 39. © 1994 by the National Association for Multicultural Education. Reprinted by permission.

into racially homogeneous groups to compile a list of the main concerns facing their group. I was in the European-American group, and it floundered. Participants discussed mainly family history and ethnic immigrant background. I suggested that we might address our White racism, but that theme was not taken up. The group tried to place itself on a parallel status with the other racial groups, defining our problems as comparable to theirs. Our Whiteness seemed to be invisible to us— we could discuss our religious, ethnic, and social class differences, but not our common Whiteness or the privileges we gain from White racism (see R. Dyer, "White," *Screen*, 1988).

• • • • • • • • • • • • •

I suspect that our privileges and silences are invisible to us partly because numerically we constitute the majority of this nation and collectively control a large portion of the nation's resources and media, which enable us to surround ourselves with our own varied experiences and to buffer ourselves from the experiences, and the pain and rage of people of color. But even still, White people do not live in a vacuum; Toni Morrison (*Playing in the dark: Whiteness and the literary imagination*, Harvard University Press, 1992) asks how Whites have managed **not** to see the "thunderous, theatrical presence" of African people in the United States (p. 13). I believe that we cling to filters that screen out what people of color try to tell us because we fear losing material and psychological advantages that we enjoy. Further, we have not yet collectively created a compelling self-identity and sense of meaning that does not entail ravenous materialism and acquisition of power over others.

By White racism (or White supremacy), I am referring to the system of rules, procedures, and tacit beliefs that result in Whites collectively maintaining control over the wealth and power of the nation and the world. For at least 500 years, Europeans and their descendants have taken huge amounts of land, wealth, labor, and other resources from peoples of color around the world. With the exceptions of small, sporadic attempts at restitution, such as that offered belatedly to Japanese American concentration camp survivors, White Americans have never returned or repaid what we have taken. We seem to have agreed tacitly to continue to reap the benefits of the past, and not to talk about it, except largely in ways that render present race relations as legitimate. Current data illustrate the continued advantages Whites enjoy. For example, a recent United Nations report ranks White Americans as having the highest standard of living in the world; Black Americans' living standard ranks 31st and Hispanic Americans' ranks 35th. Of the six nations with the highest living standard, five are predominantly White (R. Wright, "Living standard in U. S. diverse: U. N.," *Kenosha News*, 1993).

As we grow up, Whites become aware that we tend to have more than people of color, and we learn to accept and justify our own position. Until about 40 years ago, it was acceptable in White society to talk openly about presumed shortcomings of groups of color, and the presumed superior intelligence, culture, and morality of Whites. Not all Whites accepted racist beliefs, of course, but they were widely enough held to be openly verbalized.

With the Civil Rights movement, people of color challenged the morality of racism successfully enough that most Whites no longer found it acceptable to voice racist beliefs. So, we simply stopped talking openly about race relations. In general, Whites seem to believe that racism was gone once we eliminated Jim Crow laws, created an ostensibly colorblind legal system (Williams, 1991), and stopped openly saying negative things about groups of color. We maintain a worldview, however, that continues to uphold our racial privileges. We are willing to critique the psychological impact of slavery on Blacks, but not its impact on ourselves. In addition, we continue to obliterate from our historic consciousness information about racism; for example, I have learned to expect only about half of my White teacher education students to have ever heard of Jim Crow laws. ("What, then, was the Civil Rights movement about?" "Well—I'm not sure, I guess.") Groups of color have hoped that we would genuinely accept them as equals if we appreciated the intellectual sophistication of their cultural creations. Too often, however, our response is to experience "other" cultures as a tourist or colonialist would, and tacitly accept White supremacy.

Deflecting attention from White racism

Most readers are probably aware that racism is an important issue to multicultural education, and most White readers probably do talk about it from time to time. However, I would suggest that our talk does not delve into it in much depth. As a result, we tend to incorporate into multicultural education fairly simplistic notions about racism, giving attention mainly to ideas that fit within European ethnic immigrant experiences. For example, consider the following passage from a children's book about racism: "Racism is the mistaken belief by some people that their group, or race, is better than others" (A. Grunsell, *Let's talk about racism*, Gloucester Press, 1991, p. 7). While I applaud the book's effort to help children understand racism, the book barely hints at the power differential between Whites and groups of color, and subsequent control Whites maintain over most resources in the U.S. and world.

• • • • • • • • • • • • •

Having learned the ideology of individualism well, we tend to interpret racism as an individual belief rather than an institutionalized system supported by a collective worldview. This interpretation allows us to assume that we are not racist if we have an open mind. The ideology of individualism also takes our attention away from group relations and statuses, directing it instead toward equal opportunity to achieve upward mobility. On a global level, we still do not see it as problematic to assume that we are entitled to the highest standard of living in the world, and cheer ourselves on in international competition as if we were watching a football game.

Multicultural education should challenge racism, but often to Whites it provides a way of trying to project a positive image about groups of color without actually confronting White supremacy. We do this by tapping into our own European ethnic immigrant experience for guidance. According to the dominant, White American ideology, the United States is a nation of immigrants: our ancestors all came here to seek opportunity. Ethnic identity is a choice, something to add onto a common American identity. Ethnicity is a side-bar, no longer relevant to our relationships with social institutions, which are colorblind and ethnic-blind.

For example, my ancestry is largely German. In school I learned very little about German immigration and culture until taking German language classes in high school, but at home I learned some broad ideas that White people commonly learn about our own ancestry. I do not have records of my German immigrant ancestors, but I grew up learning that they as well as other immigrants chose to come to the United States for opportunity, but faced great hardships at first. My own name, Sleeter, is Anglicized; somewhere along the line my ancestors decided that identifying markers of German-ness worked to their disadvantage. In addition, my family no longer speaks German; rather than developing bilingual competence, my ancestors decided to shed the German language (as well as recollection of historic German bilingual education programs). My paternal grandmother was a good German cook; my family's Christmas celebrations retain some German customs. Physically I learned that I had inherited a strong German constitution; tempermentally, I inherited German industriousness. In my daily life, German ancestry is irrelevant to who I associate with, where I live, where I work, and so forth; it is relevant mainly to my personal family history and identification with ethnic festivals during the summer.

Now let me apply this view of ethnicity to a non-White group, say, Native Americans. To apply it accurately, I should be tribe-specific, such as applying it to Winnebagos or Navajos. Some Whites distinguish among specific tribes, many do not. What is relevant to learn about Native Americans? The list of items above suggests: how Indians immigrated to the New World, food, customs, physical characteristics, language, temperament, and folk arts. (Sounds like many multicultural curricula, which many of us do critique but still see flourishing.) These are not irrelevant items (although many Indians dispute the notion of Indian immigration to North America), but this list completely excludes more important issues. Most importantly, it evades the fact that Whites occupy Indian land; Whites benefit in numerous ways from that occupation, while Indian people live largely in a state of poverty. The most helpful stance Whites could take would be to return large amounts of good land, and stop controlling the internal affairs of Indian people.

Whites generally have no intention of doing that, however. We have learned to justify the oppression of Indian people today by viewing them as a very small, inconsequential minority; attributing their problems to pathology (such as drinking), and locating Indian people in our own consciousness in America's past rather than its present or future. We have learned, and teach our children, to regard Indians of yesterday as colorful and interesting, past wrongs as tragic, but ourselves today as lacking much responsibility. Many of us, in fact, try to show respect for Indian people in a manner similar to that in which Whites have always acted: We take what we like for our own personal use. For example, many Whites try to adopt versions of Indian spirituality; Indian themes are popularly used in interior decor; and the buying and selling of Indian artifacts is common, regardless of whether Indian people themselves are deriving any profit from this exchange.

. . . .

A *common White* understanding of ethnicity, in fact, "emerged into prominence during a period when the civil rights movement was most active and racial minorities were challenging in basic respects the fairness of the American system" (R. D.

Alba, *Ethnic identity: The transformation of White America*, Yale University Press, 1990, p. 317). White society felt threatened, and attempted to reframe ethnicity and race within our own worldview and experience. "The thrust of European-American identity is to defend the individualistic view of the American system, because it portrays the system as open to those who are willing to work hard and pull themselves over barriers of poverty and discrimination" (Alba, p. 317).

We evade discussion of racism because we do not want to give up the lifestyle, privileges, and resources that we control, and that are built on those our ancestors took from others. The very locations on which our homes rest should rightfully belong to Indian nations. Some of us are from families whose wealth was generated partly by slave labor; even if our own familial ancestors did not own slaves or exploit Mexican or Asian laborers, they still did have access to jobs, education, and other opportunities from which Whites barred people of color. To open up a discussion of White racism challenges the legitimacy of White peoples' very lives. Once we are able to say that aloud, we may be able to create a new White discourse that can contribute to a vision of a just future that actually includes all of us, and an agenda for action. But I do not believe we can do that without fully confronting the related layers and processes of White racism.

White people know a great deal about how racism works because we have observed White people intimately all our lives. By examining our own experiences critically, we are uniquely positioned to contribute insights into racism. There are many dimensions of White racism that we need to examine, such as the use of language to frame racial issues in ways that obscure racism (see T. van Dijk, *Elite discourse and racism*, Sage Publications, 1993), connections between White racism and capitalism, roots of White fears and psychological insecurities, the impact of colonialism and slavery on the White psyche, shifts over time in the forms racism takes and the way it is discussed, and factors that differentiate anti-racist Whites from the rest of us. Below I give one example of the kind of analysis in which I believe we should engage.

White racial bonding

In general, Whites stick together on common definitions of issues that involve race relations, and behave accordingly. We live largely with other Whites, socialize mainly with Whites, consume White media, vote for Whites, and so forth. Although today most Whites profess colorblindness and support for equal opportunity, in fact

we behave in a very race-conscious manner. What are some of the processes we use to build and maintain racial solidarity?

This question struck me several months ago, when I watched my White teacher education students respond to an issue. The teacher education program in which I teach has a strong emphasis on multicultural and urban education throughout its coursework. In addition, we have hired a fairly diverse faculty: of eight full-time members, four are White, three are Black, and one is Asian; in addition, our dean is Black. The dean had been working with a committee of faculty, students, school administrators and teachers, and the dean of another institution to create an alternative certification program for prospective teachers of color. It would include a paid internship in a classroom and fewer course credits than the regular program, which is long on course credits and has no paid internship. Word of the alternative program reached White students in the regular program, and within days a large segment of the White student population had mobilized to affirm a common definition of the program: It was racially biased and wrong. When I tried to direct the few students who talked with me about it toward sources of more information about the program and reasons for its need, I realized that they did not want information; they wanted validation that the program was unfair toward Whites. In a meeting between the students and the faculty, White students vented openly a degree of racism that caught us off guard; no White student rose to defend the program (although a few did silently support it). Although part of the students' anger was frustration over the length of the regular teacher education program, part of it was racial.

I began to ask myself, given the coursework and field experiences the students had had, why did the White students coalesce so strongly and quickly around a common condemnation of the alternative program? How did they know their peers would support thinly-veiled as well as overt expressions of racial hostility? Why did the supporters of the program decide to keep quiet?

We are all familiar with some of the more overt ways Whites socialize Whites to accept racism (such as TV stereotypes and expressions of prejudice). But following this experience, I began to pay attention to what I will call "White racial bonding" processes White people engage in everyday. By "racial bonding," I mean simply interactions that have the purpose of affirming a common stance on race-related issues, legitimatizing particular interpretations of groups of color, and drawing conspiratorial we-they boundaries. These communication patterns take forms such as inserts into conversations, race-related "asides" in conversations, strategic eye-contact, and jokes. Often they are so short and subtle that they may seem relatively harmless. I used to regard such utterances as annoying expressions of prejudice or ignorance, but that seems to underestimate their power to demarcate racial lines and communicate solidarity.

. . . .

Inserts into conversations may go like this. Two White people are talking casually about various things. One comments, "This community is starting to change. A lot of Mexicans have been moving in." This comment serves as an invitation to White bonding, in which the other person is being asked to agree with the implication that Mexicans create problems and do not belong here, although this has not been said directly. The other person could respond very simply, "Yeah, that's a bummer," affirming the first person's viewpoint; this could be the end of a successful exchange. Or, the other person could complain about Mexicans, the ensuing conversation taking the form of Mexican-bashing. In either case, both parties will have communicated agreement that there is a linkage between "Mexicans" and "problems," and will have defined themselves as "insiders" in a network of people who view it as acceptable to articulate a negative valuation of Mexicans. Further, they will have communicated the acceptability of supporting policies limiting Mexican access to the community. Even silence can serve as tacit acquiescence for the purpose of winning approval. P. Williams (*The alchemy of race and rights*, Harvard University Press, 1991, p. 126-8) describes in exquisite detail such an exchange in which she participated passively.

How do I know this kind of exchange serves the purpose of racial bonding? I know because if I do not give the desired response, the other person very often presses the issue much more explicitly; I also may never hear from the other person again (including relatives). For example, if I change the subject, it usually reappears but more forcefully ("Mexicans bring gang problems, you know; I'm really concerned

about the future of this community."). Sometimes I give a response I know the other person is not seeking such as, "Yes, I'm really pleased to see this community becoming more multicultural, I've been working on my Spanish." More often than not, the other person responds with a lecture on problems associated with Mexican American people, and the misguidedness of my judgment. I am usually uncomfortable when people who do not know me well ask what I teach; quite often responses such as "multicultural education" or "urban education" provoke uninvited lectures on race relations, or on their own beliefs as a White liberal (hoping for validation that we share a common viewpoint).

These kinds of interactions seem to serve the purpose of defining racial lines, and inviting individuals to either declare their solidarity or mark themselves as deviant. Depending on degree of deviance, one runs the risk of losing the other individual's approval, friendship, and company. (This usually occurs in the form of feeling "uncomfortable" around the deviant White person.) Many Whites who do not support racist beliefs, actions, or policies, but who also do not want to risk breaking bonds with other Whites, simply remain silent.

Consideration of White racial bonding has several implications. No White person is exempt from pressures from other White people to "fit in," with the price of conformity to a racial norm very often being approval and friendship. While active anti-racist Whites may not be affected by such processes, I would hypothesize that it does affect Whites who are uncertain about their own racial beliefs and loyalties. J. E. Helms (editor of *Black and white racial identity: Theory, research, and practice*, Greenwood Press, 1990), for example, posits a stage of "reintegration" in White racial identity development in which the White person, after experiencing challenges to her or his previous beliefs about race, returns to those prior, more comfortable and socially acceptable (in White circles) beliefs (see also B. D. Tatum, "Talking about race, learning about racism: The application of racial identity development theory in the classroom," *Harvard Educational Review*, 1992). We all need affective

bonds with people. Given the segregation of our society, the strongest bonds are usually with members of our own race. In order to mitigate effects of White racial bonding, potential multicultural education advocates need to develop deep personal bonds with White anti-racists and people of color.

Implications for NAME

This consideration of White racial bonding is only one example of the sorts of issues we need to unearth and examine, in order to engage in constructive change. The National Association for Multicultural Education can provide an excellent forum for such engagement, if we as Whites decide to tackle White racism.

At the 1993 NAME conference, I spent time in the materials display. What struck me was an absence of materials about racism. To be sure, there were many very useful items; like other conference participants, I took home an armload of catalogs and ordered many dollars-worth of books. But by and large, the materials framed multiculturalism as learning about "other" non-White cultures, learning about heroes and heroines of color, and learning English while retaining one's own language. The lack of critical attention to White racism in the materials reflected the silence Whites maintain about it. If we expect to see materials that help children learn to critique White supremacy, we need to engage in such critiques ourselves.

NAME has the potential for developing a strong anti-racist, anti-sexist, anti-oppression approach to multicultural education. That will not happen without White members developing a very critical and explicit examination of what we know about White racism, and how all of us can dismantle it. Some members may object that doing so will drive Whites away; they will say that many, many Whites simply will not tolerate discussion of the "r" word. I would counter, however, that the organization will attract more politically conscious educators who do wish to see multicultural education framed as anti-racism. In addition, we may develop more effective ways of engaging Whites in grappling honestly with racism.

Cultural Pluralism, Multicultural Education, and Then What?

> It seems to me that multicultural education works on improving the status dimension of inequality which supports the notion of cultural pluralism but does not touch structural issues of class and power for those who are doubly negative evaluated.

Elaine C. Hagopian

Elaine C. Hagopian is a professor in the Department of Sociology, Simmons College, Boston, Massachusetts. This article is based on her address to the National Association for Multicultural Education conference on February 10, 1994, in Detroit, Michigan.

Opening Remarks

My field is not education but sociology. Nonetheless, I hope that a sociological perspective on multicultural education will be of some value to this distinguished audience. Let me quickly spell out for you what my basic points will be. They are not dissimilar from many of your own, and especially the views of the distinguished President of the National Association for Multicultural Education, Carl A. Grant. What I hope will be new is some of the content and analysis of the issues the points reflect.

First, while my focus will be on racial and ethnic groups, class and power correlates will be accented.

Second, the results of the civil rights movement took us from desegration to visions of integration, and when the latter faltered, to recognition of diversity in the form of cultural pluralism—which nonetheless implied "structural integration." What we actually witnessed was more emphasis on cultural expression and less on structural access. Cultural pluralism as the focus of solution for the problem of inequality deflected attention from the need for structural change and access.

Third, what cultural pluralism as a policy did do, along with the negative pressures created by continuing racism/ethnism, was to encourage multicultural education as a kind of "cure-all" for the tensions of the society and to offer it as proof of our commitment to democracy.

Fourth, multicultural education at its best may create greater awareness and appreciation of all categories of people within and beyond race, ethnicity, and gender, and it may create a number of activists determined to make the wider society match the goals of multicultural

From *Multicultural Education*, Summer 1994, pp. 10-13, 38. © 1994 by the National Association for Multicultural Education. Reprinted by permission.

education, but I do not think for the immediate future that it can effect the real changes needed to provide a truly or reasonably just society. It is part of the solution, but there are too many national and international factors which presently limit its full success.

Fifth, even so, it will have a greater impact, done right, than the previous focus on cultural pluralism alone.

Analysis

Christine Sleeter and Grant in a 1987 article in the *Harvard Educational Review* define the multicultural education approach as one that:

> ...promotes cultural pluralism and social equality by reforming the school program for all students to make it reflect diversity. These reforms include school staffing patterns that reflect the pluralistic nature of American society; unbiased curricula that incorporate the contributions of different social groups, women, and the handicapped; the affirmation of the languages of non-English-speaking minorities; and instructional materials that are appropriate and relevant for the students and which are integrated rather than supplementary.

They also identify another type that embodies the above, but adds an action dimension, *i.e.*, the notion of multicultural education actually preparing "students to challenge social structural inequality and to promote cultural diversity." Theresa Perry and James W. Fraser in their book *Freedom's Plow* have phrased this somewhat differently by saying that:

> ...if a democracy which includes all of America's people is to be fostered and prefigured in this nation's education system, then multicultural education must be at the heart, and not on the margins, of all discussions about education in this country. In this situation, multicultural education becomes not a matter of simply adding new material to the school curriculum, but of fundamentally re-visioning the relationship of schooling to a democratic society.

What these definitions have in common is their focus on equality that somehow multicultural education must create and

promote. To understand what we are promoting, we need to define equality. In its absolute sense, equality means sameness of outcome. Without getting into a long discussion as to whether or not this is desirable, sameness of outcome would require a level of monitoring that a democracy would not find acceptable. Nonetheless, ever since the liberal age with its concept of citizenship and civil society emerged from the enlightenment, the idea of equality became a goal insisted upon by emancipated western society.

How then can we define it? Here I am addressing myself to racial and ethnic groups, but it could be applied to other categories as well. The following definition includes the social ingredients necessary to attain equality: a state of racial/ethnic equality exists in a polyethnic society when racial/ethnic groups enjoy nondiscriminatory status (*i.e.*, that they are valued positively at the human and cultural levels), are guaranteed those basic conditions of security and services which enable them to secure credentials to their abilities (equal-

---

Multicultural education must include internationalization of education to its approach.

---

ity of condition), and actually have unimpeded opportunity to compete for positions of power and class that have the authority to shape the conditions of life. This will still lead to inequality, but it will meet the terms of the spirit of equality, *i.e.*, that the criterion of fairness is operative.

This means that whoever falls to the bottom of class and power will do so from a relatively equal playing field; they will be statistically spread throughout the populations rather than centered in particular groups; and they will not be left without the basic securities from which their children can mount their effort to rise in the system. I will return to the concepts of status, class, and power, as well as the notions of equality of condition and opportunity, later in this analysis.

The same definition of equality holds for interstate relations, but requires agreements first between states, especially North/South states, and second, within the separate states themselves. This is a much more complex process and requires no less than a reordering of the world politically, economically, and socially. This will not happen without great resistance, and it may be utopian. Even so, it offers clear direction for the future. And here, I hasten to add that multicultural education must therefore include internationalization of education to its approach.

To assess the prospects of attaining the spirit of equality as I have defined it, and to have multicultural education serve as a lead into, and support of it in our own society without neglecting the international scene, we need to examine what we mean by western liberalism, the birthmother of modern, universal citizenship rights. Advocates of the latter allege that it alone is able to achieve democracy and hence by association, equality, especially since the failure of state socialism in the former USSR.

First, we need to understand what the western liberal model is. Actually, there are basically three western liberal models of equality. The first is the assimilation/universalist model which came out of the enlightenment tradition and is now enshrined in the U.N. Universal Declaration of Human Rights.

It is based on the assumption that the state constitution and laws recognize universal humanity and guarantee the same rights as such to all citizens to pursue their goals, that equal opportunity is therefore one of the rights which derives from universality and constitutionally guaranteed equal rights, and that participation in the societal structures will assimilate all citizens to a common world view and experience, thus eliminating any basis for negative differentiation. In short, people will be judged individually on their own merits because they are subject to universal criteria.

The second is the protection of minority rights as individual groups in polyethnic states model which was given content and focus after World War I through the League of Nations and the Minority Protection Treaties and Declarations. It was seen as an extension of liberal concepts of rights to freedom of expression. The basic assumption in this model is the right to protection and resource support by the state of all individuals as members of specific minority ethnic nations to retain their culture, language, religious practices, and identity without jeopardizing their status, access to power, and economic opportunity and mobility in the state of citizenship.

This model insisted on the liberal value of freedom of expression in group form and the right to one's own identity. "Forced" acculturation/assimilation (the first model) was seen as a violation of their rights. Nonetheless, they were also to be guaranteed the same opportunities as other citizens of the state. Other citizens and state officials saw this as special privileges for ethnic groups who wanted resources to continue their separate cultures, schools, and languages while not forfeiting the general privileges of citizenship.

This was supposed to be a positive form of separate but equal, i.e., separate culturally and somewhat structurally as well, and yet equal in terms of citizen access to positions in the wider society. Post-World War I Europe saw these treaties as a solution to the way states with various ethnic nations were formed. The treaties never really worked and some of the ethnic problems in Europe date back to these untenable arrangements.

Third, the structural integration/cultural pluralism model was developed by such thinkers as Horace Kallen. It is a variation of the rights to freedom of cultural expression whereby ethnic group members are guaranteed equal access to the common economic, political, and social structures of the polyethnic state, while at the same time being allowed and encouraged to pursue, develop, and elaborate their own ethnic cultures freely but not guaranteed fully by the resources of the state.

The problem with some of the contemporary liberal polyethnic states (the United

Multicultural education is to help prepare us for new equality, or even to help create it.

States included) is that they often adopt unconsciously more than one of these models in full or partially and in an incoherent manner, which may further exacerbate ethnic discontent. For example, in this country we use the first model when we deal with law, *i.e.*, equal treatment before the law which in fact does not work if only because of differential resources of the defendants. More, we use the cultural pluralism model (model three) in a negative way, *i.e.*, when an Arab (especially a Muslim) commits a crime, he/she is translated communally—*i.e.*, all Arabs are bad. When Congressman Joseph Kennedy met with constituents who were speaking to Palestinian rights in the Middle East, he was quoted by a constituent in the group as saying, "they [the Arabs] killed my father." Sirhan was translated into a "they, the Arabs." This is not so for mainstream whites.

More recently, President Bill Clinton addressed a Black Church in Memphis to condemn violence. Although not conscious of his actions, he chose a Black Church to speak about violence, implying that African Americans are the group that needs to be approached about the problem, rather than to a white population. Nonetheless, cultural pluralism is still put forward as positive, while those who are members of a non-majority culture are treated negatively. They were before the cultural pluralist model, but cultural pluralism makes them more visible and objects of criticism for their alleged "special treatment," especially when "they" behave deviantly.

The protection model (model two) was produced in this country as negative Jim Crow laws, and those laws envisioned total separation with access only to menial positions in the wider society and inferior separate institutions. Today, the protective part of this model was theoretically embodied in affirmative action laws more as catch-up than guaranteed protection (entitlement), but in fact affirmative action, while benefiting some, has been gradually circumvented. In part, bilingual education derives from this model.

On the whole, however, we have the ideology of the first model of individual equality before the law, coupled with cultural pluralism which is put forward positively, but used negatively, and the perceptions on the part of some in this society

that in the second model, various racial, ethnic, and gender groups have privileges not available to others. This is why we have a mess today.

. . . .

Well, okay, we have cultural pluralism as the dominant mode of relating to diversity in this country, and we are supposed to get structural access under this policy that leads to some equality. Affirmative action and equal economic opportunity are supposed to help us achieve the latter. Multicultural education is supposed to help prepare us for this new equality, or it is even supposed to help create it. But what do we have?

Our capitalist economic order is based on inequality. The question becomes one of who gets on the bottom? Because of the limited number of top positions, whoever could be kept out of the competition allowed others greater opportunity. Whether by intent or by opportunity, women, especially of color, and various racial/ethnic groups as categories, were disproportionally found on the bottom. If the spirit of equality operated, the bottom would not be consistently inhabited in a disproportional way with particular racial/ethnic groups and women of color.

When the post-civil rights legislation aimed at achieving integration to change this situation went into effect, it was challenged by sectors of society. And in and of itself, in any case, it could not meet the demands for equity by trying to put more players into the same structure, and one in which there is a shrinking job market. Hence, the focus shifted to cultural pluralism as a policy, not simply as a recognition of right to expression, but to deflect attention from the failure of structural integration. Good money was available for arts, dance, folklore, etc. to which the committed went. This made people feel good. These programs were good for self-esteem, but very little money was available for structural change to absorb people. Even so, cultural pluralism gave appearances of respect.

. . . .

Therefore, even when members of deprived groups got into positions of "power," economic or political, they were captive leaders. Who could imagine a Colin Powell using his previous position with the joint chiefs of staff to put forward the agenda of African-Americans on such matters as their disproportional death rate in Vietnam.

Can anyone really imagine Ron Brown presenting an unambiguous picture of African-American economic and health issues. No Arab-American can ever envision George Mitchell or Donna Shalala coming out forcefully for real justice in the Middle East which is tied to viewing Arab-Americans positively in this society. Or who could imagine Connie Chung doing a speakout on Asian Americans, especially those from Vietnam, Cambodia, and Laos.

Lani Guinier was refused the post of U.S. Civil Rights Attorney because she did not have the credentials for being a captive leader. She was considered a "troublemaker" because she held to her values. All of us know of at least one feminist, or an African-American, or an Hispanic-American, etc. who are defined as radical or aggressive in their views who are refused jobs because "they would not be good for our students, or co-workers, or organization." Take your pick. I myself have been locked out of teaching courses on the Middle East, my area speciality, because I believe in including the point of view of the victims as well as the victimizers in the area. None of my colleagues offered support on this matter. In short, the few who climb to the top as proof of American democracy are absorbed into the existing corporate culture. They are not able to change the structure in ways that allow cultural pluralism to mesh with social and political mobility.

To further dissect the situation in detail, I must now examine the dimensions of inequality, class, status, and power, and then I will tie the parts of my analysis together.

Class Stratification. When members of particular ethnic groups in a polyethnic society (and/or the global system of nation-states) are consistently in the low-income and high unemployment category, it becomes obvious that certain social and political processes are re-enforcing the pattern and that equal access is not a reality.

Social Status. This is often defined simply as a person's or group's position in society. Defined in this way, social status elicits little affect. However, if we understand that social location is a result of how a group is perceived by others, then we will understand social status to include other meanings. The social status of a racial/ethnic group is a derivative of the degree to which the group is valued in society in human and in cultural terms.

Ordinarily, to evaluate a group negatively in human terms correlates significantly with a negative evaluation in cultural terms. African Americans, Native Americans, and various misnamed Hispanic Americans illustrate this point. On

The type of status evaluation of ethnic/racial groups tends to correlate with class and power.

the other hand, positive evaluation, even if given grudgingly, of an ethnic group in cultural terms may neutralize overt negative human evaluation. For example, the European cultural values of education and achievement which Jewish immigrants brought with them to the United States tended to subdue, but not defeat, overt antisemitism (the human level of their status evaluation) in this country over the years. Positive cultural evaluation provided Jewish peoples with the opportunity to achieve higher ranked positions in society.

In the first case, the double negative evaluation of a racial/ethnic group not only defines its social position, but correlates significantly with class. In the second case, latent negative human evaluation has the potential for surfacing under certain conditions. However, the cultural skills and achievements of the affected group offer a constraining factor and permit the group an overall desirable social status as well as greater class mobility.

In sum, an ethnic/racial group's status position is determined by the human and cultural evaluation made by those who "count" in society, and that these evaluations are relevant to economic access and degree of class mobility, and as we shall now see, to power positions as well.

Power. There are several types of power in addition to the obvious one of political power. There is economic power supplied either by ownership of significant shares in firms or property; there is bureaucratic power stemming from managerial positions in major organizations and agencies; and there is social power stemming from the prestige and authority of professional roles.

Ordinarily, ethnic/racial groups who are doubly negative evaluated do not have easy access to positions of power. Hence the only real power route open to doubly negative stereotyped groups is to organize the group itself to develop a critical mass capable of "disrupting" society in some form. In return for ceasing and desisting, agreements with governmental and institutional officials are made calling for attempts to alter the negative images through public education, enactment of laws to gain economic access, and greater efforts to open power positions.

Those ethnic groups negatively stereotyped humanly but not culturally are able to gain positions of power by exercising their citizens' rights and meeting necessary qualifications in the "open" society. However, the more power they gain in all areas, even in the "open" society, the greater the possibility for the latent human prejudice to express itself, especially in situations where the society as a whole is undergoing difficult economic times.

While the ethnic group is able to rally through their institutions important forces and resources against attempts to dislodge them from their class and power position, the hostility toward them is expressed quite often through acts of violence, but civil society rushes to condemn such violence against groups who are culturally valued. Clearly, the type of status evaluation of ethnic/racial groups tends to correlate with class and power positions.

. . . .

The next questions we must ask are what is the solution, and what does multicultural (including international) education have to do with it? Can multicultural education produce equality? What other forces are operating that may neutralize the intent of multicultural education?

It seems to me that multicultural education works on improving the status dimension of inequality which supports the notion of cultural pluralism but does not touch structural issues of class and power for those who are doubly negative evaluated. While it does sometimes focus on class and power issues, the reality of the American social structure tends to dampen the activists as they compete in a shrinking opportunity structure.

What we need to make multicultural education work are equality of condition and opportunity mentioned in my definition of equality. We have been on the periphery in this country of establishing equality of condition, *i.e.*, the recommendation of the Social Security Commission of 1935 that a policy of guaranteed employment be put in place so as to avoid the catastrophe of the great depression; the development of a minimum wage law—though very inadequate; some unemployment coverage; low-cost housing, etc.

. . . .

Yet we have not seen these add up to even minimal maintenance of excluded peoples, never mind basic security to "level" the playing field. We have to have equality of condition, *i.e.*, guaranteed work at a level of pay that is livable, clean and decent low cost housing, health care, first class education for all without bias, reasonable support for the unemployed and handicapped, etc.

Only equality of condition will make equality of opportunity meaningful and produce the spirit of equality. These met, multicultural education's focus on creating positive status (human and cultural) could work toward achieving the spirit of equality. However, the three liberal models would have to be reformulated into a single, conscious, and positive model. Actually, this would mean that the universalist model could operate in treating people individually for jobs, political office, and before the law.

The cultural pluralism model would allow positive cultural identity without interfering in universal criteria for access to the economic and power structures. And it is assumed that the protection model would not be needed if multicultural education and equality of condition and opportunity worked well together. All of this requires fundamental change in our society calling for a socially responsible capitalism and government. Such changes assure identifying and promoting our best into all walks of life from all walks of life, while assuring those who do not attain the positions of great income and power in society a real cushion of security from which their children will have an opportunity to compete.

. . . .

These are yet not enough. We have to move to greater international agreements and equity. We need real peace and recognition of the rights of third world peoples not to be used as cheap labor. They must be guaranteed security as well. Profits must be put into a human context that includes not only basic security, but *de facto* will also cease the destruction of our environment beyond earth's ability to replenish the resources necessary for life.

So long as we remain in a competitive national and international economic mode which relies on political and military power to control people and resources as well as control international financial institutions, polyethnic states with the most excellent multicultural education will not be able to sustain in reality the values of equality promoted in school.

What this all means is that a NAFTA would not be enacted, and hence would not pit American labor against Mexicans and Mexican Americans in a racist/ethnist battle for jobs. It means that a World

Trade Center explosion would not direct hatred to Arab Americans and other Muslim groups in America.

For even if we ever get equality of condition and opportunity, and we could work out the problem of liberal models, we must ask if multicultural education focused on creating positive human and cultural statuses can work when national and international events and policies are enacted that can immediately wipe out its effects. One need only think of the treatment of Iranian-origin peoples in the United States after the Khomeini revolution and the holding of American Embassy workers as hostages in Iran for over one year that led to hostility to Iranian-origin people in the United States.

· · · · · · · · · · · · ·

Some 90 years ago, Emile Durkheim thought he could promote moral behavior in our modern industrial societies through education; and we still keep trying through liberal arts. Thankfully, we do turn out a core of students who keep the embers burning, but the reality is before us. I hope that multicultural education will be more successful. It is the right thing to do, but we need the rest of society and the world, or those who make decisions in those arenas to walk with us. Given the fact that most people live in polyethnic states and within a competitive global economic system, the efforts required to achieve the spirit of equality are enormous and complex, but the goal is worth our very best efforts.

Identity and Personal Development: A Multicultural Focus

We have known for several decades that all human affective behavior (emotional response, values assessment, etc.) is learned behavior. Anything that can be learned can be unlearned or modified. There is no more important task for any human being than learning how to define oneself as a person within a cultural, as well as global, societal context. Persons are impacted by many social forces as they interact with others in the process of forming themselves as individuals. Multicultural education can help students as well as teachers to identify those forces that affect their personal development.

The development of each person's unique conception of self (the development of one's identity as a person) is the most important developmental learning task that any of us undertake from birth to death. In the preschool, elementary, and secondary school years, each of us learns critically important cognitive and affective strategies for defining ourselves, others, and the world. Multicultural education seeks to help people develop accepting and empathic intellectual and emotional responses to other people. There has been much psychological and psychiatric research over the past few decades on the differences between prejudiced and tolerant (accepting) personalities. One opportunity educators have as they work with students in school settings is to provide good examples of accepting, tolerant behavior and to help students develop positive, affirmative views of themselves and others. Gordon A. Allport, in his classic book *The Nature of Prejudice,* commented in his chapter on "The Tolerant Personality" that we could be "doubly sure" that early instruction and practice in accepting diversity is very important in directing a child toward becoming a tolerant person. Thus, we take up the topic of personal identity development in this unit.

In the education of persons, we need to see the interconnections among such factors as gender, social class position in society, racial or ethnic heritage, and the primary cultural values that inform the way they see the world and themselves. We need to be perceptive of and sensitive to their visions of who they are and of how things are in the world. As Tracy Robinson argues so well from a counseling perspective in her article, we need to "see our clients whole." Perceptive teachers and therapists have always been aware of this. But all teachers need to be aware of it. Teachers, as well as parents and many others, are persons with whom students at all ele-

mentary and secondary grade levels must interact. It is important for teachers to be positive examples of accepting, open-minded persons capable of empathy, compassion, and concern for the well-being of each student.

We need to help students to understand themselves, to define their strengths and their concerns, and to critically encounter their own personal social reality. These are tasks all must learn to do in childhood and adolescence so that they may empower themselves to interpret and evaluate their own experience. These tasks can be integrated and effectively achieved within the intellectual mission of the school. One way to do this is by encouraging students to critically interpret and evaluate the texts they read and to be open and active in class discussion of issues. Identity development is an ongoing process. Each student needs to be able to explore the boundaries of his or her intellectual strengths and weaknesses as well as the social boundaries encountered in school and out.

Multicultural education is intended for and needed by all students in order that they will be sensitive to the many varying heritages and backgrounds through which individuals interact in our culturally pluralistic society and will forge their own conception of who they are. Why should only one cultural heritage be thoroughly taught, while all others are essentially ignored in elementary and secondary school years, in a pluralistic society whose demographics are changing so dramatically? Cultural values are of primary importance in forming a person's self-concept. This unit's articles explore various models of human interaction and the psychosocial foundations for the formation of students' knowledge bases. How students form social groups in culturally integrated school settings is explored, along with the behavioral differences among members of "loose knit" and "tight knit" social groups in desegregated school settings. The ways in which students define themselves and their possibilities as they move across or are trapped within their perceived social boundaries in school and community settings are explored. How educators can better utilize the knowledge bases of minority cultural families in assisting minority students to achieve better social integration into mainstream school settings is also examined. The importance of educators' trying to establish more effective communications linkages between students' family and cultural environments is further examined. The multiple worlds students live in and the social roles they frequently have to play, in and out of school, are another social phenomenon in the personality development of students that receives analysis in these essays.

Students live in a hierarchy of social contexts in which their racial, cultural, gender, and social class back-

grounds, as well as the degree of their personal identification with each of these factors, impact on the processes through which they make important choices leading to individual decisions regarding their own identity. Some of the research on how desegregated schools can achieve more effective degrees of intercultural socialization is also presented in this unit. Questions being studied include these: Under what circumstances may higher rates of intercultural friendship develop? How can teachers encourage students to learn each other's cultural heritages? Helping students to learn from the cultural perspectives of other groups so that all students might better comprehend alternative, diverse definitions of their social environments is a major task of multicultural education, leading to tolerant, accepting attitudes toward people of differing cultural backgrounds. Allport and several other major psychiatrists and social psychologists of past decades have taught us that prejudice and tolerance (acceptance) are learned behaviors. We can learn to be accepting, caring, compassionate persons. Yes, schools can teach to overcome prejudice. Educators are *not* powerless in the face of the prejudiced views many students bring to school from their homes.

The essays in this unit are relevant to courses in educational policy studies and leadership, cultural foundations of education, sociology or anthropology of education, history and philosophy of education, and curriculum theory and construction, among others.

Looking Ahead: Challenge Questions

What are the primary gender issues in multicultural school settings?

What should children learn about the cultural heritages and values of other children in their schools?

How do social class differences relate to misunderstandings among students?

What can educators learn from developing close communications linkages with the families of their students?

In a desegregated school, what challenges do minority students encounter that majority students do not?

How does community structure affect adolescent identity development?

What can teachers do to foster positive personal identity development in their students?

—F. S.

THE INSIDE STORY

*Counseling for tolerance in the early
years means paying attention to the way
children think and feel about the world
— and themselves.*

....

DAVID ARONSON

"Hey, what is this, *One Flew Over the Cuckoo
Nest?*" It was Meredith Kimber's first meeting with a
6th grade class she would be counseling as part of
her year-long internship with Inventing the Future, a
racism-prevention project, and Kimber was encountering more than the usual dose of suspicion. The
students were from predominantly Irish families in a
blue-collar Massachusetts town with a reputation for
insularity and xenophobia. Kimber's project was to
help children address the inner source of the violence and racism that seem to surge in the middle
school years.

A graduate of Harvard Divinity School, Kimber
was shocked by the attitudes she encountered
among many of the children. "These kids had derogatory names for everyone," she recalls. "They
used to ride the subway searching for black kids to
pick fights with. They'd come in punching each
other, calling each other 'fag.' " They initially had
little interest in pursuing an inner exploration of
their own biases.

Still, Kimber persisted. "We didn't ever tell the children what was right or wrong. Instead, we asked them
how they felt about things, trying to get them to
change. If someone said 'fag,' we said, 'OK, here's the
homosexuality issue again.'" Kimber's hope was that by
getting the children to disclose their beliefs, values and
fears, she and the other counselors on her team could
help the children overcome the irrational thinking
underlying their prejudice.

"By the end of the year, a lot of the kids had come
to accept us and were relying on us to help them think
through a lot of issues about racism, sex and violence."

Increasingly, for school counselors and psychologists, helping students become more tolerant and
accepting means starting at the very earliest ages. Even
then, however, racism may already have sprouted its
first insidious roots. Debra Van Ausdale, a doctoral student in sociology at the University of Florida, witnessed
a disturbing number of racial incidents when she
worked as a teacher's aide at Gainesville Day Care Center in Gainesville, Fla.

"When a white girl became weary pulling an Asian
girl in a wagon one day, the Asian girl hopped out and
offered to pull," Van Ausdale recalls. "The white girl
said, 'You can't pull the wagon. Only white people can
pull the wagon.'" It was, says Van Ausdale, an incident
that crystallized for her just how well her students
understood the power of racial identity.

"We often think of the early years as an age of innocence," says Dr. Kevin Dwyer, assistant executive director of the National Association of School Psychologists.
"In fact, prejudice is probably developed before children enter school — as is a predisposition to violence.

---

*School counselors, because of their
unique position, can intervene against
prejudice at every level.*

 Reprinted with permission from *Teaching Tolerance*, Spring 1995, pp. 23-29. © 1995 by the Southern Poverty Law Center.

Teaching About "Same" and "Different"

A primary source of prejudice stems from how we make sense of the world. Kids, says Don Locke, a professor of counseling at North Carolina State University, especially want the world divided into easy pieces: Good and Bad, Black and White, Boy and Girl. And they want to assign fixed meanings to each of these categories: Boys never cry; all Chinese are good at math; girls play with dolls.

"Because kids think in such absolute terms," Locke says, "they have trouble understanding how people can be similar in some ways and different in others."

One counselor was able to get at the issue of categorization in a simple way. She tells of a second grade classroom where children had begun to use racial epithets like "whitey" and "darky." She had all the children form a circle and thrust their left hand into the middle. "The extraordinary variety of shades took them all aback," she says. "They realized you couldn't just divide people into two or three racial categories, but that there was a whole rainbow of skin tones and that everyone was unique." The racial epithets immediately ceased.

During their many visits to classrooms, Locke and his colleagues have designed a more extended program that delights children while subtly changing the way they think.

This activity, aimed at younger, elementary-age children, develops children's appreciation for cultural differences through four engaging activities that build on each other. Since school counselors and psychologists are usually scheduled to visit classrooms only periodically, this one is designed to work even if the counselor's class sessions are widely spaced. All that's required is to review the previous session at the start of each new one.

Begin each session by setting rules for speaking and listening: l. We listen to and respect one another's thoughts, ideas and feelings. 2. We share, when comfortable, our own ideas, thoughts and feelings. 3. Anyone can pass a turn if they wish. Provide a supportive environment so that the students will leave the session feeling good about being like some of their classmates while also feeling good about being different from others.

• Bring in three clear bowls—one containing salt; the second, yellow corn meal; and the third, flour. Do not tell the students the contents of the containers. Ask the children to describe how each substance looks in turn. Then place the words "same" and "different" on the blackboard and write down how the contents are similar to each other and how different. Now have them do the same exercise but this time focus on how the contents *feel*.

Summarize the discussion and ask the students what other things they know about that are the same and different. Ask them to think of things that are the same and that are different for the next scheduled session. (For example, foods all nurture our bodies but have many different tastes; clothes keep us warm but are made in different styles and colors.)

• Have the students discuss what they remember from the last session, and have them share some of the things that they discovered to be the same and different.

Next, distribute plenty of play dough or plasticine of different colors to each child. Tell the children they can make anything they want. Then go around in a circle and have the students describe what they have made.

Have them discuss one way in which their item is similar and one way in which it is different from the preceding child's creation.

At the end of the session, point out that there are a lot of ways in which things are similar and a lot of ways in which they are different. Point out that every child's creation is made from the same material, yet it is different from all the others.

• Bring in two play phones. Have pairs of children take turns in front of the class making believe that it is after school and they are calling each other to discuss an imaginary new classmate. How is that child similar to them and how is he or she different? Discuss how sameness and difference affect the children's descriptions of their new classmate.

• This time, pair the students up and have them discuss themselves. Ask them for three self-descriptions, for example, "I am tall; I have a big sister; I like to read." Do the students have some traits in common and some that are unique to themselves?

Ask the students how they felt about being different from each other and how they felt about being the same. Encourage students to remember a time when they felt like they were different from others and ask them to describe their feelings. Ask them how they get along with classmates they perceive as the same and as different.

Have the students tell how they are going to work to appreciate those students whom they see as different from themselves. They may resolve to invite them to play in their game or to share in some discussion.

These activities should help the students understand how sameness and difference are part of life, and that all people are the same in some ways and different in others. In our diversity, we have strength as a community.

School forces children together who might not have had the chance to exhibit that sort of anti-social behavior before they arrive."

The psychological development of prejudice in children was brilliantly illuminated 40 years ago in the work of Gordon Allport (*see Box p. 95*). Today, school counselors have developed an effective approach to reducing prejudice in the crucial early years, when the direction of the child's emotional and psychological growth can be set for life. This approach relies less on proselytizing than on changing the way young children make sense of the world — and themselves.

Because of their training, counselors have a better understanding than most about how young children form opinions, feelings and personalities around what they see and experience. And because of their position—their "beat" is typically an entire school—counselors can intervene at every level, from advising the troubled child who may have violently expressed his or her prejudice, to developing teacher training programs, to working with parents on addressing racial tensions in the community.

Successful early intervention efforts are based on the premise that hatred and prejudice are tools of the subconscious that ease the feeling of insecurity by offering the illusion of superiority. Counselors try to offer more responsible ways to achieve emotional security.

"Giving children a positive experience of themselves, teaching them to recognize the validity of human differences, and providing them with the tools to express their emotions — all these are ways that intolerance can be counteracted," says Pat Schwallie-Giddis, associate director for the American Counseling Association.

Like strands in a rope, the various elements that Schwallie-Giddis speaks about — self-awareness, self-expression and self-esteem — are all widely recognized as intertwined aspects of the tolerant person. Children cannot freely express their emotions or feel secure with others unless they feel secure with themselves. And they can't feel good about themselves without having some understanding of who they are. Though any effort to separate these elements is necessarily artificial, they do build on and strengthen each other and can be thought of sequentially.

A child's failure to identify and express feelings leads to frustration and self-defeating behavior.

Self-Awareness and Self-Expression

School counselors can help foster children's self-awareness through exercises designed to help children see themselves and others for who they are, apart from the expectations and stereotypes that can easily color their thinking.

In one activity, called "The Me Bag," children are each given a plain brown grocery bag that they may decorate any way they choose. Then they are encouraged to fill the bag at home with things they value, things that represent what they love and feel proudest of. The next day, children get to show off what they've brought in. A recent immigrant from Bolivia may come in with an embroidered doll, for example, and another student may bring an LA Lakers cap.

Although each bag looks different, they all contain precious items. Children learn that the things that make them unique are as valuable as the things that they have in common. They learn to appreciate differences rather than fear them. And they learn to see themselves as others might see them: as individuals with their own enthusiasms and cultural traditions, neither better nor worse than others.

With an awareness of themselves as distinct individuals, children can better learn how to express their emotions in responsible and appropriate ways. The

ability to articulate feelings is one of the most difficult things for children to learn, says Kevin Dwyer of the National Association of School Psychologists — yet it is absolutely critical. "So much depends on it: how well you're able to work as a team member, how well you resist acting on impulse, how you deal with the problems you're having."

Because it is often easier to make sense of other people's feelings than of one's own, educators have found that one of the best ways to develop children's emotional expressiveness is by asking them to think about the experiences of fictional characters. Through specially designed reading programs, children learn how failing to identify and express feelings can lead to increasing frustration and self-defeating behavior. Consider the following scenarios, taken from two popular reading programs in schools today, *PUMSY: In Pursuit of Excellence* and *Kids Have Feelings, Too.*

In the first, Pumsy the dragon is having a terrible day. While her friends are out picnicking on the beach, having the best times of their lives, Pumsy is moping under a tree. Usually, her best friend Steve would come tell her to stop feeling sorry for herself. But today, he's decided to let her make her own decisions.

In the second, a little girl from the picture book *Sometimes I Feel Awful* is also having a pretty rotten time. She has invited her best friend, David, over to play. But David just sits around playing with a puzzle, while she wants to go outside and climb a tree. Maybe a good swift punch will bring him around—but, of course, that only makes David want to leave. Now the little girl—who is never given a name, and who might, therefore, be any child—is lonelier than ever.

Children listening to these stories are encouraged to think about the consequences of the characters' actions and to offer alternatives. The little girl in *Sometimes I Feel Awful* explodes in anger because she isn't able to express to David how frustrated she is feeling. One group of children in Florida had very definite ideas about how she should behave.

"She should tell him!" called out one tousle-headed boy.

"We respect individuals not because they are from another race or culture, but because they are individuals."

"Tell him what?" the boy was asked.

"That she wants to go play in the tree!" he shouted, with the certainty of a 4-year-old.

The goal of these programs is for the children to take the insights they've learned from others and apply them to their own lives. Programs that develop children's powers of self-expression give them a feeling of control over their environment and make them less likely to lash out in violence and anger.

In Hillsboro County, Fla., an early childhood program has as its guiding image a stop sign. Bright red stop sign stickers, plastered everywhere in the classroom, emphasize children's power as decisionmakers. By teaching children to stop and think before they act, the "stop sign" program encourages "smart behavior."

"So much in our society encourages children to act on impulse," Dwyer notes. "Get out a watch and time how long any single camera angle lasts in a TV show. There's rarely more than three or four seconds between cuts. Teaching kids to slow down, not to go after the immediate gratification, is essential to reducing violent outbursts, which express the very worst kind of intolerance."

Self-Esteem

Self-awareness and self-expression are stepping-stones for self-esteem. "Those persons with high self-esteem have fewer inhibitions and can relate to and accept others far more easily than those who do not," says Schwallie-Giddis. "By contrast, vengeful, intolerant behavior reflects poor self-esteem."

Self-esteem is a complicated subject that is easy to parody: "I'm OK and you're OK, but you got an 'F' on the test." And some self-esteem programs can focus so much on affirming the child's self-identity that they seem to ignore the child's own perceptions and experiences. It takes more than simply asserting the child's worth for the child to feel worthy.

True self-esteem develops out of a variety of experiences. A vital ingredient is the attention, acceptance, approval, acknowledgment and affection that a child receives from parents, primarily, but also from teachers, friends and counselors.

From these "Five A's" come feelings of competence, security, social responsibility and self-

The Ages of Intolerance

In *The Nature of Prejudice,* first published in 1954, social scientist Gordon Allport developed a powerful explanation of the psychological roots of prejudice.

Allport says that from a startlingly young age children begin learning the lessons of tolerance or intolerance—recognizing certain differences, for example, while still in diapers. There's nothing intrinsically worrisome about this. The 10- or 12-month-old baby who cries at the approach of a stranger is doing exactly what he or she is biologically programmed to do: alert Mom or Dad to the presence of a potential source of danger.

But if the parents are themselves prejudiced, the infant's reaction to a stranger of a different skin color or different physical features may be subtly reinforced, generating an apparently seamless education in bigotry that justifies itself as "natural." "My baby just doesn't like people of such and such a color," some parents may report, oblivious of their own role in shaping the child's perceptions.

By age 3 or 4, children begin to pick up on more explicit clues about in-groups and out-groups from their own family, the media and their peers. Children at this age are at the cusp of racial awareness and may be extremely curious about physical differences. Although they may use derogatory remarks,

they often have little idea what they mean. And while they may utter racist sentiments, and even use race and gender to exclude others, their opinions and attitudes haven't yet gelled.

Of all influences on the child's ideas at this age, the family is clearly the most important. "The family," wrote Allport, "supplies a constant undertone of acceptance or rejection, anxiety or security." Even parents who avoid making overt racist comments may teach their kids negative racial values. The parent's lightening grip around the child's hand or the sound of the car doors being locked shut when a group of teenage males of a different race or ethnicity passes by—these communicate the parent's attitudes about others as clearly as words do.

By age 6 or 7, children have begun to recognize that there are distinct categories of people—that the janitor belongs to a different social class from the doctor, for example. And they've also begun to understand that many of these identities, such as race, gender and ethnicity, are fixed. They recognize that social status and positive or negative qualities can be ascribed to people based on their affiliation within these groups. And they've begun to make the connections between their individual identity and their group identity.

Often the lessons children learn at this age are as much about societal hypocrisy as they are about race. Parents who mutter something about the "wrong section of town" and then deflect their child's questions about what they meant aren't teaching their child that racism is bad; they are teaching the child to be cautious about speaking his or her mind on issues of race.

By age 10 or so children may start consistently excluding others who belong to an out-group, or , if they are themselves members of a minority, to develop a complex of attitudes that include defiance, self-doubt and hostility. Children this age are an excellent barometer of societal attitudes, for, in contrast to their elders, they tend to voice racial stereotypes quite freely.

A final stage comes in the teenage years, when the child learns those subtler rules of etiquette that govern relations between people. They've learned that "prejudiced talk and democratic talk are reserved for the appropriate occasions," Allport writes. What is said between friends in the mall may never be voiced in an official forum like a classroom. "It takes the entire period of childhood and much of adolescence to master the art of ethnocentrism," Allport concludes.

discipline, as well as strongly held values. Positive self-esteem, in other words, isn't just "feeling good about yourself." Rather, it's feeling that your life matters to others and to yourself. With that feeling comes the capacity to get along with others and the desire to conform to the rules of society.

An effective self-esteem program gives children the opportunity to learn about themselves in an environment that nurtures their growth and validates their feelings. Activities that promote self-esteem begin by teaching children to recognize the thought patterns and emotional habits that have a negative impact on their self-concept. As an alternative, such programs offer affirmations of the child as a unique being whose perceptions and feelings are valuable and appreciated. Eventually, it is hoped, the child internalizes that affirmation. No longer insecure or dissatisfied, the child is able to recognize his or her own worth and respond to the worth of others.

Some counselors have used self-portraits as a way to bring out the best in children. They ask the children to draw portraits of themselves. Then, without discussing the pictures, they have each child personally compliment the others in his or her group of six to eight fellow students ("I like your smile," "I like your shoes," etc.). Then they have the children draw their self-portraits once again, and ask them what was different this time around. Did they draw happier, prettier pictures? How did it make them feel to receive compliments from others? Did receiving compliments affect their self-portraits?

"Learning to respect yourself as an individual is, in an odd sort of way, one of the best ways to learn to respect other people and other cultures," says Jackie Allen, a school counselor who works in two bilingual elementary schools in California. "That's what it's about, ultimately, respecting individuals not because they are from another race or culture, but because they are individuals."

Counseling for the Future

School counselors, therapists and psychologists already have an extraordinary range to cover. With their many other responsibilities and involvements, it's no wonder that most feel stretched too thin. They have been lobbying for greater funding to place more counselors and psychologists in the schools.

They're needed because many of the same intervention techniques that promote tolerance can help children avoid other problems, as well: violence, drug abuse, suicide, teenage pregnancy. The whole

RESOURCES

• The World of Difference Institute of the Anti-Defamation League sponsors workshops promoting diversity awareness in the classroom. The Institute's *Elementary Study Guide* is an outstanding resource packed with activities and insights to address diversity.

*Anti-Defamation League
1100 Connecticut Ave.,
Suite 1020
Washington, DC 20036
(202) 452-8310*

• The two volumes of *Thinking, Feeling, Behaving: An Emotional Education Curriculum for Children* ($25.95 each) are compendiums of classroom activities based on the principle that thinking things through rationally is one of the best ways to overcome problems. The activities focus on developing the children's emotional intelligence. (Grades 1-6 and 7-12)

*Research Press
2612 N. Mattis Ave.
Champaign, IL 61821
(217) 352-3273*

• *The Best Self-Esteem Activities for the Elementary Grades* ($24.95) offers an excellent overview of the theory behind self-esteem and emotion management for children, as well as strategies for promoting children's sense of personal agency and self-fulfillment.

*Innerchoice Publishing
P.O. Box 2476
Spring Valley, CA 91979
(619) 698-2437*

• *Counselor in the Classroom* ($19.95) gives counselors the keys to integrating the fundamental lessons of people-skills into enjoyable learning activities designed for all children.

*Innerchoice Publishing
P.O. Box 2476
Spring Valley, CA 91979
(619) 698-2437*

• *PUMSY: In Pursuit of Excellence* ($210) is an 8-week self-esteem program featuring a cuddly dragon puppet and a variety of workbooks, posters and other supporting material. This structured program develops children's emotional skills by involving them in the trials and tribulations of Pumsy, the dragon who sometimes acts up. (Ages 6-9)

*Timberline Press
P.O. Box 70187
Eugene, OR 97401
(503) 345-1771*

• *Sometimes I Feel Awful* ($8.95) is an affecting book about a young girl who's having a lousy day. The accompanying teacher's guide ($8.95) gives practical suggestions for helping children identify and express their emotions. (Ages 4-8)

*Fearon Teacher Aids
P.O. Box 280
Carthage, IL 62321
(800) 242-7272*

raft of social ills that manifest themselves with such virulence in today's schools, and that speak to the existence of so much pain and emotional distress, are to varying degrees addressed by focusing on psychological issues in early childhood.

Forty years ago, at the end of his analysis of prejudice, Gordon Allport arrived at a penetrating insight: Those who hate, he told us, are hurting. By giving children the tools to overcome the pain they feel, by listening to, caring for and comforting them, by helping to build healthier and stronger psyches, counselors can play a crucial role in arresting the dismaying rise in hatred and violence.

Like a sport that requires the coordination of various skills and muscle groups, tolerance is by its nature a complex undertaking. By isolating and strengthening the fundamental psychological components of self-esteem, self-awareness and self-expression, counselors and psychologists hope to encourage children to become healthier, more tolerant human beings.

The Intersections of Gender, Class, Race, and Culture: On Seeing Clients Whole

The author explores the multiple and dynamic intersections of gender with race, culture, and class in psychosocial identity formation to minimize the risk of homogenizing or polarizing our understanding of these characteristics.

Tracy Robinson

Tracy Robinson is an assistant professor in the Department of Counselor Education at North Carolina State University–Raleigh.

Gender, class, race, and culture are core components of each person's identity formation (Condry, 1984; Gibbs, Huang, & Associates, 1989; Good, Gilber, & Scher, 1990; Helms, 1984; Ibrahim, 1985; Katz, 1985; Lee & Richardson, 1991; Pinderhughes, 1989; Scher & Good, 1990; Sue & Sue, 1990; Ward, 1989). Erikson's (1968) concept of identity formation has been primary to psychologists' understanding of identity, which is psychosocial and refers to the continuity of the self in a developmental context and to one's relationships with others in society (Ward, 1989). Throughout the life span, identity constructs of gender, race, class, and culture shape an individual's image and ensuing reimage of self and one's place in the world.

The overall goal of this work is to promote dialogue among helping professionals concerning the pivotal role of these simultaneous intersections in affecting clients' lives, their problems, and ultimately, their empowerment. Such a conceptual framework is preferred over focusing on one aspect of identity for assessment purposes.

Concerning research, Reid and Comas-Diaz (1990) observed, "gender research typically fails to include race/ethnic concerns, . . . studies of ethnic groups often ignore gender issues" (p. 397). The interaction of gender, class, race, and culture in our society determines one's identity (Gollnick, 1991). Thus, one identity construct does not fully reveal an individual's character.

To illustrate the importance of attending to a client's multiple intersections, a case study example is used. A discussion of monoculturalism and its relationship to oblivion regarding these intersections is explored. Finally, approaches to change for training and practice are outlined.

A DEFINITION OF CONCEPTS

In this work, the term *socioeconomic class* refers to a person's (or to a group's) relative social position in a hierarchical ranking (Jaynes & Williams, 1989). Race has both biological origins and social dimensions (Pinderhughes, 1989). Although typical conceptions of race refer to non-Whites (Christian, 1989), race refers to both Whites and non-Whites. Clearly an immutable characteristic, race holds status and rank in society just as socioeconomic class, a mutable variable, does (Leggon, 1980). Gender has social categories in terms of roles and behaviors based on a biological given of sex (Renzetti & Curan, 1992). It refers to both men and women, although traditional notions of gender reference nonmales (Christian, 1989). Thus, there is an interrelationship between race, gender, and social class (Gibbs, Huang, et al., 1989). Finally, the term *culture* refers to total ways of living and refers to values, beliefs, norms, and traditions (Pinderhughes, 1989). It is enormous and central to our lives.

Reprinted with permission from the *Journal of Multicultural Counseling and Development*, Vol. 21, No. 1, January 1993, pp. 50-58. © 1993 by the American Counseling Association. No further reproduction authorized without written permission of the American Counseling Association.

Indivisible Intersections

The importance of considering the multiple intersection of class, race, culture, and gender has been raised across a variety of disciplines (see Christian, 1989; Collins, 1989; Reid & Comas-Diaz, 1990; Siegel, 1990). Such attention is warranted, considering that every human being's psychosocial identities are an embodiment of each of these and other immutable and mutable constructs.

In her discussion of gender and race, Christian (1989) suggested that ignoring these primary intersections is to treat individual constructs as if they were pure and exhaustive categories. Such a treatment implies that certain constructs can be isolated and used solely for purposes of assessment. For example, many adult men have the roles of father and husband in common. Yet, as Carrigan, Connell, and Lee (1987) maintained, the term *men in general* is puzzling because of the underlying assumption that persons who share gender are monolithic. Clearly, socialization patterns in the United States often orient men to restrict emotion and to be aggressive, competitive, and dominant (Cook, 1990; Good & Mintz, 1990; Mintz & O'Neil, 1990). Nonetheless, the experiences, issues, and concerns of a college educated African-American man from a multigenerational, middle-class background are different from those of an African-American male laborer who has a high school diploma and is from a multigenerational, working-class family.

Whereas Bronstein and Quina (1988) suggested more variability within groups than among them, in the example just provided, there is a high degree of within-group difference that can be attributed to socioeconomic class. Invariably, individual differences come into play, because each man is different from his counterparts with similar characteristics (Lee & Richardson, 1991). Yet, socioeconomic class has a direct impact on income, housing, access to medical care, children's social environment, and a host of other indicators of life-style and life quality (Gibbs, Huang et al., 1989; Jaynes & Williams, 1989). Although both men are affected by racism, class and status affect one's economic, social, and to a large extent psychological power in this society. Considering that power relates to the capacity to produce desired effects and mastery over self, nature, and other people (Pinderhughes, 1989), the relationship between power and class is evident. The type of relationship, however, is uncertain.

Although low-income status may provoke feelings of powerlessness characterized by less comfort, less gratification, insecurity, and strong tendency to depression (Pinderhughes, 1989), racism or sexism often generates similar feelings of powerlessness, even among individuals who hold middle-class status. Although class is interrelated with gender, race, and power, it is simplistic to conclude that male gender, high socioeconomic status, and being a White American is directly associated with feelings of more power, which according to Pinderhughes (1989) is characterized by less tendency to depression, more pleasure, less pain, and feelings of superiority. Likewise it is a mistake to assume that female gender, low socioeconomic status, and being a person of color is automatically associated with feelings of less power. Such a perspective is psychologically disempowering to a client although high status is typically identified with persons who are White and middle class, whereas low status is ascribed to non-White persons, ethnic minorities, and lower-class families (Gibbs, Huang, et al., 1989).

Undeniably, a disproportionate share of people living in poverty are people of color (U.S. Department of Commerce, 1990); most jobs are stratified by race, ethnicity, and gender, with women of color at the bottom of the occupational hierarchy and White men at the top (Women for Racial and Economic Equality, 1991). A full 60% of adults receiving Aid to Families with Dependent Children (AFDC) have not completed high school (Women for Racial and Economic Equality, 1991). Economic and occupational powerlessness, however, do not dictate psychological and or moral powerlessness. Moreover, economic and occupational power do not prescribe psychological and moral strength. History and contemporary reality are replete with examples of people with economic power and impoverished morals.

Pinderhughes (1989) maintained that, however ironic, accepting the reality of one's powerless position can bring a sense of power. Reframing the situation to one's advantage (through the help of a skilled counselor) and choosing not to internalize negative behaviors and attitudes of oppressive persons are acts of empowerment.

Human Characteristics as Status

Ours is a heterogenous society, however, as diverse as this nation is and has been, diversity tends to be devalued (Pinderhughes, 1989; Sue, 1990). When differences are viewed hierarchically, disdain is probable. Naturally, intolerance for difference is not compatible with multiculturalism, and diversity and multiculturalism are not synonymous.

As an ideal state and an ongoing process wherein a person is appreciative of and comfortable with racial and cultural differences (Hoopes, 1979), multiculturalism is different from racial and ethnic monoculturalism. According to McIntosh (1990), monoculturalism is single-system seeing. It assumes that people come from the same cultural system "and that its outlines are those which have been recognized by people who have the most ethnic and racial power" (p. 1). Although non-Whites represent 24% of the U.S. population (U.S. Department of Commerce, 1991), White Americans are in the numerical majority and as such have significantly influenced U.S. culture accordingly. Components of White culture that are pervasive and dominant throughout society include individualism, competition, patriarchal family structure, the Protestant work ethic, and empiricism (Sue & Sue, 1990). These values parallel the society's adherence to the experiences of upper middle-class, Euro-American, able-bodied, heterosexual men as the referent point for normalcy, regardless of race, gender, culture, and class diversity (Bronstein & Quina, 1988; Christian, 1989; Miller, 1984; Reid & Comas-Diaz, 1990). Undoubtedly, intolerance of and disdain for differences reduces humanity and impedes moral development. In counseling, such attitudes are contradictory to the goal of client empowerment.

A Case in Point

Ms. Wing is an Asian-American lawyer who comes to counseling. She presents with problems of stress, fatigue, and feelings of being overwhelmed with her multiple responsibilities at work and at home. She has two children, ages 9 and 11 years. She is also troubled because she was not promoted at the law firm where she has been employed for 6 years. During the first session of counseling she reveals that younger and less experienced White men have been promoted above her on three different occasions. Subsequently, she is beginning to doubt her capability as a professional. She is also convinced that the overtures displayed by her male supervisor are characteristic of sexual harassment.

Although it is clear that the stress Ms. Wing is experiencing is related to multiple role conflicts many women experience as mothers, professionals, and wives (Good, Gilbert, & Scher, 1990), other issues are directly related to who the client is as an Asian American. An astute counselor, regardless of his or her gender, would be sensitive to the oppressive nature of sexual harassment and its role in provoking feelings of powerlessness, increased vulnerability, and anxiety. Feeling discriminated against because of one's race or ethnicity also conjures up feelings of powerlessness, rage, and frustration. Again, an effective counselor, regardless of his or her race or ethnicity, would have the ego strength to assess this.

Despite the professional qualifications of this client who may possess many YAVIS (young, attractive, verbal, intelligent, and successful) characteristics (Pinderhughes, 1989), high levels of educational attainment, hard work, and middle-class status are not sufficient to bypass feelings of powerlessness common among people with less education and less success. In a societal context that purports to be a meritocracy and a culture in which the Protestant work ethic is endorsed, these feelings, albeit distressing, may be new for some who thought (and had been taught) that their professional

status and middle-class income would shield them from such feelings. Once again, an effective counselor would be able to coexist with this existential realization although it may evoke feelings of vulnerability in the helping professional. Pedersen (1988) reminded counselors to have balance, which is to tolerate life's inconsistencies and to learn to coexist with dissonance. Security in one's identity as a racial, gendered, cultural, and class being minimizes countertransference (Bernardez, 1987).

Silence about any of the intersections in Ms. Wing's life is akin to believing they do not exist and are thus irrelevant and dismissable. According to Fine (1987), "silencing constitutes the process by which contradictory evidence, ideologies, and experiences find themselves buried, camouflaged, and discredited" (p. 13). Although Fine was referring to the classroom event, important parallels can be made to counseling. A counselor's silence about Ms. Wing's speculations of racial and sexual discrimination could be attributed to limited exposure to clients in cross-cultural contexts. When differences are seen as contradictory, naming them or talking about them is impeded. Silence could also be linked to one of the assumptions of monoculturalism, that everyone exists in the same cultural plane and thus desires what is valued in society.

Although a prevalent tenet of feminism maintains that women need to be more assertive in a society that has socialized them to be yielding and silent, it may not be in Ms. Wing's best interest to become more assertive with her colleagues or her spouse. Lack of assertiveness and self-denial are problems for many women (Lemkau & Landau, 1986), unquestionably in this culture and arguably in non-U.S. cultures. In many Asian cultures, however, women's identities are often defined by their relationships to others more than by occupational goals (Chan, 1986; True, 1990). Furthermore, in many microcultures (e.g., Asian, Latino, American Indian, and African-American families), collective responsibility, group solidarity, and family unity are strong values and strengths, not liabilities (Sue & Sue, 1990). Thus conferring with and even deferring to some family members may be culturally representative of the important role of family in a client's culture. If only a dominant cultural lens is used to interpret behavior, bias and stereotyping ensue (Pedersen, 1988). Because all clients are shaped by a constellation of forces (Lee & Richarson, 1991; Pedersen, 1990), a monocultural approach is undoubtedly myopic.

It is not psychologically healthy for Ms. Wing to internalize a sense of personal inadequacy. If institutional racism and sexism are involved, she should be encouraged, from a behavioral perspective, to carefully document incidents when harassment takes place, investigate policy manuals concerning her rights as an employee, and pursue mediational procedures when necessary. Cognitively speaking, it may be helpful for Ms. Wing to consider her options (a change in employment, starting her own business, hiring some help with household responsibilities, marriage counseling). These and other options should be generated from a place of power as opposed to one of powerlessness. An appropriate question for a counselor to ask is, "What would Ms. Wing like to see change in her immediate situation and what action is appropriate, given who she is and who she desires to be?" Finally, Ms. Wing should be assisted in understanding that when ascribed (more than achieved) statuses are viewed as "master" status traits, a status hierarchy results. Thus, persons not traditionally associated with a role may be regarded as unsuitable candidates, regardless of professional qualifications (Leggon, 1980). That the U.S. presidency has not been occupied by any person of color or by a woman is an example. This knowledge need not impede a client's aspirations but may in fact strengthen boundaries.

On Change

The 21st century will reflect changing conceptions of gender and population growth among racial and cultural groups (Hodgkinson, 1985; Scher & Good, 1990). To empower clients and attend to them as whole persons, counselors in training and practicing counselors need to be aware of their perceptions and assumptions about differences. One possible barrier to change is that some well-meaning and highly trained counselors are oblivious to unearned privileges associated with gender, race, class, and sexual orientation (Mcintosh, 1988). Privileges refer to an "invisible, weightless knapsack of special provisions, assurances, and blank checks" (McIntosh, 1988, p. 1). As White, female, heterosexual, highly educated, and middle class, Mcintosh identified over 40 privileges that she can use on a daily basis. For example, she can easily find academic instruction that gives attention to people of her same race and class. Moreover, she recognizes that it is not necessary that she or her children answer questions about why she lives with her husband (McIntosh, 1988). Students and professionals are encouraged to identify their own personal list of privileges as a means of increasing awareness. Helpers who are aware of their own identities are less likely to be uncomfortable with differences, particularly in cross-cultural contexts (Pinderhughes, 1989). Discomfort with differences may contribute to a counselor's inability to attend to aspects of the client's identity that are different from his or her own.

Responding to Pinderhughes's (1989) questions that focus on identity may abet the process of critical thinking for both professionals and students. Included are (a) What are your feelings about being male, female, White or a person of color? (b) How do you think others

who are different from you feel? (c) What are your experiences with power or powerlessness based on any of your identity constructs? Self-inquiry is important because countertransference can occur when counselors are unaware (Bernardez, 1987; Good, Gilbert, & Scher, 1990). Finally, operating from the client's strengths, which are independent of economic or occupational indexes, promotes empowerment.

CONCLUSION

The goal of this work was to expand understanding and to encourage dialogue about the important intersections of gender, class, race, and culture. Definitions of these terms were provided. A discussion of their relationships with one another and with power was provided. A case study example illustrated the influence of these dynamics on a client's problem, process, and empowerment. A pedagogy of change was outlined and included (a) recognizing the enormity of the intersections, (b) understanding one's personal identity constructs, (c) focusing on client's strengths toward empowerment. Such strengths are not dependent on occupational and economic indexes and may emanate from cultural traditions.

REFERENCES

Bernardez, T. (1987). Gender based countertransference of female therapist in the psychotherapy of women. *Women, Power and Therapy: Issues for Women, 6,* 25–40.

Bronstein, P. A., & Quina, K. (Eds.). (1988). *Teaching a psychology of people: Resources for gender and sociocultural awareness.* Washington DC: American Psychological Association.

Carrigan, T., Connell, B., & Lee, J. (1987). Toward a new sociology of masculinity. In H. Brod (Ed.), *The making of masculinities: The new men's studies* (pp. 63–100). Boston: Allen and Unwin.

Chan, C. (1986). Teaching about Asian women's activism: The poetry of Mila Aguilar. *Women's Studies Quarterly, XVI*(1/2), 23–25.

Christian, B. (1989). But who do you really belong to–Black studies or women's studies? *Women's Studies, 17,* 17–23.

Collins, P. H. (1989). The social construction of Black feminist thought. *Signs: Journal of Women in Culture and Society, 14,* 745–773.

Condry, J. C. (1984). Gender identity and social competence. *Sex Roles, 11,* 485–511.

Cook, E. (1990). Gender and psychological distress. *Journal of Counseling & Development, 68,* 371-375.

Erikson, E. H. (1968). *Identity, youth and crisis.* New York: Norton.

Fine, M. (1987). Silencing in public schools. *Language Arts, 64,* 157–174.

Gibbs, J. T., & Huang, L. N., & Associates. (1989). *Children of color.* San Francisco: Jossey-Bass.

Gollnick, D. M. (1991). *Race, class, and gender in teacher education* (Unpublished manuscript). Washington, DC: National Council for the Accreditation of Teacher Education.

Good, G. E., Gilbert, L. A., & Scher, M. (1990). Gender Aware Therapy: A synthesis of feminist therapy and knowledge about gender. *Journal of Counseling & Development, 68,* 376–380.

Good, G. E., & Mintz, L. B. (1990). Gender role conflict and depression in college men: Evidence for compounded risk. *Journal of Counseling & Development, 69,* 17–21.

Helms, J. E. (1984). Toward a theoretical explanation of the effects of race on counseling: A Black and White model. *The Counseling Psychologist, 12,* 153–165.

Hodgkinson, H. (1985). *All one system: Demographics of education, kindergarten through graduate school*. Washington, DC: Institute for Educational Leadership.

Hoopes, D. S. (1979). Intercultural communication concepts: Psychology of intercultural experience. In M. D. Psych (Ed.), *Multicultural education: A cross cultural training approach*. LaGrange Park, IL: Intercultural Network.

Ibrahim, F. A. (1985). Effective cross-cultural counseling and psychotherapy. *The Counseling Psychologist, 13*, 625638.

Jaynes. G. D., & Williams. R. M., Jr. (1989). *A common destiny: Blacks and American society*. Washington, DC: National Academy Press.

Katz, J. H. (1985). The sociopolitical nature of counseling. *The Counseling Psychologist, 13*, 615–624.

Lee, C. C., & Richardson, B. L. (1991). *Multicultural issues in counseling: New approaches to diversity*. Alexandria, VA: American Association for Counseling and Development.

Leggon, C. B. (1980). Black female professionals: Dilemmas and contradictions of status. In L. Rodgers-Rose (Ed.), *The Black woman* (pp. 189–202). Beverly Hills, CA: Sage.

Lemkau, J. P., & Landau C. (1986). The "selfless syndrome": Assessment and treatment considerations. *Psychotherapy, 23*, 227–233.

McIntosh, P. (1988). *White privilege and male privilege: A personal account of coming to see correspondences through work in women's studies* (Working Paper No. 189). Wellesley, MA: Wellesley College Center for Research on Women.

McIntosh, P. (1990). *Interactive phases of curricular and personal revision with regard to race* (Working Paper No. 219). Wellesley, MA: Wellesley College Center for Research on Women.

Miller, J. B. (1984). The effects of inequality on psychology. In P. P. Rieker & E. H. Carmen (Eds.). *The gender gap in psychotherapy: Social realities and psychological processes* (pp. 45–51). New York: Plenum.

Mintz, L. B., & O'Neil, J. M. (1990). Gender roles, sex, and the process of psychotherapy: Many questions and few answers. *Journal of Counseling & Development, 68*, 381–387.

Pedersen, P. (1988). Ten frequent assumptions of cultural bias in counseling. *Journal of Multicultural Counseling and Development, 15*, 16–24.

Pedersen, P. (1990). The constructs of complexity and balance in multicultural counseling theory and practice. *Journal of Counseling & Development, 68*, 550–554.

Pinderhughes, E. (1989). *Understanding race, ethnicity & power: The key to efficacy in clinical practice*. New York: The Free Press.

Reid, P. T., & Comas-Diaz, L. (1990). Gender and ethnicity: Perspectives on dual status. *Sex Roles, 22*, 397–408.

Renzetti, C. M., & Curan, D. J. (1992). *Women, men, and society*. Boston: Allyn and Bacon.

Scher, M., & Good, G. E. (1990). Gender and counseling in the twenty-first century: What does the future hold? *Journal of Counseling & Development, 68*, 388–391.

Siegel, R. J. (1990). Introduction: Jewish women in therapy: Seen but not heard. *Women and Therapy. 10*(4), 14.

Sue, D. W., & Sue, D. (1990). *Counseling the culturally different: Theory and practice*. New York: Wiley.

True. R. H. (1990). Psychotherapeutic issues with Asian American women. *Sex Roles, 22*, 477–486.

U.S. Department of Commerce, Bureau of the Census. (1990). *Poverty in the U.S.: 1990. Current Population Reports*. Washington, DC: Author.

U.S. Department of Commerce, Bureau of the Census. (1991). *Statistical Abstracts of the United States*. Washington, DC: Author.

Ward. J. V. (1989). Racial identity formation and transformation. In C. Gilligan. N. P. Lyons, & T. J. Hanmer (Eds.), *Making connections: The relational worlds of adolescent girls at Emma Willard school* (pp. 215–232). New York: Troy Press.

Women for Racial and Economic Equality. (1991). *191 facts about women*. New York: Author.

CAN SEPARATE BE EQUAL?

New answers to an old question about race and schools

James Traub

James Traub's book on City College of New York, City on a Hill, *is published by Addison-Wesley.*

Forty years have passed since the U.S. Supreme Court declared, in *Brown v. Board of Education of Topeka, Kansas,* that "in the field of public education the doctrine of 'separate but equal' has no place." No single decision the Court has rendered in this century has produced so profound a social upheaval. Hundreds of lawsuits later, black and white—and sometimes Hispanic—students are being bused back and forth to desegregated schools in Buffalo, Indianapolis, Louisville, St. Louis, Milwaukee, Oklahoma City, Wilmington, Las Vegas. The South, once the stronghold of Jim Crow, is now by far the most desegregated region of the country.

But *Brown* didn't merely launch a thousand buses; by rooting the equality of black Americans in the constitutional guarantee of the equal protection of the law, the decision established civil rights as a fundamental American principle. Six months after the decision, Rosa Parks sat down in the front of a bus in Montgomery, Alabama, and the then-unknown Martin Luther King Jr. led a boycott of the city's buses. It was King, ultimately, who demanded that America make good on *Brown's* promise of simple justice and who ennobled that promise with the language of biblical salvation and the mountaintop vision of racial harmony. What *Brown* ordered was the desegregation of the schools; but what it stands for is the hope of redemption from our original sin of slavery and racism.

Redemption, of course, hasn't come. In the great cities of the Northeast and Midwest, blacks, as well as Hispanics, live in growing isolation and increasing poverty. Desegregation is swiftly becoming a dead letter in places like Milwaukee, where in a generation the schools have gone from mostly white to overwhelmingly minority. The practical barriers to desegregation are in many places so high that the moral clarity promised by *Brown*—a simple choice between segregation and integration, between racism and justice—has blurred.

The new choice, it seems, is between separate but equal and separate but unequal. This has proved to be a welcome state of affairs not only for white suburban parents frightened by the prospect of desegregation but also for black parents and activists who despair of integration or never believed in it in the first place. For them, separate but equal is not the cynical evasion the *Brown* decision sought to eradicate but a rallying cry. Black scholars like Derrick Bell have long pointed out that in *Brown* the Court didn't declare segregation an evil in itself but rather found that segregation conferred an ineradicable stigma of inferiority on black children. Now Bell and many others look on this claim as condescending and even racist. The spokesmen for all-black "academies," which have been instituted or discussed in Miami, New York, Milwaukee, Detroit, and elsewhere, insist that separation is a precondition for black self-esteem, and many blacks now look upon integration as a white plot to undermine racial pride. So desegregation, having lost its momentum, has lost its chief constituency and beneficiary class as well.

This new separate-but-equal model is disturbing for those, like me, who grew up listening to Martin Luther King and who found in the redemptive language of the civil-rights movement a virtual substitute for religious belief. It isn't only a way of schooling that's being repudiated; it's a way of living: to accept the new ideology of separatism is to accept as well the growing obsession with racial and ethnic identity, and the assumption that each group has its own truths, its own values, even its own version of history. Desegregation has proved to be so agonizing and so impractical that it now seems almost perverse to resist the suggestion that, say, we lavish funds on ghetto schools and let them develop on their own. But it is a bargain we may live to regret.

The desegregation battle is being waged in a surprising number of places. Earlier this year I paid a series of visits to Hartford, Connecticut, a city that has been struggling to improve the dismal performance of its school system (in April, in what seemed a gesture of despair, the school board announced it was considering bringing in a private company,

From *Harper's* magazine, June 1994, pp. 36-41, 44-47. © 1994 by the Harper's Magazine Foundation. All rights reserved. Reprinted by special permission.

Education Alternatives, to run the city's schools) and is currently facing perhaps the most ambitious desegregation lawsuit filed in recent years, *Sheff v. O'Neill.* Hartford has a virtually all-minority school system, surrounded by the virtually all-white systems of the suburbs, but *Sheff* is, pointedly, not about race but about isolation, and about the overwhelming poverty of the inner city. The decision in the case, filed in state rather than in federal court, is expected sometime later this year. A victory for the plaintiffs would fill Hartford's suburbs with fear and trembling, but it might also offer a new way to think about desegregation.

On a cold morning this past February, Don Carso, principal of the McDonough Elementary School in Hartford, stood outside the dilapidated red-brick pile of his school, greeting parents as they arrived with their children. Carso is a bespectacled middle-aged white man with thinning hair and a thickening waistline. It is his habit every morning to remain outside until he has saluted every last parent. McDonough is 78 percent Hispanic, 14 percent black, and almost all poor. Carso hallooed a number of fathers in sweatshirts who looked him over with sullen glares as they climbed back into their cars. "I treat them all like lawyers and doctors," Carso said, waving a cup of tepid coffee. "Most of them come around eventually."

Carso is the kind of principal pictured in the "effective schools" literature. He's omnipresent and indefatigable, he settles fights with Solomonic compromise, and he puts learning ahead of everything else. He treats McDonough like a sanctuary from the surrounding gloom. And it is—up to a point.

Construction of McDonough began in 1897; portions of the building can be mistaken for a museum exhibition of nineteenth-century urban-school design. The cafeteria, in which 800 children are expected to eat breakfast and lunch—both provided free to almost all of the children, owing to the poverty of the students—is a basement classroom furnished with a half-dozen folding tables; sunlight barely flickers in through two windows. The boys' bathroom, next door, is a dim, high chamber. Instead of sinks it has a single long trough fitted with trumpet-shaped spigots. Only a few of the toilets have doors. The school generally runs out of toilet paper before the end of the year, and Carso has had to borrow money from another school to keep his own supplied. McDonough is so overcrowded that nearly 200 children attend classes in trailers, known as "portables," set up on what used to be the playground. Another couple hundred students go to school in another building a few blocks away, the former Moylan School, which is just as old and decrepit as McDonough.

McDonough's condition, like the condition of elementary schools throughout Hartford's slums, is shameful—an example of the sort of "savage inequalities" that crusading writer Jonathan Kozol described in his book of the same name. But it only takes money to address physical neglect, and money can be a surprisingly elastic commodity. Thanks to a $205 million city bond issue, for which Carso helped drum up support, McDonough will have a new structure by 1997; Moylan, too, will be rebuilt and rechristened as a separate institution. McDonough will have an auditorium, a gym, and a cafeteria. Carso says he will make sure that his kids have just as many computers as the kids in Hartford's fancy suburbs. And he will then have a deeply troubled school in a pristine setting.

McDonough's Hispanic students, most of them Puerto Rican, tend to be recent arrivals whose parents speak little or no English. The families are nomadic, shuttling around Hartford's slums in search of an affordable apartment. Almost every morning, two or three or four kids show up at McDonough's door, standing shyly with an equally shy parent and often a friend or relative to translate; and as they arrive, other kids simply disappear. And yet, for all their mobility the children are so isolated by their families' poverty and lack of English that they might as well be living in an Appalachian hollow. After Carso finally agreed to leave the frozen tundra that was his school's front yard, we walked into the main building and ducked into a first-grade bilingual class. The kids were sitting in a circle, singing in Spanish. The teacher, Delia Bello, came over to see us while her pupils, obviously well-drilled, talked quietly to one another. Bello said that she never ceased to be amazed by how little contact the kids had with the world. "You show them some place on the map," she said, "and they say, 'It's Hartford,' Even Russia—'It's Hartford.' And it's the same with the sixth-graders. If you talk about going to the mall, they've never been to the mall. And if you talk about college, they'll say, 'What's college? I don't know anyone who's been to college.' "

By the time we got downstairs to his pocket-sized office, Carso had to make a call to Moylan. He rushed over to the phone and, still standing in front of his desk, said, "Is she okay? Has he been drinking again?" Connie's stepfather had pulled a knife on her mother and then cut the phone cord when she tried to call 911. Connie, a sixth-grader, had told the social worker at school, who suddenly realized why the girl's work had been deteriorating in recent weeks. Carso put down the phone and said, "It's not like they don't have these problems in the suburbs, too. But you can deal with it if it's isolated." He cupped his fingertips together into a globe. "In *this* world," he said, "we're very successful. But we can't control all the stuff on the outside."

"The solution isn't in the city; maybe it's in the state," Carso says. "We are saying to our neighbors, 'Take ownership of our problem' "

A few months earlier, a janitor had been chased off a snow blower and shot behind Moylan; apparently he was a gang member. Even the violence and the degraded physical setting mattered less than the children's isolation, their immersion in a dead-end world. McDonough wasn't altering the dismal trajectory these children had been handed at birth; not enough, anyway. On Connecticut's statewide reading test, 72 percent of the school's graduating sixth-graders had scored at the remedial level. In the normal course of things, they would fall farther and farther behind, just as the great majority of Hartford's public-school children would. As Carso said, "We have hundreds of little interventions going on in our school; but they're not going to produce fundamental change."

A year earlier Carso had, after much agonizing, testified for the plaintiffs in *Sheff v. O'Neill*. Carso's testimony did not make him very popular in his suburban neighborhood, where the case raises the specter of forced busing. "It wasn't even popular in my own family," he says, rolling his eyes behind thick glasses. Carso knows how deep is the hostility to mandatory desegregation; but he also believes that his kids have to be pried loose from their environment. He even thinks there's something to the idea of simply evacuating Hartford's public schools, though he also knows that inner-city parents will bridle at the insult of one-way desegregation. Carso considers separate but equal, or even separate but more than equal, a colossal mistake; for all that he believes in his school, he doesn't see how it can overcome the world beyond his fingertip globe. "The solution," he says, sitting in his tiny office during a brief moment of calm, "isn't in the city. Maybe it's in the state." Above all, Carso thinks, the solution has to lie with the wealthy suburbs that surround Hartford. "We are," he says, striking almost a pleading note, "saying to our neighbors: 'Take ownership of our problem.' "

The desegregation premise handed down from *Brown,* the premise of the stigma of inferiority, has always contained an insulting inference for many blacks. As Dr. Eddie Davis, the principal of predominantly black Weaver High School in Hartford, says, "It would be a total slap in the face to say that education can only happen in the suburban schools." Davis testified for the plaintiffs in *Sheff,* but only because, as he said, "Wherever white children [are], there are resources." Davis would be just as happy to have the resources in a segregated environment; he doesn't see isolation as a problem. And nowadays, resources do not, in fact, follow white children as they once did. Derrick Bell has argued that the great achievement of *Brown* was to make "it possible for black parents to gain an equal educational opportunity for their children wherever those children attended school."

The declining prestige of integrationism among blacks and the rise of new and sometimes virulent forms of ethnocentrism have a good deal to do with the growing acceptance of a new separate-but-equal model, but so does the hopefulness of an Eddie Davis. Davis considers himself a disciple of the "effective schools" movement, and it was the late Ronald Edmonds, a black education scholar generally considered one of the founders of the movement, who first formulated a serious pedagogic argument for the irrelevance of desegregation. Edmonds took umbrage, as he wrote in 1978, at "the conventional liberal wisdom which said that the educational salvation of black children depended on integration." A well-run school could overcome whatever disadvantages children brought with them. There was no sound reason, Edmonds concluded, to stand in the way of the many black parents who preferred "racially distinct" schools for their children.

Edmonds's precepts have been institutionalized in groups like Theodore Sizer's Coalition of Essential Schools, which takes the demographic makeup of the schools for granted and tries to infuse those schools with the values and culture that are correlated with academic success. Weaver High School, for example, works with Sizer's group, and Dr. Davis has overseen a restructuring of his ninth- and tenth-grade classes. What really matters, Davis insists, is not race or even resources but academic rigor, high expectations, strong leadership, a willingness to experiment. But when I asked Davis how much academic improvement he had seen after five years of reform, he said that there hadn't been any yet. By the time kids reached ninth grade, he admitted, it was too late. In fact, Weaver wasn't altering trajectories any more than McDonough was. The students were scoring 150 points below the state average on the SATs. Perhaps no more than 20 percent of entering ninth-graders would ultimately go on to four-year colleges.

Separate but equal may offer a salve to black pride and a comfort to white suburbanites; but there's not much proof that it works. In *The Closing Door,* Gary Orfield, a standard-bearer of white liberal integrationism, and co-author Carole Ashkinaze analyze the effects of the 1980 decision known as the Atlanta Compromise, in which that city's largely white power structure agreed to black control over the schools in exchange for an end to litigation that would have mandated desegregation throughout the metropolitan area. Here was separate but equal in laboratory form, presided over by a new black superintendent who had a national reputation as an educational reformer. Said former Atlanta mayor Andrew Young, "It was really the integration of the money to provide a quality education for all children that was black folks' goal. Racial balance was a means for achieving the goal." But despite an initial promise of success, Orfield concludes, "Huge numbers of children flunked grades and became more likely to drop out before completing high school," while "whites and middle-class blacks abandoned the city system in droves." Poor black students, in other words, were more isolated and even more deeply cut off from the opportunity to develop, than they had been before.

What happens when city schools reach funding parity with suburbs and poor kids still ride a conveyor belt to a second-class life?

Atlanta wasn't the only place where the resources, rather than the children, were desegregated. Over the last decade or so, old-style desegregation litigation has largely given way to suits seeking equal funding for poor and rich districts. Connecticut, in fact, became one of the first states to engage in tax "equalization" as a result of a 1977 case, *Horton v. Meskill.* Thirty-six states either have agreed to equalize spending or are facing litigation that would compel them to do so. As with the Atlanta Compromise, the Connecticut measure essentially allows white suburbanites to pay a modest tax in order to keep racial lines intact. Michigan's Republican governor recently supported a move by the state legislature to equalize school funding by substituting the state sales tax for the local property tax as the source of school funding, creating a separate-but-equal status quo.

But what happens when inner-city schools reach funding parity with the suburbs and the poor kids are still riding a conveyor belt to a second-class life? This is where Hartford and *Sheff v. O'Neill* comes in.

Hartford was, for many generations, a flourishing medium-sized Yankee city. It had a fine old museum, a fine old library, a riverfront, and the headquarters of several of America's largest insurance companies. Today you can spend half an hour staring at the great Trumbull tableaux of the Revolutionary War hanging in the Wadsworth Athenaeum without encountering another soul—not even a guard. You can walk down the center of a downtown avenue at 9:00 P.M. with little fear of bodily harm, at least from a car. The insurance companies are still there, but the people who work in them live in the suburbs. Like many of the old cities of the Northeast and Midwest, Hartford peaked in size soon after World War II, as first blacks from the South, then Puerto Ricans, then Caribbeans, mostly from Jamaica, flooded into the city from the orchards and the tobacco fields of the Connecticut Valley. (The local leaf is used largely to wrap cigars.) Thereafter the city lost tens of thousands of middle-class and working-class white families. Hartford's population of 140,000 is now 69 percent non-white. Hartford is, incredibly, one of the ten poorest cities in America. Connecticut's two other major cities, New Haven and Bridgeport, are among the poorest twenty. And yet Connecticut has the highest per-capita income in the United States.

It doesn't seem so very farfetched to expect the suburbs, whose wealth depends upon Hartford, to "take ownership" of some of its problems. The suggestion, in fact, has been made before. In 1965, a study team from Harvard recommended a system of "metropolitan cooperation," in which every suburban school would agree to take two students from one of Hartford's "poverty areas" into each of its classrooms. By 1974, according to the plan, the suburbs would accommodate 6,000 inner-city students, one-fifth of the city's total student population. The idea was not to desegregate the schools. At the time, Hartford's schools were almost perfectly balanced between white and non-white students. The Harvard plan, in fact, was "directed primarily to the amelioration of the effects of poverty on education," as the authors wrote. What mattered about the students in the poverty areas was not so much that they were black or Puerto Rican as that they were poor, and living in dense concentration.

The plan, though designed to be modest, wasn't modest enough; the state legislature ultimately authorized a program known as Project Concern, which never sent more than 1,300 inner-city kids to the suburbs in a year. (The number now hovers around 650.) And the opportunity for real change was quickly past. With an unexpected increase in Puerto Rican immigration, and the continuing departure of whites to the suburbs and to parochial schools, the gulf between the Hartford schools and the suburban schools—and between the city and the suburbs—widened all the more. Five years after the Harvard report, the Hartford schools were 67 percent non-white. Hartford itself was a "poverty area."

By the late 1980s, Connecticut, despite its reputation as a pasturage of the white upper-middle class, had become a powerful symbol of the Johnson-era Kerner Commission's "two nations." The state's three largest cities were well on their way to becoming mass ghettos. The next largest cities—Waterbury and Stamford—were becoming poorer and more black. In 1988, Gerald Tirozzi, then-state commissioner of education, issued an impassioned report calling school segregation "educationally, morally and legally wrong." Tirozzi's language was unabashedly, and perhaps naively, idealistic. He called on the state to initiate a desegregation planning process based on the principle of "collective responsibility"—New England communitarianism for an expanded community. Tirozzi also had the monumental incaution to suggest that the State Board of Education "be empowered to impose a mandatory desegregation plan" should the voluntary plan fail.

The moment the report appeared, Tirozzi later testified, "all hell broke loose." One state legislator called for his resignation. As Tirozzi toured the state, pleading his case, he discovered that "the very word 'mandate' conjures up a feeling between and among citizens, parents, teachers that really is very negative." Tirozzi, in short, was all but tarred and feathered. Governor William O'Neill strongly objected to mandatory solutions, and in a follow-up report the next year, Tirozzi proposed a series of voluntary measures; even the word "desegregation" was stricken from the document. Tirozzi had run up against the hard kernel of resistance to a social policy that required a serious degree of sacrifice from non-beneficiaries. That was why desegregation has always required court orders.

By openly indicting desegregation, however, Tirozzi's report persuaded a group of lawyers from the ACLU, the NAACP Legal Defense and Education Fund, and several other groups that the time was ripe to file a long-discussed class-action lawsuit. From the beginning, *Sheff v. O'Neill* was a state rather than a federal case, for the simple reason that the Supreme Court had long since foreclosed the sort of remedy the Tirozzi report had proposed. In 1974, the Court had declared, in *Milliken v. Bradley,* that Detroit suburbs could not be compelled to pool their students with the city's without a finding of segregative intent—a finding, for example, that the suburban schools had been set up to permit whites to elude integrated city schools. This effectively meant that the Court would not disturb the single most powerful impediment to further desegregation—the demographic forces that were rapidly dividing America's metropolitan areas, including Hartford, Bridgeport, and New Haven, into poor black inner cities and middle-class white suburbs. But the Connecticut constitution, like that of many states, includes guarantees of "equal" and "adequate" education for all citizens; in fact, Connecticut is unusual in that it guarantees non-segregated as well as non-discriminatory education.

Sheff represents a new generation of litigation not only because it's been brought in state court but because it does not turn on the dynamics of race and racism. The Hartford schools are now equally divided between black and Hispanic students, and *Sheff* does not argue that either group is the victim of historic discrimination. John Brittain, a University of Connecticut Law School professor and a member of the plaintiffs' team, says, "The most signal fact about Hartford is not that it's 92 percent non-white but that it's 63 percent poor." *Sheff* is about poverty, not race; it argues that poor children need access to a non-poor educational environment, rather than that black children need access to a racially integrated environment.

The trial was held in late 1992 and early 1993; post-trial hearings continued for another year. The two sides called on so many of the leading scholars in the field that the case, in effect, recapitulated the debate over desegregation, in which scarcely anything seems to get definitively settled despite staggering research. Much of the testimony detailed the stunning disparity between city and suburb. Hartford's schools are 92.1 percent non-white; the suburban districts are 92.6 percent white. In Hartford, 65 percent of the children under the age of eighteen come from single-parent households; 41 percent of parents have not graduated from high school. In Glastonbury, a nearby suburb, the figures were 14 percent and 9 percent. And socioeconomic status dictates performance: About two-fifths of Hartford students drop out before finishing high school and only 30 percent of graduates go on to attend four-year colleges. At Glastonbury High School, the dropout rate is about 1 percent, and more than half go on to a four-year college.

"Even parts of their body they didn't know," Hernandez testified. "They didn't know their underclothing, what it was called"

Some of the trial testimony was so piercing that people wept in the courtroom. Gladys Hernandez, who taught at an elementary school called Barnard-Brown, spoke of the school's grimed-over plastic windows and recalled that in twenty-three years she could never get the proper writing paper for her students. Most of the children, Hernandez said, were Puerto Rican, and spoke neither Spanish nor English properly. "They called everything a 'thing,' " she testified. "Even parts of their body they didn't know. They didn't know their underclothing, what it was called. If they had a grandparent, they didn't know that they were a grandson or a granddaughter." Once a year, Hernandez said, the school permitted her to take the children on a trip, to a zoo or a farm. "The most extraordinary thing happened when they came to the river," she testified. "They all stood up in a group and applauded and cheered, and I was aware they were giving the river a standing ovation. And they were so happy to see the beauty of the river, something that most of us go back and forth [across] and never take time to look at."

The plaintiff's expert witnesses argued that desegregation made a measurable difference in academic outcomes. Dr. Robert Crain, of Columbia University Teachers College, testified that school desegregation is correlated with later involvement in integrated colleges, neighborhoods, and workplaces. Students in Project Concern, he found, were much more likely to graduate from high school, and more likely to complete

several years of college, than were students who stayed in Hartford schools. Mary Kennedy, director of the National Center for Research on Teacher Training, cited a study of federal survey data showing that poor children in schools with high concentrations of impoverished children were twice as likely to score below the national average as poor children in low-concentration schools; the effect on non-poor students was even more pronounced. Gary Orfield cited a number of studies that showed similar effects for both black and Hispanic students. A study he conducted in San Francisco found that additional spending on the schools produced no positive effect, and possibly even a negative effect, on outcomes, whereas low-income Hispanic students who transferred to middle-class white schools did better than those who stayed behind.

There's a strikingly conservative conclusion to be drawn from the irreproachably liberal Orfield's claim: It is values and culture, not resources, that determine academic outcomes, and middle-class children bring with them to school values that produce success—self-discipline, a faith in institutions and their rules, and, above all, an expectation of success itself. Poor kids, by contrast, often reach school with the cognitive problems that come from having poorly educated or disengaged or preoccupied parents as well as with the assumptions appropriate to their experience. It wasn't only that Don Carso's students hadn't been to the mall or seen a river; they lived in a world in which middle-class success was virtually unimaginable. Eddie Davis would say that the cure for these harmful and limiting values lies in the culture of the school itself. But Carso's reluctant response was that even a well-run school cannot be impervious to the baleful influences of the world outside. And the concentration-of-poverty argument implies that all students suffer in a school where a large number of them are deeply disadvantaged.

But, of course, the inner-city children who go to a middle-class school during the day go home to their world of troubles at night. If McDonough can't shelter Connie from the effects of her chaotic home life, then is it reasonable to expect a suburban school to do much better? The defense in *Sheff* argued that neither Orfield's San Francisco study nor Project Concern showed any real correlation between desegregation and achievement, and it cited one respected study that concluded that "recent research has not lent credence" to the proposition that minority children are likely to be "influenced by their middle class peers' stronger orientation toward achievement." The state also relied heavily on the work of David Armor, a scholar who has carved out a perennial place for himself in desegregation cases by arguing that virtually all variation in academic outcome is determined by socioeconomic status. "A good strategy for improving the academic performance of students is to improve their socioeconomic conditions," Armor testified, adding that schools, of course, could not do much in that department.

Armor has been denounced as a hired gun, and his research may be questionable; but it is undeniable that neither desegregation nor school reform, nor financing, nor any intervention, weighs very heavily in determining academic outcomes compared with a student's socioeconomic status. Even so pervasive an institution as school is less influential than a child's home and family environment. Acknowledging this truth, however, doesn't make school irrelevant; what it does mean is that the way you think about school must be linked to a larger design to uproot inner-city poverty. If it's true that what makes contemporary urban poverty so intractable is what Orfield calls "the self-perpetuating cycle of racial isolation," then the larger design must involve breaking that cycle. Certainly that's the way Don Carso or Gladys Hernandez would formulate the problem. And if you accept this finding—that racial isolation and academic underachievement and poverty are inseparable—you conclude that although desegregation is only a partial solution, separate but equal is no solution at all.

The Hopewell School, in Glastonbury, is an idyllic place, set on sprawling fields that abut a seventeen-acre nature center. The classrooms are rich with computer power. Oddly enough, though, the Glastonbury schools actually spend slightly less money per capita than the Hartford schools. Much of Hartford's money, it's true, goes to security and special-ed and bilingual classes, rather than to teachers and textbooks. But Peter Maluk, Hopewell's principal, was not shedding crocodile tears when he took me on a tour of the school and pointed out all the things that Clark, his "sister" school in Hartford's slums, had and he didn't—a big library, an auditorium, a cafeteria.

The shortage of space obviously wasn't proving crippling. On the statewide math exam, 1 percent of Maluk's fourth-graders had scored in the remedial range; 89 percent had registered "excellent." His students did only a little bit worse in writing and reading. But Hopewell was not a more "effective" school than McDonough. The kids in Glastonbury were simply replicating their parents' success, as the kids in Hartford were on their way to replicating their parents' failure.

Maluk fetched a sigh and said, "There's a sense of hopelessness at times about how you reach a conclusion that works"

Peter Maluk is not unconscious of his good fortune and of the misery next door, but thinking about it makes him gloomy and fearful. He is a big man, slightly ponderous, with watery eyes. "Anything that's going to be forced is going to cause a lot of agitation," he said. He mentioned Boston; everyone in Glastonbury talked about Boston, which was only 100 miles away and whose mid-Seventies agony over forced busing had not faded from memory. When he talks about Hartford, the first thing that comes to his mind is "the gangs and the drive-by shootings." And this phrase, too, was used so often in Glastonbury that it might as well have been a single word with dashes in it. Many of these people work in Hartford, but from the way they talked about it the city might as well have been the nightmarish setting of *Blade Runner.* Maluk agrees that the kids in Hartford deserve something better; in fact, he said, he often found himself thinking of a half-serious suggestion he recalled William Buckley making in the late Sixties to the effect that poor children be

taken from their parents and placed in a more salubrious setting. But coercing the inner-city parents didn't seem like a much better idea than coercing the suburbs. Maluk fetched a sigh and said, "There's a sense of hopelessness at times about how you reach a conclusion that works."

One of Hopewell's fifth-grade teachers, Clara Dudley, who had helped forge the sister-school relationship with Clark, told me the kids from the two schools had recently had to meet at neutral locations, since many of the parents of Hopewell students were simply too freaked out by the non-stop accounts of gang violence and drive-by shootings. Even the year before, Dudley said, parents had written letters saying things like, "You warrant that the bus will drive to the front door of the school, that the children will proceed directly from the bus into the school . . ." Dudley shook her head at the pusillanimity. It was true, she admitted, that a little girl had been "abducted" across the street from the school; but the bus "always parks on the school side of the street." That must have soothed a lot of parental concern.

Glastonbury has been somewhat more willing to welcome the huddled masses of Hartford than it has been to join them. The town was one of the earliest recipients of students from Project Concern. Now there are some sixty students—from elementary through high school—attending Glastonbury schools through the program. Two Project Concern students I spoke to, both high school seniors, said that they had never experienced any racial tension at school. Other students, though, had objected when the drama club mounted a production of *Peter Pan* and all the Native Americans turned out to be African Americans. The superintendent had agreed that *Peter Pan* wasn't really an appropriate play, what with all the stereotypes.

Faced with the reality that suburban parents won't send their children to the inner city, frustrated proponents of desegregation, like Gerald Tirozzi or Don Carso, often suggest, half-seriously, that Hartford's schools, or even Hartford itself, simply be evacuated; the overwhelming imperative to free children from an imprisoning environment lends an air of plausibility even to such doomsday scenarios. A less drastic solution would be an updated form of the 1965 Harvard plan, in which thousands of Hartford students would be dispersed to the suburbs while some modest combination of suburban and inner-city students would attend urban magnet schools. This kind of one-way desegregation plan—desegregation as dispersal—has become fairly common in recent years; St. Louis, for example, has just such a system.

Such solutions don't meet the test of ideological purity. Charles Willie, a scholar who helped craft Boston's desegregation plan, has denounced one-way plans, such as that in St. Louis, as evidence of "goal displacement," in which the goal of least offensive to whites replaces that of most helpful to blacks. Why should whites, the historical beneficiary of the oppression of blacks, benefit once again from unequally shared burdens? But that raises the question of what desegregation is *for.* Is desegregation about redress, about righting ancient wrongs? If so, where does that leave Hartford's Puerto Rican immigrants or, for that matter, its Jamaicans? And what about the middle-class black suburbanites in a place like Prince Georges County, in Maryland, who see no point in traversing the area to integrate a school with middle-class whites? But if desegregation is understood, alternatively, as a means to pierce the thick walls of isolation that perpetuate inner-city poverty, then a largely one-way system isn't racist at all, though the burden may not be shared equally.

I n his State of the State speech in January 1993, Governor Lowell Weicker made a startling admission: "The racial and economic isolation in Connecticut's school system is indisputable. Whether this segregation came about through the chance of historical boundaries or economic forces beyond the control of the state or whether it came about through private decisions or in spite of the best educational efforts of the state, what matters is that it is here and must be dealt with." According to Gerald Tirozzi, Weicker had initially thought of admitting the state's guilt in *Sheff v. O'Neill.* In the end, he backed off, granting the justice of the complaint while excusing the state from actual culpability. Weicker proposed that the state do voluntarily what it might otherwise be compelled to do at the end of the judicial sword. He suggested that the state be divided into regions, and that each of these regions initiate a planning process that would result in the satisfaction of numerical goals for desegregation. It was an amazingly bold proposal; however, by the time the state legislature got through with it, the numerical goals were gone, as was the very word "desegregation."

I attended a few of the early meetings of the local advisory committees that form the base of Connecticut's voluntary process; they did not inspire hope. The Glastonbury committee, rather than devising means of bringing more minority students to the town's schools, or more minority families to the town itself, was engaged in an honest liberal dither over the supposed instances of racism, like *Peter Pan,* that made the schools inhospitable to the few minority students already there. The Hartford committee, rather than pondering the means of access to the suburban schools, was drawing up a mock-epic listing of the city's attractions, the lures with which it would snare suburban students—the parks, the symphony, the river, the municipal golf courses, "the video collection in the public library," the "fire safety company." By the end of the evening they were touting "the only methadone program in the region." It was a perfect proof of the futility of voluntary solutions, but they were doing precisely what the legislation had proposed. Even people in and around Hartford who fear the stiff goad of judicial decree generally expect the voluntary process to be a colossal waste of time.

Connecticut, then, is unlikely to desegregate of its own free will. The best that can be hoped is that should Judge Harry Hammer find for the plaintiffs in *Sheff,* he will craft a remedy with an eye to maximizing minority access to suburban schools, rather than sheer mathematical equality. In fact, John Brittain, the law professor who has worked for the plaintiffs, suggests a remedy in which up to one quarter of Hartford's students would be dispersed to the suburbs while the state would fund the construction of ten new magnet schools located in desirable sites in Hartford, including the Trinity College campus and a site near Aetna's downtown headquarters. Even then, said

Brittain, "racially identifiable" schools, both white and non-white, would remain. If this is too much collective responsibility to ask the suburbs to accept, then there's probably not much hope for desegregation.

One just criticism of mandatory-desegregation remedies is that they treat the symptom but not the disease; school desegregation, that is, has not produced residential desegregation. Blacks (and, to a lesser extent, Hispanics) are more intensely segregated than any American ethnic group has ever been, inhabiting a parallel, and very unequal, world of their own. Describing Atlanta, Gary Orfield wrote that housing patterns "defined separate educational, social and economic worlds in which young people and their families had profoundly different sets of opportunities." Orfield has little to say about the self-destructive character of ghetto life, but perhaps what is usually described as "the culture of poverty" is, in fact, "the culture of isolation."

It is vain to expect schooling by itself to cure the pathologies of the inner city. Ghetto families need access to a middle-class setting even more than their children need access to a middle-class school. The peculiar American model of the impoverished central city ringed by prosperous suburbs not only isolates the urban poor in an abandoned world but ensures that the suburbanite will feel no sense of common destiny with the city-dweller; and, of course, it denies the city access to the resources of the white-collar class that it nourishes. In a new book, *Cities Without Suburbs,* David Rusk argues that the isolation and "hyperconcentration" of the poor in our great and growing urban ghettos create conditions that are impervious to reform and that ensure further ghettoization. The old cities of the Northeast and Midwest, Rusk says, cannot save themselves through such forms of internal development as enterprise zones, school reform, and so on. "In baldest terms," he concludes, "sustained success requires moving poor people from bad city neighborhoods to good suburban neighborhoods and moving dollars from wealthy suburban governments to poorer city governments."

Separate but equal proposes to build on isolation as a source of strength; that claim sounds like an admission of defeat

---

Rusk's neo-integrationism will have to make its way in a hostile world. Many blacks now speak with an almost perverse longing of the good old days of legal apartheid, when the black community was, perforce, self-reliant and self-governing. It was also, of course, supremely unequal; and it tries the imagination to suppose that, with a fairer distribution of resources, inner-city Hartford and our innumerable other ghettos would rediscover their capacity for self-reliance. Separate but equal proposes to build on isolation, to accept it as a source of strength and solidarity. That claim, no matter how it is phrased, sounds like an admission of defeat.

And desegregation scarcely has a constituency at all among whites. Even liberals schooled on the struggle for civil rights have retreated in the face of black separatism; and the sort of "social engineering" epitomized by busing has fallen deeply out of fashion. In fact, the Democratic agenda on urban poverty has been borrowed in large part from neo-conservatives like Charles Murray, who insists that the only civil right that counts is access to the marketplace, and conservative educators like William Bennett, who believes that an infusing of character, of standards and self-discipline, is enough to save inner-city schools.

But what does all this talk about personal values, whether from the left or the right of the separate-but-equal spectrum, have to do with the children in Don Carso's class? It is not their fault that they arrive at McDonough already a year or two behind the children at Hopewell; and it's not McDonough's fault that they leave the school just as far behind, or worse. Even with more rigorous schooling and more computers, or more racial and ethnic solidarity, McDonough will not cure what ails these students. If equal opportunity means anything for these children and for others like them throughout urban America, it must mean access to a different environment.

In the forty years since *Brown,* desegregation has not become irrelevant. But the *idea* of desegregation has been shaken by a crisis of faith, and by a contraction of sympathies. A teacher at McDonough, surveying the farcical deliberations of Connecticut's voluntary process, says sadly, "There's not enough good will to go around." The remark has an ominous ring of truth.

Contradictions of Identity: Education and the Problem of Racial Absolutism

CAMERON McCARTHY

Cameron McCarthy is an associate professor in the Department of Curriculum, University of Illinois–Urbana-Champaign, Illinois.

Theorists espousing new paradigms of race-relations analysis rooted in Eurocentric and Afrocentric philosophies have contributed to the general hardening of both the popular and the intellectual discourse on inequality in schooling. A particular failing of these emergent theories of racial inequality is their tendency toward essentialist, or single-cause, explanations of minority disadvantage. That is, these educational theorists tend to explain differences in the educational, cultural, and political behavior of minority and majority youth by reference to race only.

This article offers a critique of tendencies toward dogmatism and essentialism in current educational theories of racial inequality. I argue that, paradoxically, you cannot understand race by looking at race alone. Different gender, class, and ethnic interests intersect with racial coordination and affiliation. Programmatic reforms that underestimate the powerful role of nuance, contradiction, and heterogeneity within and between racial groups in education are not likely to succeed either in reducing racial antagonism or ameliorating educational inequities.[1]

The Limits of Ethnic Affiliation

In a recent *New York Times Book Review* article, Henry Louis Gates relates a story that has made its rounds in the jazz world. The story takes the form of an answer to what Gates calls "the perennial question: Can you really tell?" The question is about racial authenticity and racial origins and whether they can predict cultural behavior and explain the meaning of style. Can you really tell who is the black one, who is the white one? Can you *really* tell? According to Gates (1991),

The great black jazz trumpeter Roy Elridge once made a wager with the critic Leonard Feather that he could distinguish white musicians from black ones—blindfolded. Mr. Feather duly dropped the needle onto a variety of record albums whose titles and soloists were concealed from the trumpeter. More than half the time, Elridge guessed wrong. (24 November, 1)

What Gates fails to mention is that this blindfold test has been conducted by *Down Beat* jazz magazine for well over a quarter century now and that white jazz musicians who take it also confuse black musicians with white ones and vice versa. The problem of racial origins and racial authenticity is a problem all around. The elusiveness of racial identity not only affects blacks; it also affects whites. Racial identities can never be gathered up in one place as a final cultural property. And, as we approach the end of the twentieth century, what seemed like stable white ethnicities and heritages in an earlier era are now entering a zone of recoding and redefinition. Michael Omi and Howard Winant (1991) put the problem of waning white ethnicity in the following terms:

Most whites do not experience their ethnicity as a definitive aspect of their social identity. They perceive it dimly and irregularly, picking and choosing among its varied strands to exercise, as Mary Waters (1990) suggests, an "ethnic option." The specifically ethnic components of white identity are fast receding with each generation's additional remove from the old country. Unable to speak the language of their immigrant forbears, uncommitted to ethnic endogamy, and unaware of their ancestors' traditions (if in fact they can still identify their ancestors as, say, Polish or Scots, rather than a combination of four or five European—and non-European!—groups) whites undergo a racializing panethnicity as "Euro-Americans." (17)

These stories of racial/ethnic instability come at a critical juncture in debates over racial inequality, racial identity, and curriculum reform in U.S. education. They also point to the crisis regarding theories of race

From *The Clearing House*, May/June 1995, pp. 297-300. © 1995 by the Helen Dwight Reid Educational Foundation. Reprinted by permission of Heldref Publications, 1319 Eighteenth Street, NW, Washington, DC 20036-1802.

and ways of thinking about race in education. But it is also, paradoxically, a time in which people talk with a peculiar racial and ethnic certainty. The world is a vast Lacanian mirror in which people who believe in racial purity and the idea of racial essence see themselves as reflections of their ancestors. It is the perfect image, the snapshot of history collected in the nuclear-family photo album. It is the story of the singular origin, the singular essence, the one, true primary cause.

The old Marxist and neo-Marxist orthodoxies of class and economic primacy in education debates are rapidly being replaced by the new panethnic cultural assertion of racial origins. The proponents of Western civilization and Eurocentrism—as well as their critics, the proponents of Afrocentrism—now argue for the heart and soul of the educational enterprise. (This is not to suggest, of course, that there is an equivalence in the deployment of material and political resources here, for, in some ways, the playing out of this conflict involves a certain encirclement of black intellectual thinking.) Conservative educators like Diane Ravitch join conservative ideologues such as George Will in insisting, for instance, that "Our country is a branch of European civilization. . . . 'Eurocentricity' is right, in American curricula and consciousness, because it accords with the facts of our history, and we—and Europe—are fortunate for that" (1989, 3). Europe, through this legerdemain, is collapsed into the United States without any difficulty. History and tradition in this country are interchangeable with those of Europe.

On the other hand, Afrocentric theorists such as Molefi Asante (1987) argue for the panethnic unity of all black people of the diaspora; he points to the origins of African people in the "spatial reality of Africa." We are in the historical moment of what Stanley Aronowitz and Henry Giroux (1991) call the "politics of clarity." The Afrocentrics and Eurocentrics argue for school reform based on the narrow limits of ethnic affiliation. For the Afrocentric, the intolerable levels of minority failure in schools have to do with the fact that minority (particularly, African American) cultural heritages are suppressed in the curriculum. Black students fail because schools assault their identities and destabilize their sense of self and agency. (A good example of this thesis is to be found in *Countering the Conspiracy to Destroy Black Boys* by Jawanza Kunjufu [1983/1985].)

For the proponents of Western civilization, Western cultural emphasis in the curriculum is colorblind. Black students fail because of the cultural deprivation that exists in their homes and in their communities. Literacy in Western civilization would be the best antidote for failure among the black poor. As E. D. Hirsch (1987) suggests, broad cultural literacy would help disadvantaged black youth enter the mainstream.

This article is a critique of the tendency toward essentialist, or single-cause, explanations of racial inequality and racial identity in education. (By *essentialism*, I refer to the tendency in current mainstream and radical writing on race to treat social groups as stable or homogeneous entities. Racial groups such as "Asians," or "Latinos," or "blacks" are discussed as though members of these groups possessed some innate and invariant set of characteristics that set them apart from each other and from "whites.") Feminist theorists such as Coco Fusco (1988) and Teresa DeLauretis (1984) have critiqued this tendency in mainstream research. Fusco (1988), for example, maintains that differences in the political and cultural behavior of minority women and men are determined by social and historical contingencies and not by some checklist of innate, biological, or cultural characteristics.

Current tendencies toward essentialism in the analysis of race relations significantly inhibit a dynamic understanding of race relations and raced-based politics in education and society. Common to these approaches to race and education, as well as some of the more recent formulations around multiculturalism, is a tendency to "undertheorize" race—racial antagonism is seen as a kind of deposit or disease that is triggered by some deeper flaw of character or society. I would like to turn the discussion of race away from the current emphasis on deprivation and away from cultural and economic essentialism. Instead, I would like to point to the fact that racial differences are produced; they are, as Edward Said (1992) points out, "the product of human work." I am therefore interested in the ways in which moral leadership and social power are exercised in the concrete and the ways in which regimes of racial domination and subordination are constructed and resisted in education.

The theoretical and pedagogical issues concerning race are complex and therefore require a relational approach to analysis and intervention in unequal relations in school. We must pay special attention to contradiction, discontinuity, and nuance within and between embattled social groups (what I have called elsewhere the process of *nonsynchrony*). These discontinuities in the needs and interests of minority and majority groups are, for example, expressed in the long history of tension and hostility between the black and the white working classes in this country. Also of crucial importance within this framework are the issues of the "contradictory location" (Wright 1978) of the "new" black middle class and the role of neoconservative black and white intellectuals in redefining racial inequality toward the ideal of a colorblind society (McCarthy 1990).

Just as important for a relational and nonessentialist approach to race and curriculum is the fact that minority women and girls have experiences of racial inequality that are radically different from those of their male counterparts. (Michelle Wallace, in her book *Invisibility Blues* [1990], calls these dynamics "negative variations.") A relational and nonessentialist approach to the discussion of racial identities allows for a more complex understanding of the educational and political behavior of minority groups. Such a complex understanding of racial inequality, focusing on the contradictory nature of racial subjectivity and identity and the dynamic intersection of race with class, gender, and nation, must be taken into account in strategies for improving race relations in schools.

Contradictions in the Experience of Race

As Michael Burawoy (1981) and Mokubong Nkomo (1984) make clear with respect to South Africa, economic divisions between the black underclass from the Bantustan and their more middle-class counterparts working for the South African state (the police, nurses, Bantustan bureaucrats, etc.) often undermine black unity in the face of racial oppression and exclusion. Similarly, in the United States, some middle-class minority intellectuals such as Shelby Steele and Thomas Sowell have spoken out against affirmative action and minority scholarship programs in higher education, suggesting that such policies discriminate against white males. A case in point is a 1990 ruling by U.S. Department of Education Assistant Secretary for Civil Rights Michael Williams, which maintained that it was illegal for a college or university to offer a scholarship only to minority students (Jaschik 1990). The irony of this situation is underlined by the fact that the assistant secretary for civil rights is a black man. In fact, without these scholarships a number of very talented minority individuals would not be able to pursue higher education. Here again, the "point man" on a policy that effectively undermines the material interests of African Americans and other minority groups is a neoconservative member of the emergent minority middle class.

Linda Grant (1984) calls attention to these discontinuities in terms of how gender operates in the classroom. Based on the findings from a study of face-to-face interactions in six desegregated elementary school classrooms in a midwestern industrial city, Grant concludes that "black females' experiences in desegregated schools . . . differ from those of other race-gender groups and cannot be fully understood by extrapolating from the research on females or research on blacks." Grant contends that the teachers (all women—three blacks and three whites) she observed did not relate to their black students and white students in any consistent or monolithic way. Grant notes particularly the way language was used in the classroom and the manner of informal exchanges between teachers and students:

> Although generally compliant with teachers' rules, black females were less tied to teachers than white girls were and approached them only when they had a specific need to do so. White girls spent more time with teachers, prolonging questions into chats about personal issues. Black girls contacts were briefer and more task related. (1984, 107)

Although these teachers tended to avoid contact with black male students, they still identified at least one black male student in each of their classrooms as a "superstar." In none of the six classrooms was any of the black girls identified as a high academic achiever. Instead, Grant maintains, black girls were typified as "average achievers" and assigned to average or below-average ability groups. Gender differences interacted with race when teachers evaluated, diagnosed, labeled, and tracked their students. Grant therefore points to a hidden cost of desegregation for black girls: "Although they are usually the top students in all-black classes, they lose this stature to white children in desegregated rooms" (1984, 109).

Beyond Dogmatism and Essentialism

The point that I want to make here, then, is that you cannot explain educational, cultural, or political behavior based on assumptions about race alone. Different gender and class interests and experiences within minority and majority groups are important in forming people's attitudes. The findings of researchers such as Grant, Nkomo, and Omi and Winant help to clarify the complex workings of racial thinking in schools. These researchers directly challenge mainstream, single-group studies of inequality that have tended to isolate race from gender and class. They also challenge accounts of inequality that suggest that you can understand the cultural behavior of minority groups based on economic location or racial origins alone. Instead, the work of these researchers underscores the need for comparative analysis of how race, class, and gender have interacted in education. Using a nonessentialist approach to the study of inequality in schooling, we see that different race-class-gender groups not only have qualitatively different experiences in schools but actually exist in a state of tension regarding each other; they actively compete with each other, receive different forms of rewards, sanctions, and evaluations, and ultimately are structured into different futures. The critical theoretical, methodological, and pedagogical tasks then, as Hall (1980) suggests, involve "radically decoding and mapping" the specific relations and nuances of particular historical and institutional contexts: "One needs to know how different groups were inserted historically, and the relations which have tended to erode and transform, or to preserve these distinctions through time . . . . Racial categories *alone* will *not* explain these" (339).

What is abundantly clear is that monolithic or homogeneous strategies of curriculum reform that attempt to ignore or avoid the contradictions of race at the institutional level will be of limited usefulness to minority youth. New approaches to race-relations reform must begin with a more sophisticated and robust concept of the dynamic relations between minority and majority students and teachers. Efforts to get beyond the essentialism and dogmatism in current theories would be a very good place to start.

The multifaceted nature of race relations requires a

many-sided response. I would like, for example, to see multicultural theorists delve into analyses of curriculum that explore critical thinking, school effectiveness, and institutional organization and to see them investigate the urban ethnographic work of researchers such as Michele Fine (1990) and Mercer Sullivan (1990), who are looking at socioeconomic contexts of urban schooling. These dynamics of race, class, and gender are interwoven unevenly into the social fabric of the United States—its educational system, economy, and state. This uneven interaction is present in the daily encounters that minority and majority people have in institutional and social settings. Thus, for example, the experience of educational inequality for a black male middle-class youth from a two-parent family is qualitatively different from that of a black working-class female from a single-parent household.

It is not enough, however, merely to critique current theoretical and programmatic approaches to race and educational reform. Contemporary discussions on schooling must emphasize the need for more inclusive, affirmative practices that take seriously the different needs, interests, and desires of minority women and men and urban working-class youth. First, we must seriously insist that urban schools meet their social contract vis-à-vis African American and Latino students and parents: a much greater effort ought to be placed on equality of access to instructional and learning opportunities and equality of educational outcomes. We need a more dynamic approach to what is learned in school that gets us beyond the essentialisms of Eurocentrism and Afrocentrism and the content-addition models of multiculturalism. Such an approach should be interdisciplinary and would emphasize heterogeneity of perspectives, intellectual challenge and debate, and vigorous interrogation of received knowledge and traditions.

Curriculum reform should mean that students have autonomy with respect to multiple sources of information rather than their having to accept corrective bits of knowledge presented as already settled truth—for example, the good realism of multiculturalism and Afrocentrism versus the bad fiction of stereotypes. Eurocentrism presents us with a similarly unwarranted, calcified vision of canonical texts and the history of the West. Ultimately, there is a desperate need for schools, school districts, and university teacher education programs to develop strategies for interpreting the urban context by closely collaborating with minority parents and communities. These strategies should lead to specific curriculum and instructional initiatives that give priority to the educational needs of disadvantaged youth.

Equally important, we must remember that contradictions in racial and identity formation also apply to whites. Much work needs to be done to understand, and to intervene in, the ways in which whites are seen as "white" in the language and the symbolic and material structures that dominate culture in the Western world. There is a need to move beyond static definitions of whites and blacks in existing research in education (Fusco 1988; Giroux 1992; McCarthy and Crichlow 1993; Roman 1993). This means, for example, that we should not continue to see all whites as the "other" of multicultural curriculum reform. In the end, it means that in every local setting, particularly in urban areas, we must find the moral, ethical, material, and political resources for a deep investment in our schools.

NOTE

1. My arguments against ethnic absolutism are presented more extensively in McCarthy, "The Problem with Origins" in Peter McLaren and Christine Sleeter, eds. *Multiculturalism and Critical Pedagogy*, SUNY Press, forthcoming.

REFERENCES

Aronowitz, S., and H. Giroux. 1991. The politics of clarity. *Afterimage 19*(3): 5, 17.

Asante, M. 1987. *The Afrocentric idea*. Philadelphia: Temple University Press.

Burawoy, M. 1981. The capitalist state in South Africa: Marxist and sociological perspectives on race and class. In M. Zeitlin (Ed.), *Political power and social theory* (Vol. 2, pp. 279–335). Greenwich, Conn.: JAI Press.

DeLauretis, T. 1984. *Alice doesn't: Feminism, semiotics and cinema*. Bloomington: Indiana University Press.

Fine, M. 1990. *Framing dropouts*. Albany: SUNY Press.

Fusco, C. 1988. Fantasies of oppositionality. *Screen 29* (4): 80–95.

Gates, H. 1991. "Authenticity," or the lesson of little tree. *New York Times Book Review* (24 November): 1.

Giroux, H. 1992. *Border crossings: Cultural workers and the politics of education*. New York: Routledge.

Grant, L. 1984. Black females' "place" in desegregated classrooms. *Sociology of Education* 57: 98–111.

Hall, S. 1980. Race, articulation, and societies structured in dominance. In *Sociological theories: Race and colonialism*, 305–45. Paris: UNESCO.

Hirsch, E. D. 1987. *Cultural literacy*. Boston: Houghton Mifflin.

JanMohamed, A., and D. Lloyd. 1987. Introduction: Minority discourse—What is to be done? *Cultural Critique* 7: 5–17.

Jaschik, S. 1990. Scholarships set up for minority students are called illegal. *Chronicle of Higher Education* 37 (15): A1.

Kunjufu, J. 1983/1986. *Countering the conspiracy to destroy black boys*. 2 vols. Chicago: African American Images.

McCarthy, C. 1990. *Race and curriculum*. London: Falmer Press.

McCarthy, C., and W. Crichlow. 1993. *Race, identity and representation in education*. New York: Routledge.

Nkomo, M. 1984. *Student culture and activism in black South African universities*. Westport, Conn.: Greenwood Press.

Omi, M., and H. Winant. 1991. *Contesting the meaning of race in the post-civil rights period*. Paper presented at the Annual Meeting of the American Sociological Association, August 23–27.

Roman, L. 1993. White is a color! White defensiveness, postmodernism, and anti-racist pedagogy. In *Race, identity and representation in education*, edited by C. McCarthy and W. Crichlow. New York: Routledge.

Said, E. 1992. Identity, authority, and freedom: The potentate and the traveler. *Transition* 54: 4–18.

Sandoval, C. 1991. U.S. third world feminism: Theory and method of oppositional consciousness in the postmodern world. *Genders*, 10, 1–24.

Sullivan, M. 1990. *Getting paid: Youth crime and work in the inner city*. Ithaca: Cornell University Press.

Wallace, M. 1990. *Invisibility blues*. New York: Verso.

Waters, M. 1990. *Ethnic options: Choosing identities in America*. Berkeley: University of California Press.

West, C. 1993. *Race matters*. Boston: Beacon Press.

Will, G. 1989. Eurocentricity and the school curriculum. *Baton Rouge Morning Advocate* (18 December): 3.

Wright, E. O. 1978. *Class, crisis and the state*. London: New Left Review.

All-Black Schools Provide Role Models: Is This the Solution?

RUSSELL BRADSHAW

Russell Bradshaw is an assistant professor in the Secondary, Adult, and Business Education Department, Lehman College, CUNY, Bronx, New York.

Traditional two-parent families in America, reflecting a worldwide trend, are in a serious state of decline (Bronfenbrenner 1991). Although disputing causes, most experts agree that children's welfare is seriously suffering from this development (Etzioni 1992; Popenoe 1988, 1993; Leach 1994; Elkind 1992). Those families with the least resources and support systems are suffering the most (Wilson 1987; Moynihan 1993[1]; Carnegie 1994), particularly African Americans and other "involuntary" minorities (Ogbu 1978; Ingrassia 1994; Gresham 1994).

Erik Erikson's psychosocial theory of development maintains that appropriate role models are necessary for children, particularly during adolescence (Powell 1983; Comer and Poussaint 1992). Yet in 1989 more than half of all black children, almost one-third of Hispanic children, and about 20 percent of white children lived in single-parent families (Lewin 1990; U.S. Census 1988). The figure for children living with a single parent who had *never* been married rose 85 percent between 1983 and 1993. In 1993, 6.3 million children were living in such homes, almost as many as the 6.8 million living with single parents who had been divorced, according to a recent U.S. Census report (U.S. Census 1993). This report also showed that the median two-parent family income was $43,578, as opposed to $9,272 for a never-married, single-parent family. This illustrates one of America's most urgent social problems: the lack of economic support and the absence of positive role models for many children, particularly inner-city black boys (Clark 1965; Rainwater and Yancey 1967; Kunjufu 1986; Moynihan 1993). An even more urgent problem is the increasing number of *zero-parent* children, concentrated in inner cities, where single mothers are becoming crack addicts, going to jail, or leaving their children for other reasons. These children now make up about 9 percent of all children (Gross 1992).

As successful minorities can now leave the inner city for the suburbs, as the traditional role of the priest or pastor in the community becomes weaker in a more secular and materialistic society, and as the extended-family network breaks down, there are few other successful male role models left to children in these families (Richman, Clark and Brown 1985; Poussaint 1987; Staples 1985; Wilson 1989; Lehmann 1991). Also, because women are usually paid less than men, most single-parent, father-absent homes are also economically disadvantaged (Model 1990; Gimenez 1990; Schmidt 1989; Etzioni 1992; Barton 1992; Popenoe 1988, 1993). A few authors, however, contend that the so-called postmodern family is actually a positive, evolutionary advancement from the repressive and binding modern (nuclear) family (Elkind 1992, 1994).

Single-Parent Minority Boys and School Discipline

One of education's most urgent concerns is closely associated with this socioeconomic development: the discipline problem in our schools (Shanker 1991, 1994). This problem is often specifically linked to students from poor, minority backgrounds, particularly boys (Fordham and Ogbu 1986; Holland 1989; Levine and Havighurst 1989; Poussaint 1987, 1990; Moynihan 1993).

These minority boys make up a disproportionately large percentage of behavioral problems and special education students (Gibson and Ogbu 1991; Racial harm 1990; Snider 1987; Gatto 1992). They are also expelled or drop out at much higher rates than other students (Le Compte 1987; Study finds 1988; Rumberger 1987; Johnson 1990; Kunjufu 1990; Shanker 1994).

Because of these correlations, educators and psychologists often assume there is a connection between discipline problems in schools and the lack of positive male role models at home (Wilkinson and O'Connor 1977; Johnson 1990; Moynihan 1993). In fact, Barton (1992) has advanced the idea of *parent-pupil ratio* in schools as being a simple measure predicting school quality.

Moynihan (1993) has attempted to summarize this research. He states that areas with higher concentrations of

From *The Clearing House*, January/February 1995, pp. 146-150. © 1995 by the Helen Dwight Reid Educational Foundation.
Reprinted by permission of Heldref Publications, 1319 Eighteenth Street, NW, Washington, DC 20036-1802.

single-parent families also have higher rates of violent crime, and the *correlation is so strong* that it supersedes the relationship between race and crime and even low income and crime. Nevertheless, Ogbu (1978) notes that in a "caste society" where race is historically linked to inferior socioeconomic position, these variables are difficult to separate.

In many cases, these "parentally disadvantaged" students bring to school the frustration, bitterness, and violence of their neighborhoods and homes (Hampton 1987; Mydans 1990; Stephenson 1993; Hobart 1994). This violence is evident even in kindergarten and elementary school (Violence rises 1990).

Mentors and Teachers As Role Models

Traditionally, the relationship between troubled young men and the lack of supportive and nurturing adult male figures in their lives has been recognized by mentoring programs such as the Big Brothers/Big Sisters of America program, Career Beginnings Program, Mentors, Inc., and 100 Black Men (Glass 1990; Marriot 1990; Freedman 1993). They link an adult male with a young man deprived of such a role model. The success of these and similar programs has been a particular source of inspiration for the current "black school" proposals.

In these schools, the adult male role model will be a major emphasis, as it has been in mentoring programs. This role model will address the lack of sex-role models and occupational role models in these boys' lives (Johnson 1990). A black male teacher or professional will counter the stereotype that black inner-city males are violent and aggressive, unemployed and unskilled, and welfare-dependent (Powell 1983).

New York, Chicago, Detroit, Milwaukee, and other cities are already developing these special "black schools" (All-male school 1991; Berger 1991; Johnson 1990). It is hoped they will positively influence school behavior and counteract boys' acting out in school because they lack a secure male role model at home. These students often end up in the criminal justice system rather than in school (Fiske 1989; Glaberson 1990; Terry 1993).

This situation indicates the need for male role models in the lives of boys. However, most psychological theories are based on the role model's being *in the family* or immediate social environment. It is a large leap to the assumption that having a role model in a distant, compulsory schoolroom for a few hours would also serve this function (Woodring 1989). Although teachers may help, they usually can't *replace* a father (Bronfenbrenner 1991; Etzioni 1992; Popenoe 1988, 1993).

Unfortunately, there is very little research on single-parent or zero-parent minority students in relationship to male role models in the classroom (Berger 1990). The few pilot studies that have been done (Holland 1989) may be reflecting a general tendency toward school improvement when *any* positive intervention is perceived by students and teachers.

However, one can turn to a related area of research to shed some light on the current debate: studies done on mentoring. Although mentoring and teaching are different, they are also similar in many ways. The research on mentoring (usually a one-on-one interaction) is more circumscribed than that on teaching, probably because it is easier to study than complex classroom interactions.

In many mentoring programs, success does *not* appear to be linked with the variables of race or sex. This result has been replicated in several programs (Alleman et al. 1987; Commonwealth Fund 1990; Marriot 1990). It is true that race, in particular, does influence *initial* pairing choices (mentors and "mentees" tend to pick each other from the same racial group [Becker and Carper 1956; Kantor 1977; Stenberg 1990]). However, these results only tend to indicate that the psychological process of identification—"likes attract likes"—is in operation. This phenomenon does not necessarily indicate that homogeneity in pairing leads to a *successful* mentoring relationship.

Caring and Being Available

The only variable that correlated with success in the program I am most familiar with—the CUNY/BOE Student Mentor Program (Bradshaw 1990)—was the *amount of time* the mentor spent with the high school student. This finding replicates Stenberg (1988), who found "availability of the mentor" to be the single most important predictor of success.

It may be hypothesized that amount of time spent with a young person represents attitudes of being available and of caring on the part of the mentor. This variable is also seen by Bronfenbrenner (1991) as being the most important in child-rearing situations in general, even superseding the existence of biological parents.

In general, therefore, the mentor research findings would seem to warn against an uncritical acceptance of the proposed schools where race and sex are the characteristics deemed most necessary for teachers. Instead, emphasis should be placed on a caring, nurturing attitude on the part of the teacher. This emphasis does not mean lowering expectations for students. It means that high goals can be achieved—even by students with low self-esteem—if based on a solid foundation of sincere concern exhibited by the teacher, as shown by Marva Collins (1982) in Chicago.

Although it is true that the ideal mentor/teacher for these students, especially boys, would be both caring *and* a member of the same sex and minority group (Stenberg 1990), this combination often proves elusive. If one is forced to choose between one or the other—between homogeneity of teacher and student or a caring attitude and availability—it appears clear that one should choose the latter. Unfortunately, in the real world, this *is* often the choice we must make.

Perhaps the most trenchant question at this point is a purely practical one: How many minority male teachers are available? Unfortunately, the answer is "not enough" (Berger 1990; Blacks disappearing 1990; Banks 1993a; Gay 1993). If we wish to address the needs of many single-parent black boys in the near future, then the model of the black male teacher is not viable: there are simply not enough black male teachers—caring or otherwise—to fill the need.

Therefore, although the current black-male schools appear to be a necessary and valuable alternative during the present acute crisis of the family, we should not delude ourselves by believing they could become a large-scale model. Nor *should* they become a model, since the issue of black segregation here is very real, as Kenneth Clark and the National Urban League have pointed out (Stevens 1990). By themselves, these schools are incapable of addressing the major, underlying causes of the problems facing black male students. We must especially find out what is causing the disintegration of American families, particularly black inner-city families.

The phenomenon of absent fathers is a problem of another order of magnitude than finding caring teachers. Even concerned teachers who try to be available for their students usually can't give the time and attention a father could. This problem must be dealt with on deeper structural levels in American society.

Social-Structure Causes

Probably the greatest problem our society faces today is the fact that most black infants are currently born to unmarried mothers, half of them to teenagers (Lewin 1990). The rate of illegitimacy has more than doubled since 1965. This situation disproportionately affects inner-city schools (Noll 1993; Weir 1993; Gay 1993; Woodring 1989).

If this social development is, in fact, the most basic indicator of many of the behavioral problems in inner-city schools, then the socioeconomic and historical causes of this dramatic demographic change must be recognized (Ogbu 1978; Model 1990; Staples 1985; Bronfenbrenner 1991; Etzioni 1992; Popenoe 1988, 1993). Extensive societal efforts will be required to eliminate this trend (Barkan 1991; Wilson 1987). For example, there is clearly some correlation between rapidly rising unemployment among young minority males in the inner city and their disinclination to get married (Model 1990; Wilson 1987; Moynihan 1993). There is also a disinclination among minority females to marry males who are perceived as having low status and low job prospects—and who may hamper them in achieving either a more secure marriage or higher welfare compensation (Poussaint 1990; Daniels 1989).

Improving the deteriorating conditions within inner-city families, and particularly black families, should be given the highest priority of all social programs in the United States. All other attempts to help black and minority students in school are doomed to be inadequate unless this basic condition is dealt with (Popenoe 1993; Moynihan 1993; Etzioni 1992). The most obvious solution is unfortunately the least implemented: creating jobs to replace the vanishing inner-city blue-collar jobs—or whatever their post-industrial equivalents would be. Keeping teenagers in school to keep them off the street, especially when potential job prospects still remain low, is not a viable solution and exacerbates school discipline problems (Wilkerson 1991; Wilson 1987; Gans 1993; Woodring 1989).

Compensatory special schools, no matter how successful, do not address the root cause of the father-absent families they are helping: poverty. This poverty is perpetuated by structural discrimination resulting in poor schools, lack of housing, jobs, and health care, and by unfortunate welfare policies (Schmidt 1989; Wilson 1987). A historical legacy of racism helps to perpetuate bias (Ogbu 1978; Banks 1993a). Continuing majority indifference to a wronged and suffering minority also lies behind the socioeconomic structures that maintain this unequal situation (Myrdal 1994; Galbraith 1992; Tobin 1992).

Realizing Our Interconnectedness

How do we overcome this unfortunate legacy? Only by all Americans' sharing a sense of oneness with the suffering of *any* group of citizens. Just as two-parent families from all races and socioeconomic classes are experiencing problems today, we must recognize that those families with the least resources will be most devastated.

We must realize that the inner-city poverty of today is almost as debilitating as the slavery that preceded it (Howard and Hammond 1985; McGrath and Weathers 1985; Wilson 1987). Black marriages and families cannot thrive under these hardships, especially when other general cultural values and pressures are already weakening the position of families and children in our society.

We must realize that even in our increasingly ego-centered modern society, *we are all interconnected.* Just as children from all groups will suffer if viable marriages and families are not reinforced and protected, so everyone will eventually suffer from any racial discrimination and poverty (Goldman 1990). In addition, minority children will soon make up a majority of all school-age children (Banks 1993b). Our futures will soon depend directly on the ability and will of America's multicultural children to pay and care for older people (Grant and Sleeter 1993); this is the so-called demographic imperative for multicultural perspectives.

A balanced multicultural curriculum in all our schools, not just in minority areas (New York State 1991), will help achieve the realization that we are all mutually dependent. Minority male teachers and mentors will also help many struggling students (Bradshaw 1990; Glass

1990; Marriot 1990). Most important, however, must be the acknowledgment by our cultural and political institutions that children thrive best in families where parents are not overly stressed and harried, where stable emotional commitments and a sense of caring are evident (Bronfenbrenner 1991; Leach 1994; Popenoe 1988).

Majority Americans must feel the same moral outrage and responsibility for the modern vestiges of slavery as many did during the Civil War (Kuzirian and Madaras 1985; Meier and Rudwick 1966). Most black people only migrated from the poverty of the rural plantation to the eventual poverty of the urban ghetto—where inner-city blue-collar and unskilled jobs have virtually disappeared (Lehmann 1991; Meier and Rudwick 1966; Wilkerson 1991; Wilson 1987). The deteriorating climate for children encountered in our mainstream society is even worse for black children. Although all minority group children suffer from cultural bias, Ogbu's "involuntary immigrant" groups, particularly African Americans, inevitably suffer the most.

The United States has never really addressed the problem that arose when slavery was abolished: How can America help restore the dignity, economic enterprise, and motivation of the only immigrant group in this country that was forced to move here against its will and then systematically subjected to discrimination for hundreds of years (Elkins 1976; DeParle 1990; Leary 1991; Lee 1990; Ogbu 1978)? Indeed, our Civil War is still being fought. Although most casualties are physically confined to the inner cities at present (Mydans 1990), its insidious influence is steadily weakening the total fabric of American democracy and making a mockery of the most powerful society in the world.

As the weakening of the family and a deteriorating cultural climate for children pervade our entire society, minority families, and black families in particular, are disintegrating at an alarming rate. Creating alternative schools that will expose children, especially boys, to positive role models will help, but certainly not cure, these deep-seated cultural and structural problems.

NOTE

1. See also recent debate on illegitimacy, when Moynihan, in July 1994, commented on the fact that nationally, 70 percent of all juveniles in state reform institutions come from fatherless homes. Moynihan pointed out that in 1950, 4 percent of all children were born out of wedlock; today that figure is about 30 percent. If this trend continues at the same rate, by 2000 over half of all children will be born to single parents. If he were a biologist, Moynihan said, he would refer to such drastic behavioral change as leading to *speciation*—the evolutionary process by which new species are formed.

REFERENCES

Alleman, E., I. Newman, H. Huggins, and L. Carr. 1987. The impact of race on mentoring relationships. *International Journal of Mentoring* (later, journal name changed to *Mentoring International*) 1(2): 20–23.

All-male school gets green light in Detroit. 1991. *New York Times* (1 March): 16.

Banks, J. 1993a. The canon debate, knowledge construction, and multi-cultural education. *Educational Researcher* (June/July): 4–14.

———. 1993b. Multicultural literacy and curriculum reform. In *Taking sides: Clashing views on controversial educational issues*. 7th ed. Edited by J. W. Noll, 219–22. Guilford, Conn.: Dushkin.

Barkan, J. 1991. Saved from the fate of the Swedes. *New York Teacher* (24 June): 19.

Barton, P. E. 1992. *America's smallest school: The family*. Princeton: Educational Testing Service.

Becker, H., and J. Carper. 1956. The development of identification with an organization. *American Journal of Sociology* 61: 289–98.

Berger, J. 1990. Pessimism lurks as schools try "affirmative action." *New York Times* (27 Feb.): B1, 3.

———. 1991. New York panel backs school for minority men. *New York Times* (10 Jan.): 1, B7.

Blacks disappearing from colleges. 1990. *On Campus* (April): 1.

Bradshaw, R. 1990. Mentoring for teacher candidates: Proceed with caution. *Mentoring International* 4(4): 18–20, 31.

Bronfenbrenner, U. 1991. Sources of competence and character: What do families do? *Family Affairs* (Winter/Spring).

Carnegie Corporation of New York. 1994. *Starting points: Meeting the needs of our youngest children*. New York: Carnegie Corporation.

Clark, K. 1965. *Dark Ghetto: Dilemmas of social power*. New York: Harper and Row.

Collins, M. 1982. *The Marva Collins approach*. Los Angeles: Jeremy P. Tarcher.

Comer, J. P., and A. F. Poussaint. 1992. *Raising black children*. New York: Plume.

Commonwealth Fund. 1990. *Research on mentoring*. T. Maloney and M. McKaughan, eds. New York: Harkness House. (Louis Harris and Associates, Inc., Survey #892010; Project directors: H. Taylor and R. Bass.)

Daniels, L. 1989. Experts foresee a social gap between sexes among blacks. *New York Times* (5 Feb.): 1, 30.

DeParle, J. 1990. Talk grows of government being out to get blacks. *New York Times* (29 Oct.): B6.

Elkind, D. 1992. Why kids have a lot to cry about. *Psychology Today* (May/June): 38–41, 80–81.

———. 1994. *Ties that stress: The new family in balance*. Cambridge: Harvard University Press.

Elkins, S. 1976. *Slavery: A problem in American institutional life*. Chicago: University of Chicago.

Etzioni, A. 1992. A "social science court" could inform debate over family values. *Chronicle of Higher Education* (7 Oct.).

Fiske, E. 1989. About education: Can money spent on schools save money that would be spent on prisons. *New York Times* (27 Sept.): B8.

Foley, D. E. 1991. Reconsidering anthropological explanations of ethnic school failure. *Anthropology and Education Quarterly* 22(March): 1.

Fordham, S., and J. Ogbu. 1986. Black students school success: Coping with the burden of "acting white." *Urban Review* 18: 176–206.

Freedman, M. 1993. *The kindness of strangers: Adult mentors, urban youth and the new voluntarism*. San Francisco: Jossey-Bass.

Galbraith, J. K. 1992. *The Culture of Contentment*. New York: Houghton Mifflin.

Gans, H. J. 1993. Scholars role in planning a "post-work society." *Chronicle of Higher Education* (9 June): B3.

Gatto, J. E. 1992. *Dumbing us down: The hidden curriculum of compulsory schooling*. Philadelphia: New Society.

Gay, G. 1993. Ethnic minorities and educational equality. In *Multicultural education: Issues and perspectives*, 2nd ed. Edited by J. A. Banks and C. A. M. Banks, 171–94. Boston: Allyn & Bacon.

Gibson, M., and J. Ogbu. 1991. *Minority status and schooling: A comparative study of immigrant and involuntary minorities*. New York: Garland.

Gimenez, M. E. 1990. The feminization of poverty: Myth or reality? *Social Justice* 17(3).

Glaberson, W. 1990. One in four young black men is in custody, study says. *New York Times* (4 Oct.): B6.

Glass, R. 1990. Opening windows for teenagers: How mentors can help. *American Educator* (Spring): 21–26, 48.

Goldman, A. 1990. Urban League leader calls equality essential to U.S. *New York Times* (30 July): 10.

Grant, C., and C. Sleeter. 1993. Race, class, gender and disability in the classroom. In *Multicultural education: Issues and perspectives*, 2nd ed. Edited by J. A. Banks and C. A. M. Banks, 65. Boston: Allyn & Bacon.

Gresham, J. H. 1994. The politics of family in America. In *Multicultural education, 1994/95: Annual editions*, edited by F. Schultz, 29–33. Guilford, Conn.: Dushkin.

Gross, J. 1992. Collapse of inner city families creates America's new orphans. *New York Times* (29 March): 1, 20.

Hacker, A. 1992. *Two nations—Black and white, separate, hostile, and unequal.* New York: Charles Scribner & Sons.

Hampton, R. 1987. Race, class and child mistreatment. *Journal of Comparative Family Studies* 18(1).

Hobart, T. Y. 1994. The horror of school violence. *New York Teacher* (21 Feb.): 9.

Holland, S. 1989. Fighting the epidemic of failure: A radical strategy for educating inner city boys. *Teacher* 1(1): 88–89.

Howard, J., and R. Hammond. 1985. Rumors of inferiority: Barriers to black success in America. *New Republic* (9 Sept.).

Ingrassia, M. 1994. Endangered family: For many African-Americans, marriage and childbearing do not go together. In *Race and ethnic relations 1994/95; Annual editions*, edited by J. Kromkowski, 147–51. Guilford, Conn.: Dushkin.

Johnson, D. 1990. Milwaukee creating 2 schools just for black boys. *New York Times* (30 Sept.): 1, 26.

Kantor, R. 1977. *Men and women of the corporation.* New York: Basic.

Kunjufu, J. 1986. *Countering the conspiracy to destroy black boys.* Chicago: African-American Images.

Kunjufu, J. 1990. Speak out: Unfortunately, separate classrooms for black males are needed. *American Educator* (1 April): 6.

Kuzirian, E., and L. Madaras. 1985. *Taking sides: Clashing views on controversial issues in American History. Volume 1, The colonial period to reconstruction.* Guilford, Conn.: Dushkin.

Leach, P. 1994. *Children first.* New York: Knopf.

Leary, W. 1991. Stress among blacks is tied to bias: Environmental may outweigh genetic factors. *New York Times* (6 Feb.): 16.

LeCompte, M. 1987. The cultural content of dropping out: Why remedial programs fail to solve the problem. *Education and Urban Society* 19: 232–49.

Lee, F. 1990. Black men: Are they imperiled? *New York Times* (26 June): B3.

Lehmann, N. 1991. *The promised land: The great black migration and how it changed America.* New York: Alfred Knopf.

Levine, D., and R. Havighurst. 1989. *Society and education.* 7th ed. Boston: Allyn & Bacon.

Lewin, T. 1990. Black children living with one parent put at 55%. *New York Times* (15 July): 17.

Marriot, M. 1990. Matching those who need guidance with those who have been there. *New York Times* (27 June): 8.

McGrath, P., and D. Weathers. 1985. Breaking the code: A new strand of black thought deals in difficult facts. *Newsweek* (21 Oct.): 84–87.

Meier, A., and E. Rudwick. 1966. *From plantation to ghetto: An interpretive history of American Negroes.* New York: Hill and Wang.

Model, S. 1990. Work and family: Blacks and immigrants from South and East Europe. In *Immigration reconsidered: History, sociology, and politics*, edited by V. Yans-McLaughlin, 130–59. New York: Oxford University Press.

Moynihan, D. P. 1993. Defining deviancy down. *American Scholar* (Winter).

Mydans, S. 1990. War in the streets: Homicide rate up for young blacks, casualties rise by 66% and approach wartime totals, federal report asserts. *New York Times* (7 Dec.): 1, 26.

Myrdal, G. 1944. *An American dilemma: The Negro problem and modern democracy.* New York: Harper Brothers.

New York State Department of Education. 1991. *One nation, many peoples: A declaration of interdependence.* Albany, N.Y.: State Department of Education.

Noll, J. W., ed. 1993. *Taking sides: Clashing views on controversial educational issues.* 7th ed. Guilford, Conn.: Dushkin.

Ogbu, J. 1978. *Minority education and caste: The American system in cross-cultural perspective.* New York: Academic Press.

Popenoe, D. 1988. *Disturbing the nest: Family change and decline in modern societies.* New York: Aldine de Gruyter.

———. 1993. Scholars should worry about the disintegration of the American family. *Chronicle of Higher Education* (14 April): A48.

Poussaint, A. 1987. Black men must organize. *Black Scholar* (May/June): 12–15.

———. 1990. Looking ahead: Problems and solutions. *Journal of Health and Social Policy* 1(4): 129–39.

Powell, G. J. 1983. *Psychosocial development of minority group children.* New York: Brunner/Mazel.

Racial harm is found in schools' tracking. 1990. *New York Times* (19 Sept.).

Rainwater, L., and W. Yancey. 1967. *The Moynihan Report and the politics of controversy.* Cambridge: MIT Press.

Richman, C., M. L. Clark, and K. Brown. 1985. General and specific self-esteem in late adolescent students: Race, gender, SES effects. *Adolescence* 20(79): 555–56.

Rumberger, R. 1987. High school dropouts: A review of issues and evidence. *Review of Educational Research* 57: 101–21.

Schmidt, W. 1989. Study links male unemployment and single mothers in Chicago. *New York Times* (15 Jan.): 16.

Shanker, A. 1991. Discipline in our schools: People are right to be alarmed. *New York Teacher* (10 June): 10.

———. 1994. Discipline by the numbers. *On Campus* (March): 9.

Snider, W. 1987. Negative peer pressure said to inhibit black student achievement. *Education Week* (25 March): 1, 14.

Staples, R. 1985. Changes in black family structure: The conflict between family, ideology, and structural conditions. *Journal of Marriage and the Family* 47: 1005–13.

Stenberg, L. 1988. *Factors associated with the professional socialization relationships of secondary male and female home economics educators.* Unpublished doctoral dissertation, Ohio State University.

———. 1990. Mentoring home economics educators: Diversity or homogeneity? *Journal of Vocational Educational Research* 15(1): 9–23.

Stephenson, J. 1993. *Men are not cost-effective: Male crime in America.* Ventura, Calif.: Diemer & Smith.

Stevens, L. 1990. "Separate but equal" has no place. *Education Week* (31 Oct.).

Study finds blacks twice as liable to school penalties as whites. 1988. *New York Times* (12 Dec.): 16.

Terry, D. 1993. More familiar, life in a cell seems less terrible. *New York Times* (13 Sept.): 1, 40.

Tobin, J. 1992. Voodoo curse: Exorcising the legacy of Reaganomics. *Harvard International Review* (Summer): 10–12.

U.S. Census. 1988, 1993. *Marital status and living arrangements: March 1988; July 1994.* Series P-20, Nr. 432. Washington, D.C.: U.S. Government Printing Office.

Violence rises in elementary schools. 1990. *New York Times* (24 April): 1.

Weir, M. 1993. Race and urban poverty: Comparing Europe and America. *Brookings Institute Review* (Summer): 23–27.

Wilkerson, I. 1991. How Milwaukee boomed but left its blacks behind. *New York Times* (19 March): 1, D22.

Wilkinson, C. B., and W. A. O'Connor. 1977. Growing up male in a black single-parent family. *Psychiatric Annals* 7(7): 356–62.

Wilson, W. J. 1987. *The truly disadvantaged: The inner city, the underclass, and public policy.* Chicago: University of Chicago Press.

Woodring, P. 1989. A new approach to the dropout problem. *Phi Delta Kappan* (Feb.).

On Being a Mexican American

It is important for Mexican Americans to accept the fact that they are a unique group at a crossroads, Mr. Mendoza points out.

Joe I. Mendoza

JOE I. MENDOZA is director of the Migrant Education Program, Ventura County Schools Office, Ventura, Calif.

I WAS born in the U.S.A., but I was born a Mexican. However, at the moment I arrived, I was not labeled as such by the doctor who delivered me. Nor did my mother and father cry out in triumph that yet another Mexican had entered the world. No, I only slowly came to the realization of who I was, in the same way all my friends did.

In the beginning I learned to be a Mexican from my relatives. We all ate the same food, and we ate it the same way. For instance, we had tortillas, frijoles, tamales, enchiladas, huevos con chorizo, and arroz as part of our daily diet. We also had chile rellenos, guacamole, pan dulce, and a Sunday dish of menudo as special treats. Back then menudo was not a singing group, but a soup for the treatment of hangovers, or so I was told.

As I grew, I shared other Mexican experiences with my friends, who, I might add, also looked like me. In other words, they were Mexicans too. They had black hair, brown skin, and slightly slanted eyes. We dressed alike, too; we wore levis or an occasional pair of corduroy pants. Most of us wore high-top shoes that laced through several small holes at the bottom and small

Illustration by Sharon Siskind

From *Phi Delta Kappan*, December 1994, pp. 293-295. © 1994 by Phi Delta Kappa, Inc. Reprinted by permission.

hooks toward the top, so that tying one's shoelaces required patience and practice. When the shoes would not tie easily, a stream of appropriate phrases was sure to follow.

We all spoke the same language, a certain form of Spanish. I say this because, as Mexicans born and raised in La Colonia, we were obligated to speak alike or suffer exclusion. For example, we sang when we spoke. It was a melodic tone that quickly identified not only who we were, but where we were from. Certain vocabulary words would identify our ethnicity, geographic origin, and specific barrio within La Colonia. Words such as "dompe" for the English word "dump," "neegle" for "nickel," and of course the ever-popular "lonche" for "lunch" told the world we were from Hayes Street. Words like "orale, carnal" for "hi, friend" and "no-'mbre" for "no, man" would identify those from Seaboard Avenue.

A shared language plus common experiences were a part of our early education. But by junior high school, I suddenly awakened to the fact that Mexicans were considered different from and even inferior to others. For the first time, I experienced segregation.

One recreation period, when we were playing our usual game of soccer, I took time out to search for a rest room. I spotted a building on the north side of the playground and ran for it. As I was about to enter, a teacher blew her whistle very loudly, freezing me on the spot. She approached me and demanded to know where I was going, who I was, and what I was doing on that side of the playground. I was dumbfounded and afraid to respond, so she took me by the ear and escorted me back across the playground to the south side. Her parting remark was a stern admonition not to cross the line and to stay with all the other Mexicans.

At that very moment I stopped, turned, and looked at the school as if for the first time. I saw a white line painted across the playground. On one side were the white children playing; on my side were the Mexicans. Then I looked at the building, which was divided in half. The office was in the center, with two wings spreading north and south — one wing for whites and the other for Mexicans. I was overwhelmed with emotions that I could not understand. I was hurt, disappointed, and frustrated. But more than anything else, I was profoundly angry.

Much later, I realized that acts of segregation, prejudice, and racism leave wounds that never heal. Scars continually remind you of the pain you suffered at the hands of people who saw you as low, ignorant, and not worthy of anyone's time or effort.

But there was always a source to turn to for emotional first aid — one's family and friends. In my own family, the matriarch was my grandmother, a short lady with gray hair that she always wore in a bun. She spoke only Spanish.

During the summer months my grandmother became my mentor and guide and would take me with her to pick various crops, especially the beautiful golden apricots in Moorpark. She would come by and call for me at 5 a.m.; we would walk a few blocks, stand at the corner with other people, and wait for a truck to pick us up.

One time when we were picking, I felt it was time to assert my "machismo." Rebelliously, I told her I was tired. But one of my grandmother's favorite phrases was *un poquito más*, which means "just a little bit more." She said this then, and I said, "I'm tired and will not move another step."

She tried to convince me to continue working by promising me "una taza de café con burrito." When my grandmother promised a cup of coffee and a burrito, I was easily persuaded to continue working. We continued picking, but after a while I announced once more that I was tired and needed to rest. My grandmother again said, "Un poquito más."

This time I stood my ground and announced that no one and nothing was going to force me to continue picking apricots. I looked my grandmother straight in the eye and said, "No!"

My grandmother responded to the challenge by clearly stating her position in two words. In Spanish, there are certain phrases that, when pronounced with a sweet melodic tone, mean one thing, but when pronounced with a low, slow, and deeper tone, mean unthinkable pain and misery. One such phrase is *mi hijo* — "my son" — or *mi hija* — "my daughter." My grandmother said, "mi hijo" in a low and long tone that could only mean impending doom.

Still, I was 12 going on 30 and decided to play the ever-popular male game of acting macho. I stood my ground and said no again, with conviction and resolve. To which my grandmother replied, with some sarcasm and still with that low, mean tone, "Oh? All right." She quickly took a branch from the ground, looked menacingly at me, and said, "Let me be sure I understood you. What did you say to me?"

Still feeling sure of my newfound independence, I responded confidently. "I said, I will not work until I've rested for as long as I want to, and that's final. There's nothing you can do to me. I don't care if you have a stick in your hand. I'll start running, and you'll never catch me. So forget it, old lady."

To which my grandmother replied, "All right, then, so be it."

I laughed and remarked, "You'll never catch me. I'm known as the eagle because I fly when I run."

"Well, then," said my grandmother, "take off, because here I come."

I began running down a row of trees, which became a blur as I ran past them, and turned to see how far back my grandmother was. To my shock and surprise, the little old lady was immediately behind me, keeping up with me step for step. I stopped running and fell to the ground in laughter.

She then stood over me, beating me with her little branch. To add insult to injury, she still had a smoking cigarette dangling from the corner of her mouth! To this day, I can see her rolling her own cigarettes — wrapping the tobacco with the dry skin of an ear of corn — and scraping the match on her backside, an embarrassing habit, I thought.

Still, I learned many important lessons about life from my grandmother that day. For example, I learned that before a man can become macho, it takes a woman to make him so.

ANOTHER LESSON I learned came much later. I had three very close friends while I was growing up. As was the custom of the time, we shared nicknames. One of my friends was left-handed, so we called him *surdo*. The other had a limp, so he was *pata*. The third one came by his name in a somewhat different fashion.

When we played cowboys and Indians, each of us had imaginary guns and rifles. The imaginary sounds that they made corresponded to the sophistication of the weapon. For example, "bang, bang" represented a common everyday weapon. But our friend would use a special sound, "talo, talo," for his special weapon. You can probably guess what his nickname was.

Nicknames can be dangerous if one does not shed them when maturity is reached. Not too long ago, I had the opportunity to serve as master of ceremonies at a banquet celebrating the election of the first Hispanic municipal judge in that city. During the introduction, I became rather emotional and reached the climax of my comments by saying, "And now, ladies and gentlemen, I am pleased to present the first Hispanic municipal judge, his honor, Talo-Talo."

He shook my hand and spoke into the microphone, "Thank you very much, four-eyes."

My being a Mexican came to an abrupt end before I entered high school. By then, my family had moved to a neighboring town about 20 miles north of La Colonia. In this town and in its high school, there were scarcely any Mexicans. In fact, I was hard pressed to find a single one, let alone a group of them. So I joined a group of Anglos and began the process of becoming "Anglocized." Or, as I later learned, "acculturated."

I had already learned to speak, read, and write English fluently and had been able to join school activities and participate in musical productions. Now in high school I was not only part of the mainstream but became active in student government and was elected president of the student body. I had embarked on a new life.

Later I entered two major institutions that ensured that I remain "Anglocized." I was drafted into the U.S. Army and then attended a university. In both worlds I was again completely removed from Mexican culture and role models, and these surroundings reinforced my belief that I had arrived. Then came the final two

major events of my evolution. I married an Anglo and began teaching school.

Wouldn't you know it, I began my teaching career in a neighborhood school that was predominantly upper-class. Not one Mexican was present, and there were no blacks or Asians. Again, I remained "Anglocized" and felt accepted. I joined the parent/teacher organization, became a Republican, and even gave up my Chevy for a Ford.

All was well, until one day I received a call from an old friend of mine who invited me to a Chicano Educators' Conference. Reluctantly, I agreed to attend. Upon my arrival at a fancy hotel, my old friend greeted me warmly. From my days as a Mexican, I recalled the traditional greeting between old friends. I prepared to offer an *abrazo* or embrace. To my surprise and chagrin, he didn't embrace but began shaking my hand. And it was not a normal handshake.

Instead, he began a series of movements with my hand and arm which I cannot describe easily. He shook my hand up and down several times, followed by clasping the palm, and then appeared to run his hand up and down my arm. In any case, he was enjoying himself so much, I just stood there and watched. I didn't have the heart to interrupt. Finally, he finished, and I was relieved. This was a "typical" Chicano handshake — but the movement was young, and I had not encountered the gesture previously.

Eventually, I became aware that I did not really fit in with this group. And yet, I could not dismiss a new feeling — that of still needing to be a Mexican. When I returned to my school, I had a different

outlook. Although I thought I had been safely "acculturated," I found I could not so easily forget my past.

DO WE "Mexicans" ever totally integrate? Can we ignore our past, our youth, and our family background? The answer appears to be no. As much as we may try to become part of the mainstream, there will always be someone or some event that will remind us of who we are and where we came from; it is usually just enough to cause most of us to stop and remember our heritage.

Today there is a menu of terms from which we may select a label. Should we select Mexican American, Chicano, Latino, or Hispanic? It is interesting to note that recently arrived Mexicans are not confused, for they know who they are. I submit that it is the members of the second or third generation in the U.S. who have problems with having to choose — or with having someone else choose for them.

It is important for society to understand that we may all look alike, but we are not alike. It is equally important for Mexican Americans to accept the fact that we are a unique group at a crossroads. We need to decide once and for all who we are and stop trying to be what we are not. We are not all Latinos or Hispanics. Instead, we possess a culture that is uniquely Mexican American. How much Mexican and how much American remains to be seen — but the question needs to be asked, then discussed, and, finally, answered as well as possible.

Respect, Cultural Sensitivity, and Communication

Promoting Participation by Asian Families in the Individualized Family Service Plan

"When I was growing up, what did my family say about people from different cultures?"

Jinhee K. Hyun
Susan A. Fowler

Jinhee K. Hyun, *Doctoral Student, and* **Susan A. Fowler** *(CEC Chapter #51), Professor and Head, Department of Special Education, University of Illinois at Urbana-Champaign.*

ASKING YOURSELF A QUESTION LIKE THIS AND EXPLORING YOUR ANSWERS MAY GO A LONG WAY TOWARD HELPING YOU UNDERSTAND YOUR OWN CULTURE. THIS IS AN IMPORTANT FIRST STEP IN LEARNING ABOUT THE CULTURES OF THE PEOPLE YOU SERVE IN EARLY INTERVENTION PROGRAMS. TEACHERS, ADMINISTRATORS, SOCIAL WORKERS, HEALTH AND CHILD CARE PROFESSIONALS— ALL ARE CLOSELY INVOLVED WITH THE FAMILIES IN THEIR PROGRAMS, AND ALL CAN BENEFIT FROM GREATER AWARENESS OF CULTURAL DIVERSITY.

This article provides suggestions for enabling families with different cultural and linguistic backgrounds to participate fully in early intervention programs. Because Asian Americans have emerged as the fastest-growing ethnic minority group in the United States (Chan, 1992), we have based most examples on the Asian culture. In addition, we recognize that diversity exists within a cultural group. Variables such as socioeconomic status, educational level, and length of residence in the United States may affect people's beliefs as much as culture itself. Therefore, each family should be viewed as a unique unit that is influenced by its culture, but not defined by it (Wayman, Lynch, & Hanson, 1990).

We hope that this article will lead to a better understanding of the ways in which cultural diversity can be acknowledged, respected, and valued in the individualized family service plan (IFSP) process. The first step is to enhance our own cultural awareness.

Enhancing Cultural Awareness

We may enhance cultural self-awareness by (a) exploring our own cultural heritage and (b) examining the attitudes and behaviors that are associated with our own culture. Listening to or recollecting stories of the eldest members of a family, such as grandparents or great-grandparents, is a first step. Examining family genealogical records, family albums, or church records is invaluable in exploring our own heritage.

One illuminating way to examine some of the behaviors, values, and attitudes identified with our own cultural heritage is to recount common sayings (e.g., "Make do with or do without" and

From *Teaching Exceptional Children*, Fall 1995, pp. 25-28. © 1995 by The Council for Exceptional Children. Reprinted by permission.

"Where there is a will, there is a way") and identify the values behind these sayings. For example, if you are from the Euro-American culture, which values individualism and independence, you may want to examine how these values affect your attitude toward an Asian family who values harmony and interdependence in a family. Moreover, if you have been raised in beliefs like "Where there is a will, there is a way," your views about disabilities may be very different from those of a person who has heard that "It's God's will" or "It's my fate."

A question like the one at the beginning of this article—"When I was growing up, what did my family say about people from different cultures?"—may also clarify your own attitudes toward people from diverse cultures. This self-awareness can help us discover potent but pervasive biases that may affect intercultural interactions.

Learning about other cultures is a life-long process, involving the following:

- Reading books or magazines about different cultures.
- Watching films or videotapes about diverse cultures.
- Interacting with friends, colleagues, or neighbors from different cultures.
- Participating in gatherings like celebration of holidays of other cultures.

Dealing with language barriers effectively can enrich your own understanding and speed the communication process.

Overcoming Language Differences—Obvious Barriers to Communication

If a family has limited English conversational skills, invite an interpreter to conferences and meetings. Ideally, the interpreter should be trained in cross-cultural interpretation, have knowledge about the early intervention system, and be proficient in both the language of the family and your language. In addition, you need to be sensitive to the family's choice of who should act as an interpreter, because the interpreter will be translating potentially confidential or privileged information by the family. In many Asian families, family matters involving a child with a disability are considered private concerns, not openly discussed with others.

A leader of the cultural community can be a rich resource for understanding the culture; because of his or her position, a community leader is usually trusted and respected by the family. In the Korean-American culture, for example, a clergyman or a priest may be a good source for a cultural mediator or guide because "between 60% and 70% of Korean-Americans are affiliated with Christian churches" (Chan, 1992, p. 196).

Other specific suggestions for effective cross-cultural communication with many Asian families include the following courtesies:

- Using Mr., Mrs., or Miss with the family name (e.g., Mr. Chen, Mrs. Lee), because only close friends in the same peer group use first names.
- Learning greeting words or other simple words (e.g., hello, thank you) in the family's language.
- Using written forms and letters in the family's language for important communications, such as information about parent rights and community resources.

Asian language is characterized by indirect and nonverbal communication styles, whereas Anglo-American language focuses on direct and verbal styles (Lynch, 1992). Many Asian families convey a lot of information through nonverbal communication, using silence and eye contact. Maintaining silence in a conversation often indicates an expression of respect. However, if silence follows active verbal responses by the family, it may indicate disagreement. Direct eye contact is usually avoided. Especially, direct eye contact with the elder is viewed as disrespectful. Given the differences in communication styles, listen carefully—and, when unsure, ask parents for clarification. Developing your listening skills is especially important in parent-professional conferences with families from diverse cultures.

Holding Effective Family Conferences

Include time for preconference preparation and consider the schedule, room arrangement, and number of participants. Families should have an opportunity to participate at the level they find comfortable. Provide alternatives to facilitate

Early Intervention and Cultural Issues

Public Law 99-457 places the family in the center of the early intervention system. A major intent of the law is to foster meaningful parent-professional partnerships to support the optimal development of infants and toddlers (Summers et al., 1990).

The issues on which families and professionals focus in providing services for these very young children often are closely related to the families' beliefs, values, and child-rearing practices (Hanson, 1992). This may present a challenge when professionals and families are from different cultures. Important issues include the following:

- The family-centered perspective may not be shared by all cultures (Hanson, Lynch, & Wayman, 1990).

- Recommendations and child-rearing practices may be misunderstood by either party (Lynch, 1992).

- Parents with different cultural and linguistic backgrounds may respond differently to the individualized family service plan (IFSP) process, depending on their understanding of the educational process and the number of barriers they encounter to their participation.

- Even though the concept of uniqueness of each family is generally acknowledged, it may not be always considered in the design of all early intervention programs (Chandler, Fowler, & Lubeck, 1986).

parent participation and then let the parents decide on their level of participation.

Careful preconference preparation can influence actual IFSP conference success. Consulting with other service providers or mediators who are familiar with and knowledgeable about the families' cultural and linguistic community should be the first step.

Helpful strategies include the following:

- Decide with the parents the time and location of the meeting and who will participate.
- Encourage parents to bring people who are important to them, such as relatives, friends, or religious leaders.
- Send a written notice of the meeting in the family's primary language.
- Determine whether families need assistance with logistics, such as child care or transportation.

We can express respect for the family by scheduling adequate time for the meeting and arranging it at times convenient for the family (Summers et al., 1990). The location of the meeting is another consideration. If meetings are conducted at home, professionals should be sensitive to different customs. In most Asian homes, it is common courtesy to remove one's shoes upon entering. If older persons or grandparents are present, it is a courtesy to greet them with a slight bow and, when seated, to avoid crossing one's legs. Asian families are likely to provide a snack or beverage, because it is their custom to offer food when visited. You may decline the offered snack or beverage, but you should express thanks for the offering.

When meetings are conducted at a center or in a public location, you should select a quiet, private place with comfortable chairs. To promote the sense of professional-parent partnership, provide all participants with adult-sized chairs; and do not sit behind a desk, separated from the parents (deBettencourt, 1987). Privacy is essential if you expect families to feel comfortable discussing personal concerns (Kroth, 1985).

In addition, consider the number of people present at the conference. Parents may feel overwhelmed and outnumbered by too many professionals at the IFSP meeting (Able-Boone, Sandall, Loughry,

& Frederick, 1990), particularly if families are from cultural backgrounds different from others present at the meeting (Lynch & Hanson, 1992). Meetings in which the professionals don't outnumber the family representatives are likely to be more comfortable and conducive to exchange of ideas for Asian families.

Developing Family Outcomes in the IFSP

We should always respect family preferences and concerns in the development of family outcomes. The family outcomes should be written in clear and nonintrusive language, considering the family's cultural background. Meaningful family involvement requires culturally acceptable family outcomes. To identify culturally acceptable family outcomes, consider the following issues:

- Who is the primary caregiver?
- What are the family's beliefs about disability?
- Who is the decision maker? (Hanson et al., 1990).

In addition, ask about daily routines, such as eating practices or sleeping patterns. Some practices may be unique to the culture; if so, the cultural values must be respected when choosing those routines for intervention. For example, if one outcome is that a child will increase her ability to feed herself, keep in mind that an Asian family whose main meal is rice and soup usually doesn't encourage very young children to self-feed but instead provides assistance during mealtime. The professional can recommend self-feeding during snack time when finger feeding is possible, rather than emphasizing self-feeding during mealtime. Professionals should also ensure that the proposed outcomes are important to the family and are realistic for them.

If outcomes involve sleeping patterns, consider that the mother-infant interaction is often characterized by close physical contact in many Asian families (Chan, 1992). Infants rarely sleep alone, and it is not unusual that children under school age sleep with their parents in the same room. If you recommend that the child sleep alone, the outcome is not likely to be acceptable to the family.

If families have a different understanding of the family outcomes, or if

Promoting Communication Between Parents and Professionals

Cultural sensitivity, clear language, and active listening are critical to ensuring shared communication in the IFSP process. Cultural sensitivity involves respecting family values, beliefs, and customs that differ from our own (Wayman et al., 1990). To infuse cultural sensitivity into all aspects of our programs, we need to do the following:

- Be aware of the extent to which our own opinions are driven by cultural values (Randall-David, 1989).
- Learn about the values of families with whom we work (Lynch, 1992).
- Whenever possible, identify members of the family's linguistic or cultural community to serve as a resource for translation or mediation (Anderson & Goldberg, 1991).

their view of their roles in implementation differs from yours, the potential for conflict may emerge. For example, a reverent regard for teachers is firmly established in Asian culture. Professionals are viewed as respected figures with the expertise and ability to offer assistance (Chan, 1992). As a result, some Asian parents may assume a dependent role rather than active partnership. Accordingly, even if family members believe that family outcomes are of no importance, they are not likely to contradict your selection of outcomes, out of respect for your opinion as a professional. However, the family may not implement the plan, if the outcomes are not important goals for the family.

By frequently reviewing the outcomes and holding informal interviews with the family, you can recognize the family's perceptions about the outcomes. Your patient and sincere attitudes toward the family may facilitate the family in being frank, addressing problems, and making decisions. Once the outcomes are realistic and acceptable for the family, they will work very hard to achieve the outcomes.

Conclusion

The extent to which parents will participate as partners with professionals in the development and implementation of the IFSP must be determined by the family itself. We must recognize and respect the individual preferences and cultural values of each family. The IFSP must be flexible to be acceptable by families. If we are to attain the collaboration and meaningful partnership intended by the IFSP, we must cultivate and maintain respect for families, for their diversity, and for their choices.

We must have *culturally sensitive* early interventions. In this article, we have suggested strategies for enabling Asian parent participation. However, each family is different, and culture-specific information cannot be assumed to apply in every situation. *The information should not be used to make generalizations that stereotype families.* Acquiring cross-culturally competent skills and attitudes can be a long process; however, a desire and

willingness to learn about different people is certainly a rewarding pursuit (Lynch, 1992). *Enthusiasm, openness, and willingness* are the most important characteristics that support meaningful partnership between professionals and culturally diverse families.

References

Able-Boone, H., Sandall, S. R., Loughry, A., & Frederick, L. L. (1990). An informed, family-centered approach to Public Law 99-457: Parental views. *Topics in Early Childhood Special Education, 10,* 100–111.

Anderson, M., & Goldberg, P. F. (1991). *Cultural competence in screening and assessment: Implications for services to young children with special needs ages birth through five.* Chapel Hill, NC: National Early Childhood Technical Assistance System. (ERIC Document Reproduction Service No. ED 370 313)

Chan, S. (1992). Families with Asian roots. In E. W. Lynch & M. J. Hanson (Eds.), *Developing cross-cultural competence: A guide for working with young children and their families* (pp. 181–257). Baltimore: Paul H. Brookes.

Chandler, L. K., Fowler, S. A., & Lubeck, R. C. (1986). Assessing family needs: The first step in providing family-focused intervention. *Diagnostique, 11,* 233–245.

deBettencourt, L. U. (1987). How to develop parent relationships. *TEACHING Exceptional Children, 19,* 26–27.

Hanson, M. J. (1992). Ethnic, cultural, and language diversity in intervention settings. In E. W. Lynch & M. J. Hanson (Eds.), *Developing cross-cultural competence: A guide for working with young children and their families* (pp. 3–18). Baltimore: Paul H. Brookes.

Hanson, M. J., Lynch, E. W., & Wayman, K. I. (1990). Honoring the cultural diversity of families when gathering data. *Topics in Early Childhood Special Education, 10,* 112–131.

Kroth, R. L. (1985). *Communicating with parents of exceptional children: Improving parent-teacher relationships.* Denver, CO: Love.

Lynch, E. W. (1992). Developing cross-cultural competence. In E. W. Lynch & M. J. Hanson (Eds.), *Developing cross-cultural competence: A guide for working with young children and their families* (pp. 35–57). Baltimore: Paul H. Brookes.

Lynch, E. W., & Hanson, M. J. (1992). Steps in the right direction: Implications for interventionists. In E. W. Lynch & M. J. Hanson (Eds.), *Developing cross-cultural competence: A guide for working with young children and their families* (pp. 355–370). Baltimore: Paul H. Brookes.

Randall-David, E. (1989). *Strategies for working with culturally diverse communities and clients.* Washington, DC: Association for the Care of Children's Health. (ERIC Document Reproduction Service No. ED 325 559)

Summers, J. A., Dell'Oliver, C., Turnbull, A. P., Benson, H. A., Santelli, E., Campbell, M., & Siegel-Causey, E. (1990). Examining the Individualized Family Service Plan process: What are family and practitioner preferences? *Topics in Early Childhood Special Education, 10,* 78–99.

Wayman, K. I., Lynch, E. W., & Hanson, M. J. (1990). Home-based early childhood services: Cultural sensitivity in a family systems approach. *Topics in Early Childhood Special Education, 10,* 56–75.

Lessons of Vancouver

Immigration raises fundamental questions of identity and values.

Andrew Phillips

If the old Canada has a refuge and a stronghold these days, it may well be in legion halls across the land. It is there that veterans, their sons and their daughters have long gathered to sip rye and ginger and simply be together—upholding proud traditions of service and remembrance. These days, though, legion branches are anything but tranquil. Many are bitterly divided over whether to admit people wearing turbans—a seemingly obscure issue that starkly underlines the pain and confusion that results when the old Canada gives way to the new. For many legionnaires uncomfortable with the changes, the issue is straightforward. Turbans, as one Halifax legion member put it last week, should not be allowed because "tradition is tradition."

These days, though, even tradition isn't what it used to be. The new Canada wears not only legion caps and hockey sweaters, but saris and smart Hong Kong suits and—yes—turbans. In our big cities, and in many small towns as well, the highest levels of nonwhite immigration ever are raising fears and testing our commitment to the ideals of multiculturalism. Poll after poll shows Canadians increasingly hostile to immigration at a time of high unemployment: almost half of those surveyed by Gallup in December said the country should accept fewer immigrants. And the polite agreement among the old-line parties not to debate the issue seriously has vanished. Instead, the loudest voices in the new House of Commons openly question both the wisdom of accepting almost a quarter of a million newcomers a year and Ottawa's two-decade-old policy of officially encouraging them to stress their separate identities rather than their common Canadian citizenship. Last week alone, Reform and Bloc Québécois MPs condemned official multiculturalism in harsher language than Parliament has heard for many years.

Because they accept 60 per cent of all immigrants, the country's three biggest cities—Montreal, Toronto and Vancouver—are being most profoundly reshaped by the newcomers from Asia, the Middle East and Latin America. But if Canada has a laboratory in which its new ethnic chemistry is being most acutely tested, it is surely Vancouver. The city's position as a magnet for Asian immigrants means that change there has been most far-reaching. In typically Canadian fashion, established (mainly white) Vancouverites have for the most part expressed their concerns only in guarded fashion. But the changes are so profound that even many who regard themselves as liberal are bound to ask themselves: Is it all going too quickly? Is the city I knew being transformed into something alien? Will my children be well served by schools increasingly geared to serving youngsters whose greatest need is simply to learn English?

Until recently, it was virtually impossible to raise those questions publicly without being accused of intolerance, or even racism. But the new Commons is bound to witness confrontations between Reform MPs who want immigration levels cut drastically, and a rookie immigration minister determined to uphold the traditional Liberal openness towards newcomers. Ironically, though, the pointed debate on immigration that seems about to begin will take place in a House that includes more visible minorities than ever before—MPs of Chinese, Japanese, Indian, Filipino and West Indian heritage. Not to mention a record three native Canadians, who might justly regard all the other 292 MPs as immigrants.

From *Maclean's* magazine, February 7, 1994, pp. 26-31. © 1994 by Maclean Hunter Publishing, Ltd. Reprinted by permission.

Chris Wood

Jack Lee has a dilemma. The 42-year-old Vancouver-area developer's shiny new $60-million hotel, shopping and community centre in suburban Richmond, B.C., is almost complete—financed largely by would-be Canadians from Lee's native Taiwan who have each put $250,000 into his project, qualifying them for citizenship under Canada's investor-immigrant entry rules. The finishing touch on the gleaming glass-and-concrete project will be a fountain near the entrance where, Lee says, water will splash from the open mouth of one fish into that of another. One of the fish will be a carp, a symbol of the Orient; the other a dolphin, representing the West. To Asians, he adds, "water is for money." Lee's quandary: "Which fish should receive it? And which should spit it out?"

The question is on many minds in Canada's fastest-growing city. Even as Vancouver enjoys the economic benefits of record levels of immigration, the city of 1.6 million finds itself straining to accommodate the needs of an increasingly multicultural population. Citizens of longer standing, meanwhile, are asking other questions: as the face of the city changes, whose values will prevail, those of traditional Vancouver—or those of the newcomers? Indeed, in a city where street names like Blenheim and Balaclava evoke a staunchly British heritage, the visibly changing population prompts an even deeper question, one that resonates across the nation. As the number of Canadians of non-European origin approaches those of the two so-called founding nations of Canada, who, ultimately, are "we" anyway?

The sensitivity and significance of the issue were driven home again last week. After federal Immigration Minister Sergio Marchi announced that refugee claimants will now be allowed to work while awaiting a ruling on their status in Canada—lifting a load from overburdened welfare systems—critics immediately charged that the decision would deprive Canadians of jobs. In British Columbia, however, another news item drove home a different economic message. Fuelled by record immigration of 76,000 people (from both inside and outside Canada) in 1993, British Columbia generated nearly two out of every three new full-time jobs in the entire country last year.

Welcome as that news was to Vancouver residents, it did little to ease the stresses that have accompanied a sharp reversal in earlier patterns of immigration from abroad. In contrast to newcomers in previous decades, most of whom arrived with little money and a humble willingness to accept whatever work was offered, many of those who now come to the city, particularly the roughly one-fifth of them who arrive from Hong Kong, possess both wealth and high expectations. Both as investors and as consumers, their growing presence has profoundly visible consequences.

Nowhere is that more evident than in the south Vancouver suburb of Richmond. The elegant compound curves of Lee's mirror-sheathed President Plaza embrace both a Sheraton Hotel, due to open in April, and the country's largest Asian-food supermarket, which is already doing business. On its shelves, Old Dutch Potato Chips share space with Korean *kim chi* and cans of grass jelly drink; a live seafood section boasts tanks of eels as well as lobster. Three floors above the shoppers, seven Buddhist nuns and monks clad in plain ochre habits are preparing to dedicate a 5,000-square-foot temple, the heart of a community centre that will offer adult education in Asian languages and crafts.

Lee's complex is just the latest addition to Richmond's increasingly Asian-influenced skyline. Immediately to the south of President Plaza sits the Aberdeen Centre: despite its Scottish name, the bustling complex of shops and restaurants is owned by investors from Hong Kong who modelled it on similar centres in that enclave of capitalism. "You feel very much at home when you go there," observes Joseph Li, a Hong Kong native who now works for Lee's President Asian Enterprises Inc. To the north of Lee's building stands the Yaohan Centre, the first Canadian link in an international chain of supermarkets and department stores owned by Japan's Wada Group. There, jewelry store owner May Leung surveyed the uniformly Asian shoppers beyond her counter one day recently and observed with unconscious irony: "We do not see many foreigners out here."

That Leung meant Canadians of European extraction would frankly appall some white Vancouverites. Many feel pushed aside by the Asian influx. "They make no effort to fit in," complains Elizabeth Campbell, who has lived in Vancouver almost all her life. She was speaking particularly of the large, boxy homes on bare lots, many of them owned by Chinese immigrants, that in the late 1980s began to displace the more modest bungalows with leafy landscaping that once defined her west end neighborhood of Kerrisdale. Locals promptly dubbed the dwellings "monster houses."

But the sentiment plainly has more general application. At Magee Secondary School in the city's west end, guidance counsellor William McNulty has witnessed the change over the past 19 years as the once overwhelmingly white, Anglo-Saxon and Protestant school body has become more than half Asian. "So far," he says of attempts to foster mutual understanding between the old group and the new, "it is a one-way street: Canadians wanting to understand the newcomers." But, McNulty adds, "Canadians do have a culture. There is a case for the Asians showing they want to understand the local culture." A straw poll of one typical office floor in downtown Vancouver, meanwhile, turned up complaints directed at the Asian newcomers from more than half the tenants. Sore points ranged from the inconsiderate rudeness of some new arrivals to the soaring price of real estate, fuelled in part by wealthy immigrants paying top dollar for the city's most desirable properties. "That's why I voted Reform [in last fall's federal election]," volunteered secretary Terri Richardson. She was attracted, she says, by that party's call for restrictions on immigration.

Some of the harshest criticism of Vancouver's increasingly Asian cast can be heard in a spacious book-lined basement office a few steps down from Water Street in the city's historic Gastown district. Red and black hand-painted letters across a window facing the street identify the office as belonging to the Procult Institute: "In service to Western cultural values." The institute's founder, former businessman Jud Cyllorn, has written and published a 490-page polemic against Canada's immigration policy called *Stop Apologizing*. "In 22 years," he argues, "we have completely changed who we are and what we believe in." According to Cyllorn, who is of Scots origin, Canada's "British culture, which is based on trust" has given way to an "Asian culture [of] individual greed." Cyllorn, whose tiny organization has little influence, insists he is not a racist. "Anything I say is not to raise hatred against anyone," he told *Maclean's*, "but only to raise disgust at our own laxity and stupidity in surrendering our country without even a whimper."

But history, and the numbers, tell a very different story, one that is both more complex and more reassuring than Cyllorn's crudely bipolar perspective. The purely European past that he evokes is a fiction. So, too, is the alarmist notion that Vancouver is on the verge of becoming a transplanted version of Asia's teeming city-states.

As a matter of record, the census of 1891 documented no fewer than 42 countries of origin among the 14,000 people living in Vancouver. Orientals even then outnumbered Caucasians from continental Europe, 840 to 560. Succeeding generations of immigrants have added dozens of additional ethnic flavors to Vancouver's multicultural mix. Until 1942, a prosperous Japanese community abutted Vancouver's traditional Chinatown; its residents were abruptly interned and their property confiscated following the bombing of Pearl Harbor (the Canadian government formally apologized in 1988 for the mistreatment).

During the two decades following the Second World War, further immigration added a vigorous Italian community to the city's east end, while the concentration of Germans along one downtown street earned it the nickname "Robsonstrasse." Greek, Indo-Pakistani, Portuguese and Filipino communities appeared during the 1960s and 1970s, and by 1990, the children of immigrants registering for school in Vancouver came from a breathtaking total of 79 countries. Now, a local joke asks what the shortest distance is between Iran and Hong Kong. Answer: Lion's Gate Bridge, which links North Vancouver, favored by the city's Iranians to downtown and old Chinatown. "Vancouver has always been a seaport," observes city councillor Jennifer Clarke. "It has always accepted waves of immigrants from anywhere, and it has always been enriched by them."

For that matter, Vancouver's Chinese are scarcely less diverse in outlook than the rest of the city's population. Many families trace their Canadian roots back more than a century to the Klondike Gold Rush or the building of the Canadian Pacific Railway—which drew thousands of Chinese immigrants to the young country as prospectors and laborers. Another wave of newcomers fled the Communist takeover of mainland China in the late 1940s and early 1950s. Still more arrived in the 1960s—many with professional qualifications. The latest group of Chinese immigrants hail mainly from Hong Kong, but many also arrive from Taiwan, Vietnam and elsewhere along the southeast Asian rim. "People like my parents," observes Sonny Wong, the 32-year-old founder of a successful marketing agency whose parents came to Canada in the early 1950s, "continue to work in Chinese-dominated businesses. All their friends are Chinese. There is a tremendous amount of ethnocentric clustering." But of himself, Wong adds: "I was educated and socialized in Western society."

At the same time, foreign immigration to Vancouver continues to be outweighed by in-migration from elsewhere in Canada. In 1993, the 41,000 in-migrants who came to British Columbia from east of the Rockies outnumbered newcomers from other countries by nearly 20 per cent. Still, the 35,000 people who came to British Columbia from outside Canada last year, three-quarters of them from Asia and most of them settling in the lower mainland, were hardly insignificant. It is unarguable that Vancouver has already changed mightily and will change still more. According to Bruce MacDonald, the author of a historical atlas of Vancouver published in 1992, residents of British heritage made up a majority of the city's population as recently as 1961. But in the most recent census, in 1991, barely 24 per cent acknowledged British heritage. They were substantially outnumbered by the nearly 30 per cent of Vancouverites who told census takers they were of Asian origin—with fully 22 per cent saying they were ethnically Chinese.

The pronounced shift in Vancouver's ethnic centre of gravity has created new strains on civic institutions as well as striking changes in what constitutes businesses as usual in Canada's third-largest city. It is not just that white business executives are signing up for classes in Asian corporate etiquette at the downtown campus of Simon Fraser University, or that virtually any hip Vancouverite can negotiate his or her way through lunch using chop sticks. At City Hall, public notices are now routinely prepared in at least five languages in addition to English: Cantonese, Punjabi, Vietnamese, Spanish and French. "If it doesn't happen," declares Philip Owen, a former councillor who won election as mayor last November, "somebody is going to be reprimanded." And since October, 1992, the city's 911 emergency line has been equipped to respond to calls for help in an even larger number of tongues, thanks to a computer link to a continent-wide network of translators.

There is no identifying sign—in any language—outside the heavily secured, cream-colored cement building just south of False Creek where a special joint squad of Vancouver city police, RCMP and officers from other nearby municipalities are grappling with a different challenge. According to Staff Sgt. Andy Nimmo, commanding officer of the Asian Gang Squad, mixed in with the tens of thousands of law-abiding immigrants who have come to Canada from various Asian nations over the decades is a tiny but potent minority of gangsters. Their victims, overwhelmingly, have been others in their own community: Asian businessmen who became targets for extortion; shopkeepers and restaurateurs shaken down for protection money; youths studying in Canada who could easily be terrorized into handing over their allowances to thugs. Until recently, however, the mainly white police forces focused most of their efforts on serving and protecting the Caucasian majority.

That began to change in 1990 after a sweeping review of police policy. It uncovered a crippling lack of confidence among many Asians in the ability of the police to protect victims and

Bridging the gap

British Columbia's lieutenant-governor, 70-year old **David See-Chai Lam,** is one of Canada's most successful immigrants. He, his wife, Dorothy, and their three daughters left Hong Kong for Vancouver in 1967. Since then, he has made a fortune in real estate, become a leading philanthropist—and in 1988 was named the Queen's representative in the province. As lieutenant-governor, Lam has been on a mission to increase understanding between established Canadians and new arrivals. "It's quite natural for people to feel uncomfortable with different people," he says. "Both sides have to gradually get used to the changes."

Lam tells established Canadians that they should not be quite so proud of Canada's reputation as a tolerant country. "Tolerant is a slightly negative word," he says. "It's like saying, 'You smell, but I can hold my breath.'" Lam says he would like Canada to celebrate its immigrants, not just put up with them.

Lam is even tougher on the new arrivals. He has little patience for complaints about minor incidents of discrimination. "Don't talk to me about discrimination," he says bluntly. "The Chinese race is one of the most discriminatory in the world. I say to them, 'Do you think you will live to see the day when in one of the provinces in China, or in any of the countries in Asia, there will be a blond, blue-eyed governor?'" And he speaks against the common practice among elderly Chinese-Canadians of having their bodies sent back to China for burial. "I tell them to go out and buy a burial plot in Vancouver," he says. "That's when they'll be really committed to Canada."

In his quest to eliminate cultural misunderstandings, Lam worries about a new problem that he fears could create antagonism. He says that children who, following Canadian custom, go door-to-door selling things like Girl Guide cookies or collecting donations for school projects no longer knock on the doors of Chinese homes. "Chinese people think that if someone comes to their door and asks for money, they are a beggar and they send them away," he says. Lam is trying to get out the word to new immigrants so they will stop unknowingly offending the youngsters—and their parents. Still, Lam says his greatest contribution has been as a symbol of change. "British Columbia has a long, long history of discrimination," he says. "To have someone of the Chinese race now occupying its most important residence, that says a lot." To both sides.

BRENDA DALGLISH

witnesses who reported crimes—fuelled by a deep-seated fear of violent reprisals from the likes of the Dai Huen Jai, a shadowy Chinese group whose name means Big Circle Boys. "Without support from victims and witnesses," Nimmo says, "there is nothing we can do." Still, he was forced to acknowledge: "Their fear is real."

Last year, Nimmo secured funding for a counterattack. He doubled the number of Chinese officers on his 28-member squad to six and in October put into service a Cantonese-language hotline for crime tips. Those and other measures have already produced some successes. "We are hearing from more people than we used to," observes Nimmo, who points to a 35-per-cent jump in arrests during 1993. In one, the victim himself wore a hidden microphone to help Nimmo's unit snare an extortionist who had extracted as much as $500,000 from visa students in the Vancouver area.

The last four years have seen Vancouver's schools similarly transform their approach to the children of immigrant families. In place of one overworked English-as-a-second-language (ESL) teaching consultant tucked away in a third-floor room at the Vancouver school board main office, the Oak Ridge Reception and Orientation Centre now greets newcomers to the city who register their children for public school. There, a multilingual staff of 10 puts prospective students and their families through a penetrating series of assessments designed not only to grade a child's grasp of English, but also to prepare youngsters for classrooms that may be very different from the ones they have left. "Many Asian students are used to rote learning," observes the centre's director, Catherine Eddy. "And they come into a class where they are supposed to break up into groups and do problem solving." For many, she adds, "this is foreign, this is weird."

One measure of the distance that Vancouver has travelled towards smoothing relations between its old and new residents can be found in the leafy and lovingly manicured precincts of Kerrisdale and South Shaughnessy. In late 1992, the neighborhoods were at the epicentre of heated debate over the right of new purchasers to raze existing homes and replace them with much larger dwellings that frequently struck established residents as glaringly out of place. In a district where many long-standing homeowners are avid gardeners, it did not help that some builders felled full-grown trees in order to accommodate the ambitious scale of the new homes, and replaced shrubs and bushes with multiple parking spaces. "It is the barrenness that upsets me," Kerrisdale resident Campbell complains of many of the new buildings. "There were old houses here before, landscaped beautifully. Now, it looks like a movie set." At the same time, the owners of the offending homes, many—although by no means all—of them newly arrived immigrants from Hong Kong, insisted that they had met existing zoning rules and had a clear right to do as they wished with their property.

A series of emotional public hearings during early 1993 led to a compromise. In exchange for permission to build houses larger than any allowed elsewhere in Vancouver, City Hall now insists that builders of new homes take into account the style of the dwellings on either side. "The houses that are being produced now," says council member Clarke, who actively resisted the encroachment of large, boxy structures into her

South Shaughnessy neighborhood, "look just great. It seems to be working."

At the same time, even many of those who express discomfort with some aspects of immigration's impact on Vancouver concede that it is largely responsible for the city's buoyant economy. Businessman John Walker, for one, complains that the need to provide ESL instruction to nearly half of Vancouver's 55,000 public school students has helped to drive up his taxes. "But in some ways," he also acknowledges, "you cannot knock [immigration]. It keeps the economy going, especially construction." Indeed, construction workers in British Columbia are enjoying good times unparalleled anywhere else in the country.

Much of that activity is visible along the north shore of False Creek. There, a company controlled by Hong Kong billionaire Li Ka-Shing is slowly transforming the former site of Vancouver's Expo 86 into what will eventually be 204 acres of parks, high-rise condominiums, marinas and public services, including a community centre anchored by a roundhouse where the first steam locomotive to cross the country on the Canadian Pacific Railway now sits in silent and imposing retirement With eight buildings completed and construction slated to begin on five more later this year, Concord Pacific Place is the largest real estate development under way in the country.

But if the money that is fuelling the activity along False Creek comes largely from the Orient, the development's Hong Kong-born president, Terry Hui, the 30-year-old son of a junior partner in the $3-billion project, bristles at the suggestion that the dominant esthetic is anything but Canadian. "It is not our vision," Hui, who is now a Canadian citizen, told *Maclean's*. "It is Vancouver's vision. It is Vancouver's taste." To bolster that claim, Concord Pacific points to more than 200 public meetings it conducted to ensure that its plans had support from Vancouver's residents.

In less visible ways, many other Vancouver businesses plainly hope to share the prosperity that the city's Asian connection has brought to its builders. The various trade councils, business forums, networking circles, institutes and foundations aimed at fostering closer commercial ties between Canada and the Orient number well over a dozen. And the Vancouver Stock Exchange announced in December that it plans to establish an Asian Board that it hopes will attract Taiwanese and Hong Kong-owned companies with operations in booming mainland China.

Economic optimism aside, strains and frictions do remain. Although immigration and race do not show up as concerns in the letters from constituents that reach Clarke's desk, taxes do. And they are being driven up, at least in part, by the need for the new services that Nimmo and Eddy champion.

Even many people of Asian heritage admit that Hong Kong's frenetic and keenly competitive culture transplants with difficulty to Vancouver's more laid-back shores. "New immigrants are different from old immigrants," says Johnny Yan, a house builder who came to Canada from Hong Kong as a child in 1967. "A few rich people always look down on others." Adds Maggie Ip, a high-school teacher who emigrated from Hong Kong 28 years ago and who was elected to Vancouver city council last November: "In Hong Kong, they never look at the long term, because they can't plan anything beyond 1997," when the British colony will revert to the control of mainland China. Adds Ip: "That kind of mentality shows in their daily life. They want something instantly—they can't wait."

If those characteristics occasionally grate on the nerves of Vancouver's more settled residents, Ip and others argue that there are still compelling reasons for patience. For one thing, the newcomers eventually adjust to the city's slower pace. After three or four years in Canada, says Ip, "they will tell you, 'This is very peaceful, we have a nice climate, there's not too much rushing.' It is almost like two different people." (For at least a few recent arrivals from Hong Kong, however, Vancouver's slower tempo has proven *too* relaxed: there is a steady, if undocumented, trickle of individuals returning to the colony, lured back by its faster-paced economy.) British Columbia's Hong Kong-born lieutenant-governor, David Lam, meanwhile, offers another argument in favor of understanding. "We have what I consider a secret weapon with the Asian community in Canada," Lam told *Maclean's*. "Everyone of them could be the beginning of the best network linkage to Asia."

In fact, Vancouver stands little danger of becoming the "Hongcouver" of Jud Cyllorn's nightmares. New arrivals from places no more exotic than New Brunswick and Manitoba will continue to find places in a richly textured ethnic fabric. That many more will also come from across the Pacific should only reinforce Vancouver's claim to be, in developer Hui's phrase, "the gateway between North America and Asia." For most people in this Pacific city, there is far more to celebrate than to fear in its Asian connection. Indeed, when Vancouver's Chinatown erupts in fireworks and dragon dancers next week in celebration of Chinese New Year, many of the faces that crowd the sidewalks will not be Oriental. They will reflect a Canada of many colors. Jack Lee's fountain, perhaps, should rightly flow in both directions.

With JOHN HOWES and BOB IP in Vancouver and BRENDA DALGLISH in Toronto

Curriculum and Instruction in Multicultural Perspective

This unit on curriculum and instruction includes concerns relative to subject matter content to be taught and pedagogical theory of practice relating to methods of instruction. All pedagogical theory is situated in philosophical assumptions regarding what is of worth to know, what is true, and what is good to either know or do. Every school curriculum is a socially situated product of a "knowledge production" process, in which those who design the curriculum choose from all that could be included in it what actually will be included. Since classroom teachers, along with whatever texts are used, are the delivery systems for a curriculum, they have the opportunity to interpret it and add their own insights to it.

It is in the area of curriculum and instruction in the elementary and secondary schools, as well as in teacher education curricula, that a fundamental transformation must occur to sensitize all young people, including those living in isolated rural and small town communities, to the multicultural reality of our national civilization. The multicultural social heritage of our civilization must be integrated into what children and young adults learn in school. There are several different approaches to multicultural educational programming in the schools. This area of study has developed steadily, in stages, since the events of the 1960s, 1970s, and 1980s forced a reassessment of our sense of social justice. Programs in some school systems merely include the study of minority cultural groups living in their own area, and this is often done through isolated, elective courses or units in required courses. This is not the approach to multicultural education that most current leaders in the field favor. Today, most people who are experienced in working with students and teachers in the development of multicultural education programming favor a more holistic, inclusive approach to the subject. This involves the infusion of multicultural themes into the entire life of the school and all course content that can be related to human social life and the ongoing struggle for social justice on the part of traditionally conceived minority groups and women. Such an inclusive approach to multicultural education seeks to help students and teachers to develop a sense of social consciousness. The sense of social consciousness, coupled with a more global and integrated conception of our social reality, will empower them to assess more critically than most of our citizens have in the past such situations as the disparity between public democratic rhetoric and the reality that some groups still have difficulty being accepted into society's mainstream.

The National Council for the Social Studies (NCSS) has developed comprehensive curriculum guidelines for the implementation of multicultural education in elementary and secondary schools. These guidelines were prepared by the NCSS Task Force on Ethnic Studies. A revised version of these guidelines was published in 1991. They reflect the developmental thinking on the part of many educators who have been involved in the implementation of multicultural programming in school systems as well as teacher education programs. One important reason to focus on multicultural education is that a democratic nation has a moral responsibility to see that minority ethnic, cultural, or religious groups are not isolated or marginalized in the social life of the nation. The educational institutions of a nation tend to be the primary places where children and young adults learn about their national history, literature, and scientific achievement. Multicultural educational content is necessary in all American schools because students, even in the most culturally isolated rural and small town settings, do learn opinions and beliefs about ethnic, cultural, and religious groups other than their own. What students learn in the informal social relations of their home communities about other social groups that are different from theirs is often factually misleading or incorrect. This is how our past sad heritage of racism and negative stereotypes of differing social groups evolved. There has been much progress in the area of civil rights in the past 40 years, but there has also been resurgent racism and intercultural misunderstanding. School is the one place children and adolescents go each day where it is possible for them to learn an objective view of the culturally pluralistic national heritage that is both their present social reality and their future one as well. All communities are linked in some way to the culturally pluralistic social reality. When students leave high school to go into military service, attend college, or attempt careers in other parts of the nation in the corporate sector, government, or the arts, they will encounter a multicultural world very different from the frequently provincial and not adequately informed social structure of their own local community or cultural groups.

Teachers should help their students to recognize and respect ethnic and cultural diversity and to value it, because it does enhance and enrich the quality of our civilization. All students should be raised to cherish the concept of equality of social and academic opportunity as part of a democracy. Children and adolescents should also be taught that they each, individually, have the right to choose to what extent they wish to identify with the activities and organized efforts of their own particular ethnic or cultural groups. Participation in ethnic group activities is voluntary in a democracy. Young people need to be taught in their school studies that they are a part of a great, unified nation, in which people of many diverse ethnic, cultural, and religious backgrounds work together to build an ever richer and more just nation-state in a world of interdependent political and economic systems. This commitment to the appreciation of cultural diversity along with social justice for all should permeate every part of the life of every school in the nation. Every youngster should grow up in such a way that, upon high school graduation, he or she will honorably, honestly believe that Thomas Jefferson and others were right to swear "eternal hostility against every form of tyranny over the mind of man." Realizing how far we have come since Jefferson's time, we should plan every school curriculum to reflect the idea that every man or woman in the nation deserves an equal educational and social opportunity. For we are brothers and sisters as coexistent citizens of a great, culturally pluralistic nation. We should not see one another as adversaries because of our differing ethnic, cultural, or religious backgrounds.

The essays in this unit reflect these concerns and provide a wide variety of perspectives on how to broaden the multicultural effort in our schools. The authors seek to incorporate more intercultural and global content and experiences into the main body of curriculum and instruction. Educators will find that, taken together, these essays provide a sound basis for understanding what multicultural curriculum and instruction should be about. They are relevant to course work in curriculum and instruction, curriculum theory and construction, educational policy studies and leadership, history and philosophy of education, and cultural foundations of education.

Looking Ahead: Challenge Questions

What are the similarities and distinctions between a "culture" and an "ethnic group"?

Why is it more effective to integrate multicultural content into all aspects of a school curriculum?

What are the varying ways in which multicultural education is defined? Which model do you prefer?

What is the rationale for the multicultural educational effort in the elementary and secondary schools? Why, or why not, should all students be exposed to it?

How can in-service teachers be better prepared to engage in multicultural instruction and learning experiences?

—F. S.

Curriculum Guidelines for Multicultural Education

Prepared by the NCSS Task Force on Ethnic Studies Curriculum Guidelines
Adopted by NCSS Board of Directors, 1976, revised 1991

Introduction

Publishing a revision of *Curriculum Guidelines for Multicultural Education* is especially appropriate and timely because of the significant increase in the nation's population of people of color that has occurred since they were published sixteen years ago. The percentage of people of color in the nation will continue to rise throughout the early decades of the next century. Indeed, the 1990 census revealed that one out of every four people who live in the United States is a person of color and that one out of every three people will be a person of color by the turn of the century. Likewise, the ethnic and racial makeup of the nation's classrooms is changing significantly. Students of color constitute a majority in twenty-five of the nation's largest school districts and in California, our most populous state with a population of thirty million people. Students of color will make up nearly half (46 percent) of the nation's school-age youth by 2020, and about 27 percent of those students will be victims of poverty.

One important implication of these demographic trends is that education in the twenty-first century must help low-income students and students of color to develop the knowledge, attitudes, and skills necessary to participate in the work force and in society. This goal is not possible without restructuring schools, colleges, and universities, and institutionalizing new goals and ideals within them. As currently conceptualized and organized, schools today are unable to help most low-income students and students of color attain these goals.

Another important implication of the demographic imperative is that students from all social groups, i.e., class, racial, ethnic, cultural, and gender, must attain the knowledge, skills, and competencies necessary to participate in public discourse and civic action with people who differ from them in significant ways. People are socialized within families and in communities where they learn the values, perspectives, attitudes, and behaviors of their primordial culture. Community culture enables people to survive. It also, however, restricts their freedom and their ability to make critical choices and to reform their society.

Multicultural education helps students understand and affirm their community cultures and helps to free them from cultural boundaries, allowing them to create and maintain a civic community that works for the common good. Multicultural education seeks to actualize the idea of *e pluribus unum* within our nation and to create a society that recognizes and respects the cultures of its diverse people, people united within a framework of overarching democratic values. A unified and cohesive democratic society can be created only when the rights of its diverse people are reflected in its institutions, within its national culture, and within its schools, colleges, and universities. A national culture or school curriculum that does not reflect the voices, struggles, hopes, and dreams of its many peoples is neither democratic nor cohesive. Divisiveness within a nation-state occurs when important segments within its society are structurally excluded and marginalized.

The changing ethnic texture in the United States has stimulated a bitter debate over the extent to which the school, college, and university curricula should be revised to reflect ethnic, cultural, and gender diversity. This polarized debate has become forensic and has generated more heat than light.

The increase of our nation's students of color and the debate over the curriculum make this an appropriate time for the National Council for the Social Studies to reaffirm its commitment to educational programs and curricula that reflect the racial, ethnic, and cultural diversity within the United States and the world. As diversity in the world grows, it becomes increasingly important for students in the United States to acquire the knowledge, skills, and values essential for functioning in cross-racial, cross-ethnic, and cross-cultural situations. For democracy to function in a pluralistic nation-state, its citizens must be able to transcend their ethnic and cultural boundaries in order to participate in public discussion and action. An important goal of multicultural education is to help students from diverse cultures learn *how* to transcend their cultural borders and engage in dialogue and action essential for the survival of our democratic political system and way of life. No goal for education is more important as we approach the threshold of the new century.

When Margit McGuire, president of National Council for the Social Studies, invited me to revise these guidelines, I asked each original author to send me his or her revisions and suggestions. I have incorporated most of the suggestions they sent me. I must assume total responsibility for this revised edition, however, because I selected the ideas to incorporate and wrote the new text. I wish to publicly thank each member of the task force for sending me thoughtful revisions and suggestions in a timely fashion. We have remained warm friends and professional colleagues for nearly two decades.

I am grateful to Charlotte Anderson and the NCSS Equity and Social Justice Committee for preparing thoughtful and

From *Social Education,* September 1992, pp. 274-294. © 1992 by the National Council for the Social Studies. Reprinted by permission.

helpful comments on an earlier draft of this revised edition of the guidelines.

This revised edition of the guidelines differs from the original in many ways. The term *multiethnic education* was used in the title and throughout the first edition; in the revised edition, *multicultural education* is used. Today, *multicultural education* is the most frequently used term to refer to the issues and concerns discussed in this document. The term *multiethnic education* has almost faded from our lexicon, a trend the task force resisted and did not foresee when the guidelines were written in 1976.

Multicultural education is also used in this edition because it more readily communicates to the new generation of readers its focus and content. Furthermore, I have tried to broaden the document's scope to include cultural groups that may not be ethnic, although ethnic groups remain the primary focus. Many of the principles, concepts, and issues discussed in the guidelines are linked to issues related to gender, class, and region—and to the intersection of these variables—as much as they are to ethnic groups and ethnicity. Also, people who are ethnic also have a gender, a social class, and a region; the intersection of these variables is an important and growing concern of multicultural theorists.

This revised edition also focuses more on race than the original does. We rarely used the word *race* in the first edition, perhaps because of our vain hope that silence would facilitate racism's disappearance. The ugly racial incidents that have occurred in our society—specifically on college and university campuses—since the guidelines were first published have eroded our hope that racism would dry up like a raisin in the sun. Racism is cyclic, and is alive and well today. Both racism and sexism must be examined seriously in any sound multicultural curriculum.

New concepts, terms, and statistics have also been incorporated into this edition. The bibliography reflects the new research and the extent to which the field of multicultural education has matured and prospered since the guidelines were first published. I hope this revision will both promote further growth and development in the field and raise the level of dialogue about multicultural education, especially among the public and within the popular media.

These guidelines are divided into four sections: A Rationale for Ethnic Pluralism and Multicultural Education, Curriculum Guidelines for Multicultural Education, The Multicultural Education Program Evaluation Checklist, plus a section of references.

The rationale section describes the view of society on which these guidelines are predicated, describes the nature of educational institutions and learners in a culturally pluralistic society, and delineates goals for school reform.

The second section describes the ideal characteristics of educational environments that are consistent with the ethnic pluralism described in the rationale. The term *multicultural education*, as used in these guidelines, does not necessarily refer to educational institutions that have mixed racial and ethnic populations, but, rather, to the idealized educational institutions and curricula that reflect and are sensitive to the ethnic and cultural diversity within the United States and the world.

The third section encourages and helps in the assessment of specific educational environments to determine how they reflect an idealized educational institution. The guidelines describe goals that each educational institution can strive to achieve and provide specific guidelines intended to clarify the meaning of the general guideline and to facilitate the assessment of educational environments.

I would like to acknowledge the Center for Multicultural Education at the University of Washington for research assistance that enabled me to find time within a hectic schedule to revise these guidelines. I am grateful to Allen D. Glenn, dean of our College of Education, for his support of the Center and my work. I thank my family—Cherry, Angela, and Patricia—for paying a high price of family time and weekends for a professional duty that I felt was a high calling.

James A. Banks, Director
Center for Multicultural Education
University of Washington
Seattle, Washington

Part One: A Rationale for Ethnic Pluralism and Multicultural Education

Three major factors make multicultural education a necessity: (1) ethnic pluralism is a growing societal reality that influences the lives of young people; (2) in one way or another, individuals acquire knowledge or beliefs, sometimes invalid, about ethnic and cultural groups; and (3) beliefs and knowledge about ethnic and cultural groups limit the perspectives of many and make a difference, often a negative difference, in the opportunities and options available to members of ethnic and cultural groups. Because ethnicity, race, and class are important in the lives of many citizens of the United States, it is essential that all members of our society develop multicultural literacy, that is, a solidly based understanding of racial, ethnic, and cultural groups and their significance in U.S. society and throughout the world. Schools cannot afford to ignore their responsibility to contribute to the development of multicultural literacy and understanding. Only a well-conceived, sensitive, thorough, and continuous program of multicultural education can create the broadly based multicultural literacy so necessary for the future of our nation and world.

In the United States, ethnic diversity has remained visible despite the acculturation process that takes place in any society made up of many ethnic groups. Although ethnic affiliations are weak for many U.S. citizens, a large number still have some attachments to their ethnic cultures and to the symbols of their ancestral traditions. The values and behavior of many U.S. citizens are heavily influenced by their ethnicity. Ethnic identification is often increased by the discrimination experienced by many because of their racial characteristics, language, or culture. Ethnic identification is also increased when significant numbers of new immigrants from the homeland arrive in the United States. Thousands of immigrants from Asia and Latin America made the United States their home during the 1980s. About 85 percent of the documented immigrants that settled in the United States between 1981 and 1989 came from Asia (47 percent) and Latin America (38 percent) (Banks 1991a, 4).

During the 1980s and 1990s, a significant increase in the population of people of color in the United States and the expression of new forms of racism stimulated a vigorous and contentious debate among educators about the extent to which the curriculum should be revised to reflect ethnic and cultural diversity. At least three major groups that participated in this debate can be identified—the Western traditionalists, the Afrocentrists, and the multiculturalists. The Western traditionalists argue that content about Europe and Western civilization should be at the center of the curriculum in the nation's schools, colleges, and universities because of the extent to which Western ideas and values have influenced the development of U.S. culture and civilization (Howe 1991; Ravitch 1990; Schlesinger 1991). The Afrocentrists maintain that it is essential that an African perspective be incorporated into the curriculum (Asante 1991). The multiculturalists believe that concepts and events should be viewed from diverse ethnic and cultural perspectives (Banks 1991a; Sleeter and Grant 1987; Tetreault 1989). The multiculturalists also argue that the conception of Western civilization taught in schools should be reconceptualized to acknowledge the debt the West owes to Asian and African civilizations (Bernal 1991). The multiculturalists also believe that the conflict inherent in the West's commitment to democratic ideals and the racism and sexism still practiced in Western societies should be made explicit in the curriculum.

The bitter debate about the extent to which issues related to race and ethnicity should be reflected in the curriculum of the nation's schools indicates that race and ethnicity are cogent forces in contemporary U.S. society. The debate over the curriculum canon is an appropriate one for a pluralistic democratic society. It reflects the extent to which various interest groups are trying to shape the national identity and culture in the United States in ways that are consistent with their views of the nation's past, present, and future.

The concept of cultural diversity embraced in these guidelines is most consistent with the position of the multiculturalists—a position that incorporates important elements of both the Western traditionalist and the Afrocentrist approaches. The multiculturalists' position contributes best to the building of a society that incorporates diversity within a cohesive and unified nation-state. Multicultural education supports and enhances the notion of *e pluribus unum*—out of many, one. To build a successful and inclusive nation-state, the hopes, dreams, and experiences of the many groups within it must be reflected in the structure and institutions of society. This is the only viable way to create a nation-state in which all groups will feel included, loyal, and patriotic.

The guidelines presented in this document are predicated on a democratic ideology in which ethnic and cultural diversity is viewed as a positive, integral ingredient. A democratic society protects and provides opportunities for ethnic and cultural diversity at the same time having overarching values—such as equality, justice, and human dignity—that all groups accept and respect. Ethnic and cultural diversity is based on the following four premises:

1. Ethnic and cultural diversity should be recognized and respected at individual, group, and societal levels.
2. Ethnic and cultural diversity provides a basis for societal enrichment, cohesiveness, and survival.
3. Equality of opportunity should be afforded to members of all ethnic and cultural groups.
4. Ethnic and cultural identification should be optional for individuals.

Characteristics of an Ethnic Group

Because this document focuses on ethnic pluralism and its implications for school reform, it is essential that we establish a working definition of *ethnic group* that reflects social sci-

ence theory and research and facilitates school reform. No one definition of the term is accepted by all social scientists or is adequate for the purpose of this document. Consequently, the working definition used herein reflects a composite of existing definitions and the results of task force discussions.

An ethnic group is distinguished from other kinds of cultural groups in the definition for this document. An ethnic group is a specific kind of cultural group having all the following characteristics:

a. Its origins precede the creation of a nation-state or are external to the nation-state. In the case of the United States, ethnic groups have distinct pre–United States or extro–United States territorial bases, e.g., immigrant groups and Native Americans.
b. It is an involuntary group, although individual identification with the group may be optional.
c. It has an ancestral tradition and its members share a sense of peoplehood and an interdependence of fate.
d. It has distinguishing value orientations, behavioral patterns, and interests.
e. Its existence has an influence, in many cases a substantial influence, on the lives of its members.
f. Membership in the group is influenced both by how members define themselves and by how they are defined by others.

The definition of *ethnic group* stated above includes some groups that are distinguished primarily on the basis of race, such as African Americans and Japanese Americans, some that are distinguished primarily on the basis of unique sets of cultural and religious attributes, such as Jewish Americans, and some that are distinguished on the basis of national origin, such as Polish Americans. The criteria for characterization, of course, frequently overlap; Japanese Americans, for example, constitute an ethnic group characterized by national, cultural, and racial origins. The definition does not include cultural or regional groups of United States origin, such as those from the Appalachian region. This exclusion does not imply that such groups do not have unique cultural experiences that have teaching implications. Although they are not the primary focus of this document, many of the guidelines are applicable to the study of regional and other kinds of cultural groups. Factors such as region, race, gender, social class, and religion are variables that cut across ethnic groups. Students must examine these factors to gain a valid understanding of the nature of racial, ethnic, and cultural diversity in U.S. society.

Characteristics of a Cultural Group

A cultural group shares behavioral patterns, symbols, values, beliefs, and other human-constructed characteristics that distinguish it from other groups. Kroeber and Kluckhuhn (1952, 161), after surveying definitions of culture, concluded that "culture consists of patterns, explicit and implicit, of and for behavior acquired and transmitted by symbols, constituting the distinctive achievements of human groups, including their embodiments in artifacts; the essential core of culture consists of traditional…ideas and especially their attached values."

Like most social scientists today, Kroeber and Kluckhuhn emphasize the intangible, symbolic, and ideational aspects of culture. Ideas, ways of thinking, values, symbols, and other intangible aspects of human life—and not tangible objects such as tools, clothing, or foods—distinguish one cultural group from another in modernized societies. Two cultural groups might eat the same foods but have different meanings and interpretations for them. It is their values, perspectives, and ways of viewing reality that distinguish cultural groups from one another in the United States, not their clothing, foods, or other tangible aspects of group life.

Principles of Ethnic and Cultural Diversity

1. Ethnic and cultural diversity should be recognized and respected at the individual, group, and societal levels.

Ethnic and cultural diversity is a social reality all too frequently ignored by educational institutions, yet it deserves open recognition. Members of ethnic and cultural groups often have worldviews, values, traditions, and practices that differ from those of the mainstream society and from those of other ethnic groups.

Even in the midst of a marked degree of assimilation and acculturation, and in spite of efforts to ignore, belittle, or eliminate some ethnic differences, many U.S. citizens have strong feelings of ethnic identity (Alba 1990). Since the civil rights movement of the 1960s and 1970s, some ethnic groups have heightened their visibility and increased their demands for equal opportunity (Alba 1990). Ethnic and cultural diversity continues to permeate life in the United States. Its persistence and our nation's changing demographics suggest that it will characterize the future (Hodgkinson 1985).

Nearly half (46 percent) of school-age youths in the United States will be people of color by 2020 (Pallas, Natriello, and McDill 1989). People of color, women, and immigrants will make up more than 83 percent of the new additions to the U.S. work force between now and the turn of the century. White men born in the United States will make up only 15 percent of the new additions to the labor force during this period (Johnson and Packer 1987).

Simply recognizing ethnic and cultural diversity is not enough. Understanding and respect for diverse values, traditions, and behaviors are essential if we are to actualize fully our nation's democratic ideals. The call for understanding and respect is based on a belief that the existence and expression of differences can improve the quality of life for individuals, for ethnic and cultural groups, and for society as a whole.

For individuals, group identity can provide a foundation for self-definition. Ethnic and cultural group membership can provide a sense of belonging, of shared traditions, of interdependence of fate—especially for members of groups who have all too often had restricted access to institutions in the larger society. When society views ethnic and cultural differences with respect, individuals can define themselves ethnically without conflict or shame.

The psychological cost of assimilation has been and continues to be high for many U.S. citizens. It too often demands self-denial, self-hatred, and rejection of family and ethnic ties. Social demands for conformity, which have harmful human consequences, are neither democratic nor humane. Such practices deny dignity by refusing to accept individuals as persons in themselves and by limiting the realization of human potential. Such demands run counter to the democratic values of freedom of association and equality of opportunity.

A society that respects ethnic group differences aims to protect its citizens from discriminatory practices and prejudicial attitudes. Such respect supports the survival of these groups and augments their opportunities to shape their lives in ways they choose. For society as a whole, ethnic groups can serve as sources of innovation. By respecting differences, society is provided a wider base of ideas, values, and behaviors that increase its capacity for creative change.

Coping with change is fundamental to the survival of culture. Adapting to new conditions is critical. Without constructive reaction to change, cultures may weaken and deteriorate. In the face of rapidly changing conditions, the United States, as a nation, has to be concerned with ensuring mechanisms for coping with change. One way cultures change is through the process of innovation: a person (or persons) introduces new ways of thinking or behaving which are accepted by society or challenge cultural views. By respecting the plurality of ethnic and cultural life-styles, and by permitting them to flourish, our national culture may expand the base of alternatives from which it can draw in responding to new conditions and new problems.

Conversely, to the extent that a culture is homogeneous, its capability for creative change is limited. When the range of tolerated differences in values and behaviors is minimal, rigidity inhibits innovation. Too much conformity and convergence is characteristic of mass culture. On the other hand, too little acceptance of common cultural values and practices can produce social disorganization. The balance is a delicate one in a culture that must face up to the challenge of changing conditions; a dynamic and pluralistic nation cannot be left without access to competing, unique, and creative ideas. Recognition and respect for ethnic and cultural differences enable society to enhance the potential of individuals and the integrity and contributions of ethnic and cultural groups, and so to invigorate the culture.

2. Ethnic and cultural diversity provides a basis for societal enrichment, cohesiveness, and survival.

The principles on which these guidelines are based seek not only to recognize and respect ethnic and cultural diversity but to establish across racial, ethnic, and cultural lines intercultural bonds that will contribute to the strength and vitality of society.

This position maintains the right of ethnic groups to socialize their young into their cultural patterns as long as such practices are consistent with human dignity and democratic ideals. Therefore, an individual's primary group associations—family relations, friendship groups, religious affiliations—may be heavily influenced by ethnic traditions. At the same time, members of ethnic groups have both the right and the responsibility to accept U.S. democratic values and to help shape the significant institutions of the larger society. Legal and educational institutions must have a strong commitment to affecting the conditions that will permit members of ethnic groups to become fully participating members of the larger society. Ethnic groups must feel that they have a stake in this society; to the extent that ethnic group members feel a sense of ownership in societal institutions, their cultural practices will reflect the inherent values of society as a whole. What is needed is a cohesive society, characterized by ethnic pluralism, wherein the self-identities of individuals allow them to say: "I am an African American (or a Polish American, or a Mexican American)—and I am an American."

Respect for ethnic differences should promote, not destroy, societal cohesion. Although separatism is not the desire of most members of ethnic groups, they strongly demand that their histories and cultures become integral parts of the school curriculum and the larger society (Asante 1987, 1991). To the extent that society creates an environment in which all ethnic groups can flourish, and in which such groups can contribute constructively to the shaping of public institutions, hostilities will be defused and the society will benefit from its rich base of ethnic traditions and cultures. In effect, unity thrives in an atmosphere where varieties of human potential are neither socially censored nor ignored, but valued.

3. Equality of opportunity must be afforded to all members of ethnic and cultural groups.

Recognition and respect for ethnic and cultural groups require legal enforcement of equal economic, political, and educational opportunity. Anything less relegates ethnic groups and their members to the inferior status that has too often limited the quality of their lives.

Ethnic and cultural groups themselves continue to demand equal participation in society as a whole. If society is to benefit from ethnic and cultural differences, it must provide for significant interactions within social institutions. To reach this goal, ethnic and cultural groups must have access to the full range of occupational, educational, economic, and political opportunities. Society will benefit from structural integration and the mutual involvement of all sorts of people in political, educational, and economic life.

4. Ethnic and cultural identification for individuals should be optional in a democracy.

Although the assimilationist ideology has dominated our national thought for two centuries, ethnicity has proved to be a resilient factor in U.S. life and culture. The centrality of Anglo-American tradition notwithstanding, many individuals continue to derive their primary identity from their ethnic group membership. At the same time, it must be recognized that widespread cultural assimilation and acculturation has taken place in U.S. society. Many individuals of white ethnic origin are no longer identified ethnically with their original or primordial ethnic group. Although a large number of these individuals have intermarried and much cultural exchange among white ethnic groups has taken place, a new collective ethnic identity has emerged among white Americans that most of them share. Alba (1990) calls this new ethnic identity and group *European Americans*.

The degree of individuals' ethnic attachments and affiliations vary greatly. The beliefs and behaviors of some individuals are heavily influenced by their ethnic culture or cultures; others maintain only some ethnic beliefs and behavioral characteristics; still others try to reject or lose, or are simply unaware of, their ethnic origins. There are also individuals of mixed ethnic origin who identify with more than one group or for whom ethnic identification may be difficult or impossible.

For many persons, then, ethnic criteria may be irrelevant for purposes of self-identification. Their identities stem primarily from, for example, gender, social class, occupation, political affiliation, or religion. Moreover, ethnic origins ought not to be romanticized. Many, though not all, who left their original homelands did so because opportunities were closed to them there. However good "the good old days" were, they are gone. The "old countries" too have been changing. Ethnicity should not be maintained artificially.

It is inconsistent with a democratic ideology to mandate ethnic affiliation. In an idealized democratic society, individuals are free to choose their group allegiances. Association should be voluntary—a matter of personal choice. In our society, however, members of some ethnic groups have this option

while others do not. Society should maximize the opportunity for individuals to choose their group identifications and affiliations.

Although a democratic society can and should protect the right to ethnic identification, it cannot insist upon it. To do so would violate individual freedom of choice. To confine individuals to any given form of affiliation violates the principles of liberty guaranteed by the basic documents upon which this nation was founded.

The Role of the School

The societal goals stated in this document are future oriented. In effect, they present a vision of our society that recognizes and respects ethnic and cultural diversity as compatible with national and societal unity rather than one that seeks to reduce ethnic and cultural differences. Further progress in that direction is consistent with the democratic ideals—freedom, equality, justice, and human dignity—embodied in our basic national documents. By respecting ethnic and cultural differences, we can help to close the gap between our democratic ideals and societal practices. Such practices are too often discriminatory toward members of ethnic and cultural groups.

It follows, therefore, that schools need to assume a new responsibility. Their socialization practices should incorporate the ethnic diversity that is an integral part of the democratic commitment to human dignity. At the same time, however, schools must help socialize youth in ways that will foster basic democratic ideals that serve as overarching goals for all U.S. citizens. The schools' goal should be to help attain a delicate balance of diversity and unity—one nation that respects the cultural rights and freedoms of its many peoples. As schools embark on educational programs that reflect multiculturalism, they must demonstrate a commitment to:
a. recognize and respect ethnic and cultural diversity;
b. promote societal cohesiveness based on the shared participation of ethnically and culturally diverse peoples;
c. maximize equality of opportunity for all individuals and groups; and
d. facilitate constructive societal change that enhances human dignity and democratic ideals.

The study of ethnic heritage should not consist of a narrow promotion of ethnocentrism or nationalism. Personal ethnic identity and knowledge of others' ethnic identities is essential to the sense of understanding and the feeling of personal well-being that promote intergroup and international understanding. Multicultural education should stress the process of self-identification as an essential aspect of the understanding that underlies commitment to the dignity of humankind throughout the world community.

The Nature of the Learner

Research indicates that individual learning styles vary, that all people do not learn in the same way. Of particular interest to multicultural education is research suggesting that learning styles may be related to ethnicity in some ways (Hale-Benson 1982; Shade 1989). On the basis of this research, schools can reject the notion that all students learn in precisely the same way. For too long, educational practices have reflected such universal views of learning and have expected all students to conform to them. Schools should recognize that they cannot treat all students alike or they run the risk of denying equal educational opportunity to all persons. Educators should be aware of behavior that is normative and acceptable in various ethnic and cultural groups. The practices of multicultural schools must be both responsive and adaptive to ethnic differences.

Goals for School Reform

Two major goals for school reform follow. Both are based on what has preceded: the principles of ethnic and cultural diversity, the role of the school, and cultural differences among individual learners.

1. Schools should create total school environments that are consistent with democratic ideals and cultural diversity.

Schools reflect their values not only in their curricula and materials, but in policies, hiring practices, governance procedures, and climate—sometimes referred to as the informal, or "hidden," curricula. It can be argued that students often learn as much about the society from nonformal areas of schooling as from the planned curriculum. Education for multiculturalism, therefore, requires more than a change in curricula and textbooks. It requires systemwide changes that permeate all aspects of school life.

2. Schools should define and implement curricular policies that are consistent with democratic ideals and cultural diversity.

Schools should not promote the ideologies and political goals of any specific group, including those of dominant groups, but should promote a democratic ideology. Too often, school curricula have promoted the interests of dominant groups and, therefore, have been detrimental to the interests of some ethnic groups. Promoting the interests of any group over those of others increases the possibility of ethnic and racial tension and conflict.

In recent years, a contentious debate has taken place about whose culture or cultures should be reflected and represented in the school and university curriculum. The debate has centered on which social science, philosophical, and literary works should constitute the canonical knowledge taught in the nation's schools, colleges, and universities.

The Western traditionalists are concerned that more content about women and people of color will result in insufficient attention to the Western roots of American civilization (Howe 1991; Ravitch 1990). Multiculturalists have pointed out that the voices, experiences, and perspectives of people of color and women are often left out or muted in many school and university courses about Western civilization and U.S. society (Lerner 1979; Sleeter and Grant 1987; Tetreault 1989). Other advocates have called for an Afrocentric curriculum for predominantly African-American schools (Asante 1987, 1990, 1991).

Curriculum transformation is necessary for the nation's schools, colleges, and universities to describe accurately the Western roots of American civilization and to depict the diversity that characterizes the West. The debt that Western civilization owes to Africa, Asia, and indigenous America should also be described in the curriculum (Bernal 1991; Diop 1974; Sertima 1988; Weatherford 1988).

The conception of Western civilization most often taught in schools, colleges, and universities should be broadened. Too often, the West is conceptualized in a narrow way to include primarily the heritage of Western European upper-class males. Yet the ideas and writings of women and people of color in

the United States are also Western. Zora Neale Hurston, Maxine Hong Kingston, Rudolfo A. Anaya, W. E. B. Dubois, Carlos Bulosan, and N. Scott Momaday—like Milton, Shakespeare, Virgil, and Locke—are Western writers. The West should also be described in ways that accurately describe the gap between its democratic ideals and realities. Western civilization is characterized by ideals such as democracy and freedom but also by struggle, conflict, and deferred and shattered dreams.

The curriculum in the nation's schools, colleges, and universities should reflect all of its citizens. When particular groups feel excluded or victimized by schools and other institutions, conflicts, tensions, and power struggles ensue. The pluralist dilemma related to the curriculum canon debate can only be resolved when all groups involved—the Western traditionalists, the Afrocentrists, and the multiculturalists—share power and engage in genuine dialogue and discussion. Power sharing is a requisite to genuine debate and conflict resolution. When groups and individuals feel victimized by the school and the larger society because of ethnicity, conflict and tension result, and struggles to gain rights occur.

Part Two: Curriculum Guidelines for Multicultural Education

1.0 Ethnic and cultural diversity should permeate the total school environment.

Effective teaching about U.S. ethnic and cultural groups can best take place within an educational setting that accepts, encourages, and respects the expression of ethnic and cultural diversity. To attain this kind of educational atmosphere, the total school environment—not merely courses and programs—must be reformed. Schools' informal or "hidden" curricula are as important as their formalized courses of study.

Teaching about various ethnic or cultural groups in a few specialized courses is not enough. Content about a variety of ethnic groups should be incorporated into many subject areas, preschool through 12th grade and beyond. Some dimensions of multicultural education, however, have higher priority in some subject areas than in others. We can identity several dimensions of multicultural education, including *content integration,* the *knowledge construction process*, and an *equity pedagogy* (Banks 1991b). In social studies, the humanities, and the language arts, content integration is often the first and most important concern. In physics, however, developing pedagogies that will help students of color and female students to excel academically might be of greater concern than content integration (Belenky et al. 1986). Students can examine how knowledge is constructed in each discipline.

Multicultural education clearly means different things in different disciplines and areas of study. To interpret or attempt to implement multicultural education the same way in each discipline or area of study will create frustration among teachers and build resistance to the concept. Nevertheless, teachers in each discipline can analyze their teaching procedures and styles to determine the extent to which they reflect multicultural issues and concerns. An equity pedagogy exists when teachers modify their instruction in ways that facilitate the academic achievement of students from diverse racial, cultural, gender, and social-class groups. This includes using a variety of teaching styles and approaches that are consistent with the wide range of learning styles found in various cultural, ethnic, and gender groups.

To permeate the total school environment with ethnic and

139

cultural diversity, students must have readily available resource materials that provide accurate information on the diverse aspects of the histories and cultures of various racial, ethnic, and cultural groups. Learning centers, libraries, and resource centers should include a variety of resources on the history, literature, music, folklore, views of life, and art of different ethnic and cultural groups.

Ethnic and cultural diversity in a school's informal programs should be reflected in assembly programs, classrooms, hallway and entrance decorations, cafeteria menus, counseling interactions, and extracurricular programs. School-sponsored dances that consistently provide only one kind of ethnic music, for example, are as contrary to the spirit and principles of multicultural education as are curricula that teach only about mainstream U.S. ideals, values, and contributions.

Participation in activities—such as cheerleading, booster clubs, honor societies, and athletic teams—should be open to all students; in fact, the participation of students from various racial, ethnic, and cultural backgrounds should be solicited. Such activities can provide invaluable opportunities not only for the development of self-esteem, but for students from different ethnic and cultural backgrounds to learn to work and play together, and to recognize that all individuals, whatever their ethnic identities, have worth and are capable of achieving.

2.0 School policies and procedures should foster positive multicultural interactions and understandings among students, teachers, and the support staff.

School governance should protect the individual's right to (1) retain esteem for his or her home environment, (2) develop a positive self-concept, (3) develop empathy and insight into and respect for the ethnicity of others, and (4) receive an equal educational opportunity.

Each institution needs rules and regulations to guide behavior so as to attain institutional goals and objectives. School rules and regulations should enhance cross-cultural harmony and understanding among students, staff, and teachers. In the past, school harmony was often sought through efforts to "treat everyone the same"; experience in multiethnic settings, however, indicates that the same treatment for everyone is unfair to many students. Instead of insisting on one ideal model of behavior that is unfair to many students, school policies should recognize and accommodate individual and ethnic group differences. This does not mean that some students should obey school rules and others should not; it means that ethnic groups' behaviors should be honored as long as they are not inconsistent with major school and societal goals. It also means that school policies may have to make allowances for ethnic traditions. For example, customs that affect Jewish students' food preferences and school attendance on certain religious days should be respected.

Equal educational opportunity should be increased by rules that protect students from procedures and practices that relegate them to low-ability or special education classes simply because of their low scores on standardized English reading and achievement tests.

It is especially important for educators to consider equity issues related to testing because many groups and individuals are pushing for the establishment of a national test or tests. Unless significant changes are made within schools and society that will enable low-income students and students of color to perform well on national tests, these students will become double victims—victims of both a poor educational system

and national tests that relegate them to inferior jobs and deny them opportunities for further education (Mercer 1989). If developed, these national tests should be constructed and used in ways that are consistent with the principles of ethnic pluralism and multicultural education described in these guidelines.

Guidance and other student services personnel should not view students stereotypically regarding their academic abilities and occupational aspirations, and students must be protected from responses based on such views. Counselors should be cautioned to counsel students on the basis of their individual potentials and interests as well as their ethnic needs and concerns. Counselors will need to be particularly aware of their own biases when counseling students whose ethnicity differs from theirs.

Schools should recognize the holidays and festivities of major importance to various ethnic groups. Provisions should be made to ensure that traditional holidays and festivities reflect multicultural modes of celebration. For example, the ways in which some American Indian tribes celebrate Thanksgiving, Orthodox Greeks celebrate Easter, and Jews celebrate Hanukkah can be appropriately included in school programs.

3.0 A school's staff should reflect the ethnic and cultural diversity within the United States.

Members of various ethnic and cultural groups must be part of a school's instructional, administrative, policymaking, and support staffs if the school is truly multiethnic and multicultural. School personnel—teachers, principals, cooks, custodians, secretaries, students, and counselors—make contributions to multicultural environments as important as do courses of study and instructional materials. Students learn important lessons about ethnic and cultural diversity by observing interactions among racial, ethnic, cultural, and gender groups in their school, observing and experiencing the verbal behavior of the professional and support staffs, and observing the extent to which the staff is ethnically and racially mixed. Therefore, school policies should be established and aggressively implemented to recruit and maintain a multiethnic school staff, sensitive to the needs of a pluralistic democratic society.

In addition, students can benefit from positive and cooperative interactions with students from various racial, ethnic, and cultural groups (Slavin 1983; Cohen 1986). When plans are made to mix students from diverse groups—whether through school desegregation, exchange programs and visits, or program assignment—extreme care must be taken to ensure that the environment in which the students interact is a positive and enhancing one (Banks 1991c). When students from different ethnic and racial groups interact within a hostile environment, their racial antipathies are likely to increase (Stephan 1985).

4.0 Schools should have systematic, comprehensive, mandatory, and continuing staff development programs.

A teacher is an important variable in a student's formal learning environment. Attention should be devoted to the training and retraining of teachers and other members of the professional and support staff to create the kind of multicultural school environment recommended in these guidelines. Sound materials and other instructional program components are ineffective in the hands of teachers who lack the skills, attitudes, perceptions, and content background essential for a positive multicultural school environment. An effective staff development program must involve administrators, librarians, counselors, and members of the support staff such as cooks, secretaries, and bus drivers. This is necessary because any well-trained and sensitive teacher must work within a supportive institutional environment to succeed. Key administrators, such as principals, must set by example the school norms for ethnic and cultural differences. The need to involve administrators, especially building principals, in comprehensive and systematic staff development programs cannot be overemphasized.

Effective professional staff development should begin at the preservice level, continue when educators are employed by schools, and focus on helping the staff members: (a) clarify and analyze their feelings, attitudes, and perceptions toward their own and other racial, ethnic, and cultural groups; (b) acquire knowledge about and understanding of the historical experiences and sociological characteristics of ethnic and cultural groups in the United States; (c) increase their instructional skills within multicultural school environments; (d) improve their intercultural communications skills; (e) improve their skill in curriculum development as it relates to ethnic and cultural diversity; and (f) improve their skill in creating, selecting, evaluating, and revising instructional materials.

Staff development for effective multicultural schools is best undertaken jointly by school districts, local colleges and universities, and local community agencies. Each bears a responsibility for training school personnel, at both the preservice and in-service levels, to function successfully within multicultural instructional settings.

Effective staff development programs must be carefully conceptualized and implemented. Short workshops, selected courses, and other short-term experiences may be essential components of such programs, but these alone cannot constitute an entire staff development program. Rather, sound staff development programs should consist of a wide variety of program components including needs assessments, curriculum development, peer teaching, and materials selection and evaluation. Lectures alone are insufficient. Ongoing changes should be made to make staff development programs more responsive to the needs of practicing professionals.

5.0 The curriculum should reflect the cultural learning styles and characteristics of the students within the school community.

Students in a school responsive to ethnic and cultural diversity cannot be treated identically and still be afforded equal educational opportunities. Some students have unique cultural and ethnic characteristics to which the school should respond deliberately and sensitively. Research indicates that the academic achievement of African-American and Hispanic students increases when cooperative teaching techniques such as the jigsaw are used (Aronson and Gonzalez 1988). Moreover, *all* students develop more positive racial and ethnic attitudes when teachers use cooperative, rather than competitive, learning activities (Aronson and Gonzalez 1988).

Research indicates that many students of color, especially those from low-income families, often have value orientations, behaviors, cognitive styles, language characteristics, and other cultural components that differ from those of the school's culture (Delpit 1988; Deyhle 1986; Fordham 1991; Fordham and Ogbu 1986; Gay 1991; Heath 1983; Hale-Benson [1982]; Shade 1989). These components often lead to

conflict between students and teachers. By comparison, most middle-class mainstream youths find the school culture consistent with their home cultures and are, therefore, much more comfortable in school. Many students, though, regardless of their racial, ethnic, or cultural identity, find the school culture alien, hostile, and self-defeating.

A school's culture and instructional programs should be restructured and made to reflect the cultures and learning styles of students from diverse ethnic and social-class groups (Banks and Banks 1989). Research indicates that the instructional strategies and learning styles most often favored in the nation's schools are inconsistent with the cognitive styles, cultural orientations, and cultural characteristics of some groups of students of color (Aronson and Gonzalez 1988; Fordham 1991). This research provides important guidelines and principles that educators can use to change schools to make them more responsive to students from diverse cultural groups. Educators should not ignore racial and ethnic differences when planning instruction; nor should they dismiss the question of racial and ethnic differences with the all-too-easy cliché, "I don't see racial differences in students and I treat them all alike." Research on cognitive styles and language and communication characteristics of ethnic groups suggests that if all students are treated alike, their distinctive needs are not being met and they are probably being denied access to equal educational opportunities (Cummins 1986; Heath 1983; Kochman 1981; Philips 1983).

Although differences among students are accepted in an effective multicultural school, teaching students to function effectively in mainstream society and in social settings different from the ones in which they were socialized, and helping them learn new cognitive styles and learning patterns, must also be major goals. The successful multicultural school helps students become aware of and able to acquire cultural and cognitive alternatives, thus enabling them to function successfully within cultural environments other than their own.

6.0 The multicultural curriculum should provide students with continuous opportunities to develop a better sense of self.

The multicultural curriculum should help students to develop a better sense of self. This development should be an ongoing process, beginning when the student first enters school and continuing throughout the student's school career. This development should include at least three areas:

1. Students should be helped to develop accurate self-identities. Students must ask questions such as who am I? and what am I? in order to come to grips with their own identities.

2. The multicultural curriculum should help students develop improved self-concepts. Beyond considering such questions as who they are and what they are, students should learn to feel positively about their identities, particularly their ethnic identities. Positive self-concepts may be expressed in several ways. The multicultural curriculum, for example, should recognize the varying talents of students and capitalize on them in the academic curriculum. All students need to feel that academic success is possible. The multicultural curriculum should also help students develop a high regard for their original languages and cultures.

3. The multicultural curriculum should help students develop greater self-understanding. Students should develop more sophisticated understandings of why they are the way they are, why their ethnic and cultural groups are the way they are,

and what ethnicity and culture mean in their daily lives. Such self-understanding will help students to handle more effectively situations in which ethnicity and culture may play a part.

Students cannot fully understand why they are the way they are and why certain things might occur in their future until they have a solid knowledge of the groups to which they belong and the effects of group membership on their lives. Multicultural education should enable students to come to grips with these individual and group relationships in general and the effects of ethnicity and culture on their lives in particular.

Looking at group membership should not undermine a student's individuality. Rather, it should add a dimension to the understanding of a student's unique individuality by learning the effects of belonging to groups. Neither are students to be assigned and locked into one group. Instead, students should be aware of the many groups to which they belong, both voluntarily and involuntarily, and recognize that at various moments one or more of these groups may be affecting their lives.

The multicultural curriculum should also help students understand and appreciate their personal backgrounds and family heritages. Family studies in the school can contribute to increased self-understanding and a personal sense of heritage, as contrasted with the generalized experiences presented in books. They can also contribute to family and personal pride. If parents and other relatives come to school to share their stories and experiences, students will become increasingly aware that ethnic groups are a meaningful part of our nation's heritage and merit study by all of us so that we can better understand the complexity of the nation's pluralistic experiences and traditions.

7.0 The curriculum should help students understand the totality of the experiences of ethnic and cultural groups in the United States.

The social problems that ethnic and cultural group members experience are often regarded as part of their cultural characteristics. Alcoholism, crime, and illiteracy, for example, are considered by many people cultural characteristics of particular racial or ethnic groups. Ethnicity is often assumed to mean something negative and divisive, and the study of ethnic groups and ethnicity often becomes the examination of problems such as prejudice, racism, discrimination, and exploitation. To concentrate exclusively on these problems when studying ethnicity creates serious distortions in perceptions of ethnic groups. Among other things, it stereotypes ethnic groups as essentially passive recipients of the dominant society's discrimination and exploitation. Although these are legitimate issues and should be included in a comprehensive, effective multicultural curriculum, they should not constitute the entire curriculum.

Although many ethnic group members face staggering sociopolitical problems, these problems do not constitute the whole of their lives. Nor are all ethnic groups affected to the same degree or in the same way by these problems. Moreover, many ethnic groups have developed and maintained viable life-styles and have made notable contributions to U.S. culture. The experiences of each ethnic group are part of a composite of human activities. Although it is true that each ethnic group has significant unifying historical experiences and cultural traits, no ethnic group has a single, homogeneous, historical-cultural pattern. Members of an ethnic group do not conform to a single cultural norm or mode of behavior, nor are ethnic cultures uniform and static.

Consequently, the many dimensions of ethnic experiences and cultures should be studied. The curriculum should help students understand the significant historical experiences and basic cultural patterns of ethnic groups, the critical contemporary issues and social problems confronting each of them, and the dynamic diversity of the experiences, cultures, and individuals within each ethnic group.

A consistently multifaceted approach to teaching benefits students in several major ways. It helps them to become aware of the commonalities within and among ethnic groups. At the same time, it helps counteract stereotyping by making students aware of the rich diversity within each ethnic group in the United States. It also helps students develop more comprehensive and realistic understandings of the broad range of ethnic group heritages and experiences.

8.0 The multicultural curriculum should help students understand that a conflict between ideals and realities always exists in human societies.

Traditionally, students in U.S. common schools have been taught a great deal about the ideals of our society. Conflicts between ideals, however, are often glossed over. Often values, such as freedom in the U.S. democracy, are treated as attainable ideals, and the realities of U.S. society have been distorted to make it appear that they have, indeed, been achieved. Courses in U.S. history and citizenship especially have been characterized by this kind of unquestioning approach to the socialization of youth. This form of citizenship education, "passing down the myths and legends of our national heritage," tends to inculcate parochial national attitudes, promote serious misconceptions about the nature of U.S. society and culture, and develop cynicism in youth who are aware of the gaps between the ideal and the real.

When ethnic studies emerged from the civil rights movement of the 1960s, there was a strong and negative reaction to the traditional approach to citizenship education. A widely expressed goal of many curriculum reformers was to "tell it like it is and was" in the classroom. In many of the reformed courses, however, U.S. history and society were taught and viewed primarily from the viewpoints of specific ethnic groups. Little attention was given to basic U.S. values, except to highlight gross discrepancies between ideals and practices of U.S. society. Emphasis was often on how ethnic groups of color had been oppressed by Anglo-Americans.

Both the unquestioning approach and the tell-it-like-it-is approach result in distortions. In a sound multicultural curriculum, emphasis should be neither on the ways in which the United States has "fulfilled its noble ideals" nor on the "sins committed by the Anglo-Americans" (or any other group of Americans). Rather, students should be encouraged to examine the democratic values that emerged in the United States, why they emerged, how they were defined in various periods, and to whom they referred in various eras. Students should also examine the extent to which these values have or have not been fulfilled, and the continuing conflict between values such as freedom and equality and between ideals in other societies.

Students should also be encouraged to examine alternative interpretations of the discrepancies between ideals and realities in the life and history of the United States. From the perspectives of some individuals and groups, there has been a continuing expansion of human rights in the United States. Others see a continuing process of weighing rights against rights as the optimum mix of values, none of which can be fully realized as ideals. Many argue that basic human rights are still limited to U.S. citizens who have certain class, racial, ethnic, gender, and cultural characteristics. Students should consider why these various interpretations arose and why there are different views regarding conflicts between the ideals and between the ideals and realities of U.S. society.

9.0 The multicultural curriculum should explore and clarify ethnic and cultural alternatives and options in the United States.

Educational questions regarding students' ethnic and cultural alternatives and options are complex and difficult. Some individuals, for a variety of complex reasons, are uncomfortable with their ethnic and cultural identities and wish to deny them. Some individuals are uncomfortable when their own ethnic groups are discussed in the classroom. Teachers need to handle these topics sensitively; they must not ignore them.

The degree of a class's resistance when studying ethnic or cultural groups is influenced by the teacher's approach to the study of diversity. Students can sense when the teacher or other students in the class are intolerant of their particular group or some of its characteristics. Students often receive such messages from nonverbal responses. The teacher can minimize students' resistance to studying their own heritage by creating a classroom atmosphere that reflects acceptance and respect for ethnic and cultural differences. Most importantly, teachers need to model their own acceptance of and respect for ethnic, racial, and cultural diversity.

Teachers should help students understand the options related to their own ethnic and cultural identity and the nature of ethnic and cultural alternatives and options within the United States. Students should be helped to understand that, ideally, all individuals should have the right to select the manner and degree of identifying or not identifying with their ethnic and cultural groups. They should learn, however, that some individuals, such as members of many white ethnic groups, have this privilege while others, such as most African Americans, have more limited options. Most persons of European ancestry can become structurally assimilated into the mainstream U.S. society. When they become highly assimilated, they can usually participate completely in most U.S. economic, social, and political institutions. On the other hand, no matter how culturally assimilated or acculturated members of some ethnic groups become, they are still perceived and stigmatized by the larger society on the basis of their physical characteristics.

Students should also be helped to understand that although individualism is strong in the United States, in reality many Americans, such as American Indians and Chinese Americans, are often judged not as individuals but on the basis of the racial or ethnic group to which they belong. While teachers may give American Indian or Chinese American students the option of examining or not examining their ethnic heritage and identity, such students need to be helped to understand how they are perceived and identified by the larger society. Educators must respect the individual rights of students, at the same time, however, they have a professional responsibility to help students learn basic facts and generalizations about the nature of race and ethnicity in the United States.

10.0 The multicultural curriculum should promote values, attitudes, and behaviors that support ethnic pluralism and cultural diversity as well as build and support the nation-state and the nation's shared national culture. E pluribus unum should be the goal of the schools and the nation.

Ethnicity and cultural identity are salient factors in the lives of many U.S. citizens. They helps individuals answer the question, Who am I? by providing a sense of peoplehood, identity, and cultural and spiritual roots. They provide a filter through which events, life-styles, norms, and values are processed and screened. They provide a means through which identity is affirmed, heritages are validated, and preferred associates are selected. Therefore, ethnicity and cultural identity serve necessary functions in many people's lives. Ethnicity and cultural identity are neither always positive and reinforcing, nor always negative and debilitating, although they have the potential for both. An effective multicultural curriculum examines all of these dimensions of ethnicity and cultural identity.

The curriculum should help students understand that diversity is an integral part of life in the United States. Ethnic and cultural diversity permeate U.S. history and society. Demographic projections indicate that the United States will become increasingly multiethnic and multicultural in the future. Consequently, schools should teach about ethnic and cultural diversity to help students acquire more accurate assessments of history and culture in the United States. Major goals of multicultural education include improving respect for human dignity, maximizing cultural options, understanding what makes people alike and different, and accepting diversity as inevitable and valuable to human life.

Students should learn that difference does not necessarily imply inferiority or superiority, and that the study of ethnic and cultural group differences need not lead to polarization. They should also learn that although conflict is unavoidable in ethnically and racially pluralistic societies, such conflict does not necessarily have to be destructive or divisive. Conflict is an intrinsic part of the human condition, especially so in a pluralistic society. Conflict is often a catalyst for social progress. Multicultural education programs that explore ethnic diversity in positive, realistic ways will present ethnic conflict in its proper perspective. They will help students understand that there is strength in diversity, and that cooperation among ethnic groups does not necessarily require identical beliefs, behaviors, and values.

The multicultural curriculum should help students understand and respect ethnic diversity and broaden their cultural options. Too many people in the United States learn only the values, behavioral patterns, and beliefs of either mainstream society or their own ethnic groups, cultural groups, or communities. Socialization is, in effect, encapsulating, providing few opportunities for most individuals to acquire more than stereotypes about ethnic and cultural groups other than their own. Therefore, many people tend to view other ethnic groups and life-styles as "abnormal" or "deviant." The multicultural curriculum can help students correct these misconceptions by teaching them that other ways of living are as valid and viable as their own.

The multicultural curriculum should also promote the basic values expressed in our major historical documents. Each ethnic group should have the right to practice its own religious, social, and cultural beliefs, albeit within the limits of due regard for the rights of others. There is, after all, a set of over-arching values that all groups within a society or nation must endorse to maintain societal cohesion. In our nation, these core values stem from our commitment to human dignity, and include justice, equality, freedom, and due process of law. Although the school should value and reflect ethnic and cultural diversity, it should not promote the practices and beliefs of any ethnic or cultural group that contradict the core democratic values of the United States. Rather, the school should foster ethnic and cultural differences that maximize opportunities for democratic living. Pluralism must take place within the context of national unity. *E pluribus unum*—out of many, one—should be our goal.

Although ethnic and cultural group membership should not restrict an individual's opportunity and ability to achieve and to participate, it is sometimes used by groups in power to the detriment of less powerful groups. Individuals who do not understand the role of ethnicity often find it a troublesome reality, one extremely difficult to handle. Multicultural curricula should help students examine the dilemmas surrounding ethnicity as a step toward realizing its full potential as an enabling force in the lives of individuals, groups, and the nation.

11.0 The multicultural curriculum should help students develop their decision-making abilities, social participation skills, and sense of political efficacy as necessary bases for effective citizenship in a pluralistic democratic nation.

The demands upon people to make reflective decisions on issues related to race, ethnicity, and culture are increasing as the nation's ethnic texture deepens. When people are unable to process the masses of conflicting information—including facts, opinions, interpretations, and theories about ethnic groups—they are often overwhelmed.

The multicultural curriculum must enable students to gain knowledge and apply it. Students need a rich foundation of sound knowledge. Facts, concepts, generalizations, and theories differ in their capability for organizing particulars and in predictive capacity; concepts and generalizations have more usefulness than mere collections of miscellaneous facts. Young people need practice in the steps of scholarly methods for arriving at knowledge—identifying problems, formulating hypotheses, locating and evaluating source materials, organizing information as evidence, analyzing, interpreting, and reworking what they find, and making conclusions. Students also need ample opportunities to learn to use knowledge in making sense out of the situations they encounter.

When curricular programs are inappropriate, teaching is inept, or expectations are low for students of some ethnic groups, and especially for those who are low-income, the emphasis in class is likely to be on discrete facts, memorization of empty generalizations, and low-level skills. Even if the names, dates, and exercises in using an index are drawn from ethnic content, such an emphasis is still discriminatory and inconsistent with the basic purpose of multicultural education. All young people need opportunities to develop powerful concepts, generalizations, and intellectual abilities when studying content related to ethnic and cultural diversity.

Students must also learn to identify values and relate them to knowledge. Young people should be taught methods for clarifying their own values relating to ethnic and cultural diversity. Such processes should include identifying value

problems (their own and others'), describing evaluative behaviors, recognizing value conflicts in themselves and in social situations, recognizing and proposing alternatives based on values, and making choices between values in light of their consequences.

Determining basic ideas, discovering and verifying facts, and valuing are interrelated aspects of decision making. Ample opportunity for practice in real-life situations is necessary; such practice frequently requires interdisciplinary as well as multicultural perspectives. Decision-making skills help people assess social situations objectively and perceptively, identify feasible courses of action and project their consequences, decide thoughtfully, and then act.

The multicultural curriculum must also help students develop effective social and civic action skills because many students from ethnic groups are overwhelmed by a sense of a lack of control of their destinies. These feelings often stem from their belief that, as in the past, they and other people of color have little influence on political policies and institutions (Ogbu 1990). The multicultural curriculum should help students develop a sense of political efficacy and become active and effective in the civic life of their communities and the nation. With a basis in strong commitments to such democratic values as justice, freedom, and equality, students can learn to exercise political and social influence responsibly to influence societal decisions related to race, ethnicity, and cultural freedom in ways consistent with human dignity.

The school, in many ways, is a microcosm of society, reflecting the changing dynamics of ethnic group situations. The school can provide many opportunities for students to practice social participation skills and to test their political efficacy as they address themselves to resolving some of the school's racial and ethnic problems. Issues such as the participation of ethnic individuals in school government, the uneven application of discriminatory disciplinary rules, and preferential treatment of certain students because of their racial, ethnic, cultural, and social-class backgrounds are examples of problems that students can help to resolve. Applying social action skills effectively, students can combine knowledge, valuing, and thought gained from multicultural perspectives and experiences to resolve problems affecting racial, ethnic, and cultural groups.

By providing students with opportunities to use decision-making abilities and social action skills in the resolution of problems affecting ethnic, racial, and cultural groups, schools can contribute to more effective education for democratic citizenship.

12.0 The multicultural curriculum should help students develop the skills necessary for effective interpersonal, interethnic, and intercultural group interactions.

Effective interpersonal interaction across ethnic group lines is often difficult to achieve. The problem is complicated by the fact that individuals bring to cross-ethnic interaction situations attitudes, values, and expectations that influence their own behavior, including their responses to the behavior of others. These expectations are sometimes formed on the basis of what their own groups deem appropriate behavior and what each individual believes he or she knows about other ethnic groups. Much knowledge about ethnic groups is stereotyped, distorted, and based on distant observations, scattered and superficial contacts, inadequate or imbalanced media treatment, and incomplete factual information. Attempts at cross-ethnic interpersonal interactions, therefore, are often stymied by ethnocentrism.

The problems created by ethnocentrism can be at least partially resolved by helping students recognize the forces operating in interpersonal interactions, and how these forces affect behavior. Students should develop skills and concepts to overcome factors that prevent successful interactions including identifying ethnic and cultural stereotypes, examining media treatment of ethnic groups, clarifying ethnic and cultural attitudes and values, developing cross-cultural communication skills, recognizing how attitudes and values are projected in verbal and nonverbal behaviors, and viewing the dynamics of interpersonal interactions from others' perspectives.

One of the goals of multicultural education should be to help individuals function easily and effectively with members of both their own and other racial, ethnic, and cultural groups. The multicultural curriculum should provide opportunities for students to explore lines of cross-cultural communication and to experiment with cross-ethnic and cross-cultural functioning. Actual experiences can be effective teaching devices, allowing students to test stereotypes and idealized behavioral constructs against real-life situations, and make the necessary adjustments in their frames of reference and behaviors. In the process, they should learn that ethnic group members, in the final analysis, are individuals, with all of the variations that characterize all individuals, and that ethnicity is only one of many variables that shape their personalities. Students will be forced to confront their values and make moral choices when their experiences in cross-ethnic and cross-cultural interactions produce information contrary to previously held notions. Thus, students should broaden their ethnic and cultural options, increase their frames of reference, develop greater appreciation for individual and ethnic differences, and deepen their own capacities as human beings.

13.0 The multicultural curriculum should be comprehensive in scope and sequence, should present holistic views of ethnic and cultural groups, and should be an integral part of the total school curriculum.

Students learn best from well-planned, comprehensive, continuous, and interrelated experiences. In an effective multicultural school, the study of ethnic and cultural content is integrated into the curriculum from preschool through 12th grade and beyond. This study should be carefully planned to encourage the development of progressively more complex concepts and generalizations. It should also involve students in the study of a variety of ethnic and cultural groups.

A comprehensive multicultural curriculum should also include a broad range of experiences within the study of any group: present culture, historical experiences, sociopolitical realities, contributions to the nation's development, problems faced in everyday living, and conditions of existence in society.

Students should be introduced to the experiences of persons from widely varying backgrounds. Although the study of ethnic and cultural success stories can help students of an ethnic group develop pride in their own group, the curriculum should include study of ethnic peoples in general, not just heroes and success stories. In addition, those outside of an ethnic group can develop greater respect for that group by learning about these heroes and successes. Moreover, in establishing heroes and labeling people as successes, teachers should move beyond the standards of the dominant society and consider the

values of each ethnic group and the worth of each individual life. An active contributor to an ethnic neighborhood may be more of a hero to the local community than a famous athlete; a good parent may be more of a "success" than a famous politician.

For optimum effectiveness, the study of ethnic and cultural group experiences must be interwoven into the total curriculum. It should not be reserved for special occasions, units, or courses, nor should it be considered supplementary to the existing curriculum. Such observances as African-American History or Brotherhood Week, Hanukkah, Cinco de Mayo, St. Patrick's Day, and Martin Luther King, Jr.'s birthday are important and necessary, but insufficient in themselves. To rely entirely on these kinds of occasions and events, or to relegate ethnic content to a marginal position in the curriculum, is to guarantee a minimal influence of ethnic studies.

The basic premises and organizational structures of schools should be reformed to reflect the nation's multicultural realities. The curriculum should be reorganized so that ethnic and cultural diversity is an integral, natural, and normal component of educational experiences for *all* students, with ethnic and cultural content accepted and used in everyday instruction, and with various ethnic and cultural perspectives introduced. Multicultural content is as appropriate and important in teaching such fundamental skills and abilities as reading, thinking, and decision making as it is in teaching about social issues raised by racism, dehumanization, racial conflict, and alternative ethnic and cultural life-styles.

14.0 The multicultural curriculum should include the continuous study of the cultures, historical experiences, social realities, and existential conditions of ethnic and cultural groups, including a variety of racial compositions.

The multicultural curriculum should involve students in the continuous study of ethnic groups of different racial compositions. A curriculum that concentrates on one ethnic or cultural group is not multicultural. Nor is a curriculum multicultural if it focuses exclusively on European ethnics or exclusively on ethnic groups of color. Every ethnic group cannot be included in the curriculum of a particular school or school district—the number is too large to be manageable. The inclusion of groups of different racial compositions, however, is a necessary characteristic of effective multicultural education.

Moreover, the multicultural curriculum should include the consistent examination of significant aspects of ethnic experiences influenced by or related to race. These include such concepts as racism, racial prejudice, racial discrimination, and exploitation based on race. The sensitive and continuous development of such concepts should help students develop an understanding of racial factors in the past and present of our nation.

15.0 Interdisciplinary and multidisciplinary approaches should be used in designing and implementing the multicultural curriculum.

No single discipline can adequately explain all components of the life-styles, cultural experiences, and social problems of ethnic groups. Knowledge from any one discipline is insufficient to help individuals make adequate decisions on the complex issues raised by racism, sexism, structural exclusion, poverty, and powerlessness. Concepts such as racism, anti-Semitism, and language discrimination have multiple dimensions. To delineate these requires the concepts and perspectives of the social sciences, history, literature, music, art, and philosophy.

Single-discipline or mono-perspective analyses of complex ethnic and cultural issues can produce skewed, distorted interpretations and evaluations. A promising way to avoid these pitfalls is to employ consistently multidisciplinary approaches in studying experiences and events related to ethnic and cultural groups. For example, ethnic protest is not simply a political, economic, artistic, or sociological activity; it is all four of these. Therefore, a curriculum that purports to be multicultural and is realistic in its treatment of ethnic protest must focus on its broader ramifications. Such study must address the scientific, political, artistic, and sociological dimensions of protest.

The accomplishments of the United States are due neither to the ingenuity and creativity of a single ethnic or cultural group, nor to accomplishments in a single area, but rather to the efforts and contributions of many ethnic groups and individuals in many areas. African American, Latino, American Indian, Asian American, and European immigrant group members have all contributed to the fields of science and industry, politics, literature, economics, and the arts. Multidisciplinary analyses will best help students to understand them.

16.0 The multicultural curriculum should use comparative approaches in the study of ethnic·and cultural groups.

The study of ethnic and cultural group experiences should not be a process of competition. It should not promote the idea that any one ethnic or cultural group has a monopoly on talent and worth, or incapacity and weakness, but, instead, the idea that each individual and each ethnic group has worth and dignity. Students should be taught that persons from all ethnic groups have common characteristics and needs, although they are affected differently by certain social situations and may use different means to respond to their needs and to achieve their objectives. Furthermore, school personnel should remember that realistic comparative approaches to the study of different ethnic and cultural group experiences are descriptive and analytical, not normative or judgmental. Teachers should also be aware of their own biases and prejudices as they help students to use comparative approaches.

Social situations and events included in the curriculum should be analyzed from the perspectives of several ethnic and cultural groups instead of using a mono-perspective analysis. This approach allows students to see the subtle ways in which the lives of different ethnic group members are similar and interrelated, to study the concept of universality as it relates to ethnic groups, and to see how all ethnic groups are active participants in all aspects of society. Studying such issues as power and politics, ethnicity, and culture from comparative, multicultural perspectives will help students to develop more realistic, accurate understandings of how these issues affect everyone, and how the effects are both alike and different.

17.0 The multicultural curriculum should help students to view and interpret events, situations, and conflict from diverse ethnic and cultural perspectives and points of view.

Historically, students have been taught to view events, situations, and our national history primarily from the perspectives of mainstream historians and social scientists sympathet-

ic to the dominant groups within our society. The perspectives of other groups have been largely omitted in the school curriculum. The World War II Japanese-American internment and the Indian Removal Act of 1830, for example, are rarely studied from the points of view of interned Japanese Americans or the American Indians forced to leave their homes and move west.

To gain a more complete understanding of both our past and our present, students should look at events and situations from the perspectives of the mainstream and from the perspectives of marginalized groups. This approach to teaching is more likely to make our students less ethnocentric and more able to understand that almost any event or situation can be legitimately looked at from many perspectives. When using this approach in the classroom, the teacher should avoid, as much as possible, labeling any perspective "right" or "wrong." Rather, the teacher should try to help students understand how each group may view a situation differently and why. The emphasis should be on understanding and explanation and not on simplistic moralizing. For example, the perceptions many Jewish Americans have of political events in the United States have been shaped by memories of the Holocaust and anti-Semitism in the United States.

Ethnicity and cultural diversity have strongly influenced the nature of intergroup relations in U.S. society. The way that individuals perceive events and situations occurring in the United States is often influenced by their ethnic and cultural experiences, especially when the events and situations are directly related to ethnic conflict and discrimination or to issues such as affirmative action and busing for school desegregation. When students view a historical or contemporary situation from the perspectives of one ethnic or cultural group only—whether majority or minority—they can acquire, at best, an incomplete understanding.

18.0 The multicultural curriculum should conceptualize and describe the development of the United States as a multidirectional society.

A basic structural concept in the study and teaching of U.S. society is the view that the United States has developed mainly from east to west. According to this concept, the United States is the product of the spread of civilization from Western Europe across the Atlantic Ocean to the east coast of what is today the United States and then west to the Pacific. Within this approach, ethnic groups appear almost always in two forms: as obstacles to the advancement of westward-moving Anglo civilization or as problems that must be corrected or, at least, kept under control.

The underlying rationale for this frame of reference is that the study of U.S. history is for the most part an account of processes within the national boundaries of the United States. In applying this frame of reference, however, educators have been inconsistent, including as part of the study of the United States such themes as pre–United States geography, the pre–United States British colonies, the Texas revolution, and the Lone Star Republic. In short, the study of the United States has traditionally included phenomena outside the boundaries of the political United States.

Yet, while including some non–United States themes as part of the traditional study of the United States, school programs have not adequately included study of the Native American, Hispanic, and Mexican societies that developed on land that ultimately became part of the United States. Nor has sufficient attention been devoted to the northwesterly flow of cultures from Africa to the United States, the northerly flow of cultures from Mexico, Latin America, and the Caribbean, the easterly flow of cultures from Asia, and the westerly flow of latter-day immigrants from Eastern, Central, and Southern Europe.

Multicultural education, from the early years of school onward, must redress these intellectually invalid and distorting imbalances by illuminating the variety of cultural experiences that compose the total U.S. experience. Multicultural education must consistently address the development of the entire geo-cultural United States—that area which, in time, was to become the United States and the peoples encompassed by that area. Moreover, the flow of cultures into the United States must be viewed multidirectionally.

19.0 Schools should provide opportunities for students to participate in the aesthetic experiences of various ethnic and cultural groups.

The study of ethnic and cultural groups should be based on more than the social sciences. Although incorporating statistical and analytical social science methodologies and concepts into the study of ethnic and cultural groups is valuable, an overreliance on these methods lacks an important part of the multicultural experience—participation in the experiences of ethnic and cultural groups.

A number of teaching materials can be used. Students should read and hear past and contemporary writings of members of various ethnic and cultural groups. Poetry, short stories, folklore, essays, plays, and novels should be used. Ethnic autobiographies offer special insight into what it means to be ethnic in the United States.

Ethnic music, art, architecture, and dance—past and contemporary—provide other avenues for experiential participation, interpreting the emotions and feelings of ethnic groups. The arts and humanities can serve as excellent vehicles for studying group experiences by focusing on these questions: What aspects of the experience of a particular ethnic group helped create these kinds of musical and artistic expressions? What do they reveal about these groups?

Studying multiethnic literature and arts, students should become acquainted with what has been created in local ethnic communities. In addition, members of local ethnic communities can provide dramatic "living autobiographies" for students; invite them to discuss their viewpoints and experiences with students. Students should also have opportunities for developing their own artistic, musical, and literary abilities, even to make them available to the local community.

Role playing of various ethnic and cultural experiences should be interspersed throughout the curriculum to encourage understanding of what it means to belong to various ethnic groups. The immersion of students in multiethnic experiences is an effective means for developing understanding of both self and others.

20.0 The multicultural curriculum should provide opportunities for students to study ethnic group languages as legitimate communication systems and help them develop full literacy in at least two languages.

A multicultural curriculum recognizes language diversity and promotes the attitude that all languages and dialects are valid communicating systems for some groups and for some purposes. The program requires a multidisciplinary focus on language and dialect.

Concepts about language and dialect derived from disciplines such as anthropology, sociology, and political science expand students' perceptions of language and dialect as something more than correct grammar. For example, the nature and intent of language policies and laws in the United States can be compared to those in bilingual nations. Students can also be taught sociolinguistic concepts that provide a framework for understanding the verbal and nonverbal behavior of others and themselves. Critical listening, speaking, and reading habits should be nurtured with special attention to the uses of language.

Research indicates that a school's rejection of a student's home language affects the student's self-esteem, academic achievement, and social and occupational mobility. Conversely, a school's acceptance and use of a student's home language improves the student's self-esteem, academic achievement, and relationships among students in a school (U.S. Commission on Civil Rights 1975). In a multicultural curriculum, students are provided opportunities to study their own and others' dialects. They become increasingly receptive to the languages and dialects of their peers. Such an approach helps students develop concepts in their own vernaculars whenever necessary at the same time promoting appreciation of home language environments.

Literacy in U.S. English is a time-honored goal of schools and should be maintained. Another important goal of the multicultural curriculum, however, is to help all students acquire literacy in a second language. Second language literacy requires students to understand, speak, read, and write well enough to communicate effectively with native speakers of the second language. Equally important, students should study the cultures of the people who use the second language. Ultimately, effective communication in the second language requires an understanding of its people and their culture.

Some students come to school speaking two languages. These students should be provided the opportunity to develop full literacy in their native language. In turn, these students and their parents can be used as resources for helping other students acquire a second language proficiency.

Second language literacy complements other areas of the multicultural curriculum. For example, approaches for studying the culture of other people are described in several of the above guidelines. As students are learning a second language, they can learn skills in interpersonal and intercultural communications. Further, because these guidelines encourage multidisciplinary approaches, second language literacy can be achieved while other areas of the language arts and the social studies are taught.

21.0 The multicultural curriculum should make maximum use of experiential learning, especially local community resources.

An effective multicultural curriculum includes a study of ethnic and cultural groups not only nationally, but locally as well. An effective multicultural curriculum must expand beyond classroom walls. Teachers should use the local community as a "laboratory" in which students can develop and use intellectual, social, and political action skills. Planned field trips and individual or group research projects are helpful. Continuous investigation of the local community can provide insights into the dynamics of ethnic and cultural groups. It can create greater respect for what has been accomplished.

It can promote awareness of and commitment to what still needs to be done to improve the lives and opportunities of all local residents.

Every member of the local community, including students' family members, is a valuable source of knowledge. There are no class, educational, or linguistic qualifications for participating in the U.S. experience, for having a culture or society, for having family or neighborhood traditions, for perceiving the surrounding community, or for relating experiences. Teachers should invite local residents of various ethnic backgrounds to the classroom to share their experiences and views with students, relate their oral traditions, answer questions, offer new outlooks on society and history, and open doors of investigation for students. Special efforts should be made to involve senior citizens in school multicultural programs both to help them develop a higher sense of self-worth and to benefit the students and the school community.

It is important that students develop a sensitivity to ethnic differences and a conceptual framework for viewing ethnic differences before interacting with ethnic classroom guests or studying the local ethnic communities. Otherwise, these promising opportunities may reinforce, rather than reduce, ethnic stereotypes and prejudices.

In study projects, students can consider such topics as local population distribution, housing, school assignments, political representation, and ethnic community activities. Older students can take advantage of accessible public documents, such as city council and school board minutes, minutes of local organizations, and church records for insight into the community. To separate the local community from the school is to ignore the everyday world in which students live.

22.0 The assessment procedures used with students should reflect their ethnic and cultural experiences.

To make the school a truly multicultural institution, major changes must be made in the ways in which we test and ascertain student abilities. Most of the intelligence tests administered in the public schools are based upon a mainstream conformity, mono-ethnic model. Because many students socialized within other ethnic and cultural groups find the tests and other aspects of the school alien and intimidating, they perform poorly and are placed in low academic tracks, special education classes, or low-ability reading groups (Oakes 1985). Research indicates that teachers in these kinds of situations tend to have low expectations for their students and often fail to create the kinds of learning environments that promote proficiency in the skills and abilities necessary to function effectively in society (Oakes 1985).

In the final analysis, standardized intelligence testing frequently serves to deny some youths equal educational opportunities. The results of these tests are often used to justify the noneducation of students of color and low-income students and to relieve teachers and other school personnel from accountability (Deyhle 1986; Mercer 1989). Novel assessment devices that reflect the cultures of ethnic youths need to be developed and used. Moreover, teacher-generated tests and other routine classroom assessment techniques should reflect the cultures of ethnic youths. It will, however, do little good for educators to create improved assessment procedures for ethnic youths unless they also implement multicultural curricular and instructional practices.

23.0 Schools should conduct ongoing, systematic evaluations of the goals, methods, and instructional materials used in teaching about ethnic and cultural diversity.

Schools should formulate attainable goals and objectives for multicultural education. To evaluate the extent to which these goals and objectives are accomplished, school personnel must judge—with evidence—what occurs in their schools in three broad areas: (1) school policies and governance procedures; (2) everyday practices of staff and teachers; and (3) curricular programs and offerings, academic and nonacademic, preschool through 12th grade. These guidelines and the checklist that follows in part 3 will help schools' evaluation programs.

Many sources of evidence should be used. Teachers, administrators, support staff, parents, students, and others in the school community ought to participate in providing and evaluating evidence.

Evaluation should be construed as a means by which a school, its staff, and students can improve multiethnic and multicultural relations, experiences, and understandings. Evaluation should be oriented toward analyzing and improving, not castigating or applauding, multicultural programs.

Part Three: The Multicultural Education Program Evaluation Checklist

Rating Strongly ◄────► Hardly at all				Guidelines
				1.0　Does ethnic and cultural diversity permeate the total school environment? 　　1.1　Are ethnic content and perspectives incorporated into all aspects of the curriculum, preschool through 12th grade and beyond? 　　1.2　Do instructional materials treat racial and ethnic differences and groups honestly, realistically, and sensitively? 　　1.3　Do school libraries and resource centers offer a variety of materials on the histories, experiences, and cultures of many racial, ethnic, and cultural groups? 　　1.4　Do school assemblies, decorations, speakers, holidays, and heroes reflect racial, ethnic, and cultural group differences? 　　1.5　Are extracurricular activities multiethnic and multicultural? 2.0　Do school policies and procedures foster positive interactions among the various racial, ethnic, and cultural group members of the school? 　　2.1　Do school policies accommodate the behavioral patterns, learning styles, and orientations of those ethnic and cultural group members actually in the school? 　　2.2　Does the school provide a variety of instruments and techniques for teaching and counseling students of various ethnic and cultural groups? 　　2.3　Do school policies recognize the holidays and festivities of various ethnic groups? 　　2.4　Do school policies avoid instructional and guidance practices based on stereotyped and ethnocentric perceptions? 　　2.5　Do school policies respect the dignity and worth of students as individuals *and* as members of racial, ethnic, and cultural groups? 3.0　Is the school staff (administrators, instructors, counselors, and support staff) multiethnic and multiracial? 　　3.1　Has the school established and enforced policies for recruiting and maintaining a staff made up of individuals from various racial and ethnic groups? 4.0　Does the school have systematic, comprehensive, mandatory, and continuing multicultural staff development programs? 　　4.1　Are teachers, librarians, counselors, administrators, and support staff included in the staff development programs? 　　4.2　Do the staff development programs include a variety of experiences (such as lectures, field experiences, and curriculum projects)? 　　4.3　Do the staff development programs provide opportunities to gain knowledge and understanding about various racial, ethnic, and cultural groups? 　　4.4　Do the staff development programs provide opportunities for participants to explore their attitudes and feelings about their own ethnicity and others'? 　　4.5　Do the staff development programs examine the verbal and nonverbal patterns of interethnic group interactions? 　　4.6　Do the staff development programs provide opportunities for learning how to create and select multiethnic instructional materials and how to incorporate multicultural content into curriculum materials? 5.0　Does the curriculum reflect the ethnic learning styles of students within the school?

5. CURRICULUM AND INSTRUCTION IN MULTICULTURAL PERSPECTIVE

Rating				Guidelines
Strongly ←		→	Hardly at all	

5.1 Is the curriculum designed to help students learn how to function effectively in various cultural environments and learn more than one cognitive style?

5.2 Do the objectives, instructional strategies, and learning materials reflect the cultures and cognitive styles of the various ethnic and cultural groups within the school?

6.0 Does the curriculum provide continuous opportunities for students to develop a better sense of self?

6.1 Does the curriculum help students strengthen their self-identities?

6.2 Is the curriculum designed to help students develop greater self-understanding?

6.3 Does the curriculum help students improve their self-concepts?

6.4 Does the curriculum help students to better understand themselves in light of their ethnic and cultural heritages?

7.0 Does the curriculum help students understand the wholeness of the experiences of ethnic and cultural groups?

7.1 Does the curriculum include the study of societal problems some ethnic and cultural group members experience, such as racism, prejudice, discrimination, and exploitation?

7.2 Does the curriculum include the study of historical experiences, cultural patterns, and social problems of various ethnic and cultural groups?

7.3 Does the curriculum include both positive and negative aspects of ethnic and cultural group experiences?

7.4 Does the curriculum present people of color both as active participants in society and as subjects of oppression and exploitation?

7.5 Does the curriculum examine the diversity within each group's experience?

7.6 Does the curriculum present group experiences as dynamic and continuously changing?

7.7 Does the curriculum examine the total experiences of groups instead of focusing exclusively on the "heroes"?

8.0 Does the curriculum help students identify and understand the ever-present conflict between ideals and realities in human societies?

8.1 Does the curriculum help students identify and understand the value conflicts inherent in a multicultural society?

8.2 Does the curriculum examine differing views of ideals and realities among ethnic and cultural groups?

9.0 Does the curriculum explore and clarify ethnic alternatives and options within U.S. society?

9.1 Does the teacher create a classroom atmosphere reflecting an acceptance of and respect for ethnic and cultural differences?

9.2 Does the teacher create a classroom atmosphere allowing realistic consideration of alternatives and options for members of ethnic and cultural groups?

10.0 Does the curriculum promote values, attitudes, and behaviors that support ethnic and cultural diversity?

10.1 Does the curriculum help students examine differences within and among ethnic and cultural groups?

10.2 Does the curriculum foster attitudes supportive of cultural democracy and other unifying democratic ideals and values?

10.3 Does the curriculum reflect ethnic and cultural diversity?

Rating					Guidelines
Strongly ◄————► Hardly at all					

10.4 Does the curriculum present diversity as a vital societal force that encompasses both potential strength and potential conflict?

11.0 Does the curriculum help students develop decision-making abilities, social participation skills, and a sense of political efficacy necessary for effective citizenship?

11.1 Does the curriculum help students develop the ability to distinguish facts from interpretations and opinions?

11.2 Does the curriculum help students develop skills in finding and processing information?

11.3 Does the curriculum help students develop sound knowledge, concepts, generalizations, and theories about issues related to ethnicity and cultural identity?

11.4 Does the curriculum help students develop sound methods of thinking about issues related to ethnic and cultural groups?

11.5 Does the curriculum help students develop skills in clarifying and reconsidering their values and relating them to their understanding of ethnicity and cultural identity?

11.6 Does the curriculum include opportunities to use knowledge, valuing, and thinking in decision making on issues related to race, ethnicity, and culture?

11.7 Does the curriculum provide opportunities for students to take action on social problems affecting racial, ethnic, and cultural groups?

11.8 Does the curriculum help students develop a sense of efficacy?

12.0 Does the curriculum help students develop skills necessary for effective interpersonal and intercultural group interactions?

12.1 Does the curriculum help students understand ethnic and cultural reference points that influence communication?

12.2 Does the curriculum help students participate in cross-ethnic and cross-cultural experiences and reflect upon them?

13.0 Is the multicultural curriculum comprehensive in scope and sequence, presenting holistic views of ethnic and cultural groups, and an integral part of the total school curriculum?

13.1 Does the curriculum introduce students to the experiences of persons of widely varying backgrounds in the study of each ethnic and cultural group?

13.2 Does the curriculum discuss the successes and contributions of group members within the context of that group's values?

13.3 Does the curriculum include the role of ethnicity and culture in the local community as well as in the nation?

13.4 Does content related to ethnic and cultural groups extend beyond special units, courses, occasions, and holidays?

13.5 Are materials written by and about ethnic and cultural groups used in teaching fundamental skills?

13.6 Does the curriculum provide for the development of progressively more complex concepts, abilities, and values?

13.7 Is the study of ethnicity and culture incorporated into instructional plans rather than being supplementary or additive?

14.0 Does the curriculum include the continuous study of the cultures, historical experiences, social realities, and existential conditions of ethnic groups with a variety of racial compositions?

14.1 Does the curriculum include study of several ethnic and cultural groups?

Rating				Guidelines
Strongly ←			→ Hardly at all	

14.2 Does the curriculum include studies of both white ethnic groups and ethnic groups of color?

14.3 Does the curriculum provide for continuity in the examination of aspects of experience affected by race?

15.0 Are interdisciplinary and multidisciplinary approaches used in designing and implementing the curriculum?

15.1 Are interdisciplinary and multidisciplinary perspectives used in the study of ethnic and cultural groups and related issues?

15.2 Are approaches used authentic and comprehensive explanations of ethnic and cultural issues, events, and problems?

16.0 Does the curriculum use comparative approaches in the study of racial, ethnic, and cultural groups?

16.1 Does the curriculum focus on the similarities and differences among and between ethnic and cultural groups?

16.2 Are matters examined from comparative perspectives with fairness to all?

17.0 Does the curriculum help students view and interpret events, situations, and conflict from diverse ethnic and cultural perspectives and points of view?

17.1 Are the perspectives of various ethnic and cultural groups represented in the instructional program?

17.2 Are students taught why different ethnic and cultural groups often perceive the same historical event or contemporary situation differently?

17.3 Are the perspectives of each ethnic and cultural group presented as valid ways to perceive the past and the present?

18.0 Does the curriculum conceptualize and describe the development of the United States as a multidirectional society?

18.1 Does the curriculum view the territorial and cultural growth of the United States as flowing from several directions?

18.2 Does the curriculum include a parallel study of the various societies that developed in the geo-cultural United States?

19.0 Does the school provide opportunities for students to participate in the aesthetic experiences of various ethnic and cultural groups?

19.1 Are multiethnic literature and art used to promote empathy and understanding of people from various ethnic and cultural groups?

19.2 Are multiethnic literature and art used to promote self-examination and self-understanding?

19.3 Do students read and hear the poetry, short stories, novels, folklore, plays, essays, and autobiographies of a variety of ethnic and cultural groups?

19.4 Do students examine the music, art, architecture, and dance of a variety of ethnic and cultural groups?

19.5 Do students have available the artistic, musical, and literary expression of the local ethnic and cultural communities?

19.6 Are opportunities provided for students to develop their own artistic, literary, and musical expression?

20.0 Does the curriculum provide opportunities for students to develop full literacy in at least two languages?

20.1 Are students taught to communicate (speaking, reading, and writing) in a second language?

Rating				Guidelines
Strongly ⟵ ⟶ Hardly at all				

20.2 Are students taught about the culture of the people who use the second language?

20.3 Are second language speakers provided opportunities to develop full literacy in their native language?

20.4 Are students for whom English is a second language taught in their native languages as needed?

21.0 Does the curriculum make maximum use of local community resources?

21.1 Are students involved in the continuous study of the local community?

21.2 Are members of the local ethnic and cultural communities continually used as classroom resources?

21.3 Are field trips to the various local ethnic and cultural communities provided for students?

22.0 Do the assessment procedures used with students reflect their ethnic and community cultures?

22.1 Do teachers use a variety of assessment procedures that reflect the ethnic and cultural diversity of students?

22.2 Do teachers' day-to-day assessment techniques take into account the ethnic and cultural diversity of their students?

23.0 Does the school conduct ongoing, systematic evaluations of the goals, methods, and instructional materials used in teaching about ethnicity and culture?

23.1 Do assessment procedures draw on many sources of evidence from many sorts of people?

23.2 Does the evaluation program examine school policies and procedures?

23.3 Does the evaluation program examine the everyday climate of the school?

23.4 Does the evaluation program examine the effectiveness of curricular programs, both academic and nonacademic?

23.5 Are the results of evaluation used to improve the school program?

5. CURRICULUM AND INSTRUCTION IN MULTICULTURAL PERSPECTIVE

Part Four: References

Alba, Richard D. *Ethnic Identity: The Transformation of White America*. New Haven, Conn.: Yale University Press, 1990.

Aronson, Elliot, and Alex Gonzalez. "Desegregation, Jigsaw, and the Mexican-American Experience." In *Eliminating Racism: Profiles in Controversy*, edited by P. A. Katz and D. A. Taylor, 301–14. New York: Plenum Press, 1988.

Asante, Molefi Kete. *The Afrocentric Idea*. Philadelphia: Temple University Press, 1987.

_____. *Kemet, Afrocentricity, and Knowledge*. Trenton, N.J.: African World Press, 1990.

_____. "The Afrocentric Idea in Education." *The Journal of Negro Education* 60, no. 2 (Spring 1991): 170–80.

Banks, James A. *Teaching Strategies for Ethnic Studies*, 5th ed. Boston: Allyn and Bacon, 1991a.

_____. "The Dimensions of Multicultural Education." *Multicultural Leader* 4, no. 1 (Winter/Spring 1991b): 3–4.

_____. "Multicultural Education: Its Effects on Students' Racial and Gender Role Attitudes." In *Handbook of Research on Social Studies Teaching and Learning*, edited by James P. Shaver, 459–69. New York: Macmillan, 1991c.

Banks, James A., and Cherry A. McGee Banks, eds. *Multicultural Education: Issues and Perspectives*. Boston: Allyn and Bacon, 1989.

Belenky, Mary F., Blythe M. Clinchy, Nancy R. Goldberger, and Jill M. Tarule. *Women's Ways of Knowing: The Development of Self, Voice and Mind*. New York: Basic Books, 1986.

Bernal, Martin. *Black Athena: The Afroasiatic Roots of Classical Civilization*. Vol. 2, *The Archaeological and Documentary Evidence*. New Brunswick, N.J.: Rutgers University Press, 1991.

Cohen, Elizabeth G. *Designing Groupwork: Strategies for the Heterogeneous Classroom*. New York: Teachers College Press, 1986.

Cummins, Jim. "Empowering Minority Students: A Framework for Intervention." *Harvard Educational Review* 56, no. 1 (February 1986): 18–36.

Delpit, Lisa D. "The Silenced Dialogue: Power and Pedagogy in Educating Other People's Children." *Harvard Educational Review* 58, no. 3 (August 1988): 280–98.

Deyhle, Donna. "Success and Failure: A Micro-Ethnographic Comparison of Navajo and Anglo Students' Perceptions of Testing." *Curriculum Inquiry* 16, no. 4 (1986): 365–89.

Diop, Cheikh Anta. *The African Origins of Civilization: Myth or Reality?* New York: Lawrence Hill and Co., 1974.

Fordham, Signithia. "Racelessness in Private Schools: Should We Deconstruct the Racial and Cultural Identity of African-American Adolescents?" *Teachers College Record* 92 (Spring 1991): 470–84.

Fordham, Signithia, and John U. Ogbu. "Black Students' School Success: Coping with the Burden of 'Acting White.'" *The Urban Review* 18, no. 3 (1986): 176–206.

Gay, Geneva. "Culturally Diverse Students and Social Studies." In *Handbook of Research on Social Studies Teaching and Learning*, edited by James P. Shaver, 144–56. New York: Macmillan, 1991.

Hale-Benson, Janice E. *Black Children: Their Roots, Culture and Learning Styles*. Baltimore: John Hopkins University Press, 1982.

Heath, Shirley Brice. *Ways with Words: Language, Life and Work in Communities and Classrooms*. New York: Cambridge University Press, 1983.

Hodgkinson, Harold L. *All One System: Demographics of Education, Kindergarten through Graduate School*. Washington, D.C.: The Institute for Educational Leadership, 1985.

Howe, Irving. "The Value of the Canon." *The New Republic* 204, no. 7 (18 February 1991): 40–47.

Johnson, William B., and Arnold E. Packer. *Workforce 2000: Work and Workers for the 21st Century*. Washington, D.C.: U.S. Government Printing Office, 1987.

Kochman, Thomas. *Black and White: Styles in Conflict*. Chicago: University of Chicago Press, 1981.

Kroeber, Alfred, and Clyde Kluckhuhn. *Culture: A Critical Review of Concepts and Definitions*. New York: Vintage, 1952.

Lerner, Gerda. *The Majority Finds Its Past: Placing Women in History*. New York: Oxford University Press, 1979.

Mercer, Jane R. "Alternate Paradigms for Assessment in a Pluralistic Society." In *Multicultural Education: Issues and Perspectives*, edited by James A. Banks and Cherry A. McGee Banks, 289–304. Boston: Allyn and Bacon, 1989.

Oakes, Jeannie. *Keeping Track: How Schools Structure Inequality*. New Haven, Conn.: Yale University Press, 1985.

Ogbu, John. "Overcoming Racial Barriers to Equal Access." In *Access to Knowledge: An Agenda for Our Nation's Schools*, edited by John I. Goodlad and Pamela Keating, 59–89. New York: The College Board, 1990.

Pallas, Aaron M., Gary Natriello, and Edward L. McDill. "The Changing Nature of the Disadvantaged Population: Current Dimensions and Future Trends." *Educational Researcher* 18, no. 5 (June/July 1989): 16–22.

Philips, Susan U. *The Invisible Culture: Communication in Classroom and Community on the Warm Springs Indian Reservation*. New York: Longman, 1983.

Ravitch, Diane. "Multiculturalism E Pluribus Plures." *The American Scholar* 54 (Spring 1990): 337–54.

Schlesinger, Arthur M., Jr. *The Disuniting of America: Reflections on a Multicultural Society*. Knoxville, Tenn.: Whittle Direct Books, 1991.

Sertima, Ivan Van, ed. *Great Black Leaders: Ancient and Modern*. New Brunswick, N.J.: Africana Studies Department, Rutgers University, 1988.

Shade, Barbara J., ed. *Culture, Style and the Educative Press*. Springfield, Ill.: Charles C. Thomas, 1989.

Slavin, Robert E. *Cooperative Learning*. New York: Longman, 1983.

Sleeter, Christine E., and Carl A. Grant. "An Analysis of Multicultural Education in the United States." *Harvard Educational Review* 57, no. 4 (1987): 421–44.

Stephan, Walter G. "Intergroup Relations." In *The Handbook of Social Psychology*, vol. 2, 3d ed., edited by Gardner Lindzey and Elliot Aronson, 599–658. New York: Random House, 1985.

Tetreault, Mary K. Thompson. "Integrating Content about Women and Gender into the Curriculum." In *Multicultural Education: Issues and Perspectives*, edited by James A. Banks and Cherry A. McGee Banks, 124–44. Boston: Allyn and Bacon, 1989.

United States Commission on Civil Rights. *A Better Chance to Learn: Bilingual-Bicultural Education*. Washington, D.C.: U.S. Government Printing Office, 1975.

Weatherford, Jack. *Indian Givers: How the Indians of the Americas Transformed the World*. New York: Fawcett Columbine, 1988.

---

*Task Force on Ethnic Studies Curriculum Guidelines

James A. Banks, Chair, University of Washington
Carlos E. Cortés, University of California, Riverside
Geneva Gay, University of Washington
Ricardo L. Garcia, University of Idaho
Anna S. Ochoa, Indiana University

Empowering Children To Create a Caring Culture in a World of Differences

Louise Derman-Sparks

Louise Derman-Sparks is Director, Anti-Bias Leadership Project, Pacific Oaks College, Pasadena, California. This article is based on her keynote address at the ACEI Study Conference in Phoenix, Arizona, April 8, 1993.

Racism, sexism, classism, heterosexism and ableism are still deeply entrenched and pervasive in society, making it very difficult for millions of children to be "Freedom's Child." What must we do as educators to ensure that all children can develop to their fullest potential—can truly become "Freedom's Child"?

Children's Development of Identity and Attitudes

Take a moment to listen to the voices of children. Members of the Anti-Bias Curriculum Task Force developed the anti-bias approach after a year spent collecting and analyzing children's thinking and trying out activities. They collected the following anecdotes:

- Steven is busy being a whale on the climbing structure in the 2-year-old yard. Susie tries to join him. "Girls can't do that!" he shouts.
- Robby, 3 years old, refuses to hold the hand of a dark-skinned classmate. At home, he insists, after bathing, that his black hair is now "white because it is clean."

- "You aren't really an Indian," 4-year-old Rebecca tells one of her child care teachers. "Where are your feathers?"
- "Malcolm can't play with us. He's a baby," Linda tells their teacher. Malcolm, another 4-year-old, uses a wheelchair.

Those voices reflect the impact of societal bias on children. Now, listen to voices of children in programs that practice anti-bias curriculum:

- Maria, 4 years old, sees a stereotypical "Indian warrior" figure in the toy store. "That toy hurts Indian people's feelings," she tells her grandmother.
- Rebecca's kindergarten teacher asks the children to draw a picture of what they would

From *Childhood Education*, Winter 1993/94, pp. 66-71. © 1993 by the Association for Childhood Education International. Reprinted by permission of the Association for Childhood Education International, 11501 Georgia Avenue, Suite 315, Wheaton, MD.

like to be when they grow up. Rebecca draws herself as a surgeon—in a pink ball gown and tiara.

- After hearing the story of Rosa Parks and the Montgomery bus boycott, 5-year-old Tiffany, whose skin is light brown, ponders whether she would have had to sit in the back of the bus. Finally, she firmly asserts, "I'm Black and, anyway, all this is stupid. I would just get off and tell them to keep their old bus."

- In the school playground, 5-year-old Casey and another white friend, Tommy, are playing. Casey calls two other boys to join them. "You can't play with them. They're Chinese eyes," Tommy says to him. Casey replies, "That's not right. All kinds of kids play together. I know. My teacher tells me civil rights stories."

Children do not come to pre-school, child care centers or elementary school as "blank slates" on the topic of diversity. Facing and understanding what underlies their thoughts and feelings are key to empowering children to resist bias. The following is a brief summary of research about how children develop racial identity and attitudes:

- As early as 6 months, infants notice skin color differences. (Katz, 1993)

- By 2 years of age, children not only notice, they also ask questions about differences and similarities among people. They soon begin forming their own hypotheses to explain the diversity they are seeing and hearing. When my daughter was 3, she commented one day, "I am thinking about skin color. How do we get it?" I launched into an explanation about melanin, which was clearly above her level of understanding. Finally, I asked her, "How do you think we get skin color?" "Magic markers!" she replied. (Derman-Sparks, Tanaka Higa & Sparks, 1980)

At my family's 1991 Passover Seder (the Seder honors the ancient Jewish Exodus from slavery in Egypt), my niece announced, "I'm half Jewish." "Uh huh," I replied (one parent is Jewish). She continued, "The Jewish people went through the water and they didn't get wet. They got to the other side. The people who weren't Jewish got drowned."

"That is what the Passover story tells us, that the Egyptian soldiers drowned," I affirmed, but her expression remained quizzical. So, I decided to ask her, "What do you think happened to the people who were half Jewish?"

"They got to the other side, too," she replied, paused and then concluded, "but they got a little bit wet." Afterward, a cousin wondered, "How did you ever think of that question?" (the Passover story does not mention people being "half Jewish").

I don't know if my question was "right" in any absolute sense, but trying to follow my niece's line of thinking, I sensed that the issue was important to her. She seemed emotionally satisfied with her solution. Moreover, it was a cognitively clever one—she got to the other side safely AND she ac-

© 1993 CLEO Freelance Photo

knowledged her identity as she understood it.

■ How we answer children's questions and respond to their ideas is crucial to their level of comfort when learning about diversity. Statements such as, "It's not polite to ask," "I'll tell you later" or "It doesn't matter," do not help children form positive ideas about themselves or

---

The following poem by Bill Martin, Jr. (1987) captures the essence of what I think it means to empower children to create a caring culture in a world of differences.

I like me, no doubt
about it,
I like me, can't live
without it,
I like me, let's shout
about it,
I am Freedom's Child.

You like you, no doubt
about it,
You like you, can't live
without it,
You like you, let's shout
about it,
You are Freedom's Child.

We need all the
different kinds of people
we can find,
To make freedom's dream
come true,
So as I learn to like the
differences in me,
I learn to like the
differences in you.

I like you, no doubt
about it,
You like me, can't live
without it,
We are free, let's shout
about it,
Hooray for Freedom's
Child!

*Reprinted by permission of SRA/Macmillan/
McGraw-Hill School Publishing Co.*

pro-diversity dispositions toward others. (Derman-Sparks & ABC Task Force, 1989)

■ Between 2 1/2 to 3 1/2 years of age, children also become aware of and begin to absorb socially prevailing negative stereotypes, feelings and ideas about people, including themselves. All children are exposed to these attitudes in one form or another, usually through a combination of sources (parents, extended family, neighbors, teachers, friends, TV, children's books, movies). (Derman-Sparks & ABC Task Force, 1989)

■ Throughout the early childhood period, children continue to construct and elaborate on their ideas about their own and others' identities and their feelings about human differences. In the primary years, children's development goes beyond the individual to include a group identity. Some researchers believe that after age 9, racial attitudes tend to stay constant unless the child experiences a life-changing event. (Aboud, 1988)

■ The research literature also points to the great damage racism, sexism and classism have on *all* children's development. Young children are harmed by a psychologically toxic environment. How they are harmed depends on how they are affected by the various "isms"—whether they receive messages of superiority or inferiority. (Clark, 1955; Dennis, 1981)

For children of color, the wounds can be overt. Often, however, they are quite subtle. Chester Pierce calls these subtle forms of racism "micro-contaminants" (Pierce, 1980). Kenyon Chan notes that these micro-contaminants "are carried by children like grains of sand, added one by one, eventually weighing children down beyond their capacity to carry the sand and to grow emotionally and intellectually to their fullest" (Chan, 1993).

Racism attacks young children's growing sense of group, as well as individual, identity. Thus, the chil-

dren are even less able to resist racism's harm. Chan cites an example: A Chinese American girl enrolled in a suburban kindergarten in Los Angeles. Her European American teacher claimed that her name was too difficult to pronounce and promptly renamed her "Mary," calling it an "American" name. This young child is forced to wonder what is wrong with her name and what is wrong with her parents for giving her such a "bad" name. And her doubts originated with the very person who is responsible for supporting and cultivating her development.

---

*R*acism attacks young children's growing sense of group, as well as individual, identity.

Moreover, as Lily Wong-Fillmore's research documents, young children who come from homes where a language other than English is spoken pay a terrible price if they experience a too-early loss of continued development in their home language. The price includes the gradual impoverishment of communication between the child and parents (and other family members) and the potentially serious weakening of the "family's continued role in the socialization of its children" (Wong-Fillmore, 1991).

White, English-speaking children also experience psychological damage. Although this issue has been less studied, the research we do have suggests some disturbing problems:

■ First, racism teaches white children moral double standards for treating people of racial/ethnic groups other than their own. This leads to the possibility of general ethical erosion (Clark, 1955) and to a form of hypocrisy that results in primary school-age children saying words that sound like acceptance of diversity, while acting in ways that demonstrate the opposite (Miel, 1976).

■ Second, children may be constructing identity on a false sense of superiority based on skin color. White children's self-esteem will be rather vulnerable if/when they come to realize that skin color does not determine a person's value.

■ Third, racism results in white children developing fears about people different from themselves. They do not gain the life skills they need for effectively interacting with the increasing range of human diversity in society and the world.

Racial stereotyping is not the only danger. Children's absorption of gender stereotypes limits their development. As young as 3 and 4, children begin to self-limit their choices of learning experiences because of the gender norms they are already absorbing. One of the negative consequences of this process is a pattern of uneven cognitive development, or "practice deficits," related to the types of activities boys and girls choose (Serbin, 1980, p. 60). Girls tend to function below potential in math and boys in expression of their feelings.

Furthermore, research on children's development of ideas and feelings about disabilities indicates that by 2 and 3, they notice, are curious about and sometimes fear people with a disability and their equipment (Froschl, Colon, Rubin & Sprung, 1984; Sapon-Shevin, 1983). Children's fears appear to come from developmental misconceptions that they might "catch" the disability, as well as from adults' indirect and direct communication of discomfort. Moreover, the impact of stereotypes and biases about people with disabilities affects primary age children's treatment of any child

who does not fit the physical "norms" of attractiveness, weight and height.

Research also suggests that young children who learn about people with disabilities through a variety of concrete activities are much more likely to see the whole person, rather than just focusing on the person's disability.

What Empowering Children To Create a Caring Culture Requires of Us

Clarity About Goals. The following goals are for *all* children. The specific issues and tasks necessary for working toward these goals will vary for children, depending on their backgrounds, ages and life experiences.

■ *Nurture each child's construction of a knowledgeable, confident self-concept and group identity.* To achieve this goal, we must create education conditions in which all children are able to like who they are without needing to feel superior to anyone else. Children must also be able to develop biculturally where that is appropriate.

■ *Promote each child's comfortable, empathic interaction with people from diverse backgrounds.* This goal requires educators to guide children's development of the cognitive awareness, emotional disposition and behavioral skills needed to respectfully and effectively learn about differences, comfortably negotiate and adapt to differences, and cognitively understand and emotionally accept the common humanity that all people share.

■ *Foster each child's critical thinking about bias.* Children need to develop the cognitive skills to identify "unfair" and "untrue" images (stereotypes), comments (teasing, name-calling) and behaviors (discrimination) directed at one's own or others' identities. They also need the emotional empathy to know that bias hurts.

■ *Cultivate each child's ability to stand up for her/himself and for others in the face of bias.* This "activism" goal requires educators to help every child learn and practice a variety of ways to act: a) when another child acts in a biased manner toward her/him, b) when a child acts in a biased manner toward another child, c) when an adult acts in a biased manner. Goal 4 builds on goal 3 as critical thinking and empathy are necessary components of acting for oneself or others in the face of bias.

These four goals interact with and build on each other. We cannot accomplish any one goal without the other three. *Their combined intent is to empower children to resist the negative impact of racism and other "isms" on their development and to grow into adults who will want and be able to work with others to eliminate all forms of oppression.* In other words, the underlying intent is not to end racism (and other "isms") in one generation by changing children's attitudes and behaviors, but rather to promote critical thinkers and activists who can work for social change and participate in creating a caring culture in a world of differences.

Preparing ourselves. Effective anti-bias education requires every teacher to look inward and commit to a lifelong journey of understanding her/his own cultural beliefs, while changing the prejudices and behaviors that interfere with the nurturing of all children. Teachers need to know:

■ how to see their own culture in relationship to society's history and current power realities
■ how to effectively adapt their teaching style and curriculum content to their children's needs
■ how to engage in cultural conflict resolution with people from cultural backgrounds other than their own
■ how to be critical thinkers about bias in their practice

- how to be activists—engaging people in dialogue about bias, intervening, working with others to create change.

Achieving these goals takes commitment and time, and is a developmental process for adults as well as for children. One must be emotionally as well as cognitively involved and ready to face periods of disequilibrium and then reconstruction and transformation.

Implementation Principles and Strategies

To create a caring culture in which children can be empowered, teachers must be "reflective practitioners" who can think critically about their own teaching practice and adapt curriculum goals and general strategies to the needs of their children.

Critical thinking. Be aware of "tourist multicultural curriculum" and find ways to eliminate tourism from your program. Tourist multicultural curriculum is the most commonly practiced approach in early childhood education and elementary school today. The majority of commercial curriculum materials currently available on the market and many published curriculum guides reflect a tourist version of multicultural education. Unfortunately, tourist multicultural curriculum is a simplistic, inadequate version of multicultural education.

In a classroom practicing a tourist approach, the daily "regular" curriculum reflects mainstream European American perspectives, rules of behavior, images, learning and teaching styles. Activities about "other" cultures often exhibit the following problems:

- *Disconnection*: Activities are added on to the curriculum as special times, rather than integrated into all aspects of the daily environment and curriculum.
- *Patronization*: "Other" cultures are treated as "quaint" or "exotic." This form of tourism does

not teach children to appreciate what all humans share in common.

- *Trivialization*: Cultural activities that are disconnected from the daily life of the people trivialize the culture. A typical example is multicultural curriculum that focuses on holidays—days that are different from "normal" days. Children do not learn about how people live their lives, how they work, who does what in the family—all of which is the essence of a culture. Other forms of trivialization include: turning cultural practices that have deep, ritual meaning into "arts and crafts" or dance activities, or asking parents to cook special foods without any further lessons about the parents' cultures.
- *Misrepresentation*: Too few images of a group oversimplifies the variety within the group. Use of images and activities based on traditional, past practices of an ethnic group rather than images of contemporary life confuse children. Misusing activities and images that reflect the culture-of-origin of a group to teach about *the life of cultures in the U.S.* conveys misconceptions about people with whom children have little or no face-to-face experience.

In sum, tourist multicultural curriculum does not give children the tools they need to comfortably, empathetically and fairly interact with diversity. Instead, it teaches simplistic generalizations about other people that lead to stereotyping, rather than to understanding of differences. Moreover, tourist curriculum, because it focuses on the unusual and special times of a culture and neglects how people live their daily lives, does not foster children's understanding and empathy for our common humanity. Moving beyond tourist multicultural curriculum is key to our profession's more effective nurturing of diversity.

Incorporate multicultural and anti-bias activities into daily curriculum planning. Diversity and anti-bias topics are integral to the entire curriculum at any education

level. One practical brainstorming technique for identifying the numerous topic possibilities is "webbing."

Step one is determining the center of the "web." This can be: 1) an issue raised by the children (e.g., a person who is visually impaired cannot work); 2) any number of traditional preschool "units" (e.g., my body, families, work); 3) High/Scope's (Weikart, 1975) "key experiences" (e.g., classification or

---

Critical thinking and activism activities should rise out of real life situations that are of interest to children.

---

seriation); 4) any of the traditional content areas of the primary curriculum (science, math, language arts, physical and health curriculum).

Step two involves brainstorming the many possible anti-bias, multicultural issues that stem from the subject at the web's center. *Step three* involves identifying specific content for a particular classroom based on contextual/developmental analysis. *Step four* involves listing possible activities that are developmentally and culturally appropriate for your particular class.

Cultural Appropriateness: Adult/Child Interactions

Effective teaching about diversity, as in all other areas, *is a continuous interaction between adults and children.* On the one hand, teachers are responsible for brainstorming, planning and initiating diversity topics, based on their analyses of children's needs and life experiences. On the other hand, careful attention to children's thinking and behavior, and to "teachable moments," leads educators to modify initial plans.

Find ways to engage children in critical thinking and the planning and carrying out of "activism" activities appropriate to their developmental levels, cultural backgrounds and interests.

Critical thinking and activism activities should rise out of real life situations that are of interest to children. The purpose of such activities is to provide opportunities for children, 4 years old and up, to build their empathy, skills and confidence and to encourage their sense of responsibility for both themselves and for others. Consequently, activities should reflect *their* ideas and issues, not the teacher's. The following two examples are appropriate activism activities.

In the first situation, the children's school did not have a "handicapped" parking space in their parking lot. After a parent was unable to attend open school night because of this lack, the teacher told the class of 4- and 5-year-olds what had happened and why. They then visited other places in their neighborhood that had "handicapped" parking and decided to make one in their school lot. After they did so, they then noticed that teachers were inappropriately parking in the "handicapped" spot (their classroom overlooked the parking lot), so they decided to make tickets. The children dictated their messages, which their teacher faithfully took down, and drew pictures to accompany their words. They then ticketed those cars that did not have "handicapped parking" plaques in their windows.

In the second example, a class of 1st- through 3rd-graders visited a homeless shelter and talked to the director to find out what people needed. They started a toy and blanket collection drive, which they promoted using posters and flyers. They visited several classrooms to talk about what they were doing. They also wrote to the Mayor and the City Council to say that homeless people needed more houses and jobs.

Parents and Family Involvement

Find ways to involve parents and other adult family members in all aspects of anti-bias education. Education and collaboration with parents is *essential.* Educators have to be creative and ingenious to make this happen. Parents can help plan, implement and evaluate environmental adaptations and curricular activities. They can serve on advisory/planning committees with staff, provide information about their lifestyles and beliefs, participate in classroom activities and serve as community liaisons. Teachers can send home regular short newsletters to share ongoing plans and classroom activities, and elicit parent advice and resources. Parent meetings on child-rearing and education issues should also incorporate relevant diversity topics.

When a family member disagrees with an aspect of the curriculum, it is essential that the teachers listen carefully and sensitively to the issues underlying the disagreement. Objections may include: 1) family's belief that learning about differences will "make the children prejudiced" ("color-blind" view), 2) parent's belief that teaching about stereotyping and such values belongs in the home, not at school, 3) family members' strong prejudices against specific groups.

Staff need to find out all they can about the cultural and other issues that influence the family's concerns, and then work with family members to find ways to meet their needs while also maintaining the goals of anti-bias education. The techniques for working with parents on anti-bias issues are generally the same as those used for other child development and education topics. The difference, however, lies in the teachers' level of comfort about addressing such topics with other adults.

Teacher Education and Professional Development

Teacher training must incorporate liberating pedagogical techniques that:

- engage students on cognitive, emotional and behavioral levels
- use storytelling to enable students to both name and identify the ways that various identity contexts and bias have affected their lives
- use experiential activities that engage learners in discovering the dynamics of cultural differences and the various "isms"
- provide new information and analysis that give deeper meaning to what is learned through storytelling and experiential activities
- create a balance between supporting and challenging students in an environment of safety, not necessarily comfort.

The most useful way to work on our own development is to join with others (staff, or staff and parents) in support groups that meet regularly over a long period of time. By collaborating, sharing resources and providing encouragement, we can work on our self-awareness issues, build and improve our practices, strengthen our courage and determination and maintain the joy and excitement of education.

In sum, children of the 21st century will not be able to function if they are psychologically bound by outdated and narrow assumptions about their neighbors. To thrive, even to survive, in this more complicated world, children need to learn how to function in many different cultural contexts, to recognize and respect different histories and perspectives, and to know how to work together to create a more just world that can take care of all its people, its living creatures, its land.

Let's remember the African American novelist Alice Walker's call to "Keep in mind always the present you are constructing. It should be the future you want" (Walker, 1989, p. 238).

References

Aboud, F. (1988). *Children and prejudice.* London: Basil Blackwell.

Chan, K. S. (1993). Sociocultural aspects of anger: Impact on minority children. In M. Furlong & D. Smith (Eds.), *Anger, hostility, and aggression in children and adolescents: Assessment, prevention, and intervention strategies in schools.* Brandon, VT: Clinical Psychology Publishing.

Clark, K. (1955). *Prejudice and your child.* Boston: Bacon.

Dennis, R. (1981). Socialization and racism: The White experience. In B. Bowser & R. Hunt (Eds.), *Impacts of racism on White Americans* (pp. 71-85). Beverly Hills, CA: Sage.

Derman-Sparks, L., Tanaka Higa, C., & Sparks, B. (1980). Children, race, and racism: How race awareness develops.

Bulletin, 11(3 & 4), 3-9.

Derman-Sparks, L., & ABC Task Force (1989). *Anti-bias curriculum: Tools for empowering young children.* Washington, DC: National Association for the Education of Young Children.

Froschl, M., Colon, L., Rubin, E., & Sprung, B. (1984). *Including all of us: An early childhood curriculum about disability.* New York: Educational Equity Concepts.

Katz, P. (May, 1993). *Development of racial attitudes in children.* Presentation given to the University of Delaware.

Martin, B., Jr. (1987). *I am freedom's child.* Allen, TX: DLM Teaching Resources.

Miel, A. (1976). *The short-changed children of suburbia.* New York: Insitute of Human Relations Press.

Pierce, C. (1980). Social trace contaminants: Subtle indicators of racism in

TV. In Withey & Abelis (Eds.), *Television and social behavior.* New Jersey: Lawrence & Erlbaum.

Sapon-Shevin, M. (1983). Teaching young children about differences. *Young Children, 38*(2), 24-32.

Serbin, L. (1980). Play activities and the development of visual-spatial skills. *Equal Play, 1*(4), 5.

Walker, A. (1989). *The temple of my familiar.* New York: Pocket Books.

Weikart, D. (1975). *Young children in action.* Ypsilanti, MI: High Scope Press.

Wong-Fillmore, L. (1991). Language and cultural issues in early education. In S. L. Kagan (Ed.), *The care and education of America's young children: Obstacles and opportunites. The 90th yearbook of the National Society for the Study of Education* (pp. 3-49). Chicago: University of Chicago Press.

"The Party":
Role Playing to Enhance Multicultural Understanding

Ellen N. Junn

Ellen N. Junn is an associate professor of child development at California State University, Fullerton.

Tell me and I will forget. Show me and I will remember. Involve me and I will understand." This adage aptly summarizes the power that experiential involvement has for promoting deeper, more lasting forms of learning or understanding. Indeed, research by social psychologists (Fazio & Zanna, 1981) indicates that direct, active experience may be crucial for altering attitudes and beliefs. Thus, as a way of introducing new students to course material on prejudice and ethnic identity formation, I used an exercise that immersed them in role playing that forced them to experience first-hand the effects of stereotyping.

"The Party" is a role-playing activity that has been used on a number of college campuses including University of California at Berkeley and Stanford University[1] as part of their programs to enhance multicultural understanding among residence hall students. I adapted this strategy for use with seventy-five entering students in a one-unit Ethnic Studies course as part of a Summer Bridge Program for underrepresented students at California State University at Fullerton.

This exercise is most effective for use with groups no larger than thirty-five with one group facilitator, and it requires from sixty to ninety minutes (roughly ten minutes for instructions and role playing and an hour for discussion). Few materials are required other than sticky labels of cultural stereotypes for participants (e.g., Asian male computer science student, white female sorority member, African American male athlete, lesbian student, Jewish female student, etc.) and a discussion handout with questions for individuals and small groups to address following the role playing.

Three female upper division undergraduate teaching assistants (who had experienced the exercise at an earlier training session) led smaller "break out" groups of twenty-five students. The group facilitator set the tone by indicating that: (a) "The Party" was a short role-playing exercise that would be used to explore the similarities and differences among cultures in an everyday setting and to highlight related material in the lecture part of the ethnic studies course; (b) All students were urged to participate actively in the role playing for maximal benefit; (c) Students were also cautioned to expect that they may experience some strong emotions due to the experiential nature of role playing, but that these emotions and experiences

would be processed during the discussion period.

The activity began with asking students to imagine that they are eager to meet other students at a campus "party." Next, the facilitator affixed a label representing a cultural stereotype on each participant's forehead, taking pains to select stereotypes that did not match a particular participant (e.g., affixing "white female sorority member" on a non-white male). Although students could read the labels of others at the party, they did not know which label the facilitator had affixed to their own forehead. The goals of each participant were: (a) to try to meet and talk to as many participants at the "party" as possible; (b) to respond and relate to others at the party based on their stereotyped labels—in other words, after viewing someone else's label, students were encouraged to make stereotyped conversational comments, even if they did not believe in those stereotypes; and (c) to make a guess as to what label they were wearing by the end of the role-playing session based only on the comments made to them during the "party."

Following the ten-minute role playing, students were given a handout to answer first individually, then in small groups for the processing discussion. The handout included questions such as, "What is your

From *College Teaching*, Summer 1994, pp. 109-110. © 1994 by the Helen Dwight Reid Educational Foundation. Reprinted by permission of Heldref Publications, 1319 Eighteenth Street, NW, Washington, DC 20036-1802.

label's gender/culture?" "What were the most frequent comments made to you and how did these comments make you feel?" "Do you share these same stereotypical views and why or why not?" "Who did you feel most comfortable with at the party?" "What did you learn from this exercise?" etc. After people had completed the questionnaire, the facilitator asked them to convene in small groups of four or five students to discuss their responses on the handout, and reminded them that during their discussions, they should listen closely to each other and should be fair, open, and sensitive to others in the group. Groups then reported back in a general class discussion of students' reaction to the exercise and the insights gained as they related to course material on stereotyping, prejudice, and strategies to counteract stereotyping.

Student Response

Students responded very favorably to this experience. There were clear signs of excitement, curiosity, and amusement as group facilitators described the exercise to students. Student interaction during the role playing was extremely lively, active, and very often humorous—virtually all students appeared to be enjoying the "party." There was frequent laughter, joking, and high levels of animation and involvement. Indeed, students' accuracy at guessing their own stereotypic labels was very high (averaging 82% for culture and 68% for gender). Although the role-playing sessions were generally characterized by mirth and glee, students' subsequent discussions and reflections on the exercise were, by contrast, serious.

At the end of the ethnic studies course, participating students completed a brief questionnaire to assess the value of this activity using a scale of 1 = "very useless or unenjoyable" to 5 = "very useful or enjoyable." Students found the entire "party" exercise quite enjoyable (mean rating = 4.0, standard deviation = 0.96). When asked to rate the usefulness of the role playing for helping them to experience and understand stereotyping and prejudice, students responded very positively (mean rating = 4.1, standard deviation = 0.94). Similarly, students rated the subsequent classroom discussions as useful for furthering their understanding of stereotyping and prejudice (mean rating = 4.1, standard deviation = 0.92).

Finally, when students were asked to respond in writing to what they learned about the topic of prejudice and about themselves or others, the following comments were typical: "I loved it! [the exercise] I learned that stereotypes and prejudice are everywhere and it can be hard for anyone to get over it." "The best part was that I experienced a view within people that I never was able to understand before. It was very emotional for me." "It made me realize how prejudiced I am sometimes—I learned that many times we stereotype without knowing it." "It gave me an understanding of racism." And, "People are all the same—we shouldn't stereotype each other—we have the power to eradicate prejudice, but it'll take lots of effort and education from every individual."

Judging from students' enthusiastic response to this experiential classroom exercise, "The Party" appears to be an effective, simple, and evocative vehicle for sensitizing students to issues related to cultural or ethnic diversity. In fact, this strategy can be modified easily to focus on other forms of understanding such as differences due to age, ableness, social class, etc. Some additional suggestions for instructors include: (1) foster a responsive, safe classroom environment by maintaining a warm and positive attitude throughout discussions; (2) avoid singling out non-majority students as spokespersons for their particular ethnic group; (3) be prepared to use flexible and sensitive communication and negotiation skills should potentially derisive issues arise; (4) permit some measure of honest, appropriate self-disclosure about your own ethnic or cultural experiences because research indicates that instructors who do so are more effective when dealing with multicultural students and issues (Scollon, 1981); and (5) familiarize yourself with the increasing number of resources addressing the topic of university teaching regarding issues of diversity (Banks, 1993; Junn, in press; Wurzel & Holt, 1991).

Whether students or faculty are consciously aware of it or not, each of us brings into the classroom a wealth of unique, personal cultural knowledge. By tapping this rich resource, students not only deepen their understanding of the influence of social, historical, and political forces for cultural diversity, they have the potential to view themselves and the world from more complex perspectives. It is this enriched sense of self in relation to larger contexts that sets the stage for powerful possibilities as these students leave our colleges to navigate their personal and professional worlds. Viewed from this perspective, taking up the challenge of educating for diversity represents an important opportunity for all.

NOTE

1. A facilitator manual with instructions for "The Party" exercise as well as others can be obtained for $25 by writing to Ms. Edith Ng, University of California at Berkeley, Staff Affirmative Action Office, Project DARE, 2199 Addison Street, Suite 641, Berkeley, CA 94720, telephone: 510-643-7464.

REFERENCES

Banks, J. A. 1993. The canon debate, knowledge construction, and multicultural education. *Educational Researcher* 22(5): 4–14.

Fazio, R. H., and M. P. Zanna. 1981. Direct experience and attitude-behavior consistency. In *Advances in experimental social psychology,* edited by L. Berkowitz, Vol. 14. New York: Academic Press.

Junn, E. in press. Enhancing diversity understanding through experiential classroom exercises: Issues and techniques. In *Changing college classrooms: New teaching and learning strategies for an increasingly complex world,* edited by D. Halpern. San Francisco, Calif.: Jossey-Bass.

Scollon, R. 1981. *Teacher's questions about Alaska Native education.* Fairbanks, AK: University of Alaska Center for Cross Cultural Studies. (ERIC Document Reproduction Service No. ED 238 661)

Wurzel, J. S., and W. Holt. 1991. Teaching aids for multicultural education. *Communication Education* 40(3): 288–291.

Classrooms Without Borders

Kathleen Ralph

Kathleen Ralph is Assistant Professor, California State University, Fullerton.

By the year 2020, one out of every two students in the United States will be a person of color (Banks, 1991). In order to reflect this change, the classroom should become a forum that permits students of all ethnic and cultural groups to fully develop their talents. Educators must help students understand their own cultures and help free them from any cultural boundaries in order to appreciate others' cultures. In order to do this, educators need to select literary works that reflect the perspectives, experiences and values of all ethnic and cultural groups. We should become students ourselves by re-examining the issues that animate history and interacting with cultural art on its own terms.

Multicultural education should not merely address literacy, but also should contribute to interethnic understanding. When multicultural literature becomes an integral part of the curriculum and teachers act as models and guides, classrooms will become arenas for open exchange. Literature and related discussions permit students to read, think and become actively engaged with the texts. As a consequence, it will be easier for students to cross cultural borders.

Crossing cultural borders may involve conflict, but we need to confront those conflicts. Gerald Graff (1990) suggests that although traditional education theory assumes that instructors have to resolve or avoid conflicts, students would benefit more from discovering what connections and contrasts emerge when controversies are brought out in the open and discussed. The point is not to delete the classics, but rather to teach them in relation to texts that challenge them. The result is a continuing dialogue that does not force a consensus. Change and conflict do not have to lead to divisiveness. Instead, diversity can enhance student involvement in the curriculum.

Students need guidance to help them seek this personal experience in literature. The greatest challenge the language arts teacher faces is finding ways to connect the realities of the classroom to the literature being read. According to Louise Rosenblatt (1976), traditional classes tend to insulate students from the impact of literature. The primary instruction emphasis has been on identifying literary elements such as plot, setting and character description. Students cannot truly experience literature when classroom discussions of literature exclude personal impact in favor of the intellectual response. In order to extract meaning from literature, students need to connect what is in the text to their life experiences.

Students are empowered through collaboration. Power should not be a fixed quantity parceled out by the teacher. In contrast to the traditional classroom, the collaborative classroom generates power that is shared by all the participants in the learning environment. Multicultural literature is a primary vehicle for power-generating dialogues. The literary work becomes the shared body of experience that allows students to respond from the perspectives of their individual cultural backgrounds. The teacher uses thought-provoking questions to enhance students' connections to literature and to establish a relationship of cultural equality between students and teacher.

Multicultural Literature in the Classroom

Teachers must first help students examine their own cultural backgrounds. Some students are very knowledgeable about their ethnic and cultural heritage, while others identify so strongly with mainstream culture that they fail to see how behaviors, attitudes and beliefs reflect their own cultures. All of us belong to many cultural groups simultaneously, whether consciously or unconsciously. In addition to membership in ethnic cultures, our cultural identities can also be linked to subcultures defined by religion, socioeconomic class, nationality, geographic region, age and gender. Multicultural literature offers opportunities for personal reflection and identification with many cultures. In *Taking Sides* (Soto, 1991), a Hispanic teenager, Lincoln Mendoza, struggles to cross socioeconomic and

From *Childhood Education*, Annual Theme Issue, 1995, pp. 90-92. © 1995 by the Association for Childhood Education International. Reprinted by permission of the Association for Childhood Education International, 11501 Georgia Avenue, Suite 315, Wheaton, MD.

urban/suburban cultural borders when he moves to a new school. Students can learn to cope with their own cultural identity confusions by reading about characters facing similar issues.

When introducing literature to students, the teacher needs to find a balance between giving background information prior to reading the text and letting students make personal initial connections with the literature. Providing too much background information inhibits the student from seeking a personal response to the text. On the other hand, background information might be needed to entice the reader into the literary work's rich cultural world. Accurate background information prevents a student's prejudices and stereotypes from coloring the text and encourages him to sample texts that may be slightly beyond the borders of his current capabilities.

When students first enter an unfamiliar cultural milieu, the teacher can provide sensory input that creates a backdrop for the story. The sights, sounds and flavors of a culture can be experienced by calling upon community resources. A setting can be created using slides, videotapes, photographs and other visual media. Language, music and other performing arts help introduce students to a culture's people. Food-related experiences can forge links among cultures (e.g., *Everybody Cooks Rice*, Dooley, 1991), while simultaneously acknowledging subtle or not-so-subtle differences. Teachers should permit children to choose whether or not to taste new foods. It is more important for students to understand the role of food in a culture and to realize that all cultures see their own foods as "normal." A study of *Sadako and the Thousand Paper Cranes* (Coerr, 1977) offers students a view of Japanese culture, as well as an awareness of its peace theme. *Amelia's Road* (Altman, 1993) introduces students to the daily life of Mexican-American migrant families. Teachers can help students bridge the gap between the familiar and the unfamiliar by carefully orchestrating the flow of background information.

The ability to look at one's own cultures objectively is a challenge for most students and adults because they tend to be insulated by family and communities. Jean Fritz's (1982) autobiographical children's novel, *Homesick: My Own Story*, documents her adjustment from her early childhood in China to living in rural Pennsylvania. As a daughter of Christian missionaries, she spent her formative years in China insisting that she was "American." At 12, she returned to the United States only to realize that some of her new classmates perceived her to be more Chinese than American. Like many bicultural students, Fritz found that she needed to resolve cultural conflicts, while valuing the richness of having lived in two cultures. After reading this work, classroom discussions could focus on identifying the differences between their own cultures and those of the literary characters. Objectively viewing one's culture from the perspective of another culture might be a second, more sophisticated, step. Novels such as *In the Year of the Boar and Jackie Robinson* (Lord, 1984) and *Children of the River* (Crew, 1989) chronicle first-generation immigrants' perspectives of mainstream "American" culture.

Confronting prejudice indirectly through literature is often easier than asking students to reflect on their present-day prejudices. Upper elementary students reading Mildred Taylor's *Roll of Thunder, Hear My Cry* (1976) or younger students reading Taylor's *Mississippi Bridge* (1990) can learn about the injustice of the Deep South in the 1930s, allowing them to view their own situations from an historical perspective. Teacher-led discussions and activities can guide the students toward personal responses that illuminate their own beliefs and biases. Similarly, discussions of homelessness and illegal immigration can be enhanced by reading *Fly Away Home* (Bunting, 1991) and *Lupita Manana* (Beatty, 1981). Issues that may appear at first to be clear-cut and easily solved gain complexity when stereotypes are questioned through fiction.

One of the values of being able to see commonalities across cultures is the avenue this attitude creates for establishing lines of communication with people of diverse cultures. Knowing that one shares a common interest sets the stage for finding other areas of compatibility. Children across the nation and the world share similar physical and psychological characteristics that can become springboards for exploration and discussion. All children need shelter and food. Most children are nurtured in some type of family setting and participate in play. Books such as *A Country Far Away* (Gray, 1988) and *Hopscotch Around the World* (Lankford, 1992) illustrate the universality of play. *How My Family Lives in America* (Kuklin, 1992) gives young readers opportunities to compare home situations and activities among recent immigrant families. *Bread, Bread, Bread* (Morris, 1989) explains the role of bread as a cross-cultural staple of life, while illustrating the variety that is the richness of cultural diversity. Cultural differences can be valued within a framework of a shared cultural bond. Teachers should help students understand that while cultures do have representative attributes, not all people from a particular culture embrace all its attributes. More accurate stereotypes are still stereotypes.

Celebrating ethnic holidays as a strategy for learning about diverse cultures has been heavily criticized in recent years. Such token celebrations are justifiably criticized when they are used to perpetuate inaccurate stereotypes. Some teachers ask students to participate in the celebrations without explaining the historical and cultural significance of the event. Cinco de Mayo, for example, is frequently celebrated in schools in order to cover Mexican culture. Although the event may have become more of a Mexican-American holiday, many teachers erroneously equate it with the United States' Independence Day. For some teachers, it is also the *only* time that Mexican culture is introduced into the curriculum. Celebrations of ethnic holidays should not encompass the totality of multicultural education. To deny the importance of holiday observances for cultures and for children in particular, however, is also a disservice. Most children learn about their family customs and cultural heritage from celebrations and young children often perceive holidays as the most important days of the year. Children's literature selections such as *Pablo Remembers: The Fiesta of the Day of the Dead* (Ancona, 1993), *Seven Candles for Kwanzaa* (Pinkley, 1993) and *Lion Dancer: Ernie Wan's Chinese New Year* (Waters & Slovenz-Low, 1990) can support teacher efforts to attach meaning to the artifacts and tangible elements of culture.

Communication and Community Among Teachers of Literature

In order to effectively teach cultural diversity, teachers must be able to cultivate critical thinking skills and the ability to mediate the emotions associated with controversial subject matter. Because the teacher needs to present multicultural literature from a balanced perspective, she must think through her own responses to sensitive subjects prior to the class session. By doing so, she can promote student involvement, while simultaneously anticipating pitfalls.

As the most powerful influence in the classroom, the teacher provides the links to multicultural literature. Professional development programs where multicultural literature is read and discussed on an adult level can help teachers reexperience their own reactions and connections to diverse cultures

Relegating multicultural literature to the classroom deprives teachers of forming a personal bond with it. Literature programs provide teachers with opportunities to renew themselves, read adult texts and reflect on their personal response. Immersing oneself in text without looking for formal literary structures allows the reader to focus on reading's potential for pleasure and personal insight. Through collaborative exchanges, teacher-learners can anticipate barriers to crossing cultural borders and thus increase the likelihood of creating viable bridges within their own classrooms.

By sharing their own reading processes and teaching strategies, teachers as learners are able to see different perspectives. Often, teachers can be isolated from the view that all personal responses to literature are equally valid because in the classroom the teacher's perspective is often viewed as the only acceptable one.

Developing a personal philosophy of multicultural education does not happen in isolation. The process is enhanced by the stimulation and interaction available within a community of ethnically and culturally diverse teachers from various school districts and grade levels. School and district staff development sessions abound with informal opportunities to reflect on and confront cultural barriers. Literature circles among faculty members could readily be developed. Ultimately, what happens in individual classrooms is guided by the teaching philosophies of individual teachers. To be successful, institutional change must begin with the classroom teacher.

Teachers need to turn classrooms into lively forums of open multicultural exchange. They must select materials that help students not only understand another culture's point of view, but also see their own culture from an outsider's perspective. Faculty must be willing to use literary works from outside the canon in order to prepare students to live in their increasingly diverse society. They must challenge students to become engaged with, and reflect on, the material they read. Students will become multiculturally sensitive in these classrooms without borders. They will be able to participate vicariously in different ways of living and they will be liberated from the narrow confines of their particular circumstance.

References

Banks, J. (1991). Multicultural education: For freedom's sake. *Educational Leadership, 49*(4), 32-36.
Graff, G. (1990). Teach the conflicts. *The South Atlantic Quarterly, 89*:I, Winter.
Rosenblatt, L. (1976). *Literature as exploration.* New York: Modern Language Association.

For Further Reading:

Jay, G. S. (1991, March). The end of "American" literature: Toward a multicultural practice. *College English, 53*, 3.
Morrison, T. (1992). *Playing in the dark: Whiteness and the literary imagination.* New York: Vintage Books.

Children's Literature
Illustrated Books

Altman, L. (1993). *Amelia's road.* New York: Low & Low.
Ancona, G. (1993). *Pablo remembers: The fiesta of the Day of the Dead.* New York: Lothrop, Lee & Shepard.
Bunting, E. (1991). *Fly away home.* New York: Clarion.
Dooley, N. (1991). *Everybody cooks rice.* Minneapolis, MN: Carolrhoda.
Gray, N. (1988). *A country far away.* New York: Orchard.
Lankford, M. (1992). *Hopscotch around the world.* New York: Morrow & Company.
Morris, A. (1989). *Bread, bread, bread.* New York: Lothrop, Lee & Shepard.
Pinkley, A. (1993). *Seven candles for Kwanzaa.* New York: Dial.
Waters, K., & Slovenz-Low, M. (1990). *Lion dancer: Ernie Wan's Chinese New Year.* New York: Scholastic.

Novels

Beatty, P. (1981). *Lupita Manana.* New York: Beech Tree Books.
Coerr, E. (1977). *Sadako and the thousand paper cranes.* New York: Dell.
Crew, L. (1989). *Children of the river.* New York: Dell.
Fritz, J. (1982). *Homesick: My own story.* New York: Dell.
Kuklin, S. (1992). *How my family lives in America.* New York: Bradbury.
Lord, B. B. (1984). *In the Year of the Boar and Jackie Robinson.* New York: Trumpet Club.
Soto, G. (1991). *Taking sides.* San Diego: Harcourt Brace.
Taylor, M. (1976). *Roll of thunder, hear my cry.* New York: Bantam.
Taylor, M. (1990). *Mississippi bridge.* New York: Bantam Skylark.

Teaching:

The Challenge of Change;
Reclaiming Democracy through Schooling

Sudia Paloma McCaleb

Sudia Paloma McCaleb is Director of Teacher Education at the New College of California, 777 Valencia Street, San Francisco, California 94110

Many educators across the country are beginning to rethink old assumptions about "minority" or "non-dominant" cultures and about the ways in which we educate culturally and linguistically diverse populations. It is unlikely that there will be any real, deep, or lasting changes in public schooling until the nature of teacher education itself begins to change radically. This is the story of a small progressive college in San Francisco and a Federal grant (Title III) it received to develop and begin a new Teacher Education/Credential Program. The College had the opportunity to start from the beginning, rather than to reform or to cosmetically reorganize an already existing program.

New College of California in San Francisco made the decision to adopt as its basic teacher education program the new Bilingual, Crosscultural, Language and Academic Development (CLAD/BCLAD) credential recently developed by the state of California. This credential emphasis integrates inclusive multicultural and bilingual teaching perspectives and pedagogies.

New College has endorsed diversity and multiculturalism from its inception. Its programs emphasize innovative and interactive pedagogy and the vital importance of education to a democratic and just society. Undergraduates are encouraged to put their social principles into practice in their working lives. The college's administrators and faculty were enthusiastic and hopeful about beginning in teacher education at a time when a

profound societal awareness of the need for educational change and reform exists.

We began by engaging in informal dialogues with educators across the state who represent a variety of perspectives. Our guiding question was, "What should a new teacher education program look like? What is needed?" The following summary of comments provided us with some serious beginning thoughts for the initiation of the program:

First Year Teachers
"I am learning a lot of what I need to know from other teachers in my school and 'in-services' which are covering areas I never learned about in my teacher education program. They didn't prepare me for the reality of classroom teaching."

Veteran Teachers
"I learned everything on the job, nothing in teacher education."

School Principals Receiving New Teachers
"They need classroom management and organizational skills or they'll drown."

District Superintendent
"I'm tired of the quality of teachers being sent by standard credential programs. They are not interactive and problem-posing enough. They copy what they see traditional veteran teachers doing."

Enlightened Faculty in Schools of Education
"If you're starting from scratch do it right! You know what needs to happen.

Don't blow the opportunity. Don't just train the new teachers to 'fit in' to what already exists in the schools or we'll never see any change. Present the whole picture in the beginning and then return to the pieces all throughout the year."

The recent report from California Tomorrow, "Embracing Diversity" (Olsen & Mullen, 1990) gave us much to reflect on. It presents a teacher-generated summary of four major areas of competency required to teach effectively in classrooms which integrate immigrant and students born in the United States. The list included,

1. Competency in Language Development;
2. Competency in Building and Teaching an Inclusive Curriculum;
3. Competency in Establishing a Climate Supportive of Diversity;
4. Knowledge of the Cultures and Backgrounds of the Students.

As we began to create and develop our program we were also inspired and guided by Nieto's (1992) definition of multicultural education as a "process of comprehensive and basic education for all students." In interacting with a culturally diverse student population, teachers today are challenged to find ways to create partnerships in learning with their students, families, and communities. These partnerships have the potential to nurture literacy and academic achievement in the schools, while validating and celebrating students' home culture and language.

THE COLLEGE COMMITMENT TO A DIVERSE TEACHING FORCE

New College has a strong commitment to increase the numbers of culturally and

From *Multicultural Education*, Spring 1995, pp. 16-23. © 1995 by the National Association for Multicultural Education. Reprinted by permission.

New College credential students engage in interactive science exploration. —Photo by Vincent William

linguistically diverse teachers in the profession. (At the present time, approximately 85 percent of students in the nation's teacher education programs are Anglo women). During the first year of the Teacher Credential Program, New College offered a 50 percent tuition grant to all bilingual and teachers of color who demonstrated potential for becoming excellent teachers. This comprised more than half of the beginning class of 25 candidates. State and national exams that have served as gate-keeping mechanisms for the profession were not used to exclude potential teacher candidates since these have been shown to be culturally and linguistically biased. Additional ways of evaluation, such as demonstrated commitment to youth, community service, and subject area knowledge were emphasized for entrance. Support systems were developed to assist students to pass the exams required before completing the credential.

This article describes how New College is implementing a broad multicultural vision with extensive pedagogical goals in a year-long Elementary Teacher Credential program. The article

focuses primarily on innovative aspects of the program. Components of the program design which are in all standard teacher education programs are not discussed. We created innovative, integrated program structures, institutional supports, and pioneering program components to actualize our vision of the new understandings and skills teachers would need for the culturally diverse 21st century schools.

PRE-PROGRAM READER

Students are required to complete a reader before entering the program. This provides the incoming cohort of students a common text for reflection and discussion. If teachers do not have a strong philosophical vision and theoretical foundation, their practice will be shaky and their teaching direction vague. Through the readings a strong multiculturally inclusive perspective is presented and many of the current educational debates are introduced.

The reader is available approximately two months before the program starts

and begins with James Baldwin's essay, "A Talk to Teachers." Also included are a series of articles about multiculturalism and diversity, language issues and bilingualism, literacy development, cooperative learning, participatory research, critical pedagogy, environmentalism and the struggle for environmental justice among people of color in urban communities. Issues of family literacy are fully developed. The reader ends with a letter by Medicine Grizzlybear, "An Indian Father's Plea," in which a Native American father introduces his son to his new teacher. He encourages the teacher to put aside any deficit assumptions concerning his child's lack of skills and get to know his son. Using this approach, the teacher discovers the multiple forms of knowledge the child possesses, knowledge gained by living close to the earth while being nurtured by the traditional cultural practices of his people.

Students are asked to write personal interpretive reflections about each article. Through their readings and writings students begin to see that education is not a politically neutral endeavor. There are many important issues to think about that affect how children grow up and how they are educated in our schools. The dialogue among students and faculty is rich and lively from day one.

THREE WEEK INTENSIVE: A LOOK AT THE BIG PICTURE

The actual program begins in August with a Three Week Intensive session. The goal is to introduce many of the philosophical, instructional, "management", and subject content areas that will be studied in depth during the year. Students are asked to prepare for the first day of class by bringing two items; a visual item that can be hung on the wall and some kind of personal artifact. Both objects are to have personal or cultural meaning for the student and are used as a way to introduce themselves to the group—their learning cohort, with whom they will be learning and working throughout the year. This activity, and many of the subsequent activities are designed to model an inclusive pedagogical practice which connects the develop-

ment of literacy in the classroom to each student's home and community.

Among the wall hangings this summer were travel and political posters, family photographs, and a painting done in kindergarten by one student and saved for 25 years by her mother. Written across the painting were the words, "I will not be quiet in class." Lucy remembered doing the drawing after being scolded by the teacher. Tara, a student artist, brought an oil painting of the kitchen of her childhood home. "When I was growing up, there were rats in my kitchen." How did the group respond to Tara's painting? How can or should teachers respond to the pain that students may bring into the classroom? Through the sharing of cultural artifacts, a group book was produced in which every student contributed an illustrated page with a descriptive sentence. The book was named, "These Are a Few Of My Favorite Things." Elisa, a native of Puerto Rico, brought a hand-crafted statue depicting a woman grinding corn. Her sentence was "*Siempre en la lucha*" [Always in the struggle] which she said

represented the life force of all the women in her family.

PROGRAM VISIONS AND GOALS

During the Three Week Intensive and throughout the year everything is linked to the following seven philosophical and pedagogical goals:

1. Celebrating Diversity; Unlearning Prejudice
Teachers need to reflect on their own schooling and cultural experiences in order to acknowledge and understand the perspective that they bring to the profession. In recognizing that there are multiple perspectives which must be affirmed and embraced, teachers increase their capacity for compassion and can more equitably educate all students.

Teachers frequently display a lack of awareness about people different from themselves. They need the self understanding and the skills to be able to counteract the low self-esteem many students bring to school because of inter-

Drawing by New College credential candidate Elisa Garcia which she introduced as her artifact from Puerto Rico.

nalized oppression. Teachers must ask themselves, "What baggage am I bringing along with me? How can my own conscious or unconscious prejudice and even ignorance about 'otherness' limit my effectiveness as a teacher to all my students?"

During the first week everyone participates in two days of a "Celebrating Diversity; Unlearning Prejudice" workshop. A skilled facilitator, using a compassionate approach, helps students to share their cultural experiences and also to recognize the inequalities which members of the group have experienced in life due to race, class, or gender. The goal of the facilitator is to build allies among future educators, across groups, by helping them to recognize their commonalities and differences. This experiential process of self and group discovery is essential for those who will be working with diverse groups of students and their families.

Assumptions about Family Realities
Following the diversity training days, a set of assumptions that are commonly held by many educators about "minority" students and their families are presented. (Auerbach, 1990). One assumption is

that children who do not speak English at home are at a disadvantage academically. Another is that good readers only come from homes where adults read. Students discuss these assumptions and share counter-evidence that they have found in their own experience to contradict these commonly held assumptions. It is important for future teachers to have this discussion because the views that they hold about their students and their families may not only negatively label children but also will set unjustifiably low academic expectations for them.

2. Building Communities of Learners
Teachers must learn how to humanize the teaching environment and develop their classrooms as "communities of learners" (McCaleb, 1994).

As candidates acquire deeper levels of understanding about their own past, present, and future realities they are better able to create a learning environment in their classrooms in which all students feel listened to, validated, and empowered as both individual and collaborative learners. Students who know that their realities and identities are valued at school do not have the same need to resist or reject school learning as those who feel their identities are being demeaned or excluded.

Cooperative Learning, "Complex Instruction," "Tribes"
It is clear from the research and our own work with classroom teachers and diverse student groups that children attain higher achievement levels when they learn in the context of cooperative classrooms. We must view cooperation as including not only classroom practice but also as a necessary skill for productive work and democratic citizenship in the future. During the Three Week Intensive, students are introduced to "Complex Instruction" or "Finding-Out Descubrimiento." This is a model for cooperative learning, developed at Stanford University (Cohen, 1986) which looks at power issues within groups and works towards balanced learning groups where responsibilities are clearly shared as the members work to attain a common goal. Students are also introduced to "Tribes: A Process for Social Development and Cooperative Learning" (Gibbs, 1987). Collaboration among teachers, students, and their families and communities in ways that embrace the diversity of cultures and languages that families pass onto their children is a major aspect of building communities of learners. This collaboration extends beyond the classroom and breaks down the

New College Family Literacy Program: —Photo by Vincent William
students learn strategies to facilitate home/school literacy partnership.

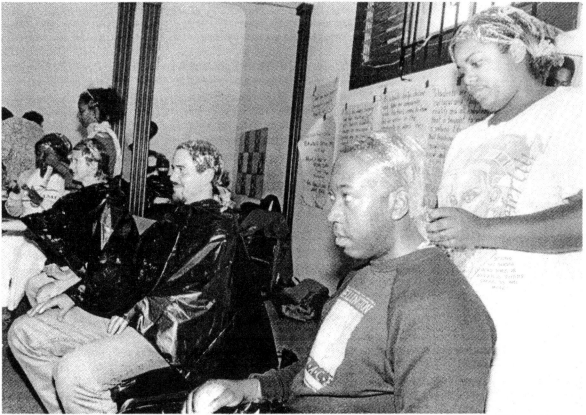

Mask-Making workshop at New College—   —Photo by Vincent Williams
learning how to integrate the arts across curriculum.

walls between the school and the community.

3. Working with Families through Family Literacy

Teachers must gain the experience and skills needed to work with families in collaborative relationships and to develop curricula that include and affirm family concerns and cultural values. Teachers must discover that through living and observing everyone learns to read the world before reading the word (Freire, 1970). This understanding and the instructional strategies involved to translate it into practice are essential for educating all students.

One of the major innovative features of the program is the creation of a Family Literacy Center at the College. It is located in San Francisco's Mission District—home to many Mexican and Central American immigrants. The Center not only offers a service to the surrounding community and to the schools in which student teachers are working but also provides a facility where teacher education students acquire strategies for working with families around issues of

literacy development. They learn the mechanics of how to create successful programs. Family literacy, as we define it, is the collaboration between the family, community, and school in support of the student's emerging literacy skills.

The Center experience is considered an essential component of the methods courses in Literacy Development and Social Studies. Sessions are also included which focus on Family Math, Hands-On Science and Ecology. Several of our first year students were talented musicians; this led to the development of a Family Literacy Band. We learned that the way in which we welcome families and the enthusiasm and generosity expressed by the program participants makes families want to return. At the end of sessions, parents shared their feelings:

"Ustedes saben porque regresamos. Es por el amor y la dedicación que sentimos aquí de los maestros en el programa y también por primera vez en la vida sentimos que como padres de familia somos importantes en la educación de nuestros hijos . . . que nosotros los padres tenemos algo importante de enseñar." [Do you know why we keep coming back? It's because of the love and dedication we

feel here from the teachers in this program and also because for the first time in our lives we feel that we are important in the education of our children and that we as parents have something to teach them].

Over the course of the year, students work with parents, many who have limited years of formal schooling themselves. Teachers come to see both children and their families as writers, authors, and experts about their own lives. Sessions always integrate art, singing, and hands-on experiences with literacy development as students facilitate small groups by using children's literature as a point of departure for discussion of important common life issues and concerns.

In the first year we chose to conduct the sessions in Spanish, which is the primary language in the surrounding community. This was initially viewed by the program faculty as a way to support and raise the status of the Spanish language in the community. This helped the children to develop a strong primary language foundation in order to become potentially more successful in English. Several students felt that the Center presented a perfect opportunity to bring together the multiple cultural and linguistic groups in the community and to begin to build bridges in the community with the children as the focus. They suggested that the sessions be conducted bilingually.

4. Teachers as Researchers

The concept of "teachers as researchers" must be developed through participatory or action research. This will enable future teachers to come to know and respect the communities in which they teach. Teachers cannot be expected to enter a classroom or a community with all the necessary knowledge and answers but must be co-learners along with their students, their families, and the communities from which they come.

During the Three Week Intensive students discussed the basic principles of participatory research. "Participatory research is a philosophical and ideological commitment which holds that every human being has the capacity of knowing, of analyzing and reflecting about reality so that she becomes a true agent of action in her own life" (Ada & Beutel 1991, p.8). By attempting to break down the established power roles between researcher and participants, both agents become co-participants in a dialogue.

The researcher, who in this case is the teacher, the students, or both, invites the participants to speak or write about and critically reflect on their thoughts. The participants may be other students in the classroom or members of the family or community. As teachers and students through dialogue, writing, and illustration, establish partnerships of co-researchers, more meaningful participation in the lives of all results. This classroom research is particularly appropriate for students and parents from culturally and linguistically diverse backgrounds because their voices have seldom been heard or documented.

To learn the process, during the Three Week Intensive students engage in a short research project among themselves; a community of future teachers. The current group of students formulated their own research question. "What obstacles stand in the way of teachers implementing a multicultural curriculum?" Through dialogues with each other, they explored their own cultural and educational experiences growing up and spoke of their dreams and visions as teachers. Collectively they explored the common themes and concerns that arose. On the final day of the Three Week Intensive

each group presented its findings and formulated a plan for creative action as future teachers.

During the Fall semester, the candidates' research skills are expanded and their understanding of the potential instructional benefits of the process grow as they begin their second research project. They are asked to engage in dialogue with two different parents of children in the public schools. (At least one of the two is to be of a culture or language group other than their own). They are to explore three areas: (a) The educational experiences of the parents, (b) the parent's view of their child's present schooling experiences, and (c) the parent's view of the potential for building bridges between the home and the school.

Participatory research invites parents to tap into their internalized and traditional sources of knowledge and wisdom while contributing to their children's education. Teachers are acquiring the skills to listen and to seek out the experiences and opinions of the families which can help in the creation of an authentic text for classroom learning.

5. Integration of Music and the Arts

Music and the arts must be integrated into all methods courses so that future teachers may appeal to the diverse learning modes of children and teach to the whole child.

We are not all artists and musicians but as teachers we can all promote and facilitate the arts. We involve ourselves with music as a way to learn about and experience the richness of diverse cultures. Part of the New College vision is that teachers emerging from this program will be bridge builders in their schools and communities. They will be able to recognize common forms of oppression experienced by all groups that are not part of the dominant culture and will develop ways to work together for the common good of equitably educating all children.

During the Three Week Intensive we chose to focus on bringing together the African American and the Latino experiences through Afro-Cuban music and movement because it is common in urban schools to witness an ongoing struggle between the African American and the Latino populations. An Afro-Cuban musicologist presented the dual influences on Cuban music (African and Spanish) and also taught call and response songs

and dances. Students also worked with a multicultural music educator who taught songs which helped future teachers to begin to build their own classroom repertoire. This approach enhances the ability to build classrooms as inclusive communities.

All credential students learn silkscreening, an empowering art form. They are asked to purchase a silk screen which becomes one of their tools of the trade. They learn a simple method for making posters with their students. The posters can speak about any theme being studied and include printed words and opinions students may wish to express. This year, most of the students during their field placements took turns borrowing additional screens from their peers and experimented in their classrooms.

6. Development of Personal Philosophy

Students need to formulate their own philosophy and vision of critical pedagogy and transformative education and see themselves as agents working towards positive change in the schools, the community, the society and the world.

The central pedagogies of transformative or critical education are dialogue and problem posing. The problems are real-life concerns that the students engage in for critical reflection. Through this process, students come to see and understand how they exist in the world. The teacher is present not only as an observer and a guide but also as a co-participant in an on-going dialogue.

Mary Poplin (1991) emphasizes that critical pedagogy is concerned primarily with ways to educate citizens to "live responsibly in a free and democratic state." In a transformative classroom students are encouraged to develop their own voices in interaction with the voices of others and to participate in the democracy of the classroom. Throughout the year, teacher candidates participate in a process which focuses on learning how to provide multiple opportunities in their classrooms for the development of student voices. Teachers must be seen as "transformative intellectuals" (Giroux, 1989) and must be given time to plan and reflect with others about the theory that informs their practice. Students need to believe that they can make a difference in the world, but first teachers must believe that they can make a difference.

7. Societal and Political Context

Teachers must understand the societal and political context of the institution of schooling and develop an understanding of how the history and structures of schooling have impacted ethnically and linguistically diverse students.

New teachers soon discover that the basic structures of roles and relationships in school systems are generally more bureaucratic than collaborative. Schools are expected to produce "winners and losers." These assumptions are reinforced by testing, tracking, and accountability practices. Cummins (1989) proposes that real changes in schools will begin to take place only when the relationships of power begin to change, that is, when the voices of parents, community, and teachers are heard and the direction of the schools reflects a collaborative vision and effort.

For transformative educators, a discussion of schools is very much intertwined with a discussion of society in general and democracy specifically. Teaching practices that include only one group's knowledge might serve to silence rather than empower the students who are living in cultural worlds that exist outside of the dominant culture. While at school, unless care is taken, these students may learn that they don't count and that their histories and ideas are unimportant.

ONGOING QUESTIONS

Several key questions guide the program:

1. How do we maintain a balance between the transmission of information and the importance of dialogue in a teacher education program when there is so much to learn and less than one year in which to accomplish it?

2. How do we engage in a reflective and in-depth learning process when many students, for economic reasons, need to continue working and thus become overwhelmed by the process itself?

3. How does the teacher education process itself become an instructional model and an inspiration for future teachers in their own work?

4. How can students gain experience in new ways of teaching when there are so few appropriate practice environments available to them?

CONCLUSION

These are the major concerns we have for the education of our teachers. Machado poetically expressed, *"Caminante, no hay camino, se hace camino al andar."* [Traveler, there is no road, we make the road by walking.] These words affirm our belief that there is no set way or formula to be followed. If we as educators fully commit ourselves to the process and respond authentically to what we see and understand emerging, we can recreate our schools and offer our students and ourselves multiple opportunities in our lives.

This process is not an easy undertaking. In our first year we made mistakes, learned, and grew a great deal from that experience. We hope that this presentation of our infant program will inspire a dialogue among teacher educators. We would appreciate hearing from you.

REFERENCES

Ada, A. F. & Buetel, C. 1991. Participatory research as dialogue for action. Unpublished Manuscript. University of San Francisco.

Auerbach, E. 1990. *Making Meaning Making Change.* Boston, MA: University of Massachusetts.

Baldwin, J. 1988. A talk to teachers. In R. Simonsons & S. Walker (Eds.), *Multicultural Literacy.* St. Paul, MN: The Graywolf Annual Five.

Cohen, E. 1986. *Designing Groupwork: Strategies for the Heterogeneous Classroom.* New York: Teachers College, Columbia University.

Gibbs, J. 1987. *Tribes; A Process for Social Development and Cooperative Learning.* Salt Lake City, UT: Publisher's Press.

Giroux, H. 1989. Rethinking education reforms in the age of George Bush. *Phi Delta Kappan, 70,* 728–730.

Lake, R. (Medicine Grizzlybear) *Teacher.* September 1990. pp. 50–53.

McCaleb, S. P. 1994. *Building Communities of Learners: A Collaboration Among Teachers, Students and Family, and Community.* New York: St. Martin's Press.

Olsen, L. & Mullen, A. 1990. *Embracing Diversity.* San Francisco, CA: California Tomorrow.

Poplin, M. 1991. The two restructuring movements: Which shall it be? Transformative or reductive? Manuscript submitted for publication.

Special Topics in Multicultural Education

The themes touched on in this unit relate to real, dynamic elements in the great multicultural mosaic of North America. There are always areas of concern that demand our sincere attention, such as the stereotypes of particular cultural groups and the relations between cultural groups attempting to survive and thrive in our complex, structured society. The members of every cultural group wish to express their experiences in society in their own voices. This is a basic right of any cultural group in a true democracy.

Each year we focus in this unit on selected special topics that have been of particular interest to those who live or work in multicultural settings. Other articles have a direct bearing on issues of equality of educational opportunity that are of concern to many educators. There are so many outstanding articles to choose from that we have difficulty deciding which ones to include each year, due to the space limitations of a single volume.

The important changes in the demographic composition of the United States referred to in unit 1 are reexamined in the light of their implications for educators. We also examine the struggle to empower both youth and adults to develop their own visions of the world as they become literate persons defining their own understanding of their life situations. What children and teenagers learn from their out-of-school neighborhood environments is also of interest to teachers.

Important issues are yet to be resolved in multicultural studies in education; however, the dialogue on these issues is spirited. This is as it should be. More and more eloquent voices are being raised to challenge prevailing stereotypes of particular cultural groups. For instance, Native American and Asian American scholars are eloquently challenging popular misconceptions of their cultural heritages. Another demographic dynamic of great interest to many persons is that not only is the United States becoming amazingly more multicultural, but there is a continuing increase in the number of intercultural marriages. Multicultural (or bicultural) families still face many mixed signals from many people. Although social acceptance of intercultural marriage seems to be increasing, many bicultural and biracial couples continue to face poignantly challenging receptions in society. Another dynamic is that several cultural minorities in the United States are involved in the complex, and sometimes painful, resolution of historic misperceptions of one another. Some cultural minorities share their lives as Americans with other cultural minorities whose interests include histories of antagonistic stereotypes and misperceptions of one another, as well as conflicting political and cultural interests in the Near East, Europe, and Asia. There is thus an ongoing dialogue within and among those cultural minority groups who believe their national and international interests to be challenged by other cultural minorities as well as by mainstream American society. The issues relating to acceptance of all cultural groups as equal participants in democratic social structures are still with us. The struggle to win acceptance of cultural diversity as a source of national strength and national cultural wealth continues. Respect for the rights of all citizens as individuals is a necessary theme in our schools.

Educators who work in the area of multicultural education are concerned with research into how students can succeed in school and transcend the impact of socioeconomic inequality and feelings of powerlessness. Educators are also documenting the causes of school failure as part of the process of developing the knowledge base to prevent or minimize it. Of great importance is discovering how at-risk minority students can overcome feelings of low self-esteem and develop positive, workable strategies for working through their problems in school. The students of each racial, cultural, or religious minority group have had their own special historical and sociocultural experiences with mainstream school curriculum. Multicultural education seeks to help all students to locate or situate their lives in the context of their developing individual identities within a pluralistic social order.

Teachers, even experienced ones, need continuing inservice preparation and training in order to learn the many skills needed to work with diverse school populations.

The essays in this unit are relevant to courses in educational policy studies, multicultural education, and cultural foundations of education.

Looking Ahead: Challenge Questions

How will demographic changes in American society impact on the public schools?

How does a teacher empower students? How does a teacher develop a sense of social consciousness in students?

What are concerns of Native Americans regarding how they are portrayed in the media?

What can we learn from the Native American experience?

How can educators counter the out-of-school curriculum learned by youth in urban ghettos?

Why did so much resegregation occur as the nation attempted to desegregate?

Why do Asian American educators take issue with the stereotype of the "model minority"?

What should every American student know about the Holocaust?

How great a problem is anti-Semitism in America? What can be done to combat it?

What special challenges confront bicultural and biracial families?

—F. S.

The Dynamic Demographic Mosaic Called America

Implications for Education

Leobardo F. Estrada

University of California, Los Angeles

There is a simple and recognized association between demographic growth and education. An increase in children requires more classrooms, more teachers, and more resources. Less obvious is the relationship between changes in the composition of families. It is the household that relates to schools as the basis of taxpayer support, as the unit that makes up neighborhood, and also as the site that determines for the most part which school will be attended. Needless to say, the number of children in a household compounds the effects that a household will have on local schools, for it is households with children that place intense demands on the schools. Finally, the concentration of households with children in certain areas focuses these effects on particular places.

Higher education, although less constrained by space, has a different relationship to its students as individuals. Nonetheless, universities recognize that the success of their students is associated with the relationship between their students and their families.

The numerical changes are visually evident in the changing cultural landscape—significant changes in the fabric and texture of the nation. For educators, it is these demographic changes that are more crucial. In sum, numbers help us to plan for the future.

TRENDS IN POPULATION GROWTH: CHANGING DEMOGRAPHICS

The U.S. population in 1990 stood at 249 million.[1] During the decade of the 1980s, the non-Hispanic population grew by 7% compared to 53% for the Hispanic population. Differential growth rates like these are significant in considering future school-age populations.

Between 1990 and 2005, the total U.S. population is expected to increase by about 11%. The K–12 population (from age 5 to 17) in 1990 was 53.2 million, and the traditional college-age population (from 18 to 24 years old) was 19 million. It is expected that, by the year 2005, these school-age groups will increase by 4.7% and 1.3%, respectively (see Table 1).

These modest growth trends for the United States mask the underlying differential in growth for minority populations. From 1990 to 2005, the population of African-Americans is expected to grow by 21% and the population of Latinos by 33%, compared to a 7.7% growth rate for the White population. Likewise, among the K–12 population, African-American and Latino populations will exceed the growth of the White population (11% for African-Americans and 20% for Latinos, compared to 9.2% for Whites). Among traditional college-age populations, African-Americans will increase 9.3%, and Latinos will increase by 40%, compared to −2.5% for the White population. Among school-age children, minority growth will exceed that of the majority population by a factor of 3:1.

In 1990, minority populations as a whole represented one of every four U.S. residents; however, among the school-age population, minority youth represented one of every three U.S. school-age youth.

TABLE 1
Summary of Growth by Race and Ethnicity

	1990		2005	
	Number	*1980-1990 % Growth*	*Number*	*1990-2005 % Growth*
Total	248,710	9.8	274,884	10.5
White	199,686	6.0	225,048	12.7
Black	29,986	13.2	36,816	22.7
Latino[a]	22,354	53.0	30,795	37.8
Other	9,805	45.1	13,020	32.8
K-12				
White	34,476		37,118	7.6
Black	6,838		7,889	15.4
Latino	5,428		6,848	26.1
18-24				
White	17,193		21,188	23.2
Black	3,642		4,198	15.3
Latino	3,127		3,599	15.1

a. The Latino population may be of any race.

From *Education and Urban Society,* Vol. 25, No. 3, May 1993, pp. 231-245. © 1993 by Sage Publications, Inc. Reprinted by permission of Corwin Press, Inc.

TABLE 2
Fast-Growing States and the Ranking of
Population for Blacks, Latinos, and Asians

| | State Rank for Group | | | 1980-1990 |
	Black	Latino	Asian	% Growth
Nevada	33	8	7	50.1
Alaska	41	21	5	36.9
Arizona	31	4	19	34.8
Florida	4	7	22	32.7
California	2	2	2	25.7
New Hampshire	43	39	32	20.5
Texas	3	3	14	19.4
Georgia	5	32	23	18.6
Utah	42	15	13	17.9
Washington	27	18	3	17.8

As will be noted in Table 2, there is a direct relationship between state population growth over the last decade and the proportion of state population represented by Latinos and Asians. Latinos and Asians, as the two fastest-growing ethnic/racial groups in the United States, fuel the growth rate of these states.

As indicated by the state data, where Hispanics, Asians, and African-Americans are concentrated in large numbers, growth invariably increased in the 1980s and is likely to continue growing in the near future. The exceptions to this pattern are New Hampshire and Utah, which grew rapidly despite the low levels of minority representation in the two states.

THE HISPANIC POPULATION
OF THE UNITED STATES

Among the fastest-growing ethnic/racial groups in the United States, the Latino population numbered 22.4 million persons in 1990 (not counting the 3.5 million persons residing in Puerto Rico), which represents an increase of 53% over the 1980 figure of 14.6 million. As a result, the proportion of Latinos in the total population rose from 6% in 1980 to 9% in 1990. In 1990, 6 of every 10 Latinos said that they were of Mexican origin, making them the largest Hispanic group in the United States. Mexican-origin persons totaled 13.5 million persons, an increase of 54% over the last decade. Persons of Puerto Rican origin constitute 2.7 million persons, representing 12% of all U.S. Latinos. The slower growth of the Puerto Rican population, like that of the Cuban population, reflects a slower level of immigration but is, nevertheless, impressive compared to the growth of non-Latino groups. The category of "Other Hispanics," representing primarily Central and South American groups, grew by 67%, reflecting the high levels of immigration engendered by political and economic turmoil in their countries of origin.

With these high levels of growth, it is not surprising to find that the projections for Latinos indicate that the Latino population may reach 30 million by the year 2000, 49 million by 2020, and 80.7 million by 2050 (see Table 3).

In 1990, Latinos composed 9% of the U.S. population. These projections indicate that, by the year 2000, Latinos are likely to represent 11% of the population, rising thereafter to 15% by 2020 and possibly 21% by the year 2050. These figures are a stark reminder that Latino growth is truly impressive within a nation characterized by slow and stable growth.

THE CAUSES OF MINORITY GROWTH

Youthfulness

The causes of minority growth have been recognized for some time. The first is the youthfulness of minority populations. For example, Latinos are about 8 years younger than the non-Latino population. Youthfulness affects growth in two ways. First, a higher proportion of youthful women are likely to be in the childbearing age. Hispanic women, for example, represent 9% of the U.S. population, but they account for 12% of all births in the United States. When fertility is higher, as is the case particularly for Hispanic women, these higher proportions translate into more children for the near future. Currently, about 35% (8 million) of Latinos are below age 18, compared to 26% in the total U.S. population. By the year 2020, about 31% of Hispanics will he below the age of 18, compared to 22% of the total U.S. population.

Second, youthfulness results in a higher proportion of pre-teens yet to move through the childbearing ages. As these preteens move through the childbearing ages over the next 15 years, there will be more children in the far future as well. There is yet another aspect of youthfulness: A population that receives a sizable number of immigrants at the youthful working ages will "remain young" as the downward pressure on the median age balances out the upward pressure of the aging process.

Higher rates of fertility for minorities, particularly Hispanics, has the effect of restructuring the population from "below." The restructuring process is visible by the growing percentages of Hispanic, Asian, and Black public high school enrollments.

Immigration

Minority population growth, particularly among Asian and Latino populations, is fueled by continued immigration. During the last decade, the United States was the desired destination for 3.5 million immigrants from Asia, Mexico, and other Latin American nations.

The United States has historically been a recipient country for immigration. The amount of immigration has varied somewhat over time, but the largest difference in immigration has not been in magnitude but rather in the composition of immigrants.

Prior to 1960, the vast majority of immigrants were from Canada, Great Britain, and other European nations. As indicated in Table 4, since 1980, the vast majority of immigration has been from Mexico, other Latin American nations, and

TABLE 3
Projections of the Hispanic Population
of the United States (in Millions)

Year	Hispanic Population
1970	9.1
1980	14.6.
1990	22.4
1992	24.0
2000	30.0
2020	47-54
2050	74-96

TABLE 4
Origins of Foreign-Born in the United States, 1990 and 1980

| | | 1990 | | | | 1980 | |
Rank	Place	No. (Thousands)	%	Rank	Place	No. (Thousands)	%
	United States	19,767	100.0		United States	14,080	100.0
1	Mexico	4,298	21.7	1	Mexico	2,199	15.6
2	Philippines	913	4.6	2	Germany	849	6.0
3	Canada	745	3.8	3	Canada	843	6.0
4	Cuba	737	3.7	4	Italy	832	5.9
5	Germany	712	3.6	5	United Kingdom	669	4.8
6	United Kingdom	640	3.2	6	Cuba	608	4.3
7	Italy	581	2.9	7	Philippines	501	3.6
8	Korea	568	2.9	8	Poland	418	3.0
9	Vietnam	543	2.7	9	USSR	406	2.9
10	China	530	2.7	10	Korea	290	2.1
11	El Salvador	465	2.4	11	China	286	2.0
12	India	450	2.3	12	Vietnam	231	1.6
13	Poland	388	2.0	13	Japan	222	1.6
14	Dominican Republic	348	1.8	14	Portugal	212	1.5
15	Jamaica	334	1.7	15	Greece	211	1.5
16	USSR	334	1.7	16	India	206	1.5
17	Japan	290	1.5	17	Ireland	198	1.4
18	Colombia	286	1.4	18	Jamaica	197	1.4
19	Taiwan	244	1.2	19	Dominican Republic	169	1.2
20	Guatemala	226	1.1	20	Yugoslavia	153	1.1

Asian countries. Immigration has typically been regarded as a positive element. It is a common premise that immigration is a self-selecting process that brings risk-taking, highly motivated, and entrepreneurial individuals in search of opportunity. Many U.S. residents today are descendants of parents who were ambitious enough to move here and succeed in obtaining an economic foothold.

As indicated in Table 5, Hispanic foreign-born persons are concentrated in just a few of the states of the Union. This uneven distribution intensifies the impact of immigration on specific states and, within them, specific localities.

The primary countries of origin of Latinos are indicated in Table 6. Mexico remains, by an overwhelming margin, the primary source of Latino immigration; yet, despite its magnitude, the base population of Mexican-origin persons born in and residing in the United States exceeds immigrants by a margin of 2:1. The other countries listed represent more recent immigration, as indicated by the high levels of "foreign-bornness" of the total population.

Finally, in the same manner that the Latino population is distributed in a concentrated manner, Latino foreign-born also arrive in the United States and distribute themselves in distinct patterns.

Immigrants are typically young, the majority being concentrated in the youthful working ages. If their numbers are large, immigration can reconstruct the population from the "middle."

TABLE 5
Hispanic Foreign-Born by State, 1990

	Total Hispanic	Hispanic Foreign-Born	% Hispanic Foreign-Born
United States	21,900,089	7,699,820	35.2
California	7,557,550	3,295,826	43.6
Texas	4,294,120	1,105,591	25.8
New York	2,151,743	711,069	33.1
Florida	1,555,031	893,018	57.4
Illinois	878,682	352,302	40.1
New Jersey	720,344	268,090	37.2
Arizona	680,628	173,280	25.5
New Mexico	576,709	58,004	10.1
Colorado	419,322	46,021	11.0
Massachusetts	275,859	71,203	25.8
Pennsylvania	220,479	31,343	14.2
Washington	206,088	60,993	29.6
Connecticut	203,511	32,659	16.0
Michigan	189,915	26,690	14.0
Virginia	155,353	75,420	48.6
Ohio	131,983	16,888	12.8
Nevada	121,346	48,156	39.7
Maryland	119,984	60,802	50.7
Oregon	110,606	37,185	33.6
Georgia	101,379	43,450	42.9
Indiana	95,363	16,250	17.0
Louisiana	90,609	32,783	36.2
Kansas	90,289	20,406	22.6

TABLE 6
Hispanic Foreign-Born by Country of Origin

	Total Population	Foreign-Born	% Foreign-Born
Mexican	13,393,208	4,447,439	33.2
Cuban	1,053,197	750,609	71.3
Dominican	520,151	356,971	68.6
Central American			
Costa Rican	57,223	48,264	84.3
Guatemalan	268,779	232,977	86.7
Honduran	131,066	114,603	87.4
Nicaraguan	202,658	171,950	84.8
Salvadoran	565,081	472,885	83.7
Other Central or South American	7,010	6,339	90.4
South American			
Argentinean	100,921	97,422	96.5
Bolivian	38,073	33,637	88.4
Chilean	68,799	61,212	89.0
Colombian	378,726	303,918	80.2
Equadorian	191,198	147,867	77.3
Peruvian	175,035	152,315	87.0
Uruguayan	21,996	21,628	98.3

The United States is currently in one of its periods of nativism in which the voices calling for more restrictive immigration policies are the loudest. However, historical data confirm that, despite these cycles of anti-immigration sentiment, the United States requires immigration in order to grow and finds it economically desirable. Immigrants are highly motivated to mainstream into the economic society. This is evidenced by the 1.7 million individuals who took advantage of the amnesty provisions of the Immigration Reform and Control Act, allowing long-term residents to regularize their status. The hysteria against immigration can best be understood by recognizing the concentrated nature of immigration—one half of all Hispanic foreign-born residents reside in California, New York, and Florida (see Table 7). Not surprisingly, it is in these areas of the country that immigration issues are felt with such high levels of intensity.

Combining the restructuring process of immigration with the process of population restructuring from below attributable to the differential fertility mentioned earlier, the U.S. population is undergoing a dramatic shift in composition, with its impacts felt most in geographic areas of the United States where Asians and Hispanics are the most populous and where immigrants have settled.

Today, 1 of every 8 U.S. residents is African-American, 1 of every 11 U.S. residents is Latino, and 1 of every 34 U.S. residents is Asian or Pacific Islander. By the turn of the century, 1 of every 3 U.S. residents will be African-American, Latino, or Asian.

The primary conclusion that can be drawn from the information on population growth is that minority populations will continue to grow into the new century and beyond and that the educational demands required by this growing population will challenge educators to understand the nature of this growth.

CHILDREN AND HOUSEHOLD FORMATION

How families arrange themselves into households will condition the effects of future growth. Table 8 reminds us of the dynamic manner in which families arrange and rearrange patterns of living. Over the last two decades, the trend has been

TABLE 7
Primary State of Residence of
the Hispanic-Origin Groups, 1990

Mexican		Puerto Rican		Cuban		Salvadoran	
CA	6,070,637	NY	1,046,896	FL	675,786	CA	338,769
TX	3,899,518	NJ	304,179	NJ	87,085	TX	58,128
AZ	619,435	FL	240,673	NY	77,016	NY	47,350
IL	612,442	IL	147,201	CA	75,034	MD	19,122
NM	329,233	MA	146,015	OH	45,911	NJ	16,817
Guatemalan		Nicaraguan		Honduran		Colombian	
CA	159,177	FL	79,056	CA	30,284	NY	107,377
NY	21,995	CA	74,119	NY	26,169	FL	83,634
IL	16,017	NY	11,011	FL	23,900	NJ	52,210
FL	13,558	TX	7,911	VA	23,537	CA	41,562
TX	11,724	LA	4,935	TX	10,622	TX	16,295
Peruvian		Equadorian		Argentinean		Dominican	
CA	45,885	NY	89,838	CA	30,620	NY	357,868
NY	32,161	NJ	27,572	FL	14,226	FL	34,268
FL	24,777	CA	26,953				

TABLE 8
Changes in Family Composition 1970 and 1990 (in Percentages)

Family Households	Married Couple		Male Householder		Female Householder	
	1970	1990	1970	1990	1970	1990
White	89	83	2	4	9	13
Black	68	50	4	6	28	44
Latino	81	70	4	7	15	23

TABLE 9
Persons per Household, 1990

Group	Persons per Household
White	2.63
Owner	2.75
Renter	2.43
Black	2.87
Owner	3.14
Renter	2.68
Latino	3.44
Owner	3.56
Renter	3.36

a move toward single parenthood. This trend is found among all ethnic/racial groups.

An increase in single parenthood has influenced the decrease in average household size. Furthermore, household size is expected to decline even further with the expected increases in unmarrieds, childless couples, and lower levels of fertility for traditionally high-fertility minority populations, including Latino women.

Latinos continue to be characterized by larger than average families, in part because of higher fertility. As indicated in Table 9, the largest families are those in owner-occupied housing, a pattern similar to other ethnic/racial groups. Recent studies indicate that fertility among women from all ethnic and racial groups is decreasing and converging around the rates for White women. However, the highest fertility is found among foreign-born Latinas. With continued immigration, the fertility of Latinas will converge at a much lower rate.

Population growth occurs either from immigration, which has been shown to be high for Latinos, or from fertility, which remains higher (although at a decreasing rate) for Latinas. Thus it is not surprising that the Latino population is undergoing rapid growth. However, it is important to recognize the wide variation among those high growth rates. There exist important differences between native and foreign-born Latinos, first and subsequent generations of Latinos, and borderland and interior-residing Latinos, as well as distinct patterns that are conditioned by socioeconomic and educational attainment. For example, recent census results indicate that interethnic inter-marriage rates continue to increase among Latinos. The implications of these high rates of intermarriage are unclear for future growth rates, although a reasonable assumption is that they will moderate growth. In 1990, about one of every three Cuban and Puerto Rican marriages was an intermarriage, compared to about one of every five marriages for Central and South Americans and one of every six marriages for Mexican-origin persons.

Despite these variations, in general, where Latinos reside, household formation is high, fertility is above the average, more

TABLE 10
Families by Number of Children Under 18,
1970 and 1990 (in Percentages)

Group	Number of Children Under 18			
	None	1	2	3 or more
White				
1970	45	18	18	19
1990	53	20	18	9
Black				
1970	39	18	15	29
1990	41	25	19	14
Latino				
1970	30	20	19	31
1990	37	23	21	19

Group	Number of Children Under 6		
	None	1	2 or more
White			
1990	78	15	7
Black			
1990	72	19	9
Latino			
1990	65	23	12

children are found in families (see Table 10), and the size of households is likely to be above the average as well.

REGIONAL CONCENTRATION OF GROWTH

Future growth will be concentrated in particular areas—those with concentrations of minority populations—intensifying education needs in certain places. Differential regional growth has been ongoing for over a century. In brief, the Southwest has experienced dramatic growth, whereas the Northeast and Midwest have experienced low rates of growth. Not surprisingly, it is in these high-growth regions that educational demands continue to require year-round schools to alleviate overcrowded classes, teacher shortages, school facility construction, and expansion of higher education institutions. Equally important are the educational strategies and tactics required to manage lack of growth. Retrenchment strategies, decisions regarding school closures, the redeployment of staff, and the need to redefine the mission of institutions are equally challenging when the goal is to maintain quality and be fair to all concerned.

TABLE 11
Growth of Population by Region (in Millions)

Region	1970	1980	1990	1970-1990 % Change
Northeast	49.1	49.1	50.8	3.5
New England	11.8	12.3	13.2	11.9
Middle Atlantic	37.2	36.8	37.6	1.1
Midwest	56.6	58.9	59.7	5.5
East North Central	40.3	41.7	42.0	4.2
West North Central	16.3	17.2	17.7	8.6
South	62.8	75.4	85.4	36.0
South Atlantic	30.7	37.0	43.6	42.0
East South Central	12.8	14.7	15.2	18.8
West South Central	19.3	23.7	26.7	38.3
West	34.8	43.2	52.8	51.7
Mountain	8.3	11.4	13.7	65.1
Pacific	26.5	31.8	39.1	47.6

Within the regions noted in Table 11 are numerous metropolitan areas where Latinos are concentrated. These represent the kinds of places where educational decision makers must deal with growth within the context of declining revenues.

These metropolitan areas are more than geographic areas; they represent places where Latinos are a visible presence in the community as well as in the schools (see Table 12). In many of these areas, Latinos overlap significantly with Asians, American-Indians, and African-American concentrations. These urban areas also contain high proportions of immigrants in search of an economic foothold, high numbers of non-English speakers, as well as the usual issues of all cities—community safety, lack of affordable housing, shrinking base of manufacturing jobs, growing number of homeless, deteriorating infrastructure, traffic congestion, and poverty.

SOCIOECONOMIC CONDITIONS OF LATINOS

Latinos have a low educational attainment compared to those who are non-Latino. Only about one half (53%) of Latinos 25 years and older report completing high school, compared to 82% of non-Latinos. Only 9% have graduated from college, compared to 22% of non-Latinos. Nonetheless, the decade of the 1980s was, in retrospect, a decade of educational progress for Latinos.

Low educational attainment is responsible in large part for higher levels of unemployment among Latinos. For example, in March 1992, 11.3% of Latinos were unemployed compared to 6.5% of non-Latinos. The jobs that Latinos hold are also more likely to be vulnerable to economic dislocations. Latino men are more likely to be employed in lower-paying, less stable, and

TABLE 12
Most Hispanic Metropolitan Areas, 1980-1990

Area	Number (Thousands)	1980-1990 Change (%)	% of Total Metro
Los Angeles, CA	4,779	26.4	32.9
New York, NY	2,779	3.1	15.4
Miami, FL	1,062	20.8	33.3
San Francisco, CA	970	16.5	15.5
Chicago, IL	893	1.6	11.1
Houston, TX	772	19.7	20.8
San Antonio, TX	620	21.5	47.6
Dallas-Ft. Worth, TX	519	32.6	13.4
San Diego, CA	511	34.2	20.4
El Paso, TX	412	23.3	69.6
Phoenix, AZ	345	40.6	16.3
McAllen, TX	327	35.4	85.2
Fresno, CA	237	29.7	35.5
Denver, CO	226	14.2	12.2
Philadelphia, PA	226	3.9	3.8
Washington, DC	225	20.7	5.7
Brownsville, TX	213	24.0	81.9
Boston, MA	193	5.0	4.6
Corpus Christi, TX	182	7.3	52.0
Albuquerque, NM	178	14.4	37.1
Sacramento, CA	172	34.7	11.6
Tucson, AZ	163	25.5	24.5
Austin, TX	160	45.6	20.5
Bakersfield, CA	152	34.8	28.0
Tampa, FL	139	28.2	6.7
Laredo, TX	125	34.4	93.9
Visalia, CA	121	26.9	38.8
Salinas, CA	120	22.5	33.6
Stockton, CA	113	38.4	23.4

more hazardous occupations than are non-Latinos. Most Latino men are employed in service, machine operations, precision production, and farming. Non-Latino males are more likely to be employed in managerial-professional and technical-sales occupations. Latina workers are more similar to non-Latina workers, although they are more likely to work in factories as machine operators and less likely to hold managerial-professional positions.

Given this job structure, it is not surprising to find that Latinos have lower incomes than do non-Latinos. The median family income of Latinos ($23,400) was about $14,000 less than non-Latino White families. Conversely, Latino families are more likely to he poorer than non-Latino families. About 26% of Latino families were below the poverty level in 1991 compared to 10% of non-Latino White families. Poverty disproportionately affects children. About 41% of Latino children live in poverty compared to 13% of non-Latino children.

CONCLUSIONS

For the Latino population, educational attainment represents a critical foundation for that community's struggle for self-determination. To participate fully in the U.S. economy, to engage forcefully in civic activity, requires basic skills in literacy, training in English as a second language, affordable child care, and opportunities to move into the economic mainstream.

The Latino population is numerically too large to have its needs ignored, and the educational enterprise must be responsive to the demographic context of change. Decades of neglect and wishful thinking that Latinos would not differ substantially from prior immigrant groups must come to an end. Investment in the educational enterprise demands that a large portion be devoted to the needs of Latino children and youth currently in the schools and to the needs of those who will be there over the next decades.

NOTE

1. Discussion in this and following sections is based on U.S. Bureau of the Census (1990, 1991, 1992a, 1992b, 1922c).

REFERENCES

U.S. Bureau of the Census. (1990). *The foreign born population in the United States: 1990* (CPH-L98). Washington, DC: U.S. Government Printing Office.

U.S. Bureau of the Census. (1991). *Statistical abstract of the United States: 1991* (111th ed.). Washington, DC: U.S. Government Printing Office.

U.S. Bureau of the Census. (1992a). *Current population reports: Hispanic population of the United States: March 1991* (pp. 20–455). Washington, DC: U.S. Government Printing Office.

U.S. Bureau of the Census. (1992b). *Population projections of the United States by age, sex, race, and Hispanic origin: 1992 to 2050* (pp. 25–1092). Washington, DC: U.S. Government Printing Office.

U.S. Bureau of the Census. (1992c). *Statistical abstract of the United States: 1992* (112th ed.). Washington, DC: U.S. Government Printing Office.

Black Hawk's *An Autobiography:*

The Production and Use of an "Indian" Voice

Mark Wallace

Mark Wallace is a Professor in the Department of English at George Washington University in Washington, D.C.

What are the conditions under which Native American voices are first allowed to emerge in texts for white Americans? Perhaps no nineteenth century text raises this question more powerfully, or shows the ground of contest more clearly, than *Black Hawk: An Autobiography.* When it appeared in 1833, *An Autobiography* was the first text in United States history to claim to present the unmediated voice of an unassimilated Indian. However, not only was its voice mediated, but it was restrained by whites before it was even conceived. The voice of Black Hawk in *An Autobiography,* and white responses to that voice, tell us much about how Native American and other non-white voices became textualized within white American systems of discourse in the nineteenth and twentieth centuries. The questionable composition of the text, the responses of white historians and scholars, and the structure of its narrative are evidence of the cultural methods, assumptions, and limits under which Black Hawk's "voice" had to pass before it would be allowed to make its presence felt.

Until very recently *Black Hawk: An Autobiography* has received little attention as a literary text. It has been used almost exclusively by historians, as additional evidence for understanding the events to which it refers, and the historical context of those events. Recent scholarship has changed this situation. Arnold Krupat's books *For Those Who Come After: A Study of Native American Autobiography,* and *The Voice in the Margin: Native American Literature and the Canon,* make a case for *An Autobiography* as a unique work, the only "fully developed instance of Indian autobiography" in the nineteenth century (Krupat 1985:53). Even Krupat's work, though, tends to skirt close reading of the text's voice. Instead, he contextualizes *An Autobiography* within the larger cultural and discursive frames white American discourse has applied to texts claiming to represent a Native American viewpoint.

Neil Schmitz's article "Captive Utterance: Black Hawk and Indian Irony" gives the closest reading to date of *Black Hawk: An Autobiography* as a text. Schmitz reads the text for how "Black Hawk effectively speaks against . . . Anglo-Indianist constraints," revealing the ways in which Black Hawk repeatedly resists the discursive frame that white America attempts to impose on his voice (Schmitz 1992:1). Schmitz sees *An Autobiography* as "defiant, litigious, maledictory," a "resisting text" whose "contrary logic" consistently contests both Anglo-Indianist discourse and the actions of white Americans (Schmitz 1992:2).

Yet whatever resistance to white America Black Hawk achieves by resisting white impositions on the text, Black Hawk's tale remains the story of a defeated warrior just released from prison, and close attention must be paid to the shackles placed even on his voice. If one wishes to treat *An Autobiography* as text and not merely as historical record, it is important to look at how Black Hawk resisted the voice that the text's white writer, John B. Patterson, attempted to impose on him, and at the characteristics of the voice that Patterson claimed belonged to Black Hawk.

The Sauk warrior Black Hawk spent the winter of 1832–1833 jailed at Jefferson Barracks, south of St. Louis, along with several other Native Americans involved in the uprising that has become known as the Black Hawk War. The group was transported east to Washington, D.C., to appear before President Andrew Jackson. After informing Black Hawk and the others that they were to be kept in jail, Jackson went on to say that he meant to enforce peace both between the tribes that lived in the region of the Sauk and Fox,[1] and between Indians and whites. Black Hawk gave his word that he intended to remain at peace, although he had no real choice in the matter. After the meeting, he spent six weeks as a prisoner in Fortress Monroe in Virginia, where his image was painted by a number of Americans including George Catlin[2] and Robert Sully. Black Hawk and the other imprisoned Native Americans were escorted on a "tour" of United States cities en route to their release in Illinois, a trip that was probably intended to impress them with the hopelessness of fighting so powerful a nation as the United States (pp. 4–18).[3]

In each city, Black Hawk drew large audiences who came to see the Indian who had caused the American government so much trouble. By coincidence, he visited several cities at the same time as Andrew Jackson and the crowds that turned out to see Black Hawk were nearly as large as those for the war hero president (p. 12). In his defeat Black Hawk had become a celebrity and his defiance of the government, now under control, had become reason for public fascination rather than hate or fear.

Soon after his release, Black Hawk is reported to have approached a U.S. interpreter for the Sauk and Fox, the half-

From *American Indian Quarterly*, Fall 1994, pp. 481-494. © 1994 by the University of Nebraska Press. Reprinted by permission.

French half-Potawatomi[4] Antoine Leclaire, with the "desire to have a History of his Life written and published" (p. 41). According to Leclaire, Black Hawk did this so that:

> the people of the United States (among whom he had been travelling, and by whom he had been treated with great respect, friendship and hospitality,) might know the causes that had impelled him to act as he has done, and the principles by which he was governed (p. 41).

Leclaire told Patterson Black Hawk's story, and *An Autobiography* appeared in 1833. The second edition appeared in 1882, in which Patterson heightened the prose of the first edition into romantic ornateness and added a number of fanciful stories that the historical record shows to be untrue (pp. 36–37). The first edition to attempt to put *An Autobiography* in a historical context appeared in 1916 and contained an introduction by Milo Milton Quaife (Preface). The currently authoritative edition was edited by Donald Jackson and appeared in 1955. This edition restored *An Autobiography* to its 1833 form and added appendices and an introduction describing the Black Hawk War and details of the text's production.

Writing in *For Those Who Come After,* Krupat is careful to restrict what he means by a "fully developed" Indian autobiography. His definition of "the principle constituting . . . Indian autobiography" is that of "original bicultural composite composition" (Krupat 1985:31). That is, Indian autobiography is a literary form that comes into being through the contact of two cultures. More particularly, it is a form of which each textual example is biculturally produced:

> Strictly speaking, therefore, Indian autobiography is a contradiction in terms. Indian autobiographies are collaborative efforts, jointly produced by some white who translates, transcribes, compiles, edits, interprets, polishes, and ultimately determines the form of the text in writing, and by an Indian who is its subject and whose life becomes the content of the "autobiography" whose title may bear his name (Krupat 1985:30).

By invoking the principle of "original bicultural composite composition," Krupat means to exclude from the category of "fully developed" Indian autobiographies those "autobiographies by 'civilized' or christianized Indians whose texts originate with them and contain, inevitably, a certain bicultural element, yet are not compositely produced" (Krupat 1985:31).[5] One may question Krupat's suggestion that only "compositely produced" Indian autobiographies are "fully developed." Nonetheless, the way in which *An Autobiography* was produced does mark it as a text unique to its time.

Krupat sees *An Autobiography* as arising partly out of an American literary tradition he calls the western autobiography. According to Krupat, western autobiography exists in opposition to the eastern tradition of autobiography, which is composed of texts written by cultured men of letters (Franklin's *Autobiography* is an example of the latter). Western autobiography is often "anti-literary," written from the point of view of men who, according to Krupat, "in comparison to the European or American easterner, seemed to be 'Indians,' men of action not letters, hunters and warriors, not preachers or farmers, neither book-keepers nor book-writers" (Krupat 1985:42).[6] This western autobiographical tradition includes autobiographies of Daniel Boone, Davy Crockett, and Kit Carson, and tends to privilege oral storytelling over writing, at least as much as possible in a written form. Thus these western, often illiterate "authors" tell their stories in what seems a written approximation of their speaking voice. On first glance this is what seems to happen in Black Hawk's autobiography as well. The difference is that in this case one reads "the unprecedented instance of an Indian speaking for himself"—the first time in American history that a non-English speaking Indian is supposedly allowed to speak for himself in a text (Krupat 1985:50).

As Krupat's discussion of the bicultural composition of Indian autobiography implies, however, it is ultimately impossible to determine to what extent *An Autobiography* can be said to be an expression of Black Hawk's voice, or even his attitude. Whether Black Hawk dictated *An Autobiography* (something that, according to Donald Jackson, seems likely but cannot be determined), the words that appear in the text are not the ones he spoke, but rather are translated for the white audience for whom the book was intended (p. 31–36). Black Hawk's original words are long since lost. Because those words are lost, *An Autobiography* is a translation for which no original exists. As Krupat says of Crashing Thunder's autobiography, and could have said just as easily of Black Hawk's, "We have no one's spoken words, however much we may be urged to believe that the Indian has been allowed to speak for himself, but only written words, and words in English" (Krupat 1985:105).

The cultural makeup of the three men supposedly involved in the text's composition provides an excellent metaphor for the text's inadequacy as the expression of an "authentic" Indian voice. Black Hawk, a Sauk Indian, tells his story to a half-Indian, half-white translator who symbolizes in his own person the point at which Native American and white cultures meet. It is the translator who tells the story to the white writer. Without this cross-cultural cooperation (assuming that Black Hawk dictated it), the text would not have appeared. It is this cultural mixing, this struggle for the control of voice, that previous writings on *An Autobiography* have ignored, tried to deny, or used to prove the text inauthentic and so invalid.[7]

It is hardly an accident that *An Autobiography* emerges only after Black Hawk's defeat. The appearance of what is supposedly Black Hawk's voice in white American discourse may be evidence of Black Hawk's "having his say" on the events of the war, but it is also evidence of his defeat: The only power remaining to him is to become textualized. Even the title, *An Autobiography,* asserts that this is the story of an individual and not the story of a people, undermining Black Hawk's authority to speak for the Sauk Nation. Black Hawk did not speak English and he did not *want* to speak English. In one sense, the victory he did not achieve against the whites could have been symbolized by the extent to which his voice could have existed on its own terms, not as part of white American discourse. It is clear that the Black Hawk in *An Autobiography* realizes he is powerless except as a voice within white American discourse. Patterson explains this in his introduction:

> Several accounts of the late war having been published, in which he [Black Hawk] thinks justice is not done to himself or [his] nation, he determined to make known to the world, the injuries

his people have received from the whites—the causes which brought on the war on the part of his nation, and a general history of it throughout the campaign. In his opinion, this is the only method now left him, to rescue his little Band—the remnant of those who fought bravely with him—from the effects of the statements that have already gone forth (p. 44).

Far from presenting an "authentic" Native voice speaking from within a Native culture to other Native voices, *An Autobiography* presents a cross-culturally produced "Indian" voice that is responding to white voices in the language of the whites. It is addressed to them, and it is dedicated to the white general (General Atkinson) who defeated Black Hawk in the Black Hawk War. *An Autobiography* represents that moment at which Black Hawk becomes a voice within white American discourse, and as such the text is perhaps the final mark of the destruction of whatever autonomy had remained to him. As Krupat writes, "defeat is the enabling condition of Indian autobiography" (Krupat 1985:48).

It is as a similar mark of defeat that the celebrity status that Black Hawk achieved on his journey through white America becomes significant. By the end of the war, Black Hawk's story is, as Schmitz points out, "safely exploitable" (1992:6). Even now in the United States it is typical of those who have been "defeated" (in war or another endeavor) to publish memoirs and speak of their experiences. In doing so they become the living symbols of those experiences. The celebrity status often granted such figures provides a measure of the power they have lost elsewhere. In a general way one can say that the extent of one's fame after one's defeat is often equivalent to one's previous notoriety, now that one is no longer dangerous.[8] Krupat writes, "For it is only when the Indian subject of an autobiography acknowledges his defeat, when he becomes what Patterson calls a 'State-prisoner,' that he can appear as a 'hero' " (Krupat 1985:49).

Even the appearance of a Native American speaking in his or her own voice within white American discourse would have seemed a radical act to white Americans of the 1830s. As Krupat points out, earlier attempts by such men as Samuel Drake, B.B. Thatcher and Benjamin Drake to write Indian biography had never allowed the subject of those biographies to speak for themselves, and thus supported "the belief that the 'savage' has no intelligible voice of his own, that the 'civilized' man of letters must speak for him if he is to be heard at all" (Krupat 1985:51). Patterson's refusal to admit that he has created Black Hawk's voice—he says that he "does not consider himself responsible for any of the facts, or views, contained in it"—is not due solely to an attempt to hide the coercive nature of the text. This refusal also is due to a more radical desire to allow a Native American to speak in his own unmediated voice, although this is in practice firmly limited by the Anglo-Indianized voice forced on Black Hawk (p. 45; Krupat 1985:46). In addition, Krupat points out, Patterson refers to Black Hawk's story as "the life of a Hero" and not a savage. One can see that to white Americans of the time, *An Autobiography* seemed a truly dangerous book (p. 44). As Phillip Fisher's book *Hard Facts* suggests, it is only the cultural space opened by work like Patterson's that allows later

works to criticize and expand on that earlier effort. Fisher speaks most particularly about the ways successful "popular forms" of art can transform the "national mind" and then be absorbed so quickly into a nation's consciousness that they come "rapidly to seem an entrenched burden" that serves "as a barrier to the intelligent perceptions that they themselves had initially made possible" (Fisher 1985: 20–21). Although *An Autobiography* was not successful in the same way as the books Fisher discusses (such as *Uncle Tom's Cabin),* it does seem to open a cultural space that makes possible later criticisms of its failings.

However, one must always keep in mind the larger historical frame of Native American voices in white American discourse: the defeat, removal, and absorption of Native Americans by white America. *An Autobiography* emerges in the very decade in which, as Krupat says, "Indian removal . . . became a national, not merely a local, priority" (Krupat 1985:36). Whatever radicality *An Autobiography* may have in terms of the history of white American discourse, it must be remembered that discourse had the final say about what the text became. In terms of Native American discourse, the book remains evidence of defeat, however valiant and contestatory.

The 1955 edition of *An Autobiography* includes many authenticating apparatuses. It includes comments, primarily by white American voices, that intend to prove the extent to which *An Autobiography* is outside white American discourse and an authentic expression of an "Indian" voice. Donald Jackson's introduction to the 1955 edition, with its maps and illustrations, appendices, indexes, and notes on the text, must be included as one of these apparatuses, despite its far greater sophistication to the authenticating apparatuses that appear in the original 1833 edition. Jackson attempts to authenticate the text, though not as an absolute and unmediated expression of Black Hawk's point of view. Instead he tries to determine, according to historical methods, the ways in which the text is accurate or inaccurate, authentic or inauthentic. Secondly, he attempts to establish the "proper" historical context in which to look at the text, framing it in a network of historical events. Finally, he tries to establish the text as interesting to scholars or other readers interested in a Native American viewpoint on events that have more usually been described by whites—an admirable goal that is marred only by certain cultural biases and assumptions.

The 1833 edition of *An Autobiography* contains a number of other authenticating apparatuses, all of them attempting to establish that the text of *An Autobiography* a legitimate and absolute expression of Black Hawk's voice and viewpoint. The first of these is a certification on the part of the interpreter, Antoine Leclaire. Leclaire asserts that *An Autobiography* is originally and legitimately Black Hawk's idea and, by implication, that it is not his (Leclaire's) idea, or the idea of the writer Patterson. He asserts also that he and Patterson have accurately reproduced Black Hawk's story:

I do hereby certify, that Ma-ka-tai-me-she-kia-kiak, or Black Hawk, did call upon me, on his return to his people in August last, and express a great desire to have a History of his Life written and published. . . . In accordance with his request, I acted as Interpreter; and was particularly cautious, to understand distinctly the narrative of Black Hawk throughout—and have examined the work carefully since its completion—and have no hesitation in pronouncing it strictly correct, it all its particulars (p. 41).

Following this certification is Black Hawk's dedication to Brigadier General Atkinson, the man in charge of the American forces which defeated Black Hawk in the war. Interestingly, the dedication appears first in a phonetic transcription of Black Hawk's language into the Roman alphabet, and then the full translation into English appears on the opposite page. If the presence of what is supposedly Black Hawk's language is intended to further authenticate the text, it is not a strategy that works. If one did not want to believe that the text was Black Hawk's—and many people did not (pp. 32–33)—the presence of a phonetic transcription of Black Hawk's language does not prove the text's authenticity. It could not have been written by Black Hawk himself, any more than the full translation could.

Lastly, there appears an "advertisement" from Patterson, who refers to himself as "the editor," that is, as someone who organizes the text after its writing. Patterson explains for Black Hawk the reasons Black Hawk dictated *An Autobiography;* and says that the "facts which he states" are "worthy of attention," though he carefully restricts which facts he means to those "respecting the Treaty of 1804, in virtue of the provisions of which the Government claimed the country in dispute, and enforced its arguments with the sword" (pp. 44–45). He closes by again stressing that the text is one told by Black Hawk, and in so doing he disavows his responsibility for what *An Autobiography* says:

> The Editor has written this work according to the dictation of Black Hawk, through the United States' Interpreter, at the Sac and Fox Agency of Rock Island. He does not, therefore, consider himself responsible for any of the facts, or views, contained in it—and leaves the old Chief and his story with the public, whilst he neither asks, nor expects, any fame for his services as an amanuensis (p. 45).

In the 206 pages of Jackson's 1955 edition, only 134 pages, roughly 65 percent, are devoted to Patterson's translation of Black Hawk's account. If one considers that those pages include numerous pictures as well as Jackson's lengthy footnotes, it is clear that even within the textual space reserved for Black Hawk to speak (mediated by a translator and a writer), white voices are overwhelming, even if those voices claim only to establish the importance of Black Hawk's words. The presence of such authenticating voices is a common element of both Indian and slave narratives of the nineteenth century. Only the presence of authoritative white voices claiming that the text is authentic can prevent those narratives from being written off as inauthentic hoaxes, though many commentators did just that.[9]

Black Hawk consistently speaks of the whites, French or British or American, in the third person, an appeal, as Schmitz points out, to "disinterested justice" (Schmitz 1992:4). The strategy of addressing justice itself and speaking of whites in the third person allows Black Hawk a more politically effective way to gain sympathy for his cause. He can say "the whites have done this" rather than "you have done this." This is not to say that Black Hawk is speaking to anyone other than whites; his intended audience is clear. If he addresses them

indirectly, it is because he believes that it is more useful to speak to their abstract feelings about justice than it is to directly attack their behavior, which he had promised not to do.

The narrative framing of *An Autobiography* makes it even more clear that the text is intended as a story of white and Indian interaction. The text begins with Black Hawk's story of the first meeting of members of his tribe with white men; a meeting between his great-grandfather and the French. It ends with a description of Black Hawk's journey as a captive through the major cities of white America, before he is finally released at Rock River, Illinois. One could describe the book as a sort of Dante's Inferno, although Black Hawk's reaction to white society is somewhat more ambivalent than Dante's reaction to Hell. Black Hawk appears as much impressed as horrified by what he witnesses. After detailing the destruction of his army, ancestral village, and much of his tribe, Black Hawk describes his encounter with white society as a sort of hell into which he has to move deeper and deeper before he can emerge. The difference between the texts is that Dante emerges into spiritual triumph. Black Hawk emerges a defeated man, however defiant, whose way of life has been destroyed, and who calls for a "friendship" in which he clearly has no faith (p. 154). Hell does far less damage to Dante than the United States does to Black Hawk.

However, as Krupat points out, *An Autobiography* is in many ways based on the forms of comedy rather than tragedy. Black Hawk's defeat appears not as the result of his own failings but as simply inevitable. Krupat writes:

> [F]rom the point of view of Patterson and his contemporary readers, the structure of Black Hawk's life is not tragic at all, but comic, the sad comedy of "civilization" progressing to a happy ending in which the red-skinned "blocking characters" are overcome; "the normal response of the audience . . . is 'this should be'" (Krupat 1985:69).

An Autobiography is written in a plain style, primarily narrating Black Hawk's experiences with whites. It describes the Sauk's wars with the whites and with other Native American tribes. Black Hawk speaks at length of the various agreements that are used to take advantage of his tribe. The text operates in ways similar to nineteenth century slave narratives. It gives witness to the reality of events or social conditions by saying, "I was there and this is what I saw and did." This provides a "subjective" eyewitness description of events that can call up a more sympathetic response than the "objective" numbers and dates. Of course, Black Hawk as he appears in the text is not presenting an unbiased account of the events he describes; he is justifying his cause.

One of the standard elements of many slave narratives and Indian biographies and autobiographies is a section describing the culture and day-to-day life of the group.[10] A similar formulaic element appears in the middle of Black Hawk's narrative, suspending it for more than seven pages (pp. 100–107). Black Hawk describes what his village (Saukenak) looked like before the whites came, what his people eat and how they come to have that food, how they treat their dead, and lastly their dances and celebrations. While the information provided on those pages is insightful, it must be remembered that such a section did come to be a formulaic element of culturally strange texts within white American discourse. Its appearance also represents an acceptable documentary format.

On more than one occasion, the plain narrative gives way to the elegiac tone which is a feature of the "Indian" discourse within white American discourse. This tone bewails the fate of the Indians and accuses white Americans of immorally bringing about that fate:

> Why did the Great Spirit even send the whites to this island, to drive us from our homes, and introduce among us poisonous liquors, disease and death? They should have remained on the island where the Great Spirit first placed them. But I will proceed with my story (p. 69).
>
> But, how different is our situation now, from what it was in those days! Then we were as happy as the buffalo on the plains—but now, we are as miserable as the hungry, howling wolf in the prairie! But I am digressing from my story (p. 101).

As those two passages show, in almost every case in which Black Hawk begins to rise to this elegiac tone, he quickly restrains himself. As with his appeals to abstract justice, this seems partly due to Black Hawk's promise to remain at peace with the whites, both in word and deed.[11] But it seems, as well, an excellent strategy for complaining about the very people who are going to read the book. Black Hawk airs the complaint but then holds back from saying too much. In so doing he speaks the complaint but not to the point that it might inhibit white sympathy. At the same time, he makes himself look like an honorable and reasonable man, capable of self-restraint and keeping his word.

As well as these elegiac laments, the text also includes a number of moments at which Black Hawk pauses to philosophize, and to make moral judgments on the absurdities of white culture. The following passage is a well-known one, expressing an attitude that became typical within white American discourse of Native American attitudes toward land ownership:

> My reason teaches me that land cannot be sold. The Great Spirit gave it to his children to live upon, as far as is necessary for their subsistence; and so long as they occupy and cultivate it, they have the right to the soil—but if they voluntarily leave it, then any other people have a right to settle upon it. Nothing can be sold, but such things as can be carried away (p. 114).

At other moments Black Hawk criticizes the absurd behavior of whites. For instance, the following passage points out the callousness of whites toward the death in war of their own men, whose dying seems less important than following "proper" methods of battle:

> I explained to them the matter the British and Americans fought. Instead of stealing upon each other, and taking every advantage to kill the enemy and save their own people, as we do (which, with us is considered good policy in a war chief,) they march out, in open daylight, and fight, regardless of the number of warriors they may lose! After the battle is over, they retire to feast, and drink wine, as if nothing had happened; after which, they make a statement in writing, of what they have done—each party claiming the victory! and neither giving an account of half the number that have been killed on their own side. They all fought like braves, but would not do to lead a war party with us. Our maxim is, "to kill the enemy, and save our own men" (p. 80).

The moments in the text in which Black Hawk's "native common sense" points out the absurdities of the whites'

supposedly more "civilized" behavior must be questioned, because of the ways in which those moments set up clear distinctions between Native American behavior and "civilized" behavior. That is, although Black Hawk is capable of seeing through the behavior of the whites, the voice that emerges in the text consistently presents itself as incapable of understanding the complexity of white "civilized" behavior. Black Hawk's comments on the absurdities of white society can be seen, then, as another culturally-biased way of establishing the authenticity of Black Hawk's voice for white Americans. Such comments establish that the difference between Native Americans and whites remains inviolable, because even powerful Native American heroes are ultimately unable to comprehend white civilization.

That the text is attempting to enforce such a distinction becomes particularly clear in what is perhaps its most cynical and racist element; the translation of some of Black Hawk's words into English words that attempt to create a "quaint" Indian colloquialism. This fake colloquialism purports to show Black Hawk's inability to understand the terms (discursive and cultural) on which white America exists. Black Hawk speaks of alcohol as "bad medicine," of American cities as "big villages" and American women as "squaws," and finally he describes American editors and journalists (i.e. including Patterson himself) as "village criers" (pp. 90, 172–73, 179). There is no good reason to translate Black Hawk's words into this fake, Indian-colloquial English; a more accurate English word would serve just as well.[12] Translating certain words in this way, then, must be seen as a method of stressing Black Hawk's cultural separateness, his inability to understand anything except in his own "primitive" terms.

Along with this racist translation, the translation of Black Hawk's religious and political values may be similarly biased. In his essay "Two Concepts of Authority," William Miller points out that religion in Fox culture was conceptualized very differently from European religious systems. In European systems:

> [T]he ultimate locus of supernatural power rests in a supreme being situated in an elevated location. Below him are a series of subordinate supernatural beings, arranged in a persisting and orderly hierarchy, each possessing considerable power but less than that of the supreme being from whom their power derives, or flows. . . . At some point in this system the power-flow breaks through to an earthly system (Miller 1955: 279).

The earthly system then does its best to replicate this supernatural hierarchy.

In Fox culture, on the other hand, the God-figures (which include "all varieties of natural phenomena") exist within the world, not above it, and their power is not rigorously hierarchical, but instead shifts, as a result of the always temporary possession of a "generalized essence of supernatural power" known as Manitu (Miller 1955:279). This "horizontal" power does not contain the same permanent, "vertical" hierarchical power relationships that characterize European religious systems. These shifting relationships carry over into the relationships between members of the Fox tribe and include all tribal and family relationships. The term "father," for instance, simply does not hold the same hierarchical connotations for the

Fox that it does for Europeans. "That the Fox calls his principal deity 'my nephew' is as revealing as the fact that the European calls his principal deity 'my father' " (Miller 1955:281).

Black Hawk's spiritual beliefs are not a matter of record, and whatever the close relation between the two tribes, he was Sauk and not Fox. However, throughout *An Autobiography* Black Hawk refers to white generals and politicians as "father," and on occasion "great father," and he also refers at times to a single god that he calls "the great spirit" (pp. 47–51).[13] It is possible that Black Hawk spoke this way so as to address white men in terms they could understand, and Patterson may have had a limited understanding of the complexities of Native American life. Black Hawk's concepts of religion and politics—consistently based on a hierarchical system—seem unlikely to have been his.[14]

What does Black Hawk say is left for him at the end of *An Autobiography*? What does white America want there to be left for him? Nothing but going home to die: "A few more moons, and I must follow my father to the shades!" (p. 180). *An Autobiography*; then, falls off into Black Hawk's silence, and the silence of his tribe: That this final silence is a cliched element of "Indian" voices in white American discourse robs it of the power to condemn white American culture outside of the ways white America is willing to hear itself condemned.

NOTES

1. The Sauk and Fox are both originally Central Algonquin tribes that share many cultural and linguistic traits. The Fox were an independent tribe until they began fighting the French in the early 18th century. The severity of the French attacks, which seriously decimated the numbers of the Fox tribe (Michael Green estimates that the population of the Fox had been reduced to around 100 people), drove the Fox into close contact with the Sauk, who lived in the area of Green Bay in the early 1730s. To escape the French, both tribes moved to what is now Iowa, and Black Hawk's village of Saukenak may have been founded around 1733. In the 1740s the Sauk and Fox returned to the Wisconsin area, and it was not until the 1780s that they settled more thoroughly the land around the Rock River in Illinois that they occupied at the time of the Black Hawk War. In the years after the Black Hawk War, the Fox began to separate from the Sauk, in particular with the refusal of the Fox to join the Sauk in removing from Iowa to Kansas following the treaty of 1842. For a discussion of the relationship and eventual separation of the Sauk and Fox tribes, see Green 1983: 129–140. For even greater detail (though offensively racist and biased) regarding the movement of the Sauk and Fox tribes up to the time of the Black Hawk War, see *Sac, Fox, and Iowa Indians* 1974, 1:123–161.
2. For a discussion of how Catlin's portrait of Black Hawk "feminized" Black Hawk and attempted to rob him of his masculine, warrior image, see Sweet 1993:475–499.
3. All page numbers without other citation refer to *Black Hawk: An Autobiography* [1833] 1955.
4. The Potawatomi were a Central Algonquin tribe like the Sauk and Fox. Their relationship with the Sauk and Fox dates back at least to 1616, when all three tribes lived around the Upper Great Lakes. The Potawatomi and Sauk were closely allied through much of their history. However, during the Black Hawk War the Potawatomi refused to aid Black Hawk and his people with warriors or corn, although the Potawatomi's own dissatisfaction with the United States led at roughly the same time to their last acts of violence against whites. For a thorough history of the Potawatomi see Clifton 1977. For their relationship with the Sauk and Fox see in particular Clifton 1977:6, 62, 232–235.
5. For a list of Native American biographies not restricted to those of "original bicultural composite composition" see Brumble 1981.
Timothy Sweet further distinguishes Black Hawk's *An Autobiography* from the autobiographies of assimilationist Indians "such as Samson Occom and William Apes, who in their autobiographies voice the dominant white discourses of salvationism and progressivism in attempting to produce narratives of assimilation" (Sweet 1993:481).

6. See also Krupat's discussion of western autobiography (Krupat 1985:40–43).
7. See for instance Jackson's quote of Thomas Ford's *History of Illinois*, which appeared in 1854. After denying that Black Hawk knew anything about *An Autobiography*, Ford goes on to undermine Laclaire's authority by referring to him as a "half-breed," suggesting that because of his racial make-up Laclaire is compromised, corrupt, and cannot be trusted (p. 32).
8. The recreation of Richard Nixon in the post-Watergate years as an "elder statesman" of American politics is one of the most celebrated recent examples of "celebrity" status of this sort. It must be remembered that while Nixon was often called upon late in his life to comment on American politics, he no longer had the power to affect events.
9. A fascinating Jacksonian era example of how a white voice was used to establish the authenticity of a slave narrative is Frederick Douglass's *Narrative of the Life of Frederick Douglass* (1845), which originally appeared with an authenticating preface by William Lloyd Garrison. Douglass's later autobiographies, which appear after his falling out with Garrison over Garrison's pacifism and desire to dissolve the Union, and when Douglass himself has gained more authority as a spokesman on slavery, do not contain this preface. In fact, *My Bondage and My Freedom* (1855) replaces Garrison's introduction with an introduction by a black abolitionist. See Michael Meyer's introduction in *Frederick Douglass: The Narrative and Selected Writings* (Douglass 1984:xxiii–xxvii).
10. For instance, Jacksonian era slave narratives such as *Narrative of the Life of Frederick Douglass* and *Narrative of the Life and Adventures of Henry Bibb* (1850), among countless others, contain sections that attempt to describe the day-to-day life of slaves.
11. See for instance p. 176 and Jackson's footnote No. 132 for one example of what this promise consisted of, and one particular result of it.
12. This is not to say any single English word would be a perfect way of translating what Black Hawk supposedly said. As Walter Benjamin points out in the "Task of the Translator," "Fidelity in the translation of individual words can almost never fully reproduce the meaning they have in the original" (Benjamin 1968:78). However, translating Black Hawk's tale into standard English would at least avoid blatant racism, and since Black Hawk's original telling of the story is lost (assuming it ever existed), Benjamin's suggestion that "The task of the translator consists in finding that intended effect upon the language in which he is translating which produces in it the echo of the original" simply is not possible in this case (Benjamin 1968:76).
13. The use of such words recurs throughout the text.
14. The information provided in *Sac, Fox and Iowa Indians, Vol. 1* does state that "The Indians [Sauk and Fox] believe in one great and good spirit who superintends and commands all things" (*Sac, Fox and Iowa Indians* 1974, 1:218). But this is contradicted by Miller's assertion that "the Fox pantheon lacks any supremely placed deity" (Miller 1955:281). Miller's information seems far more reliable and less racist than that in the other text, in which a subsection titled "General Manners and Customs" begins with the sentence, "The Sauk Indians never eat human flesh except some individual might do it by way of Bravado in revenge for the loss of a relative," and also includes the phrase, "An Indian in love is a silly looking mortal "(*Sac, Fox and Iowa Indians* 1974, 1:219, 220).

REFERENCES

Benjamin, Walter. 1968 *Illuminations*. New York: Harcourt, Brace & World.
Black Hawk 1955 *An Autobiography*, ed. Donald Jackson. Urbana, Illinois: University of Illinois Press [1833].
Brumble, David H. 1981 *An Annotated Bibliography of American Indian and Eskimo Autobiographies*. Lincoln, Nebraska: University of Nebraska Press.
Clifton, James A. 1977 *The Prairie People: Continuity and Change in Potawatomi Indian Culture 1665–1965* Lawrence, Kansas: The Regents Press of Kansas.
Douglass, Frederick 1984 *Frederick Douglass: The Narrative and Selected Writings*. New York: The Modern Library.
Fisher, Phillip 1985 *Hard Facts*. New York: Oxford University Press.
Green, Michael C. 1983 " 'We Dance In Opposite Directions': Mesquakie (Fox) Separatism from the Sac and Fox Tribe." *Ethnohistory* 30:3:129–140.
Krupat, Arnold. 1985 *For Those Who Come After: A Study of Native American Autobiography*. Berkeley, California: University of California Press.
Miller, William B. 1955 "Two Concepts of Authority." *American Anthropologist* 57:256–283.
Sac, Fox and Iowa Indians, Vol 1. 1974 New York: Garland Publishing Corp.
Schmitz, Neil. 1992 "Captive Utterance: Black Hawk and Indian Irony." *Arizona Quarterly* 48:4: 1–18.
Sweet, Timothy. 1993 "Masculinity in the Life of Black Hawk." *American Literature* (65:3:475–499).

Behind the Model-Minority Stereotype: Voices of High- and Low-Achieving Asian American Students

Stacey J. Lee

Stacey J. Lee is an assistant professor in Educational Policy Studies at the University of Wisconsin-Madison.

This article examines the complex relationship between Asian American student identity(ies) and perceptions regarding future opportunity and attitudes toward schooling. The article argues that identity and attitudes toward schooling are not static, as some have argued, but are negotiated through experiences and relationships inside and outside of school. Data for this article were collected as part of a larger ethnographic study on Asian American high school students. ASIAN AMERICAN, MODEL-MINORITY STEREOTYPE, HIGH SCHOOL STUDENTS, MINORITY ACHIEVEMENT

Asian American students are commonly depicted as academic superstars or model minorities. According to the model-minority stereotype, Asian Americans are successful in school because they work hard and come from cultures that believe in the value of education. Scholars and the popular press have contrasted the success of Asian American students to the under-achievement of other minorities.

In an attempt to understand differential achievement among minority groups, cultural ecologists have pointed to the ways in which identity, historical experiences, and perceptions of opportunities affect school performance (Gibson 1988; Matute-Bianchi 1986, 1991; Ogbu 1978, 1983, 1987, 1989, 1991; Suárez-Orozco 1989, 1991). Ogbu distinguishes between what he calls voluntary and involuntary minorities (Ogbu 1989). He defines voluntary minorities as immigrants who voluntarily come to this country (e.g., Asian Americans) in search of a better life and involuntary minorities as those who were incorporated into the United States through slavery or conquest (e.g., African Americans, Mexicans, Hawaiians, etc.). Ogbu argues that differences in achievement levels between voluntary and involuntary minorities are related to their respective perceptions regarding future opportunities and their perceptions and responses to schooling (Ogbu 1987:313). According to Ogbu, voluntary minorities tend to do well in school because they see schooling as a necessary step to social mobility. They see themselves as guests in the United States who must live by the host's rules. Furthermore, they interpret the cultural and language barriers that they face in the United States as things that they must overcome in order to succeed there. On the other hand, because of persistent economic and social discrimination, involuntary minorities do not believe in the possibility of social mobility. These minorities reject the dominant culture and develop an oppositional culture. In short, Ogbu argues that involuntary minorities underachieve in school because they view schooling as a threat to their oppositional cultures and identities.

Ogbu's framework provides important insight into the relationship between a group's perception of schooling and that group's achievement in school, but his categories promote the stereotype that Asian Americans are a monolithic group with shared achievement levels and shared attitudes toward schooling. In short, while the cultural ecological perspective points to significant intergroup differences, it does not uncover the

From *Anthropology & Education Quarterly,* December 1994, pp. 413-429. © 1994 by the American Anthropological Association. Reprinted by permission. Not for further reproduction.

equally significant intragroup differences. One result is that Asian Americans are once again seen as model minorities whose diverse and complex experiences remain hidden.

This article will attempt to lift the veil of the model-minority myth and reveal the lives of the students behind the stereotype. Through excerpts from ethnographic interviews we will hear what Asian American students have to say about their identity, schooling, and the model-minority stereotype. Like the cultural ecologists, I address the relationship between students' perceptions of opportunities, their perceptions of schooling and students' achievement, but I also focus on intragroup differences among Asian American high school students. The article will examine how different groups of Asian American students define themselves in terms of ethnic/racial identity and how their different identities influence their attitudes toward schooling and their achievement.

BACKGROUND OF THE STUDY

Data for this article were collected as part of a larger ethnographic study on the development of identity among Asian American high school students. The fieldwork was conducted at a school that I call Academic High School. The fieldwork consisted of participant observations, interviews, and analysis of site documents. The quotations used in this article are verbatim transcriptions from interview tapes. Academic High is a public, coeducational high school located in Philadelphia. Admission to Academic High is open to students throughout Philadelphia on the basis of grades and standardized test scores. During the 1988–89 school year when this data was collected, there were 2050 students enrolled at Academic High. The racial makeup of the student population was: white (45%); African American (35%); Asian American (18%); and Latino (2%). Although there were a few American-born Asian students at the school, the Asian American population consisted primarily of students from Cambodia, Laos, Korea, Taiwan, Vietnam, Hong Kong, and China.

ACHIEVEMENT AMONG ASIAN AMERICANS AT ACADEMIC HIGH

During my first days of fieldwork at Academic High School, teachers and administrators were eager to show me that their Asian students were doing well (that is, that they were model minorities). Teachers pointed to the bulletin board in the main corridor which listed the names (many Asian) of the top ten students in each graduating class, in order to show me that Asians did well at Academic High. An overview of such indicators of academic achievement as academic awards, and enrollment in Advanced Placement (AP), Honors, and Mentally Gifted classes suggested that at least some Asian Americans at Academic High were successful. The class of 1990 had six Asian American students ranked in the top ten, a fact that led students to nickname the class the "Asian class."

Despite the high proportion of Asian students who are at the top of the academic rankings, a thorough examination of the rankings illustrates that not all Asian American students are successful. During the 1988–89 school year, 15 Asian students were deselected from Academic High because of weak academic performance and sent back to their neighborhood schools. Of the 18 students in the class of 1989 who were deemed ineligible to graduate with their class, three (16%) of them were Asian. These three students eventually received Academic High diplomas after completing summer school classes. In the class of 1989 one out of the four students who were ineligible to receive an Academic High diploma was Asian. All four of these students were deselected from Academic High and transferred back to their neighborhood schools. In addition to these students with serious academic troubles, the successful students told me that there were many Asian students who "just get by."

While a survey of class rankings and other statistics told me that Asian American students experienced varying levels of achievement, these facts could not tell me who the different students were or what they thought about schooling. In order to find out whether achievement levels are related to identity and perceptions of schooling, I set out to uncover the stories behind the numbers.

ASIAN AMERICAN IDENTITIES AT ACADEMIC HIGH SCHOOL

When I arrived at Academic High, I was told that Asian American students had split themselves into two major groups: Koreans in one group, and all other Asians in another group. I found this observation, as a gross generalization, to be true. While Asians from China, Hong Kong, Laos, Cambodia, Vietnam, and Taiwan expressed a panethnic identity usually referring to each other as Asian, Koreans identified solely as Korean and never as Asian or Asian American. However, Asian students who shared a panethnic identity did not make up a single identity group but divided themselves into three identity groups: Asian, Asian new wave, and Asian American. Thus the Asian American students at Academic High divided themselves into four identity groups: Koreans, Asians, Asian new wavers, and Asian Americans. Each identity group had a unique perspective on schooling which influenced their experiences at Academic High. Matute-

Bianchi (1986) discovered similar variations among Mexican American students in her study.

KOREANS

Korean students identified solely as Koreans and not as Asians or Asian Americans. They rarely socialized with Asians from other ethnic backgrounds and even took steps to distance themselves from the other Asian students at Academic High. Korean students formed their own separate club (the Korean Students' Association) and refused to participate in the Asian Students' Association (ASA). They explained to me that Koreans were "superior" to other Asians. Korean students' notions regarding Korean superiority were based on their belief that Southeast Asians were poor and unsophisticated. The majority of the Korean students at Academic High were children of merchants, and they thought of themselves as being middle class. Korean students criticized Southeast Asians for being "welfare sponges," and they ridiculed them for wearing "tacky" clothing. In writing about Asian American panethnicity, Espiritu (1992) noted that social- and economic-class differences have historically limited the development of a pan-Asian identity. At Academic High, the Korean students used social class as a marker of difference.

Koreans' attempts to distance themselves from other Asians were motivated by their efforts to get closer to whites. Korean students told me that their parents instructed them to socialize only with Koreans and whites. Peter Choe said:[1]

> When I first came to [the] U.S., they said I should get— should hang out with American kids so I could get Americanized. So, I hang out with American kids.

When I asked Peter to define what he and his parents meant when they used the term *American,* he and his Korean friends responded in unison with "White! Korean parents like whites." They said that their parents believed that "learning American ways" was essential to success in the United States and that by socializing with whites they could learn "American ways." It is important to point out that Korean students recognized that not all whites have equal social status and that they targeted the more socially elite groups as their role models. Thus the white upper-middle-class students, often referred to as "Chestnut Hillers" or "Chestnut Hill types," were the ones whom the Koreans chose to emulate. Specifically, the Korean students looked to the "Chestnut Hill types" to find out what kind of clothes to wear and where to buy them.

Although, Korean students were taught to emulate their white middle-class peers while at school, their parents also encouraged them to maintain their Korean identities at home and in the Korean community. Mrs. Kyung Clark, the only Korean teacher at Aca-

demic High, promoted the strategy of a dual identity among her students. For example, she encouraged her students to speak Korean when they were among Koreans, but she also encouraged them to adopt "American names" to use among "Americans." This strategy of maintaining a dual identity is similar to the strategy of "accommodation without assimilation" that Gibson describes the Punjabis adapting in California (1988). In both cases the parents and the immigrant communities promote the adaption of "American" values while at school and the maintenance of traditional values at home.

Koreans believed school success was the other ingredient necessary for social mobility in the United States. According to many Korean students, success would be a high-paying job in business, or a career as a doctor, lawyer, or engineer. Students often stated that their parents decided to come to the United States because of the educational opportunities for children. Some students spoke of the responsibility and guilt that they felt for their parents' sacrifices. As a result, Korean students worked hard in school. But despite the group's positive attitude toward schooling, achievement among Korean students varied. Korean students with limited English proficiency experienced the greatest academic difficulty.

One response that Korean students had to differential achievement within the Korean student population was that the higher achievers would help the lower achievers. Kay Row, a high-achieving Korean 11th grader, had been in the United States since she was very young and was more comfortable speaking English than Korean. Kay explained that she felt it was her responsibility to use her English language skills to help younger Korean classmates who had problems at Academic High. Another way that Koreans responded to differential achievement among Koreans was to promote the model-minority image. Jane Park made this statement to a few of her Korean peers:

> American kids have this stereotype, like, [that] we're smart. We are smarter. I mean, I don't think it's a stereotype—Look at our report cards. We are better, and we have to show it.

When I asked Jane about the low-achieving Koreans, she stated that Koreans were "still smarter." Jane and her friends believed that by being like model minorities Koreans could earn the respect of whites and move up the social ladder.

ASIANS

Students who identified as Asian represented a range of Asian ethnicities and a range of social-class backgrounds. This group included American-born Chinese, immigrants from Hong Kong and Taiwan, and Southeast Asian refugees. These students believed that all Asians regardless of ethnicity shared common experiences in the United States. In addition to their Asian identity, these students also identified with their specific ethnic group. Loosely speaking, students would stress their Asian identity in interracial situations and would stress their specific group affiliations within Asian circles.

Of all the Asian American students at Academic High, the Asian-identified students most closely resembled the quiet, polite, and hardworking student exemplified by the model-minority stereotype. I often found these students studying before-school and during lunch periods. Asian-identified students dreamt of jobs in medicine, engineering, computer science, or other science-related fields. These students told me that their parents had taught them that doing well in school was important in order to do well in this country. Although these students believed in the value of hard work, they also seemed to accept that discrimination would limit their potential. They did not challenge discrimination but instead altered their expectations to fit what they perceived to be their opportunities. For example, most Asian-identified students believed that their Asian "accents" would keep them from doing certain things in the United States, but none questioned the fairness of this discrimination. One Asian identified informant told me that, although he wanted to be a lawyer or politician, he planned to be an engineer because of his "accent."

Like the Korean students, Asian-identified students were motivated to work hard because they felt obligated to their families for the sacrifices that they had made. Asian-identified students spoke about their desire to get good jobs in order to help support their parents. Suárez-Orozco (1989) reports similar achievement motivation among students from Central America. Although the students who identified as Asian worked hard and held positive attitudes toward schooling, these students ranged from high achievers to low achievers. The experience of the low achievers suggests that positive attitudes and hard work do not necessarily guarantee school success.

High Achievers
Thai Le is a high-achieving student who identifies as Chinese and as Asian. Ranked number three in his class, Thai has always been an exemplary student. Thai takes AP and Honors classes and earns straight As. In elementary school, his academic talent allowed him to skip two grade levels. During his junior year at Academic High, his academic prowess won him a full scholarship to participate in a special summer program at Carnegie Mellon University.

Thai explained that his mother has always encouraged him and his sister to do well in school. He explained that he did not have any chores around the house because his primary responsibility was to get good grades. Thai's mother, a cosmetology student, dreams that her children will become white-collar professionals who will achieve the American dream. Thai's family came to the United States as refugees from Vietnam. Thai told me that his family had lost everything to communism and that he planned to help his family regain their economic security. His plans were to do well in school, win a scholarship to a prestigious university, get a good job, and make a lot of money in order to support his parents.

Although Thai's mother has high expectations for her son, she has warned him that as a Chinese person he must choose his career carefully. Thai explained that his mother counseled him against a career that would require public speaking because he has a Chinese accent. Thus, while Thai would like to be a lawyer and a politician, he says that he plans to be an engineer.

Mei Mei Wong, another high-achieving student, identifies as both Taiwanese and Asian. Like others who identify as Asian, Mei Mei works hard in school and believes that her hard work will one day pay off in the form of a good job. Mei Mei often worried that she would not succeed. By many standards, Mei Mei is a highly successful student. Within five years of coming to the United States, Mei Mei had already earned academic success at an elite American high school. She is ranked in the top ten of her class, takes Honors and AP classes, plays in the orchestra, and is a member of the softball team. Her academic prowess won her the honor of attending the 1989 Pennsylvania Governor's School for agriculture. Despite this success, Mei Mei is uneasy. In the following quotation, Mei Mei talks about how the model-minority stereotype has affected her sense of self:

> They [whites] will have stereotypes, like, we're smart—They are so wrong; not everyone is smart. They expect you to be this and that, and when you're not—[shakes her head]. And sometimes you tend to be what they expect you to be, and you just lose your identity- just lose being yourself. Become part of what-what someone else want[s] you to be. And it's really awkward too! When you get bad grades, people look at you really strangely because you are sort of distorting the way they see an Asian. It makes you feel really awkward if you don't fit the stereotype.

Mei Mei's statement illustrates the pressure that the model-minority stereotype places on Asian students to achieve. Mei Mei's statement points to the way that the stereotype influences how she sees herself. Despite her success, Mei Mei often spoke of her "poor" performance. Mei Mei's teachers and her non-Asian classmates were all aware of Mei Mei's fear of failure. Because the model-minority stereotype sets the parameters for "good" and "acceptable" behavior, students like Mei

Mei may fear that a failure to live up to these standards would mean being perceived as "unacceptable."

Low Achievers

Like their high-achieving counterparts, the low-achieving students who identified as Asian worked hard in school and believed that schooling was the key to a secure future. I stumbled upon my first group of low-achieving Asian-identified students during my initial weeks at Academic High, but since these students fit my stereotype of model achievers rather than my image of academically troubled students, it took me weeks before I made my discovery.

Ming Chang was one of these seemingly model achievers who turned out to be a low achiever. When I met Ming, he was eating lunch with a group of extraordinarily quiet Asian males. when I arrived at their table, they acknowledged me and then quickly went back to playing chess. Their behavior fed into my stereotype of quiet and studious Asian students. Since they did not talk to me, I decided to tell them a little about my research. They told me that they were all from Cambodia (ethnic Chinese or Cambodian). Since I had not met many students from Cambodia, I asked them whether or not they would agree to be interviewed. Although nobody refused, it was clear that they were not eager to talk to me.

At the end of their lunch period, Ming lingered for a few moments and then suddenly began to tell me all about his escape from Cambodia and the recent death of his brother. Ming explained that these incidents had sapped him of his energy. It was with this rather dramatic disclosure that Ming and I began our relationship. I followed him to classes and ate lunch with him and his group on a regular basis. Despite all of this contact and the fact that he regularly shared information about how he was feeling, I had little information about his academic achievement. In my mind, Ming was a diligent and quiet student. He seemed to fit the image of a model minority.

It was Ming's government teacher, Brian Johnson, who finally told me about Ming's academic problems. Ming was on the verge of failing government—a major course needed for graduation. Mr. Johnson approached me about Ming because he felt that he could not reach him and thought that I might have some advice. In his words, "I just don't know what to do. He won't come to [group] tutoring sessions, and he won't come to me for help. We don't have problems personally. . . . In fact, Ming talks to me about his personal problems all of the time." When I spoke to Ming about his problems in government, I learned that he was also failing his English class and that he was having problems in physics. The most surprising fact, however, was not that he was having academic difficulty but that many of his peers assumed that Ming was academically

successful. On at least one occasion a member of the ASA tried to recruit Ming as a tutor for their peer-tutoring program.

When I suggested to Ming that he attend the tutoring sessions, Ming shook his head and said that he would not even consider attending these sessions. Ming said that it would be embarrassing to reveal his academic difficulties and that Asians did not talk about their problems. In his words:

> You know, Asians don't talk about their problem—We just keep it inside—My father would kill me if I talk about stuff.

Ming was referring to the Asian ethos that states that an individual's first loyalty is to his/her family and that "bad" behavior (i.e., disclosure of failure) on the part of an individual shames the entire family (Sue and Sue 1971).

The ironic thing, however, was that Ming often spoke to non-Asians about his personal problems. The stories about his experiences in Cambodia and his experience as a refugee were well known among teachers. Why, then, did Ming feel comfortable sharing these stories and not feel comfortable asking for academic help? In order to answer this question it is crucial to consider the difference between revealing stories of personal trauma and information about academic problems.

Stories of Cambodia evoked everything from respect to pity from his teachers and non-Asian peers. Refugee stories conform to the image of Asians as long-suffering people who struggle against the odds to achieve. In short, stories of personal struggle support the model-minority image depicted by the popular press during this period. The 1987 *Time* article that characterized Asians as "whiz kids" who overcome incredible odds to succeed in school is one example of the articles that glorified the model-minority image (Brand 1987). Although many of the articles that appeared in the 1980s recognized the potential danger of the model-minority stereotype, the articles continued to cast Asian Americans as academic stars who achieve success through sheer effort (Osajima 1988). These articles ignored the problems of Asian American students who are low achievers. It should be noted that Ming and other Asian American students at Academic High were aware of the model-minority image depicted in the popular press and that some students spoke specifically about the "whiz kid" piece in *Time*. Many of my Asian American informants expressed pride in the whiz-kid image. I would argue that Ming's reluctance to seek academic support was based on his desire to live within the boundaries of the model-minority stereotype. Since academic failure clearly contradicts the model-minority stereotype, Ming felt that admitting his academic failure would cause his family to lose face (be ashamed). In the end, Ming's refusal to seek help for his academic difficulties perpetuated his academic problems and left him feeling isolated and depressed.

Ming's academic problems were related to his difficulties with English. Ming had been in the English for Speakers of Other Languages (ESOL) program in middle school and during his ninth-grade year at Academic High. Although he was deemed eligible for mainstreaming, he still had trouble with reading and writing. During the remainder of the year I met several Asian-identified students who were having academic difficulties related to their problems with the English language. Like Ming, these students tended to be rather quiet, and hesitant about reaching out for academic support. They often spoke about their inability to communicate in English. Thus, in addition to the limits that the model-minority stereotype places on these students, another explanation for their reluctance to ask for help might be their discomfort with any interaction that requires verbal interaction in English. Thus, their problems became self-perpetuating.

ASIAN NEW WAVERS

Most of the students who identified as new wavers were Southeast Asian refugees from working-class and poor families. New wavers had a panethnic identity similar to students who identified simply as Asian. New wave students were named after the new wave music that many of these students were said to like. The new wavers were easily identifiable because they almost always wore black clothes and spiked up their hair. The other Asian American students described new wavers as the students who "liked to party."

Unlike the students who simply referred to themselves as Asian, the new wavers did not see school as the key to success in the United States. In fact, the new wave students were almost flamboyant in their disrespect for academic achievement. Like the lads in Willis's study (1977), the new wavers refused to conform to the rules required for academic success (e.g., regular attendance, studying). Their primary goals were to get around the school rules and to pass their classes without having to do much work. When asked what they planned to do after high school, most new wavers responded with vague plans to work or attend community college. Although some spoke of getting high-paying jobs, they did not have concrete ideas about how to achieve these goals. Matute-Bianchi (1986) reported similar findings among some Mexican-descent students.

Another way that new wavers differed from those who identified as Asian was that they were peer oriented. While Korean- and Asian-identified students emphasized family obligation, the new wavers were most concerned with what their peers thought. New wave students understood that non-Asians stereotype Asians as good students or nerds, and they believed

that these images prevented Asians from gaining social acceptance among non-Asians. In an attempt to be accepted by non-Asians, new wave students rejected all behaviors associated with nerds. One new wave girl told me that her new wave friends often cut classes in order to be "more American . . . more cool." Other new wavers simply told me that they wanted to be "cool." They defined cool people as those who are fashionable dressers, good dancers, partygoers, and popular, especially with the opposite gender. These students told me that cool people are not supposed to be overly concerned with academic achievement or rules. In short, cool people know how to have fun, a definition that is in direct contrast to the model-minority stereotype of Asians.

I learned that new wavers often socialized on the southeast lawn of the school grounds before, during, and after school. Although male students outnumbered female students on the southeast lawn, girls were generally present. I met Lee Chau, an ethnic Chinese from Vietnam who identified himself as Asian and socially new wave at an ASA bakesale. Lee sat at the bakesale for three class periods in a row. Although he did not work at the bakesale, he used it as an excuse to miss his classes. We chatted informally about his ideas about Academic High and about my research. Personable from the beginning, Lee invited me to a dance party at a local club that weekend. Although I did not attend the party, Lee agreed to show me life on the southeast lawn.

As an informant, Lee proved to be rather colorful. Since he was often truant, it was difficult to schedule appointments with him. But because he held high status on the southeast lawn, his acceptance of me proved to be helpful in my efforts to gain the trust of his buddies. Lee was popular among his male and female peers. An athlete, Lee is well built and, according to his friends, "able to handle himself." In his own words, "I'm not a wimp. I can defend myself. A lot of Asians can't fight; so they have to go around in gangs. They're small. You know Asian guys." During his junior year at Academic High, Lee and another Asian-American male were the victims of a racially motivated attack that took place at a subway station near school. Although Lee was able to get away with minor injuries, this incident confirmed his belief that he had to be able to protect himself.

As a car owner, Lee earned extra status. During the spring, his car stereo provided music for the group on the southeast lawn. In addition to musical entertainment, cars provided students with a means of escape. This is what Lee told me when I asked him about his "extracurricular adventures."

SL: What do you do when you cut class?
Lee: You know, we hang on the southeast lawn. Sometimes, if enough cars are available, we go places. Last year a lot of Asians owned cars, and we used to drive to

Atlantic City to shoot pool. If we go, you could come with us. Sometimes we just go to the Gallery [a shopping mall near Chinatown] and eat.

On the day that I tailed Lee, we spent most of the day on the southeast lawn, where he smoked, listened to music, played volleyball, and talked.

Unlike Ming, Lee's academic problems were not related to problems with English. Lee simply did not go to his classes or do his work. His teachers described him as "bright but lazy." Veronica Jefferson, his math teacher, said, "Oh, Lee's a character. He's not like my other Asian students. . . . He's capable of doing better, but he didn't bother to take a test. He's getting a D, and his attitude is 'I'm passing.' " This laissez faire attitude earned him a place in the bottom quarter of his class.

Lee explained that he did not care about his grades at Academic because he did not have any intentions of going on to college. His plans included a stint in the U.S. Navy, where he would learn a mechanical skill. For Lee, the biggest attraction to the navy, however, was not the vocational training or the idea of serving his adopted country but the fact that it offered him an opportunity to develop his boxing skills. Lee's athletic abilities set him apart from most other Asians. In addition, Lee had been in fights with non-Asians. Athletic prowess is not typically included in the stereotype of Asian men. In fact, the model-minority stereotype creates an image of Asian men as small weak men who develop their minds while ignoring their physical development. Hence, we have Lee's comment about not being a "wimp" and his disparaging remark about Asians who "can't fight." Lee's rejection of school was influenced by his desire to emphasize his physical strength.

Kevin Ng was another new waver who bragged about his academic weaknesses. He was ethnic Chinese from Vietnam. Kevin had been a high achiever during his elementary and middle school years. During elementary school, Kevin received the ultimate legitimation of his intellectual abilities—the mentally gifted (MG) label. At Academic, however, Kevin adopted a low-maintenance attitude toward his schooling. He went to class only when it was absolutely necessary (tests) or when it struck his fancy, and he did the minimum amount of studying in order to pass his classes.

Kevin often joked that his favorite subject was lunch. In his words, "I never cut lunch!" During the second semester of his senior year, the only classes that Kevin attended on a regular basis were mechanical drawing and Spanish. He explained that he went to mechanical drawing because he liked it and that he went to Spanish in order to "flirt with all the girls." During this same report period, Kevin received grades that ranged from a B in mechanical drawing to a D in elementary functions. Kevin proudly reported that he had received a D in elementary functions despite the fact that he had cut this class 40 times.

According to Kevin, the best way to get through school was to do the minimum amount of work and to have the maximum amount of fun. In his opinion, high academic achievers were missing out on the fun. Kevin explained that he was "more relaxed" about school than other Asians were because he knew that there was "more to life than studying." Kevin criticized his Asian peers for not being able to get along with non-Asians. He believed that studying and doing well in school prevented Asians from being accepted by non-Asians. Kevin wanted to be accepted by non-Asians and believed that being less fixated on school would help him. Despite his efforts, I never observed him socializing with any non-Asian students. Kevin spent all of his lunch periods socializing with other Asian males.

The peer orientation of new wavers was likely influenced by the negative experiences they had with adult authority figures in the United States. For example, new wavers complained of being unfairly hassled by police. In this quotation, a new waver complains about experiences that he and his friends have had with security guards at a local mall:

The security there—I think they're prejudice[d]. So, every time we stand around, not in the way of other people, still they tell us to "move along or else I['m] gonna throw you out." They did not tell the Americans to pass along. They only pay attention to us.

Because of experiences with police and security guards, these students come to school suspicious of all authority figures, including teachers. Soloman (1992) asserts that negative experiences with authority outside of school can leave students with latent resistance.

New wave students complained that teachers were insensitive to them. They spoke of teachers whom they thought were "anti-Asian." For their part, teachers seemed to view new wavers as Asian students who had gone wrong. Erickson (1987) has written about the importance of trust between teacher and student in creating positive educational experiences. The new wavers did not trust the teachers to be fair, and the teachers did not trust that the new wavers wanted to learn. The experiences that the new wavers had with adults inside and outside of school confirmed their belief that they could only depend on each other.

The new wavers' social experiences in school may also have contributed to their resistance. As noted earlier, new wavers like Lee and Kevin had rather tenuous relations with non-Asians. In addition, Korean and high-achieving Asian-identified students viewed new wavers with contempt. The problems that they had with their Asian and non-Asian peers further encouraged new wavers to stick to themselves.

The case of the new wave students suggests that students' identities and responses to schooling are constantly being negotiated. Ogbu's exclusive concentration on what students bring to school because of their particular minority status (i.e., voluntary or involuntary) overlooks this fact. The new wavers' experiences with their peers, their teachers, and adult authorities outside of school all contributed to their resistance.

ASIAN AMERICANS

The smallest group of Asian American students consisted of those who identified themselves as Asian American. As a group these students were diverse in terms of ethnicity, social class (working class and merchant class), and length of time in the United States (4 to 12 years). Like the Asians and the new wavers, Asian Americans socialized primarily with other Asian American students and expressed a panethnic identity. Like the high-achieving Asians, Asian American-identified students worked hard and did well in school. Their motivation for working hard was the belief that education would give them the tools to fight racism. These students spoke about studying law, journalism, film, and ethnic studies in college.

Unlike Asians and new wavers, Asian Americans were outspoken about racism. Although students who identified as Asian and those who identified as new wave spoke about experiences with discrimination, neither group seemed to feel empowered to challenge or question white authority. The Asians dealt with discrimination by emulating model-minority behavior, and the new wavers responded by resisting behavior that promoted school success. On the other hand, Asian Americans fought racism directly. One of the ways that they fought racism was by speaking out about the model-minority stereotype.

Xuan Nguyen is an example of a student who identified as Asian American. Xuan took Honors classes in English and social studies and was a student in the mentally gifted program. Additionally, she was one of the first Asian students at Academic High to be a National Merit Scholarship semifinalist. Born in Vietnam, Xuan came to the United States in 1975 with the first wave of Vietnamese refugees. Xuan is the kind of student that teachers raved about. She is a bright and conscientious student who is not afraid to speak her mind. Upon my arrival at Academic High, the principal asked Xuan to serve as my first student "guide" through Academic High. He described Xuan as a "neat kid" with leadership ability. The following are Xuan's comments regarding the model minority.

> I used to go into classes, and if you don't do that well in math or science, the teacher is like, "What are you? Some kind of mutant Asian? You don't do well in math . . ." You see, I'm not that good in math. I also find that a lot of my friends become upset if they're not good students. . . . I don't think it's right for them to have to

feel defensive. And for people who are doing well, it's just like, "Oh, they (Asians) didn't have to work for it. . . . They're just made that way."

Xuan points to how the stereotype affects high- and low-achieving students. Xuan's understanding of how the model-minority stereotype affects low achievers is based partly on her own experiences. An average math student, Xuan has often been made to feel like a low achiever simply because she does not fit the stereotype of the Asian math genius.

Another factor that distinguishes students who identify as Asian American from others with a panethnic identity is that Asian Americans see themselves as American and Asian. For them, being Asian American means forging a new identity based on their Asian and American experiences and identities. In Xuan's words,

> I have experiences that are similar to other Asians that live in America: that my culture is not all Asian and it's not all American. It's something entirely different. And it's not like some people say, that it's a mixture. It's like a whole different thing. When I say I'm Asian American, I feel like I establish a root for myself here. May parents think of themselves as Vietnamese because their roots are in Vietnam. Being Asian American is like a way to feel I belong.

By establishing "roots" in the United States, Xuan feels entitled to the things that other Americans are entitled to have. Unlike her parents and the students who identify as Asian or new wave, Xuan does not see herself as a visitor who must adapt to the host's demands.

CONCLUSIONS

The data presented in this article supports Ogbu's assertion that perceptions regarding future opportunities and attitudes toward schooling are linked. Unlike Ogbu's work, this work points to variation within a minority group. Korean students and Asian-identified students held positive attitudes toward schooling based on their belief that education would help them to achieve social and economic advancement. Both groups attempted to live up to the model-minority standards. Korean students and Asian-identified students were motivated by a sense of guilt and responsibility to their families. High- and low-achieving Asian identified students experienced anxiety as a result of their efforts to live up to the standards of the model-minority stereotypes. Students unable to do well academically felt depressed and embarrassed. This embarrassment prevented them from seeking necessary academic attention. New wave students resisted any behavior that encouraged academic achievement. Their resistance challenges the cultural ecological position that, as a group, recent arrivals to the United States hold positive folk theories of success. Furthermore, the new wave identity suggests that identity is not something simply located in minority status (i.e., voluntary or involuntary) but something negotiated through lived experiences. Students who identified as Asian American were high achievers who worked hard in school. Although they did not believe that education would guarantee them equal opportunity, the Asian Americans believed that education would allow them to more effectively fight racism and other social inequalities. The Asian America-identified students' continued efforts in school, despite their perception of racism, challenges the cultural ecological position that minorities either downplay racism and embrace schooling or perceive limited opportunities based on racism and resist schooling. Asian American-identified students saw school success as a necessary part of resisting racism.

In short, this study, like the work of Trueba, Cheng, and Ima (1993), suggests that there is variability within groups in Asian American achievement. The experiences and attitudes of the various Asian-American identity groups at Academic High School point to the complexity of Asian American achievement. Asian Americans do not see themselves as being the same, they do not share a common attitude regarding future opportunities, and they do not share a common attitude toward schooling. If we are to move beyond a stereotypic image of Asian Americans and understand the diversity of Asian American experiences, more ethnographic studies on Asian American students are necessary.

NOTES

1. All names used in this article are pseudonyms.

REFERENCES CITED

Brand, David. 1987. The New Whiz Kids: Why Asian Americans Are Doing So Well, and What It Costs Them. Time 130(9):42–51.

Erickson, Frederick. 1987. Transformation and School Success: The Politics and Culture of Educational Achievement. Anthropology and Education Quarterly 18(4):335–356.

Espiritu, Yen Le. 1992. Asian American Panethnicity: Bridging Institutions and Identities. Philadelphia: Temple University Press.

Gibson, Margaret. 1988. Accommodation without Assimilation: Sikh Immigrants in an American High School. Ithaca: Cornell University Press.

Lee, Stacey. 1991. Ethnic Identification and Social Interaction: A Study of Asian American High School Students in Philadelphia. Doctoral dissertation, School of Education, University of Pennsylvania.

Matute-Bianchi, Maria. 1986. Ethnic Identities and Patterns of School Success and Failure among Mexican-Descent and Japanese American Students in a California High School: An Ethnographic Analysis. American Journal of Education 95(1):233–255.

_____ 1991. Situational Ethnicity and Patterns of School Performance among Immigrant and Nonimmigrant Mexican Descent Students. In Minority Status and Schooling: A Comparative Study of Immigrant and Involuntary Minorities. M. Gibson and J. Ogbu, eds. Pp. 205–247. New York: Garland Press.

Ogbu, John. 1978. Minority Education and Caste: The American System in Cross-Cultural Perspective. New York: Academic Press.

_____ 1983. Minority Status and Schooling in Plural Societies. Comparative Education Review 27(2):168–190.

_____ 1987. Variability in Minority School Performance: A Problem in Search of an Explanation. Anthropology and Education Quarterly 18(4):312–334.

_____ 1989. The Individual in Collective Adaption: A Framework for Focusing on Academic Underperformance and Dropping Out among Involuntary Minorities. In Dropouts from School: Issues, Dilemmas, and Solutions. L. Weis, E. Farrar, and H. Petrie, eds. Pp. 181–204. Albany, NY: SUNY Press.

_____ 1991. Immigrant and Involuntary Minorities in Comparative Perspective. In Minority Status and Schooling; A Comparative Study Immigrant and Involuntary Minorities. M. Gibson and J. Ogbu, eds. Pp. 333. New York: Garland Press.

Osajima, Keith. 1988. Asian Americans as the Model Minority: An Analysis of the Popular Press Image in the 1960's and 1980's. In Reflections on Shattered Windows: Promises and Prospects for Asian American Studies. G. Okihiro, S. Hune, A. Hansen, and J. Liu, eds. Pp. 163–174. Pullman: Washington State University Press.

Soloman, R. Patrick. 1992. Black Resistance in High School: Forging a Separatist Culture. Albany, NY: SUNY Press.

Suárez-Orozco, Marcelo. 1989. Central American Refugees and U.S. High Schools: A Psychosocial Study of Motivation and Achievement. Stanford, CA: Stanford University Press.

_____ 1991. Immigrant Adaptation to Schooling: A Hispanic Case. In Minority Status and Schooling: A Comparative Study of Immigrant and Involuntary Minorities. M. Gibson and J. Ogbu, eds. Pp. 37–61. New York: Garland Press.

Sue, Stanley, and Sue, Derald W. 1971. Chinese-American Personality and Mental Health. Amerasia Journal 1(2):39–46.

Trueba, Henry, Li-Rong Lily Cheng, and Kenji Ima. 1993. Myth or Reality: Adaptive Strategies of Asian Americans in California. Washington, DC: Falmer Press.

Willis, Paul. 1977. Learning to Labor: How Working Class Kids Get Working Class Jobs. New York: Columbia University Press.

Multicultural Education: Reflections on Brown at 40

Debbie G. Thomas, *University of Kentucky;*
Phil Chinn, *California State University at Los Angeles;*
Fran Perkins, *University of Kentucky, and*
David G. Carter, *Eastern Connecticut State University*

INTRODUCTION

In 1954, *Brown v. Board of Education of Topeka, Kansas* (*Brown I*) was heralded as the landmark decision representing the dawning of a new era in American society and its educational system. With *Brown,* the Supreme Court ended the systematic educational apartheid that had for so long upheld the constitutionality of separate and unequal educational systems in the United States. Although the decision was intended to ignite immediate nationwide educational reform to end segregation, the winds of change did not blow into many schools until some 15 to 20 years after *Brown.* Clearly, the Court's admonishment to the states to proceed "with all deliberate speed" was not readily heeded (*Brown II,* 1955).

The promise of igniting change offered by *Brown* was stalled largely because many schools considered themselves flame-retardant and staunchly rejected the Court's mandates. Despite promised legal repercussions, many school officials vowed never to comply (Rowan, 1993). With the support of local authorities, some succeeded in delaying compliance and yielded only as a result of military force imposed by the President of the United States. Eventually, even those schools that considered themselves the most resistant and impenetrable, most notably Central High School in Little Rock, Arkansas, ultimately succumbed to the educational reform started by *Brown* (*Cooper v. Aaron,* 1958).

As discussed more fully in other articles in this issue of the *Journal of Negro Education,* the struggle to implement the spirit and the letter of *Brown* continued for years (Gordon, 1994; Russo, Harris, & Sandidge, 1994; Stefkovich & Leas, 1994). Students of color soon discovered, however, that the new dawn promised by *Brown* was an eclipse with prolonged darkness and little light. The monocultural, Eurocentric curriculum continued in force, and many school systems complied only in nontransformative ways. Although judicial opinions succeeded in declaring school segregation illegal, their mandates stopped short of ensuring that the students would be afforded the equal quality educational opportunities they needed to excel. As a result, few if any structural or curricular changes were made to turn schools into educational environments in which students of all hues could thrive.

Phillip (1994) submits that although "sociologists, educators, and civil rights advocates agree that the *Brown* decision has yielded a lot that is worthwhile . . . as its 40th anniversary is acknowledged, many view the occasion as one for introspection rather than celebration" (p. 9). This article undertakes the task of introspection. Focusing on multicultural education in the context of *Brown,* it presents a discussion of ongoing educational inequities in American schools since the Court's decision in this landmark case and offers a model for the effective implementation of multicultural education in our pluralistic society.

BROWN AND THE DEVELOPMENT OF MULTICULTURAL AWARENESS IN OUR NATION'S SCHOOLS

Reflections on *Brown*

As Phillip (1994) notes, "desegregation of the nation's schools has been a difficult equation to solve" (p. 13). Though *Brown* outlawed the physical separation characteristic of segregated schools, it fell short of addressing the psychological separation that even today prevents some students who differ racially from the mainstream from bridging cultural gaps. Merely placing students of color in physical proximity to Whites did not result in eradication of the educational disparities perpetuated by segregation; provisions for equal access were not coupled with provisions for equal quality. Four decades after *Brown,* inequities persist at many levels of our nation's educational system (Orfield, 1993; Weinberg, 1994). Moreover, White flight—the exodus of Whites from the cities to the suburbs and exurbs from the 1960s to the present—has resulted in urban classrooms largely populated by students of color whose socioeconomic status is lower than that of their White counterparts. Consequently, despite legal mandates to end segregation, these students are being educated in classrooms that bear a striking resemblance to those in place prior to *Brown* and that result in "textbook cases of the neglect and inequality *Brown* was intended to erase" (Phillip, 1994, p. 13).

In a 1993 report, Orfield notes that "for the first time since the Supreme Court declared school segregation in the South unconstitutional in 1954, the public schools in that region have turned back toward greater segregation" (p. 1). Not only is this development particularly alarming because the South has been the nation's most integrated region since 1970, Orfield adds, but also because "segregation by race is strongly related to segregation by poverty" (p. 1). In a discouraging commentary on the nation's educational status quo, he concludes that "the country and its schools are going through vast changes without any strategy. The civil rights impulse from the 1960s is dead in the water and the ship is floating backward toward the shoals of racial segregation" (p. 2).

Problem-based Approaches to Multiculturalism

Since *Brown,* the U.S. legal system has helped to promote multiculturalism by making schools and programs more readily available to an increasingly culturally and ethnically diverse population. Mattai (1992) briefly chronicles the rise and fall of numerous efforts to ensure inclusion of the diverse cultures that comprise this nation in its educational curricula and practices. According to Mattai, "the agitation of ethnic minorities in the sixties [1960s] gave impetus to the escalating momentum in demands for genuine incorporation of ethnic minorities" (p. 66). This was achieved largely through the ethnic populations' staunch resistance and rejection of assimilationist ideologies. Although contemporary efforts to implement multicultural education in our nation's schools indicate that significant strides have been made since *Brown,* much remains to be done.

Banks and Banks (1993) describe multicultural education as:

> . . . an educational reform movement designed to change the total educational environment so that students from diverse racial and ethnic groups, both gender groups, exceptional students, and students from each social-class group will experience equal educational opportunities in schools, colleges and universities. (p. 359)

The American Association of Colleges for Teacher Education (AACTE) (1973) maintains that multicultural education is an approach that values cultural pluralism and rejects the view that schools should seek to melt away cultural differences or merely tolerate cultural pluralism. Educational institutions should therefore strive to preserve and enhance cultural pluralism by endorsing the principle that there is "no one model American" (p. 264). According to the AACTE, effective implementation of multicultural education should have four major objectives:

> . . . [to teach] . . . values which support cultural diversity and individual uniqueness; [to encourage] . . . the qualitative expansion of existing ethnic cultures and their incorporation into the mainstream of American socioeconomic and political life; [to support] . . . explorations in alternative and emerging life styles; and [to encourage] . . . multiculturalism, multilingualism . . . (p. 264)

Given these definitions, however, and despite presumably good intentions, many educators tend to employ ill-conceived approaches to implementing multicultural education. These approaches often have deleterious effects on students and serve only to perpetuate the very inequities that *Brown* was designed to eliminate. This is especially evident in three common methods for implementing multicultural education. These can be characterized as the missionary approach (sometimes referred to as the messiah complex), the minstrel approach, and the tolerance approach.

Educators operating from a missionary posture view their efforts as somehow rescuing or saving "culturally deprived" or economically disadvantaged students of color (Delpit, 1992; Ogbu, 1992). These educators believe that without their intervention poor students of color are destined to lead "broken" lives because their cultural backgrounds do not provide them with the skills needed to survive in the majority culture. Such educators see themselves as somehow saving these students from their disadvantaged communities rather than becoming more knowledgeable of the communities and working with them in a joint effort to teach their students more effectively. Such negative perceptions often result in lowered or nonexistent teacher expectations and crippling, self-fulfilling prophecies for students of color. Delpit (1992), describing the inevitable conflict that can occur when students' home culture differs from their school culture and that of their teachers, notes that children of color do not come to school already at risk, but are more likely to be placed at risk upon arrival at school. She maintains that educators often fail to acknowledge issues that result from the incongruity between the students' home and school cultures. Such neglect, can lead to a detrimental misreading of students' aptitudes, intentions, or abilities as well as to inappropriate and ineffective modes of instruction and discipline that conflict with and are inconsistent with students' home cultures. Instead of operating from the perception that the students themselves are deficient, Delpit suggests that educators should scrutinize the instruction and curricula in order to assess and correct inadequacies there. Rather than do so, however, most U.S. educators tend to view culturally diverse students as deficient and attempt to assimilate them by trying to fit them into a dominant cultural model that is not their own (Burstein & Cabello, 1989).

The minstrel approach yields equally detrimental outcomes because educators' attempts at multicultural inclusion result in the perpetuation of caricature images of non-majority cultures. Often the image projected results from an overreliance on superficial and distorted sources such as biased textbooks and media images that are replete with negative stereotypes or blatant omissions of accurate and positive images of minorities. When the tolerance theme undergirds educators' approaches to multicultural education, students generally learn to merely endure the presence of persons who are culturally different without learning the importance of valuing individual differences (Nieto, 1992, 1994). If educational equity is the primary goal of cultural inclusiveness in education, then educators cannot allow themselves to be content with superficial attainment of "politically correct tolerance" or simply "putting up with each other" just enough to "get by." Mere tolerance does not equate with transformation.

Faced with the formidable challenges of meeting the diverse educational needs of their students, educators must reconsider existing curricular and instructional practices such as ability grouping or tracking, which tend to be discriminatory rather than inclusive. In this context, educators cannot afford to trivialize or marginalize multicultural education. It is essential for educators to recognize the merits and significance of multicultural education as a means of ensuring that all students are afforded an equal opportunity to learn and excel academically in a culturally diverse society. In their efforts to meet the demands inherent in a multicultural *perestroika,* educators must strive to develop and enhance their multicultural education awareness, knowledge, attitudes, and skills. Only then can they expect to design and implement effectively the inclusive pedagogy needed to meet the needs of all learners. Such a pedagogy must be multicultural rather than monocultural in content and delivery.

DIVERSE: A MODEL APPROACH

Using the acronym "DIVERSE," we suggest a foundation upon which efforts to implement multicultural education can be based. Specifically, multicultural education is pedagogy that is (1) *D*emocratic, (2) *I*ntegrative/Inclusive, (3) *V*aluing, (4) *E*quitable, (5) *R*elationally Enhancing, (6) *S*ocially Relevant and Reconstructive, and (7) *E*xperiential. These seven components are described in more detail below.

Pedagogy that is Democratic
Democratic principles and ideals have historically served to undergird this nation. Hilliard (1992) aptly maintains that "respect for diversity is the hallmark of democracy" (p. 13). Thus, in accordance with America's democratic creed, educators can be held accountable for making the necessary provisions to ensure that the educational needs of all students are met. Similarly, Greene (1985) notes that because the educational system in the U.S. exists in a democracy, educators are obligated to enable and even empower students of all races, religions, genders, ages, and abilities to participate in and maintain articulate, meaningful roles in society. Given the diversity that has historically characterized this nation, it was at best remiss on the part of the framers of the Constitution not to record these educational assurances at the country's inception. Present-day educators have before them an opportunity to correct this omission. When effectively implemented, multicultural education has the potential to do this and more. Educators can be empowered to design curricula and instruction that include rather than exclude consideration of their student's differing cultural identities. Students can be empowered to retain their cultural identities rather than relinquish them in futile attempts to assimilate into a culture that is not their own and that devalues them by relegating them to "subcultural" status.

Banks (1992) holds that multicultural education is effectively "giving voice to the voiceless" (p. 21). Greene (1985) argues that all persons should be considered in their particularity and concreteness and not forced to assimilate into an identity that not only is not their own but that effectively silences or replaces their voices. Such silencing of individual voices is counter to the purposes and intents of multicultural education. Multicultural education affords educators the opportunity to conduct and orchestrate a chorus so that all are empowered to participate and contribute while each voice maintains its distinctness. Indeed, the resulting chorus will be music to many ears[,] even those which were impenetrable by and imperceptive to "different" voices.

Pedagogy that is Integrative/Inclusive
Integrative and inclusive pedagogical considerations ensure that tokenistic, piecemeal, or segmented inclusion is unacceptable. Educators who are content with the use of curricular design and instruction limited to mere superficial inclusion only succeed in perpetuating and promoting negative cultural stereotypes. Such perpetuations reinforce erroneous intercultural and intracultural perceptions. To avoid this pitfall, it is vital for educators to strive to design and implement curricula and instruction that are permeated with multicultural rather than monocultural perspectives. This entails recognizing the detrimental effect that can result for students of all races and ethnicities when a Eurocentric model is adhered to with only tokenistic mention of other cultures. When such an ethnocentric model is utilized, educators systematically convey to learners that all cultures other than the "mainstream" culture being promoted are to be relegated to a subcultural status.

Projections indicate that the minority population will become the "new majority" population in many parts of the nation (Heflin, 1991; Hodgkinson, 1988; Williams, 1992). As the demographics continue to shift, many educators will find themselves among the "new minority" population in their classrooms. Therefore, the tendency by educators to promote a Eurocentric model that excludes and omits consideration of non-Europeans will become increasingly unacceptable. No longer will educators be allowed to systematically impose their cultural identities on students whose cultural identity differ from their own, nor will they be able to demand that their students be bicultural while they remain monocultural.

Pedagogy that Values Diversity
Valuing the cultural diversity inherent in our pluralistic society is crucial. Educators can make provisions in their design and implementation of curricula and instruction to ensure that the diversity characterizing our nation's overall population is valued in culturally homogeneous and heterogeneous classrooms alike. Students must not be expected to leave their cultural identity outside of the school environment. Instead, educators must strive to ensure that all students are embraced and welcomed into the school and classroom. It is a commonly observed domestic practice to greet visitors to one's home by placing a welcome mat outside the door. Educators are encouraged to make similar necessary provisions so that students not only feel welcome in the school and classroom, but that they continue to be welcomed and embraced throughout their years of schooling.

Coincidentally, the welcome mat analogy has limited applicability for educational settings. It is not intended to suggest that students be expected to pause at the classroom entrance to discard their cultural identities such as when individuals pause at the door of a home to rid themselves of the debris on the bottoms of their shoes. After all, that which is collected by the students on their "walk through life" before, during, and after they enter the classroom is relevant for determining what their educational needs are and how they might best be met. Further, the analogy is not intended to perpetuate the fallacy that students of color should be viewed as visitors to the school and classroom. On the contrary, students are the schools' raison d'être.

This heightened appreciation of diversity in the classroom holds much promise beyond the confines of the school environment. Perhaps students who are empowered to value diversity in the microcosmic school environment will be empowered to value diversity in the larger macrocosmic society, yet another premise consistent with the principles of a democratic society.

Pedagogy that is Equitable and Empowering

Educational excellence and equity are not mutually exclusive; excellence need not be sacrificed for equity. Indeed, in a culturally pluralistic society, the opposite might be argued: one is not attainable unless the other is achieved. In the United States today, educators who subscribe to curricular and instructional principles that promote the exclusion rather than the inclusion of multiculturalism are, in effect, condemning their students to very limited access to both educational equity and excellence. Rather, educators must design and implement curricula and instruction so that all students will have a greater chance of receiving an equitable education. This, in turn, will empower more students to realize academic excellence as well as success in the society-at-large.

Pedagogy that is Relationally Enhancing

Multicultural education must promote the development and maintenance of positive cross-cultural relationships within and beyond the confines of the classroom. An instructional model that continues to be heralded as a viable means of achieving enhanced cross-cultural relations is cooperative learning, which has been shown to promote positive interdependence, individual accountability, face-to-face interaction, small group development, and social skill development (Johnson, Johnson, Holubec, & Roy, 1984). When properly implemented, cooperative learning holds promise for enhancing cross-cultural relations (Johnson et al., 1984).

Pedagogy that is Socially Relevant and Reconstructive

Socially relevant and reconstructive pedagogy enables students to engage in learning experiences that are not bound by sole adherence to traditional modes of instruction and that are relevant to their lives outside of the classroom and school environment. Thus, curricular and instructional practices must be structured around real-life experiences. Moreover, the learning experiences that students have in school should not prepare them to accept passively whatever circumstances society offers them. Rather, students must be guided to challenge unjust practices that infringe upon their rights and/or the rights of others. They must also be shown how to analyze and constructively critique the societal status quo and determine for themselves whether it is acceptable to them or in need of reconstruction.

Socially relevant and reconstructive pedagogy challenges all students, not just those deemed "high-ability" according to often discriminatory criteria, to develop more complex cognitive processing abilities so that they can become more critical thinkers. Recommended pedagogical innovations include nongraded classrooms, team teaching, concept-based curricula, and heterogeneous groupings.

Pedagogy that is Experiential

Students must be provided ample opportunities to become actively engaged in learning. This can be accomplished via pedagogical practices that encourage simulated experiences in class and school and structured field experiences. Such experiential learning helps students to make the necessary connections between what they learn in class and what has occurred or is occurring in real life. When this is accomplished, students might come to view getting an education not so much as preparation for life as it is a life in and of itself.

CONCLUSION

Notwithstanding the difficulties associated with the implementation of *Brown,* the benefits of the changes it wrought have far outweighed the sometimes trying periods of transition experienced as American society progressed from segregation to desegregation (Russo, Stefkovich, & Harris, 1993). What remains is for the spirit of diversity to be carried forward by linking the legal principle of equal educational opportunities for all with the development of a truly inclusive pedagogy. This requires policy makers and educators to transform existing curricula so that they reflect equitably the cultural and ethnic diversity that characterizes this nation (American Council on Education & Education Commission of the States, 1988; Harris, Heid, Carter, & Brown, 1991; Hodgkinson, 1983; Williams, 1992). Moreover, a full assessment of educators' approaches to multicultural education is crucial to eliminating potential roadblocks that might hinder the full transformation and effective implementation of this pedagogical strategy.

In the tradition of African American scholars such as Carter G. Woodson (1933) and W. E. B. DuBois (1953), *Brown* laid the foundation for contemporary efforts to develop and implement multicultural education in American schools. Perhaps school desegregation might have been more effective if multicultural education had been a seed or prerequisite rather than a fruit or after-product of *Brown.* The tensions of integration might have been eased if efforts had been made before, during, and after *Brown* to implement a culturally inclusive pedagogy in U.S.

schools. Instead, educators presently find themselves in a quandary over how best to implement the type of education that should have been in place at the onset of such nationwide reform.

Supreme Court Justice Thurgood Marshall admonished all Americans to accept the challenge of making a positive difference. His challenge holds particular significance for the nation's educators. *Brown* was an epochal decision that laid the foundation for achieving educational equity by forcing open the doors of American schools to all learners, regardless of race, creed, or color. It also established a base for the creation and implementation of multicultural education. However, four decades have passed since the Court's decision was handed down, and the leadership of our nation's schools have yet to build upon this foundation and ensure that all learners receive an equitable education. The proposed DIVERSE model, which moves multicultural education from its present peripheral standing to one of central focus, offers criteria to help advance these efforts so that the passage of another four decades does not find our nation maintaining the status quo and lamenting the lost opportunities of *Brown*.

REFERENCES

American Council on Education and Education Commission of the States. (1988). *One-third of a nation: A report of the Commission on Minority Participation in Education and American Life.* Washington, DC: American Council on Education and Education Commission of the States.

American Association of Colleges for Teacher Education Commission on Multicultural Education. (1973). No one model American. *Journal of Teacher Education, 24*(4), 264–265.

Banks, J. A. (1992). It's up to us. *Teaching Tolerance, 1*(2), 20–35.

Banks, J. A., & Banks, C. M. (1993). *Multicultural education: Issues and perspectives* (2nd ed.). Boston: Allyn & Bacon.

Brown v. Board of Education, Topeka, 347 U.S. 483 (1954).

Brown v. Board of Education, Topeka, 349 U.S. 294 (1955).

Burstein, N. D., & Cabello, B. (1989). Preparing teachers to work with culturally diverse students: A teacher education model. *Journal of Teacher Education, 40*(5), 9–16.

Cooper v. Aaron, 358 U.S. 1 (1958).

Delpit, L. (1992). Education in a multicultural society: Our future's greatest challenge. *Journal of Negro Education, 61*(3), 237–249.

DuBois, W. E. B. (1953). *The souls of Black folk.* New York: Blue Heron Press.

Gordon, W. M. (1994). The implementation of desegregation plans since *Brown. Journal of Negro Education, 63*(3), 310–322.

Greene, M. (1985). The role of education in a democracy. *Educational Horizons, 63,* 3–9.

Harris, J. J., III, Heid, C. A., Carter, D. G., & Brown, F. (Eds.). (1991). *Readings on the state of education in urban America.* Bloomington, IN: Indiana University Press.

Heflin, J. (1991). Demographics in the United States from now to the year 2000. In J. Harris, III, C. A. Heid, D. G. Carter, & F. Brown (Eds.), *Readings on the state of education in urban America* (pp. 57–66). Bloomington, IN: Indiana University Press.

Hilliard, A. (1992). Why we must pluralize the curriculum. *Educational Leadership, 49*(4), 12–16.

Hodgkinson, H. (1983). Guess who's coming to college? *Academe, 69*(2), 13–20.

Johnson, D., Johnson, R., Holubec, E., & Roy, P. (1984). *Circles of learning.* Alexandria, VA: Association for Supervision and Curriculum Development.

Mattai, R. (1992). Rethinking the nature of multicultural education: Has it lost its focus or is it being misused? *Journal of Negro Education, 61*(1), 65–77.

Nieto, S. (1992). *Affirming diversity: The sociopolitical context of multicultural education.* New York: Longman.

Nieto, S. (1994). Affirming solidarity and critique: Moving beyond tolerance in multicultural education. *Multicultural Education, 1*(4), 9–12, 35–38.

Ogbu, J. U. (1992). Understanding cultural diversity and learning. *Educational Researcher, 21*(8), 5–14.

Orfield, G. (1993). *The growth of segregation in American schools: Changing patterns of separation and poverty since 1968.* Alexandria, VA: National School Boards Association Council of Urban Boards of Education.

Phillip, M. (1994). *Brown* at 40: Reassessing the case that changed public education in the United States. *Black Issues in Higher Education, 10*(23), 8–14.

Rowan, C. (1993). *Dream makers, dream breakers: The world of Justice Thurgood Marshall.* Boston: Little, Brown.

Russo, C., Harris, J. J., III, & Sandidge, R. (1994). *Brown v. Board of Education* at 40: A legal history of equal educational opportunities in American public education. *Journal of Negro Education, 63*(3), 297–309.

Russo, C. J., Stefkovich, J. S., & Harris, J. J., III. (1993). Multicultural curricula and the legal system: An evolving perspective. *New Directions in Educational Reform, 1*(1), 47–54.

Stefkovich, J. A., & Leas, T. (1994). A legal history of desegregation in higher education. *Journal of Negro Education, 63*(3), 406–420.

Weinberg, M. (1994). Diversity without equality = oppression. *Multicultural Education, 1*(4), 13–16.

Williams, B. (1992). Changing demographics: Challenges for educators. *Intervention in School and Clinic, 27*(3), 157–163.

Woodson, C. (1933). *Mis-education of the Negro.* Washington, DC: The Associated Publishers.

The Road to Auschwitz:

What's So Funny About Schindler's List?

Bernard Beck

Bernard Beck is a Professor in the Department of Sociology at Northwestern University, Evanston, Illinois, and an actor with Second City *in Chicago.*

Steven Spielberg knows how to make movies that please people, or so everyone believes. His film essay on a provocative episode of the Holocaust, *Schindler's List*, was widely praised. Even those commentators who were displeased or doubtful agreed that the movie was effective at manipulating audience sentiments. The most common criticisms, when there were any, blamed him for being too facile and effective with the techniques of popular movie making.

It was natural for educators to try to use the movie as a tool of instruction for American students about the Holocaust and all the important lessons our generation has decided it must teach us; about the horrible consequences of prejudice, hostility against minorities, uncritical conformism, indifference to the fate of outsiders, and the failure of political courage. The Holocaust is the unmatchable horror and the modern Hollywood movie is the state-of-the-art horror show. So it was a scandal when a school audience of African-American young people received the movie with hilarity. The context of multicultural education revealed some paradox in the work, a paradox unexpected after a history of winning Oscars and honors. It was all the more agonizing because it seemed to show American Black disrespect for an event regarded by American Jews as defining their peoplehood.

To belong to a people is a serious business. We use culture to represent that seriousness to ourselves and others: Treating cultural matters seriously is a way of showing respect for the people whose culture it is. Silence is one of the strongest ways of taking things seriously, and breaking silence about an important subject is one of the most daring things we can do in culture. But silence is also dangerous; it may lead us to forget and neglect that serious business.

It should not be a surprise that sacred matters present cultural paradoxes. Both to speak and to be silent are dangerous, outrageous, and intolerable. The matters that define us and preoccupy us as a definable people are sacred cultural questions, and the uniqueness of those questions is what makes a people distinctive.

Making movies, on the other hand, is a profane and irreverent enterprise—especially commercial, cosmopolitan movies addressed to whom it may concern. Especially "Hollywood" movies. Although our contemporary feeling about movies recognizes their emotional power, their capacity to impress, persuade, and move us, we are suspicious of that power in our more grown-up, responsible moods. The movies, in America, are about entertainment, about making money, about consumption of marketed pleasures. When movies are about sacred matters, they embody a fundamental contradiction. They communicate loudly, vividly, even promiscuously, about things that should be treated with respectful silence. At the same time, they present the opportunity to send a profound message out to a mass audience, a message that is most likely to be heard and attended to.

This contradiction is familiar to us through the conventions of religious movies, such as the Bible epics that were C.B. DeMille's stock in trade. The obligatory avoidance of explicit portrayals of Jesus (as in *Ben-Hur*) or God (as in *The Ten Commandments*) demonstrates how difficult it is to be reverential and entertaining at the same time. It is always safe to be suspicious of the facile, maudlin religiosity of such works. A religious movie is always a trap, as the strong reaction against Martin Scorsese's *The Last Temptation of Christ* shows.

For Jews, the Holocaust is a sacred matter on many levels. For 50 years, it has been understood to be a problem for interpretation. Those who speak about it with the greatest moral authority, the survivors, have endowed it with transcendent meaning: It may not be explained; it may not be recovered from; it may not be assimilated to ordinary theories of human action. It must be regarded as unique and unknowable. At the same time, it must be regarded as paradigmatic and instructive to all humanity. It is fundamental to the efforts of contemporary Jews to explain to themselves what it means to be Jewish. It also dominates the

From *Multicultural Education*, Spring 1995, pp. 13-15. © 1995 by the National Association for Multicultural Education. Reprinted by permission.

claims they make on the attention of non-Jews.

So Jews are concerned with any cultural representation of the Holocaust; they examine its meaning for them and its meaning to non-Jews. What does it say to us, and what does it say about us? Underlying these questions is another loaded question: Who dares to say anything about the Holocaust, what do they want, and what are they doing to us? Every year at Passover, Jews observe the season with a Seder, a ceremony that focuses on the retelling of the Exodus from Egypt, emphasizing that the story explains and confirms the existence of the Jewish people. What is formalized in the Seder is also expressed in the continuing cultural exploration of the Holocaust. It is an exploration of the meanings that Jews will give to their Jewishness. It is an exploration that each individual Jew may do, that Jews may do with (and against) one another, and that Jews may do in the presence of and for the instruction of non-Jews. A movie about the Holocaust is always an exercise in multicultural education for Jews, whatever the explicit apology for the movie may be.

Many peoples have such central themes and events that they treat as defining of their identity and their legitimacy. A significant aspect of claiming to be a people is the assertion of proprietorship over an element of culture, a form of expression, an episode of history. A vital and powerful people can demand to be consulted and respected whenever the world at large presumes to understand, explain, or participate in such a defining cultural enterprise. As the Holocaust is for Jewish self-consciousness, so is the history of slavery for African-Americans or the history of European conquest for Native Americans. For outsiders to mention it is troublesome; for insiders to deal with it is to invite criticism from their fellows.

The cultural repertoire produced about the Holocaust for half a century, often by Jews and sometimes by non-Jews, has become massive. Each generation has raised anew the questions and produced additional material, taking form as historical or scientific research, artistic and philosophical comment. There is a long and significant history of films about the Holocaust from many different countries, including Alain Resnais's *Night and Fog* from France, *The Shop on Main Street* from Czechoslovakia, and Claude Lanzmann's long and powerful documentary *Shoah*, to name a few. We can also remember popular American movies like *The Diary of Anne Frank*, *The Pawnbroker*, *Julia*, *Sophie's Choice*, and the television mini-series *Holocaust*.

Schindler's List is different in important ways. It is, perhaps, the most popular, successful, and effective movie ever made about the Holocaust. High on the list of reasons why people have been impressed with this movie is their belief that it will have a salutary impact on some target audience. It is not only that people have had a positive response to their own viewing of the movie but also that they expect it to make an impression on some others who need a lesson. In other words, even before it was introduced into any school curriculum, the audience for *Schindler's List* was thinking of it as a tool of multicultural education.

The Holocaust was a long, complex event involving millions of people all over the world. There are countless stories to be told about it, including the rise of modern European Anti-Semitism, the institution of the Nazi persecution of Jews, the imposition of the Final Solution, the creation and decimation of the ghettoes of Eastern Europe, the operation of the death camps, the growth of resistance, the flight of refugees, liberation, and many more. The story of Oskar Schindler is a peculiar one to occupy such a central place in our contemporary view of the Holocaust.

Many critics have wondered whether this story should be treated as so important. Why would the book about Schindler's activities make such an impression on a huge-

ly successful, assimilated Jewish movie maker who had never before concerned himself with themes of Jewish identity or history? Why would he treat the project with the care and respect he has testified to? Why would the result be so honored in comparison to all the other cultural products dealing with the Holocaust?

Schindler was a small-scale German entrepreneur of no particular power or importance, a member of the Nazi Party who made business opportunities for himself in the midst of war and genocide. He established a successful business using the labor of Jews who were, to begin with, his slave workers. In the process, he kept them alive. At the war's end, he had managed to save an incredible number of people, at the cost of his profits from the business. Along the way, he had become a savior of Jewish victims, like some other non-Jews now called "righteous Gentiles" by Jews, but unlike most people in the Nazi world, for reasons that the book and movie explore without satisfying us with a pat explanation.

What is wrong with this picture? Although we can observe in passing some important themes, such as the injustice and inhumanity of the genocide against the Jews of Europe and their suffering and courage in the face of it, the movie is focussed on the slippery maneuvers of Schindler, his survival and the success of his enterprise under dangerous conditions, the transformation of his feelings, his complex relations with his workers and the Nazi officials who held the fate of all of them in their hands. In the midst of a great historical occurrence of death and misery to an entire people, this movie has a. happy ending, one which was true but highly unusual. And the agent of this deliverance is not a member of the group that is so involved with this story that defines their contemporary identity, but an oddball member of the oppressive group. Why is he so interesting?

I do not propose to offer a clever answer to this question. Instead, I intend to present something I believe will be more useful, a discussion of some themes and issues of contemporary relevance that are raised by the movie. So a viewing of the movie can be the basis for a continuing dialogue about them.

Separation and Inclusion

This is a movie made by a Jew about a matter sacred to modern Jews. But is it a Jewish treatment of a Jewish question? Perhaps the movie can be seen as the contribution by a Jew who defines himself as a member of a multicultural, diverse, and cosmopolitan world to a dialogue about responsibility, participation, and courage. It may be a reflection of the common (although by no means universal) position of Jews in American society—prosperous, resourceful, accomplished. While Jews in America and the world must still face the challenges of minority status, hostility, prejudice, and outbreaks of hate, their moral challenges are more likely to look like Schindler's than like those facing his Jewish proteges. Spielberg has not preoccupied himself with the plight of the victims of cultural persecution, but with the obligations of someone found among those who are spared. **Living in a multicultural world raises not only questions about differentiated identity and the preservation of distinctive culture, but also the construction of common identity and the creation of a culture of mutual care.** The lessons of the Holocaust from its victims and for them may be more about forbearance and rescue than about resistance and survival. Jews are still victims in the world, but the recurrences of genocide in the modern world have involved people in Cambodia, Bosnia, El Salvador, Rwanda, Angola and other places, where anti-semitism is not the issue but where Jews, like others, may need to be involved.

Strength and Weakness

Jews have found in the Holocaust a painful challenge that has much in common with the cultural preoccupations of other minority groups in many modern societies. Focusing on injustice may bring an awareness of weakness, vulnerability, and helplessness, as well. An overriding concern of groups trying to define their own legitimacy and honor their own virtues is nowadays called "empowerment." The word suggests to us the importance of feeling strong and capable. We abhor the suggestion that we may be unable to command respect, that we may depend, like Blanche DuBois in *A Streetcar Named Desire*, "on the kindness of strangers."

Spielberg has rubbed the noses of his audience, particularly his Jewish audience, in the fact that they required the emerging good will of an unlikely friend to survive. In the midst of a cosmic tragedy, in which courage, culture, and humanity were destroyed over and over, some were saved, not by their own virtue, but by the almost whimsical intercession of a nobody. This disturbing idea is all the more disturbing to members of a triumphal capitalist, individualist, and litigious society whose deepest wisdom has transformed the Golden Rule into "when the going gets tough, the tough get going."

Who Is the Hero?

Movies are popular entertainments that are more concerned with sentiment than with history. They have more in common with parables than reports. We emerge from the movie theater more responsive to an experience than to information. And the experience is as though from the point of view of some particular person. In the long, varied history of popular movies about minorities, underdogs, and subcultures, that is to say, movies about "them," it is typical to have one of "us" play the part of protagonist. The movie is from "our" point of view. "We" are the dominant group members from whose ranks come the movie makers and the hero characters in stories about outsiders. That is the mass culture's way of dealing with multicultural situations.

So the hero of *Broken Arrow,* a 1950s movie about the Apache chief Cochise, is the white scout who befriends the Apaches, played by Jimmy Stewart. The heroes of several movies of recent years about the struggle against Apartheid in South Africa have been sympathetic white liberals. In the popular, award-winning movie about the civil rights movement, *Mississippi Burning,* the hero is a white FBI agent. There is a familiar variant of this pattern which has noble members of out-groups serving as idealized adjuncts to the development of the main characters who belong to dominant groups. Decades of European popular culture have employed the stock figures of saintly black folks and wise Jews to catalyze the stories of white main characters. In a similar way, this year's movie *Quiz Show,* based on the television scandals of the 1950s, deals with the struggles of the Jewish contestant Herbert Stempel to bring respectability for his people through success on the quiz show of the title. But the central figure of the movie is Charles Van Doren, the WASP.

In *Schindler's List,* the Jewish workers being saved from destruction are not the protagonists; the movie is not made from their point of view. Instead, it is the tall Aryan Schindler, even though he is no Viking hero, whose perspective is presented. The sympathetic figure of the Jew played by Ben Kingsley is the familiar out-group sidekick. However, this is a movie made by a Jew about one of the most important defining moments of Jewish history. Why has this Schindler-centered story been chosen to explore the Holocaust?

Oddly enough, Schindler, as he is constructed by Spielberg, is very much like a familiar, stock Jewish character of popular culture—the clever, inventive, ingratiating merchant who survives by wit rather than power, rather like the Jewish title character of Franz Werfel's play,

Jacobowski and the Colonel (brought to the screen as *Me and the Colonel,* with Danny Kaye). The Aryan performing a Jewish role is a mirror image of the modern figure of the "non-Jewish Jew," the emancipated apostate who plays a pivotal role in the history of Western thought. Although the usual distinguished examples include Spinoza, Marx, Einstein, and Freud, Spielberg himself may be considered a candidate for this designation. This turnabout may remind us that there are some approaches to defining group-based individual identity that emphasize cosmopolitan universalism and that see it as a positive result of living in Diaspora.

Conclusion

At first sight, *Schindler's List* appears to be a peculiar kind of Holocaust movie for a Jewish filmmaker to produce and to gather so much honor, notwithstanding its obvious technical competence. In spite of the facile elements available to the director, the peculiar choice of a central character leads to a cheerful tone and a distance from the victims portrayed.

Perhaps the laughter of students, whose real lives are full of daily peril, at a story of how people who are weak and threatened survive anyway will bring us an unexpected insight. This movie shows the unlikely circumstances that saved the lives of hundreds when powerful forces tried to destroy them; it might really be a comedy.

New Colors

Mixed-race families still find a mixed reception

Melissa Steel

Melissa Steel is a senior at Williams College and is planning a career in education. She interned at Teaching Tolerance during the summer of 1994.

In late February 1994, the principal of Randolph County High School in eastern Alabama held an assembly of all juniors and seniors to talk about the upcoming prom. Among the students in the auditorium that day was Revonda Bowen, president of the junior class and the prom committee. She had worked hard planning and raising money for the prom, unaware that Principal Hulond Humphries had plans of his own for the big event.

At the assembly, Humphries asked how many of the students were planning to bring a date of another race to the dance. When more than a dozen students raised their hands, Hemphries threatened to cancel the event. Revonda, whose mother is black and father is white, felt that Humphries' stance against interracial dating put her in a particularly difficult situation. "Who am I supposed to go with?" she asked the principal.

"That's the problem," he reportedly replied. "Your mom and dad made a mistake." What he was trying to do, he supposedly added, was to prevent others from making the same "mistake."

What started as a casual remark in an obscure Alabama high school quickly became national news. Humphries announced the day after the assembly that the prom would go on after all, but the damage was already

done. Revonda and her parents decided to bring a lawsuit against the principal and the school board charging Humphries with "willful derogation of (Revonda's] civil rights." The Randolph County School Board quickly agreed to settle Bowen's lawsuit for $25,000, although it found itself embroiled in a costly, high-profile dispute with the U.S. Justice Department over other possible civil rights violations in the school system.

The Revonda Bowen case illuminated more than the troubling racial divisions in our country's schools. It also brought to national attention the kind of struggles that many children of multiracial families face in their daily lives.

As the child of a black Ghanaian mother and a white American father, I felt keenly the irony of Revonda's question, "Who am I supposed to go with?" It was another variation of the kind of question I—like many other Americans of mixed heritage—have struggled with for years. And as the numbers of families like mine and Revonda Bowen's increase, the question of where we multiracial kids fit in becomes more urgent.

The number of interracial couples in America has increased by 78 percent since 1980. One in every 50 marriages is now between people of different races. In addition to interracial marriages, there were over 8,000 foreign and transracial adoptions in 1992 alone, according to estimates from the National Council on Adoption.

Yet, despite their increasing significance, multiracial families are often made to feel unwelcome or abnormal.

All too often, families that cross racial boundaries are alienated from their disapproving relatives or suffer abuse from intolerant strangers. "Think about the poor children!" is the warning given to interracial couples—a warning that reflects the common assumption that transracial relationships are inherently problematic. The near invisibility of multiracial families in the media only reinforces such negative attitudes. In my experience, however, it's not the children of multiracial families who are the source of the problem; the problem stems from society's thinking that they should be pitied.

Revonda Bowen's experience, while extreme, is not uncommon. School is one of the main arenas in which multiracial children must deal with other people's assumptions about their families. Lauren, a 10th grader from Atlanta, Ga., remembers other kids in her predominantly black elementary school asking her questions about what it was like to have a white father. "They have stereotypes of what a white person's like, so they'd ask [things like], 'How does he talk?' and 'What kind of clothes does he wear?' "

Zorah, an 8-year-old from the same area, was once told by another girl who saw her family that black daddies weren't allowed to be with white mommies. Reactions like these from other kids can make many multiracial children feel different and alone.

Their feeling of social isolation is often reinforced in junior high school, a time when students begin exploring their own identities by singling out those they perceive as different. Jesse,

   Reprinted with permission from *Teaching Tolerance*, Spring 1995, pp. 44-49. © 1995 by the Southern Poverty Law Center.

the adopted Asian American son of a white family, remembers his experience in a predominantly black Washington, D.C., school. "In middle school . . . every kid has problems with identity. And mine were compounded by the fact that not only was I a minority, but I didn't fit into the Asian community, [because] my entire family was white. I knew I wasn't white either, and I didn't have any direction to go. . . . I was a misfit."

The number of interracial families in America has increased by 78 percent since 1980.

My own experiences at this age were just as confusing. When I was in elementary school, my family lived in the Ivory Coast, in West Africa. At the international school I attended, the students came from all over the world. Everybody's family was different, so I never felt that my own family was special or unique.

Moving to Washington, D.C., in 5th grade changed that comfortable feeling. Suddenly, I found that I was expected to be just like all the other African American girls in my predominantly white class. But, having been raised by a white man and a West African woman, largely outside of the U.S., I actually had very little exposure to African American culture, and I didn't fit in very well with the girls who had. I was an outsider to them in all the little ways that matter in 5th grade: I'd never heard of Double Dutch, I couldn't play Spades or jacks, and I didn't even know the difference between "break-dancing" and "popping." I was African and I was American, but I was not African American.

I found that I had more in common with some of the white girls in my class, but here, too, I wasn't totally at home. We may have talked more alike and dressed more alike, but my hair was a mystery to them, as was my life in Africa and the issues I was dealing with growing up black in America.

Throughout middle school and high school, I got used to being unable to identify completely with my white friends, while feeling somehow guilty because I wasn't what my black classmates expected me to be. I gradually realized that my problems were more the result of divisions in American society than of deficiencies in my biracial upbringing, but that didn't help much as the time. I felt stuck in the middle.

For some people, the messages they receive from others during this time can lead to years of painful self-doubt. Jesse, now a 24-year-old graduate student in secondary education, remembers an incident in 8th grade when a math teacher humiliated him in front of the class, insinuating that he should be doing better in algebra because he was Asian.

"I think that incident shaped a lot of how I saw myself in a racial context in this society," Jesse says, explaining that the teacher's statement confirmed his feeling that no matter how hard he tried to fit in, he would always fail. His self-confidence was so deeply undermined that he actually failed three classes in 8th grade, setting a self-defeating trend that would last throughout high school. After years of working through the negative messages he'd received about his identity, Jesse wishes that teachers had been more sensitive to the issues he was struggling with and had helped him address them earlier.

Marisa, a biracial college student, also found that other people's perceptions of her deeply affected her sense of identity as she was growing up. The daughter of a Japanese woman and a Mexican man, she went to school in an almost completely white Southern California environment where people were constantly trying to pigeonhole her. If she got good grades or played an instrument, it was because she was Asian. But when she told classmates that she was part Mexican, they were surprised that she was "so smart."

This constant sterotyping made Marisa unhappy with her non-white identity. It was only when she left home for college that Marisa discovered that not only did she not have to

try to be "white," but she could embrace both of her heritages by identifying as a multiracial person of color. Now she realizes that "it would have been great to have had people be interested in my two cultures . . . instead of [my] having to change everything I was to try to fit in."

Some children from multiracial families have an easier time, especially if they find a group they can identify with. Lauren, whose mother is black and father is white, explains that she doesn't have any problem being interracial in her school. Most of her close friends are black, and her interracial identity is basically accepted by them. She does note that there is pressure to choose one side or the other, which can sometimes be a little isolating. "There's not a big group of mixed kids, so it's not like you can hang with people who are like you. But," she adds, "I don't really mind being different."

Although I was raised to be proud of both my heritages, a it wasn't until pivotal trip to Ghana with my mother that I came to terms with not always being able to fit in. It was the summer after my sophomore year in high school, and I looked forward to more than simply seeing my Ghanaian family again after a four-year absence. In America, I had learned that no matter how I chose to identify myself, I was inevitably perceived as black. So I expected that with my black family and other Ghanaians, I would finally find my niche—at least in terms of my appearance.

But instead, as I walked the streets of the capital city and smaller villages with my mother, I was stared at openly. And I kept hearing the word "Oburoni"—murmured by strangers as I passed by, yelled by excited children as they trailed behind me down a village road, or playfully tossed at me in conversation with a family member or acquaintance. When I asked my mother what it meant, I was amazed to learn that in Twi, her language, "Oburoni" meant, literally, "white person." Ghanaians saw me as more white than black!

Shades of Gray: The Conundrum of Color Categories

Please choose one: American Indian or Alaskan Native, Asian or Pacific Islander, black, white. Of Hispanic Origin or Not of Hispanic Origin. Like a game of musical chairs, traditional racial categories always seem to leave someone out.

Today, the government requires racial categorization for statistical purposes — to monitor and enforce civil rights legislation, and to ensure that businesses and public programs comply with equal opportunity provisions in housing, employment and education. But with a population that is constantly changing, statistics regarding race can be arbitrary and imprecise.

The game of fitting people into categories has been played throughout history. The country's first census, in 1790, divided the population into four groups: free white males, free white females, slaves, and other persons (including free blacks and Indians). By the early 19th century, the census specified that slaves were to be identified with a "B" if they were black and an "M" if they were mulatto.

In 1815, Thomas Jefferson tried to nail down the science of racial categorization. He devised an intricate algebraic equation *(see below)* to show that "one fourth Negro blood, mixed with any portion of white, constitutes the mulatto."

To guarantee that mixed-race children of slaveholders would be included in the slave population, the "one-drop rule" was promoted in the antebellum South. The one-drop rule evolved out of the premise that each race had its own blood type and that a single drop of "Negro blood" was sufficient to define a person as black. It was, scientifically speaking, nonsense — but it got the slaveholders out of having to recognize that many of their enslaved progeny were basically white. Today it is estimated that between 75 percent and 95 percent of blacks could define themselves as something other than black because of their mixed heritage.

In the 19th century, the rise of Darwinian theory gave impetus to a new trend — "scientific racism." Some scientists devoted their entire careers to measuring skull sizes and shapes, seeking physical evidence of a racial ranking that would validate their prejudices. Other scientists measured body parts — from calf muscles to jaws to lips to noses — in an attempt to prove that "inferior" races resembled apes. But no matter what they measured or how many numbers they crunched, the scientists weren't able to come up with the evidence they were seeking. So, quite often, they made it up. The "science" of 19th-century racialists is shot full of wishful thinking, spurious reasoning and outright fraud.

The one-drop rule endures to some extent today. Many people of mixed black-and-white ancestry encounter more acceptance in the black community and therefore define themselves as black. But others of mixed heritage are no longer willing to adhere to this rule because they are determined to acknowledge the diversity of their heritage. Many times, how they identify themselves depends on how they feel at the moment. As one biracial student admitted: "If my mom yelled at me in Spanish this morning, I feel Hispanic; if I went out last night and listened to rap, I feel black." Or as another said: "What category I check depends on my mood."

One proposed solution is the addition of a "multiracial" category to the census and other forms. Opponents to the proposal argue that a new category is just a continuation of the divisions and categorizations that have bedeviled us for so long. They contend such a category would deprive the government of its ability to fight racial discrimination. Some even contend that the multiracial category would constitute an extension of the one-drop rule because nearly anyone could say "I've got one drop of something — I must be multiracial."

Advocates of the multiracial category view such objections as relatively unimportant. As one college professor explained, the addition of a multiracial category "has the potential for undermining the very basis of racism, which is its categories."

The debate over racial categories is bewildering because it is based on ever-changing social standards rather than scientific evidence. In fact, anthropologists tell us that we are nearly all multiracial. If we were to be perfectly accurate, we would all check the box marked "Other."

— *Glenda Valentine*

WHAT CONSTITUTES A MULATTO?

by Thomas Jefferson

Let the first crossing be of 'a,' pure Negro, with 'A,' pure white. The unit of blood of the issue being composed of the half of that of each parent, will be $a/2 + A/2$. Call it, for abbreviation, h (half blood).

Let the second crossing be of h and B, the blood of the issue will be $h/2 + B/2$, or substituting for $h/2$ its equivalent, it will be $a/4 + A/4 + B/2$ call it q (quarteroon) being 1/4 Negro blood.

Let the third crossing be of q and C, their offspring will be $q/2 + C/2 = a/8 + A/8 + B/4 + C/2$, call this e (eighth), who having less than 1/4 of a, or of pure Negro blood, to wit 1/8 only, is no longer a mulatto, so that a third cross clears the blood.

From these elements let us examine their compounds. For example, let h and q cohabit, their issue will be $h/2 + q/2 = a/4 + A/4 + a/8 + A/8 + B/4 = {}^3a/8 + {}^3A/8 + B/4$ wherein we find 3/8 of a, or Negro blood ...

That revelation opened my eyes to the irony of my situation. I was exactly as much white as I was black, but—depending on what side of the Atlantic Ocean I was on—people only saw one of those two colors in me. I realized that there was nothing arbitrary about my personal identity. I knew who I was, and that knowledge remained constant. What was arbitrary was other people's constructions of race and how they perceived me. Figuring this out didn't clear up all my problems overnight, but it did make me feel more secure. I was proud to have the ability to differ from the expected.

And that may be the key for many children of mixed heritage: to be proud of being different. We represent the kind of difference that defies people's prejudices. After all, each multiracial child is the product of a small act of one race reaching out to another—something that we seem to have so much difficulty doing on a national scale.

Peggy Gillespie, a Massachusetts woman who co-designed a photographic exhibit featuring multiracial families, agrees. Herself the white mother of an adopted biracial child, she explains the value of her exhibit as an educational tool: "With so much racial conflict in society, this exhibit provides examples of individuals who have created lives together where race is not a barrier to love."

Another School's Reality

The authors describe mainstreaming at the Dowling Urban Environment Learning Center in Minneapolis — a fully inclusive, racially mixed, general education magnet school for grades K-6 that is not cheap to operate but that is well worth the cost.

························

Jeffrey Raison, Lee Anna Hanson, Cheryl Hall, and Maynard C. Reynolds

JEFFREY RAISON is the principal of Dowling Urban Environment Learning Center, Minneapolis, where LEE ANNA HANSON is a special education teacher and CHERYL HALL is an integration specialist. MAYNARD C. REYNOLDS is a senior research associate at the National Center on Education in Inner Cities at Temple University, Philadelphia, and professor emeritus of educational psychology, University of Minnesota, Minneapolis. The research reported in this article was supported by a grant from the Office of Educational Research and Improvement of the U.S. Department of Education, through the National Center on Education in Inner Cities. However, the opinions expressed are those of the authors.

IN THEIR article "Mainstreaming: One School's Reality," which appeared in the September 1994 *Kappan*, Lawrence Baines, Coleen Baines, and Carol Masterson reported on Coats Middle School, where "mainstreaming was achieved every day under . . . absurd conditions and worse." The situation they described was clearly the result of inadequate communication, misgovernance, and poor allocation of resources. The "reality" of mainstreaming at Coats Middle School was, according to the authors, dreadful.

Yet other mainstreamed schools have different and more positive realities. The Dowling Urban Environment Learning Center in Minneapolis is one example. A decade ago Dowling was changed from a special school for disabled students to a fully inclusive, racially mixed, general education, urban environment center for grades K-6. Although it is a magnet school for the south side of the city, some students are transported from the north side because parents have chosen to send them to Dowling. More than 95% of the student population is bused.

The 450 students who attend Dowling range in age from 4 to 13 and come from five different racial/ethnic backgrounds. The students, needless to say, are not separated by racial/ethnic categories in any school program. Twenty-one percent of the students receive special education. (Fifty of them have multiple physical or cognitive disabilities, and 13 lower-grade students have severe emotional and behavioral disabilities; some of the most medically fragile students in the state of Minnesota attend the school.) The number of learning-disabled students is probably below district averages, owing to early intervention and collaboration between regular and special education teachers.

Dowling is an inclusive school in which thoughtful planning, much hard work, and continuous improvement are in evidence. The school has a clear purpose, there are few signs of emotional exhaustion among its staff members, and depersonalization is kept to a minimum. The levels of satisfaction are high for everyone: staff, students, and parents. Such schools do not just happen. The principal supports a strong conceptual framework and maintains a clear vision of what the school is about and where it is headed. Leadership is shared by the principal and faculty members. Decisions are made by those who are closest to the individuals that the decisions affect.

Coats Middle School, by contrast, appears to be a school where few (if any) persons are in charge, where power seems to rest with someone "out there," and where the levels of satisfaction are very low. Baines and his co-authors report that, in response to a survey, every teacher except one at Coats Middle School indicated that "mainstreaming had . . . deleterious effects for most students" and "contended that mainstreaming had increased the amount of stress in their lives."

In a recent survey conducted by the Minneapolis Public Schools, 100% of the Dowling staff members indicated that they like working at the school. (Citywide, 92% of the teachers reported that they like working at their schools.) Furthermore, measurements of children's achievement show that mainstreaming at Dowling has had no deleterious effects. In fact, children who have attended the school continuously over several years (there is an annual student turnover of about 7%) make substantial progress.

In 1991 the services for mildly disabled and low-achieving children at Dowling were restructured to emphasize team teaching and integrated delivery of compensatory services within mainstream classes. A "collaborative teacher" is assigned to each grade level, and he or she provides

From *Phi Delta Kappan*, February 1995, pp. 480-482. © 1995 by Phi Delta Kappa, Inc. Reprinted by permission.

services by academic need area rather than by label. At the same time, in order to extend the restructuring goal, the staff initiated "20/20 analysis," an assessment technique developed by the National Center on Education in Inner Cities at Temple University.[1] Data are reported for the 20th and 80th percentiles as well as for the median. This procedure permits the staff to focus on the margins of achievement.

In 1991 the CAT Total Reading test was given to all students at Dowling. For Dowling students the 20th percentile on national norms was 18, the median was 50, and the 80th percentile, 78. These figures indicate that, for the school as a whole, the distribution of reading scores was remarkably similar to that of the national norm group. From 1991 to 1993, all indicators of reading achievement showed definite improvement. The improvement in CAT Math Concept scores from 1990 to 1992 was even greater.

High achievers are not neglected in the school. They are regularly challenged by such offerings as advanced computer techniques, higher-order thinking skills (HOTS), drama and art, and accelerated versions of all subject matter included in urban education. Many low-achieving students follow individualized education programs that are planned carefully by teachers and parents and that are used systematically.

One of the most moving sections of the article on Coats Middle School was the story of "Sabrina," the seventh-grader with cerebral palsy who needs help to go the bathroom. At Dowling "Becky" also needs help with toileting. She has been diagnosed with Rubinstein-Taybi Syndrome (congenital skeletal and organic defects), facial and hand disfigurements, and moderate mental disabilities. Although her physical needs differ from Sabrina's, we tell Becky's story here because it demonstrates how a problem similar to the one at Coats was handled at Dowling.

Becky started at Dowling as a 4-year-old, left for a couple of years, and returned as a first-grader. She was placed in a general education class with an educational assistant who provided supports for her as well as for another student. Becky also received services from a special education resource teacher and from speech, occupational, and physical therapists. This staffing arrangement was maintained through grade 3. At that time it became clear to the members of the team managing Becky's case that they were having difficulty meeting her needs. She was not yet toilet trained (despite several earlier attempts) and had become disruptive in class (speaking out, behaving inappropriately, and wandering around the room). The resource teacher consulted with a special class teacher to provide a more meaningful curriculum for Becky and to help toilet train her. With the participation of an educational assistant and the cooperation of her parents, Becky was toilet trained within two weeks.

WHY IS THE Dowling experience with mainstreaming so different from that observed at Coats Middle School? The Dowling community knows that inclusive schools need much focused work, a strong staff, and strong leadership. Indeed, the banner at the entrance to the building proclaims the school motto: "I Am the Solution!" — and everyone means it. Leadership and problem solving are shared. Everyone has a piece of the action. The principal has many functions: teacher, coach, cheerleader, strategic planner, facilitator, listener, customer service representative, and member of the team. All staff members are assumed to be creative and are expected to put forth new ideas and practices. Research is considered an important resource. The school is well-staffed. High-quality education leading to healthy, strong patterns of learning is the goal. Inclusive education is a part of that process.

Dowling is not cheap. In fact, it is quite expensive to operate. The leadership team seeks grants from local foundations and the U.S. Department of Education for new and extraordinary needs when appropriations are insufficient. The worth of the school, however, is reflected in the achievements of the students, the satisfaction of the parents, and the long-term benefits to the community.

1. Maynard Reynolds, Andrea Zetlin, and Margaret Wang, "20/20 Analysis: Taking a Close Look at the Margins," *Exceptional Children*, February 1993, pp. 294-300.

How School Materials Teach About The Middle East

Barry Rubin

This report is part of a series, The Education for Democracy Papers: How School Materials Teach and Misteach World Affairs, *published by the Education for Democracy Project, a joint venture of the American Federation of Teachers and Freedom House. Other papers in the series focus on Asia, Africa, Latin America, and the former Soviet bloc.*

The Education for Democracy Papers *were inspired by the belief that schools must purposely impart to their students the learning necessary for an informed, reasoned allegiance to the idea of a free society. The values and behaviors upon which democracy rests must all be taught and learned and practiced. They cannot be taken for granted or regarded as merely one set of options against which any other may be accepted as equally worthy. The struggles of people around the globe and across the centuries to win, preserve, and extend their freedom should be a central theme in the study of history and world affairs. Students who learn of the struggles of democrats in Africa, Asia, Europe, and Latin America will be in a better position to understand the worth and fragility of our own democracy and to recognize and appreciate the principles that underlie it. Students who have seen how difficult it has been throughout history to secure human rights will be less likely to take those rights for granted and more willing to work to preserve and extend them.*

Some time ago, the Education for Democracy Project asked Barry Rubin to examine the way the Middle East is presented in the textbooks used by American high

The Education for Democracy Papers *series is edited by Joshua Muravchik, resident fellow at the American Enterprise Institute and author of* Exporting Democracy *and* The Uncertain Crusade.

Funding for The Education for Democracy Papers *was provided by the United States Institute of Peace. The opinions, findings, and conclusions or recommendations expressed in* The Education for Democracy Papers *are those of the authors and do not necessarily reflect the views of the United States Institute of Peace.*

schools, with a special eye to how they address the topics of democracy and human rights. We asked him to evaluate whether students who read these textbooks would be prepared to understand events as they unfolded in one of the most complicated regions in the world. His assessment follows.

Mr. Rubin, who teaches at Tel Aviv and Hebrew Universities, is often called upon to help explain events in the Middle East on news and public affairs television programs. He has taught at Georgetown University and Johns Hopkins School of Advanced International Studies and is the author of 13 books, including Cauldron of Turmoil: America in the Middle East, Istanbul Intrigues, *and* Revolution Until Victory? The Politics and History of the PLO.

It should be noted that, while the materials reviewed date from the 1980s and 1990, textbooks have long shelf lives and undergo major revisions only once in a long while. The world having changed dramatically since the last generation of textbooks was published, they are due to be substantially revised. And we at the Education for Democracy Project believe that Mr. Rubin's evaluation will be very helpful for all those involved in textbook preparation, selection, and use—in other words, the entire educational community.

A GOOD TEXT about a distant part of the world should give the student a sense of both those things that are familiar and those that seem strange. It will show that all human beings share certain desires, concerns, and rights, but that different cultures often interpret these differently, leading people to behave differently.

A good text will hide the sins and errors of neither the United States nor other governments. It will not shrink from explaining the repressive, often ruthless nature of dictatorships, the horrors of terrorism, or the fanaticism of extreme ideologies. It will not, in the interest of tolerance, ignore the intolerance in other societies.

The textbooks used in most high schools in the Unit-

Reprinted with permission from *American Educator,* Summer 1994, pp. 18-25. © 1994 by the American Federation of Teachers.

ed States are careful about giving a fair presentation of the Middle East's religions and cultures and avoiding ethnocentrism, in the traditional sense of the word. These books, examined for this survey, do not view Middle Eastern, Arab, or Islamic cultures as inferior to the West, nor do they portray them in terms of derogatory stereotypes.

Most of the information in the textbooks is accurate and possibly superior to what was available in texts in the past. Each work deals at length with such matters as the origins and nature of Islam; the different economic systems and lifestyles in the desert, village, and town; the origin and location of the different countries; the variety of ethnic and religious communities; and the basic history of the area. Although their focus is concentrated on presenting the Arab world, the texts make a reasonable effort to cover the region's non-Arab states—Iran, Israel, and Turkey.

But when inaccuracies and political biases appear in these texts they tend to be in one direction. This can be summarized as apologizing for, legitimating, or prettifying revolutionary, nationalist, and leftist regimes. There is virtually no discussion of such democratic rights as freedom of speech, freedom of the press, and the right to form independent organizations.

Wallbank's *History and Life,* for example, tells students that from independence until now, "Egypt, Syria and Iraq benefitted from strong leadership" (p. 732), without describing in any meaningful way what "strong leadership" means. Beers' *World History: Patterns of Civilization,* tells students, "In 1971, a Baath military officer, Hafez al-Assad became president [of Syria]." It says not a word about *how* he became president. And it says only this about his domestic rule: "Under Assad, the Syrian economy prospered as both agriculture and industry expanded. The government built a railroad network linking cities, ports, and farming areas" (p. 766). In fact, Assad and other dictators have despoiled their countries, prosecuted ruinous wars, and employed demagoguery, often anti-American, to enhance their own power. But students would gain little appreciation of those facts from their textbooks.

Understanding Middle East Regimes

The texts under review manifest the traditional American political characteristics of naivete and romanticism. They tend, for example, to conflate nationalism, populism, and democracy. They reflect the American conventional wisdom which assumes that nationalism is progressive and implicitly democratic, since "the nation" consists of "the people." A populist government, outspoken on behalf of the poor and downtrodden, is also commonly thought of as democratic. To this are added the assumptions that political change comes from the bottom up and that each government represents its people, with the exception of monarchies and other conservative governments.

Few positive statements can be found in these texts about conservative regimes which are, it seems, assumed to be anti-nationalist and anti-populist and therefore less "authentic" than the nationalist/populist radical regimes. Rarely are the democratic freedoms of speech,

press, and association used as a basis for making judgments. The assumption appears to be that these are completely irrelevant.

Examples of these assumptions can be found throughout the textbooks. Beyer's *Eastern Hemisphere,* for example, begins a section about the fall of the Ottoman Empire with the subhead: "People Wanted Change" (p. 356). It is true that *some* people living under the Sultan's rule wanted change, but an American student is likely to read this as "the people" when in fact the authors of change were a small elite of officers who constituted but one of several contending groups.

Elsewhere in that book (p. 365), a Saudi "leader" is quoted as saying that "we" are masters of our own affairs and will decide to whom oil is exported. But the identity of the "we" in this and other cases is not explored.

Hagans' *The World Today* tells students that many people who lived in Ottoman and Persian lands in the early 20th century "did not want to be ruled by anyone foreign" (p. 250). But as the text itself ambiguously implies, few of the subject Moslems came to look upon the Ottomans, their fellow Moslems, as foreign until long after Ottoman rule had ended.

Newhill's *Exploring World Cultures* gets off on a better foot, saying, "Traditionally, politics in the Middle East has involved clashes among opposing rulers or ruling families. The majority of the people were not involved in these struggles," except for occasional village revolts (p. 87).

Unfortunately, the book offers this only as a description of traditional society. It says that with nationalism came increasing support for "new political concepts coming from the West—ideas of freedom, independence, national sovereignty, and social equality." But this statement fails to convey how little has actually changed. The masses are still rarely involved in politics; they are the audience called on to applaud the vanguard parties, military officers, and dictators who act in their name. And in Arab political terminology, "freedom" usually refers not to the rights of the citizen but to the rights of the state; social equality—never a serious policy in Arab states—is translated into a highly bureaucratized and statist socialism.

Tortured Typologies

Mistaken assumptions lead to confused descriptions of the political systems of the Middle East. *Exploring World Cultures,* for example, presents a bizarre typology of Middle East governments that confuses more than it clarifies: "Some Middle Eastern countries like Turkey are moving toward a Western-style democracy. Others, like Egypt, have developed a one-party government dedicated to social reform. Jordan and others have remained as monarchies" (p. 87).

Although this list seems intended as exhaustive, it actually accounts for few non-royal Middle Eastern governments. Except for Turkey—basically a democracy since 1950 despite some breakdowns—it is hard to think of any Moslem country in the Middle East "moving toward" democracy. In the few countries where elections have been held, anti-democratic Islamic fundamentalists have made major gains. The fear that such extremists would gain power has led rulers in Egypt to fix the elections and in Algeria to cancel them altogether. It is also misleading for the text to couple one-party rule with social reform. To be sure, there is plenty of one-party rule in the Middle East, but it rarely accompanies social reform. A case could be made, in fact, that for such social reforms as providing education and medicine, the monarchies have done better than the one-party states. This is not because they are monarchies but because most of them are wealthy from oil. Moreover, it is misleading to lump together all one-party regimes: Egypt has tolerated pluralism for more than a decade; Iraq and Syria are rigid tyrannies.

Exploring World Cultures is not the only text that has trouble with typologies. *Eastern Hemisphere* lists Iraq, Algeria, Egypt, and Israel as republics; Syria as a dictatorship; Oman an absolute monarchy; Kuwait a constitutional monarchy; and the United Arab Emirates a sheikdom (pp. 330-31). In fact, the differences among these three monarchies—presented as three distinct types—are nominal, while those among the four "republics" could hardly be larger. And while it is good to see Syria described as a dictatorship, Iraq is no less of one. It would be far more informative to tell students that all of these countries except Israel are essentially dictatorships, that Egypt is the most tolerant and that some, say Kuwait and the United Arab Emirates, are much less brutal than Syria and Iraq.

Hagans' *The World Today* also has trouble describing the political systems in the Middle East. It introduces the subject after saying that although Kemal Ataturk, the founder of modern Turkey, reduced the power of Islamic religious leaders, army commanders "still have much power." The book goes on to explain that "a number of other countries in the Middle East have governments much like Turkey's. Egypt, the Sudan, Algeria, and Syria all have governments with some democratic features and some army influence" (p. 251). This is a very strained comparison. The Turkish military has assumed power three times in the last 65 years, but restored democratic practice on each occasion. Egypt, although allowing different parties, has never had a truly honest election; Algeria has been a one-party state for 30 years; and whatever "democratic features" Syria has (in the best formalist tradition, it does have a parliament and allows different parties to participate in the government coalition), these are only window dressing for a military dictatorship.

Good Dictators

These tortured typologies display an important feature in common: They fail to draw a clear distinction between freedom and tyranny, democracy and dictatorship. They rarely discuss the treatment of citizens, the degree of liberty, or the level of competency of political regimes. If regimes are nationalist with modernizing aspirations, they seem preferable to traditionalist regimes. Thus, Wallbank's *History and Life* can say, "Syria and Iraq ... turned to dictatorships in order to establish order and encourage progress in their communities" (p. 732).

While these books devote a great deal of space to eco-nomic issues, none of them mentions the devastating economic failure of the "progressive" regimes in Syria, Iraq, Algeria, Egypt, or Libya. On the rare occasions when the texts address questions of human rights, they do not discuss the rights of all citizens but of minority groups. Even in this category, though, much is left out. There is no hint of the Syrian government's massacre of several thousand religious dissidents at Hama. The Iraqi government's murderous chemical weapons attack on the Kurdish town of Halabja is mentioned at most as a Kurdish accusation, although the grim facts have been amply confirmed. Indeed, there is almost no discussion in any of these works of any act of repression by any radical regime. Nor is there any discussion of what it is like to live in a repressive dictatorship.

The Nasser regime has been widely criticized in Egypt for more than a decade for its shortcomings in foreign policy (intervention in Yemen, provocation of the 1967 war with Israel) and domestic policy (concentration camps, torture, damage to the economy, wiretapping). Nonetheless, Nasser's legacy is often presented to American students in admiring terms. Nasser was a reformer who instituted land reforms, built industry, and improved the life of Egypt's peasants, says Newhill's *Exploring World Cultures* (p. 91). He was a "popular leader" who "help[ed] Egypt's poor ... promoted land reforms, encouraged industrialization, and developed the country's natural resources," says *History and Life* (pp. 720, 732).

History and Life does a better job than some in comparing the prerevolutionary and postrevolutionary governments of Iran: "A violent revolution in Iran replaced the dictatorial shah with an Islamic dictatorship led by the Ayatollah Khomeini" (p. 738). In contrast, *The World Today* reports that "the shah's officers tortured, imprisoned, and murdered people to hold on to power" (p. 257). This is true, but it is misleading to say this and not say that the same behavior was at least as common under the Khomeini regime.

Another weakness of the texts is their exaggeration of the practical impact of pan-Arabism. The idea of an Arab world united in the face of Western slights and challenges is perhaps the most venerable misperception of Middle East politics. These books perpetuate it. Although *Exploring World Cultures* has a fairly balanced discussion of the ups and downs of Arab unity (p. 89), a student relying on any of the other texts would believe that Arabs almost always support each other.

Arabs do feel a sense of group identity and solidarity, but the political reach of these sentiments is short. Arab politics has less often been characterized by unity than by rivalries among states, clans, and leaders. The pan-Arab dream has been exploited for the benefit of individual leaders or states by the likes of Nasser, its greatest popularizer, or, more recently, Saddam Hussein. Still, it is no nearer realization than when it was first dreamt.

Students would be served better by texts that describe the emerging local identities within the individual states, the use of Arab nationalist rhetoric to justify dictatorship and subversion of neighbors on the part of governments, and the gap between the theory and practice of pan-Arabism.

Invisible Terrorists,
Radicals as Moderates

In presenting the Arab-Israeli conflict, the tone of the texts is balanced and dispassionate, but their substance tends to be skewed. None of the most widely used texts mentions Arab terrorism against Israel. Few discuss the refusal of the Arab states to recognize Israel, and not one offers a single example of a hardline statement against Israel by any Arab ruler or leader. The PLO itself is ignored to a remarkable extent, and its long-held goal of destroying Israel is reported nowhere except in *History and Life,* which explains that this is a goal that Yasser Arafat foreswore in 1988.

The effect of the textbooks is to undercut the idea that Israel has a real security problem. Thus, Israel's past need to occupy territories and retain a large army, and its longstanding policy to refuse to negotiate with the PLO are rendered as totally irrational. Although this situation has now been altered, it did characterize an era of more than 40 years and created the current situation in the region. The problem here is not a matter of political belief or of a specific viewpoint but a failure to present one side of the conflict.

Beers' *World History* explains that the Arabs attacked Israel in 1948 because "Arab nations supported the demands of Arabs in Palestine for self-determination" (p. 769). The Arab nations and the Arabs of Palestine, however, defined "self-determination" as ruling the entire country. The Jews, supported by the UN plan, favored the partition of Palestine into Jewish and Arab states. The Israeli side on this and other issues is simply never presented.

World History's account of the 1967 War is equally misleading: "The simmering conflict flared into war again in 1967. Both sides had been building up their armed forces. Fearing an Arab attack, Israel struck first in a surprise move" (p. 770). What precipitated war in 1967 was not "both sides," but Egypt's mobilization on the border, its unilateral expulsion of UN peacekeeping forces that had separated the two sides, its announcement of a naval blockade choking off Israeli shipping in direct violation of the 1948 armistice, and direct threats of war by President Nasser. At the time, American opinion was virtually unanimous that these actions made Egypt the aggressor, although Israeli forces did strike first. Future generations will see it differently if they are raised on texts such as this.

For all its flaws, *World History* is not nearly as biased as Hantula's *Global Insights.*

Global Insights introduces the Arab-Israeli conflict by explaining that the land "used to be called Palestine, and Muslim and Christian Arabs and Jews lived there. Then, on May 14, 1948, the Jewish state of Israel was created on Palestinian land. The Arabs, however, did not want a Jewish state on land that once belonged to Jews and Arabs, Muslims and Christians, alike. As a result, conflict broke out between the Arabs and the Jews" (p. 561). This makes it sound as if the Jews alone, who the text elsewhere says consider themselves "the chosen people" (p. 586), destroyed a paradise of inter-communal harmony. In contrast to Jewish particularism, "Many Palestinians feel that their hopes can be fulfilled only by returning to their land and by creating a democratic nonreligious Palestinian state" (p. 562).

With each ensuing war, *Global Insights* says, "the Israelis occupied new territories, which the Arabs want back. They also want the several million Palestinians who fled during the fighting to have their homes and lands returned to them" (p. 618). This greatly exaggerates the number of refugees and, more importantly, the book makes no mention of what Israelis might seek in return. *Global Insights* presents a critical view of the Camp David agreements (pp. 618, 621) without discussing the fact that the Palestinians rejected a treaty that contained a mechanism for the return of territories. Even more striking is that the book does not mention the PLO, the terrorist incidents at the time, the PLO's alliance with the USSR, Arab and PLO statements calling for Israel's destruction, or Israel's return of the Sinai in exchange for peace with Egypt.

Thus, when the text finally mentions (p. 621) that some Israelis want the occupied territories as a security belt, this desire appears quite irrational. Israeli greed seems the only cause of continued conflict.

The text occasionally mentions Israel's position on one issue or another, but usually as a straw man quickly knocked down. As if to leave no doubt about where truth lies, it includes a page-long pedagogic exercise in "distinguishing between warranted and unwarranted claims" (p. 567). In it, all of the examples of unwarranted claims are sentences containing the Israeli view. One example is so amazing that it must be quoted in full: "The Israelis believe that their security would be threatened if they admitted into Israel persons who have been their enemies and who object to the 'Jewishness' of the state." The text continues: "This statement is a prediction that might very well prove to be true. However, since the persons to which [sic] the Israelis object have not actually been admitted to the country yet, at this point in time, there is no way of proving if the claim is true or not. Therefore, it is an unwarranted claim."

In other words, Israel must let in millions of historically hostile Palestinians, and then we will see if they were right in fearing them. This kind of reasoning is biased to the point of being ludicrous. One text that incorporated the Israeli perspective in its presentation was Wallbank's *History and Life*—in its 1987 edition. However, in its 1990 edition, the section on the Arab-Israeli conflict was revised to present a very different picture. The earlier version began with a heading, "The state of Israel faced a hostile Arab world" (p. 685). This was replaced by "The Arab-Israel conflict challenged the entire region" (p. 729). After World War II, said the earlier edition, "Britain proposed that Palestine be partitioned (geographically divided) between Arabs and Jews, but the Arabs denounced partition" (p. 686). This explanation for the failure to reach a solution has been replaced in the later version with this: "Because Jews made up only one-third of the population of Palestine in 1945, an independent government that was based on a democratic vote would have meant a government dominated by Arabs. The Jews were opposed to living under this type of government" (p. 729). There was virtually no chance of such a government, regardless of Jewish opinion.

Both versions mention the refugees generated by the war of 1948, but the older version stressed the failure of Arab states to absorb these people (p. 687), while the new version stresses Israel's failure to readmit them (p. 729). The older version devoted a few sentences to the thousands of Jews who fled the Arab lands at this time (p. 687), but all such references are omitted from the new version.

Each version presents the PLO in a single paragraph, but there is a remarkable difference in the image conveyed. Here are the two paragraphs in their entireties.

Old version:

In 1964, the heads of the Arab states created an umbrella organization for the various Palestinian Arab groups and called it the Palestine Liberation Organization (PLO). The PLO said that it was a government in exile and that it spoke for all Palestinian Arabs. It refused to recognize the existence of Israel and demanded that an Arab state be established in its place. In the next few years, the PLO began to acquire money and arms from various Arab states and the Soviet Union (p. 687).

New version:

In 1964, the heads of the Arab states recognized the Palestine Liberation Organization (PLO) as the only legitimate representative of the Palestinian people. The PLO is an umbrella organization for various Palestinian Arab guerrilla groups and service organizations. In addition, later that year the PLO received observer status at the UN to speak for Palestinian issues (p. 730).

The events described in the new paragraph actually took place in 1974.

In describing the onset of the 1967 war, the old version said:

The hostility of the Arab world toward Israel continued undiminished. In 1967, Egypt closed the Strait of Tiran to Israeli shipping and mobilized its troops in the Sinai. President Nasser called for a general Arab war, declaring that "our objective will be to destroy Israel." Thinking that Egypt, Syria, and Jordan were about to attack, Israel struck first (p. 687).

This has been replaced in the new edition with a more succinct version: "… in 1967[,] Egypt, Syria, and Jordan began to mass their troops along the Israeli border. Israel, sensing an invasion, decided to strike first" (p. 730).

The lack of detail in the latter version makes the events difficult for students to understand. And such a brief statement still managed a factual error: Jordan did not mobilize on the border.

Although no one change is egregious (apart from factual errors), the final result of all the changes is to give the impression of a unified Arab world rightly aggrieved by unilateral, unjustified Israeli actions.

Whitewashes and Scapegoats

The flaws in the treatment of the Arab-Israeli issue carry over into some of the portrayals of the Lebanese civil war. Hantula's *Global Insights* for some strange reason portrays the civil war as resulting in large measure from inflation. Then it says, "In 1976, the Lebanese government and other Arab states asked the Syrian government to help restore peace. Syria sent troops, and order was restored" (pp. 623-24). While it is true that Syria did obtain an Arab sanction for its action, Damascus occupied two-thirds of Lebanon, usurped the central government's sovereignty, silenced the free press, and killed many civilians. Syrian officers involved themselves in drug smuggling. And the civil war did not end.

This whitewash becomes coherent when the book goes on to suggest that violence resumed only because of Israel's invasion in 1982. The Israeli attack, it says, "destroyed many villages and left tens of thousands … homeless" (p. 624). To illustrate this point, it presents a long excerpt from an article by an American doctor (a PLO sympathizer) who says: "We could not find a single structure intact—nor a single person—in the formerly Christian town of Damur." The reader can only conclude that Israel was the culprit. But, as has been amply and often documented, Damur was besieged, looted, and destroyed by the PLO's radical Lebanese allies and some of its member groups years before Israel drove the PLO out in 1982.

Another book, Hagans' *The World Today*, states that soon after the Lebanese civil war began in 1975 other countries became involved: "Israel sent troops to help one group. Syria sent troops to help several other groups" (p. 260). This seems evenhanded, but from 1976 until 1982 there were some 20,000 Syrian troops in Lebanon and no Israelis. The Israeli attack was a single episode, however harsh, whereas Syrian intervention has been enduring. After 1984, there were still 20,000 Syrians in Lebanon and perhaps 200 Israeli soldiers in the far south. The book states that by 1984 several countries, including the United States, sent troops. But this expeditionary force (U.S., French, British) had left by then. More important, Syria comes across in all this as only one of a number of countries involved in Lebanon, rather than what it is: its occupier.

On the whole, the texts are not much better at presenting the 1980s war between Iraq and Iran. *The World Today* states simply that war "broke out" between Iran and Iraq (p. 259), inexplicably avoiding the more informative formulation, Iraq invaded Iran. It mistakenly says that the main cause of the war was a conflict between the Sunni and Shi'a branch of Islam (p. 260). *Global Insights* gives as the reason for the war the fact that the Khomeini regime in Iran was fundamentalist while Iraq was secular (pp. 627-28).

Actually, there were two major causes of the war. The first was Iraq's fear that Iran would win the loyalty of Iraq's large Shi'a population and persuade them to revolt. The second was Iraq's ambition to dominate the Persian Gulf and the Arab world. *History and Life* is the only text reviewed here that provides the second reason (p. 734). The others tend to leave readers unprepared to think of

Iraq as an aggressive country. *Global Insights* reproduces an article from *National Geographic* which goes on at length about the high standard of living in Iraq and the relatively elevated status of women (pp. 628-29). While this is not altogether inaccurate, it is presented in the absence of any discussion of Iraqi repression and leaves a falsely favorable image of Saddam Hussein's regime.

Although the texts resort to less "West-bashing" than one might have found in earlier years, here and there the tendency lingers. For example, *Eastern Hemisphere* explains that by working too closely with the British an Egyptian king (presumably Farouk) angered nationalists (p. 363). This conforms to the stereotype that imperialism allied with reaction and was opposed by nationalists. Reality is more complicated. The British often supported liberal forces in Egypt. At times they were closer to the populist Wafd party than to the palace. In addition, Egyptian nationalists had some sympathy for the king as a victim of British imperialism. Moreover, the most egregious instance of British intervention came during World War II to eliminate pro-Axis tendencies in high Egyptian circles, including the king and some of those "angry" nationalists.

Global Insights says, "Many Middle Easterners fought and died for independence" from European rule (p. 603). Actually, with the exception of Algeria's war against France (which is not mentioned in this text), there was very little bloodshed. A long passage about Syria would lead one to believe that the French loosed a bloodbath there (p. 605-6) whereas, in the main, independence was granted peacefully. Again, the stereotype—heroic freedom fighters against recalcitrant imperialists—is the explanation implied in the absence of specific knowledge.

Factual Errors and Sloppiness

In addition to these thematic flaws, the texts suffer from a number of factual errors. Not all of them are substantive, but they display a sloppiness that reflects very poorly on the research, writing, editing, and evaluation methods used.

A few examples illustrate the problem. In *Eastern Hemisphere* the birth of Islam is given in a chart as in the 500s, a century too early (p. 328), while the caliphs' rule in Baghdad is given as between 700 and 1100 (it should be between 750 and 1258). The Ottoman Empire is said to have begun in the 1500s, but this date is about three centuries too late. (Perhaps the authors were thinking of the period of the Ottoman domination over the Arab world.)

The same book tells us that nationalism in the Middle East began in Turkey in 1919 (p. 357), when a nationalist government had already ruled that country for almost a dozen years. In Iran, we are told, nationalism developed because of Reza Shah and that this monarch "turned his country into a modern nation" (p. 358). Actually, a strong sense of nationalism never developed in Iran, and Reza Shah's effort to transform Iran was a failure for which his son would pay dearly at the time of the Islamic revolution.

The same source says that the PLO "has fought against Israel for more than 40 years" (p. 366), but the PLO was founded in 1964. Golda Meir's name is given as "Mier" (p. 368).

The World Today puts the UN partition of Palestine in 1946 (p. 252), not 1947. It informs us that members of Israel's parliament are elected every four years (p. 253), but Israel is a parliamentary system in which elections must be held at least every four years. The text says that, "Many people suspect" that a fundamentalist group murdered Egyptian President Anwar el-Sadat (p. 258), when this is a fact no one has ever disputed. Two pages later we read that in the 1970s many Palestinian Moslems arrived as refugees in Lebanon (p. 260). The correct date is 1948, although PLO gunmen did come from Jordan in 1970-71.

Newhill's *Exploring World Cultures* places the war in Jordan between the Jordanian army and the PLO in 1971 (p. 91), whereas it occurred in 1970. On the same page Saudi Arabia is misspelled. The same book explains that in 1979 religious leaders overthrew the shah of Iran and "returned the country to Islamic rule" (p. 91), although it had never known such rule before.

Conclusion

In the main, these books are good introductions to Islam, and the geography, culture, and early history of the Middle East. But they do a poor job of dealing with contemporary issues. Just how poor a job they do can be seen when the texts are held up to events that have occurred since they were published. It would be foolish to expect textbooks to predict correctly future events. But good historians have a head start in understanding events as they unfold. Students whose only knowledge of the Middle East was from these texts would more often be handicapped in understanding current events. A student who learned from the textbooks that war "broke out" between Iraq and Iran because of the religious differences between Sunnis and Shi'as (*The World Today*, p. 260) or between Iraq's secularism and Iran's fundamentalism (*Global Insights*, pp. 627-28) would have been very puzzled by the Iraqi invasion of Sunni Kuwait.

Students who learned only of the intransigent Israelis whose concern about security seemed irrational were probably equally puzzled by the eagerness of the Israeli government and population to sign a peace accord as soon as the PLO agreed to recognize formally the existence of Israel.

A student who dutifully studied the description of the ruling Baath parties in Iraq and Syria as supporters of "Arab socialism," which had previously been described as emphasizing "mutual help, social justice and charity" (*Exploring World Cultures*, pp. 90, 92), might be confounded to learn of massacres of civilian populations by the governments of Iraq and Syria.

The overriding fault in these textbooks is that, in an effort to be open-minded, students are taught to approach the world innocently. "Leaders"—with little examination of how they become leaders—are taken at their word. If they say they are for progress, then they are for progress, no matter what that progress may look like.

6. SPECIAL TOPICS IN MULTICULTURAL EDUCATION

Although the goal of such well-intended preaching is to teach an acceptance of others, it is profoundly misleading. To teach a certain amount of skepticism toward the preachments of foreign cultures and governments, and about the distinction between claims and reality, would perform a greater service.

BIBLIOGRAPHY

Beers, Burton, *World History: Patterns of Civilization*. Englewood Cliffs, N.J.: Prentice Hall, 1988. pp. 686-703.

Lots of facts reeled off with insufficient attention to making them interesting. Also suffers from a biased presentation of the Arab-Israel conflict and an indulgence for politically correct dictators.

Beyer, Barry K., et al., *Eastern Hemisphere: The World Around Us,* New York: Macmillan Publishing Company, 1990. pp. 327-71.

A broad, generally good overview introduces the geography and history of the Middle East in understandable terms, though occasionally careless. Rather naive, however, on the modern period, seeking to be both fair and to avoid controversy. Emphasis on parallels among societies.

Hagans, Gloria P., et al., *The World Today.* Lexington, Mass.: D.C. Heath & Co., 1987. pp. 227-63.

Beginning with a discussion of geography and climate, goes on to survey regional history through Middle Ages and through the 19th century. Lots of teaching suggestions and a section on oil. Relatively short portion on contemporary issues regarding Arab-Israel conflict and Lebanese civil war.

Hantula, James Neil, et al., *Global Insights.* Columbus, Ohio: Merrill Publishing Company, 1987. pp. 686-703.

The longest Middle East section of any text examined. Frequent quotes from primary sources make the book livelier. It tries to address the experiences of the common people, social life, and family structure. With these strengths, however, it also tends to be more partisan on contemporary issues.

Mazour, Anatole G., et al., *People and Nations: A World History.* Revised Edition. Orlando, Fla.: Harcourt Brace Jovanovich, 1987.

A relatively straight and succinct narrative focusing on political issues, especially international relations.

Newhill, Esko E., et al., *Exploring World Cultures*. Lexington, Mass.: Ginn & Co., 1986. pp. 63-95.

A more social and economic approach to the region with no historical background. Somewhat spotty coverage of contemporary issues and a formalistic presentation on existing political systems with little analysis.

Wallbank, T. Walter, et al., *History and Life.* Fourth Edition. Glenview, Ill.: Scott, Foresman and Co., 1990. pp. 720-39.

Brief, topical presentations on climate and geography, and short presentations on each country. Sprightly and readable, but watch out for dramatic ideological differences between the third edition and the fourth.

The AAUW Report: How Schools Shortchange Girls — Overview —

— Why a Report on Girls? —

The invisibility of girls in the current education debate suggests that girls and boys have identical educational experiences in school. Nothing could be further from the truth. Whether one looks at achievement scores, curriculum design, or teacher-student interaction, it is clear that sex and gender make a difference in the nation's public elementary and secondary schools.

The educational system is not meeting girls' needs. Girls and boys enter school roughly equal in measured ability. Twelve years later, girls have fallen behind their male classmates in key areas such as higher-level mathematics and measures of self-esteem. Yet gender equity is still not a part of the national debate on educational reform.

Research shows that policies developed to foster the equitable treatment of students and the creation of gender-equitable educational environments can make a difference. They can make a difference, that is, if they are strongly worded and vigorously enforced.

V. Lee, H. Marks and T. Knowles, "Sexism in Single-Sex and Coeducational Secondary School Classrooms," paper presented at the American Sociological Association annual meeting, Cincinnati, OH, August 1991; S. Bailey and R. Smith, *Policies for the Future,* Council of Chief State School Officers, Washington, DC, 1982.

Neither the *National Education Goals* issued by the National Governors Association in 1990 nor *America 2000,* the 1991 plan of the President and the U.S. Department of Education to "move every community in America toward these goals" makes any mention of providing girls equitable opportunities in the nation's public schools. Girls continue to be left out of the debate—despite the fact that for more than two decades researchers have identified gender bias as a major problem at all levels of schooling.

Schools must prepare both girls and boys for full and active roles in the family, the community, and the work force. Whether we look at the issues from an economic, political, or social perspective, girls are one-half of our future. We must move them from the sidelines to the center of the education-reform debate.

A critical step in correcting educational inequities is identifying them publicly. The *AAUW Report: How Schools Shortchange Girls* provides a comprehensive assessment of the status of girls in public education today. It exposes myths about girls and learning, and it supports the work of the many teachers who have struggled to define and combat gender bias in their schools. The report challenges us all—policymakers, educators, administrators, parents, and citizens—to rethink old assumptions and act now to stop schools from shortchanging girls.

Our public education system is plagued by numerous failings that affect boys as negatively as girls. But in many respects girls are put at a disadvantage simply because they are girls. *The AAUW Report* documents this in hundreds of cited studies.

When our schools become more gender-fair, education will improve for all our students—boys as well as girls—because excellence in education cannot be achieved without equity in education. By studying what happens to girls in school, we can gain valuable insights about what has to change in order for each student, every girl and every boy, to do as well as she or he can.

What Do We Teach Our Students?

• The contributions and experiences of girls and women are still marginalized or ignored in many of the textbooks used in our nation's schools.
• Schools, for the most part, provide inadequate education on sexuality and healthy development despite national concern about teen pregnancy, the AIDS crisis, and the increase of sexually transmitted diseases among adolescents.

Reprinted with permission from *The AAUW Report: How Schools Shortchange Girls,* 1992. © 1992 by the American Association of University Women Educational Foundation, 1111 16th Street, NW, Washington, DC 20036.

• Incest, rape, and other physical violence severely compromise the lives of girls and women all across the country. These realities are rarely, if ever, discussed in schools.

Curriculum delivers the central messages of education. It can strengthen or decrease student motivation for engagement, effort, growth, and development through the images it gives to students about themselves and the world. When the curriculum does not reflect the diversity of students' lives and cultures, it delivers an incomplete message.

Studies have shown that multicultural readings produced markedly more favorable attitudes toward nondominant groups than did the traditional reading lists, that academic achievement for all students was linked to use of nonsexist and multicultural materials, and that sex-role stereotyping was reduced in students whose curriculum portrayed males and females in non-stereotypical roles. Yet during the 1980s, federal support for reform regarding sex and race equity dropped, and a 1989 study showed that of the ten books most frequently assigned in public high school English courses only one was written by a woman and none by members of minority groups.

The "evaded" curriculum is a term coined in this report to refer to matters central to the lives of students that are touched on only briefly, if at all, in most schools. The United States has the highest rate of teenage childbearing in the Western industrialized world. Syphilis rates are now equal for girls and boys, and more teenage girls than boys contract gonorrhea. Although in the adult population AIDS is nine times more prevalent in men than in women, the same is not true for young people. In a District of Columbia study, the rate of HIV infection for girls was almost three times that for boys. Despite all of this, adequate sex and health education is the exception rather than the rule.

Adolescence is a difficult period for all young people, but it is particularly difficult for girls, who are far more likely to develop eating disorders and experience depression. Adolescent girls attempt suicide four to five times as often as boys (although boys, who choose more lethal methods, are more likely to be successful in their attempts).

Despite medical studies indicating that roughly equal proportions of girls and boys suffer from learning disabilities, more than twice as many boys are identified by school personnel as in need of special-education services for learning-disabled students.
U.S. Department of Education, Office for Civil Rights, 1988.

Perhaps the most evaded of all topics in schools is the issue of gender and power. As girls mature they confront a culture that both idealizes and exploits the sexuality of young women while assigning them roles that are clearly less valued than male roles. If we do not begin to discuss more openly the ways in which

ascribed power—whether on the basis of race, sex, class, sexual orientation, or religion—affects individual lives, we cannot truly prepare our students for responsible citizenship.

These issues are discussed in detail and the research fully annotated in Part 4/Chapters 1 and 3 of The AAUW Report.

How Do Race/Ethnicity and Socioeconomic Status Affect Achievement in School?

• Girls from low-income families face particularly severe obstacles. Socioeconomic status, more than any other variable, affects access to school resources and educational outcomes.
• Test scores of low-socioeconomic-status girls are somewhat better than for boys from the same background in the lower grades, but by high school these differences disappear. Among high-socioeconomic-status students, boys generally outperform girls regardless of race/ethnicity.
• Girls and boys with the same Math SAT scores do not do equally well in college—girls do better.

In most cases tests reflect rather than cause inequities in American education. The fact that groups score differently on a test does not necessarily mean that the test is biased. If, however, the score differences are related to the validity of the test—for example, if girls and boys know about the same amount of math but boys' test scores are consistently and significantly higher—then the test is biased.

A number of aspects of a test—beyond that which is being tested—can affect the score. For example, girls tend to score better than boys on essay tests, boys better than girls on multiple-choice items. Even today many girls and boys come to a testing situation with different interests and experiences. Thus a reading-comprehension passage that focuses on baseball scores will tend to favor boys, while a question testing the same skills that focuses on child care will tend to favor girls.

These issues are discussed in detail and the research fully annotated in Part 3 of The AAUW Report.

Why Do Girls Drop Out and What Are the Consequences?

• Pregnancy is not the only reason girls drop out of school. In fact, less than half the girls who leave school give pregnancy as the reason.
• Dropout rates for Hispanic girls vary considerably by national origin: Puerto Rican and Cuban American girls are more likely to drop out than are boys from the same cultures or other Hispanic girls.
• Childhood poverty is almost inescapable in single-parent families headed by women without a high school diploma: 77 percent for whites and 87 percent for African Americans.

In a recent study, 37 percent of the female drop-outs compared to only 5 percent of the male drop-outs cited "family-related problems" as the reason they left high school. Traditional gender roles place greater family responsibilities on adolescent girls than on their brothers. Girls are often expected to "help out" with caretaking responsibilities; boys rarely encounter this expectation.

There has been little change in sex-segregated enrollment patterns in vocational education: girls are enrolled primarily in office and business-training programs, boys in programs leading to higher-paying jobs in the trades.

U.S. Department of Education, 1989.

However, girls as well as boys also drop out of school simply because they do not consider school pleasant or worthwhile. Asked what a worthwhile school experience would be, a group of teenage girls responded, "School would be fun. Our teachers would be excited and lively, not bored. They would act caring and take time to understand how students feel. . . . Boys would treat us with respect. If they run by and grab your tits, they would get into trouble."*

Women and children are the most impoverished members of our society. Inadequate education not only limits opportunities for women but jeopardizes their children's—and the nation's—future.

These issues are discussed in detail and the research fully annotated in Part 2/Chapters 4 and 6 of The AAUW Report.

The research reviewed in this report challenges traditional assumptions about the egalitarian nature of American schools. Young women in the United States today are still not participating equally in our educational system. Research documents that girls do not receive equitable amounts of teacher attention, that they are less apt than boys to see themselves reflected in the materials they study, and that they often are not expected or encouraged to pursue higher level mathematics and science courses. The implications are clear; the system must change.

We now have a window of opportunity that must not be missed. Efforts to improve public education are under way around the nation. We must move girls from the sidelines to the center of educational planning. The nation can no longer afford to ignore the potential of girls and young women. Whether one looks at the issues from an economic, political, or social perspective, girls are one-half of our future.

Significant improvements in the educational opportunities available to girls have occurred in the past two decades. However, twenty years after the passage of Title IX, the achievement of sex- and gender-equitable education remains an elusive dream. The time to turn dreams to reality is now. The

current education-reform movement cannot succeed if it continues to ignore half of its constituents. The issues are urgent; our actions must be swift and effective.

— The Recommendations —

Strengthened Reinforcement of Title IX Is Essential.

1. Require school districts to assess and report on a regular basis to the Office for Civil Rights in the U.S. Department of Education on their own Title IX compliance measures.
2. Fund the Office for Civil Rights at a level that permits increased compliance reviews and full and prompt investigation of Title IX complaints.
3. In assessing the status of Title IX compliance, school districts must include a review of the treatment of pregnant teens and teen parents. Evidence indicates that these students are still the victims of discriminatory treatment in many schools.

Teachers, Administrators and Counselors Must Be Prepared and Encouraged to Bring Gender Equity and Awareness to Every Aspect of Schooling.

4. State certification standards for teachers and administrators should require course work on gender issues, including new research on women, bias in classroom-interaction patterns, and the ways in which schools can develop and implement gender-fair multicultural curricula.
5. If a national teacher examination is developed, it should include items on methods for achieving gender equity in the classroom and in curricula.
6. Teachers, administrators, and counselors should be evaluated on the degree to which they promote and encourage gender-equitable and multicultural education.
7. Support and released time must be provided by school districts for teacher-initiated research on curricula and classroom variables that affect student learning. Gender equity should be a focus of this research and a criterion for awarding funds.
8. School-improvement efforts must include a focus on the ongoing professional development of teachers and administrators, including those working in specialized areas such as bilingual, compensatory, special, and vocational education.
9. Teacher-training courses must not perpetuate assumptions about the superiority of traits and activities traditionally ascribed to males in our society. Assertive and affiliative skills as well as verbal and mathematical skills must be fostered in both girls and boys.
10. Teachers must help girls develop positive views of themselves and their futures, as well as an understanding of the obstacles women must overcome in a society where their options and opportunities are still limited by gender stereotypes and assumptions.

---

*As quoted in *In Their Own Voices: Young Women Talk About Dropping Out,* Project on Equal Education Rights (New York, National Organization for Women Legal Defense and Education Fund, 1988), p. 12.

The Formal School Curriculum Must Include the Experiences of Women and Men From All Walks of Life. Girls and Boys Must See Women and Girls Reflected and Valued in the Materials They Study.

11. Federal and state funding must be used to support research, development, and follow-up study of gender-fair multicultural curricular models.

12. The Women's Educational Equity Act Program (WEEAP) in the U.S. Department of Education must receive increased funding in order to continue the development of curricular materials and models, and to assist school districts in Title IX compliance.

13. School curricula should deal directly with issues of power, gender politics, and violence against women. Better-informed girls are better equipped to make decisions about their futures. Girls and young women who have a strong sense of themselves are better able to confront violence and abuse in their lives.

14. Educational organizations must support, via conferences, meetings, budget deliberations, and policy decisions, the development of gender-fair multicultural curricula in all areas of instruction.

15. Curricula for young children must not perpetuate gender stereotypes and should reflect sensitivity to different learning styles.

Girls Must Be Educated and Encouraged to Understand That Mathematics and the Sciences Are Important and Relevant to Their Lives. Girls Must Be Actively Supported in Pursuing Education and Employment in These Areas.

16. Existing equity guidelines should be effectively implemented in all programs supported by local, state, and federal governments. Specific attention must be directed toward including women on planning committees and focusing on girls and women in the goals, instructional strategies, teacher training, and research components of these programs.

17. The federal government must fund and encourage research on the effect on girls and boys of new curricula in the sciences and mathematics. Research is needed particularly in science areas where boys appear to be improving their performance while girls are not.

18. Educational institutions, professional organizations, and the business community must work together to dispel myths about math and science as "inappropriate" fields for women.

19. Local schools and communities must encourage and support girls studying science and mathematics by showcasing women role models in scientific and technological fields, disseminating career information, and offering "hands-on" experiences and work groups in science and math classes.

20. Local schools should seek strong links with youth-serving organizations that have developed successful out-of-school programs for girls in mathematics and science and with those girls' schools that have developed effective programs in these areas.

Continued Attention to Gender Equity in Vocational Education Programs Must Be a High Priority at Every Level of Educational Governance and Administration.

21. Linkages must be developed with the private sector to help ensure that girls with training in nontraditional areas find appropriate employment.

22. The use of a discretionary process for awarding vocational-education funds should be encouraged to prompt innovative efforts.

23. All states should be required to make support services (such as child care and transportation) available to both vocational and prevocational students.

24. There must be continuing research on the effectiveness of vocational education for girls and the extent to which the 1990 Vocational Education Amendments benefit girls.

Testing and Assessment Must Serve as Stepping Stones Not Stop Signs. New Tests and Testing Techniques Must Accurately Reflect the Abilities of Both Girls and Boys.

25. Test scores should not be the only factor considered in admissions or the awarding of scholarships.

26. General aptitude and achievement tests should balance sex differences in item types and contexts. Tests should favor neither females nor males.

27. Tests that relate to "real life situations" should reflect the experiences of both girls and boys.

Girls and Women Must Play a Central Role in Educational Reform. The Experiences, Strengths, and Needs of Girls From Every Race and Social Class Must Be Considered in Order to Provide Excellence and Equity for All Our Nation's Students.

28. National, state, and local governing bodies should ensure that women of diverse backgrounds are equitably represented on committees and commissions on educational reform.

29. Receipt of government funding for in-service and professional development programs should be conditioned upon evidence of efforts to increase the number of women in positions in which they are underrepresented. All levels of government have a role to play in increasing the numbers of women, especially women of color, in education-management and policy positions.

30. The U.S. Department of Education's Office of Educational Research and Improvement (OERI) should establish an advisory panel of gender-equity experts to work with OERI to develop a research and dissemination agenda to foster gender-equitable education in the nation's classrooms.

31. Federal and state agencies must collect, analyze, and report data broken down by race/ethnicity, sex, and some measure of socioeconomic status, such as parental income or education. National standards for use by all school districts should be developed so that data are comparable across district and state lines.

32. National standards for computing dropout rates should be developed for use by all school districts.

33. Professional organizations should ensure that women serve on education-focused committees. Organizations should utilize the expertise of their female membership when developing educational initiatives.

34. Local schools must call on the expertise of teachers, a majority of whom are women, in their restructuring efforts.

35. Women teachers must be encouraged and supported to seek administrative positions and elected office, where they can bring the insights gained in the classroom to the formulation of education policies.

A Critical Goal of Education Reform Must Be to Enable Students to Deal Effectively with the Realities of Their Lives, Particularly in Areas Such as Sexuality and Health.

36. Strong policies against sexual harassment must be developed. All school personnel must take responsibility for enforcing these policies.

37. Federal and state funding should be used to promote partnerships between schools and community groups, including social service agencies, youth-serving organizations, medical facilities, and local businesses. The needs of students, partic-

ularly as highlighted by pregnant teens and teen mothers, require a multi-institutional response.

38. Comprehensive school-based health- and sex-education programs must begin in the early grades and continue sequentially through twelfth grade. These courses must address the topics of reproduction and reproductive health, sexual abuse, drug and alcohol use, and general mental and physical health issues. There must be a special focus on the prevention of AIDS.

39. State and local school board policies should enable and encourage young mothers to complete school, without compromising the quality of education these students receive.

40. Child care for the children of teen mothers must be an integral part of all programs designed to encourage young women to pursue or complete educational programs.

**The AAUW Report:
How Schools Shortchange Girls**

A startling examination of how girls are disadvantaged in America's schools, grades K–12. Prepared by the Wellesley College Center for Research on Women, the book includes recommendations for educators and policymakers, as well as concrete strategies for change. 128 pages/1992. $14.95 AAUW members/$16.95 nonmembers. Bulk prices available.

For Vision and Voice:
A Call to Conscience

We look forward to the near-term future of multicultural education with a fair degree of optimism, yet we are aware that there are serious challenges before us. The winds of prejudice are blowing across the land; concern regarding immigration is at a high level. Yet this concern was present in all earlier decades in American history when rates of immigration were running high. There is much work to be done to accomplish the goals of multicultural education. There is, however, great hope that these goals will be achieved as our population moves steadily forward toward becoming ever more multicultural. We are becoming less and less like western Europe and more and more a unique national wonder such as Earth has not seen before. The next 30 to 40 years will bring that vision into reality.

We need a vision for the future of our schools that includes a belief in the worth and dignity of all persons. We need to clarify this vision in such a way that it has a holistic character, which takes into account our culturally pluralistic social reality. As part of this effort to construct a vision for our social future in which we embrace our great multicultural reality, we need to consider the French revolutionary concept of fraternity, and its female counterpart, sorority. Fraternity and sorority refer to brotherhood and sisterhood. Our multicultural peoples need to bond together as brothers and sisters who care for and are committed to one another's well-being. A new birth of fraternity and sorority in our national life will enable us to truly care about what happens to one another. Teachers need very much to communicate that sense of caring to the young people who attend our schools, for they are our social future. The teaching profession needs a good dose of fraternity and sorority as well. Teachers need to work together in solving problems and supporting one another's professional efforts on behalf of students.

The future of teaching and learning from a multicultural perspective should include more emphasis on cooperative learning strategies that encourage students to develop a sense of community, which will transcend competition with one another and create a sense of trust and caring among them. We need to stop making students compete with one another, and encourage them to work together. The future should see more emphasis on competition with self and caring community with others. Along with this emphasis on building a sense of community among our students, teachers need to work as a community of concerned brothers and sisters who care about each other's professional responsibilities and autonomy as classroom decision makers. There needs to be more sharing of experience, knowledge bases, and expertise among teachers. They need to learn to team together and teach together more than in the past, and they need the professional autonomy (independence of professional judgment) to do so at their own discretion and not because someone told them to.

More democratization of the day-to-day governance structures of schools is needed, so that competent teachers can enjoy the same levels of professional autonomy as their colleagues in teacher education. A multicultural vision of the future of education embraces the concept that the strengths and talents of all students need an optimum, best possible development. The problems and weaknesses of all students need resolution and assistance. Teachers have a commitment to the optimum educational development of each student. Teachers need to see young people as a treasured human resource whose needs for safety, health, and cognitive and affective development are to be met by their best efforts as educators. A multicultural vision of our educational future includes acceptance by educators of an expanded conception of their responsibility to their students, including a commitment to each student's optimum development as a person; we will see our clients whole. Although students' intellectual development is our primary goal, teachers will see schooling as having a therapeutic mission as well. Diverse cultural backgrounds and learning styles will be accepted and nurtured in a national community of shared educational interests.

The future will also see less dependence on standardized, systemwide, behavioral objectives and more emphasis on permitting teachers at the local school level to develop models for assessing whether or not their students are achieving their educational goals. There will be more informal, teacher-customized approaches to evaluation of student learning and less reliance on rigid statewide, standardized learning objectives. Individual school faculties will be permitted to modify their schools' learning objectives for their students, and students will receive more individualized assessment and feedback on their progress in school.

Finally, a multicultural vision of future education includes a strong commitment to develop a powerful, critical sense of social consciousness and social responsibility between teachers and students. Students will be encouraged, and assisted, to define and to reconstruct as necessary their personal worlds, empowering them to see the world as it is and to make it better if they can. The educational settings of society are important terrain in the struggle to reconstruct public life along more egalitarian and just social policy lines. A multicultural vision of our educational future encourages teachers to adopt a pedagogy of liberation that champions the development of critical social awareness among students and that empowers them to evaluate critically all that they may experience. Education will have a liberating intent; the goal will not just be to teach children to reason critically. It will be to teach children to reason critically in the light of a clear vision of social justice worthy of all of their rights as citizens to achieve its fulfillment in public life. The struggle to see a multicultural vision for our schools adopted by the teaching profession will continue to be closely aligned with the broader struggle for civil liberties and human dignity.

Looking Ahead: Challenge Questions

What would be possible if schools permitted teachers more autonomy in how they assess their students?

What can teachers do to help students develop a sense of social consciousness and social responsibility?

Why would it help teachers and students to develop a "language of possibility" as part of the development of their critical reasoning skills?

What do "transformative intellectuals" or "teacher prophets" actually do in their elementary and secondary classrooms?

How can teachers help students to develop their talents and to develop a vision of hope for themselves? How can teachers help students to develop a sense of public service?

What are the most important challenges confronting multicultural educators as we enter a new century?

—F. S.

Home Was A Horse Stall

Jim Carnes

Yumi Ishimaru was used to picking up and moving on. In 1905, at the age of 20, she left Yamaguchi, Japan, for San Francisco to marry a man she had only seen in a picture. After being detained with other "picture brides" for medical tests at Angel Island, Yumi reached the mainland, met Masajiro Kataoka, and found him shorter than she had expected.

Masajiro, also from Yamaguchi, operated a restaurant off Fillmore Street. After they were married, Yumi went to work as a housekeeper for an American family. Before long, she was expecting her first child. The Kataokas' prospects looked good.

But the great earthquake of April 1906 destroyed Masajiro's restaurant and left the young couple homeless. They lived for a while in a tent in Sacramento Park, then later in a succession of small apartments. Yumi gave birth to a daughter that summer.

Masajiro decided not to rebuild his restaurant. He was tired of city life, of the mobsters who pressured honest businessmen to pay for "protection." He and Yumi and their new baby left San Francisco, and Masajiro made a fresh start as a tenant farmer. He saw a bright future in strawberry farming and hoped one day to own some land.

In 1913, the state of California dashed Masajiro's hope of ever owning his own farm. A new law denied the right of land ownership to anyone who was not eligible to become a U.S. citizen. And, according to the federal Naturalization Law of 1790, only white immigrants were permitted to become naturalized citizens. Although the California alien land law didn't mention the Japanese or any other group by name, its intent was obvious. Ever since the Gold Rush of 1849, white workers in the Western states had seen Asians arrive in increasing numbers to find a place in the American economy. During hard times, competition for jobs brought racial tensions to the surface.

Only white immigrants were permitted to become naturalized citizens.

In 1906, the San Francisco school board segregated all Japanese, Chinese and Korean children into an "Oriental" school. When the Japanese government protested, Pres. Theodore Roosevelt offered a deal: He would reverse the school policy if Japan agreed to let only professionals of certain categories emigrate to the United States. The so-called Gentlemen's Agreement prevented an international confrontation, but bias against the Japanese in California increased. The 1913 alien land law was designed to make people like Yumi and Masajiro Kataoka permanent outsiders.

Farm life was hard work for the Kataokas. Yumi and Masajiro eventually had six children, and all of them had chores to do before and after school. Tsuyako, the youngest daughter, was born in 1918. She got her nickname, "Sox," from white friends who couldn't pronounce her real name. The nickname made her feel more American. Sox remembers that there was no Saturday or Sunday or Monday in the strawberry business, only Workday. And she remembers that no matter how difficult and tiring the labor, her mother was usually singing.

In 1932 Masajiro began renting farmland from a Mrs. Perkins, a strong-willed pioneer rancher whose family owned one of the largest rose nurseries in the world. Mrs. Perkins didn't make Masajiro sign a contract for the land. She even let him build his own house on it. She hired Sox's older sister, Nobuko, to work in her big ranch house. Nobuko got her nickname, "Nee," from the Perkins children, who were tall for their ages and considered her tiny. Nee cooked and cleaned and performed many more tasks than were expected of her, such as chopping firewood. In fact, she was such a vigorous worker that after she married and moved away, everyone else Mrs. Perkins hired seemed lazy by comparison.

Masajiro Kataoka died in late 1940. In keeping with Buddhist tradition, Yumi had his body cremated. Since he had always wanted to see Japan again, Yumi and Nee decided to take his ashes back for burial in Yamaguchi. They went in the late fall of 1941. At that time, World War II was raging in Europe, and many feared that conflict would soon erupt between the U.S. and Japan. Nee and her mother got back to California just before that fear came true.

On Sunday morning, December 7, 1941, Sox, her sister Lillian and their mother were riding in the car. A special bulletin on the radio announced that the Japanese had mounted a surprise air attack on the U.S. Naval base at Pearl Harbor, Hawaii. The girls translated the news for Yumi. "This is

Reprinted with permission from *Teaching Tolerance*, Spring 1995, pp. 50-56. © 1995 by the Southern Poverty Law Center.

terrible," Yumi said to them in Japanese. Because she was an Issei ("first generation" Japanese immigrant), she was not a U.S. citizen. Her native country was now the enemy.

Sox and Lillian knew that their lives were about to change. They were Americans, born on American soil. They listened to the same music, followed the same fashions, pledged allegiance to the same flag as everyone else. But now they wondered how other Americans would treat them. They wondered if the storekeepers would still sell them food. Over the next few weeks, shops in towns around the area began posting signs telling Japanese customers to stay away. Old hostilities found new expression in the name of patriotism. There were scattered incidents of violence against Japanese Americans and their property.

The Kataokas had a mailbox at the post office in Centerville. Every morning, Sox went in to pick up the mail. After the Pearl Harbor attack, the postmaster began holding the family's mail at the window instead of putting it in the box, so that Sox had to come and ask him for it. This way, he could ask her questions, such as "How do you feel about the bombing?" or "What do you think is going to happen to you people?" Sox hated this daily confrontation. She kept her answers short and left as quickly as possible.

The question about what was going to happen was partially answered on February 19, 1942. Pres. Franklin D. Roosevelt on that day issued Executive Order 9066, establishing "military areas" along the West Coast and limiting the activities of "any or all persons" within them. Two months later, Civilian Exclusion Order No. 27 narrowed the focus of the restrictions by announcing that "all persons of Japanese ancestry, both alien and non-alien," would be "excluded" from the West Coast. Even Nisei ("second generation"), or those born in America to Japanese parents, were now unwelcome. The order disrupted the lives of 112,000 people, two-thirds of them U.S. citizens.

Evacuation orders posted on telephone poles and public buildings declared that Japanese Americans had one week to prepare to leave their homes. In the meantime, they had to abide by an 8 p.m. curfew and get permits to travel.

The instructions didn't tell people where they would be going, but they did tell them what to bring: only the bare necessities, like clothing and linens and soap. When someone said they could take what they could carry in two hands, the Kataokas took this literally. They had never owned suitcases, so they got a permit to go to a nearby town and buy two each—flimsy cardboard ones, outrageously priced.

Deciding what to pack was easy; getting rid of the rest was not. Anything obviously Japanese could be interpreted as a sign of collaboration with the enemy. Yumi Kataoka burned her family's Japanese books and letters, advertising calendars from Japanese businesses, even her certificates from a Japanese bank. Many people burned family keepsakes such as photographs and antique kimonos.

As for their other possessions, the evacuees had two choices: either leave them to be stolen or sell them at the going rate. One of Yumi's sons sold two cars, a long-bed truck and a Caterpillar tractor for a fraction of their worth. The Kataokas got $15 for their piano, and Sox was so happy to see it going home with someone that she gave the buyer all her sheet music and even threw her tennis racket into the bargain. Some people in the valley refused to trade their brand new stoves or refrigerators for pocket change, so they stored them in the Japanese school building, in hopes of retrieving them when the war was over.

May 9, 1942, was leaving day. A few days beforehand, Mrs. Perkins got in touch with Nee and told her to bring her whole family to the ranch house for a farewell breakfast. The invitation meant a lot to the Kataokas because most of the other white people they knew had shunned them. That morning, Mrs. Perkins ushered them into her beautiful formal dining room. The long table was set with her best

china and crystal and silver. She usually had someone to cook and serve meals for her, but this time she did everything herself. When Nee and Sox offered to help her bring the food out, she told them that now it was her turn to serve.

After breakfast, Mrs. Perkins drove the Kataokas in her Oldsmobile to the grounds of the Japanese school, where buses were waiting. The fellow who ran the local hamburger stand was the only other white person who came to say goodbye. It hurt Sox's feelings that her close friends didn't show up, but she decided the reason was that they were afraid.

Yumi Kataoka had moved her family many times, but never like this. The bus let them out at Tanforan Racetrack in San Bruno, Calif. No one knew what to expect. None of the Kataokas had even been to a racetrack before. Inside, military policemen searched each person. All suitcases were opened and ransacked. A nurse peered into every eye and down every throat.

On the infield of the track stood new, army-style barracks. Sox said that she wanted to stay in those, but the officer said they were for mothers with infants. He led the Kataokas around back to the stables: Their new home was a horse stall.

The building contained two back-to-back rows of 10 stalls each. Five adults—Sox and her three brothers and their mother—had a 9- by 20-foot enclosure to share. Manure littered the dirt floor. The walls had been recently whitewashed, but carelessly, so that horsehair and dirt were smeared in. And the walls reached only halfway to the roof—there were no ceilings. The nearest bathroom was a long walk away.

Sox worried about how her mother would take such humiliation. She was proud of Yumi for keeping the hurt hidden, for acting as if this were just another move. She knew that keeping the family together was Yumi's biggest concern.

The officers passed out cloth sacks for everyone to fill with hay for mattresses. In the dark stall that night, listening to the noises of all the other

7. FOR VISION AND VOICE: A CALL TO CONSCIENCE

people, Sox couldn't fall asleep. She couldn't stop wondering what any of them had done to deserve being penned up like animals. She couldn't believe this was happening in America.

It didn't take Sox long to learn the local routine, including how early she had to get up to find an empty tub in the laundry shed. Her brothers washed dishes in the mess hall. There were long lines everywhere—for the toilets, for the laundry, for food. As clothing wore out, people shopped by mail from the Sears Roebuck catalog.

Occasionally, Mrs. Perkins came to visit. When she saw the damp dirt floor of the drafty stall, she went home and ripped up the linoleum from the Kataokas' kitchen and brought it to them. She didn't want Yumi's rheumatism to get worse. Another time, she took Sox's broken wristwatch to have it repaired.

For four long months, daydreams and small acts of kindness made their internment bearable. Every night, Sox wondered what the next day would bring. There was very little official news about the government's plans, so rumors were the main source of information. Late in the summer a rumor went around that the Japanese were going to be moved inland, to a concentration camp in the desert. Everyone started ordering high-top boots from the catalog—there were scorpions and snakes out there. According to some people, once they got to the new location, the government was going to drop a bomb on them.

Some of the rumors turned out to be true. At the end of the summer, Sox, Yumi and the other Japanese were packed into buses and driven east into the desert. Sox had never seen a place as dry and dusty and lifeless as Topaz, Utah. It looked like the surface of the moon. But when she saw the rows and rows of new barracks, some of them still unfinished, she could have kissed the ground. She reasoned that if the government was spending the time and money to build housing for her people, then it must not be planning to kill them.

The Kataokas' new quarters measured 20 by 24 feet—a little roomier than the horse stall and a lot cleaner. A single naked light bulb hung from the ceiling. In the corner stood a potbellied stove. By stringing up a few sheets, family members could carve out the illusion of privacy. The communal bathroom had six toilets and no doors.

There were no chairs or tables. People scoured the construction site for materials. In just a short time, many families skillfully fashioned whole sets of furniture from orange crates and scrap lumber. Later, some residents laid out beautiful rock gardens on the barren ground.

Even in this strange new environment, much about camp life was familiar—the crowded living space, the boredom, the long lines for every necessity. But Sox began to notice changes in the people around her. In the dining hall, children made friends quickly and sat together in groups. The family meal—a central part of Japanese life—was losing its importance. A deeper toll resulted from unemployment: Fathers, no longer breadwinners, began to lose their self-respect and, sometimes, the respect of their families. Everyone was aimless now. Everyone was a small step from stir-crazy.

Camp residents had to pull together to avert despair. They formed social clubs and choirs and sports teams. They started newsletters to share information and ideas.

Sox had the good fortune to get a job as assistant block manager. She was responsible for looking after about 200 people in 72 rooms. The managers met every morning to discuss the needs of their residents. Extremes of climate caused many problems, since temperatures often reached well below zero in the winter and over 100 in the summer months. Food was another source of complaint. The animal innards such as liver, gizzard, tongue, brains and chitterlings that made up much of the meat ration were foreign to the Japanese diet. Sox found them sickening. When the quality of meat improved after a while, Sox decided

DOCUMENT

CONFIDENTIAL

After some Japanese Americans attempted to challenge the internment policy in the courts, the War Relocation Authority included the following statements in a confidential internal memo on August 12, 1942.

The action taken with respect to Japanese in this country is justifiable on the grounds of military necessity for several reasons.

1. All Japanese look very much alike to a white person — it is hard for us to distinguish between them. It would be hard to tell a Japanese soldier in disguise from a resident Japanese. The danger of infiltration by Japanese parachutists, soldiers, etc. is, therefore, reduced and the chances of detecting any attempt at infiltration are increased.

2. The Japanese Government has always tried to maintain close ties with and control over Japanese people in this country with the result that many of them have never really been absorbed into American life and culture. Many Japanese-Americans have been educated in Japan. Many, believers in Shintoism, worship the Emperor and regard his orders as superior to any loyalty they may owe the United States. Therefore, the action has reduced the danger of successful invasion by removing an element of the population which had never been assimilated and which might not successfully withstand the strong emotional impulse to change loyalties or give way to their true feelings in the event that Japanese troops should land on our shores.

US and THEM
SPECIAL EXCERPT

DOCUMENT

"A GRAVE INJUSTICE"

On August 10, 1988, Congress enacted a law granting restitution payments for civilians interned during World War II.

SECTION. 2. Statement of the Congress

(a) With Regard to Individuals of Japanese Ancestry. — The Congress recognizes that, as described by the Commission on Wartime Relocation and Internment of Civilians, a grave injustice was done to both citizens and permanent resident aliens of Japanese ancestry by the evacuation, relocation, and internment of civilians during World War II. As the Commission documents, these actions were carried out without adequate security reasons and without any acts of espionage or sabotage documented by the Commission, and were motivated largely by racial prejudice, wartime hysteria, and a failure of political leadership. The excluded individuals of Japanese ancestry suffered enormous damages, both material and intangible, and there were incalculable losses in education and job training, all of which resulted in significant human suffering for which appropriate compensation has not been made. For these fundamental violations of the basic civil liberties and constitutional rights of these individuals of Japanese ancestry, the Congress apologizes on behalf of the Nation.

that the project director must have figured out that her people were human.

The block manager meetings gave Sox and the others some sense of value. But everywhere they looked, barbed wire and police patrols and curfews and watchtowers with armed guards constantly reminded them of their status.

"Americanism is not, and never was, a matter of race or ancestry."

The word around camp was "Don't go near the fence." Most of the military policemen were fresh out of combat duty, and they did not hesitate to use their weapons. At Topaz one day, a man was picking some wildflowers along the barbed wire. A guard yelled "Halt!" but the man was hard of hearing. He kept on picking and was shot. And once, a grandfather playing catch with his grandson went to retrieve the ball from just beyond the fence. The guard who killed him told authorities that the old man had tried to escape.

As the war in Europe and the Pacific intensified, the government realized that many potentially able soldiers were sitting idle in the camps. In early 1943 Pres. Roosevelt wrote to the Secretary of War and contradicted his earlier Executive Order: "Americanism is not, and never was, a matter of race or ancestry. Every loyal American citizen should be given the opportunity to serve this country . . . in the ranks of our armed forces."

By means of a "loyalty questionnaire," Uncle Sam began recruiting Nisei. In all, more than 30,000 Japanese Americans joined the service during the war. Others protested that they wouldn't serve until their families were allowed to return to the West Coast. About 300 so-called "no-no

boys" refused to pledge their loyalty and were jailed for draft resistance. The questionnaire was also used as a means of releasing internees into the work force. In the camps, this process—however objectionable—stirred the first hopes of freedom.

On November 11, 1944, Pres. Roosevelt lifted the Civilian Exclusion Order. A month later, the government announced that the internment camps would be closed within a year.

Sox married a young man named Tom Kitashima in August 1945, just as the bombing of Hiroshima and Nagasaki brought the war to its conclusion. The camp supervisor offered her a job helping to process the closure of the camp. But since he didn't have a job for Tom, Sox said she couldn't stay. Even so, the supervisor found her a good position in San Francisco.

A few nights before Sox and Tom were set to leave Topaz, the supervisor and his wife invited them out for dinner and a cowboy movie in the town of Delta, 16 miles from the camp. There were rules against this kind of socializing, but the white couple didn't seem to care. The supervisor also gave them a blanket for the cold train ride to San Francisco—the government was using old dilapidated railroad cars to relocate the internees. On an October morning in 1945, Sox repacked the suitcase she had been living out of for three years and four months.

Yumi Kataoka, now 60 years old, prepared to move one more time. People were heading in all directions—there was nothing left to go back to. Yumi joined a large group headed for a housing center at Richmond, Calif. In time, Yumi and her scattered children heard reports from the valley that used to be their home. The Japanese school building had been emptied of all the stored appliances. The house that Masajiro had built on Mrs. Perkins' place was gone now, along with all the little things the family had left behind.

Turning the Tide:

A Call for Radical Voices of Affirmation

Bakari Chavanu

Bakari Chavanu is a teacher at Florin High School in Sacramento, California.

Reading essays by the Black feminist thinker, writer, and teacher, bell hooks, in which she speaks of the "awareness of the need to speak, to give voice to the varied dimensions of our lives..." (1989. p. 13) reminds me of my younger days in high school when I fortunately became aware of a distinctive existence of the Black voice in literature and consequently in my own life.

Bused, but not necessarily integrated, into a traditional white high school during the mid 1970s, I reflect now—as I didn't realize then—how this forced integrated school was unprepared for a different culture of students who came loaded with our own distinctive experiences and ignorance to the purpose of attending a predominantly white institution. But as far as I could tell, the first year of integration was not met with physically violent resistance on the part of White students or their parents. I even doubt that myself or the other Black students attending the school at the time were aware of Little Rock or what blood had been shed for us to attend. We were simply indifferent to attending because we could not go to one of the predominantly Black schools on the northeast side.

As I look back on it, high school was a kind of senseless four years of my life. The image of fellow students sleeping at their desks during class constantly comes to mind. So many of my Black peers in my graduating class made conscious and unconscious decisions to not take school seriously. We participated in forms of reckless indifference—skipping classes, refusing to do course assignments or homework, talking back to instructors, and laughing off three-day suspensions which to us meant a vacation. We came to school with little or no missions to fulfill.

I don't wish to make blanket generalization about every Black student at this forcibly integrated school. Some Black students, depending largely on their family background or where they grew up, actually made good grades and wound up, like myself, attending college (albeit through much trial and error and certainly not by design). One year, the school even elected a Black male as student body president; however, many of us didn't make much of it because we knew his light skin and growing up in the white community surrounding the school gained him quite a few votes.

There were also a handful of Black teachers and a Black vice-principle. We brought with us our amateur Michael Jacksons, Stevie Wonders, Roberta Flacks, all-pro ball players, and theatrical jazz dancers. But when I say the physical resistance to our presence at John Marshall was not met with violent resistance, I don't mean such was true in the curriculum of the classroom.

As a literature and writing teacher today, I am keenly aware of the cultural silence that exists in most classrooms. When I look back on my high school years, I am painfully aware of how important voice is to culture. Fundamentally, little has changed since I sat behind a classroom desk over ten years ago. The literature curriculum back then rarely spoke powerfully or meaningfully to any students, especially us Black students. Many of us just didn't know that we existed in books which again served to remove us from any sense of purpose in attending an integrated school. In fact, as with the vast majority of Black and other minority students today, the literature and school curriculum was downright insulting and harmful in ways many teachers and society will never understand.

But it was in my junior year that I stumbled across the voice of a writer who helped change forever my sense of Blackness and how much larger life was than the bus ride to John Marshall. It was probably on a Sunday afternoon listening to the Black radio station that I heard an album recording of Nikki Giovanni reading one of her poems set to jazz music—no better way to capture the mind of a teenager.

For the first time, I really heard poetry and felt the presence of a Black voice which was not singing, even though Black singing voices were also important to me. (Even today, Black music remains unconsidered as an important form of communication worth studying.) I grasped hold of Giovanni's words as something valuable, new, bold, and culturally me. The next day I went out and purchased her album. Later, reading a book of her poems and her "extended autobiographical statement on my first 20 years of being a Black poet," titled *Gemini* (1971), lead me to other Black literary voices and, above all to an appreciation of reading.

Unfortunately, my experience is something not easily brought to students. Teachers who care about wanting their students to love reading and writing relish moments when a student takes hold of a book without being motivated by grades or the promise of a diploma. I value deeply the importance of my students discovering the power the written word and the power of their own individual and cultural voices. As bell hooks points out, however, so much in the American hegemony serves to silence voices of women, the working class, and non-European people. "Silence," she understands and clarifies, "is the condition of one who has been dominated, made an object; talk is the mark of freeing, of making one subject" (1979).

Black students who are met with literary core works like *Huckleberry Finn*, *To Kill a Mockingbird*, or even *Of Mice and Men* don't hear powerful Black voices. They hear passive, stuttering voices dominated by a white power structure. It is no wonder that so many Black students are captivated by Malcolm X. For them, he is subject, speaking his mind—boldly, intelligently, and with conviction. Rarely, if ever,

From *Multicultural Education*, Fall 1995, pp. 23-24. © 1995 by the National Association for Multicultural Education. Reprinted by permission.

do students hear radical voices in the classroom—voices that speak to the joys, frustrations, and aspirations of the Black community.

Today, with the conservative control of education, students hear what I call politically passive voices in and outside the classroom. Teachers and the curriculum they are compelled to teach are either silent in their ignorance of the cultures in their classroom, or they are too passive or reluctant, for fear of reprisal, to share voices that may not belong to the dominate mainstream America—the white elite.

Today, for sure, a well developed and complex tradition of literature by people of African, Native American, and Asian descent is grounded and growing so much so that you have to step over it to avoid it. These post-colonial voices must be heard by all students if we are going to challenge them to see American society and the world as it really is. Far too many institutions—including education—exist to confuse and make students complacent about the issues and systems of the domination historically maintaining hundreds of years of race, class, and gender oppression.

I witnessed with dismay, for instance, how easily my students, taking their perspectives from the media, espoused the propaganda that the "riot" in Los Angeles was nothing more than hoodlums gone out of control. Only when I read to them a quote by Malcolm X (1991, p 29) about the motivations and tactics behind urban rebellions did they stop to rethink the message they received from the television.

The work of Malcolm X, Giovanni, and other Black writers and cultural workers I now realize were for me when I was growing up voices that constructively challenged the status quo and how the world, especially the Black world, is traditionally viewed. Theirs was and continues to be a voice of affirmation. As June Jordan has pointed out, "affirmation of Black values and lifestyle within the American context is, indeed, an act of protest" (1974).

How can students witness or hear about the racism and other forms of injustices they see acted out and are so often impacted by and not feel a sense of rage, indifference, or an innate feeling of protest? If and when they are silent about what they see around them, it is only because they are never led to constructively confront, dialogue, study, and reflect on the various forms of resistance struggles to dismantle oppressive infrastructures of racism, poverty, sexism—road blocks in so many people's lives. What they confront day after day are silent voices—passive, indifferent, and many times hostile.

In her essay on "coming to voice," hooks concludes by saying:

> To understand that finding a voice is an essential part of liberation struggle—for the oppressed, the exploited a necessary starting place—a move in the direction of freedom, is important for those who stand in solidarity with us. That talk which identifies us as uncommitted, as lacking critical consciousness, which signifies a condition of oppression and exploitation is utterly transformed as we engage in critical reflection and as we act to resist domination. (1979, p 17)

More teachers must become role models who "engage in critical reflection," even when it means often teaching against the grain. During the last presidential election, I was asked by my students the inevitable question of who I would vote for. I had avoided the question more than a few times when it was previously asked, until I thought I had the time to explain my response. I told them I didn't plan on voting. Many of them appeared shocked. How could I be a role model, one of them retorted, if I, myself, did not vote? I emphatically said that voting was not the only way to voice your opinion; that in fact not voting made a statement.

What they were getting from me was an oppositional view that for some of them was new and to others demonstrated outright contempt for the "democratic" process in America. But I understood before answering the question that the dominate ideology under which they were being taught did not put an emphasis on the radical tradition that had brought about various reforms in this country (very few fundamental changes in this country have been initiated in the voting booth). Nor had they been made aware of alternative political parties and their agendas. Again they were simply co-opted by the mainstream elite. I informed them that I was not advocating that voting is a waste of time, but that they should be as knowledgeable as they can of the various ways change comes about, and thus not to automatically, at such a young age, resign themselves to just one option.

As the struggle increases to expose, clarify, and dismantle forms of domination in this country and throughout the world, I think students growing up in oppressive/exploitive cultures will increasingly feel alienated and indifferent toward public education. They will, as many of my minority students have done in my classroom, speak out and make interrogations about the absence or silence concerning the cultural experiences that have shaped their lives and the people of their communities. Lecturing them about meeting the challenges of the "real world" in which they must learn to fit into rather than change will motivate only a minority of Black students—and perhaps that is by design in a system that has maintained itself on the back of fundamental inequalities.

I believe students really want to learn. But they must be heard. They must be exposed to various voices, especially literary and critically conscious voices speaking to the world they see falling apart around them. Frederick Douglas must be read along side Mark Twain. The voices of the civil rights, Black power, and African liberation movements must be understood and made just as important as the American revolution, the death of John F Kennedy, and the concept of America as the leader of the free world. Contemporary Black feminist or womanist writers—indeed female writers and cultural workers in general—must be equally a part of a core curriculum as the works of Jane Austin. Radical voices worldwide must play a part in making education truly multicultural and meaningful for all students.

References

Giovanni, Nikki. 1971. *Gemini*. Indianapolis, IN: Bobbs-Merrill Co.

hooks, bell. 1989. *Talking back: thinking feminist / thinking black*. Boston, MA: South End Press

Jordan, June. March, 1974. On Richard Wright or Zora Neale Hurston: Notes toward a balancing of love and hatred. *Black World*. p. 5.

X, Malcolm. 1991. *Malcolm X talks to young people*. New York: Path Finder Press.

KNOCKING ON HEAVEN'S DOOR

Surrounded by death and dying, the children of the South Bronx speak with painful clarity about the poverty that has wounded but not hardened them.

Jonathan Kozol

Jonathan Kozol is the author of many books, including Savage Inequalities *and* Rachel and Her Children. *His first book*, Death at an Early Age, *won the National Book Award.*

Over the course of a year, beginning in the summer of 1993, Jonathan Kozol made regular visits to a neighborhood in the South Bronx known as Mott Haven, one of the nation's poorest. Two-thirds of the local residents are Hispanic, one-third black. Thirty-five percent are children. Drug abuse, AIDS, murder, life-consuming fire are part of every day life. In this new book, Amazing Grace: The Lives of Children and the Conscience of a Nation, *Kozol, with sparing eloquence, lets the people themselves—the children, parents, teachers, and pastors—tell their own stories. Here, in an excerpt, he visits a local elementary school, P.S. 65, where only seven of 800 children do not qualify for free lunches. "Five of those seven," the principal tells Kozol, "get reduced-price lunches because they are classified as only 'poor,' not destitute."*

"What are these holes in our window?" asks a 4th grade teacher at P.S. 65 in a rapid drill that, I imagine, few of those who read this will recall from their own days in school.

"Bullet shots!" the children chant in unison.

"How do police patrol our neighborhood?" the teacher asks.

"By helicopter!" say the children.

"What do we do when we hear shooting?"

"Lie down on the floor!"

In the lunchroom, I talk with a serious-looking boy in the 6th grade, named Damian, who tells me he does not live with his parents. I ask him who takes care of him.

"My grandma," he replies.

"Where does your mother live?"

"She lives in Harlem."

"Why don't you live with her?"

"She gave me to my father."

"Why don't you live with your father then?"

"My father is in prison."

A teacher has told me that Damian is considered the top student in his class. I ask him if he knows what he would like to do when he grows up.

"X-ray technician," he replies without conviction.

After lunch, I ask the children in his 6th grade class to tell me what they hate or fear the most in life.

Several children answer, "Dying." One boy says, "The rats that have red eyes." A small girl with curly hair and large round plastic glasses says she is most afraid "of growing up," but when I ask her why, she says, "I don't know why." The only white boy in the class and in the school, an immigrant from Russia, says, "What I hate most is the unfairness on this earth."

I ask the children to tell me something they consider beautiful.

Virtually every child answers, "Heaven."

"What," I ask, "is heaven like?"

"A peaceful place with only the innocent," one child says.

"Where is heaven?"

Rolling her eyes and pointing above her at the ceiling, a child with a ponytail, named Anabelle, replies, "Upstairs."

"How far upstairs?"

"Oh, very far!" she answers.

"Where is the other place?"

"Downstairs," she replies, pointing with her finger at the floor.

I ask again, "How far downstairs?"

"All the way down!" she says, like someone giving orders to an elevator operator.

Before I leave the class, I ask the children if they'd speak of something wonderful or beautiful, not in the after-

From *Teacher Magazine*, October 1995, pp. 28-31, 34-35. Excerpted from *Amazing Grace: The Lives of Children and the Conscience of a Nation* by Jonathan Kozol. © 1995 by Jonathan Kozol. Reprinted by permission of Crown Publishers, Inc.

life but here on earth. Several girls say, "Flowers." One of them says, "My mother," and another says, "My baby brother." One child says, "Myself." Anabelle, one of the smallest children in the 6th grade, answers, "My pet mouse." The boy from Russia answers, "Life itself. Being alive is wonderful."

The affirmation heard in certain of these voices, and the merriment in others, are, however, anything but universal in this school, which serves 800 of the poorest children in the South Bronx—many of whom are also known to be lead-poisoned—and which ranks 627th out of 628 New York City elementary schools in reading scores.

"So many of our children," says one teacher, "walk with their fists clenched and with scowls on their faces. I see a boy come in. I say, 'Good morning,' but he walks right by. I think, 'What can we teach this boy today?'"

"One boy named Alexander looks down at the floor and mutters when his father's name is mentioned. He seems ashamed of him. There's so much bitterness within his eyes."

At the same time, the teacher says, despite this bitterness or shame, many of the children also seem to love their fathers. "There was gunfire last week during recess. When it stopped, we saw the man who had been shot. He was facedown across the street, covered with blood. Several of the children said, 'Oh God! It's my daddy! Is it my daddy?' It wasn't anybody's father that I know of, but you can see from this why children you've been meeting speak so frequently of heaven."

The notion of "trauma" as an individual event, he and other teachers say, does not really get at what they feel is taking place because these things are happening so often. "'Traumatization' as an ordinary state of mind is closer to the fact of things for some, though not for all, the children," says another teacher. "They lead the life most people only read about. A little one speaks to me, and I have tears in my eyes."

I ask if she makes referrals to a clinic or a hospital in cases where a child's state of mind particularly alarms her. She sighs and says, "We do. But every place is overbooked. You make the referral. Then you wait for months...."

"A 13-year-old boy," she says, "came in one day during the winter in a despondent state of mind. I've never come across a child more depressed. He sat here and he said, 'I want to die.' We reached his mother. She took him to Lincoln hospital. They did a brief assessment, then turned him right around."

I ask, "What does that mean?"

"It means that they did nothing for him," says the principal, who is sitting with us in the teacher's room.

"A week later," says the school psychologist, "the mother took him back. This time, he got a blood test, whatever that was for, and was released again. They told the mother she would hear. But she heard nothing.

"Eight weeks after we referred him, he had still received no medication and no treatment. I told the hospital, 'This boy has suicidal ideation. He's in crisis.' But this is the way it is. They say, 'We'll see him in four weeks or so.' Then—nothing."

I mention Damian, the boy who said he wanted to be an X-ray technician when he grows up, although he had said it with a shrug. I tell the psychologist that I had wondered why, if he's one of the best students, he would not have had in mind at least the possibility that he'd become a doctor.

"Many of the ambitions of the children," she replies, "are locked in at a level that suburban kids would scorn. It's as if the very possibilities of life have been scaled back. Boys who are doing well in school will tell me, 'I would like to be a sanitation man.' I have to guard my words and not say anything to indicate my sense of disappointment. In this neighborhood, a sanitation job is something to be longed for."

At 2 p.m., a terrific, rhythmic sound of clapping fills the gym of P.S. 65, as 18 girls in 4th, 5th, and 6th grade go through a cheerleading routine. A few of the girls are fairly tall and look grown-up. Others, like Anabelle, who spoke of her pet mouse during the class discussion, still look like little kids. Small and skinny, full of pep, her big white T-shirt hanging down over her jeans, she snaps her fingers, stamps her feet, swings her ponytail back and forth, then claps her hands with a live-wire frenzy and a big, bright smile in her eyes. "If all this energy could be stored up somehow," a teacher says, "and used in just exactly the right way, I bet these little girls could lick the world."

The same energy is still there later in the schoolyard as the girls do double Dutch and other jump-rope games.

Grandma, grandma
Sick in bed
Called the doctor
And the doctor said:
Get the rhythm in the hands!
Get the rhythm in the head!

A number of teachers and some parent volunteers are standing by the side to supervise the children as they swing the ropes and chant the rhymes, some of them passed down for six or seven generations from grandmothers to their children and grandchildren.

Shake it to the east!
Shake it to the west!
Shake it to the one
that you love best!

The rhymes, combining mischief, challenge, and flirtation, fill the pleasant air of afternoon with innocence and fun.

I can do the hoochie coochie
I can do the split
Bet you five dollars
You can't do this!

Ten or 12 boys in the schoolyard, attracted by my tape recorder, seem overly eager to tell me of some recent murders they have seen.

"A man over there in front of the church shot another man," a 9-year-old announces. "The man he shot was a teenager. I guess he knew him, so he shot him."

"How many times did he shoot him?"

"Seven times," he answers.

"How close were you when this happened?"

"He did it to him right in front of my face," the boy replies.

"My friend's mother was killed," reports another boy. "She uses cocaine. She overdosed and died. It happened in his house."

"Where is his house?"

"On St. Ann's Avenue," he says.

"His father died of a shot in the heart," he adds.

"Where did his father die?"

"On Cypress Avenue."

There isn't much emotion in their voices. They speak of these events the way that people speak of things they've seen on television. I ask the boys to lift their hands if any of them have asthma. Three of their hands go up.

"Do you have someone in your family who has asthma?" Half the hands go up.

"What do they do," I ask, "when they can't breathe?"

"Go to the hospital, get some shots," one boy replies.

A small boy eyes me mysteriously and says in a half-whisper, "I got three quarters in my pocket." He squeezes his hand into his pocket and brings out the coins to show me. His mother, he says, gives him a quarter every morning. "When I get another quarter, I will have a dollar."

"What are you going to do with the dollar?"

"I'm going to buy a hot dog."

A blaring voice from a police car, which is moving slowly past the school, temporarily drowns out the voices of the children. "We are trying to locate a 4-month-old infant who is missing from her home," the magnified voice from the patrol car says. "If you have any information on this child, please telephone the following number...." The patrol car moves on toward a modern-looking homeless shelter, one of two shelters in the blocks behind the school.

As class lets out at 3 p.m., the sidewalk in front of P.S. 65 is filled with mothers and grandmothers waiting to escort their children and grandchildren to their homes. Some of the older children slip loose from the other kids and enter a bodega on the corner of the street. A toddler with a canvas backpack that looks almost as big as he is says goodbye to another toddler, hugs her awkwardly, then reaches up to take his grandmother's hand.

As long as I have visited in inner-city schools like P.S. 65, I have always found the sight of children coming out at 3 o'clock, their mothers and grandmothers waiting to collect them, tremendously exciting and upsetting at the same time. The sheer numbers of the children, the determination of the older women to protect them, and the knowledge that they cannot really be protected in the face of all the dangers that surround them fill a visitor with foreboding. You wish that while they were in class, someone with magic powers had appeared and waved a wand and turned the world outside the building into fields of flowers.

Sympathy for these children, though movingly expressed in some news stories, is not of the magnitude one would expect within a richly cultivated city. One of the most popular radio talk-show hosts in New York City, who refers to African blacks as "savages" and advocates eugenics in America, recently wondered aloud, during a monologue about black people, "how they multiply like that," then answered, "It's like maggots on a hot day. You look one

minute and there are so many there.... You look again and wow! they've tripled." These are not unusual statements these days on the radio in New York City. It often seems as if the hatred for black women in particular is so intense

---

I ask the children to tell me what they hate or fear the most in life. Several children answer, 'Dying.' One boy says, 'The rats that have red eyes.' A small girl says she is most afraid of 'growing up,' but when I ask her why, she says, 'I don't know why.'

---

that there is no longer any sense of prohibition about venting the same hatred on their children.

"I didn't breed them. I don't want to feed them," says a woman cited in the *The New York Times*. The woman, who lives in Arizona, is speaking of Mexican children who enter border towns illegally; but the sentiment is not unlike the one you hear repeatedly in New York City from a number of the talk-show hosts whose scorn for children of black and Hispanic people, frequently conveyed with searing humor, seems to stir the deepest, most responsive chords among white listeners.

The sparklingly happy little girl, named Anabelle, who had explained to me where heaven is ("upstairs"), sees me opposite the school and walks right up and tells me, "Hi! Do you remember me?"

I ask her where she lives, and when she says, "Two blocks away," I ask if I can walk her home, so we can talk a little more. As we walk, I ask her to tell me more about her images of heaven. "Tell me everything. Who gets to go there? What's it like? What happens to the ones who don't get in?"

She seems more than willing to comply.

"People who are good go up to heaven," she begins in a singsong voice, as if this part is obvious. "People who are bad go down to where the Devil lives. They have to wear red suits, which look like red pajamas. People who go to heaven wear a nightgown, white, because they're angels. All little children who die when they are young will go to heaven. Dogs and kittens go to animal heaven. But, if you loved an animal who died, you can go and visit with each other on the weekend. In heaven you don't pay for things with money. You pay for things you need with smiles."

I ask her, "Can a pet mouse go to heaven too?"

"I don't know about a mouse," she answers. "He's quite small."

She tells me that she also has a dog and cat and parakeet. "If I had my own house, I would have nine animals. Cats in one room. Dogs in another. I would have a room for every animal, and I'd put pillows for them on the floor. My mother will not let me do it."

I tell her I'm not surprised by that.

"If I had my own house I would do it."

I ask the names and ages of her animals. When she gets to her parakeet, she says, "He's 59."

"How old are you?"

"I'm only 11," she replies.

She adds that she had another bird before she got the parakeet but that he died the year before. "When he died," she says, cupping her hands and looking into them, "he died in my hands." She smiles, however, as she says this, and does not look sad.

I ask if she says prayers at night.

"I do."

"Who do you pray for?"

"I pray for my dog and cat."

"What do you pray?"

"I pray for them to stay right next to me all night and wake me up if I have a bad dream."

"Do you have many bad dreams?"

"Many!" she replies.

"How do you know when you are in heaven?" I ask her, finally.

"You'll see an archway made of gold," she answers.

I meet Anabelle again a few days later. She has two quarters in her hand to buy a pineapple *coquito*. I go to the corner with her, and I get a pineapple *coquito* too. It's a beautiful day. She stands with me eating her icie and chatters about nothing of importance for a while.

Being treated as a friend this way by children always feels like a great privilege. It seems like something you just wouldn't have the right to hope for. Why should this child trust a stranger who can come into her world at will and leave it any time he likes? Why should she be so generous and open? In the drabness of the neighborhood, her friendliness seems like the sunshine that has not been seen in New York City during many months of snow and storm and meanness.

Anabelle's images of heaven give me a delightful feeling that I rarely have in New York City. I speak of these kinds of things as often as I can, and of the feelings children voice for animals they love, because I think they show us something very different from the customary picture we are given of a generation of young thugs and future whores. There is a golden moment here that our society has chosen not to seize. We have not nourished this part of the hearts of children, not in New York, not really anywhere.

Anabelle is, by any odds, one of the most joyful children I have ever met. There is seldom any hint of sorrow in her voice. Only once, when she told me of children at her school whose mothers or fathers or older sisters had died recently of AIDS, did she become quite solemn. I asked her how the children who are orphaned seem to handle what they have gone through.

"They cry. They suffer. People die. They pray," she answered softly.

A block from P.S. 65, I run into Cliffie, the little boy who was concerned about the "burning bodies" in the medical waste incinerator built on Locust Avenue. He's sitting on a high brick wall as I come up the street.

As I approach, he shows no particular surprise at seeing me again after eight months but asks me, "Do you see that wall back there, behind this yard?"

I say I do.

"This man I saw, he buried another man back there. The man he buried was alive."

"Is that true?"

> 'Many of the ambitions of the children,' one psychologist explains, 'are locked in at a level that suburban kids would scorn. Boys who are doing well in school will tell me, "I would like to be a sanitation man." I have to guard my words. In this neighborhood, a sanitation job is something to be longed for.'

"The man was alive! And then, when I went back in there, I saw a dead dog and I saw this little, little bottle with a purple top. The man was moving. I saw his fingers sticking out. There was a crucifix, and it was moving too."

I ask him, "Did you try to dig him out?"

"No!" he says. "It was too gross! I put more dirt on top of him so he would not get out. I asked him, 'Are you still alive?' But he said no."

He says this in a cheerful voice, adding, "People pee in there and bring their dogs to doodle on his grave."

"I think you're making this up," I say.

He doesn't contest my statement but slips down adeptly from the wall and reaches up and takes my hand and walks with me in the direction I was heading.

"Long ago," his mother tells me later, "one of the hospitals used to use that plot of land to bury people who had nobody to claim their bodies. There used to be markers on the graves, but they've been gone for years." She wonders if he may have heard this story and inflated it into his fable of the moving hand.

If it is true that children often make up fables to explain the things that trouble them or things they fear, then there is certainly sufficient reason for the many legends that some of the children have created in Mott Haven. Month after month, they witness shootings and police raids, hear of bodies found in trash chutes, other bodies found in elevator shafts, and always, and predictably, they see the consequences of life-taking fires.

The fires sometimes come so close together that the names and ages of the victims soon dissolve into a vague scenario of sadness that can seem uncomfortably abstract. "FIERY TOMB FOR TWO BRONX KIDS," reads a headline in the *Daily News*. "NO ESCAPE," reads a second headline. "TRAPPED TOT KILLED IN APARTMENT BLAZE," reads a headline one day later. "APARTMENT FIRE KILLS BRONX BOY," reads a headline on the next day. "BRONX APARTMENT BLAZE KILLS MOM AND SON," reads a fourth headline for another fire in Mott Haven.

The last of these fires, in which a mother and her child died together, took place in a building I have often passed in walking from the train to St. Ann's Church. The building is across an airshaft from another building where the child's uncle and grandmother lived. The grandmother and uncle, awakened by the fire, watched the flames consume the mother and the boy. The mother was last seen standing with the child in her third-floor window, screaming, "Mami! Mami! I can't get out!"

"The fire got bigger," says the uncle of the boy. Then "they became quiet," and then "we couldn't see them anymore." A photograph taken while the fire blazed shows a thin Hispanic man standing in the street outside the building, cradling a beagle puppy in his arms and looking upward with dark, shadowed eyes.

The boy who died, a 10-year-old, was, like his mother, believed to be somewhat retarded. A woman who works in a hardware store one block from where he lived tells me he used to come into her store to say hello. "He had a round face, like a Mexican boy," she says. "He'd pick up a key chain or some other little thing that didn't cost a lot, and he might ask me, 'Can I have it?' I would tell him, 'Take it!' His mother watched him like a hawk. She'd stand outside the door and wait 'til he came out.

"On the day before the fire, he came in and handed me a dollar bill. He asked me, 'Would you change it for five dollars?' I told him, 'I can't do that, Papi!' He looked up at me as if he was confused. 'Why can't you do it?' I explained, 'One dollar and five dollars aren't the same.' He gave me a look that made me laugh, as if he thought that I was fooling him. I asked him, 'Papi, what do you need five dollars for?' He said he wanted to buy a baseball at the store across the street.

"The store got crowded then. I couldn't talk. He gave me another look and went back out the door. Later, I learned that he went up the line of all the other stores and asked them all the same thing: Would they change one dollar for five dollars? That's when I knew that there was something wrong. Two days later, when I learned that he was dead, I wished that I had gone and bought the baseball for him. I wish that I could go and buy him 20 baseballs. A baseball's not a big thing for a boy who has so little."

"The boy who burned to death," a 3rd grade teacher at P.S. 65 recalls, "was sitting right there, right in that chair, the afternoon before he died."

I ask if it's true that the boy and his mother were retarded.

"No," she says. "That was the 138th Street fire. This is the boy who died on 140th Street. This boy was a little one. That boy there was older."

In order to keep these different children clear in my own mind, I finally had to make a map of the South Bronx and put it on the wall over my desk, placing a marker on each block in which a child died, using one symbol for death by fire, one for death by accident, and one for death by gunshot.

"This little boy was in a special class because he had a learning disability," the teacher says. "His regular teacher had to go to a meeting after lunch that afternoon, so I was asked to keep him here until the end of school.

"One of the things that makes me sad is that I didn't spend as much time with him as I would have liked. It was one of those hectic afternoons. I never had a chance to stop and just sit down with him and chat. The only thing that I recall is that this boy right here"—she gestures at a fat boy sitting near the door—"kept teasing him, and I finally had to interfere.

"One of the other boys, a sensitive child named Domingo, had befriended him. He made a date to visit him and play with him that afternoon. But Domingo had to stay late for some reason. By the time he got there to the house, he saw the child's body carried out."

"How old was this boy?" I ask.

"Eight years old," the teacher says.

"Was he the only victim?"

"No," she says. "His mother's in a coma at Jacobi Hospital. Another child, a 5-year-old, is dead. Two of the other children are in critical care." She then lifts one hand over her face and starts to cry.

Leaving the school, I walk three blocks to see the apartment building where this child died. A garbage bag is billowing from one of the upper windows, charred and open. It isn't apparent if the family has moved out. With the mother and two children in the hospital, however, that does not seem likely.

A few doors away, my attention is arrested by one of the most unusual memorials that I have seen in the South Bronx. In bright white paint against a soft beige background is a painting of a large and friendly looking dog, his tail erect, his ears alert for danger. Above, in yellow letters, I read "MOONDOG," which appears to be the nickname of the person who has died. "Gone is the face.... Silent is the voice.... In our hearts we'll remember," reads the epitaph.

As I am standing on the sidewalk copying these words, a plump Hispanic woman rises from the stoop nearby and comes up to my side.

"Is this where he died?" I ask.

"Yes," she answers. "He was shot right there, inside the door."

"Why was he killed?"

"He was protecting a woman who was pregnant."

"Did the woman live?"

"The woman lived. She's fine."

"Did the baby live?"

"The baby's doing fine."

"How old was the man who died?"

"He was almost 21," she replies.

I ask her how he got his nickname.

"He loved dogs. He used to bring them home." Her voice is jovial and pleasant.

"Did you know him well?"

"He was my son," she says.

Nearby, in the afternoon sun, dozens of children are playing in a playground flecked with broken glass. Puerto Rican music with a pounding salsa rhythm fills the air. In the distance is the jingling music from an ice cream truck, parked at the corner of Brook Avenue. Under a basketball hoop without a net, a number of teenage boys are warming up before a game.

At 5 p.m., I stand at the corner of East 139th Street and St. Ann's Avenue. Tall iron bars have been installed around the space where Children's Park once stood. There is no one enjoying the space inside the bars, which will remain an antiseptic fortress for a year to come, but it is, for now at least, defensible against drug dealers. At some of the local bodegas, store owners are installing stronger, more protective barriers to fend off bullets; bulletproof vests are also becoming part of their work uniforms. So the bodegas soon will be a little more defensible as well.

All the strategies and agencies and institutions needed to contain, control, and normalize a social plague—some of them severe, others exploitative, and some benign—are, it seems, being assembled: defensible stores, defensible parks, defensible entrances to housing projects, defensible schools where weapons-detectors are installed at the front doors and guards are posted, "drug-free zones" in front of the schools, "safety corridors" between the schools and nearby subway stations, "grieving rooms" in some of the schools where students have a place to mourn the friends who do not make it safely through the "safety corridors," a large and crowded criminal court and the enormous new court complex now under construction, an old reform school (Spofford) and the new, much larger juvenile prison being built on St. Ann's Avenue, an adult prison, a prison barge, a projected kitchen to prepackage prison meals, a projected high school to train kids to work in prisons and in other crime-related areas, the two symmetrical prostitute strolls, one to the east, one to the west, and counselling and condom distribution to protect the prostitutes from spreading or contracting AIDS, services for grown-ups who already have contracted AIDS, services for children who have AIDS, services for children who have seen their mothers die of AIDS, services for men and women coming out of prison, services for children of the men and women who are still in prison, a welfare office to determine who is eligible for checks and check-cashing stores where residents can cash the checks, food stamp distribution and bodegas that accept the stamps at discount to enable mothers to buy cigarettes or diapers, 13 shelters, 12 soup kitchens, 11 free food pantries, perhaps someday an "empowerment zone," or "enterprise zone," or some other kind of business zone to generate some jobs for a small fraction of the people who reside here: all the pieces of the perfectible ghetto, the modernized and sometimes even well-served urban lazaretto, with civic-minded CEOs who come up from Manhattan maybe once a week to serve as mentors or "role models" to the children in the schools while some of their spouses organize benefit balls to pay for dinners in the shelters.

All these strategies and services are needed—all these and hundreds more—if our society intends to keep on placing those it sees as unclean in the unclean places. "In real-

ity, it *is* a form of quarantine," says Ana Oliveira, who directs an agency that serves ex-prison inmates who have AIDS, "not just of people who have AIDS but of people who have everything we fear, sickness, color, destitution—but it has been carried out in ways that seem compatible with humane principles.

"We don't have 'pass cards' in New York. Black women who have AIDS don't have to clip a photo ID to their dress. You don't need a permit to cross over at the magic line of 96th Street. We just tell you the apartment that's available is in Mott Haven, or East Tremont, or Hunts Point. 'That's where we can serve you best. Here's a referral number. Call this agency. They'll help you to get settled....' That's what I mean by 'humane principles.' For those who work within these agencies, as I do, it appears benevolent. And, of course, once you accept the preconditions, all these things are absolutely critical."

One of the humane principles of which she speaks is present, it appears, here at the former site of Children's Park. The city has apparently tried hard to make this into a "good" corner. By smashing the benches and the shelter where drug needles once were given out, and flushing out the last remaining symbols of a local drug lord, it has created something clean and modern-looking, metal, geometric, which will someday be transformed into a pleasant place for children. The part of the drug trade that once flourished here has moved both up and down the street, a number of blocks in each direction. The needle exchange is now in a new location, just four doors from P.S. 65.

A few of the people who once frequented the park, however, are standing on the sidewalk looking through the bars. A woman I have seen here several times and who, I am told, is HIV-infected holds a pack of Winstons in one hand, a single cigarette in the other. In a voice that is a bit peremptory and gruff, she asks me for a match.

Lighting the match and holding it for her as she cups her hands, I ask her something that, I realize, even as I say it, must strike her as somewhat strange. "What do you call this place?"

She looks perplexed. "What do I call *what* place?" she asks.

"This place here—what do you call it?"

"This place here?" she shrugs. "This here is the ghetto."

When she sees me taking out my pen, she says it louder, "GHETTO," and then spells it.

I ask, "Why do you live here?"

She looks around her at the street and shrugs again. "This is where poor peoples *lives*," she says. "Where else you think poor peoples goin' to be? You a professor? You wants to meet poor peoples, you come to the ghetto."

She seems frustrated by my question, no doubt with good reason. She walks away, repeating my words in a sarcastic voice and heads for St. Benedict the Moor, a residence for people in drug treatment, with a soup kitchen on its ground floor, which is just next door.

After she leaves, I leave the corner also and walk to St. Ann's, where vespers have begun. The pastor's clear and calming voice fills the chapel of the church, in which six people from the neighborhood have come to pray. It isn't my religion, but it lends a sense of blessed peace and sanity to my evening.

Investing in Our
CHILDREN:
A Struggle for America's Conscience and Future

"Too many young people of all races and classes are growing up unable to handle life, without hope or steady compasses to navigate a world that is reinventing itself technologically and politically at a kaleidoscopic pace."

Marian Wright Edelman

Ms. Edelman is president of the Children's Defense Fund, Washington, D.C.

THE 1990S' STRUGGLE is about the U.S.'s conscience and future. Many of the battles will not be as dramatic as Gettysburg or Vietnam or Desert Storm, but they are going to shape this nation's place in the 21st century. Every American in this last decade of the last century of this millennium must struggle to redefine success in the U.S., asking not "How much can I get?," but "How much can I do without and share?"; not "How can I find myself?," but "How can I lose myself in service to others?"; not just how I can take care of me and mine, but how I can help as one American to strengthen family and community values and help this great nation regain her moral and economic bearings at home and abroad.

When I was growing up, service was as essential as eating and sleeping and going to church and school. Caring black adults were buffers against the segregated outside world which told me that, as a black girl, I wasn't worth anything and was not important. However, I didn't believe it because my parents, teachers, and preachers said it wasn't so. The childhood message I internalized, despite the outside segregation and poverty all around, was that, as God's child, no man or woman could look down on me, and I could look down on no man or woman.

I couldn't play in segregated playgrounds or sit at drugstore lunch counters, so my father, a Baptist minister, built a playground and canteen behind our church. Whenever he saw a need, he tried to respond. There were no black homes for the aged in South Carolina at that time, so my parents began one across the street, and our entire family had to help out. I didn't like it a whole lot of the time, but that is how I learned that it was my responsibility to take care of elderly family members and neighbors, and that everyone was my neighbor.

I went everywhere with my parents and the members of my church and community who were my watchful extended family. The entire black community took responsibility for protecting its children. They reported on me when I did wrong, applauded me when I did well, and were very clear as adults about what doing well meant. It meant being helpful to others, achieving in school, and reading. We all finally figured out that the only time our father wouldn't give us a chore was when we were reading, so we all read a lot.

Children were taught, by example, that nothing was too lowly to do and that the work of our heads and hands were both valuable. As a child, I went with an older brother—I was eight or nine or 10 and remember the debate between my parents as to whether I was too young to go help clean the bedsores of a poor, sick woman—but I went and learned just how much the smallest helping hands can mean to a lonely person in need.

Our families, churches, and community made kids feel useful and important. While life often was hard and resources scarce, we always knew who we were and that the measure of our worth was inside our heads and hearts, not outside in material possessions or personal ambition. We were taught that the world had a lot of problems; that black people had an *extra* lot of problems, but that we could struggle and change them; that extra intellectual and material gifts brought with them the privilege and responsibility of sharing with others less fortunate; and that service is the rent each of us pays for living—the very purpose of life and not something you do in your spare time or after you have reached your personal goals.

I am grateful for these childhood legacies of a living faith reflected in daily service, the discipline of hard work, and stick-to-itiveness—a capacity to struggle in the face of adversity. Giving up, despite how bad the world was outside, simply was not a part of my childhood lexicon. You got up every

From *USA Today Magazine,* March 1993, pp. 24-26. © 1993 by the Society for the Advancement of Education. Reprinted by permission.

morning and did what you had to do, and you got up every time you fell down and tried as many times as you had to until you got it right. I was 14 the night my father died. He had holes in his shoes, but he had two children who graduated from college, one in college, another in divinity school, and a vision that he was able to convey to me even as he was dying in an ambulance—that I, a young black girl, could be and do anything, that race and gender are shadows, and that character, self-discipline, determination, attitude, and service are the substance of life.

What kind of vision are we conveying to our children today as parents, political and business leaders, and professionals? Our children are growing up in an ethically polluted nation where instant sex without responsibility, instant gratification without effort, instant solutions without sacrifice, getting rather than giving, and hoarding rather than sharing are the too frequent signals of our mass media, popular culture, and political life.

The standard of success for far too many Americans has become personal greed, rather than common good. The standard for striving and achievement has become getting, rather than making an extra effort or service to others. Truth-telling and moral example have become devalued commodities. Nowhere is the paralysis of public or private conscience more evident than in the neglect and abandonment of millions of our shrinking pool of youngsters, whose futures will determine our nation's ability to compete economically and lead morally as much as any child of privilege and as much as any other issue.

We need to understand that investing in our children is not investing in a special interest group or helping out somebody else—it is absolutely essential to every American's well-being and future. Only two out of every 10 new labor force entrants in this decade will be white males born in the U.S. As an aging population with a shrinking pool of kids, we don't have a child to waste—we need every one of them. We either can decide to invest in them up front and give them a sense of nurturing and caring adults that are part of a community and a society that guarantees them a future, or we can continue to fear them, build more and more prisons, and worry about them shooting at us. We don't have a choice about investing in our children, only when we are going to invest and whether it's going to be positive or negative investment.

Every 16 seconds of every school day, as we talk about a competitive workforce in the future, one of our children drops out of school. Every 26 seconds of every day, an American child runs away from home. These are not just poor or black children—they are all of our children. This is not something affecting just a few families—these are national problems. Every 47

seconds, a youngster is abused. Every 67 seconds, a teenager has a baby. We produce the equivalent of the city of Seattle each year with children having children. Every seven minutes, a child is arrested for a drug offense. Every 30 minutes, one of our children is charged with drunken driving. Every 53 minutes, in the richest land on Earth, an American child dies because of poverty.

It is disgraceful that children are the poorest Americans and that, in the last year alone, 840,000 youngsters fell into poverty and that there has been a 26% increase since 1979 in poverty among children. The majority of poor youngsters in America are not black and not in inner cities. They are in rural and suburban areas and in working and two-parent families. A lot of folk who were middle class last year around the country are now in poverty and on food stamps. It can happen to any of us.

We are in a sad state when the American Dream for many middle-class young people has become a choice between a house and a child. They are worrying about how their offspring are going to make it through college, pay off their higher education loans, and get off the ground and form families. We have to begin investing in all of our kids and all of our families. I believe we have lost our sense of what is important as a people. Too many children of all races and classes are growing up unable to handle life, without hope or steady compasses to navigate a world that is reinventing itself technologically and politically at a kaleidoscopic pace. Too many are growing up terribly uncertain and fearful about the future.

Despite the global realities the nation faces and a lot of the economic and moral uncertainty of the present, there are some enduring values we have lost sight of. I agree with poet Archibald MacLeish that there is only one thing more powerful than learning from experience and that is *not* learning from experience. It is the responsibility of every adult—parent, teacher, preacher, professional, and political leader—to make sure that youngsters hear what adults have learned from the lessons of life. Author James Baldwin wrote some years back that children really don't ever do what we tell them to do, but they almost always do what we do.

Americans have to move away from the idea of being entitled to something because they are men, or wealthy, or white, or black. It is time to come together to work quietly and systematically toward building a more just America and ensuring that no child is left behind. We should resist quick-fix, simplistic answers and easy gains that disappear as fast as they come. I am sick of people talking big and making great promises, then not following up and getting it done. Too often, we get bogged down

in our ego needs and lose sight of deeper community and national needs.

Family values vs. hypocrisy

As a nation, we mouth family values we do not practice. Seventy countries provide medical care and financial assistance to all pregnant women and to children—the U.S. is not one of them. Seventeen industrialized nations have paid maternity/paternity leave programs—the U.S. is not one of them. In 1992, Pres. George Bush vetoed an unpaid leave bill that would have allowed parents to stay at home when a child is sick or disabled. We need to stop the hypocrisy of talking about families when all our practices are the opposite. It is time for parents to have a real choice about whether to remain at home or work outside the home without worrying about the safety of their children.

Many families have had to put a second parent into the workforce in order to make ends meet. Even when both parents work, a vast number are not able to meet their basic housing and health care needs.

The new generation of young people must share and stress family rituals and values and be moral examples for their children, just as this generation must try even harder to be. If people cut corners, their children will too. If they are not honest, their children will not be either. If adults spend all of their money and tithe no portion of it for colleges, synagogues or churches, and civic causes, their children won't either. If they tolerate political leaders who don't tell the truth or do what they say, their children will lose faith as too many are doing in the political process.

If we snicker at racial and gender jokes, another generation will pass on the poison that our generation still has not had the will to snuff out. Each of us must counter the proliferating voices of racial, ethnic, and religious division that separates us as Americans. It's important for us to face up to, rather than ignore, our growing racial problems, which are America's historic and future Achilles' heel. Whites didn't create black or brown people; men didn't create women; Christians didn't create Jews—so what gives anybody the right to feel entitled to diminish another?

We need to ask ourselves as Americans—how many potential Martin Luther King, Jrs. or Colin Powells, Sally Rides or Barbara McClintocks our nation is going to waste before it wakes up and recognizes that its ability to compete in the new century is as inextricably intertwined with poor and non-white children as with its white and privileged ones, with girls as well as its boys? As Rabbi Abraham Heschel put it, "We may not all be equally guilty for the problems that we face, but we are all equally responsible" for building a decent and just

7. FOR VISION AND VOICE: A CALL TO CONSCIENCE

America and seeing that no child is left behind.

People who are unwilling or unable to share and make complicated and sometimes hard choices may be incapable or taking courageous action to rebuild our families and community and nation. Nevertheless, I have great hopes about America and believe we can rebuild community and begin to put our children first as a nation. It is going to require that each of us figure out what we're going to be willing to sacrifice and share.

Many whites favor racial justice as long as things remain the same. Many voters hate Congress, but love their own Congressman as long as he or she takes care of their special interests. Many husbands are happier to share their wives' added income than share the housework and child care. Many Americans deny the growing gap between the rich and the poor, and they are sympathetic and concerned about escalating child suffering as long as somebody else's program is cut.

Americans have to grow up beyond this national adolescence. Everybody wants to spend, but nobody wants to pay. Everybody wants to lower the deficit, but also to get everything that they can. We have to ask ourselves how we're going to come together as a people to begin to make sure that the necessities of the many are taken care of and that every child gets what he or she needs to achieve a healthy start in life. If we're not too poor to bail out the savings and loan institutions, if we're not too poor to build all those B-2 bombers, we're not too poor to rescue our suffering children and to ensure that all youngsters get what they need.

In a time of economic uncertainty and fear about the future, of rising crime, rising costs, and rising joblessness, we must never give in to the urge to give up, no matter how hard it gets. There's an old proverb that says, "When you get to your wits end, remember that God lives there." Harriet Beecher Stowe once said that, when you get into a "tight place and everything goes against you, till it seems as though you could not hang on for a minute longer, never give up then, for that is just the place and the time when the tide will turn."

We can not continue as a nation to make a distinction between our children and other people's kids. Every youngster is entitled to an equal share of the American Dream. Every poor child, every black child, every white child—every child living everywhere—should have an equal shot. We need every one of them to be productive and educated and healthy.

Let me end this article with a prayer, written by a schoolteacher in South Carolina. She urges us to pray and accept responsibility for children who sneak popsicles before supper, erase holes in math workbooks, and never can find their shoes, but let's also pray and accept responsibility for children who can't bound down the street in a new pair of sneakers, who don't have any rooms to clean up, whose pictures aren't on anybody's dresser, and whose monsters are real. Let each of us commit to praying and accepting responsibility for children who spend all their allowance before Tuesday, throw tantrums in the grocery store, pick at their food, shove dirty clothes under the bed, never rinse out the tub, squirm in church or temple, and scream in the phone, but let's also pray and accept responsibility for those children whose nightmares come in the daytime, who will eat anything, who have never seen a dentist, who aren't spoiled by anybody, who go to bed hungry and cry themselves to sleep all over this rich nation. Let's commit to praying and accepting responsibility for children who want to be carried and for those who must be carried. Let's commit to protecting those children whom we never give up on, but also those children who don't get a second chance. Let each of us commit to praying and voting and speaking and fighting for those children whom we smother, but also for those who will grab the hand of anybody kind enough to offer it.

AAUW (American Association of University Women), report of, on gender discrimination in education, 219–223
ability grouping, 63
academic discipline, multicultural education as, 71–75
acceptance, diversity and, 61–62
action response, to deconstruction, 58
adolescence, prejudice and, 10
aesthetic experiences, in multicultural education, 147, 152, 172
affirmation, multicultural education and, 59–65
affirmative action, 86
Afrocentrism, 111, 112, 114, 136, 139
Allport, Gordon, 93, 95, 97
American GI Forum, 7
anti-bias curriculum, 155–161
anti-Semitism, 145, 146, 156
Arab people, discussion of, in social studies textbooks, 212–218
art, teaching as, 41–42
Asante, Molefi, 112, 137, 139
Asian Americans, 7–8, 22, 45, 47, 69, 87, 100–101, 135, 143, 146, 157, 162, 165, 231; during World War II, 226–229; Individualized Family Service Plan for, 123–126; as model minority, 188–196; in Vancouver, BC, 127–131. See also demographics
assimilation, 61, 137, 198; intermarriage and, 26–27
assimilation/universalist model, of equality, 85
Atlanta Compromise, 105
Autobiography, An (Black Hawk), 182–187

"banking" approach to education, 31
Banks, James A., 10, 55, 59, 68, 141, 164, 198, 199; on multicultural education as academic discipline, 71–75; on curriculum guide for multicultural education, 134–135
behavior disorders, inclusion and, 35
Bell, Derrick, 103, 105
bicultural actors, teachers as, 48
bilingual education, 15, 16, 18–19, 49, 62, 63, 64, 104, 108, 166, 167
Black Hawk, autobiography of, 182–187
blacks, 6, 7, 9, 16, 45, 47, 48, 60, 68, 69, 86, 99, 103, 109, 114, 136, 141, 146, 188, 200, 202, 203; all-black schools for, 115–119; literature of, 230–231; in South Bronx, NY, 232–237. See also demographics
Boas, Franz, 71, 72
borrowed words, in English, 20–21
Brittain, John, 107, 109
Brown, Ron, 86–87
Brown v. Board of Education, 7, 103, 105, 110, 197–201
"browning of America," 45
Bullivant, Brian M., 67, 68

California, immigration to, 22–25
Canada: Asian immigration to, 127–131
Carso, Don, 104–110
change agents, teachers as, 49
change and continuity, as curricular theme, 62–63
children: all-black schools and, 115–119; anti-bias curriculum for, 155–161; household formation and, 179; inclusion

and, 34–37; intermarriage and, 26–27; prejudice in 10; in the South Bronx, NY, 232–237; tolerance and, 92–97; urban, teachers of, 40–44
Civil Rights Act of 1964, 7, 8, 9
civil rights movement, 6, 80, 83, 103, 137
Civilian Exclusion Order No. 27, 227, 229
class stratification, in polyethnic societies, 87
Clinton, Bill, 17, 86
cognitive processing, cultural discontinuities and, 47
colleges, prejudice in, 38–39
coming of age, as curricular theme, 62–63
communication, patterns of, cultural discontinuities and, 48
communities of learners, classrooms as, 170–171
conceptual webbing, multicultural education and, 55
Constitution, U.S., 6
content integration, in multicultural education, 139
cooperative learning, multicultural education and, 10–11, 170
craft, teaching as, 41–42
critical thinking, multicultural education and, 159, 160
critique, multicultural education and, 58, 59–65, 172
cultural brokers, teachers as, 48–49, 50
cultural context teaching, multicultural education and, 46, 48
cultural discontinuities, multicultural education and, 46–47
cultural group, definition of, 68, 136–137
cultural literacy, 76
cultural pluralism, multicultural education and, 83–89
cultural self-disclosure, 69–70
culture, definition of, 76, 98
curriculum: anti-bias, 155–161; guidelines for multicultural, 134–154

Davis, Eddie, 105, 107
deconstruction, multicultural education and, 57, 58
decontextualization, of multicultural education, 56, 61
demographics, changes in student, 45–51, 134, 176–181
desegregation, school, 103–110, 197–201
developmentally appropriate curriculum, multicultural education and, 57
dictators, discussion of, in textbooks regarding the Middle East, 214
discipline, single parent families and, 115–116
disconnection, in multicultural education, 159
discourse competency, 76
DIVERSE model, of multicultural education, 199–200, 201
Dowling Urban Environment Learning Center (Minneapolis, MN), 210–211
dropouts, girls as school, 220–221
Dubois, W. E. B., 139, 200
Dwyer, Kevin, 92–93, 94, 95

e pluribus unum, multicultural education and, 134, 136, 143–144
early intervention, 210; cultural issues and, 123–126

Eastern Hemisphere: The World Around Us (Beyer), discussion of Middle East in, 212–218
Education for All Handicapped Children Act, 34–37
education, importance of, for Native Americans, 12–14
Ellis Island, NYC, immigration and, 22, 23
English: borrowed words in, 20–21; as official language for U.S., 15–17
equity pedagogy, in multicultural education, 139
Erikson, Erik, 98, 115
ESEA (Elementary and Secondary Education Act), 18
ESL (English as a Second Language), 61, 64, 130, 131, 153, 181, 193
essential schools, 105
essentialism, 112
ethnic group, definition of, 136
ethnic pluralism, multicultural education and, 135–136
ethnic self-disclosure, 69–70
ethnocentrism, 213
equal protection clause, of the Fourteenth Amendment, 6
equality, models of, 85–86
Eurocentrism, 111, 112, 114, 197
European Americans, 138
evaded curriculum, 220
experiential learning, multicultural education and, 147–148, 200
Exploring World Cultures (Newhill), discussion of Middle East in, 212–218

factual errors, in social studies textbooks discussing the Middle East, 217
family literacy, 171–172
family values, 239–240
feminism, 100, 112
Fifteenth Amendment, to the Constitution, 6
First Amendment, to the Constitution, 38
Fourteenth Amendment, to the Constitution, 6
Freire, Paolo, 31, 171
functional contexualization, of multicultural education, 56

gender discrimination, in education, 219–223
gender, identity formation and, 98–102
genocide, Schindler's List and, 202–205
Gentleman's Agreement, 226
Giovanni, Nikki, 230, 231
girls, and gender discrimination in education, 219–223
Global Insights (Hantula), discussion of Middle East in, 212–218
Grant, Carl, 55, 59, 73, 83, 84, 139
Guns 'n' Roses, prejudice in lyrics of, 38–39

harmony, as value in Asian culture, 124
Hartford, CT, school segregation in, 103–110
Hawley, Willis D., 9–11
hidden curriculum, 31, 139
Hirsch, E. D., 76, 112
Hispanics, 6, 7, 16, 18, 45, 48, 60, 69, 87, 88–89, 103, 104, 107, 108, 109, 114, 115, 120–122, 135, 141, 146, 165–166, 171, 188; immigration of, to California,

22–25; in South Bronx, NY; 232–237. *See also* demographics
History and Life (Wallbank), discussion of Middle East in, 212–218
Holocaust, *Schindler's List* and, 202–205
hooks, bell, 230, 231
Horton v. Meskill, 105
HOTS (higher-order thinking skills), 211
household formation, children and, 179
human rights, 143

identity formation: in adolescence, 10; gender and, 98–102
ideology, urban teachers and, 40–44
IFSP (Individualized Family Service Plan), 123–126
immigration, 8, 15, 17, 18, 45, 62–63, 77, 80, 135, 136, 146, 165; Asian, to Vancouver, BC, 127–131; to California, 22–25; demographics and, 177–179
inclusion, 34–37, 57, 167, 198, 199, 204; magnet schools and, 210–211
Indian Removal Act of 1830, 146
individual and collective responsibility, as curricular theme, 62–63
infusion, 55–56, 57, 58, 73–74, 75
intelligence testing, standardized, 148
interdependence, as value in Asian culture, 124
intermarriage, 26–27, 206–209
interrogation, multicultural education and, 58
inverse growth patterns, of multicultural education, 54–56
issues-centered education, 31

Jackson, Donald, 183, 184
Jews: discussion of, in textbooks regarding the Middle East, 215–216; *Schindler's List* and, 202–205
Jim Crow laws, 80

Kerner Commission, 106
King, Martin Luther, 7, 9, 61, 103, 145
knowledge reconstruction, multicultural education and, 58, 139
Krupat, Arnold, 182, 183, 184, 185

language: borrowed words in English, 20–21; English as official U.S., 15–17
language discrimination, 145
League of Nations, 85
learned helplessness, multicultural education and, 46, 48
learning styles, ethnic diversity and, 141–142, 149–150
least restrictive environment, inclusion and, 35
Leclaire, Antoine, 183, 184–185
LEP (limited English proficiency), 18–19, 47
literacy: family, 171–172; multilingual, 147, 152–153
literature: black, 230–231; children's multicultural, 32–33, 164–166
LULAC (League of United Latin American Citizens), 7

magnet schools, 210–211
mainstreaming, 210–211
Mead, Margaret, 72, 76–77
medically fragile children, inclusion and, 35
mental retardation, inclusion and, 35
Middle East, discussion of, in social studies textbooks, 212–218

Milliken v. Bradley, 106
Minneapolis, MN, Dowling Urban Environment Learning Center in, 210–211
Minority Protection Treaties and Declarations, 85
minstrel approach, to multicultural education, 198
misrepresentation, in multicultural education, 159
missionary approach, to multicultural education, 198
mixed-race families, 206–209
model minority, Asian Americans as, 188–196
monocultural education, 60, 99, 197
Moynihan, Daniel Patrick, 115–116
Mujica, Mauro, 15, 16
multiracial families, 206–209
music, prejudice in, 38–39

NAFTA (North American Free Trade Agreement), 24, 88
NAME (National Association of Multicultural Education), 82, 83
Native Americans, 18–19, 41, 69, 76, 86, 136, 143, 146, 168, 203, 204, 231; and autobiography of Black Hawk, 182–187; importance of education for, 12–14
Naturalization Act of 1790, 7, 227
Nazi Germany, *Schindler's List* and, 202–205
New College of California, teacher education program at, 167–173
New York, poor children of South Bronx, 232–237
Nieto, Sonia, 55, 167; on tolerance in multicultural education, 59–65
Nineteenth Amendment, to the Constitution, 6
nonsynchrony, 112
normalization, inclusion and, 35
nuclear family, 115

official language, English as U.S., 15–17
Ogbu, John, 116, 118, 188, 195
Omi, Michael, 111, 113
operational bridging, between multicultural education theory and practice, 55
Orfield, Gary, 105, 107, 108, 109, 198

Parks, Rosa, 61, 103, 156
patronization, in multicultural education, 159
Patterson, John B., 182, 183–184
People and Nations: A World History (Mazour), discussion of Middle East in, 212–218
Philippines, 8
picture brides, 226
polyethnic states model, of equality, 85–86, 87
postmodern family, 115
poverty, 48, 99, 117, 118, 148, 220; and children of South Bronx, NY, 232–237; urban teachers and, 40–44
power, ethnic groups and, 87–88
powerlessness, racism and, 99, 100, 145
prejudice: in children, 10; in colleges, 38–39; unlearning, 169–170
problem solving, cultural discontinuities and, 47
problem-posing education, 31
Project Concern, 106, 107, 108
Proposition 187, California's, 17, 22, 23

protection model, of equality, 86

racial intermarriage, 26–27
racism, whites and, 79–82
REI (Regular Education Initiative), 34
religion: intermarriage and, 26–27; Native American, 186–187. *See also* Jews
researchers, teachers as, 172
respect, multicultural education and, 62–63
role models, all-black schools and, 115–119
role playing, in multicultural education, 162–163
Roosevelt, Franklin, 227, 229

scapegoats, in textbooks discussing the Middle East, 216–217
Schindler's List, 202–205
schools, segregation in, 6–7, 103–110, 197–201
Schwallie-Giddis, Pat, 94, 95
science, teaching as, 41–42
scientific racism, 208
segmented marketing, multicultural education and, 48
segregation, school, 6–7, 103–110, 197–201
self-esteem, tolerance and, 95–96
self-identification, 138
separate but equal, school segregation and, 103–110
sexual harassment, 100
Shalala, Donna, 87
Sheff v. O'Neill, 104–110
single-parent families, 179; discipline and, 115–116
situational competence, multicultural education and, 46, 47–48
Sizer, Theodore, 105
Skinner, B. F., 43
slavery, 6, 185, 188, 203
Sleeter, Christine, 55, 59, 73, 84, 139; on white racism, 79–82
sloppiness, in social studies textbooks discussing the Middle East, 217
Smith, Lamar, 17
social distance, multicultural education and, 46
social status, inequality and, 87
social studies textbooks, discussion of Middle East in, 212–218
socioeconomic class: definition of, 98; school achievement and, 220
solidarity, multicultural education and, 59–65
Soloman, R. Patrick, 194
South Bronx, NY, poor children of, 232–237
Sowell, Thomas, 113
Spanish-American War, 8
special education, inclusion and, 34–37
speech, freedom of, music lyrics and, 38–39
Spielberg, Steven, *Schindler's List* and, 202–205
Steele, Shelby, 113
Stempel, Herbert, 204
Stephenson, Karin, 26, 27
Stowe, Harriet Beecher, 240
stress and anxiety, multicultural education and, 46, 47
structural integration/cultural pluralism model, of equality, 85–86
Suarez-Oroco, Marcelo, 191
Sullivan, Mercer, 114
Sully, Robert, 182
Sumner, William G., 71

Supreme Court, 6, 8, 103, 106. *See also Brown v. Board of Education*

Taba, Hilda, 72
Taylor, Mildred, 165
teachers: inclusion and, 34–37; multicultural professional education for, 30–33, 45–51, 66–70, 71–75, 140–141, 149, 167–173; urban, 40–44
textbooks, discussion of Middle East in social studies, 212–218
Thatcher, B. B., 184
Thirteenth Amendment, to the Constitution, 6
Thomas, William I., 71
Tirozzi, Gerald, 106, 108, 109
tolerance, multicultural education and, 59–65, 92–97, 130, 199
tourist multicultural curriculum, 159
Toward a Common Destiny (Hawley and Jackson), 9–11
tracking, academic, 62, 64
transformation, multicultural education and, 57, 58, 74–75, 172, 198
trivialization, in multicultural education, 159

typologies, inaccurate, in social studies textbooks regarding the Middle East, 213–214

United Nations Universal Declaration of Human Rights, 85
urban teachers, 40–44

values, cultural discontinuities and, 47
Van Doren, Charles, 204
Vancouver, British Columbia, Asian immigration to, 127–131
vocational education, gender discrimination in, 222
Voting Rights Act, 6

Walker, Alice, 160
WEEAP (Women's Educational Equity Act Program), 222
Weicker, Lowell, 109
Werfel, Franz, 204
Wesley, Charles H., 72
western liberal mode, of equality, 85, 136, 139
whites: racism and, 79–82. *See also* demographics

whitewashing, in textbooks discussing the Middle East, 216–217
Will, George, 112
Wilson, Pete, 17, 23
Winant, Howard, 111, 113
Wong-Fillmore, Lily, 157
Woodson, Carter G., 72, 200
work habits, cultural discontinuities and, 47
World History: Patterns of Civilization (Beers), discussion of Middle East in, 212–218
World Today, The (Hagans), discussion of Middle East in, 212–218
World War II: *Shindler's List* and, 202–205; treatment of Asian Americans during, 226–229

X, Malcolm, 230, 231

Young, Andrew, 105
youthfulness, as cause of minority growth, 177

zero-parent children, role models for, 115–119
zero-reject policy, inclusion and, 35

Credits/ Acknowledgments

Cover design by Charles Vitelli

1. The Social Contexts of Multicultural Education
Facing overview—United Nations photo.

2. Teacher Education in Multicultural Perspective
Facing overview—Dushkin Publishing Group/Brown & Benchmark Publishers photo.

3. Multicultural Education as an Academic Discipline
Facing overview—Photo by Pamela Carley.

4. Identity and Personal Development
Facing overview—Photo by Cheryl Greenleaf.

5. Curriculum and Instruction in Multicultural Perspective
Facing overview—AP/Wide World photo by Carlos Osorio.

6. Special Topics in Multicultural Education
Facing overview—Photo by Pamela Carley.

7. For Vision and Voice
Facing overview—United Nations photo by John Isaac.

PHOTOCOPY THIS PAGE!!!*

ANNUAL EDITIONS ARTICLE REVIEW FORM

■ NAME: _____ DATE: _____

■ TITLE AND NUMBER OF ARTICLE: _____

■ BRIEFLY STATE THE MAIN IDEA OF THIS ARTICLE: _____

_____

■ LIST THREE IMPORTANT FACTS THAT THE AUTHOR USES TO SUPPORT THE MAIN IDEA:

_____

_____

_____

_____

_____

■ WHAT INFORMATION OR IDEAS DISCUSSED IN THIS ARTICLE ARE ALSO DISCUSSED IN YOUR
TEXTBOOK OR OTHER READING YOU HAVE DONE? LIST THE TEXTBOOK CHAPTERS AND PAGE
NUMBERS:

_____

_____

_____

_____

_____

_____

■ LIST ANY EXAMPLES OF BIAS OR FAULTY REASONING THAT YOU FOUND IN THE ARTICLE:

_____

_____

_____

_____

■ LIST ANY NEW TERMS/CONCEPTS THAT WERE DISCUSSED IN THE ARTICLE AND WRITE A SHORT
DEFINITION:

_____

_____

_____

_____

*Your instructor may require you to use this Annual Editions Article Review Form in any number of
ways: for articles that are assigned, for extra credit, as a tool to assist in developing assigned papers, or
simply for your own reference. Even if it is not required, we encourage you to photocopy and use this
page; you'll find that reflecting on the articles will greatly enhance the information from your text.

ANNUAL EDITIONS: MULTICULTURAL EDUCATION 96/97
Article Rating Form

We Want Your Advice

Here is an opportunity for you to have direct input into the next revision of this volume. We would like you to rate each of the 46 articles listed below, using the following scale:

1. **Excellent: should definitely be retained**
2. **Above average: should probably be retained**
3. **Below average: should probably be deleted**
4. **Poor: should definitely be deleted**

Your ratings will play a vital part in the next revision. So please mail this prepaid form to us just as soon as you complete it.
Thanks for your help!

Annual Editions revisions depend on two major opinion sources: one is our Advisory Board, listed in the front of this volume, which works with us in scanning the thousands of articles published in the public press each year; the other is you—the person actually using the book. Please help us and the users of the next edition by completing the prepaid article rating form on this page and returning it to us. Thank you.

Rating	Article	Rating	Article
	1. Diversity without Equality = Oppression		25. All-Black Schools Provide Role Models: Is This the Solution?
	2. Toward a Common Destiny		26. On Being a Mexican American
	3. The Importance of Education . . . and How His Education Helped Turn the Tide for Indian People		27. Respect, Cultural Sensitivity, and Communication
	4. One Nation, One Language		28. Lessons of Vancouver: Immigration Raises Fundamental Questions of Identity and Values
	5. Tongue-Tied in the Schools		29. Curriculum Guidelines for Multicultural Education
	6. A "Glorious Mongrel"		30. Empowering Children to Create a Caring Culture in a World of Differences
	7. Go North, Young Man		
	8. Intermarried . . . with Children		31. "The Party": Role Playing to Enhance Multicultural Understanding
	9. Why Do We Need This Class? Multicultural Education for Teachers		32. Classrooms without Borders
	10. Questions and Answers about Inclusion: What Every Teacher Should Know		33. Teaching: The Challenge of Change; Reclaiming Democracy through Schooling
	11. Time to Talk Back		34. The Dynamic Demographic Mosaic Called America
	12. The Ideology of Star Teachers of Children in Poverty		35. Black Hawk's *An Autobiography*: The Production and Use of an "Indian" Voice
	13. Building Cultural Bridges: A Bold Proposal for Teacher Education		36. Behind the Model-Minority Stereotype: Voices of High- and Low-Achieving Asian American Students
	14. Bridging Multicultural Theory and Practice		
	15. Affirmation, Solidarity, and Critique: Moving beyond Tolerance in Multicultural Education		37. Multicultural Education: Reflections on *Brown* at 40
	16. Multicultural Education: A Movement in Search of Meaning and Positive Connections		38. The Road to Auschwitz: What's So Funny about Schindler's List?
			39. New Colors
	17. Multicultural Education as an Academic Discipline		40. Another School's Reality
	18. Multicultural Education and Culture Change: An Anthropological Perspective		41. How School Materials Teach about the Middle East
	19. White Racism		42. The AAUW Report: How Schools Shortchange Girls
	20. Cultural Pluralism, Multicultural Education, and Then What?		43. Home Was a Horse Stall
	21. The Inside Story		44. Turning the Tide: A Call for Radical Voices of Affirmation
	22. The Intersections of Gender, Class, Race, and Culture: On Seeing Clients Whole		45. Knocking on Heaven's Door
	23. Can Separate Be Equal?		46. Investing in Our Children: A Struggle for America's Conscience and Future
	24. Contradictions of Identity: Education and the Problem of Racial Absolutism		

(Continued on next page)

ABOUT YOU

Name _____ Date _____

Are you a teacher? ❏ Or student? ❏

Your School Name _____

Department _____

Address _____

City _____ State _____ Zip _____

School Telephone # _____

YOUR COMMENTS ARE IMPORTANT TO US!

Please fill in the following information:

For which course did you use this book? _____

Did you use a text with this Annual Edition? ❏ yes ❏ no

The title of the text? _____

What are your general reactions to the Annual Editions concept?

Have you read any particular articles recently that you think should be included in the next edition?

Are there any articles you feel should be replaced in the next edition? Why?

Are there other areas that you feel would utilize an Annual Edition?

May we contact you for editorial input?

May we quote you from above?

ANNUAL EDITIONS: MULTICULTURAL EDUCATION 96/97

BUSINESS REPLY MAIL

First Class   Permit No. 84   Guilford, CT

Postage will be paid by addressee

**Dushkin Publishing Group/
Brown & Benchmark Publishers**
Sluice Dock
Guilford, Connecticut 06437

No Postage
Necessary
if Mailed
in the
United States